1,000 BEST MOVIES ON DVD

PETER TRAVERS

MOVIE CRITIC FOR *Rolling Stone*

1,000
BEST
MOVIES
ON DVD

WENNER BOOKS, NEW YORK

Editor: Nicholas Weir-Williams
Assistant Editor: Robert Land
Cover Design: Doyle Partners
Text Design: Mayapriya Long, Bookwrights Design

Library of Congress Cataloging-in-Publication Data
Travers, Peter.
 The 1,000 best movies on DVDs / Peter Travers.
  p. cm.
 Includes index.
 ISBN 1-932958-52-5
 1. Motion pictures—Catalogs. 2. Video recordings—Catalogs. 3. DVD-Video discs—Catalogs. I. Title: 1,000 best movies on DVD. II. Rolling stone (San Francisco, Calif.) III. Title.
 PN1998.T64 2005
 016.79143'75—dc22
                    2005020419

Wenner books are available for special promotions and premiums. For details contact Michael Rentas, Manager, Inventory and Premium Sales, Hyperion, 77 West 66th Street, 11th Floor, New York, NY 10023, or call 212-456-0133.

FIRST EDITION

10 9 8 7 6 5 4 3 2 1

To Robyn,
with love for a thousand reasons

CONTENTS

INTRODUCTION

*L*et's go straight to the question at the heart of this book: Why is it called The 1,000 Best Movies on DVD and not The 1,000 Best Movies period? Blunt answer: Because in these pages, the quality of the DVD picture and the digital sound counts just as much as the quality of the film. That's right. If the movie scores but the disc sucks (Elvis' *Jailhouse Rock*), it's off the list. If the disc scores but the movie sucks (Oliver Stone's *Alexander*), it's off the list. This is a book for a DVD generation that wants terrific films, transferred to disc in peak condition, and with the added value of bonus features that wrap you up in a movie in ways that are impossible to achieve at the multiplex or on television. That means DVD Special Editions, uncut and uncensored, with deleted scenes, outtakes, alternate endings, behind-the-scenes documentaries, trailers, photo galleries, blooper reels, hidden surprises and commentaries from directors and actors. To watch, say, *The Lord of the Rings* trilogy on DVD or the *Alien Quadrilogy* or the *Star Wars* sextet is to experience those showiest of shows to the fullest.

This book is a selective guide to the best of the best. And it's fully loaded. As the film critic for *Rolling Stone* since 1989 and a lifelong movie fanatic, I've done the genre-jumping groundwork. Every kind of movie is in this book, be it a timeless classic, a rebel newcomer, a sci-fi fantasy, a blockbuster epic, a suspense thriller, a sexy farce, a screwball comedy, a delicate human drama, a kickass action powerhouse, a horror show, a film noir, a musical, an artful anime, a provocative documentary or a guilty pleasure. (Look for movies listed by subject in the back of the book.) The standard for making it into the Top 1,000 has nothing to do with size or snob appeal: the movie has to be alive, you have to feel its pulse. No clunkers here. No undeserved blockbusters (*Fantastic Four, The Day After Tomorrow*, the collected works of Michael Bay). No dull, sappy Oscar winners (*Gandhi, Around the World in 80 Days, The Sound of Music, A Beautiful Mind*). No films whose reputations have gone moldy. Have you watched *Life Is Beautiful* lately—what were we thinking?

But selection is just the starting point. Since the advent of DVD in 1997, the content on each disc has grown in reach and ambition. Besides reviewing each of the 1,000 movies on the list, there are the following areas to consider:

Picture: Whenever possible, I avoided geek-speak about aspect ratios. Most widescreen movies are letterboxed for DVD, meaning you'll see black bars on the top and bottom of your screen on a standard TV monitor. If the package your DVD comes in lists the aspect ratio as 1.85:1, the bars will be smaller than if the aspect ratio is 2.35: 1. On a widescreen television, most DVDs are encoded for 16:9 playback, an enhancement that makes the black bars disappear. That peak performance is referred to as an anamorphic widescreen transfer. What is decidedly non-peak is a pan-and-scan DVD transfer, which trims the top, bottom and sides of a film image to squeeze it on a standard TV screen. In this book, you can assume the best about any aspect ratio unless I tell you otherwise. Fullscreen versions of older movies cause fewer problems unless the picture is worn from age. The words *remastered* and *restored* indicate those problems have been addressed on the DVD.

Sound: Those who think sound is less important than picture are kidding themselves. A DVD movie that lands too harshly or too softly on the ears takes you out of the experience. Dolby Surround is the standard. But for the big-ticket items, such as *Jurassic Park*, you want to hear those dinosaurs roar. Most Special Edition DVDs offer two premium sound choices, requiring two front speakers, two rear speakers, a center-channel speaker and a subwoofer. The 5.1 channel Dolby Digital track came first, followed by DTS, which really pumps out that bass. Of course, you don't need either to enjoy *Napoleon Dynamite* or other low-budget movies that nonetheless require a skilled hand at audio mixing. Older movies, with mono tracks that can pop and wheeze from wear-and-tear, benefit greatly from a remastered soundtrack on DVD.

Special Editions: Maybe you think there's only one DVD for every movie. No way. Studios define a hit DVD by how many times they can sell it to you. For example, if you go online to find *Terminator 2*, you'll find the movie all by itself, then *Terminator 2: The Ultimate Edition*, and also something called *T2–Extreme DVD*. What do you do? Is *Ultimate* better than *Extreme* or vice versa? *Extreme* is actually the one you want. This book will tell you why, but it's a jungle out there. There are times when several companies release the same DVD. Criterion, justly prized for its superior DVD transfers, went head to head with MGM on the DVD for *This Is Spinal Tap*. But MGM gets the edge, which I'll explain when you tap into the *Tap* entry.

Hot Bonus: I use the term *hot* advisedly because all DVD extras are not created equal. The typical DVD produced today can have from one to eight hours of bonus material. Reviewing that material is more than a challenge, it's a mosh pit. Don't worry, I'm here for you. The only extras I mention in this book are the ones worth seeing and hearing. You don't need to know about the hype that crowds so many discs, except to avoid it. On the *Ocean's Eleven* DVD, George Clooney informs us that the movie works because the script is so good. Thanks George, for nothing. And let's ring a leper's bell for those discs that try to pass off promotional filler—mostly interviews from softball talk shows— as incisive commentary. This book notes only hype-free bonus materials that replace scam with substance. No one needed that deleted scene of a clueless Samuel L. Jackson in *Star Wars: Attack of the Clones*. On the other hand, the extra dose of Harvey Keitel in *Pulp Fiction* is a nutso treat. The most common extras, besides deleted scenes and outtakes, are documentaries about the making of the movie. Those shot on set are generally much preferable to those shot as part of the film's promotion, when actors and filmmakers go out on the TV circuit under the watchful eyes of publicists who guard their every word. This is the DVD equivalent of spam and should be outlawed. And what of those bare-bones DVDs that offer a mere trailer and a few production notes? For me, they are acceptable only if the DVD transfer offers knockout picture and sound.

Audio Commentaries: Sometimes actors and directors will speak on camera about making the film. More often they will provide audio commentary, allowing you to hear them discuss each scene as it plays. With participants who do this well—Ridley Scott, Martin Scorsese, Francis Coppola, Robert Rodriquez—these commentaries add up to a master class in filmmaking. Others seem to be asleep or worse. On the *Meet the Parents* DVD, Robert De Niro joins director Jay Roach but barely speaks, even when asked.

DVD Documentaries: True fans will treasure any footage of the actors and directors on the set as the film is being made. The new rage is for retrospective documentaries that reunite cast and crew years or decades later to talk about what went down. Since time tends to loosen tongues, there's a lot of mischief in these puppies. Check out Paul Newman and Robert Redford going at it on the 25th Anniversary Edition of *Butch Cassidy and the Sundance Kid*.

Easter Eggs: The mystery category. It refers to bonus extras that aren't listed on the DVD box. You have to go on a hunt just as you would for Easter eggs (get it?). That means you have to press a bunch of buttons and directionals on your DVD remote, often driving yourself crazy in the process, to find things as dull as extra pages of DVD credits. Skip those. The Easter Eggs I've included in the book are really worth the effort. On the *Reservoir Dogs* DVD, you'll get to see the notorious ear-slicing scene re-enacted with puppets. And on the . . . well, why should I tell you now?

Key Scenes: DVD fanatics often refer to scenes that are "demo quality," meaning they can be used on family and friends to demonstrate just how powerfully their home-theater system can deliver picture and sound. You can start with the T-Rex attack in *Jurassic Park*, move on to the freeway chase in *The Matrix Reloaded*, show Alan Cumming's shape-shifting Nightcrawler invade the White House in *X2: X-Men United*, and stun them with the harrowing chopper attack on a Vietnamese village in *Apocalypse Now*—a combination of image-and-sound design (Wagner's "Ride of the Valkyries" provides the thundering musical accompaniment) that still inspires jaw-dropping awe. In films without special effects, the Key Scene is often a moment that can evoke the entire movie, such as Kim Novak emerging from the shadows as a living ghost in *Vertigo* or the first sight of Anthony Hopkins as Hannibal Lecter, stone still in his cell and scary as Satan in *The Silence of the Lambs* or John Wayne silhouetted in a doorway, forever shut off from life, at the end of *The Searchers*. My picks for these scenes are meant to stir you up about a movie and its meanings. It's the talking that helps keep good movies alive and the expertly transferred DVD that keeps us talking.

It is now officially the golden age for watching movies at home. VHS is dead and Laser Disc is deader. DVD is king. No less an authority than the *New York Times* reports that because of DVD "Americans are changing how they watch movies." In the last five years, movie attendance has inched up by 8.1 percent while sales and rentals of DVDs during that same time period have soared to 676.5 percent. Last year, movies collected $9.5 billion at the box office while DVDs cashed in at $21 billion. Not only is the tail wagging the dog, it's bringing the puppy to its knees. A hit movie on DVD can roughly double the business that it did in theaters. Hollywood studios can afford to take risks on big-budget films because DVD revenues make up for potential box-office slack. Sixty percent of American homes with a TV set also have a DVD player. Sales are soaring for home-theater units with multi-channel surround-sound systems and high-definition, flat-screen TVs, as well as rear-projection screens that can stretch to seventy inches.

Thanks to DVDs, the wow factor has passed from the multiplex to the home. DVD technology is so accessible right now that you don't even need a high-end system to white-knuckle the couch when the Great White shark first heaves out of the briny deep in the 30th Anniversary DVD edition of *Jaws*. You'll feel the punches that Brad Pitt throws in *Fight Club*, duck the flying asteroids along with Han Solo in *Star Wars: A New Hope*, hit the STILL button on your DVD remote to study the montage of bare butts and bouncing breasts in *The Wedding Crashers*, and experience the heat of bloody battle from Helm's Deep in *The Lord of the Rings: The Two Towers* to Normandy beach in *Saving Private Ryan*. Even more surprising is what a great DVD transfer can do with quiet—the hush before the final revelation in *The Sixth Sense*, the play of color and light in *The Red Shoes*, the nearly silent scene of drowned bodies floating in the water in *Titanic*, the unheard whisper between Bill Murray and Scarlett Johansson in *Lost in Translation*, and the erotic fever dreams of Alfred Hitchcock's *Vertigo* and David Lynch's *Mulholland Dr.* Sound, in all its digital glory, adds just as much as picture does to the engulfing experience of movies on DVD. It can start small—the intercut whirs of fans and helicopters at the opening of *Apocalypse Now* and that whizzing bullet Keanu Reeves dances around in *The Matrix*—and climax in the crash-and-boom symphonies of James Cameron's *Terminator 2* and Steven Spielberg's *War of the Worlds*. The great movie scores—Bernard Herrmann's screaming violins in *Psycho*, Jerry Goldsmith's haunting sax in *Chinatown*—feel enriched on disc. When the sound mix works on DVD, well, give a listen to Jimi Hendrix in *Woodstock*, sending the stragglers home to the scorched remains of "The Star Spangled Banner," and you'll see what I mean.

A word here for the DVD detractors. We may indeed be missing something here, like the shared experience of watching a movie in a theater with—to quote Billy Wilder's *Sunset Boulevard*—"all those wonderful people out there in the dark." But the great Wilder didn't live to see those wonderful people tripping over him in the dark while carrying popcorn boxes and soda containers big enough to hold a DVD player or to hear them talking on cell phones as the movie begins and not just during those maddening commercials theater owners now foist on us to make back some of the money they lose to the Hollywood studios that gouge them for the lion's share of ticket revenues. No wonder that couch at home is starting to look mighty cozy.

Some argue that DVD is a maturing business, that in the future studio hype-masters will have to work harder to persuade us to buy DVDs in a competitive world of video-games, TiVo and Internet obsession. The upshot is: DVDs will have to offer us more and charge us less. I'm still trying to figure out a downside to that one.

Face it: DVD is the best toy a kid ever had for deconstructing movies from the best seat in the house. Those shiny little discs have colonized our living spaces, our computers, our camcorders, the backseats of our cars and even our iPods if talk of the video iPod comes to fruition. As to the question of what's missing on DVD, the big hurt for me is Bernardo Bertolucci's *The Conformist*, a hugely influential film bursting with the kind of color and sound design that begs for a dazzling DVD transfer. And I'm getting impatient for John Huston's *African Queen*, Orson Welles' *Magnificent Ambersons* and his *Chimes at Midnight*, Vincente Minnelli's *Some Came Running*, Billy Wilder's *Ace in the Hole*, Jean-Pierre Melville's *Le Samourai*, Sidney Lumet's *Prince of the City*, Prince's *Sign 'o' the Times*, and Kenji Fukasaku's *Battle Royale*. We get Madonna at her worst in *Swept Away* on DVD and we don't get W.C. Fields at his peak in *David Copperfield*—what's up with that? Still, these are rare exceptions to the rule that if you want it, you can have it on a fully loaded DVD. This book is for those who want it, for those film junkies and rookies who demand to know about the 1,000 movies on DVD that get it right, including the bells and whistles. Dig in.

PETER TRAVERS
SEPTEMBER 2005

A.I.: Artificial Intelligence (Special Edition) (2001)

Starring: Haley Joel Osment, Jude Law

Directed by: Steven Spielberg

This sci-fi tale of a killer robot child (Osment) with a Pinocchio dream to be a real boy was a box-office disappointment owing to a bizarre collaboration between Spielberg and a dead man. That would be Stanley Kubrick, who planned to make the film for twenty years. When Kubrick died in 1999, Spielberg picked up the pieces to create a schizoid wreck of a movie that still casts a potent spell. Spielberg champions human triumph; Kubrick (*Dr. Strangelove, A Clockwork Orange*) was drawn to darkness. But there is no doubting the film's visual astonishments, which come through thrillingly on disc.

Hot Bonus: The behind-the-scenes featurette fills in all the details of what Kubrick wanted and where Spielberg went his own way.

Key Scene: Manhattan underwater, while robot boy watches from the tip of a skyscraper.

Abyss, The (Two-Disc Special Edition) (1989)

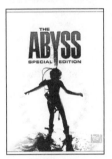

Starring: Ed Harris, Mary Elizabeth Mastrantonio

Directed and written by: James Cameron

Eight years before he sank the *Titanic*, director-writer Cameron warmed up with this relentlessly exciting and unfairly underrated tale of a civilian underwater oil-rig commandeered by the navy to help rescue a nuclear sub gone to a watery grave in the Caribbean. Harris stars as the rig foreman, and Mastrantonio kicks ass as his boss and about-to-be-ex-wife. Their relationship mirrors the one between Cameron and producer Gale Ann Hurd, his former wife, and gives the film an added emotional kick. But it's the Oscar-winning visual effects—watch out for aliens—and the mounting claustrophobia—the actors did their own diving—that pin you to your seat.

Hot Bonus: The double digipack, with its startlingly vibrant sound and DVD picture, offers the original theatrical release and a special edition with nearly half an hour of extra footage. And for sheer fun, you can't beat the optional pop-up captions that explain how each special effect was created.

Key Scene: There is tragic beauty in the moment when the divers move through the sub as drowned bodies float by in an eerie mockery of death.

Adaptation (Superbit) (2002)

Starring: Nicolas Cage, Meryl Streep, Chris Cooper

Directed by: Spike Jonze; **written by:** Charlie Kaufman

Screenwriting that's this smart, inventive, passionate, and rip-roaringly funny is a rare species. So all praise to Kaufman, reteaming with *Being John Malkovich* director Jonze, to tell the story of a balding, paunchy, self-loathing screenwriter (Cage) who wants to adapt a nonlinear book by a *New Yorker* writer (Streep) about a toothless Florida orchid breeder (Cooper). Cage also plays the writer's extroverted twin who adds things to the script—sex, guns, car chases—that his brother vowed to avoid. Cage is a double-barreled marvel; Streep runs with the rich comic material—just watch her trip out with a dial tone; and Cooper won a deserved Oscar.

Hot Bonus: This is a Superbit DVD, an encoding process that reallocates space on the disc normally used for bonus features to optimize picture and sound, which here adds to the enjoyment of how Jonze runs amok with visuals, from time travel to a cameo from Charles Darwin and a quickie nature lesson on how flowers adapt. Few scripts toss more challenging balls in the air, and Jonze juggles them all with an artful, light-stepping ease.

Key Scene: Cage at his keyboard, promising himself coffee and a muffin if he can cough up ideas. I don't know a writer who hasn't been there.

Adventures of Robin Hood, The (Two-Disc Special Edition) (1938)

Starring: Errol Flynn, Olivia DeHavilland, Alan Hale, Basil Rathbone

Directed by: Michael Curtiz

Forget Kevin Costner's 1992 vanity production and seize this spectacular DVD transfer with the picture restored to such Technicolor glory that it looks like it was made yesterday. Flynn buckles his swash with witty dash as Robin robs from the rich to give to the poor. DeHavilland is the perfect Maid Marian. And Hale's Little John leads Robin's merry men in tights against the sniveling sheriff of Nottingham (Melville Cooper).

Hot Bonus: The retrospective look at the filming can't match the documentary on Technicolor, that now sadly defunct process that produced unparalleled eye candy. This DVD is Exhibit A.

Key Scene: Robin's fencing duel with the evil Sir Guy of Gisbourne, superbly played by Rathbone under the inspired direction of Curtiz.

After Hours (1985)

Starring: Griffin Dunne, Rosanna Arquette

Directed by: Martin Scorsese; **written by:** Joseph Minion

Dante has nothing on Scorsese, who sees a hot night in the Big Apple as only slightly less terrifying than an express run through the nine circles of hell. The film's co-producer Dunne gives a career performance as a bachelor bored with his job as a computer programmer and nights alone with his cable TV. At a coffee shop, a babe (Arquette) invites him to her friend's loft in SoHo. And so begins Dunne's waking nightmare—murder for him, mirthful for us. Scorsese, working with ace cameraman Michael Ballhaus, finds comic poetry in SoHo's rain-splattered streets and fun in such details as the cannonball velocity of keys thrown from a loft window. It's a small, but superbly crafted film, expertly captured on DVD.

Hot Bonus: Scorsese talking a mile a minute on the commentary track offers a lesson in filmmaking that the "making of" documentary only hints at.

Key Scene: Arquette's monologue about her husband, a *Wizard of Oz* freak who can't reach orgasm without shouting, "Surrender, Dorothy."

Age of Innocence, The (1993)

Starring: Daniel Day-Lewis, Michelle Pfeiffer, Winona Ryder

Directed by: Martin Scorsese

Scorsese—the raging bull of directors—bursts into the china shop that is Edith Wharton's 1920 novel. He roughs things up, though nothing gets shattered except our preconceptions. Though a century apart, Scorsese and Wharton are both experts in New York's tribal warfare. Behind the elegant facade of Wharton's characters is a calculated cruelty that Scorsese's goodfellas could easily recognize. Society is determined to wipe out the budding relationship between a lawyer (Day-Lewis) and a countess (Pfeiffer), the married cousin of the lawyer's fiancée (Ryder). And all this must be done without the slightest indication that behind the polite courtesies lies a conspiracy carried out with the formality of an execution. Ryder won a Oscar nomination for showing the killer inside the girl.

Hot Bonus: The trailer is about it, but seeing this film in all its letterboxed glory marks the DVD as a visual feast in which Scorsese and cinematographer Michael Ballhaus ravish the senses.

Key Scene: The opera house. It starts on close-ups of small details: the singer's painted mouth, the gardenia in the lawyer's lapel, the blur of jewels and clothes seen through opera glasses. Then the full view as the countess extends her fan across the expanse of the theater, and we catch our breath in amazement.

Aguirre: The Wrath of God (1972)

Starring: Klaus Kinski

Directed and written by: Werner Herzog

No doubt, Don Lope de Aguirre (Kinski) and his sixteenth-century Spanish conquistadors endured the tortures of the damned as they traversed the Amazon River jungle, dodging cannibals and poison arrows in search of El Dorado, that mythical city of gold. Shooting in the Amazon, director Herzog put his cast and crew through a modern version of hell. The result, as the DVD attests, is a film of ferocious beauty and terror. And Kinski's flipped-out performance as the crazed-with-greed Aguirre made this German film a contender for the cult status it has now indelibly achieved.

Hot Bonus: Herzog's commentary is a behind-the-scenes catalogue of catastrophes—many due to Kinski, who had the habit of beating people who got in his way.

Key Scene: The stunning opening shot with the camera pulling back and back further to reveal the vast numbers of men trying to navigate the impossible jungle.

Air Force One (Superbit) (1997)

Starring: Harrison Ford, Gary Oldman, Glenn Close

Directed by: Wolfgang Petersen

Russian terrorists, led by a vicious Oldman, take over the president's plane and hold his wife and daughter hostage while the big man sneaks around the jet looking for solutions. Ford makes

a natural-born commander-in-chief, and he's plenty pissed off. That's all you need for 125 minutes of riveting escapism.

Hot Bonus: The sound mix alone puts you right in the action, but Petersen's descriptions of how close the real Air Force One resembles its movie replica deepens the action.

Key Scene: The prez and the cell phone—a big laugh amid the mayhem.

Airplane! (1980)

Starring: Robert Hays, Leslie Nielsen, Peter Graves, Lloyd Bridges
Directed by: Jim Abrahams, David Zucker, Jerry Zucker

This parody has outlived the three dead-serious *Airport* films from the 1970s that it so delightfully skewers. Hays is the fill-in pilot on a flight from L.A. to Chicago in which nearly everyone is poisoned by their fish dinners. "Passengers Certain to Die!" reads one remarkably timely newspaper headline. Viewers are certain to laugh, especially at the antics of the older cast members, notably Bridges as a glue-sniffing air traffic controller.

Hot Bonus: The disc has a Dolby Digital track soundtrack it never had in theaters. Another good sign: the film's three directors keep cracking up on the commentary track, remembering every detail, including a priceless cameo from Ethel Merman.

Key Scene: Each veteran actor has a killer-laugh moment. Bridges is a riot as a glue-sniffing bureaucrat. But it's Graves as a pederast pilot ("Do you like gladiator movies, Joey?") who steals the show.

Akira (Two-Disc Special Edition) (1988)

Starring: Voices of Jimmy Flanders, Drew Thomas, Barbara Larsen
Directed by: Katsuhiro Otomo

Otomo's wild animated ride popularized Japanese anime in America, and this DVD qualifies as a gift to fans and newcomers alike. The plot, based on a Japanese comic book (*manga*), is a sci-fi adventure about teen bikers in a futuristic Tokyo, circa 2019, and the mysterious Akira—a child with psychic powers that can bring on an apocalypse.

Expect dazzling sights but no kid stuff. The film's gore and profanity may shock the uninitiated.

Hot Bonus: A way to stop the picture and get an English explanation of every detail in an image not explained by dialogue.

Key Scene: The clown gang at war.

Alexander Nevsky (1938)

Starring: Nikolai Cherkasov
Directed by: Sergei Eisenstein

Eisenstein, the great Russian director of silent films (*Battleship Potemkin, October*) took his first shot at the sound era with this thirteenth-century tale of how Prince Nevsky (a heroic Cherkasov) and his army beat back invading Teutonic knights and Tartars. Eisenstein loaded on the timely propaganda by presenting the prince as a precursor to Joe Stalin in his battle against the Nazis. Party butt is kissed, but the spectacular battle scenes, choreographed to the music of Sergei Prokofiev, make up for it. In a word: Wow.

Hot Bonus: Criterion has brought the black-and-white picture back from the death of scratches, hisses, and pops. David Bordwell offers historical commentary, but it's the feature on how the film was restored that dazzles.

Key Scene: The winter battle on frozen Lake Peipus in 1242 with the combatants wielding axes and spears as the ice terrifyingly cracks.

Ali (Director's Cut) (2001)

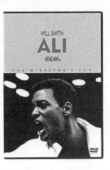

Starring: Will Smith, Jamie Foxx, Jon Voight
Directed by: Michael Mann

Why settle for just the movie when the DVD brings you director Mann's own take on his much-misunderstood biopic of Muhammad Ali? Mann and Will Smith—in an Oscar-nominated career performance—catch "the Greatest" among heavyweights in the act of discovering himself as an African

American, a Muslim, an athlete, a husband and father, a political activist, and a cultural icon. Unducked controversies include the loss of his title when he refused the Vietnam draft, his exploitation by black Muslim leadership, and the womanizing that plagued three marriages. Jamie Foxx excels as cornerman Drew "Bundini" Brown, as does Jon Voight as ABC sportscaster Howard Cosell. *Ali* is unwieldy in length and ambition, but Mann and Smith deliver this bruiser with the urgency of a champ's left hook.

Hot Bonus: In addition to Mann's pungent commentary, there are added and revised scenes that make the film seem fuller and richer than it was in theaters.

Key Scene: The Rumble in the Jungle bout with George Foreman in Zaire is a thriller, but the killer is the opener with the champ reviewing his early life in a warmup run choreographed to Sam Cooke singing in a Harlem club.

Alice Doesn't Live Here Anymore (1974)

Starring: Ellen Burstyn, Kris Kristofferson, Diane Ladd, Alfred Lutter
Directed by: Martin Scorsese

Scorsese uses *Wizard of Oz* imagery to kick off this story of a widowed mother (Burstyn, splendid and Oscar crowned) who hits the metaphorical yellow-brick road with her smartass twelve-year-old son (Lutter). Purpose? To start a singing career. End result? Waiting tables at an Arizona diner and being romanced by a rancher (Kristofferson). What could have been a sitcom weepie—it actually did become one, starring Linda Lavin—is energized by Scorsese's eye for the telling visual and a cast including Diane Ladd as a waitress pal and Jodie Foster as another smartass kid.

Hot Bonus: The commentary by Scorsese and Burstyn—who hired the then-newcomer to direct her on the advice of Francis Coppola—is a vigorous treat.

Key Scene: Burstyn singing and playing unremarkable cocktail piano at a roadside dump while Scorsese swoops around her with his camera as if he had just happened upon the rarest species in songbirds.

Alice's Restaurant (Special Edition) (1969)

Starring: Arlo Guthrie, Pat Quinn, James Broderick
Directed by: Arthur Penn

Once upon a time in the 1960s, Arlo Guth-

rie—son of folk legend Woody Guthrie—wrote a hit record ("The Alice's Restaurant Massacree") about that hippie time, about dodging the Vietnam draft, about nurturing a social conscience, and about hanging out at a restaurant. Penn turned the song into a defining film of the sixties with Arlo as himself, sleeping with a teen groupie (Shelley Plimpton), getting arrested for littering and hanging out at a restaurant in Stockbridge, Massachusetts, run by Alice (Quinn) and her husband Ray (Broderick, Matthew's father).

Hot Bonus: The R-rated version of the film, not seen in theaters, plus nonstop commentary from Arlo that is nearly as entertaining as the movie.

Key Scene: A funeral in the snow, set to Joni Mitchell's "Song to Aging Children," a time-capsule moment immortalized on disc.

Alien Quadrilogy

Starring: Sigourney Weaver
Directed by: Ridley Scott, James Cameron, David Fincher, Jean-Pierre Jeunet

There are few DVD packages more ambitious than this nine-disc monster, which includes all four movies, storyboards, cast screen tests (it's a kick watching Weaver get into her Ripley character for the first time), and forty-five (count 'em) hours of unseen footage. All the directors are interviewed, including Vincent Ward (*The Navigator*), who bailed out of *Alien³*. It's no secret that the final two chapters (*Alien³* and *Alien: Resurrection*) aren't up to the first two blockbusters. But watching them together will fry your eyeballs and stimulate your imagination.

Hot Bonus: They just don't stop. My favorite is the interview with H. R. Giger, who created the alien—as slimy and scary a creature as movies have ever seen—and owns up to a fear of worms and snakes.

Key Scene: Here we go—

Alien (1979)—The classic yuck moment when the alien busts out of John Hurt's chest and skitters across the room like a bloody, chomping fetus.

Aliens (1986)—Weaver (who won a justified Oscar nomination as Best Actress for this one) facing off with the alien queen out to grab a young girl (Carrie Henn) and snarling, "Get away from her, you bitch!"

Alien³ (1992)—The moment (watch for it) when you realize that director Fincher (*Seven, Fight Club*) is treating the alien threat as an AIDS metaphor.

Alien: Resurrection (1997)–Thanks to screenwriter Joss Whedon (*Buffy the Vampire Slayer*), the worst of the series at least has a sense of humor. As a cloned Ripley shoots at other replications of herself, one of the guys watching cracks, "Must be a chick thing."

All About Eve (1950)

Starring: Bette Davis, Anne Baxter, George Sanders, Marilyn Monroe
Directed and written by: Joseph L. Mankiewicz

Nominated for a record fourteen Oscars (it won Best Picture), this literate and hilarious take on the vipers of the New York theater scene may seem an unlikely candidate for major DVD restoration. It's all talk, right? Wrong. Mankiewicz moved his camera with masterly precision–check the party scene in which a never better or more diva-ish Davis utters the immortal line, "Fasten your seatbelts, it's going to be a bumpy night"–and the refreshed black-and-white cinematography makes the dialogue shine like new.

Hot Bonus: A documentary features time-of-release interviews with Davis and Baxter, who played the conniving Eve, that still crackle with tension.

Key Scene: I can't think of one that isn't. But any utterance of Sanders, as an acid-tongued critic, is to be savored. He intros a starlet (a very young Monroe) as "a graduate of the Copacabana School of Dramatic Arts."

All About My Mother (1999)

Starring: Cecilia Roth, Marisa Paredes, Penélope Cruz
Directed and written by: Pedro Almodóvar

Almodóvar's Oscar winner has been called the Spanish *All About Eve*, as a mother (Roth) searches for a new life after her teen son is run down by a car and killed while chasing after an autograph from a theater diva (Paredes). Almodóvar's films always burst with color and light, beautifully captured on disc, that help define characters, such as the nun (Cruz) with AIDS who is now pregnant by the same man who sired Roth's dead son.

Hot Bonus: Almodóvar talks, always a pleasure.

Key Scene: Watching the mother and the actress solidify a bond typifies the maturity and depth found in the director's later work.

All That Heaven Allows (1955)

Starring: Rock Hudson, Jane Wyman
Directed by: Douglas Sirk

Sirk stopped making movies in 1959, but the symbolic way he played with light and shadow was made for DVD, especially in this special edition done by the masters at Criterion. The plot is pure *Desperate Housewives* soap opera, as a widow (Wyman) falls for her hunky young gardener (Hudson). It's not flesh, but moral hypocrisy that the film exposes, a topic so timely that Todd Haynes filmed his own 2002 homage, *Far From Heaven*, with Julianne Moore.

Hot Bonus: The look of the film is bonus enough, but the late German director Rainer Werner Fassbinder, who did his own tribute to the film in 1974's *Fear Eats the Soul*, is heard from in a striking illustrated essay.

Key Scene: It's hard to resist Sirk's satire of the coming of television, when a salesman gives the widow this pitch: "All you have to do is turn the dial and you have all the company you want right there on the screen. Drama, comedy, life's parade at your fingertips."

All That Jazz (1979)

Starring: Roy Scheider, Jessica Lange, Ann Reinking
Directed and co-written by: Bob Fosse

Broadway legend Fosse tells his own story as dancer-director-choreographer-horndog with Scheider at his peak as Fosse alter ego Joe Gideon, a talent energized by booze, pills, screwing, and constant threats (Lange plays the angel of death) from his overtaxed heart. Fosse died shortly after the film wrapped, giving an already surreal musical an added jolt. The excellent DVD transfer makes this underrated film ripe for rediscovery.

Hot Bonus: Scheider's commentary is a mite self-congratulatory, but the clips of Fosse himself at work on the film are a priceless eight minutes.

Key Scene: The opening number with the dancers, set to George Benson's "On Broadway," is every thrilling thing the film of A *Chorus Line* is not.

All the King's Men (1949)

Starring: Broderick Crawford, Mercedes McCambridge, John Ireland
Directed and written by: Robert Rossen

The full-screen, black-and-white transfer of this Oscar-winning political drama, based on Robert Penn Warren's Pulitzer Prize–winning novel, is a thing of power and beauty. Crawford is dynamite as the corrupt, self-proclaimed hick of a senator, modeled on Louisiana's Huey Long, who flatters and exploits the common man and betrays his closest allies, stunningly played by Ireland and McCambridge. No wonder Sean Penn did the remake. What a role.

Hot Bonus: A trailer that brings back the era in a two-minute burst.

Key Scene: The political speech that sounds like George W. on steroids ("Now listen to me, you hicks. Yeah, you're hicks too. . . . I'm going to stay in this race. I'm on my own and I'm out for blood").

All the President's Men (1976)

Starring: Robert Redford, Dustin Hoffman, Jason Robards Jr.
Directed by: Alan Pakula

A superb transfer of a superb film about the investigation of the Watergate break-in by *Washington Post* reporters Bob Woodward (Redford, the WASP straightarrow) and Carl Bernstein (Hoffman, the Jewish noodge.) William Goldman's script cleverly moves from specific to universal truths, and Pakula directs with the same eye for reporting detail that helped Woodward and Bernstein bring down the Nixon White House. Robards as *Post* editor Ben Bradlee says a mouthful ("Nothing's riding on this except the First Amendment, freedom of the press, and maybe the future of the country").

Hot Bonus: A Watergate timeline is a big help for the uninitiated. The DVD received a big boost in 2005 when Deep Throat, the mysterious top-level snitch played by Hal Holbrook, was revealed to be then-FBI number-two man, Mark Felt.

Key Scene: The zoom-up from the reporters doing their quiet research to the Washington building they're in to the view of the nation's Capitol as a symbol of the enormity of the stakes facing Woodward and Bernstein.

Almost Famous (Untitled–The Bootleg Cut) (2000)

Starring: Billy Crudup, Kate Hudson, Patrick Fugit, Frances McDormand
Directed and written by: Cameron Crowe

Director Crowe won an Oscar for the script he based on his career as a teen journalist hitting the road with a band for *Rolling Stone* magazine. Fugit excels as the fifteen-year-old journo with an interfering mother (the brilliant McDormand) who keeps getting between the kid's attempts to win a groupie (a luminous Hudson) away from the band's lead singer (Crudup, in a role stupidly rejected by Brad Pitt). It's all happening on the bootleg, with thirty-six minutes added to the theatrical version, turning a solid movie into something harder, something that sticks.

Hot Bonus: More rock, coke, and groupies, plus a great deleted scene: Kyle Gass of Tenacious D playing a radio DJ who falls asleep on an open mike while interviewing band members, who take fun advantage of the situation.

Key Scene: The band shaking off their exhaustion on the tour bus by singing along to Elton John's "Tiny Dancer." Crowe says that most rock movies leave out how much musicians love the music. Not this movie.

Amadeus (Director's Cut) (1984)

Starring: F. Murray Abraham, Tom Hulce, Elizabeth Berridge, Jeffrey Jones
Directed by: Milos Forman

Twenty no-fat minutes have been added to the theatrical release of this Oscar winner, based on Peter Shaffer's funny and profound play about a presumed rivalry between musical prodigy Wolfgang Amadeus Mozart (Hulce, fine except for his exaggerated hyena laugh) and Antonio Salieri (Abraham, flawless), the envious, genius-free court composer to Emperor Joseph II (Jones, a delight). The film's production looks far more lush than it did on the original DVD, and the Dolby sound kicks in as never before.

Hot Bonus: An hourlong retrospective documentary on the second disc brings home details about the filming in Prague before the fall of communism. But hearing Mozart in 5.1 Dolby digital is reward enough.

Key Scene: On his deathbed, Mozart dictates his Requiem to Salieri. It is one of the screen's most successful attempts at depicting genius.

Amelie (2001)

Starring: Audrey Tautou, Mathieu Kassovitz
Directed and co-written by: Jean-Pierre Jeunet

A visual astonishment, expertly captured on disc, about a shy French waitress (the inimitable Tautou) who decides to help the good and punish the wicked, and in the process falls in love with a stranger (Kassovitz).

Hot Bonus: The two-disc set is loaded with valuable insights into Jeunet's visual style, and his use of computer-generated images and lenses that distort reality into his own magical vision of truth.

Key Scene: The quick-cut montage that illustrates Amelie's childhood from conception to adulthood is an eye-popper, especially the moment when a suicidal jumper leaps off a church tower and kills a principal character.

American Beauty (Special Edition) (1999)

Starring: Kevin Spacey, Annette Bening, Wes Bentley, Mena Suvari
Directed by: Sam Mendes

This Academy Award winner is a comedy of shocking gravity about a failed marriage between an unemployed exec (Spacey at the top of his game) and his adulterous wife (Bening). Director Mendes and screenwriter Alan Ball (*Six Feet Under*) made Oscar-winning debuts playing with stylistic quirks (Spacey narrates from the grave) that try to make the film work as farce, tragedy, thriller, fantasy, sitcom, skin flick, and moral fable. It does. Even better, the DVD transfer captures every delicate, risky move.

Hot Bonus: The talk between Mendes and the film's late cinematographer Conrad Hall cuts to the heart of the film's unique look, from the rose petals that fall on the naked body of Spacey's cheerleader fantasy (Suvari) to the videos shot by the boy drug pusher (Wes Bentley) next door.

Key Scene: The video the boy shoots of a plastic bag being whipped around by the wind in an empty parking lot. "This bag was, like, dancing with me," he says. "And that's the day I knew there was this entire life behind things." It's the life behind things that *American Beauty* catches as Mendes whips the audience around from humor to horror to something poetic and humane.

American Friend, The (1977)

Starring: Dennis Hopper, Bruno Ganz, Nicholas Ray, Sam Fuller
Directed and co-written by: Wim Wenders

For a film made decades ago, the transfer to DVD is altogether stunning. Working from the Patricia Highsmith novel, *Ripley's Game* (remade in 2002), director Wenders (*Wings of Desire*) pits American Tom Ripley (Hopper) against the German art restorer (Ganz) he sets up for the kill.

Hot Bonus: Compelling commentary from Hopper and Ganz, who describes acting with two great American directors, Ray (*Rebel without a Cause*) and Fuller (*The Big Red One*), cast as villains.

Key Scene: The murder on the train. Your nails will be chewed.

American Graffiti (1973)

Starring: Ron Howard, Cindy Williams, Richard Dreyfuss, Candy Clark
Directed and co-written by: George Lucas

Before *Star Wars* infected him with event-movie disease, Lucas, then twenty-eight, came up with this memorably modest take on California hot-rodders and teen queens facing their high school graduation over one defining night in 1962. The look of the movie, as the gang hangs around the neon-lighted Mel's Drive-In, is primitive as befits its low budget, and Lucas has admirably resisted spiffing it up. And hearing those period tunes, from "Sixteen Candles" to "The Book of Love," hasn't lost any of its pleasure.

Hot Bonus: Lucas talking about his own life as inspiration for the film.

Key Scene: The girl in the white Thunderbird, played by the then-unknown Suzanne Somers, mouthing "I love you" to a thrilled Dreyfuss.

American History X (1998)

Starring: Edward Norton, Edward Furlong
Directed by: Tony Kaye

Norton's Oscar-nominated performance as a neo-Nazi in Venice, California, who goes to prison, gets straightened out, and tries to reform his younger brother (Furlong) is the motor that makes this film a powerhouse. Director Kaye alternates between scenes in color and black-and-white that maintain their excitement on the disc.

Hot Bonus: Three deleted scenes, but the DVD would have benefited from a commentary track in which Kaye explained how the studio took the film away from him and released its own version.

Key Scene: The arrest of Norton, his hands folded behind his head and a gleam of pure defiant evil in his eyes that, once seen, cannot be forgotten.

American Pie (Unrated: Collector's Edition) (1999)

Starring: Jason Biggs, Chris Klein, Thomas Ian Nicholas, Eddie Kaye Thomas, Seann William Scott, Shannon Elizabeth, Alyson Hannigan, Tara Reid

Directed by: Paul Weitz

Accept no R-rated substitutes or the two limp sequels directed by hacks. Weitz gives this teen sex farce about four high school seniors who vow to lose their virginity before graduation a sense of humor and, get this, humanity. You won't find that in *American Pie 2* or *American Wedding*.

Hot Bonus: Outtakes on the unrated version lift the gross level and the laughs. And Biggs seems more interested than ever in having carnal knowledge of his mom's apple pie. As his dad, the invaluable Eugene Levy delivers an expression of shock worthy of a freeze frame.

Key Scene: Anything Scott does as the obnoxious Stifler is a keeper. But it's the erotic union of Thomas and Stifler's mom (Jennifer Coolidge at her wicked, winking best) that burns in the memory.

American Psycho (Unrated) (2000)

Starring: Christian Bale, Willem Dafoe, Reese Witherspoon, Chloë Sevigny
Directed by: Mary Harron

The sex and gore of Bret Easton Ellis's 1991 novel has been infused with satire by director Harron as she tells the story of Patrick Bateman (a buff and perversely brilliant Bale), a Wall Street trader with a fiancée (Witherspoon) and disturbingly violent urges that put a detective (Dafoe) on his tail. It's yuppie materialism, not flesh, that feels the edge of Harron's blade.

Hot Bonus: Bale's comments on his role seem defensive. The real bonus here is the shimmering evocation of Reagan-era excess on the transfer.

Key Scene: Not the grisly stuff, like the head in the fridge. It's Bateman and his fellow traders (killers all) comparing business cards with an erotic urgency no woman could engender.

American Splendor (2003)

Starring: Paul Giamatti, Hope Davis, Judah Friedlander

Directed and written by: Shari Springer Berman and Robert Pulcini

The story of underground comic-book writer and legendary curmudgeon Harvey Pekar is the framework for a remarkably funny, touching, and innovative film in which the reliably amazing Giamatti plays Pekar interacting with the man himself and the comics he writes about his drudgery as a clerk in a Cleveland, Ohio, veterans hospital. Davis is equally good playing his third wife Joyce, who shares his life and his ramshackle house crammed with jazz LPs.

Hot Bonus: Pekar contributes a wryly funny twelve-page comic book entitled "My Movie Year," a parallel to "My Cancer Year," the comic book he wrote after being diagnosed with lymphoma in 1990.

Key Scene: A conversation about jelly beans between Giamatti and Friedlander, as Pekar's ultimate nerd friend Toby, that is picked up by the real Pekar and the real Toby. Confusing? Nah. It works like a charm. The same goes for the movie.

American Werewolf in London, An (Collector's Edition) (1981)

Starring: Griffin Dunne, David Naughton, Jenny Agutter

Directed and written by: John Landis

A hip horror flick from *Animal House* director Landis gets the class-A transfer it deserves. Dunne and Naughton are American students who encounter a werewolf on the British moors. Dunne finds himself undead and looking progressively ghoulish, while Naughton is hospitalized with a bite. Landis maintains the delicate balance between horror and humor, and the soundtrack is laced with amusingly apt tunes, such as "Blue Moon," "Moondance," and "Bad Moon Rising."

Hot Bonus: An interview with makeup artist Rick Baker, whose werewolf creation still has bite after all these years.

Key Scene: The first meeting between men and monster. It's scary and real enough to advise viewing the DVD before the next full moon.

Anatomy of a Murder (1959)

Starring: James Stewart, Lee Remick, Ben Gazzara, Joseph Welch

Directed by: Otto Preminger

You won't find many films, shot in black-and-white with mono sound, that hit the eye and ear as sharply as this still-exciting courtroom drama. Stewart gives one of his best performances as a Michigan lawyer defending a soldier (Gazzara) on trial for killing a man he says raped his sluttish wife (a spectacular Remick). One of the kicks of DVD is being able to rediscover a director like Preminger, a real wild man, here at his peak.

Hot Bonus: Duke Ellington's jazz score is one of the film's major virtues, and a series of publicity photos set to his music makes for a sublime extra.

Key Scene: Non-actor Welch—a no-bull lawyer at the Joe McCarthy hearings—plays the Judge with an irresistibly sly wit, much in evidence when he holds up pink panties entered as evidence in the case.

Anchorman: The Legend of Ron Burgundy Giftset (Unrated Edition and Wake Up, Ron Burgundy) (2004)

Starring: Will Ferrell, Christina Applegate, Steve Carell, Paul Rudd

Directed by: Adam McKay

Ferrell in a two-disc giftset, loaded with extras, how do you resist that? You don't. As Ron Burgundy, the blow-dried idiot who reigns as the polyester prince of a local news station in San Diego, Ferrell is pure comic mischief. It's the 1970s, and a plucky female reporter (Appelgate) is eying Ron's anchor perch. This is a man who tells her that San Diego is a German term for a whale's vagina. The jokes are hit and miss, but Ferrell is the go-to guy if you want to laugh yourself silly.

Hot Bonus: Lots of extras, but only the outtakes count. The half hour of deleted scenes collected on disc two is presented as a second movie (*Wake Up, Ron Burgundy*), and it's as funny as anything in the first one.

Key Scene: Ron and his macho news team doing an impromptu close-harmony rendition of "Afternoon Delight."

... And God Created Woman (1956)

Starring: Brigitte Bardot, Jean-Louis Trintignant

Directed by: Roger Vadim

Back in the 1950s, France had its own Marilyn Monroe, the sex kitten Bardot. Her director husband Vadim showed her off (literally) to the world in this international hit, which starts with Bardot nude sunbathing in St. Tropez and moves on from there. Plot? There's nothing more than excuse after excuse for BB to drive men mad. In this dazzling, widescreen digital transfer from the usually highbrow Criterion Collection, she does it again.

Hot Bonus: A restoration demonstration shows how years of faded prints have been sweated over to bring Bardot back to her resplendent glory.

Key Scene: The Bardot mambo, in an open shirt—and oh those bongos!

Angel Heart (Special Edition) (1987)

Starring: Mickey Rourke, Robert De Niro, Lisa Bonet

Directed by: Alan Parker

The voodoo really gets to you in this eye-popping transfer of a film that faced censorship problems for a sex scene between

Rourke and Bonet that involved bodily fluids and dripping chicken blood. It's all here uncut. And so is the story of a New York detective (Rourke) hired by a mystery man (De Niro) to find a client who reneged on his contract. The case takes Rourke to New Orleans, where this devilish thriller takes seductive hold.

Hot Bonus: There's a ton of stuff on voodoo, but hearing Rourke vainly attempt a comprehensible commentary is its own comic opera.

Key Scene: The fun and fright of watching De Niro, as Louis Cyphre (hint, hint), finally revealing who the hell he is.

Angels in America (2003)

Starring: Al Pacino, Meryl Streep, Mary-Louise Parker, Jeffrey Wright

Directed by: Mike Nichols

Officially, it's not really a movie since this landmark film version of Tony Kushner's Pulitzer (and every other prize)–winning play was made for HBO. But this is my book, and I can break a few rules. Director Nichols equals his best work, and that includes *The Graduate, Who's Afraid of Virginia Woolf,* and *Closer,* in bringing Kushner's stage work about the plague of AIDS in the Reagan era to vibrant cinematic life. Pacino, as lawyer Roy Cohn, and Streep, in four roles including a male rabbi, give career performances. This immaculately produced DVD (on two discs) is time-capsule worthy.

Hot Bonus: Having all 352 uncut minutes is bonus enough.

Key Scene: Pacino, as the dying Cohn, being visited by Streep, as the ghost of executed spy Ethel Rosenberg, is gallows humor with a lasting sting.

Annie Hall (1977)

Starring: Woody Allen, Diane Keaton, Tony Roberts, Christopher Walken

Directed and co-written by: Woody Allen

Have movies ever produced a funnier or more bittersweet romantic comedy? None that I know of. The Woodman's signature film managed to beat *Star Wars* for the Best Picture Oscar. Out of the thinnest premise—a love that doesn't pan out between

Jewish gag writer Alvy Singer (Allen) and WASP princess Annie Hall (Keaton at her la-di-da pinnacle)—Allen crafted a film in which even the throwaway jokes defined character. "You're what Grammy Hall would call a real Jew," Annie tells Alvy, who burns silently.

Hot Bonus: Woody doesn't do extras, but the crisp transfer on the MGM disc, after years of bad TV prints, is all you could ask for.

Key Scene: Alvy meeting Annie's family, including her suicidal brother (a priceless Walken) and the Grammy who sees him as a rabbi. The great thing about Annie Hall on DVD is that every scene is so nice to come home to.

Any Given Sunday (Director's Cut) (1999)

Starring: Al Pacino, Jamie Foxx, Cameron Diaz

Directed by: Oliver Stone

A pulverizing look at pro football—a coach (Pacino at full throttle) butts heads with a team owner (Diaz, surprisingly strong) and an egomaniacal quarterback (Foxx, best in show)—that makes up for what it lacks in subtlety by Stone's down-and-dirty action on the field. You can hear the bones crunching on this DVD. Stone removed some scenes that dragged the pace and added about five minutes of adrenaline. This is the cut you want.

Hot Bonus: Stone's commentary on how he accomplished the football scenes is pungent and informative, and he takes a few gratuitous slaps at film critics that are very entertaining.

Key Scene: Pacino psyching up himself and his team by constantly running Stanley Kubrick's slave-uprising epic *Spartacus* on a giant TV screen. The comparison of football and gladiatorial battle actually works.

Apartment, The (1960)

Starring: Jack Lemmon, Shirley MacLaine, Fred MacMurray

Directed and co-written by: Billy Wilder

"Billy Wilder grew a rose in a garbage pail," Lemmon said about this tale of love that blooms in the moral vacuum of corporate America. Good call. Lemmon, the Tom Hanks of his day, found his signature role in this Best Picture Oscar–winner about C. C. Baxter, a junior exec who sucks up by loaning his apartment to horndog bosses looking for a place to take their pickups for a night. Wilder, the master cynic, also proved himself a master romantic as Baxter falls for Fran Kubelik (MacLaine, never better), an elevator operator driven to a suicide try when her married boss (MacMurray is smarmy perfection) won't leave his wife.

Hot Bonus: Watching the original trailer is a kick, but the sharp widescreen transfer of this black-and-white classic is a gift.

Key Scene: The final card game when Lemmon declares his love and MacLaine makes her blunt line ("Shut up and deal") resonate with bliss.

Apocalypse Now Redux (2001)

Starring: Martin Sheen, Marlon Brando, Robert Duvall

Directed and co-written by: Francis Ford Coppola

Coppola and editor Walter Murch have remixed and digitally remastered their Vietnam epic—one for the ages when it comes to the moral battles of war—from original raw footage and restored forty-nine minutes. This is the untamed *Apocalypse Now* that Coppola envisioned in 1979 before mental pressures made him fear he had created something too long, too weird, and too morally demanding for the masses. The film is still chaos, and as such it is an apt reflection of the war it depicts. As Captain Willard (Sheen) begins his trip up river to Cambodia to "terminate with extreme prejudice" the mad renegade Colonel Kurtz (Brando), the film moves with less velocity but with a greater sense of purpose. From the opening—a jungle burning with napalm and the Doors playing "The End"—to a climax of hallucinatory devastation, this is a masterwork that also stands as a reference for the miracles that a DVD can accomplish in rendering superb sound and image.

Hot Bonus: What isn't? There's more of the peerless Duvall as the surf-lovin', bomb-droppin' Lieutenant Colonel Kilgore ("I love the smell of napalm in the morning"). And Brando's Kurtz, once a dead weight of clanking metaphor ("The Horror! The Horror!"), resonates more fully in scenes that show him reading *Time* magazine aloud and mocking American intelligence operations in the age of Nixon. The longest addition involves the French plantation where Willard and his men stop for a burial. The scene was cut originally because these French sophisticates, who dress formally for dinner in the jungle, were thought to stop the movie cold. Hardly. The family patriarch (Christian Marquand) explains his claim on the country in a monologue that burns with the fury

and folly of imperialism. Coppola has reached the finish line of his film at last and crafted one of the greatest DVDs of all time. It smells like victory.

Key Scene: Kilgore's helicopter attack on a village, set to the rumble of Wagner's "Ride of the Valkyries," is pow and profundity unleashed.

Apollo 13 (Anniversary Edition) (1995)

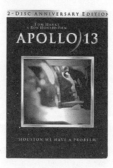

Starring: Tom Hanks, Kevin Bacon, Gary Sinise, Ed Harris

Directed by: Ron Howard

A decade after its release, Ron Howard's heartfelt, hold-your-breath film about a failed 1970 NASA moon shot received the first-class DVD treatment it deserves. With empathetic Hanks as head astronaut Jim Lovell, Paxton as Fred Haise, and Bacon as Jack Swigert—a last-minute replacement for an ailing Ken Mattingly (Gary Sinise)—the film takes a refreshingly no-bull approach to what happens when an oxygen tank explodes and the famous call is made: "Houston, we have a problem."

Hot Bonus: The archival footage of the real mission.

Key Scene: Intersecting the disaster in space with Harris, in the mission control room, trying to bring the men home and famously telling his crew: "Failure is not an option."

Army of Darkness (Boomstick Edition) (1993)

Starring: Bruce Campbell, Embeth Davidtz, Marcus Gilbert

Directed and co-written by: Sam Raimi

The third part in Raimi's *Evil Dead* trilogy gets the full treatment in this director's cut of the film about Ash (Campbell, square-jawed and hiply hilarious), a hardware-store drudge who gets transported back to King Arthur's fourteenth-century court along with a trusty chainsaw and his '73 Oldsmobile. It's a comic-horror version of Mark Twain's *Connecticut Yankee*, and this DVD adds fifteen minutes of mayhem—rough stuff from the director who treads more gently with the *Spider-man* series.

Hot Bonus: The original ending is presented separately with scrappy commentary from Raimi and Campbell.

Key Scene: The battle with the skeletons—no contest.

As Good As It Gets (1997)

Starring: Jack Nicholson, Helen Hunt, Greg Kinnear

Directed and co-written by: James L. Brooks

The Oscar-winning performances of Nicholson and Hunt—he as an obsessive-compulsive novelist with a mean streak, she as a waitress who falls for him against all her better instincts—are alone worth owning this emotionally volatile comedy. But the ability you have on disc to repeat a scene makes the accomplishment of Brooks's script even more impressive.

Hot Bonus: Nicholson, Hunt, and Kinnear, as a gay neighbor, join Brooks in a free-for-all commentary that digs deeper than you might think into director Brooks's reason for having his actors do take after take.

Key Scene: Hunt taking on Nicholson at her restaurant for making the wrong remark about her sick son. Her rage is a beautiful thing, and his stricken visage is suitable for framing.

Asphalt Jungle, The (1950)

Starring: Sterling Hayden, Louis Calhern, Sam Jaffe, Marilyn Monroe

Directed by: John Huston

One of the great crime films—from the W. R. Burnett novel about a jewel heist gone wrong—gets a crisp DVD transfer that makes it seem like new. Huston's nail-tough direction has aged like good whiskey. And oh, those actors: Jaffe as the mastermind who declares that "crime is a left-handed form of human behavior," Hayden as the hardass who wants his own horse ranch, and Calhern as the crooked lawyer with a thing for blondes, one of them being Monroe in a knockout cameo.

Hot Bonus: A superb archival interview in which Huston intros the film.

Key Scene: The safecracking can still make your palms sweat.

Assault on Precinct 13 (New Special Edition) (1976)

Starring: Austin Stoker, Darwin Joston, Laurie Zimmer

Directed by: John Carpenter

The starry, spiffed-up 2005 remake, with Ethan Hawke and Laurence Fishburne, defeats the purpose of Carpenter's cheapie original—a primitive, no-stars, seat-of-the-pants suspense thriller in which a few cops and a policewoman must join with two death-row inmates to protect an abandoned Los Angeles precinct from attack by a faceless street gang. The film is a prime example of how much tension can be generated on a low budget. That's why it's still a cult classic.

Hot Bonus: Carpenter's commentary is astute and funny, especially when he talks about the film as a modern take on the 1959 Howard Hawks western *Rio Bravo* with John Wayne and Dean Martin.

Key Scene: The infamous ice-cream killing, in which a gang sniper takes out a little girl just as she complains to her daddy that the ice-cream man gave her the wrong flavor: "I wanted vanilla twist," she says. Then boom. The remake never approaches anything as assaultive to moral values.

At Close Range (1986)

Starring: Sean Penn, Christopher Walken

Directed by: James Foley

This movie about an abandoned son (Penn) who gets a visit from his gangster father (a seductively dangerous Walken) deserves more than the bare-bones packaging it gets here. But be grateful it's here at all. And stick with it as Penn, whose character peroxides his hair and nibbles his toenails, gets sucked into the family business by his demon of a daddy.

Hot Bonus: The emergence of the film from its murky, badly cropped and poorly edited appearances on late-night TV.

Key Scene: Penn, watching in horror, as Walken casually drowns a harmless informer in a swamp. Raising a silencing finger to his grinning mouth, Walken asks for his son's complicity in evil. It's an image that ranks with the most chilling in film memory.

Atlantic City (1980)

Starring: Burt Lancaster, Susan Sarandon, Robert Joy

Directed by: Louis Malle

The DVD captures the sepia-toned haze through which director Malle views this gambling city as it rises from the ashes of ruin. Lancaster crowned a distinguished career as an aging numbers runner who gets one last shot at a jackpot, not to mention romance with Sarandon, playing a young oyster bar waitress whose drug-dealer husband (Joy) is murdered by the mob, freeing her and Lancaster to seize his stash and their chance. John Guare's script is a model of characterization in a film that stands with the best of its decade.

Hot Bonus: The scene selection menu that lets you go right to the moment when Sarandon stands naked in her window.

Key Scene: Lancaster, on the boardwalk, telling Joy about the good old days of rackets, whoring, and guns. "The Atlantic Ocean was something then," he says, staring wistfully out to sea and his past. Great stuff.

Austin Powers: International Man of Mystery (Special Edition) (1997)

Starring: Mike Myers, Elizabeth Hurley, Seth Green
Directed by: Jay Roach

Half the jokes don't work, but the ones that do—groovy, baby! And the bright look and set design of this raunchy farce—the first of the trilogy about a cryogenically frozen sixties Brit spy, Austin Powers (Myers), thawed out in the present to face the villainous Dr. Evil (also Myers, and doubly hilarious)—can make your eyes pop.

Hot Bonus: Myers and director Roach discuss their influences from James Bond to the films of Richard Lester (*A Hard Day's Night*).

Key Scene: Myers and sexpot Hurley in a nude scene that manages to hide all the naughty bits and plays twice as naughty for doing so. Oh, behave!

Austin Powers: The Spy Who Shagged Me (Special Edition) (1999)

Starring: Mike Myers, Heather Graham
Directed by: Jay Roach

Funnier than the first and just as colorful with Dr. Evil going back to the sixties to steal Austin's mojo. Myers, brilliant in both roles, adds a third character: Fat Bastard, a grotesque Scotsman who weighs a metric ton. It's, well, too much. Graham is a genuine hottie as Felicity Shagwell (a name that pays tribute to all Bond girls, especially Pussy Galore, who received her own tribute in the first *Powers* flick, which featured Alotta Fagina). Verne Troyer nails most of the laughs as Mini-Me, a pint-sized clone of Dr. Evil, who worries: "Is he giving off a creepy Oompa Loompa vibe?"

Hot Bonus: Nearly twenty minutes of deleted scenes, which play just as fast and loose as those they left in the movie.

Key Scene: Dr. Evil going on *The Jerry Springer Show* to work out father issues with his teen son Scott (the terrific Seth Green).

Austin Powers in Goldmember (Special Edition) (2002)

Starring: Mike Myers, Beyoncé Knowles, Michael Caine
Directed by: Jay Roach

The third and splashiest chapter in the series, meaning huge, elaborate, and overproduced, as in the opening segment with cameos from Tom Cruise, Gwyneth Paltrow, and Steven Spielberg. No matter. Myers has created an immortal screen character in the toothy Austin, who must rescue his swinger dad (Caine in top form) from Goldmember (also Myers), a Dutch villain who eats the skin that flakes off his body. Less icky is Foxxy Cleopatra, the shagadelic agent played with Pam Grier sass by Knowles.

Hot Bonus: The deleted scenes are delicious, none more so than Caine singing the theme from *Alfie*, the 1966 film that made him a star.

Key Scene: Austin hitting on two Japanese babes, Fook Mi and Fook Yu, reps the kind of small, gross, infantile joke that makes the movie such fun.

Aviator, The (Two-Disc Special Edition) (2004)

Starring: Leonardo DiCaprio, Cate Blanchett, Alec Baldwin, Alan Alda
Directed by: Martin Scorsese

Scorsese's Oscar movie is a big, juicy, high-flying epic, gorgeously rendered on DVD. The nearly three-hour film spins through the early life (1927–47) of Texas tycoon Howard Hughes (a turbocharged DiCaprio), the hotshot pilot, aviation pioneer, junior movie mogul, and boob-crazed seducer whose obsessive-compulsive disorders left him a germaphobic hermit, holed up naked with vials of his own urine. What you don't get in *The Aviator* is a Scorsese film cut from his own dark obsessions like *Raging Bull*, *Taxi Driver*, and *GoodFellas*. But the scenes of Hughes directing his aerial spectacle *Hell's Angels* or hooking up with the young, fiery Katharine Hepburn (a superb Blanchett) or taking on Pan Am's chief (Baldwin) and his Senate flunky (sleazed to perfection by Alda) help Scorsese make magic.

Hot Bonus: Scorsese talks, and since he's our greatest living director, that is always worth a careful listen.

Key Scene: The film's scary, surreal, thrilling high comes with Hughes's 1946 test flight of the XF-11, which ends with him crashing in Beverly Hills and sustaining injuries that worsen his mental disorders. When a rescue crew asks him who he is, he replies, "I'm the aviator."

Baadasssss! (2003)

Starring: Mario Van Peebles, Khleo Thomas, Ossie Davis
Directed by: Mario Van Peebles

Back in 1971, Melvin Van Peebles wrote, produced, directed, and starred in *Sweet Sweetback's Baadasssss Song* (also available on DVD), an X-rated cheapie that hit box-office pay dirt by capturing the rage African American audiences felt toward the white establishment. In *Baadasssss*, Melvin's son, Mario Van Peebles (*Ali, Panther*), reconstructs the making of that seminal film by directing, co-writing and starring—quite credibly—as Melvin in *Baadasssss!* The son doesn't flinch from his dad's faults, right down to Melvin casting a thirteen-year-old Mario (Thomas) as a boy getting his first taste of sex in a whorehouse. The film is technically raw, but the sight of Van Peebles playing his father at a potent moment in movie history exerts a potent fascination.

Hot Bonus: A featurette on "The Birth of Black Cinema" is just the background you need before watching the film.

Key Scene: Mario, playing his father, directing the barely pubescent young actor playing him to do a sex scene on camera.

Babe (Special Edition) (1995)

Starring: James Cromwell, Magda Szubanski
Directed by: Chris Noonan

The little pig movie that could—it was Oscar nominated as Best Picture and won the big prize from the snooty National Society of Film Critics—comes to DVD with all its storybook charm captured in widescreen. Babe, the Australian pig who wants to be a sheepdog, goes to live with Farmer Hoggett (the delightful Cromwell) and his wife (Szubanski) and has adventures with animals, real and computer-generated. The 1998 sequel, *Babe: Pig in the City*, lost the charm—so treasure this one.

Hot Bonus: The "making of" feature really shows how animals and animatronics can be blended seamlessly.

Key Scene: Babe's big moment at the sheep-herding contest and the love and pride Farmer Hoggett puts into the throwaway line: "That'll do, pig."

Backbeat (Special Edition) (1994)

Starring: Stephen Dorff, Ian Hart, Sheryl Lee, Gary Bakewell
Directed by: Iain Softley

Get back to a time when the Beatles were unknown, untamed rude boys of barely legal age, a time when the Brit band was chasing fame in the grimy basement clubs of Hamburg, Germany. Their talents were raw; ditto their tempers. Paul McCartney (Bakewell) can't figure why John Lennon (Hart) wants no-talent Stu Sutcliffe (Dorff) playing bass for the Beatles. Lennon's rage intensifies when Sutcliffe starts shagging Astrid Kirchherr (Sheryl Lee), an arty German photographer who encourages Lennon's best mate to quit the band for a serious career as a painter. This potent DVD transfer makes you believe you really are there, back in the early 1960s, when the lads left Liverpool to play the rathskellers.

Hot Bonus: A provocative conversation with Kirchherr (her photos of the Beatles are justly famous) that fills in a few blanks left by the film.

Key Scene: The music is the film's gift. Instead of tapping into old Beatles records, producer Don Was gathers a onetime-only band to deliver the goods while the actors go deftly through the motions. You're hearing drummer Dave Grohl, bassist Mike Mills, and guitarists Thurston Moore and Don Fleming. On vocals, it's Dave Pirner for McCartney and Greg Dulli for Lennon. The early Beatles sound isn't reproduced; it's reimagined.

Back to School (1986)

Starring: Rodney Dangerfield, Sally Kellerman, Keith Gordon
Directed by: Alan Metter

Any movie that offers the late, great Dangerfield in a lead role gets respect in my book. The excuse of a plot casts the comic as a millionaire who enrolls in college to discourage his son (Gordon) from dropping out. Rodney finds love—with lit prof Kellerman—and tons of one-liners. About his conceited ex-wife: "When we make love, she calls out her own name."

Hot Bonus: A booklet on Dangerfield is a real keeper.

Key Scene: Dangerfield getting so hot-under-the-collar hearing Kellerman's reading of Molly's erotic soliloquy from James Joyce's *Ulysses* that right there in class he yells out, "Yes! Yes! Yes!"

Back to the Future: The Complete Trilogy (1985, 1989, 1990)

Starring: Michael J. Fox, Christopher Lloyd, Lea Thompson, Crispin Glover

Directed by: Robert Zemeckis

The wildly imaginative fantasy and its two sequels make up a definitive, extra-loaded DVD package. Fox gives a career performance as Marty McFly, an eighties teen zapped back to the fifties in a time machine created from a DeLorean by a mad scientist (Lloyd). There the unborn Marty finds his teen dad (Glover, an eccentric joy) and mom (Thompson, a flirty pleasure). *Part II*, set in 2015, and *Part III*, set in the Old West of 1885, boast the technical wizardry Zemeckis brings to the party, but the trilogy's heart is in *Part I*.

Hot Bonus: Zemeckis and co-writer Bob Gale talk you through the highs and lows of all three films.

Key Scene:

Part I: Marty turning his dad (the scene-stealing Glover, much missed in the sequels) from nerd to Mr. Confident.

Part II: The flying skateboard chase.

Part III: Marty, adopting the name Clint Eastwood, running away from a gunfight, only to hear the crowd roar: "Clint Eastwood is the biggest, yellow-bellied coward in the West."

Bad Day at Black Rock (1955)

Starring: Spencer Tracy, Robert Ryan, Lee Marvin, Ernest Borgnine

Directed by: John Sturges

It's taken forever to get Sturges's neglected masterpiece to DVD. It's worth the wait. Tracy gives a nail-tough performance as a stranger in a black suit who comes to a western town to unbury a dirty secret and gets threatened by the nasty likes of Borgnine, Ryan, and Marvin. "You look like you need a hand," says Marvin to the one-armed Tracy. The film's widescreen vistas (idioti-

cally cropped on TV versions) do justice to a pungent mystery.

Hot Bonus: A piece on Sturges that makes you want to see more of his work.

Key Scene: Tracy's face-off with Borgnine: "You're not only wrong, you're wrong at the top of your voice."

Bad Education (2004)

Starring: Gael García Bernal, Fele Martínez, Javier Cámara

Directed by: Pedro Almodóvar

This story of two priest-abused boys who become lost men (Bernal and Martínez) is Almodóvar's most personal film to date—raw with his own feelings about sex, sin, the Catholic Church, and the healing power of cinema. The film hides its complex structure under the shimmering surface of a decadent film noir—each nuance caught on the DVD transfer. Bernal gives a juicy, jolting performance as the prime object of the priest's abuse, a transvestite working clubs with his pal (the hilarious Cámara) and blackmailing the priest for his sins. He is the corrupt soul of a mesmeric movie that offers temptations impossible to resist.

Hot Bonus: Almodóvar speaks.

Key Scene: The pubescent boys go to a movie house and jerk each other off while watching Spanish sex icon Sarita Montiel. That's Almodóvar to a T: hand on crotch, eyes on a distant dream.

Bad Lieutenant (1992)

Starring: Harvey Keitel, Frankie Thorn

Directed by: Abel Ferrara

The ultimate collaboration between wild men Keitel and Ferrara comes to DVD, as it must, in the NC-17 version, not the R-rated wussy cut shown in theaters. Keitel amazes as the Big Apple cop and lapsed Catholic who drinks, drugs, and whores like he's out to prove God's nonexistence. It's only when he meets a nun (Thorn) who forgives the men who brutally raped her that he begins to construct a moral vision of an immoral world.

Hot Bonus: Read the profile on Ferrara, and treat yourself to more of his films. This is a tormented talent to whom attention must be paid.

Key Scene: Keitel stopping two women for a driving infraction—a brutally erotic interrogation that turns into a vision of hell in miniature.

Bad Santa (Unrated Widescreen Edition) (2003)

Starring: Billy Bob Thornton, Bernie Mac, Tony Cox, Lauren Graham
Directed by: Terry Zwigoff

If you've had it with feel-good holiday sludge, hook up with the combustibly nasty *Bad Santa*, especially now that its nastiness has been upped by five minutes of badder footage for the DVD, which could become a Christmas perennial for Scrooges of all ages. Thornton is sinfully funny as the booze-swilling, hooker-screwing department-store Santa who hates the product-whoring "little shits" who sit on his lap. Why does he do it? He and his elf partner (Cox) rob the malls every year. Their new target is a store run by a prissy manager (the late John Ritter) and a hardass detective (Mac, hilarious just eating an orange). But then Santa meets a fat kid (Brett Kelly) and a sexy barkeep (Graham, pissing on her goody *Gilmore Girls* image), and the script starts throwing softballs. Until then, Thornton and director Zwigoff deck the halls with comic toxicity.

Hot Bonus: What—the extra five minutes isn't enough?

Key Scene: Thornton's Santa raging like a demon when a kid dares to interrupt his meal.

Badlands (1973)

Starring: Martin Sheen, Sissy Spacek
Directed by: Terrence Malick

One of the great American cult films gets the keen-eyed treatment it deserves on DVD. Rhodes scholar Malick was twenty-nine when he made his striking directorial debut with this feature about a young couple—Kit (Sheen), twenty-five, and Holly (Spacek), fifteen—who go on a killing spree in the Midwest. Inspired by the 1958 true story of Charles Starkweather and Caril Fugate, the film finds its true subject in an affectless, celebrity-driven society where Holly devours movie magazines and Kit fancies himself the new James Dean. Sheen and Spacek have never been better.

Hot Bonus: The disc also presents the widescreen film in a full-screen format that adds rather than distracts from the story's impact.

Key Scene: Kit systematically executes a basketball with Holly as witness.

Bananas (1971)

Starring: Woody Allen, Louise Lasser
Directed and co-written by: Woody Allen

One of Allen's throwaway early comedies, and twice as precious for that. The Woodman stars as Fielding Mellish, a Manhattan neurotic who gets involved in the politics of a banana republic in order to get in the pants of an activist (Lasser, then Mrs. Allen). The widescreen transfer looks terrific.

Hot Bonus: Look for Sylvester Stallone, who shows up briefly as a hood.

Key Scene: My favorite is when shy Fielding tries to avoid embarrassment by bringing a skin magazine to the register sandwiched between two respectable publications. No deal. The counterman yells to the back of the store: "How much is *Multiple Orgasms?*" Woody's red face is perfect.

Band of Outsiders (1964)

Starring: Anna Karina, Sami Frey, Claude Brasseur
Directed by: Jean-Luc Godard

Criterion does a standout job of bringing Godard's full-screen, black-and-white take on American pop culture, especially gangster films, to DVD. The plot, about two criminals (Frey and Brasseur) who come on to a girl (Karina) they meet at an English-language class and plot with her to steal money from the apartment where she lives, is just a starting point for Godard to trip out in the style of the French New Wave on the possibilities of cinema.

Hot Bonus: A fascinating interview with Karina, who was married to Godard and starred in seven of his films as muse and object of exploitation.

Key Scene: The romantic trio taking a nine-second run through the Louvre.

Band Wagon, The (Two-Disc Special Edition) (1953)

Starring: Fred Astaire, Cyd Charisse, Jack Buchanan
Directed by: Vincente Minnelli

Arguably the greatest movie musical after *Singin' in the Rain*, this MGM beauty is a glorious DVD package. The transfer does full justice to the vocal magic and dancing genius of Astaire, playing a fading film star out to conquer Broadway with the help of an avant-garde director (Buchanan). Leggy Charisse partners with Astaire for a magical "Dancing in the Dark." And director Minnelli, with the help of a perfect score by Howard Dietz and Arthur Schwartz, shows how a musical should be done. That's entertainment.

Hot Bonus: The director's daughter, Liza Minnelli, offers heartfelt recollections from the set. She was six at the time.

Key Scene: Astaire and Buchanan, dressed to the nines and softshoeing to "I Guess I'll Have to Change My Plan," define screen elegance.

Barbarella (1968)

Starring: Jane Fonda, John Phillip Law, Milo O'Shea
Directed by: Roger Vadim

Eye-popping colors and set design—and, oh yeah, a mostly naked Fonda—distinguish the DVD transfer of this sci-fi fantasy about a forty-first-century space babe who mixes it up with an angel (Law) and various villains and creatures.

Hot Bonus: The French track, which lets you see how well Fonda—married to Vadim at the time—spoke the language of love.

Key Scene: No contest. It's Fonda's slo-mo strip over the opening credits to the film's "Barbarella psychedela" title song.

Barry Lyndon (1975)

Starring: Ryan O'Neal, Marisa Berenson, Patrick Magee
Directed by: Stanley Kubrick

If looks were everything, Kubrick's version of Thackeray's novel about a poor eighteenth-century Irish laddieboy (O'Neal) trying to crash the British nobility would be one of the greatest films of all time. But at 183 minutes, the film drags. No matter. The sheer size, scope, and beauty of the production—it's all there on DVD—puts complaints to rest.

Hot Bonus: The scene access menu on your DVD player will never come in handier than it does here, allowing you skip the dull spots and enjoy the high points of John Alcott's spectacular camerawork.

Key Scene: The sumptuous dinner, lit only by candles.

Barton Fink (1991)

Starring: John Turturro, John Goodman, Michael Lerner
Directed by: Joel Coen

Wrapped in plain paper and no bigger than a typically swelled Hollywood head, the box looks ordinary. It's not. This is a movie from the Coen brothers, who do not traffic in the mundane. The box figures in the climax of the partly hilarious, partly horrific, totally mesmerizing film. Charlie (Goodman), a good-natured traveling salesman, has entrusted the mystery parcel to Barton Fink (Turturro), a creatively blocked screenwriter who lives next door to him in a shabby Los Angeles hotel, circa 1942. With perverse glee, the Coens never let us see what's in the box. But they drop dark hints.

Hot Bonus: Eight deleted scenes with the same atmospheric punch you find on the rest of this expert DVD transfer.

Key Scene: Barton's meeting with studio chief Jack Lipnick—a vibrant monster in the expert hands of Lerner—who gives him a week to write a wrestling picture. "We need that Barton Fink feeling," says Lipnick. He means sentimental goo, the kind that the Coens reject to create a tale that encompasses betrayal, murder, genocide, world war, and Adolf Hitler.

Basic Instinct (Collector's Edition/Unrated) (1992)

Starring: Sharon Stone, Michael Douglas
Directed by: Paul Verhoeven

This is one charged-up erotic thriller—gory, lurid, brutally funny, and without a politically correct thought in its unapologetically empty head. Director Verhoeven's cinematic wet dream delivers the goods, especially on this unrated DVD, which allows Stone, as a bisexual mystery writer, and Douglas, as a San Francisco cop who tries to nail her as an ice-pick serial killer, to go at it with naked abandon. Joe Eszterhas got a whopping $3 million for his script, which leaves you computing the monetary value of such lines as "She's got that *magna cum laude* pussy on her that done fried up your brain." The film is a must for horny pups of all ages.

Hot Bonus: Camille Paglia's defense of the film as a feminist tract must be heard to be believed.

Key Scene: Stone's police interrogation, in which she uncrosses her legs to reveal that she is NOT wearing underwear, is already infamous and a great way to test the freeze-frame button on your DVD remote.

Batman (1989)

Starring: Michael Keaton, Jack Nicholson, Kim Basinger
Directed by: Tim Burton

Time has only burnished the dark beauty of director Burton's first go at the Caped Crusader, and the DVD explores the shadows of Gotham City with striking results. Keaton is astounding, finding the humor and the pain in socialite Bruce Wayne, a schizophrenic, sexually hung-up manic depressive who gets off by climbing into bat drag with built-in muscles to take revenge on evildoers for the murder of his parents. Basinger is blonde—that's all—as Vicki Vale. But Nicholson, as the villainous Joker, is a wild, warped wonder, cackling, "Wait till they get a load of me." Indeed.

Hot Bonus: Production notes detail the history of the DC Comics character, created by Bob Kane. It's just the intro the movie deserves.

Key Scene: The final haunting glimpse of Batman standing alone.

Batman Returns (1992)

Starring: Michael Keaton, Michelle Pfeiffer, Danny DeVito
Directed by: Tim Burton

This is the second and last of the *Batman* films directed by Burton and starring Keaton as the Dark Knight. It's here that our hero meets its match, not in DeVito's Penguin—he's way overdone—but in Pfeiffer's Catwoman, the ultimate kitten with a whip. Halle Berry played the character with disastrous results in 2004, but Pfeiffer, whose lusty licking of Batman's face may arouse kinky thoughts, is no bimbo in black leather. She's a force of feline nature. To the crashing chords of Danny Elfman's score, Burton trots out every gimmick, from a Batskiboat to a Penguin umbrella-copter. But the best gimmick is neurosis: Batman and Catwoman, unable to function without dressing up their psychic wounds in fantasy, are a dysfunctional Romeo and Juliet. They lead us back into the liberating darkness of dreams.

Hot Bonus: For the full Batman experience, get *The Batman Legacy*, a four film gift set, featuring Burton's *Batman* and *Batman Returns*, plus two further sequels, chaotically directed by Joel Schumacher: *Batman Forever* (1995) with Val Kilmer in the lead and *Batman & Robin* (1997) with George Clooney in the tights and Chris O'Donnell as the Boy Wonder. But only the bat magic in the Burton films counts.

Key Scene: "How could you—I'm a woman," says Catwoman to Batman when he slugs her, meeting his apology with a kick in the groin. Meow.

Batman Begins (Two-Disc Special Edition) (2005)

Starring: Christian Bale, Katie Holmes, Liam Neeson, Michael Caine
Directed by: Christopher Nolan

This stripped-down prequel grounds the Batman legend in reality. If Tim Burton lifted the DC Comics franchise to gothic splendor and Joel Schumacher buried it in campy overkill (a Batsuit with nipples), then credit *Memento* director Nolan for resurrecting Batman as Bruce Wayne, a screwed-up rich kid. Nolan shows us what Bruce was doing before he put on his Bat drag, accessorized with lethal toys, and learned to kill like a vigilante. Bruce dumps Princeton and his virginal girl (Holmes) and heads for the Himalayas to ninja-train with Ducard (Neeson). Back in Gotham, Bruce links up with Alfred (Caine) and scientist Lucius (Morgan Freeman) to create a new identity.

The buildup is steadily engrossing. That's because Nolan keeps the emphasis on character, not gadgets. Gotham looks lived in, not art directed. And Bale, calling on our movie memories of him as a wounded child (*Empire of the Sun*) and an adult menace (*American Psycho*), created a vulnerable hero of flesh, blood, and haunted fire.

Hot Bonus: A making-of documentary and commentary from Nolan.

Key Scene: The birth of the Batmobile. Bruce asks if it comes in black and—whoosh—fans are free to go batty.

Battle of Algiers, The (1965)

Starring: Yacef Saadi, Jean Martin, Brahim Haggiag

Directed by: Gillo Pontecorvo

It looks like a documentary, filmed in black-and-white, about Algeria's revolt from colonial France in events that occurred between 1954 and 1957. But Pontecorvo's stunning and influential film—definitively presented by Criterion—was done with actors and locals on actual locations to re-create events and present an urgent portrait of revolution and terrorism that captures the bruised humanity on both sides. It resonates even more today.

Hot Bonus: The three-disc package overflows with them. It's riveting to hear American directors, such as Spike Lee, Oliver Stone, and Steven Soderbergh, discuss the role of this film—once accused of being a terrorist primer—on their own work and the many other films that imitated it.

Key Scene: The bomb in the café—a portrait of devastation in miniature.

Battleship Potemkin (1925)

Starring: Alexander Antonov, Vladamir Barsky

Directed by: Sergei Eisenstein

If silent films make your eyes glaze over, here's your cure. Eisenstein, the Russian master, was only twenty-seven when he released this shockingly immediate film about a real-life ship mutiny in 1905 when the *Potemkin*'s czarist commander ordered ten of his men shot for refusing to eat rot-ting meat. When the crew revolts and the people of Odessa (the *Potemkin* was anchored offshore) turn out to offer support, all hell breaks loose. Eisenstein's use of montage and editing was as revolutionary as his subject.

Hot Bonus: Hearing the Dmitri Shostakovich score restored to its glory.

Key Scene: The massacre by Cossack troops of men, women, and children on the Odessa steps is arguably the most famous scene in movie history.

Beauty and the Beast (Restored Edition) (1946)

Starring: Jean Marais, Josette Day

Directed by: Jean Cocteau

You don't know what visual beauty is till you see Cocteau's magical telling of the ancient fairy tale about a girl (Day) who gives herself to a beast (Marais) to save her father and finds the soul of a prince she can truly love. From Henri Alekan's luminous camerawork to the smoke that emanates from the Beast's hands after he has murdered, the film casts a spell.

Hot Bonus: The Criterion remaster is the best version of the film yet, and one of the extras features a visit to the French locations where this masterpiece was filmed. You'll want to book your own trip.

Key Scene: The Beast's candelabras, reaching from the walls.

Beauty and the Beast (Two-Disc Platinum Edition) (1991)

Starring: The voices of Robby Benson, Paige O'Hara, Angela Lansbury

Directed by: Gary Trousdale and Kirk Wise

The disc with the only animated film ever to be Oscar nominated as Best Picture offers three versions of the beguiling musical romance, with its now-classic score by Alan Menken and Howard Ashman. That includes a "work-in-progress" version that shows how the film went from rough sketches to fully realized animation. The late Jerry Orbach voices Lumiere the candlestick with his unique panache. But it's the knockout visuals, stunningly rendered on the DVD, that make this one a natural for repeated viewings.

Hot Bonus: An entire additional disc is devoted to "making of" features, with a fascinating segment on how the musical numbers were recorded.

Key Scene: Belle dances with Beast as a teapot, warmly voiced by Lansbury, sings the immortal title song about a "a tale as old as time."

Beetlejuice (1988)

Starring: Michael Keaton, Winona Ryder, Alec Baldwin, Geena Davis

Directed by: Tim Burton

Keaton's makeup took home its own Oscar—deservedly—he looks like a demon on speed. The plot concerns a dead couple (Baldwin and Davis) who haunt their own New England house when strident New Yorkers move in with their goth daughter (Ryder). It's Keaton's demon who teaches them how to scare off the intruders. He's an unholy comic terror, and the DVD catches the way his skin color ranges from parchment-pale to sickly, *Exorcist*-vomit green.

Hot Bonus: You can isolate Danny Elfman's evocative, hugely entertaining score and play it all by itself.

Key Scene: Keaton getting his head shrunk in hell, presided over by a chain-smoking caseworker, hilariously deadpanned by Sylvia Sidney. "Hey, you're messing up my hair," he yells. "Come on, whoa, whoa, stop it. Hey, this might be a good look for me."

Before Sunrise (1995)

Starring: Ethan Hawke and Julie Delpy

Directed by: Richard Linklater

Jesse (Hawke), an American traveling in Europe, has one night of sex and conversation in Vienna with Celine (Delpy), the French beauty he meets on a train. To some, the film is meandering and talky. To others (me included), the film is bliss, a rebel experiment by the two terrific actors and a gifted director Linklater (*Slacker*) to create life as it happens—and screw the Hollywood gloss. Impossibly, the film seems ever more intimate on DVD than it did in theaters, casting a spell only a fool would want to break.

Hot Bonus: An alternate French soundtrack so you can hear the radiantly appealing Delpy speak in her native tongue.

Key Scene: The lovers on the grass in a park at night.

Before Sunset (2004)

Starring: Ethan Hawke and Julie Delpy

Directed by: Richard Linklater

A sequel that picks up nine years after *Before Sunrise*. Jesse, now a best-selling author, is giving a reading at a bookstore in Paris. Celine, now an environmental activist, walks in. The conversation continues for ninety minutes, in real time, before Jesse must catch a plane home to his wife and son. Linklater follows the lovers—who had promised to reunite in Vienna in six months and never did—from café to park to boat to Celine's apartment. Those who hungered to see more of these two than the glimpse Linklater provided in his animated 2001 film *Waking Life* will be mesmerized. There is something uniquely unforgettable in the way Linklater, Hawke, and Delpy (equal collaborators on the script) find nuance, art, and eroticism in words, spoken and unspoken.

Hot Bonus: A trailer that shows clips from both movies and makes your mouth water for a continuation. And don't make us wait another nine years.

Key Scene: Delpy scores a tour de force as Celine re-creates a Nina Simone concert that leaves Jesse entranced. You will be, too.

Beguiled, The (1971)

Starring: Clint Eastwood, Geraldine Page

Directed by: Don Siegel

Eastwood plays a wounded Union soldier being hidden and cared for in a Confederate school for girls, run by a sexually frustrated headmistress, implosively played by Page. You've probably never heard of this underrated gem, which makes the widescreen DVD all the more valuable for Siegel's erotically angled direction and steamy atmospherics.

Hot Bonus: A trailer that seems to be for another movie, as if the studio didn't want to let audiences know what they were in for.

Key Scene: The amputation—say no more.

Being John Malkovich (Special Edition) (1999)

Starring: John Cusack, Cameron Diaz, Catherine Keener, John Malkovich

Directed by: Spike Jonze

The crazy-ass imaginations of director Jonze and screenwriter Charlie Kaufman hit you like a blast of pure oxygen. It's all here on the DVD: The puppeteer (Cusack) who discovers a portal into the mind of actor Malkovich, played by Malkovich himself and he's never been better, and charges two hundred dollars to take a quick trip inside. What happens to the puppet man and his dowdy wife (Diaz—yes, Diaz) and his hottie accomplice (a delicious Keener) defies description. But this one-of-a-kind movie of constant astonishments will make you laugh hard and long.

Hot Bonus: A three-minute interview with Jonze that reveals almost nothing but exerts a perverse fascination.

Key Scene: Malkovich entering his own head and freaking out at the universe of him inside, all saying: Malkovich! Malkovich! Malkovich!

Being There (1979)

Starring: Peter Sellers, Shirley MacLaine, Melvyn Douglas

Directed by: Hal Ashby

An illiterate, TV-addicted gardener (Sellers at his peak) is taken for a genius, first by a dying power-broker (Douglas in an Oscar-winning role) and his love-starved wife (MacLaine) and then by the world. Director Ashby and screenwriter Jerzy Kosinski, adapting his own story, craft a savage, nuanced satire. And the camera wizardry of Caleb Deschanel, strikingly evident on the DVD, creates a world suspended between reality and fantasy.

Hot Bonus: A profile of Ashby and his films (*The Last Detail, Shampoo, Coming Home*) sets you up to appreciate an underappreciated talent.

Key Scene: Sellers saying the line that made the film stick: "I like to watch."

Believer, The (2001)

Starring: Ryan Gosling, Summer Phoenix, Billy Zane

Directed and written by: Henry Bean

Danny Balint, played with passionate fervor by newcomer Gosling, is a young New York Jew—yeshiva-educated—who becomes a bullying, skinheaded, swastika-wearing neo-Nazi. Writer-director Bean, a conservative Jew from Philadelphia,

took heat for crafting a how-to guide for anti-Semitism. But Danny believes that hate is the Jews' only defense against annihilation—or worse, assimilation. As Bean sees it, hate is how Danny shows his love. Loosely based on the story of Daniel Burros, a Ku Klux Klan leader who killed himself when a *New York Times* reporter revealed he was a Jew, the film boldly aligns itself with Danny's conflicted heart. In Gosling, Bean has found the perfect actor for his dare-anything movie—just the DVD for audiences looking for cinematic provocation.

Hot Bonus: Bean's commentary is as potent as his film.

Key Scene: In flashbacks, we see the young Danny deriding his Talmud instructor for teaching that God asking Abraham to kill his son Isaac was a test of faith. To Danny, who sees Isaac as being "traumatized, a putz the rest of his life," the tale reveals God as "a power-drunk madman" who wants to make Jews afraid: "Let him crush me like the conceited bully that he is. Go ahead!" Danny's dare to God is the crux of the film.

Belle du Jour (1967)

Starring: Catherine Deneuve, Jean Sorel, Michel Piccoli

Directed by: Luis Buñuel

The glorious Deneuve seized the role of her career as the doctor's bride who dreams—or is she dreaming?—that she spends her afternoons working to fulfill kinky male fantasies in a Paris whorehouse. Mexico's Buñuel, directing his first film in color, proves himself a master of comic surrealism.

Hot Bonus: A talk about the film's symbols by Buñuel scholar Julie Jones.

Key Scene: The opener, in which Deneuve's character is driven to the woods and stripped, strung up, and whipped by her husband's carriage driver.

Bend It Like Beckham (2002)

Starring: Parminder Nagra, Keira Knightley, Jonathan Rhys-Meyers

Directed and co-written by: Gurinder Chadha

Teenage Jess (a terrific Nagra) idolizes Brit soccer star David Beckham. She plays amateur soccer in London behind the back of her Indian family and with the help of her tomboy pal Jules (Knightley, at the start of her fame as the sexiest tomboy beanpole on the planet). Then they both fall for their Irish coach (Rhys-Meyers). Co-writer and director Chadha juggles all the angles with flair and fairness. Like Nagra and Knightley, the movie is a sweetheart.

Hot Bonus: Chadha's commentary ups the fun of the movie.

Key Scene: The climactic sighting of Beckham himself.

Ben-Hur (Four-Disc Collector's Edition) (1959)

Starring: Charlton Heston, Stephen Boyd, Hugh Griffith, Haya Harareet

Directed by: William Wyler

Wyler's biblical epic that took a record eleven Oscars, including Best Picture, until *Titanic* tied it in 1997. I still can't believe Heston won the Oscar as Best Actor for his hamboning in the title role as a Jew enslaved by the Romans and forced to do battle with his boyhood friend Messala (Boyd, far more forceful than Heston). But this new special edition brings the epic to DVD life, making the previous edition a candidate for use as a Frisbee. It's the movie's historical re-creations of the time of Christ, filmed over ten months at Rome's Cinecittà Studios, that dazzle on this four-disc killer-diller, which is packed with extras, including commentary from Heston and a new documentary with such directors as George Lucas and Ridley Scott, speaking about the film's significance.

Hot Bonus: The comments from Gore Vidal, who collaborated on the script, regarding the inside joke on the set—shared with Boyd but not Heston—that Messala was hot for Ben-Hur. Boyd played it that way, and looking for those homoerotic wink-winks will get you over the dull spots.

Key Scene: The forty-minute chariot race can still leave you breathless.

Best in Show (2000)

Starring: Christopher Guest, Eugene Levy, Fred Willard, Catherine O'Hara

Directed and co-written by: Christopher Guest

Waggish fun like this is too good to miss. Guest and co-writer Levy take on canines and more hilariously their neurotic owners in this satire of dog shows. Many Guest players from *Waiting for Guffman* and *A Mighty Wind* are in place with blue ribbons going to Willard as an emcee, Parker Posey and Michael Hitchcock as a yuppie couple, and Jennifer Coolidge as a rich geezer's wife in hot lesbo love with her poodle handler (Jane Lynch). Repeated viewings on DVD only make the jokes seem funnier.

Hot Bonus: Deleted scenes, just as delicious as the entree.

Key Scene: The dog show itself, hosted by the great Willard with a high-comic obliviousness. "How do they miniaturize dogs anyway?" he asks his nonplussed co-commentator Jim Piddock. Later, he conjectures that a bloodhound would stand a better chance at the prize if he wore a Sherlock Holmes hat and smoked a pipe. It's time-capsule stuff.

Better Tomorrow, A (1986)

Starring: Chow Yun-Fat, Leslie Cheung, Ti Lung

Directed by: John Woo

The Hong Kong action thriller that kicked off Woo's career gets a spiffed-up treatment from Anchor Bay that puts the imported version in the shadows. The story hinges on two brothers: the older (Ti Lung) runs a counterfeiting operation with his pal (Chow Yun-Fat, the international star-to-be in a supporting role); the younger (Leslie Cheung) is a cop caught between duty and family. Woo's signature—sentiment and slo-mo violence with hoods in long trenchcoats like Alain Delon wore in *Le Samourai*—is all over the film.

Hot Bonus: An English track is available if you can't stand reading subtitles.

Key Scene: The restaurant shootout with blood spurting in all directions.

Beverly Hills Cop (1984)

Starring: Eddie Murphy, Judge Reinhold, John Ashton, Ronny Cox

Directed by: Martin Brest

The first and best of the *Cop* trilogy stars a dynamite Murphy, flashing his radiantly lewd grin as Axel Foley, a young Turk on the Detroit force who horns in on Beverly Hills police turf to nose out the killer of his buddy. At a swank art gallery, he talks his way past an espresso-sipping sleazo (a side-splitting cameo from Bronson Pinchot) to find clues to the murder. Director Brest's quirky camera eye keeps this eighties' comic caper fresh and fun.

Hot Bonus: Brest offers a first-rate walk through the film, explaining how Murphy stepped into the role at the last minute for—yikes!—Sylvester Stallone and improvised to shape the role to his comic needs.

Key Scene: Murphy's first meeting with the BHPD, from Cox as chief to Reinhold and Ashton as subordinates. They look like bank tellers with manners to match. "This is the cleanest police car I've ever been in in my life," says Axel. "The thing's nicer than my apartment."

Bicycle Thief, The (1948)

Starring: Lamberto Maggiorani, Enzo Staiola

Directed by: Vittorio De Sica

Most people know the title and the film's rep as a peak of Italian neo-realism. But is it watched? Not nearly enough. The lovely DVD transfer from Image should change all that. It delivers the story of a working-class father (Maggiorani) in postwar Rome who loses the bicycle he needs to makes his living as a billposter. On one long Sunday, the man and his son (the heartbreaking Staiola) hunt the thief who stole the bicycle, even into a whorehouse. The simple purity of De Sica's direction is a thing of beauty.

Hot Bonus: If you're allergic to subtitles, the DVD provides an English version dubbed from the original Italian.

Key Scene: The ending is devastating, but the moment in which the father slaps his son has been known to make grown men weep.

Big (1988)

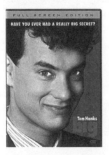

Starring: Tom Hanks, Elizabeth Perkins, Robert Loggia

Directed by: Penny Marshall

You want the widescreen, not the full-frame edition of this bracing, brightly colored comedy about a twelve-year-old boy who says, "I wish I were big," to a carnival machine and winds up as a thirty-five-year-old, played by Hanks, who was Oscar nominated as Best Actor. Hanks never makes a false move, even when the script sets him up with a lady exec (Perkins) who wants to share his bunk bed. "OK," he says, "but I get to be on top."

Hot Bonus: Hanks works so well with director Marshall, you expect to hear them talk on the DVD. No dice. Just a trailer that sells the movie as something crass, which Hanks and Marshall make sure it's not. Go figure.

Key Scene: Hanks and Loggia, as his boss, playing chopsticks on a walking piano at a Manhattan toy store just about defines the term "infectious joy."

Big Chill, The (15th Anniversary Edition) (1983)

Starring: Kevin Kline, Glenn Close, Jeff Goldblum, William Hurt

Directed by: Lawrence Kasdan

The close-to-the-bone movie for baby boomers gets the royal DVD treatment. Maybe the 30th Anniversary Edition will give us the deleted scenes with Kevin Costner as the guy who commits suicide, leaving seven of his aging college friends, now married or paired off, to ponder death. Close won the film's only Oscar nomination for acting, but Goldblum won the most laughs as a sixties activist now writing gossip for *People*.

Hot Bonus: A heated discussion with Kasdan and the actors about whether Close's character would have really offered up the sexual services of her husband (Kline) so their lawyer pal (Mary Kay Place) could have a baby.

Key Scene: An entire generation is conjured up when the friends gather to do dishes and boogie to "I Heard It Through the Grapevine."

Big Fish (2003)

Starring: Billy Crudup, Ewan McGregor, Albert Finney, Jessica Lange

Directed by: Tim Burton

Who better than Burton, with his flair for fables, to direct the tale of a man who makes up his life as he goes along? That man is Edward Bloom (a brilliant Finney), a salesman who is dying. His wife (Lange), has called their son, Will (Crudup), home to Alabama. Will, a journalist who has made his career by serving facts straight, hates his father for constructing myths to hide behind. It's the myths, of course, that most reveal the real Edward. And Burton wisely builds his movie around them. McGregor steps in to play the young Edward, and the tall tales begin—all preserved on this magical DVD. As the son learns to talk to his father on the father's terms and still see him clearly, the film takes on the transformative power of art.

Hot Bonus: The segment on how Burton brought his fable to life on camera is amazing, but don't watch if you prefer to keep illusion alive.

Key Scene: The son carrying his father, the big fish, down to the water.

Big Lebowski, The (Collector's Edition) (1998)

Starring: Jeff Bridges, Julianne Moore, John Goodman, Steve Buscemi

Directed by: Joel Coen

One of my favorite Coen brothers movies—it gets better each time you see it, so owning the DVD is essential. All hail the Dude, played by Bridges in a performance that belongs in the acting pantheon. The pot-bellied, ponytailed, pot-smoking Dude, real name Jeff Lebowski, mostly bowls with his buddies Walter (Goodman) and Donny (Buscemi) and sometimes Jesus (an unmissable John Turturro), a pervert in a hairnet. Then the Dude is mistaken for a wheelchair-bound philanthropist, also named Lebowski, and his adventures begin, involving porn, kidnapping, living erotic art (performed by Moore), and other outrageous acts to be savored. It's a Coen world. Live in it.

Hot Bonus: Joel and Ethan, his writer-producer brother, speak. As usual, the information they offer is useless. As usual, it's hugely entertaining.

Key Scene: A hood pees on the Dude's rug, forcing its removal and saddening the Dude no end: "That rug really tied the room together."

Big Night (1996)

Starring: Tony Shalhoub, Stanley Tucci, Campbell Scott, Isabella Rossellini

Directed by: Stanley Tucci and Campbell Scott

A feast of a film done on a low budget with a menu featuring top-grade acting, writing, and direction. Set in the late 1950s, the story focuses on two Italian-immigrant brothers, Primo (Shalhoub)

and Secondo (Tucci), who nearly go broke by opening a restaurant, the Paradise, in New Jersey. Primo is the purist; he despises customers who expect spaghetti and meatballs. Secondo is almost ready to sell out like the lucrative eatery across the street that carries out what Primo calls "the rape of cuisine." Instead, the brothers spend their last dime on a big night with the blowout meal in this pungent meditation on art and business.

Hot Bonus: The revelation of the film as a family affair: Tucci wrote the script with his cousin Joseph Tropiano, drawing on their family roots in Italy. And Tucci co-directed with childhood pal Scott, who plays the small role of a salesman

Key Scene: The finale, done in silence, as the brothers make and share a simple omelet in a moment of reconciliation that subtly pierces the heart.

Big Red One, The (Restored) (1980)

Starring: Lee Marvin, Mark Hamill, Robert Carradine

Directed by: Sam Fuller

Fuller, the cigar-chomping, B-movie maestro behind *Pickup on South Street, Shock Corridor,* and *The Naked Kiss* (he died in 1997 at eighty-five), tried for years to make this World War II epic about the First Infantry Division in which he served. His dream project, starring a nail-tough Marvin as the sarge who led his men from North Africa into Europe between 1942 and 1945, finally hit theaters in 1980, but in a severely cut form. Film critic Richard Schickel spearheaded this 2004 version, which added forty-five minutes of footage that helped to restore the film's mythic size. Some of the seams still show, but watching Fuller roar on DVD is an indisputable thrill.

Hot Bonus: Schickel on the restoration.

Key Scene: The revelation that a Nazi sniper is really a ten-year-old boy, who gets a spanking from a German officer.

Big Sleep, The (1946)

Starring: Humphrey Bogart, Lauren Bacall, Martha Vickers, Elisha Cook Jr.

Directed by: Howard Hawks

"I like that—I'd like more," says Bacall to Bogart, when he kisses her. Bogie and Bacall made such a great screen team that audiences barely noticed the glaring holes in the plot when Bogart as private detective Philip Marlowe tried to figure out who killed who. Now DVD comes to the rescue by providing both the release version of the classic film on one side of the DVD and the more coherent original version on the other side.

Hot Bonus: Robert Gitt of UCLA analyzes the differences between both versions. One unanswered question: William Faulkner contributed to this adaptation of Raymond Chandler's novel, but no one remembers who wrote Bogart's immortal line about Bacall's nympho sister (Vickers): "She tried to sit on my lap while I was standing up."

Key Scene: The sexual sparking when Bogart compares Bacall to a racehorse and says, "You've got a touch of class, but I don't know how far you can go." And she answers, "A lot depends on who's in the saddle."

Big Wednesday (1978)

Starring: Jan-Michael Vincent, William Katt, Gary Busey

Directed and written by: John Milius

The years and DVD technology have been kind to Milius's surfing epic, gorgeously shot by Bruce Surtees, about twelve years in the life of hotheaded hero Vincent and his two Malibu pals, Katt and Busey. Phallic symbols abound, and Milius—a former lifeguard and surfer—jams in his heated feelings on men, guns, sex, surfboards, and war—in this case, Vietnam.

Hot Bonus: An interview with Milius, who lives and breathes for his subject and can really talk a good game.

Key Scene: The boyhood friends, uniting as men, to catch the big wave.

Bill & Ted's Most Excellent Collection (Three-Disc Special Collection) (1989, 1991)

Starring: Keanu Reeves and Alex Winter

Directed by: Stephen Herek and Peter Hewitt

Awesome, dude. The DVD gift set includes 1989's *Bill & Ted's Excellent Adventure* and 1991's *Bill & Ted's Bogus Journey*, plus a bonus disc of special features. The movies, which are damn near interchangeable, bring back every tacky thing we loved about Bill (Winter) and Ted (Reeves, at his pre-*Matrix* funniest) as they travel back in time in

the first movie and to heaven and hell in the sequel, which plays like outtakes from the original.

Hot Bonus: "A History Lesson in Three Minutes or Less" is a quick montage of bios of the historical figures, from Joan of Arc to Lincoln, that Bill and Ted meet. This is followed by "A History Lesson in Six Minutes or More," which is exactly the same montage played really slowly for slower learners.

Key Scene: They are all key, man. But watching Keanu confront Socrates in the first film is a mindmeld you don't easily forget.

Billy Elliot (2000)

Starring: Jamie Bell, Julie Walters, Gary Lewis

Directed by: Stephen Daldry

The DVD, like the movie, really dances. Set in 1984 in a British mining town, where eleven-year-old Billy (Bell, a true find) sees dancing as a way out, this sleeper hit won an Oscar nomination for Daldry as Best Director and a Best Supporting Actress nod to Walters as the teacher who encourages Billy's dreams of ballet over the objections of his widower dad (Lewis).

Hot Bonus: A featurette on Bell preparing for his dancing role.

Key Scene: Billy literally bouncing off the walls of his town as he leaps and stomps in a dance of defiance to the Jam's "Town Called Malice."

Billy Jack (1971)

Starring: Tom Laughlin, Delores Taylor

Directed by: Tom Laughlin

A cult movie that still needs to be seen to be believed—that's what DVD is all about—as half-breed Billy Jack (Laughlin) guards the rights of Native Americans on an Arizona reservation with the help of a good woman (Taylor, Laughlin's wife) and his own karate-chopping feet. Laughlin took the movie to the public in a campaign that rivals Mel Gibson's on *The Passion of the Christ*, another brutal movie that preaches peace.

Hot Bonus: Laughlin and Taylor tell you how to reach them any time of the night or day at billyjack.com. Punishment gluttons only are advised to check out *The Billy Jack Ultimate Collection*, which includes this movie; its 1967 prequel, *Born Losers*; and two sequels, 1974's *The Trial of Billy Jack* and 1977's *Billy Jack Goes to Washington*.

Key Scene: You won't forget any of them, but the massacre of the wild mustangs to the tune of Coven's "One Tin Soldier" beats all.

Billy Madison (1995)

Starring: Adam Sandler, Darren McGavin, Bridgette Wilson

Directed by: Tamra Davis

Stupidity unleashed, and irresistible to fans of Sandler before he got ambition. Sandler's Billy is a rich kid, content to jerk around with his buddies (Norm MacDonald, Steve Buscemi, and Chris Farley) until—plot point—he must return to grade school and pass or his dad (McGavin) will lose the family business. Luckily, that still leaves room for pee-your-pants jokes.

Hot Bonus: Deleted scenes, as hilariously infantile as those in the movie.

Key Scene: Nudie magazine day around Billy's pool.

Bird (1988)

Starring: Forest Whitaker, Diane Venora

Directed by: Clint Eastwood

The life of saxophone genius Charlie Parker, played with a soul-scarring ache by Whitaker, is delivered as an intricate jazz riff by director Eastwood. The DVD deftly negotiates the shadows as Parker moves from his childhood in Kansas City to life on the road, a troubled interracial marriage to Chan Richardson (Venora is sensational), a suicide attempt, and a drug habit that led to Parker's death in 1955 at thirty-four.

Hot Bonus: The music, remastered in Dolby Digital and available to play alone on a separate DVD track, features Parker's own sax solos with new backup from contemporary musicians.

Key Scene: Parker's reaction to word of his daughter's death. Shattering.

Birdcage, The (1996)

Starring: Robin Williams, Nathan Lane, Hank Azaria, Gene Hackman

Directed by: Mike Nichols

In Americanizing the smash French comedy *La Cage Aux Folles*, director Nichols magically avoids the pitfalls. Maybe it's the move of the drag club from St. Tropez to Miami's South Beach, which glows like an art deco paradise on the DVD, that makes it work. Or maybe it's the infectious comic teamwork of Lane, as the drag performer, and Williams, as his lover and manager, that does the trick. The movie also offers the kick of Azaria as a near-naked gay housekeeper and Hackman (yes, Hackman!) in drag.

Hot Bonus: An eight-page booklet that describes the origins of the material is helpful, though I would have killed to hear Nichols discuss the film with his former comedy partner Elaine May, who wrote the deft script.

Key Scene: Williams trying to teach Lane to walk like John Wayne.

Birds, The (Collector's Edition) (1963)

Starring: Tippi Hedren, Rod Taylor, Jessica Tandy, Suzanne Pleshette

Directed by: Alfred Hitchcock

By now, everyone knows the story of Hitchcock's landmark thriller about unexplained bird attacks in a small California coastal town. The fun in watching it again on this splendidly produced collector's edition is to go deeper into the film's symbols as the birds begin to focus on Hedren as the spoiled socialite out to snag bachelor Taylor by using a pair of lovebirds to seduce him away from mom Tandy and schoolteacher Pleshette.

Hot Bonus: A "making of" documentary is a must for Hitchcock fans, though the suspense master, despite his dry humor, always avoided discussing the profundities lurking beneath his tales.

Key Scene: The crows gathering in a playground, Hedren in the attic, the seagulls trapping her in a phone booth (remember those?). But these are famous moments. This time watch the customers in the diner reacting to the siege as a microcosm of what fear does to us as a society.

Birth (2004)

Starring: Nicole Kidman, Cameron Bright, Lauren Bacall, Danny Huston

Directed by: Jonathan Glazer

Glazer (*Sexy Beast*) invests his film with a haunting visual poetry that transfers extremely well to DVD. It's a mesmerizing mind-teaser. What the film is not is kiddie porn, despite huffy reactions to a scene in the deluxe Manhattan apartment of Anna (Kidman), a grieving widow for ten years who is about to remarry. She is in her bath when ten-year-old Sean (the eerily effective Bright) climbs in the tub and announces that he is the re-incarnation of her dead husband. Anna's mother (Bacall) is alarmed. And Anna's fiancé (Huston) attacks the kid. But, ever so slowly, Anna begins to believe. And the film takes hold as a fierce psychological drama.

Hot Bonus: A segment on how Glazer and his ace director of photography, Harris Savides, created an atmosphere that stays alive to every possibility.

Key Scene: At a concert, while the orchestra swells with Wagner's Die Walküre, the camera just fixes on Kidman, who lets the emotions the boy has brought out in Anna play across her face in an acting tour de force.

Birth of a Nation, The (Special Edition) (1915)

Starring: Lillian Gish, Miriam Cooper, Wallace Reid
Directed by: D. W. Griffith

Griffith's powerhouse silent epic of the Civil War, a precursor to *Gone With the Wind* and every blockbuster that followed in Griffith's pioneering wake, is often ignored in history books. Has age made it stodgy and irrelevant? Not a bit. It's the film's racism that embarrasses and angers—still. In the process of inventing cinema, Griffith—the son of a Confederate officer—painted a heroic portrait of the Ku Klux Klan as protectors of whites against rampaging blacks, marring the film's second half about the Reconstruction. As art, the film holds. As politics, it's an abomination.

Hot Bonus: Footage showing Griffith at work.
Key Scene: The re-creation of Lincoln's assassination has never been bested.

Black Christmas (Anniversary Edition) (1974)

Starring: Margot Kidder, Keir Dullea, Olivia Hussey, John Saxon
Directed by: Bob Clark

A criminally underseen scare flick, set in a sorority house around the holidays. Since you never see the psycho who stalks the girls, it's fun to watch the movie again—and again—on DVD trying to pick up clues. Kidder, in her pre–Lois Lane days, has a high time sassing back to the killer's obscene calls. Another coed, played by Hussey, gets

pregnant, which maddens her musician boyfriend (Dullea, never more bug-eyed). Saxon is the cop who counts the bodies as they pile up, except that one in the attic.

Hot Bonus: Interviews with Saxon and director Clark that clear up some mysteries while leaving others deliciously ambiguous.

Key Scene: That girl's body in the attic, wrapped in plastic, her mouth agape while the killer whispers his kinky mantra of "lick, lick, lick" and repeating the name, "Billy, Beeleee!" It's really frickin' scary.

Black Hawk Down (Collector's Edition) (2001)

Starring: Josh Hartnett, Ewan McGregor, Eric Bana, Sam Shepard
Directed by: Ridley Scott

Director Scott (*Gladiator*) takes a documentary approach to the factual material in Mark Bowden's best seller about the botched 1993 U.S. incursion into Mogadishu, Somalia. The afternoon operation was supposed to last an hour, in and out. As part of a U.N. peacekeeping mission, more than one hundred of America's elite Delta Force and Task Force Rangers were ordered to enter Mogadishu in Humvees, trucks, and Black Hawk choppers, kidnap two top lieutenants of a Somali warlord, and get the hell out. Showing why it didn't happen, Scott creates a war epic as gut-wrenching as any ever filmed. Save for a few cornball speeches, *Black Hawk Down* ignores politics and star grandstanding to pitch audiences into the pitiless heat of battle. This huge $90 million undertaking is a personal best for producer Jerry Bruckheimer, a triumph for Scott, and a war film of prodigious power.

Hot Bonus: Of all the valuable commentaries and "making of" features on this monumental three-disc package, the one in which officers and soldiers who were there compare the movie with their memories is a stunner.

Key Scene: The aftermath: Fifteen hours later, with two Black Hawks down, eighteen soldiers killed and seventy-three injured, the chaos that left several hundred Somalis dead could hardly be imagined. But Scott does just that, making the parallels to Afghanistan striking and horrific.

Black Narcissus (1947)

Starring: Deborah Kerr, David Farrar, Kathleen Byron, Sabu

Directed by: Michael Powell and Emeric Pressburger

Criterion's dazzling color transfer of this seminal film is a gift. Anglican nuns, led by Sister Clodagh (Kerr), attempt to build a school and hospital in a Himalayan castle that once served as a bordello. Sexual undercurrents rise to the surface when a government agent (Farrar) stirs up the sisters. Shot mostly on soundstages, this Powell-Pressburger film, buoyed by the camerawork of Jack Cardiff, creates an atmosphere of hothouse eroticism.

Hot Bonus: Powell's conversation with his ultimate fan, director Martin Scorsese, is alone worth the price of the DVD.

Key Scene: Byron should have won a best supporting Oscar as Sister Ruth, and the moment when she unleashes her feelings for Farrar's agent proves it.

Black Orpheus (1959)

Starring: Breno Mello, Marpessa Dawn, Léa Garcia

Directed by: Marcel Camus

Criterion does it again by bringing the vibrant color and sharpness of this Oscar-winning Brazilian film back from the murky mold of VHS. Set in the slums of Rio de Janeiro during Carnival—with hypnotic music by Antonio Carlos Jobim and Luiz Bonfá—the film is an update on the legend of Orpheus and Eurydice, as a streetcar conductor (Mello) falls for a beautiful stranger (Dawn) being pursued by a man disguised as Death.

Hot Bonus: Four precious minutes of previously unseen footage.

Key Scene: The descent into Hades for love.

Black Stallion, The (1979)

Starring: Kelly Reno, Mickey Rooney, Teri Garr

Directed by: Carroll Ballard

One of the most exquisite-looking films ever made, with cinematography by Caleb Deschanel that pushes DVD technology to the limits to capture. Based on the book by Walter Farley, the movie—directed with perfect simplicity by Ballard—tells the heartfelt story of a boy (Reno), a horse trainer (the superb Rooney), and the black stallion that enters and envelops their lives.

Hot Bonus: The pause button on your remote is all you need to admire images that are suitable for framing.

Key Scene: The shipwreck—have tissues handy.

Blade II (Two-Disc Special Edition) (2002)

Starring: Wesley Snipes, Ron Perlman, Kris Kristofferson

Directed by: Guillermo del Toro

Yes, there are three *Blade* movies—the first in 1998 and the third, *Blade: Trinity* in 2004. Forget the others—they're dull and duller. *Blade II*, from *Hellboy* director del Toro, is the one that fires on all cylinders to give your DVD system a workout. Snipes, as the half-human, half-vampire Blade, is so into the role this time that the good time he's having is contagious. It's overkill, sure, but what else do you want in a vampire flick?

Hot Bonus: The two-disc platinum package is loaded with great stuff, but del Toro's foul-mouthed commentary is unmissable.

Key Scene: Blade catching a speeding sword in his hands—way cool.

Blade Runner (Director's Cut) (1982)

Starring: Harrison Ford, Rutger Hauer, Sean Young, Daryl Hannah

Directed by: Ridley Scott

A classic, plain and simple. Set in a rainy, wasted twenty-first-century Los Angeles (hey, that's now), the movie—based on sci-fi legend Philip K. Dick's *Do Androids Dream of Electric Sheep?*—focuses on Ford's Deckard, a former cop who gets back into action to kill rebel replicants who want to he human. Young is particularly good as . . . oh, why spoil it? It's the atmosphere that counts here, and director Scott sparks his crew to visual miracles.

Hot Bonus: The director's cut dispenses with the explain-all narration from Ford's character that marred the original version. And there's a new ending that deepens the film noir mood and mystery. All to the good.

Key Scene: The death of the replicant villain played by Hauer after saving Deckard's life. Audiences didn't need the narration in which Deckard intoned: "Maybe in those last moments, he loved life more than he ever had before. Not just his life—anybody's life. My life." Hauer infused all that into his performance, which the director's cut allows to stand on its own.

Blair Witch Project, The (1999)

Starring: Heather Donahue, Michael Williams, Joshua Leonard

Directed by: Daniel Myrick and Eduardo Sánchez

This may be the crappiest-looking and worst-sounding frightflick in this book, but no DVD collection would be complete without it. Set up to look like a camcorder video made by an amateur (Donahue) and her two male assistants (Williams and Leonard), the film is a joke that grabs you anyway. The footage is allegedly all that's left of the three filmmakers after their trip into the Maryland woods to shoot a documentary on the legendary Blair Witch. Know what? It's as scary as hell, and not being able to really see the things that go bump in the night adds to the terror level.

Hot Bonus: The behind-the-scenes commentary from the directors is informative, but the "fake" documentary about the making of the "fake" movie is even more fun.

Key Scene: Donahue's face, dripping snot, and lit by a flashlight—out there in the woods screaming her bloody head off.

Blazing Saddles (Thirtieth Anniversary Edition) (1974)

Starring: Cleavon Little, Gene Wilder, Harvey Korman, Madeline Kahn

Directed and co-written by: Mel Brooks

Great idea to celebrate the lasting hilariousness of Brooks's western spoof by giving it a prime, bonus-packed DVD makeover that makes the jokes seem funnier. Little is the black sheriff hired to drive the white folks away and let the villainous Hedley Lamarr (Korman) run a railroad through town. Wilder is a hoot as an alcoholic gunfighter, but the scene-stealer is Kahn as Lili Von Shtupp,

the Teutonic saloon singer who unzips the sheriff's fly to learn if it's true what thay say about black men. "It's twue," she cries. "It's twue."

Hot Bonus: Brooks's commentary track is a one-man comedy extravaganza.

Key Scene: To watch the cowboys eat beans by the campfire is to see a simple fart joke lifted to the level of epic.

Blob, The (1958)

Starring: Steve McQueen, Aneta Corsaut, Earl Rowe, Robert Fields

Directed by: Irvin S. Yeaworth Jr.

Silly can't begin to sum up this teen horror flick about an alien force disguised as an ever-expanding spoonful of red Jell-O that attacks a small-town by covering it with goo. McQueen—pushing thirty but playing a teen hero—is the whipped cream of cool on this B-movie hit given a class-A treatment by Criterion. It's hard to believe the blob ever looked this good.

Hot Bonus: Commentaries about McQueen in his pre-star days prevail, but producer Jack H. Harris spends so much time denying the theory that the red blob wasn't meant to symbolize the Commie threat of the 1950s that you can't help looking for moments that prove Harris wrong, such as . . .

Key Scene: The blob eats the diner, a symbol of America under siege.

Blood Simple (1984)

Starring: Frances McDormand, John Getz, Dan Hedaya, M. Emmett Walsh

Directed by: Joel Coen

As the debut of director Joel Coen and his producer brother Ethan, this exercise in film noir is a must. The brothers, who co-wrote the script and shot it on a shoestring budget ($1.5 million), have tweaked a few things for the DVD, but essentially it's the story of a Texas bar owner (Hedaya), his roving wife (McDormand, fab as usual), the bartender (Getz) she slips out with, and the fat detective (Walsh) whom the husband hires to kill the cheating lovers. The Coens give the detective genre a good shaking up.

Hot Bonus: The introduction to the film by Kenneth Loring is mostly a put-on. What counts is the sharp DVD transfer that allows you to watch how the Coens give terrifying dimensions to simple things, such as a football, a fan, and a newspaper tossed against a window.

Key Scene: The climax is a gruesome gag worthy of Hitchcock, and Walsh's last chilling laugh is the stuff of bad dreams.

Bloody Sunday (Widescreen Collector's Edition) (2002)

Starring: James Nesbitt, Tim Pigott-Smith, Nicholas Farrell
Directed by: Paul Greengrass

Shot in documentary style, this stunning re-creation of the events on January 30, 1972, when British soldiers and Irish peace marchers hit a violent impasse in Derry, Northern Ireland, has the impact of a punch in the gut. Using a handheld camera, director Greengrass puts you right in the middle of the senseless massacre that helped fuel a new cycle of violence.

Hot Bonus: Ivan Cooper, the organizer of the march, compares the movie to what he saw. And actor James Nesbitt, whose shattering performance as Cooper drives the film, adds his own provocative thoughts.

Key Scene: It's all one scene, really, that comes together with devastating impact when U2 sings the title song at the end.

Blow (Infinifilm Edition) (2001)

Starring: Johnny Depp, Penélope Cruz, Franka Potente, Paul Reubens
Directed by: Ted Demme

Go for broke. That's what small-town New England hick George Jung did when he began smuggling Colombian cocaine into the United States and raked in more than $100 million during the 1980s as the gringo Pablo Escobar. And that's what Depp, who is dynamite as Jung, and Demme, who directs this biopic with badass bravado, do with Blow. They put their butts on the line for the true story of a scumbag (Jung is in the slammer until 2014). And they've wrapped that story in a fever dream of a film—the DVD catches every lurid turn—that encapsulates four decades of drug-fueled hedonism in terms that are both intimate and epic. It's a movie and a half.

Hot Bonus: Director Demme talks with the real Jung in his prison cell, an interview that resonates tragically in the light of Demme's death from a cocaine-induced heart attack in 2002. He was thirty-eight.

Key Scene: Jung watches as Escobar (Cliff Curtis) casually murders a police informant. The effect is bone-chilling, but not enough to deter George. With the help of his California connection, hairdresser Derek Foreal—Reubens, out of Pee-Wee's Playhouse with a vengeance, is shockingly good—George is soon up the nose of Hollywood's elite and responsible for 85 percent of the cocaine traffic in America.

Blow Out (1981)

Starring: John Travolta, Nancy Allen, John Lithgow, Dennis Franz
Directed by: Brian De Palma

Director De Palma seizes attention from the opening scream and holds it until the final goosebump. If the title recalls Antonioni's 1966 film Blow-Up, it's no accident. Instead of a photographer stumbling on a murder in a London park, it's a sound-effects technician (Travolta in peak form) who witnesses what may be a political killing on a deserted bridge near Philadelphia. There are echoes of Chappaquiddick as Travolta rescues a hooker (Allen) from a rapidly submerging car. De Palma stretches credibility, but his visual wizardry matched with his moral challenge pull you in.

Hot Bonus: The widescreen and standard versions of the film are included.

Key Scene: Listening, with the Travolta character, to the sounds he recorded of the car before, during, and after its plunge from the bridge.

Blow-Up (1966)

Starring: David Hemmings, Vanessa Redgrave, Sarah Miles
Directed by: Michelangelo Antonioni

Since imagery is everything in this iconic Antonioni film about a swinging London photographer (Hemmings) who finds that the pix he snapped of a woman (a wickedly sexy Redgrave) in a park may hold the clues to a murder, the quality of DVD transfer needed to be good. It is. Now you can stare at those photos, freeze-frame them, and play detective in ways Antonioni never imagined in pre-DVD 1966.

Hot Bonus: An expert commentary on Antonioni from Peter Brunette.

Key Scene: That moment in his studio when Hemmings studies a blow-up of one of his park photos and sees something in the background that looks very much like a hand holding a gun. Or does it?

Blue Velvet (Special Edition) (1986)

Starring: Kyle MacLachlan, Isabell Rossellini, Laura Dern, Dennis Hopper

Directed and written by: David Lynch

The second-greatest movie of the 1980s (after *Raging Bull*) has finally emerged from the cult ghetto to take its place as a masterpiece. The Special Edition DVD gives full due to Lynch's surreal, erotically charged atmosphere as he shows the violent perversion festering just under the surface of small-town America. This kinky twist on *Alice in Wonderland* starts when good guy Jeffrey (MacLachlan) falls down a rabbit hole to hell while investigating a murder. There he meets and has S&M sex with a voluptuous night-club singer (Rossellini, never more haunting) held captive by a drug-pushing psycho (Hopper at his nutso peak). It ends when Lynch, justly Oscar nominated, lets these two worlds collide as a naked Rossellini barges into the ordered home of Jeffrey's girl (Dern) to announce: "He put his disease in me." You've never seen anything like it in your life.

Hot Bonus: A documentary that skips past hype to delve deeply into how Lynch uses imagery to define character.

Key Scene: MacLachlan in the closet, watching Rossellini, and catching carnal, scary glimpses that illuminate the raw voyeuristic power of film.

Bob & Carol & Ted & Alice (1969)

Starring: Natalie Wood, Elliott Gould, Dyan Cannon, Robert Culp

Directed by: Paul Mazursky

What was envelope-pushing in 1969—one hip couple, Bob (Culp) and Carol (Wood), introducing a less hip couple, Ted (Gould) and Alice (Cannon), to the virtues of wife-swapping—seems dated now. But it's no less charming, thanks to a talented cast and Mazursky's flair for satirizing hipsters. Gould and Cannon were both Oscar nominated, but Wood, who drowned in 1981, had a dark-eyed beauty to which this DVD does full justice.

Hot Bonus: Gould, Cannon, and Culp join Mazursky for a lively commentary that speaks with wicked humor about changing sexual mores.

Key Scene: The four of them in bed, deciding whether to have group sex or to go see Tony Bennett.

Bob Roberts (Special Edition) (1992)

Starring: Tim Robbins, Giancarlo Esposito, Alan Rickman, Brian Murray

Directed and written by: Tim Robbins

This slashingly funny political satire adds up to a hat-trick victory for Robbins, its writer, director, and star. His senatorial candidate Bob Roberts is seen exclusively through the lens of a British documentarian (Murray). Bob is a folk-singing fascist yuppie hawking dreams to an electorate all too easily distracted from the real issues. If a reporter (Esposito) gets too close to Bob's dark side, his sleazy campaign manager (Rickman) knows how to take covert action. Robbins's target is the rise of image over issues. It doesn't matter what your platform is; it's how you sell it.

Hot Bonus: Tart commentary from Robbins and Gore Vidal, who plays Bob's rival, the liberal incumbent, with irresistible blowhard charm.

Key Scene: The barbed song parodies—written by Robbins and his brother David—sound sharper than ever on the DVD, especially Bob's proposal for bringing justice to drug dealers: "Hang 'em high for a clean-living land."

Body Heat (1981)

Starring: Kathleen Turner, William Hurt, Richard Crenna, Mickey Rourke

Directed and written by: Lawrence Kasdan

Age has not dulled the sparks given off by Turner and Hurt in this sizzling, set-in-steamy-Florida take on the 1946 film noir, *The Postman Always Rings Twice*. The plot—will Turner convince lawyer Hurt to kill her husband (Crenna)?—hardly matters. Neither does the supporting cast, although Rourke steals his scenes as an arsonist. It's the way Turner, in her slinky movie debut, wraps her mouth around Kasdan's overripe dialogue: "You're not too smart, are you?" she asks Hurt. "I like that in a man."

Hot Bonus: The trailer, without a word of dialogue, gets the heat across.

Key Scene: Turner stares so smolderingly at Hurt through a window that he smashes the glass with a chair to get at her. Body heat, indeed. And on this DVD, you can really feel it.

Bonnie and Clyde (Reissue) (1967)

Starring: Warren Beatty, Faye Dunaway, Gene Hackman, Estelle Parsons

Directed by: Arthur Penn

Here's a groundbreaking gangster film with an ad campaign ("They are young. They are in love. They kill people") that drove prudes nuts as it drew in the nation's youth. Accused in 1967 of glamorizing the real-life Bonnie Parker (Dunaway) and Clyde Barrow (Beatty) as Robin Hoods who robbed banks to give to the Depression-era poor, the film actually rubs your face in the hard reality of violence. In combining slapstick and gravity, Penn brought a French New Wave energy to the movie that is still being imitated. Beatty and Dunaway hit career highs, Hackman excelled as Clyde's brother Buck, and Parsons won an Oscar as Buck's wife. And look out for Michael J. Pollard a C. W. Moss, a mechanic seduced by the Barrow gang. "What you doing, boy?" asks Bonnie as he looks under her hood. "Dirt in the fuel line," he says, adding a twinkle, "blowin' it away." This DVD transfer, catching the vividness of Burnett Guffey's camerawork, will blow you away.

Hot Bonus: The reissue presents the film in the preferred letterboxed version, not the full-screen format of the earlier Warner Bros. DVD that robbed the film of its size and scope.

Key Scene: The slow-motion massacre of Bonnie and Clyde by gunfire hasn't lost its shock-and-awe impact.

Boogie Nights (Two-Disc Special Edition) (1997)

Starring: Mark Wahlberg, Burt Reynolds, Julianne Moore, Heather Graham

Directed and written by: Paul Thomas Anderson

What sounds like a tacky peek into the inner workings of the porn industry in the late seventies, is actually a film about family. Just don't think Disney, since the teen busboy hero (Wahlberg) rises to X-rated fame on the size of his dick and his apt new name, Dirk Diggler. The mother figure for Dirk is a porn queen (Moore), the father is porn director Jack Horner (Reynolds, Oscar

nominated). The extended family includes Rollergirl (Graham), who does everything, even sex, on skates. The Brady Bunch they ain't. The seventies recreation, superbly rendered on the DVD right down to the leisure suits and disco moves, is meant to show the illusion of glamour that helps these alleged seventies swingers buy into the fantasy. Wahlberg gives a breakout performance, but Anderson, then twenty-seven, proved himself a young master with this tumultuous two-and-a-half-hour evocation of sex in the seventies.

Hot Bonus: The ten deleted scenes on disc 2 don't add up to much, but Anderson's commentary on the changes in porn really do deliver.

Key Scene: Dirk, fueled by drugs and arrogance, has walked out on Jack ("You're not the king of me!") and into the house of a drug-addled tycoon (Alfred Molina) who blares Rick Springfield's "Jessie's Girl" and holds a gun to Dirk's head while his assistant tosses lit firecrackers. Talk about a whole world exploding in microcosm.

Born on the Fourth of July (Special Edition) (1989)

Starring: Tom Cruise, Willem Dafoe, Caroline Kava, Raymond J. Berry

Directed by: Oliver Stone

Teenager Ron Kovic joined the marines, went to Vietnam to be a hero, and came back in a wheelchair to tell how his illusions about God, country, and manhood were shattered along with his spinal cord. Under the pile-driving, Oscar-winning direction of Stone, Cruise gives a deeply felt performance that takes us on a grueling journey, moving Kovic through therapy and his involvement with the antiwar movement. That's a lot to cram in. Events are compressed, and subsidiary characters are swallowed up. But Stone and Cruise do more than show what happened to Kovic. They show why it still urgently matters.

Hot Bonus: Honest talk from Stone about where his film veers from fact.

Key Scene: Kovic shouting "Penis! Big fat fucking erect penis!" at his mother (Kava), who hates the blunt words he uses to describe what he's lost.

Bottle Rocket (1996)

Starring: Owen Wilson, Luke Wilson, Andrew Wilson, James Caan

Directed by: Wes Anderson

The droll originality that Texas-born director Anderson perfected in *Rushmore* and *The Royal Tenenbaums* is shown here at its root stage in his little-known debut film. It's a comic caper about a slacker named Dignan (Owen Wilson, Anderson's writing partner), who springs his pal Anthony (Luke Wilson) from an asylum so they can embark on a series of burglaries for Mr. Henry (Caan) with rich kid Bob (Robert Musgrave) driving the getaway car. A third Wilson, Andrew, plays Bob's older brother. The film, expanded from a short, looks great on the DVD, capturing a complex color scheme that changes as the friends bungle one job after another.

Hot Bonus: Check out the short, which runs thirteen minutes.

Key Scene: The flirtation between a Paraguayan hotel maid (Lumi Cavazos) and Anthony perfectly encapsulates the film's offbeat humor. "You really have good posture," he tells his non-English-speaking lady love.

Bound (1996)

Starring: Jennifer Tilly, Gina Gershon, Joe Pantoliano

Directed and written by: Andy and Larry Wachowski

Before they thought of *The Matrix*, the brothers Wachowski made their feature debut with this lesbian crime caper. It's outrageous fun. Tilly plays Violet, the moll of Caesar (Pantoliano, whose scene stealing is felony worthy), a Chicago mobster who knows where $2 million is stashed. Gershon plays Corky, an ex-con who gets hot and heavy with Tilly, practically at first sight. That $2 million is their ticket out, and if you can unsteam your eyes from the hot lesbo action—Bill Pope's resonant camerawork comes through thrillingly on the DVD—the plot takes some twists you don't see coming.

Hot Bonus: The Wachowskis, who became hermits after *The Matrix* hit, talk freely about the fun they had. It's infectious.

Key Scene: "Caesar, I'm leaving!" Violet announces. "Why?" he whines. "Did I use a good towel?" It's moments like this—and they're frequent—that make this baby worth repeat viewings.

Bourne Identity, The (Widescreen Extended Edition) (2002)

Starring: Matt Damon, Franka Potente, Chris Cooper, Clive Owen, Julia Stiles

Directed by: Doug Liman

Based on Robert Ludlum's 1980 bestseller about an amnesiac (Damon at his best) who may be a master spy, this thriller is powered by brains as well as brawn. After being pulled out of the sea with two bullets in him, Damon's character goes on the run, along with an impulsive hottie (Potente, superb), trying to avoid various assassins and wondering how the hell he knows how to kill. Director Liman—the hip skipper of *Swingers* and *Go*—makes all the familiar dirty business seem fun.

Hot Bonus: The Extended Edition has segments on the CIA and amnesia, but it's the alternate beginning and ending that hook you.

Key Scene: The car chase through the streets of Paris will kick out the jams in your home theater, but I prefer the cat-and-mouse confrontation between Damon and Owen, as a rival assassin known as The Professor.

Bourne Supremacy, The (Widescreen Edition) (2004)

Starring: Matt Damon, Franka Potente, Joan Allen, Brian Cox, Julia Stiles

Directed by: Paul Greengrass

Even with Greengrass in for director Doug Liman, this sequel (also based on a Robert Ludlum bestseller) leaves you panting for more. It's a globe-trotting, butt-kicking, whiplash-paced action movie. Damon is better the second time around in what may become his signature role: Jason Bourne, an amnesiac C.I.A. assassin who wants to come in from the cold, even if his superiors (Allen plays one made of steel) have other ideas. Director Greengrass (*Bloody Sunday*) spins a handheld camera from India to Naples to Berlin to a killer car chase in Moscow with shotgun urgency. Plot details are irrelevant. Just grab your remote and let the movie work you over.

Hot Bonus: Ten minutes of deleted scenes, and they're good ones.

Key Scene: The bridge chase, and the DVD has a bonus features that takes this chase apart to see how it ticks.

Bowling for Columbine (Special Edition) (2002)

Directed and written by: Michael Moore

Moore's volcanically funny and scary documentary about gun obsession in America deservedly won the Oscar and sparked heated debate. Good for Moore, who deserves his title as filmdom's feistiest provocateur.

Hot Bonus: My favorite is Moore explaining his Oscar acceptance speech, which drew boos, and which the typically scared and hypocritical Academy refused to allow Moore to use on this DVD.

Key Scene: Moore's interview with actor and National Rifle Association spokesman Charlton Heston is admittedly harsh. Heston is frail and addled, but the clips of the actor taking a pro-gun stance in Colorado just weeks after the Columbine High School massacre justify Moore's verbal assault.

Boxcar Bertha (1972)

Starring: Barbara Hershey, David Carradine, Barry Primus

Directed by: Martin Scorsese

Written off at the time as a *Bonnie & Clyde* wannabe, Scorsese's second feature (done under the low-budget, rush-job mantle of producer Roger Corman) springs to life on DVD. There's more here than gore and sex and a frequently naked Hershey as a Depression-era Arkansas farm girl who gets involved with rebel union organizer Carradine and a life of crime. Scorsese's raw energy resonates in every frame. After seeing *Bertha*, indie film god John Cassavetes told Scorsese to "make a movie about something you really care about" next time. That film, 1973's *Mean Streets*, kicked off a volcanic directing career.

Hot Bonus: Scorsese crams the story of the real-life Bertha Thompson with offbeat movie references that are joy to hunt out. Watch for the *Wizard of Oz* homage set in, of all places, a whorehouse.

Key Scene: Scorsese's cameo in said whore-house will thrill film buffs, but it's the bloody climax, presaging *Taxi Driver*, that grabs you.

Boys Don't Cry (1999)

Starring: Hilary Swank, Chloë Sevigny, Peter Sarsgaard

Directed by: Kimberly Peirce

Swank won her first Oscar for playing Teena Brandon, a girl who moves from Lincoln, Nebraska, to Falls City to pass as a boy. In 1993, Teena was raped and murdered by the men she fooled. Director Peirce, in a smashing debut, crafts a shockingly intimate and deeply affecting film about the roots of sexual role playing. And Swank's indelible performance is aided immeasurably by the resonant Sevigny (nominated as Best Supporting Actress) as Lana, the woman with whom Teena falls in love. The DVD does full justice to Jim Denault's cinematography as his camera plunges into the light and the ugly shadows of small-town America.

Hot Bonus: Peirce's commentary avoids self-congratulation to focus on how she fought to find the joy and humanity in a tragic story.

Key Scene: The heartstopping moment in which Teena confesses her real sexual identity to Lana and feeling wins over shock.

Boyz N the Hood (Anniversary Edition) (1991)

Starring: Cuba Gooding Jr., Ice Cube, Laurence Fishburne, Morris Chestnut

Directed by: John Singleton

At twenty-three, Singleton became the first and (at this writing) only African American to be nominated for an Oscar as Best Director. This Anniversary Edition DVD brings out the strengths of his achievement. In telling the story of three friends growing up in the hood of South Central Los Angeles, Singleton catches signs of hope that survive amid the drive-by shootings, police harassment, and chopper surveillance. Gooding is Tre, the child of divorce whose father (Fishburne) fights to save him from the too-young parenthood that traps Ricky (Chestnut) and the life of crime that destroys Ricky's brother Doughboy (Ice Cube, in the film's best performance). Yes, the film is flawed by preachiness, but Singleton's vision seems as potently fresh as the day he envisioned it.

Hot Bonus: A documentary, *Friendly Fire: The Making of an Urban Legend*, is a cogent reminder of how Singleton made history on a bare-bones budget of $6 million.

Key Scene: Fishburne's lecture on sex to his son about how any punk kid can get laid, "but only a real man can raise his children" cuts to the heart of the film's theme about fathers and sons.

Bram Stoker's Dracula (Superbit Collection) (1992)

Starring: Gary Oldman, Winona Ryder, Anthony Hopkins, Keanu Reeves

Directed by: Francis Ford Coppola

In retelling the story of the blood-sucking vampire, the most faithful version yet to Stoker's book, Coppola is less concerned with plot logic than extravagant style. *The Godfather* director is drunk on what his camera can do, beginning with the many forms Oldman's Count Dracula takes as he leaves Transylvania for London to reclaim his lost love Mina (Ryder). Even Reeves enters into the spirit of things as Mina's ill-fated fiancé who gets a memorable visit from the Count's undead, barebreasted wives. Oldman's orgasmic expression when Reeves cuts himself shaving is just one of the film's many gorgeously crazed images.

Hot Bonus: The Superbit encoding process is all you need, producing knockout DVD image and sound (oh, that thundering bass).

Key Scene: The Count pursuing Mina at a London exhibition of a newfangled thing called movies. As the actors weave around the images projected on the screen, Coppola celebrates the immortality of cinema itself.

Braveheart (1995)

Starring: Mel Gibson, Sophie Marceau, Catherine McCormack

Directed by: Mel Gibson

This thirteenth-century epic, which won five Oscars including Best Picture and Best Director for Gibson, who stars as Scottish freedom fighter William Wallace, still gets dissed as *Die Hard* in a kilt. But there's no debating Gibson's skill at lacing this rouser with sorrow and savagery. All the film's sweep is captured on the DVD, which takes the measure of a hero with a taste for blood to match his taste for honor. Wallace is an inspiring, unsettling role, and Gibson plays him, aptly, like a gathering storm.

Hot Bonus: The detailed behind-the-scenes feature is called *A Filmmaker's Passion*, which Gibson would echo to much controversy and no Oscar glory in 2004's *The Passion of the Christ*.

Key Scene: Wallace stirring his fatigued soldiers to action. In most historical films, the stationary star manages to move multitudes with a throaty whisper. Gibson jettisons the Hollywood fakery. Riding among the men, his face streaked with woad (a blue dye used to terrify the enemy) and his voice hoarse from yelling. Wallace is a demon warrior. An indelible image.

Brazil (Three-Disc Special Edition) (1985)

Starring: Jonathan Pryce, Kim Greist, Robert De Niro, Katherine Helmond

Directed by: Terry Gilliam

This Criterion release is one glorious DVD package and just what Gilliam's daring, demented, and demanding futuristic fantasy deserves. The clerk hero (Pryce) uses his dull job to fantasize about himself as a winged savior of a gorgeous blond (Greist). Set in England in a future where technology is king, but everything is on the fritz—De Niro contributes a priceless turn as a duct repairman—the film allows Gilliam to paint this bleak universe with darkly comic visuals that leave you shaken.

Hot Bonus: Want a good scare? The DVD includes the shortened, sweetened 94-minute cut of the 142-minute film that the studio wanted to release before the suits were shamed into following Gilliam's vision.

Key Scene: My favorite is the one in which terrorists swing across Art Deco towers like high-tech Tarzans as bombs reduce one part of an elegant restaurant to rubble while diners merrily continue to munch.

Breakfast at Tiffany's (1961)

Starring: Audrey Hepburn, George Peppard, Patricia Neal, Mickey Rooney

Directed by: Blake Edwards

Hepburn's star shine is ultra-bright on this DVD. She plays Holly Golightly, the backwoods girl who comes to New York to pass as a sophisticate and ends up falling for a writer (Peppard) being kept by an older woman (Neal). Hepburn gives this glossy version of Truman Capote's far harsher novella a touching gravity, as when she tells the writer she has a case of the mean reds. "Suddenly you're afraid and you don't know what you're afraid of. Well, when I get it, the only thing that does any good is to jump into a cab and go to Tiffany's." Tourists still go to New York to do the same.

Hot Bonus: The film's charming original trailer with Hepburn speaking right into the camera.

Key Scene: What else? Hepburn singing Henry Mancini's Oscar-winning ballad "Moon River" with heartbreaking simplicity.

Breaking the Waves (1996)

Starring: Emily Watson, Stellan Skarsgård

Directed by: Lars von Trier

Watson, the luminous British actress in an Oscar-nominated performance, plays Bess, a virginal lass living in a remote village in Scotland during the 1970s. Bess shocks her strict Calvinist community by marrying Jan (Skarsgård), a lusty Scandinavian oil rigger who suffers a paralyzing accident that leads Bess to have degrading sex with strangers. The DVD brings out the raw beauty of Robby Müller's cinematography (a handheld camera is used to sensational effect). Danish maverick von Trier has crafted an allegory that needs some explaining. Watson goes straight to the heart.

Hot Bonus: Production notes that will get you up to speed on von Trier's mad mix of spirituality and perversion. "The strength of my films," he says, "is that they are easy to mock." They are also hard to forget.

Key Scene: Bess's introduction to sex by Jan has an uncommon carnal intimacy. She rubs his belly, brushes her fingers through his pubic hair and plays with his penis as if she's just discovered sex, which, of course, she has.

Breathless (1960)

Starring: Jean-Paul Belmondo, Jean Seberg

Directed by: Jean-Luc Godard

The film that kicked off the French New Wave and Godard's revolutionary career looks back at the Hollywood gangster film to reinvent cinema. The young Belmondo does his best Bogart as a Parisian hood who steals a car, kills a cop, and hooks up with an American girl (Seberg, an underrated actress from Iowa—dead of a drug overdose twenty years after this iconic performance) who beds and

betrays him. The DVD resonates with Godard's on-the-run exhilaration, shooting his film in black-and-white on the streets of Paris and banging together ideas (comedy and tragedy, art and philosophy, sex and death) for the giddy hell of it.

Hot Bonus: Insightful commentary from film scholar David Sterritt.

Key Scene: The climax with Belmondo staggering from a gunshot wound and that impassive, haunting last look from Seberg as he calls her "bitch."

Bride of Chucky (1998)

Starring: Jennifer Tilly, Brad Dourif

Directed by: Ronny Yu

Chucky Gets Lucky.

The fourth and the wicked-funniest in the *Child's Play* series about Chucky the killer doll takes its cue from the classic *Bride of Frankenstein*. Tilly is at her squeaky-voiced nuttiest as the moll who not only repairs the busted doll possessed by the spirit of her dead lover (voiced by Dourif), but becomes a doll herself. Don't ask, just enjoy the jolts and the jokes dished out by Hong Kong action director Yu. It's a pure DVD guilty pleasure.

Hot Bonus: Tilly goes into irresistibly kinky detail on the commentary track.

Key Scene: The doll sex between Chucky and his bride. "Do I have a rubber?" says Chucky, miffed at the question. "Look at me—I am rubber."

Bride of Frankenstein, The (1935)

Starring: Boris Karloff, Elsa Lanchester, Colin Clive, Ernest Thesiger

Directed by: James Whale

The original 1931 *Frankenstein* with Karloff as the monster is a horror classic. Amazingly, this sequel is even better. It's a tribute to Whale's mastery at blending humor and heartbreak in the guise of a scare flick. When Dr. Frankenstein (Clive) reluctantly joins with Dr. Pretorius (Thesiger, who must be seen to be believed) to create a bride for the monster, the result is Lanchester,

who achieves screen immortality with her electrified hair and jerky movements. The sets, costumes, and camerawork, lovingly parodied by Mel Brooks in *Young Frankenstein*, are DVD nirvana.

Hot Bonus: A documentary on the creation of the film, narrated by *Gremlins* director Joe Dante, is a history lesson in horror cinema.

Key Scene: The laugh-and-cry moment when the bride sees her groom-to-be for the first time and shouts, "Eeeek!" in rejection.

Bridge on the River Kwai, The (Two-Disc Special Edition) (1957)

Starring: Alec Guinness, William Holden, Sessue Hayakawa

Directed by: David Lean

The winner of seven Oscars, including Best Picture, is a landmark war film set in Burma in 1943. Prisoners of war, led by a British colonel (Guinness), are forced by the Japanese commander (Hayakawa, superb) to build a bridge as a morale exercise while guerilla forces, led by a roguish Holden, are sent to destroy it. Lean's brilliant epic about the madness of war has been transferred to DVD in pristine condition with no attempts to juice up image and sound. Why argue with perfection?

Hot Bonus: This edition shoots the works on extras, notably a retrospective documentary that pulls no punches about a troubled production .

Key Scene: The destruction of the bridge. Guinness won the Best Actor Oscar, and you can see why just in his reading of the line, "What have I done?" right before all hell breaks loose.

Bridges at Toko-Ri, The (1954)

Starring: William Holden, Grace Kelly, Frederic March

Directed by: Mark Robson

DVD saves this unfairly neglected war film from oblivion. Holden stars as a WW2 navy pilot, now a family man married to the beauteous Kelly, called back into active duty in Korea. Based on James Michener's novel, the movie delivers both action and provocative insights into U.S. military policy.

Hot Bonus: The trailer, which seems to be hyping a different movie.

Key Scene: The bombing of the five bridges of Toko-Ri helped the movie win an Oscar for special effects. But the real drama is on Holden's face just before the bombing as he reluctantly faces what he believes is certain death.

Bring Me the Head of Alfredo Garcia (1974)

Starring: Warren Oates, Isela Vega, Gig Young, Robert Webber

Directed by: Sam Peckinpah

A criminally underrated Peckinpah classic finally makes it to DVD with all its surreal, gonzo brilliance intact. Oates gives the performance of his life as Bennie, an American bar pianist who hightails it to Mexico to collect a million-dollar bounty by bringing back the head of Alfredo Garcia, the stud who impregnated the daughter of the wrong tycoon. Young and Webber play two gay hitmen, and Vega is the hooker who tells Bennie that Garcia is already dead, necessitating a trip to the cemetery to dig up and decapitate the body. The film is an existential meditation on manhood and its loss, and as pure a look as exists into the head of its director, a working alcoholic with a genius for showing how violence defines character.

Hot Bonus: Insightful commentary by Peckinpah scholars Paul Seydor, Garner Simmons, and David Weddle, though the notorious deleted scene in which Oates allegedly has sex with Vega's dead body is not included.

Key Scene: Oates in the car talking to the head, as flies buzz about.

Bringing Up Baby (Two-Disc Special Edition) (1938)

Starring: Katharine Hepburn, Cary Grant
Directed by: Howard Hawks

When asked to define screwball comedy at its peak, here's your answer. Hepburn plays a fast-talking heiress with a pet leopard (that's Baby) and a dog who steals a dinosaur bone from a shy paleontologist she falls for hard, not surprisingly since he's played by Grant. Hawks brings out the zany best in his stars, and this digitally remastered DVD lets them sparkle anew after years of faded TV prints and drab videos.

Hot Bonus: Peter Bogdanovich, who directed his own tribute to Baby with 1972's *What's Up, Doc?*, talks you through Hawks, Grant, Hepburn, and 1930s comedy in a commentary that is a model of scholarly wit.

Key Scene: The collapse of the dinosaur bones is famous, but it's hard to forget Grant's answer when he's asked why he's wearing a fetching negligee: "Because I just went gay all of a sudden."

Broadcast News (1987)

Starring: Holly Hunter, William Hurt, Albert Brooks, Jack Nicholson
Directed and written by: James L. Brooks

This smart, funny satire of TV news may lack the punch of *Network*, but it still gets in its licks. The plot spins around Jane, a principled TV news producer (Hunter) in Washington, who relates deeply to Aaron, a serious reporter (Brooks, no relation to the director, is sublimely funny and touching), but is sexually drawn to Tom, a Ken doll anchorman (Hurt) who has to be fed lines through an earpiece. All the actors are terrific, including Nicholson as a preening star anchor from New York. The DVD shrewdly preserves the film's bright, TV-friendly look, the better to surprise us with the comic bite of Brooks's script.

Hot Bonus: A trailer that hits exactly the right notes.

Key Scene: Aaron getting his chance in the anchor chair and perspiring like a marathon runner. Brooks delivers the line, "This is more than Nixon ever sweated," with bone-dry humor.

Broadway: The Golden Age (2003)

Starring: Carol Burnett, Jerry Orbach, Barbara Cook, and dozens of others
Directed and written by: Rick McKay

From *Ain't It Cool News* to *Variety*, the reviews were rapturous for McKay's magical treasure hunt of a movie. He grew up in the 1960s in Indiana, so far from Broadway that he had to create it in his imagination. When McKay finally saw live theater in New York, many stars had moved on. So he set out to find them with his camera and his unstoppable passion. That's the movie, and it's one for the time capsule. McKay recorded more than 250 hours of interviews with legends too numerous to mention and added archival footage, from the voice of Marlon Brando onstage in *A Streetcar Named Desire* to John Raitt in *Carousel*. The DVD is a permanent record of how McKay distilled their memories into two hours of spun gold.

Hot Bonus: A sneak preview of *Broadway: The Next Generation* that will have you salivating.

Key Scene: At the end, the feisty stage legend Elaine Stritch scolds, "For Christ's sake, Rick, don't you have enough?" Not nearly.

Buena Vista Social Club (1999)

Starring: Ry Cooder
Directed by: Wim Wenders

It couldn't be simpler: Guitarist Cooder gathered a group of Cuba's legendary musicians and singers and recorded a Grammy-winning album. Director Wenders followed up by filming a documentary of the Buena Vista Social Club in concert interspersed with members, well into their eighties, telling the stories of their lives. The DVD will be music to your ears.

Hot Bonus: Additional concert footage, plus narration from Wenders that he omitted from the theatrical version of the film.

Key Scene: The audience in modern Havana reacting to seeing these veterans again after so many years.

Bugsy (1991)

Starring: Warren Beatty, Annette Bening, Harvey Keitel, Ben Kingsley
Directed by: Barry Levinson

Beatty tears into the role of Bugsy Siegel, the family man gangster who ran the West Coast rackets in the 1940s, wore elegant clothes, and screwed the sexiest women, notably starlet Virginia Hill

(Bening, whose sizzle with Beatty was for real—they married the following year). Siegel even had ambitions to act, but his big dream was to build a gambling palace—the Flamingo—in the desert of Las Vegas. Directed in high style by Levinson, the film owes much to the actors—Kingsley and Keitel, playing mobsters, were Oscar nominated along with Beatty—and even more to James Toback's boldly perceptive script that is less an indictment of the dark side than a black-comic look at our continuing fascination with it.

Hot Bonus: A trailer that evokes the gangster films Bugsy Siegel prized.

Key Scene: The vain Bugsy taking a break during a brutal fight to give himself an appreciative once-over in a mirror.

Bull Durham (1988)

Starring: Kevin Costner, Susan Sarandon, Tim Robbins

Directed and written by: Ron Shelton

"I believe in the church of baseball," says Sarandon's Annie Savoy in one of the most memorable opening lines in movies. This major movie about the minor leagues focuses on the Durham Bulls of North Carolina. Annie loves the team so much, she chooses one player a year to school in the art of literature and sex. This summer's candidates are Nuke LaLoosh (Robbins), a horny but brainless pitcher, and Crash Davis (Costner), a seasoned catcher. Shelton gets all the details right as writer and debuting director. The DVD image is so authentically funky you can practically smell it, and the three leads perform at the top of their games.

Hot Bonus: Shelton, who spent five years in the minors, delivers a richly detailed commentary track that adds much to the movie.

Key Scene: Costner's "I Believe" speech, which ends with the line, "I believe in long, slow, deep, soft, wet kisses that last three days," and ends with Sarandon uttering, "Oh my." Now that's baseball.

Bullets Over Broadway (1994)

Starring: John Cusack, Dianne Wiest, Jennifer Tilly, Chazz Palminteri

Directed and co-written by: Woody Allen

One of the best comedies of Allen's later period, it's as much a moral meditation as it is dazzling fun. Allen, who doesn't act in the film, casts Cusack as his younger alter-ego, a laughably serious playwright in the Roaring Twenties who is forced to cast a gangster's moll (Tilly, delicious) in a play starring a grand dame (Wiest, in an Oscar-winning tour de force). Allen spoofs his own early pretentiousness (think *Interiors*) through the moll's bodyguard (a dynamite Palminteri). "You don't write like people talk," says the hood, a primitive with talent and the passion to kill for his art. With rueful wisdom, Allen has crafted his first movie in which art is no excuse.

Hot Bonus: The widescreen transfer does glorious justice to the film's period allure.

Key Scene: "Don't speak," says Wiest to Cusack when he won't see things her way. Then, with a ravishing Central Park as her backdrop, she turns him into silly putty. In Woody's world, Manhattan is always the best seducer.

Bullitt (Two-Disc Special Edition) (1968)

Starring: Steve McQueen, Jacqueline Bisset, Robert Vaughn

Directed by: Peter Yates

The DVD makes this iconic McQueen cop flick, set in San Francisco, look as cool as the day it was made. The plot, about the cop's battle with a devious politician (Vaughn at his sleaziest) and his love for a good woman (Bisset) is merely an excuse to see McQueen in action.

Hot Bonus: A "making of" special that shows McQueen, then thirty-eight, doing as many of the driving stunts as the insurance company would allow. He would die at fifty, but Bullitt helped make his screen memory indelible.

Key Scene: The car chase up and down those Frisco hills—director Yates used handheld cameras—started a movie tradition that has never been equaled, though I'll take arguments about *The French Connection*.

Butch Cassidy and the Sundance Kid (Special Edition) (1969)

Starring: Paul Newman, Robert Redford, Katharine Ross

Directed by: George Roy Hill

The DVD of this fact-based western wants to show off Newman as Butch and Redford as Sun

dance like prime studs at a thoroughbred convention. At that it succeeds beautifully. It's a fact-based tale about how our two train-robbing antiheroes, along with Sundance's schoolmarm squeeze (Ross), left the Old West in 1905 to rob banks in Bolivia. But for all the sassy dialogue in William Goldman's script and all the zoomy-woozy camera tricks in director Hill's bag, this film flies on one thing: star power.

Hot Bonus: It's great to hear Newman and Redford looking back and bitching up a storm about the lousy reviews the film received at the time.

Key Scene: The jump off the cliff into the river with Sundance confessing he can't swim and Butch saying, "Don't worry, the fall will probably kill you anyway."

Cabaret (Special Edition) (1972)

Starring: Liza Minnelli, Joel Grey, Michael York, Helmut Griem

Directed by: Bob Fosse

Wilkommen to what many believe is the last truly great movie musical, which arrives on DVD looking as fresh and divinely decadent as the day Fosse reconceived the stage version for the screen. American chanteuse Sally Bowles (Minnelli, dazzling for the ages) works the sleazy Kit Kat Klub in Berlin as the Nazis come to power and she slips into a sexual three-way with a Brit writer (York) and a German baron (Griem). Grey excels as the leering emcee, and the stinging score by John Kander and Fred Ebb is augmented with such nifty newies as "Mein Herr" and "Money, Money."

Hot Bonus: A behind-the-scenes look at the making of the film is coupled with a retrospective documentary in which Minnelli and others consider the film's impact. Fosse, who died in 1987, won the Best Director Oscar over heated competition from *The Godfather*'s Francis Coppola.

Key Scene: Minnelli and Grey both won Oscars and both electrify, but the moment that sticks longest is the "Tomorrow Belongs to Me" number in which a patriotic anthem sung by soldiers and citizens in a German beer garden becomes a ringing and chilling triumph of the Nazi will.

Caddyshack (Collector's Edition) (1980)

Starring: Rodney Dangerfield, Bill Murray, Chevy Chase, Ted Knight

Directed by: Harold Ramis

This is *not* classic comedy, but with Dangerfield as a gross, newly rich member of a swank golf club, Knight as the stuffed shirt he offends, Chase as a Zen golf pro, and especially Murray as one nutty groundskeeper who chases a gopher and gets turned on by female golfers of a certain age, the laughs keep coming. The DVD looks tacky, just as it should.

Hot Bonus: The outtakes, especially the one with Murray and Chase.

Key Scene: The turd in the swimming pool—I'll say no more.

Caged Heat (1974)

Starring: Erica Gavin, Juanita Brown, Barbara Steele

Directed by: Jonathan Demme

Long before Demme won an Oscar for directing *The Silence of the Lambs*, he began his career with this Big Momma of a women-in-prison movie. It has since spawned a cult, and for good reason. Demme, working for B-movie giant Roger Corman, not only got the "girls" into a cellblock and into the showers, he snuck in a feminist message about empowerment.

Hot Bonus: An interview with Corman, who gave then new directors such as Demme, Scorsese, and Coppola a chance to work fast, cheap, and loose and show what they could do. Demme showed plenty.

Key Scene: The intro of Steele as the wheelchair-bound prison warden.

Caine Mutiny, The (1954)

Starring: Humphrey Bogart, Van Johnson, Fred MacMurray, José Ferrer

Directed by: Edward Dmytryk

Bogart grabbed the last great role of his career as Queeg, the by-the-book skipper of a World War II minesweeper cursed with name of "Caine." When Queeg goes nuts with the pressure of command, a few of his good men, led by Maryk (John-son) and the Iago-ish Keefer (MacMurray, he should have had the Oscar nomination that went to Tom Tully in the nothing role of the ship's for-mer captain), stage a mutiny. The result is a pip of a court-martial with Ferrer superb as the lawyer who destroys Queeg on the stand.

Hot Bonus: Nothing but a gorgeous DVD trans-fer. I'll take it.

Key Scene: Queeg on the stand, sweating, turn-ing steel balls in his hand and muttering crazily about the strawberries. Bogart's genius was to make you understand and almost admire a man you hate.

Camp (2003)

Starring: Tiffany Taylor, Anna Kendrick, Alana Allen

Directed and written by: Todd Graff

Shot by first-time director Graff in twenty-three days on a shoestring with an unknown cast, the movie is a blast of exuberant fun. The teens at Camp Ovation are self-proclaimed show freaks who have no idea who Neil Young is. Graff at-tended the Camp (Stagedoor Manor in Loch Shel-drake, New York) that the film is based on and where it was shot. The climactic number, "Here's Where I Stand," is a rouser. Sung by Jenna (the sensational Taylor), the song is a burst of defiance and joy. You can feel it all on the DVD.

Hot Bonus: The documentary that tells you about these Camp kids.

Key Scene:. The revenge that Fritzi (a terrific Kendrick) takes on bombshell Jill (Allen) for treat-ing her like a slave. It involves a household poi-son, much puking, and Fritzi replacing Jill onstage to sing "The Ladies Who Lunch." You'd laugh hearing this teenager sing Sondheim's caustic cry of middle-age angst, if she didn't do it with such showstopping conviction.

Cape Fear (Collector's Edition) (1991)

Starring: Robert De Niro, Nick Nolte, Jessica Lange, Juliette Lewis

Directed by: Martin Scorsese

Scorsese tackles suspense with this tale of Max Cady (De Niro, Oscar nominated for the role), a nutjob who gets out of prison and plots revenge against the lawyer (Nolte) who framed him and the lawyer's wife (Lange) and their hottie teen daughter (Lewis). The movie looks great on this widescreen DVD. Scorsese doesn't exactly im-prove on the 1962 Cape Fear with Robert Mit-chum as Cady, but he does expand things to ex-

amine issues of sin, guilt, and redemption—you know, make a Scorsese movie.

Hot Bonus: The behind-the-scenes stuff on the Collector's Edition is rich in detail, but give your-self a bonus by rewatching the original Cape Fear before getting into this one. The differences speak volumes.

Key Scene: Cady, posing as a teacher, con-fronts the lawyer's daughter in the basement of her school. He strokes her hair and softly kisses her, and she responds with a mixture of fear and excitement. It's a seductively chilling moment, hypnotically played by De Niro and Lewis.

Capturing the Friedmans (2003)

Directed by: Andrew Jarecki

This brilliant and unnerving documentary comes to DVD in a bonus-packed two disc set. It's a modern horror story. The Friedmans—husband Arnold, a teacher; his wife, Elaine; and their three sons, David, Seth, and Jesse—lived in Long Island, New York, in 1987, when the police broke down the front door and battered the family with accu-sations that Arnold, who taught computer class-es in the family basement, had molested many of the young boys in his charge. Jesse, eighteen, is also implicated. Director Jarecki uses interviews with the Friedmans and investigators, bolstered by home movies made by David, the eldest son who works as a professional clown, to dig into a dis-turbed family psyche where the only thing out of reach is the truth.

Hot Bonus: More on the case, including com-pelling new evidence, witnesses, and uncut foot-age of the prosecution's star witness.

Key Scene: The home movie of the last Fried-man family meeting before Arnold goes to jail is the cinematic equivalent of an open wound.

Carnal Knowledge (1971)

Starring: Jack Nicholson, Ann-Margret, Candice Bergen, Art Garfunkel

Directed by: Mike Nichols

Director Nichols would return to the theme of sex as war in 2004's Closer, but you can still feel the sting in his film of Jules Feiffer's savagely witty script. Nicholson is a male sexual predator and Garfunkel is his weak acolyte. The film—cap-tured on DVD in all its toxic glow—follows them from college to middle age. Bergen, at her best, and Ann-Margret, justly Oscar-nominated, are two of the women they try to destroy. Nicholson had never before used his potent charm for such dar-ingly ugly purposes.

Hot Bonus: The letterboxing of the film. The

cropped version is also presented to let you see the damage TV does to the film's brilliant design.

Key Scene: Nicholson, sitting in a bath towel, verbally reducing Ann-Margret to emotional rubble. You wince, but you can't turn away.

Carnival of Souls (1962)

Starring: Candace Hilligoss, Sidney Berger, Herk Harvey

Directed by: Herk Harvey

Director Harvey made this surreal, low-budget (thirty-thousand-dollar) chiller in an abandoned amusement park that extended into Utah's Great Salt Lake. The Criterion DVD brings back all the haunting beauty of the black-and-white cinematography as Mary (Hilligoss) survives drowning when a car plunges into a river and begins to see (or does she?) the souls of the dead.

Hot Bonus: The Director's Cut of the film, running eighty-three minutes, five minutes more than the theatrical release, is included, along with a documentary of the 1989 reunion of the cast and crew that may answer your nagging questions about this cult phenom.

Key Scene: Mary's first realization that the people around her aren't real.

Carousel (1956)

Starring: Shirley Jones, Gordon MacRae
Directed by: Henry King

The darkest story that Rodgers & Hammerstein ever set to music is also arguably their best. Horndog carousel barker Billy Bigelow (MacRae) falls for the virginal Julie Jordan (Jones, at her loveliest), a millworker in a Maine fishing village. He gets her pregnant, gets himself dead in a robbery, and ends up begging heaven for a last chance to see his wife and now-grown daughter. Frank Sinatra started the film as Billy—his classic recording of the famous "Soliloquy" survives—but walked off when asked to do two different widescreen versions of the film. The CinemaScope version released in theaters has been gorgeously preserved on the DVD.

Hot Bonus: A Movietone newsreel covering the film's premiere.

Key Scene: Billy's ghost standing alongside his wife at their daughter's graduation, saying: "I loved you, Julie. Know that I love you." This is corn served up by masters.

Carrie (Special Edition) (1976)

Starring: Sissy Spacek, Piper Laurie, William Katt, John Travolta

Directed by: Brian De Palma

"If I concentrate hard enough, I can move things," says Carrie (Spacek) to her religious fanatic momma (Laurie). I'll say. Carrie's telekinetic powers take on a lethal side when she gets a dream date (Katt) to her high school prom only to learn that her classmates, led by Travolta, have a dirty trick planned involving pig's blood and rampant humiliation. De Palma directs this brutal tale—the best screen adaptation of Stephen King after *The Shining*—with wicked wit and stunning lyricism. Spacek and Laurie were Oscar nominated, and this DVD proves the film has stood the test of time.

Hot Bonus: With King on the evolution of the story, Spacek on acting it, and De Palma on directing it, you wouldn't think that a featurette about the making of Broadway's *Carrie: The Musical*—a flop for the ages—would top everything. It does.

Key Scene: The prom, of course, but that last-minute shock is a keeper.

Casablanca (Two-Disc Special Edition) (1942)

Starring: Humphrey Bogart, Ingrid Bergman, Paul Henreid, Claude Rains

Directed by: Michael Curtiz

As time goes by, it's still the definitive movie love story. And this special edition of the Oscar winner shows off Arthur Edeson's black-and-white cinematography to stunning advantage. Bogart is at his iconic best as Rick, a club owner in Morocco who finds his conscience when he finds his lost love (Bergman, never more radiant), and helps her and her Resistance leader husband (Henreid) escape the Nazis. For those who think the problems of three little people don't amount to a hill of beans in this crazy world, here's proof to the contrary. If this DVD is your first encounter with *Casablanca*, this will be the beginning of a beautiful friendship.

Hot Bonus: Ten minutes of deleted scenes, and funny and touching reminiscences from Bogart's widow, Lauren Bacall, their son Stephen, and Bergman's daughters, Pia Lindstrom and Isabella Rossellini.

Key Scene: "Here's looking at you, kid."

Casino (Tenth Anniversary Edition) (1995)

Starring: Robert De Niro, Sharon Stone, Joe Pesci

Directed by: Martin Scorsese

Scorsese's epic tale of mob infiltration of Las Vegas during the 1970s finally gets the bonus-packed DVD treatment it deserves. Based on Nicholas Pileggi's nonfiction book, the film weaves visual poetry out of warped ambitions. De Niro is miscast as Sam, the Jewish hood who runs the casino for the mob. Pesci is typecast as Nicky, his hotheaded hit-man pal. And the Oscar-nominated Stone steals the movie as Ginger, the ex-showgirl Sam marries and Nicky screws, playing Iago to Sam's Othello. Scorsese misses Shakespearean grandeur, but hits the mark when he's working an obsession: watching Sam watching the money.

Hot Bonus: Seeing Scorsese run the Riviera Hotel (called the Tangiers on screen) like a general. Plus deleted scenes and production material.

Key Scene: The lusciously fluid sequence, which tracks the flow of cash from gambler to bagman. Nearly the entire first hour of Casino could pass for a documentary on how money is won, lost, counted, and skimmed.

Cassavetes, John: Five Films (The Box Set)

Starring: Gena Rowlands, Peter Falk, Seymour Cassel, Ben Gazzara

Directed and written by: John Cassavetes

Criterion's eight-disc set of five films from one of the founding fathers of independent cinema qualifies as a DVD event. Cassavetes, who died at fifty-nine in 1989, was an actor, writer, and director so fed up with the Hollywood mainstream that he decided to make his own low-budget, harsh, admittedly over-the-top indies to get audiences to relate honestly to films again. Watch these five films with an eye to how his influence is still being felt:

• *Shadows* (1959)—His directing debut was an emotionally loaded love story between a woman (Lelia Goldoni), trying to pass for white, and a Caucasian man (Anthony Ray) that stands as the rawest example of Cassavetes' talent.

• *Faces* (1968)—After two unsatisfying attempts to direct within the star-driven studio system—1961's *Too Late Blues* with Bobby Darin and 1963's *A Child Is Waiting* with Judy Garland and Burt Lancaster—Cassavetes returned to his barebones approach to create this searing study of infidelity in which a husband (John Marley) has a night with a hooker (Gena Rowlands, Mrs. Cassavetes off-screen) while his wife (Lynn Carlin) takes home a hippie stud (Seymour Cassel). With Cassel and Carlin winning Oscar nominations, the Cassavetes reputation began its rise.

• *A Woman under the Influence* (1974)—Oscar called again with nominations for Cassavetes as Best Director and the reliably superb Rowlands as Best Actress for playing an L.A. wife and mother unraveling mentally with no help and a little push from her blue-collar husband (the excellent Peter Falk).

• *The Killing of a Chinese Bookie* (1976)—This is the film that separates the Cassavetes enthusiasts from the mere admirers. It's a thriller paced like a character study about the owner of a strip joint (Cassavetes pal and acting giant Ben Gazzara) who can erase his gambling debt in exchange for a murder. It may take two or three viewings, but it grows on you.

• *Opening Night* (1977)—Another tour de force for Gena Rowlands as a stage actress having a meltdown on the opening night of her play, *The Second Woman*, due to the death of a fan. Cassavetes plays her co-star in the play; he's a fitting bystander to this tribute to the art of his wife and the transcendent power of acting, which he built his films to honor.

Hot Bonus: The restoration demonstration that shows how these films were brought back to life on DVD.

Key Scene: The first frame of *Shadows*, which started Cassavetes on a career that labeled him genius and tyrant, often at the same time.

Cast Away (Double Digipack) (2000)

Starring: Tom Hanks, Helen Hunt

Directed by: Robert Zemeckis

It's all Hanks, as a FedEx systems engineer whose goal is time management—even in planning his marriage to Hunt. Then he ends up lost and alone on a deserted island when his plane crashes and he has to play *Survivor* for four years without a team. It seems unfair now that Hanks lost the Best Actor to Russell Crowe (*Gladiator*), so funny and moving is his performance, which shines all the more on this immaculately produced two-disc package.

Hot Bonus: A featurette on Wilson, the volleyball that Hanks talks to throughout the film. Wilson never got his due as a supporting actor.

Key Scene: Zemeckis can claim to have directed one of the scariest plane crashes in movie history. You'll duck and sweat watching it on the DVD.

Cat People (1942)

Starring: Simone Simon, Kent Smith, Jane Randolph

Directed by: Jacques Tourneur

It's what you don't see that scares you in the long-awaited DVD of producer Val Lewton's most famous scare flick. Director Tourneur works by indirection as Balkan sketch artist Irena Dubrovna (the mysterious Simon) marries architect Oliver Reed (Smith) but won't go all the way because sex brings out the cat in her—the dangerous kind. When Smith confides in a friend, Alice (Randolph), jealous Irena's claws come out. On DVD, the film has the effect of a wisp of smoke that grows thick enough to choke you. Paul Schrader's 1982 color remake, while not uninteresting, hits you over the head with the sex and gore. Tourneur is out to haunt your dreams.

Hot Bonus: There's audio commentary from Simon, who died in 2005, but the real treat is the inclusion of *The Curse of the Cat People*, the 1944 sequel that is equally charged with moody atmospherics.

Key Scene: Simon terrorizing Randolph at a deserted indoor swimming pool.

Catch-22 (1970)

Starring: Alan Arkin, Buck Henry, Richard Benjamin, Martin Balsam

Directed by: Mike Nichols

This widescreen DVD makes a strong case for reevaluating the film version of Joseph Heller's best-seller about the insanity of war. Critically reviled at the time, the film now seems bitingly relevant. Arkin is the perfect choice for Yossarian, the World War II bombardier who thinks it's crazy to drop any more bombs, but because it's sane to think that way he can't be sent home on the grounds that he's crazy. That's Catch-22. Henry, who wrote the script, joins Benjamin, Balsam, and a cast of crazies that includes Orson Welles as a general whose standard command is: "Take him out and shoot him!" Nichols delivers the kind of laughs that stick in your throat.

Hot Bonus: A sharp and informative discussion of the film with Nichols and *Traffic* director Steven Soderbergh.

Key Scene: The gut-spilling moment when we realize why the bombardier is crying for help, though the planes taking off at dawn runs a close second.

Charade (1963)

Starring: Cary Grant, Audrey Hepburn, Walter Matthau

Directed by: Stanley Donen

You can't go wrong putting the impossibly glam Grant and Hepburn in a mystery-romance set in an impossibly glam Paris. And with Criterion rescuing the film from the hell of faded broadcast prints, *Charade* runs off the DVD with the bracing freshness of Henry Mancini's score.

Hot Bonus: Donen and screenwriter Peter Stone sharing war stories about the shooting. It's too bad they hadn't yet seen Jonathan Demme's *The Truth About Charlie*, a ham-fisted remake that makes the original shine anew.

Key Scene: Hepburn to Grant: "Do you know what's wrong with you?" He: "No, what?" She (swooning): "Absolutely nothing."

Chariots of Fire (Two-Disc Special Edition) (1981)

Starring: Ben Cross, Ian Charleson, Ian Holm

Directed by: Hugh Hudson

Now that dust has settled over this inspirational British drama about the track competition in

the 1924 Paris Olympics beating Warren Beatty's *Reds* in an upset for the Best Picture Oscar, it's nice to see *Chariots* getting the royal two-disc treatment. Director Hudson's film hasn't looked this good since it opened. Cross plays Harold Abrahams, the English Jew whose reaction to anti-Semitism was to push himself to run harder and faster. Charleson plays Eric Liddell, an evangelical Christian who ran to glorify God. As for Holm, he stole his scenes and an Oscar nomination as Sam Mussabini, the Italian-Turkish track coach.

Hot Bonus: *Wings on Their Heels* is a stirring documentary that also catches us up on what happened to Abrahams and Liddell.

Key Scene: No contest—it's the opening run on the beach set to the music of Vangelis that has been much imitated and parodied.

Chasing Amy (Special Edition) (1997)

Starring: Ben Affleck, Jason Lee, Joey Lauren Adams
Directed and written by: Kevin Smith

Smith's third film as a writer-director-actor is a rude blast of sexual provocation. It's a love story between two cartoonists: Alyssa (Adams), a lesbian, and Holden (Affleck), a straight guy. See my point? Even Holden's roommate, Banky (Lee), is appalled, as are Alyssa's lesbian friends. Holden isn't jealous of women, but when he hears of Alyssa's former affairs with other men, he freaks out. To resolve his confusion, he invites Alyssa and Banky to join him in a three-way. Affleck, Adams, and Lee bring out all the humor and hurt in Smith's characters.

Hot Bonus: Ten deleted scenes, plus outtakes.

Key Scene: When Jay (Jason Mewes) and Silent Bob (Smith) show up. The duo is featured in nearly all Smith movies, but never with more pointed fun than here, as Silent Bob explains to Holden what it means to be chasing an Amy, a symbol of someone you're not meant to catch. Wisdom, man.

Chicago (Three-Disc Razzle-Dazzle Edition) (2002)

Starring: Renée Zellweger, Richard Gere, Catherine Zeta-Jones, Queen Latifah
Directed by: Rob Marshall

The Oscar-winning Best Picture looks like a million on this extra-packed DVD. Some people rip on this razzle-dazzler because the characters aren't lovable. Grow up. Based on Bob Fosse's Broadway smash, this musical kills. Literally. Its 1920s gold diggers, Roxie (Zellweger) and Velma (Oscar winner Zeta-Jones), both reached for a gun when their men done them wrong. But with the help of a slick lawyer, Billy Flynn (Gere), they plan to get out of the prison run by Matron Mama Morton (Latifah is a sassy wonder) by appealing to the mercy of the court and the tabloids. Broadway director Marshall makes a smashing debut in features, presenting the musical numbers as fantasies. Even when Roxie abuses her doormat husband, Amos (John C. Reilly), Zellweger wins our hearts. The cast gives its all to the John Kander and Fred Ebb score and dance with flair. Did they have help in the editing? Probably. But who cares when you're having this much fun?

Hot Bonus: The deleted musical number "Class," featuring Zeta-Jones and the Queen, should never, ever have been deleted.

Key Scene: The "Cell Block Tango," in which all the leggy ladies on Murderer's Row sing and dance about the crimes that landed them in jail.

Children of Paradise (1945)

Starring: Jean-Louis Barrault, Arletty, Pierre Brasseur
Directed by: Marcel Carné

As one of the best films ever made about the theatrical experience, Carne's masterpiece, shot in secret during the Nazi occupation of France, fully deserves its restoration to glory at the hands of Criterion. The film—set in Paris in the early nineteenth-century—actually parallels the French Resistance in the story of a mime (the great Barrault) who won't admit impediments to his true love for the fickle woman (Arletty), who is also desired by his polar opposite, a verbally gifted Shakespearean thespian (Brasseur).

Hot Bonus: A restoration demonstration that will stun you.

Key Scene: The first glimpse of the children of paradise, the poor people who watch the plays and life from the distance of the galleries.

China Syndrome, The (Special Edition) (1979)

Starring: Jane Fonda, Jack Lemmon, Michael Douglas
Directed by: James Bridges

A TV reporter (Fonda) and a freelance cameraman (Douglas, who also produced) are doing a story on a nuclear power plant just as a crisis arises. Thanks to quick thinking from a plant engineer (a no-nonsense Lemmon, Oscar nominated), a meltdown is averted. That's when the engineer decides to share some dark secrets with the media. This potent thriller, looking and sounding sharper than ever on DVD, was prophetic of the Three Mile Island crisis that occurred just weeks after the film opened.

Hot Bonus: New interviews with Fonda and Douglas that deal with their reactions when the film's nightmarish fantasy became a reality.

Key Scene: Lemmon's face seconds before he believes all is lost.

Chinatown (1974)

Starring: Jack Nicholson, Faye Dunaway, John Huston
Directed by: Roman Polanski

Politics, incest, and murder involving water rights in 1930s Los Angeles add up to one of the greatest films of all time. Yet the flawlessly acted, written (by Robert Towne), and directed (by Polanski) *Chinatown* doesn't get nearly the DVD treatment it deserves. Though the digital sound is first-rate, the better for Jerry Goldsmith's ravishing score to get inside your head, the image is less crisp than it should be. And in a DVD world where special features are lavished on litter like *Catwoman*, this classic gets the one-disc once-over. No matter. It's a must-have DVD, just to watch a peak-form Nicholson as private eye Jake Gittes, nosing into the business of newly widowed Evelyn Mulwray (Dunaway, haughty and haunting) and her perverse tycoon daddy Noah Cross (the peerless Huston). "See Mr. Gittes," Cross tells Jake, "most people never have to face that fact that at the right time and the right place they are capable of anything." Drawing on Watergate, Polanski ends his film in a darkness where no one can fight City Hall and win. The film's last line reverberates: "Forget it, Jake, it's Chinatown."

Hot Bonus: Retrospective with Polanski, Towne, and producer Robert Evans. But where's Nicholson? I wanted more, more, more.

Key Scene: When Dunaway explains: "She's my sister and my daughter."

Chopper (2000)

Starring: Eric Bana
Directed by: Andrew Dominik

A DVD for one of those quiet nights when your stomach is settled and you can stand the gut-churning violence in this fictionalized but diabolically funny story of Mark "Chopper" Read (Bana), an Australian folk hero who actually wrote books about killing and mutilating assorted drug dealers and lowlife scum. The DVD catches every chop and blood spurt with alarming verisimilitude. Chopper could talk his way out of anything—almost. Bana, beefed up and scarily brilliant, has so far never matched his impact here.

Hot Bonus: An interview with the real Mark Read.

Key Scene: Chopper reading the love letters he gets from female fans.

Christmas Carol, A (Deluxe Special Edition) (1951)

Starring: Alastair Sim, Patrick Macnee
Directed by: Brian Desmond-Hurst

The Charles Dickens classic about the Christmas reformation of the miserly, miserable Scrooge has been remade to death. But there is only one screen Scrooge who does Dickens justice, and that is Sim, a Scottish actor whose sour face hid reserves of high hilarity. This DVD has been remastered from the original negative discovered in England, so why they also included an appalling colorized version of the film is beyond me. Accept no substitutes for the black-and-white film, which preserves Sim's definitive portrayal (shamefully not Oscar nominated), and is worth watching in any season.

Hot Bonus: Macnee, who plays the young Jacob Marley, does an introduction that sets up the film nicely.

Key Scene: Scrooge waking up on Christmas morning. Sim does a little happy dance that deserves placement in a time capsule.

Cinema Paradiso (The New Version) (1988)

Starring: Philippe Noiret, Salvatore Cascio, Jacques Perrin

Directed and written by:
Giuseppe Tornatore

Just after World War II, in a small Sicilian town, a boy named Salvatore (Cascio) strikes up a friendship with a Alfredo (Noiret, a master), a theater projectionist who must remove kissing scenes from any movie he shows. As the years pass, Salvatore learns lessons in art and life from Alfredo that serve him well later when he (played by Perrin) becomes a filmmaker. Sentimental blather for those who don't love cinema and paradise for those who do, the film gets immaculate treatment on the DVD, which presents the new version of the film (the Director's Cut) at 173 minutes and also the release version, 50 minutes shorter, that won the Oscar for Best Foreign Film in 1989. The new version, which develops characters and adds immeasurably to the film's emotional gravity, is much preferred.

Hot Bonus: An English-dubbed track if you hate reading subtitles.

Key Scene: That four-hankie moment when the grown Salvatore runs a reel of all those love scenes that Alfredo had to cut.

Citizen Kane (Two-Disc Special Edition) (1941)

Starring: Orson Welles, Joseph Cotten, Everett Sloane, Ruth Warrick

Directed and co-written by: Orson Welles

The American Film Institute (and practically everyone else) calls Welles's debut film—a fictionalized take on publishing tycoon William Randolph Hearst—the best movie ever made. No big complaints here, except all that academic posturing makes watching it seem like eating peas because they're good for you. The surprise for newcomers is what a fun blast it is. Welles, twenty-five at the time, treated the camera like a toy he could use to create magic. He did. From the script by Welles and Herman J. Mankiewicz and the deep-focus photography of Gregg Toland and the music of Bernard Herrmann and the editing of Robert Wise to the resonant acting of Welles in the title role right down to the smallest parts, *Kane* is the film of a young man high on the exhilaration of what a movie could do. And this DVD, delivering the film in all its pristine glory, lets you feel that exhilaration anew.

Hot Bonus: On the second disc, the documentary *The Battle Over Citizen Kane*, provides you with all the background you need on Hearst and Welles.

Key Scene: An impossible choice, they all are. But I'll pick that final look at Rosebud—the most famous symbol in movies—going up in flames.

Citizen Ruth (1996)

Starring: Laura Dern, Swoosie Kurtz, Mary Kay Place, Burt Reynolds

Directed and co-written by: Alexander Payne

The first film from director Payne (*Sideways*), who co-wrote the script with Jim Taylor, stars a stingingly funny Dern as Ruth Stoops, a pregnant, unwed, and unfit mother less concerned with her four kids than what new hazardous vapor she can inhale—glue or patio sealant, Ruth isn't fussy. That's when both sides of the abortion debate decide to recruit Ruth for their cause, and Payne gleefully tweaks pro-lifers and pro-choicers with wicked satirical relish. The DVD sets off Dern's tour de force like a jewel and shows that Payne had an eye for character detail even back in the beginning.

Hot Bonus: Juicy commentary from Payne and Taylor.

Key Scene: Ruth's "Oh God, help me!" reaction when she hears the police suggest that she should be spayed.

City Lights (1931)

Starring: Charlie Chaplin, Virginia Cherrill

Directed by: Charlie Chaplin

If you think silent movies are not for you, try this classic in which Chaplin's Little Tramp falls for a blind flower girl (Cherrill) and develops a magnificent obsession to find the money for an operation that will restore her sight. Slapstick, involving the girl mistaking the tramp's vest for her ball of wool, fuses with delicate feeling on a DVD that restores Chaplin's images to their former glory and adds a contemporary orchestration of the score.

Hot Bonus: Rehearsal footage of Chaplin working out a scene.

Key Scene: When the flower girl, who can now see, recognizes her hero.

City of God (2002)

Starring: Alexandre Rodrigues, Leandro Firmino da Hora

Directed by: Fernando Meirelles and Kátia Lund

Sometimes a movie comes along that just floors you, its images burn so deeply. You will see just how deeply on this vivid DVD. On the slum streets (called *favelas*) of Rio de Janeiro, children walk the streets in gangs, trading jokes and drugs, carrying guns and smiling when they use them. It's just a short walk from the resorts that coddle the tourist trade. The only miracle is living past your teens. Oscar-nominated director Meirelles moves this two-hour film, spanning the 1960s to the 1980s, with whiplash velocity. Among the cast of young amateurs, most impressive are Rodrigues as Rocket, who uses his interest in photography to bust out of the *favela*, and Firmino da Hora as Little Zé, a killer bred without a shred of conscience.

Hot Bonus: A documentary, *News From a Personal War*, that looks at the hard facts behind the film.

Key Scene: In a film of battering audacity, no shock hits harder than the way that Meirelles—remember the name, he's that good—choreographs murder to a dance beat, an exuberant form of kiddie recreation.

City of Lost Children, The (1995)

Starring: Ron Perlman, Daniel Emilfork, Joseph Lucien

Directed by: Jean-Pierre Jeunet and Marc Caro

Jeunet, who co-directed with Caro, has an eye for surreal visuals that is made for DVD. Even when the plot—about a circus strongman (Perlman) out to save a child from a kidnapping ring led by a disembodied brain (voiced by Jean-Louis Trintignant, no less)—is sometimes impossible to follow, the images will hold you in thrall.

Hot Bonus: A commentary track in which Jeunet, talking with Perlman, clears up a few of the mysteries.

Key Scene: The attack of malevolent Santas in the opener.

Clear and Present Danger (Special Collector's Edition) (1994)

Starring: Harrison Ford, Donald Moffat, Anne Archer

Directed by: Philip Noyce

The best of Ford's movies as Jack Ryan, the C.I.A. agent created by novelist Tom Clancy. Don't look too deep into the plot about a businessman friend of the U.S. president (Moffat) who gets involved in a Colombian drug cartel. Just watch Ford play hardass and Noyce direct action sequences that play like gangbusters on DVD.

Hot Bonus: The behind-the-scenes stuff shows how the action was staged, and with DTS sound you can feel the bullets whiz past your head.

Key Scene: Ford dressing down the president is high drama indeed.

Clerks (Three-Disc Anniversary Edition) (1994)

Starring: Brian O'Halloran, Jeff Anderson, Jason Mewes, Kevin Smith

Directed and written by: Kevin Smith

Three discs may seem a bit much for a grungy, low-budget comedy in black-and-white about a New Jersey convenience-store clerk (O'Halloran) and his pal (Anderson) who runs the video rental dump next door. But if you think that, you don't know Smith, who can coax laughs out of a still photo gallery. Disc 1 has the theatrical version with commentary. Disc 2 offers the unrated version with comments to match. And Disc 3 is loaded with extras, including TV spots with the inimitable Jay (Mewes) and Silent Bob (Smith).

Hot Bonus: Deleted scenes that are just as funny as what Smith left in.

Key Scene: The *Star Wars* monologue about the perils of being a contractor on the Death Star in a tie with the customer who has sex with a corpse.

Cliffhanger (Special Edition) (1993)

Starring: Sylvester Stallone, John Lithgow, Janine Turner

Directed by: Renny Harlin

Listening to Stallone spout bad dialogue, partly written by him, is no pleasure. But watching Stallone and a crew of brave stunt men throw themselves into the spectacular mountain-climbing action makes for a thrill-packed DVD. Stallone is part of a rescue operation in the Rockies (the film was actually shot in the Italian Alps) that turns into a trap involving bad guys led by a sneering Lithgow. Harlin directs the opening scene, in which Stallone vainly tries to rescue a babe hanging precipitously over an abyss, with palm-sweating skill.

Hot Bonus: A terrific piece on how the stunts were done shows that Stallone often put his own ass on the line.

Key Scene: I winced the most watching Stallone murder a villain with the name of Travers. It kept making me think of all the bad reviews I'd given Stallone's movies. This time, was it personal?

Clockwork Orange, A (Remastered) (1971)

Starring: Malcolm McDowell, Patrick Magee, Adrienne Corri

Directed by: Stanley Kubrick

Getting the remastered unrated version of Kubrick's futuristic film, vividly adapted from the Anthony Burgess novel, is a cause for celebration. McDowell gives the performance of his career as Alex, the young hood who leads his droogs on a spree of ultraviolence, breaking into homes and attacking women for a "a bit of the old in-out." That is until Alex is captured and brainwashed into reforming. Is the cure worse than the disease? That's the question that will haunt you long after you watched the DVD.

Hot Bonus: If you buy this DVD as part of the Stanley Kubrick Collection, containing seven other Kubrick landmarks, you get a new full-length documentary made by Kubrick assistant Jan Harlan, *Stanley Kubrick: A Life in Pictures*, that provides valuable and prickly insights into his work.

Key Scene: The rape scene set to the sounds of Gene Kelly warbling "Singin' in the Rain." It's a shocker—then and now.

Close Encounters of the Third Kind (Collector's Edition) (1977)

Starring: Richard Dreyfuss, Melinda Dillon, Carey Guffey, Francois Truffaut

Directed by: Steven Spielberg

This DVD—a model of image and sound—stands as the definitive version of Spielberg's wondrous sci-fi film about aliens who kick no ass. For the blood-and-guts crowd, that translates into wussy drivel. But the film's humanism is its distinction. Dreyfuss plays the lineman who sees the light and is driven mad by visions until a little boy (Guffey) and his mother (Dillon) help him believe. The final meeting of man and extraterrestrial, set to a memorable John Williams score, is tremendously moving.

Hot Bonus: Among the deleted scenes is a look inside the spaceship that Spielberg included in a 1998 version of the film that left too little to the imagination. The film plays better without it.

Key Scene: The landing of the mothership, a moment of thunderous DTS sound that will give your subwoofer the ride of its life.

Closer (Superbit) (2004)

Starring: Julia Roberts, Jude Law, Clive Owen, Natalie Portman

Directed by: Mike Nichols

Nichols orchestrates this film version of Patrick Marber's 1997 play about sex as a weapon of mass destruction into a master class on the art of directing. He makes impossible demands on the actors, and they meet every one. Roberts plays Anna, a photographer who cheats on her doctor husband, Larry (Owen) with Dan (Law). Larry takes out his rage on Dan's stripper girlfriend Alice (Portman). Owen, Oscar nominated, gives the role a raw intensity. Portman, also Oscar nominated, digs deep into the bruised core of her character. They locate something unexpected in *Closer*: a grieving heart.

Hot Bonus: The Superbit process, usually provided only for action epics, makes every moment in the film as crisp and penetrating as the dialogue.

Key Scene: Roberts and Owen battling over Law. "What does his semen taste like?" he demands. "Like yours, only sweeter," she says, cutting him no slack and delivering Roberts from the safety of her Hollywood comedies.

Clueless (The Whatever Edition) (1995)

Starring: Alicia Silverstone, Stacey Dash, Brittany Murphy

Directed by: Amy Heckerling

This sweetly barbed sendup of modern high school life made a star of Silverstone, who looks DVD-delectable as Cher, sixteen, a virgin who is less interested in sex, drugs, and rock & roll than power shopping. Director Heckerling's clever script functions as a lunatic update of *Emma*, the 1815 Jane Austen novel about a girl like Cher with "a disposition to think too well of herself." As if. Cher is a major dis queen ("Did I miss something? Is big hair back?"), a knack she's taught her best friend, Dionne (Dash). Cher rules the school, until she does a makeover on grungy transfer student (Brittany Murphy), whose later rebellion spells Cher's downfall.

Hot Bonus: A retrospective look at the cast is eye-opening, as are the comments from Heckerling.

Key Scene: The intro to Cher's bedroom, which houses a computer with browse and dress me controls and a mismatch warning.

Coal Miner's Daughter (Collector's Edition) (1980)

Starring: Sissy Spacek, Tommy Lee Jones, Beverly D'Angelo, Levon Helm

Directed by: Michael Apted

With all the fuss over Spacek's Oscar-winning performance as country legend Loretta Lynn (Sissy did her own singing and darn well), people tend to forget that the movie is a superior biopic with sterling performances from Jones as Loretta's complex husband, D'Angelo as her singing mentor Patsy Cline, and Helm as her coal miner daddy. The DVD is especially good at catching the color and feel of Lynn's roots in Butcher Holler, Kentucky, to contrast with her showbiz rise at the glitzy Grand Ole Opry.

Hot Bonus: Spacek, Jones, director Apted, and Lynn herself all contribute illuminating insights on the film and its impact.

Key Scene: The onstage breakdown helped get Spacek her Oscar, but the film's family roots cut to the heart when Lynn's daddy (Helm, of the Band, plays the role with understated artistry) says goodbye with the words: "You're my pride, girl, my shinin' pride."

Cold Mountain (Two-Disc Collector's Edition) (2003)

Starring: Nicole Kidman, Jude Law, Renée Zellweger, Natalie Portman

Directed by: Anthony Minghella

Written off because it didn't live up to its Best Picture Oscar expectations, this film version of Charles Frazier's lofty novel—it's really *The Odyssey* set during the Civil War—comes through beautifully on DVD. Law plays Inman, a wounded Confederate soldier so tormented by the fighting that he heads home on foot to the woman he left behind. She is Ada, and as embodied by the radiant Kidman she looks remarkably untouched by the hell of war—one of the valid criticisms against the film, especially when Ada works a farm with Ruby, a rough-spoken hellraiser played by Zellweger, who won the Oscar for Best Supporting Actress. What sticks, after watching this epic again on DVD, is the way director Minghella probes what it takes for a divided America to heal its wounds.

Hot Bonus: The material about making the film in rainy Romania.

Key Scene: Inman's night of warmth and violence in the cabin of a lonely war widow, incisively played by Portman.

Collateral (Two-Disc Edition) (2004)

Starring: Tom Cruise, Jamie Foxx

Directed by: Michael Mann

Director Mann's crime film is a headspinning ride with the devil through a Los Angeles night. As Vincent, a contract killer hired by a drug cartel to off five trial witnesses in the ten hours between dusk and dawn, Cruise takes his game to a new level. Matching him is Foxx as Max, the cabdriver Vincent forces into chauffeuring him on his murder spree. Foxx, Oscar nominated as Best Supporting Actor, fires up the screen, and his teamwork with Cruise is a thing of beauty as Mann orchestrates action, atmosphere, and bruising humor with a poet's eye for urban darkness.

Hot Bonus: A report on how Mann and cinematographers Paul Cameron and Dion Beebe shot 80 percent of the film on high-definition digital video to penetrate the L.A. darkness. The camerawork is groundbreaking.

Key Scene: Three coyotes crossing in front of Max's cab in mockery of the city's thin hold on civilization.

Color of Money, The (1986)

Starring: Paul Newman, Tom Cruise, Mary Elizabeth Mastrantonio

Directed by: Martin Scorsese

Scorsese's fine and flashy sequel to 1961's *The Hustler*, directed by Robert Rossen, brings back Newman as pool shark Fast Eddie Felson. Good move. Newman won his first Oscar and Scorsese moves the camera around a pool table like a general plotting war strategy—those shots are made for DVD. So is just looking at Newman. Then sixty-one, he hadn't lost his looks; he had improved upon them. His acting isn't lazy; it's eager and feral as Fast Eddie trains a new hotshot (Cruise) only to wind up taking on the kid himself.

Hot Bonus: The perfect replication of the film's vibrant images in widescreen format.

Key Scene: "Sometimes if you lose, you win," says Newman, teaching Cruise how to dump a game. What makes it crackle is the way Scorsese shows how the old pro wins back his innocence by corrupting the kid.

Commitments, The (Two-Disc Collector's Edition) (1991)

Starring: Andrew Strong, Johnny Murphy, Robert Arkins

Directed by: Alan Parker

How to film Roddy Doyle's comic and affecting novel about a Dublin band trying to bring soul music to Ireland? Audition three thousand musicians and pick the top twelve to play the Commitments. British director Parker lucks out. The dozen unknowns he's chosen make a joyful noise, which the Dolby Digital audio track does proud. Strong, a beefy dynamo of sixteen, plays a piggish singer with the voice of a fallen angel. The fiftyish Murphy plays the trumpet player, a lying coot who galls the boys by shagging the three sexy backup singers, played by Angeline Ball, Bronagh Gallagher, and Maria Doyle. The film's best performance comes from Arkins, twenty-one, as the band's flinty manager. His face expressively mirrors the band's changing fortunes.

Hot Bonus: The looking-back report on how the film was made hits home.

Key Scene: When the Commitments allow their feelings to seep into the music in "Mustang Sally" and "In the Midnight Hour."

Contempt (Two-Disc Special Edition) (1963)

Starring: Brigitte Bardot, Jack Palance, Michel Piccoli, Fritz Lang

Directed by: Jean-Luc Godard

Criterion gives the deluxe DVD treatment to Godard's fable about a young wife—Bardot, the French babe supreme—who feels contempt for her screenwriter husband (Piccoli), who is called in to doctor a script based on Homer's *The Odyssey* for a great German director (Lang as himself). She ends up having an affair with the film's crass producer (Palance). Godard's film, shot in Italy by the brilliant Raoul Coutard to a haunting score by Georges Delerue, simmers with artistic and sexual betrayals. Godard, who plays the role of Lang's assistant, is still incensed that Frank Sinatra and Kim Novak, his first choices for the leads, turned him down flat.

Hot Bonus: An interview with Godard and Lang that bristles.

Key Scene: The opening, which gives Bardot full exposure.

Conversation, The (Special Edition) (1974)

Starring: Gene Hackman, Cindy Williams, Frederic Forrest

Directed and written by: Francis Ford Coppola

The quietly devastating film that Coppola directed between the first two *Godfather* films receives a striking DVD transfer that confirms its place as a film landmark. Hackman is at the top of his game as Harry Caul, a surveillance expert who is hired by a stranger (Robert Duvall in an unbilled cameo) to follow an adulterous wife (Williams). When Harry suspects a murder plot, he commits the ultimate no-no and gets involved. The film asks profound questions about privacy that still resonate, and the techno-geek lair where Harry works, lives, and hides remains an imaginative wonder.

Hot Bonus: Coppola's comparison between Harry's voyeuristic work and his own job as a film director.

Key Scene: The moment, evoking an aural version of Antonioni's photographic *Blow-Up*, when Harry isolates sounds from a tape he made in a crowd and pieces together an emotional story.

Cool Hand Luke (1967)

Starring: Paul Newman, George Kennedy, Strother Martin, Jo Van Fleet

Directed by: Stuart Rosenberg

Newman is the essence of cool as Luke, a rebel who is sentenced to a chaingang in the Deep South for drunkenly destroying a row of parking meters. The DVD is so crisp that you can see the sweat on Newman and fellow prisoner Dragline (Kennedy, who won a Best Supporting Actor Oscar) as they wipe it off under the command of a sadistic boss (Martin is nasty perfection) whose mantra is: "What we've got here is failure to communicate." Luke won't give in, even when his momma (Van Fleet, superb) talks to him from the back of a pickup truck. Director Rosenberg delivers a fierce funny drama when he doesn't overdo the Christ analogies.

Hot Bonus: Production notes reveal that this Southern drama, sharply photographed by Conrad Hall, was actually filmed in Stockton, California.

Key Scene: Luke winning the egg-eating contest.

Crash (2005)

Starring: Matt Dillon, Sandra Bullock, Don Cheadle, Ryan Phillippe

Directed by: Paul Haggis

Racism collides with its targets during one thirty-six-hour period in Los Angeles. Alive with bracing human drama and blistering wit, the film benefits from the strong directing debut of Haggis, the screenwriter of *Million Dollar Baby*. Haggis and co-writer Bobby Moresco weave many stories (too many) into the narrative. But the rage sticks, as do the emotions underlying it. And the DVD allows for re-viewing certain moments after the shock settles. The district attorney (Brendan Fraser) and his wife (Bullock, strikingly uncongenial) are carjacked at gunpoint by two black men (Ludacris and Larenz Tate). At home, the wife orders the locks changed and then changed again because a Mexican (the remarkable Michael Pena) did the first job. A black TV director (Terrence Howard), getting a blow job from his wife (Thandie Newton) while driving home, is stopped by two white cops. One officer (Dillon) gropes the wife to humiliate the husband, while the other cop (a standout Phillippe) watches helplessly. A Persian store owner (Shaun Toub), taken for an Arab, buys a gun for protection. Cheadle plays a detective who ties these stories together when he finds a dead body in the road. Despite its preachy moments, *Crash* is a knockout. In a cinema world starved for ambition, why kick a film with an excess of it?

Hot Bonus: DVD introduction by Haggis, who offers commentary with Cheadle and Moresco. Plus, *Crash: Behind the Scenes*.

Key Scene: The astonishing second encounter between Dillon and Newton.

Cries and Whispers (1972)

Starring: Liv Ullmann, Ingrid Thulin, Harriet Andersson, Kari Sylwan

Directed and written by: Ingmar Bergman

If you want evidence of how much Swedish legend Bergman owes his great cinematographer Sven Nykvist, this DVD can stand as Exhibit A. Nykvist won a deserved Oscar for bringing a shimmering beauty to this harsh, haunting tale of three

sisters: Andersson is dying, Ullmann is unfaithful to her husband, and Thulin is so turned off by the man she marries that she mutilates her vagina with broken glass. It's a servant (the magnificent Sylwan) who holds the family together as the specter of death hovers.

Hot Bonus: A rare interview with Bergman that delves deeply into his views about love and death and the bond of family.

Key Scene: The climactic flashback to the sisters in happier times.

Crimes and Misdemeanors (1989)

Starring: Woody Allen, Martin Landau, Anjelica Huston, Alan Alda

Directed and written by: Woody Allen

The Woodman's last masterpiece to date tells of an eye doctor (Landau) who arranges the murder of his mistress (Huston, mesmerizing) after she threatens to squeal to his wife. In a parallel story, a documentarian (Allen) does a feature on an obnoxious Hollywood hotshot (Alda at his best) and sabotages the creep by splicing in footage of Mussolini. Moral crises are the core of the film, which MGM has transferred in a version much preferable to the earlier Image DVD. Allen gives us a world in which God lets crimes and misdemeanors go unpunished. The film hasn't dated a bit.

Hot Bonus: A trailer that actually indicates what the film is about.

Key Scene: The filmmaker's sister is set up on a date with a man in prison. "But only for inside trading," says a friend, "and when he gets out he'll be rich." The line gets the desired laugh, the kind that sticks in the throat.

Crimes of Passion (Unrated) (1984)

Starring: Kathleen Turner, Anthony Perkins, John Laughlin

Directed by: Ken Russell

A kinky treat for Russell fanatics with the hot action spiffed up for DVD as Turner plays a prim fashion designer who moonlights as a hooker named China Blue, not for the money but because she needs the attention. As a preacher with bizarre erotic fantasies, Perkins makes his *Psycho* character seem like the model of well-adjusted humanity. And Laughlin is the young husband whose contact with China Blue changes his life. It's all one big, bad, wicked frolic with Turner at her most uninhibited.

Hot Bonus: Six extra minutes, included the infamous moment with China Blue, a cop, and the cop's nightstick.

Key Scene: Turner sucking Laughlin's bare toes and moving up to his crotch has become a classic on the fetish circuit.

Crimson Tide (1995)

Starring: Denzel Washington, Gene Hackman
Directed by: Tony Scott

It's a submarine movie with all the clichés that implies. But Washington is implosively exciting as a navy officer trying to stop the sub captain (Hackman chewing scenery in high style) from firing nuclear missiles at Russia. Director Scott has Dariusz Wolski's camera do handstands to stir up the action. And the 5.1-channel Dolby Digital is ever-ready to rumble.

Hot Bonus: To make up for the lack of extras, I'll tell you that an uncredited Quentin Tarantino juiced up the dialogue. Just listen to the crew jabbering about Silver Surfer comics books. It's *Pulp Fiction* at sea.

Key Scene: The mutiny will shiver your timbers.

Crouching Tiger, Hidden Dragon (2000)

Starring: Chow Yun-Fat, Michelle Yeoh, Zhang Ziyi
Directed by: Ang Lee

This work of daredevil cinematic artistry was robbed of the Best Picture Oscar by *Gladiator*. Think I'm nuts? Watch this pristine DVD, in which Lee, the Taiwanese director, sweeps us into martial-arts miracles in a China that he says "never existed except in my boyhood fantasies." The movie begins with two lovers who have never acted on their feelings: Mu Bai, the noble warrior portrayed by Hong Kong film legend Chow Yun-Fat, and security officer Yu Shu Lien (Yeoh invests the role with power and romantic yearning). When Jen (Zhang Ziyi, a knockout), the teen daughter of the district governor, steals Mu Bai's sword, the Green Destiny, the plot kicks in. Here is the best-acted film in the martial-arts canon, and the classiest—hell, Yo-Yo Ma does the weeping cello solos—and its slant on feminist empowerment makes it the most unique.

Hot Bonus: Lee and co-screenwriter James Schamus offer commentary that adds depth and historical context.

Key Scene: The fights—all choreographed by *The Matrix* master Yuen Wo-Ping, who put the actors on wires that were later erased digitally—reach their peak in swooping action and delicate beauty when Jen finally crosses swords with Mu Bai in a bamboo forest, each perched on branches seventy feet off the ground. It's a visual stunner for the DVD time capsule.

Croupier (1999)

Starring: Clive Owen, Kate Hardie, Alex Kingston
Directed by: Mike Hodges

Owen excels as Jack Manfred, a writer wannabe who takes a job as a croupier at a London casino, where he can observe people as subjects for his novel. Behind his cards, Jack is invincible. Or so he thinks. Screenwriter Paul Mayersberg risks tainting *Croupier* with literary pretensions, especially when Jack narrates the film in the voice of Jake, a character in his novel. But the narration is stingingly delivered by Owen, whose performance radiates seductive cool. Jack breaks the rules of the game by sleeping with Bella (Hardie), a croupier with a drug habit, but it's Jani (Kingston), a femme fatale, who really penetrates Jack's façade. Director Hodges tightens his grip without missing any chance for twisted humor.

Hot Bonus: The crisp presentation of this low-budget film is bonus enough.

Key Scene: The robbery that threatens to turn Jack into one of the suckers.

Crow, The (Collector's Series) (1994)

Starring: Brandon Lee, Ernie Hudson, Michael Wincott
Directed by: Alex Proyas

You catch your breath at the entrance of the late Brandon Lee. As rock guitarist Eric Draven, dead for a year when we first meet him, Lee busts out of the cold cemetery ground and howls in rage at the thugs who killed him and his fiancée.

A crow stands watch as his link to life. This dazzling fever dream of a movie offers a double resurrection: Draven is back, and so, for two haunting hours, is Lee. On March 31, 1993, eight days before *The Crow* was due to wrap, Lee was accidentally shot and killed while filming Draven's murder. If you're ready to dismiss *The Crow* as crass exploitation, get one thing straight: It's not. Based on a 1980s comic-book series by James O'Barr, the film—set against a stunning backdrop of urban decay—stays faithful to its darkly poetic source. As Draven wreaks havoc, cinematographer Dariusz Wolski films the carnage in whiplash style to a blistering soundtrack that includes the Cure, Stone Temple Pilots, and Nine Inch Nails. Credit Australian director Proyas for pulling the elements into a hypnotic package that will haunt you for a good long time on this collector's DVD.

Hot Bonus: A behind-the-scenes featurette doesn't make Lee's death scene any easier to watch. Though the gun was loaded with blanks, the metal tip of a dummy bullet had become lodged in the gun's barrel. The metal tip was propelled into Lee's abdomen. Lee died twelve hours later; he was twenty-eight. Lee's father, martial-arts legend Bruce Lee, was thirty-two when he died of a brain edema in 1973 in production on *Game of Death*. In a horrific irony, the elder Lee played an actor who is shot when hoods replace fake bullets with real ones.

Key Scene: Among the indelible images is Draven thrashing his guitar on the rooftops of this implacable nightmare city.

Crucible, The (1996)

Starring: Daniel Day-Lewis, Winona Ryder, Joan Allen, Paul Scofield
Directed by: Nicholas Hytner

The late Arthur Miller's second-most-famous play (after *Death of a Salesman*) is this tale of the Salem witch trials, circa 1692, which Miller likened to the communist witch hunts perpetrated by Sen. Joe McCarthy in the 1940s and 1950s. At the time of the film's release, Miller—then eighty-one—talked to me with boyish zest of working with director Hytner on recrafting *The Crucible* as a $25 million film that would allow startling imagery to resonate with his language and burst the bounds of the stage. That it did. That it does again on DVD. All the actors excel, notably Day-Lewis as the farmer who won't sacrifice his honor to save his life. "Because it is my name," he says. "Because I cannot have another in my life."

Hot Bonus: A still timely talk with Miller and Day-Lewis on the film's denunciation of persecution masked as piety—take that, Christian right!

Key Scene: When fifteen sex-starved teenage girls gather in the Salem forest at night to work out their Puritan repression. Some tear off their clothes and dance naked. Guilt over being caught drives the girls into a frenzy of false accusations. The devil made them do it.

Crumb (1994)

Starring: Robert Crumb
Directed by: Terry Zwigoff

An astonishing documentary about the life and twisted times of a skinny, four-eyed, sex-obsessed misanthrope with no weapons to fire back at the society that rejected him save one: R. Crumb, Robert to his cronies, is the underground artist who has been using the comics to zap hypocrisy since his acidhead days in the San Francisco of the sixties. He is famous for drawing Fritz the Cat, the Keep on Truckin' logo, and the cover art for the Big Brother and the Holding Company LP *Cheap Thrills*. Through frank interviews with Crumb, his friends, lovers, wives, children, colleagues, critics, and the dysfunctional Catholic family that spawned him, Zwigoff crafts a shockingly intimate portrait.

Hot Bonus: Slim pickings, except for the clever trailer.

Key Scene: The confession: "I'd be in jail or a mental institution by now if I didn't draw that stuff," says Crumb, who admits he is sometimes embarrassed by his work, though he'd never dream of censoring it.

Crying Game, The (Collector's Edition) (1992)

Starring: Stephen Rea, Jaye Davidson, Miranda Richardson, Forest Whitaker
Directed and written by: Neil Jordan

There's a jolting revelation midway through this high-wire act from Irish director

Jordan. You may want to hit the still-frame button on your DVD remote. The film concerns the kidnapping of a British soldier, Jody (Forest Whitaker), by IRA cohorts and lovers Jude (Richardson) and Fergus (Rea). Fergus grants Jody's dying wish by visiting a London hairdresser named Dil (Davidson), the "wee black chick" Jody loved. Fergus finds Dil, passes himself off as a Scot, and replaces Jody in Dil's affections. For all the characters, hiding behind race, sex, and politics is no longer possible. Rea and Davidson are incomparably good in a darkly funny and affecting film.

Hot Bonus: Lucid commentary from Jordan, who deservedly won the Oscar for Best Original Screenplay.

Key Scene: The revelation: it will help explain why Davidson was Oscar nominated as Best Supporting Actor.

Dancer in the Dark (2000)

Starring: Björk, Catherine Deneuve, Vladica Kostic

Directed and written by: Lars von Trier

Bizarre doesn't begin to describe what happens to Björk in this unique musical from Danish maverick von Trier, who boldly casts the Icelandic diva as Selma, a Czech immigrant on the verge of blindness. Selma slaves in a sixties-era rural-America sink factory to support her ten-year-old son, Gene (Kostic), who will also go blind if Selma can't pay for an operation. Selma sings and dances through it all—Björk, possessed of a face the camera embraces, composed the songs—until murder charges land her on death row. Hoo-boy, but cheers to the DVD for getting von Trier's vision just right.

Hot Bonus: The commentary from jetphobic von Trier—he won't fly anywhere, much less the United States, so he shot his film in Sweden—tells how he set up more than one hundred digital cameras to film the musical numbers.

Key Scene: Selma's dance with the dead man she's been accused of murdering.

Dances With Wolves (Two-Disc Special Edition) (1990)

Starring: Kevin Costner, Mary McDonnell, Graham Greene

Directed by: Kevin Costner

It's easy to mock Costner's I-can-do-it-all western in which the director and co-producer cast himself as a suicidal Civil War officer who learns

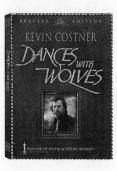

about the meaning of existence by going to live among the Lakota Sioux. And when you consider that Costner and his epic beat Martin Scorsese's *GoodFellas* for the Best Picture Oscar, blood tends to boil. But this two-disc DVD is a reminder of how good the movie looks and sounds.

Hot Bonus: Alert to gluttons for hearing the Lakota language while reading English subtitles: Nearly an hour of extra footage has been put back into a film that already ran three hours.

Key Scene: The buffalo stampede is DVD demonstration quality.

Dangerous Liaisons (1988)

Starring: Glenn Close, John Malkovich, Michelle Pfeiffer, Uma Thurman

Directed by: Stephen Frears

Close and Malkovich—costumed sumptuously in the silks and brocades of the eighteenth century—are doing a period piece. But don't expect *Masterpiece Theatre* gentility—this puppy has claws. British playwright Christopher Hampton puts real heat into his adaptation of the 1782 epistolary novel by Choderlos de Laclos. And director Frears puts the actors on a high boil. Malkovich as the Vicomte and Close as his former mistress, the Marquise, now engage in a cruel form of sexual gamesmanship. To win a night in bed with the Marquise, the Vicomte must please her by deflowering a fifteen-year-old virgin (Thurman) and turning a religious married woman (Pfeiffer) into an adulteress. Pfeiffer provides the only human warmth in this igloo. The DVD makes sure that nastiness has never looked so ravishing.

Hot Bonus: Notes on the history of the piece.

Key Scene: An angry Malkovich tells Close that her refusal to sleep with him will constitute a declaration of war. All right, says Close, as the camera zooms in on her sharklike smile, "wa-a-a-a-r." Close stretches the word to at least five delicious syllables.

Dangerous Lives of Altar Boys, The (2002)

Starring: Kieran Culkin, Emile Hirsch, Jena Malone, Jodie Foster

Directed by: Peter Care

Co-produced by Foster, this artful and surprising film of Chris Fuhrman's 1970s-era novel also features the actress as Sister Assumpta, an Irish nun with a peg leg and zero tolerance for trouble. Which is what she gets from altar-boy pals Tim (Culkin), who wants to sic a cougar on her, and Francis (Hirsch), who works with Tim on a brutal, kinky comic strip featuring Nunzilla. First-time director Care crafts something darkly funny and touching from a coming-of-age fable that might have drifted into formula without deeply felt performances from Culkin and Hirsch and dazzling animation from Todd McFarlane (*Spawn*) that brings the boys' comic fantasies to jolting life on a suitable-for-framing DVD.

Hot Bonus: Animation illustrations.

Key Scene: At the zoo.

Darkman (1990)

Starring: Liam Neeson, Frances McDormand, Larry Drake

Directed by: Sam Raimi

This high-camp hoot of a horror film from *Evil Dead* director Raimi is so far over the top that it qualifies as a DVD guilty pleasure. Neeson stars as Dr. Peyton Westlake, a scientist on the verge of marrying his lawyer girlfriend (McDormand), and making a breakthrough in creating synthetic skin. When the evil Durant (Drake) breaks into Westlake's lab and burns the owner, the doc makes use of his own invention. "I'm everyone and no one, everything and nothing," he says. "Call me Darkman."

Hot Bonus: Nothing much, but I will tell you to look out for *Evil Dead* hero Bruce Campbell in a climactic cameo.

Key Scene: Darkman dangles from the ladder of Durant's helicopter as it swings across the city, trying to shake him loose. This leaves the actors emoting wildly just to keep up with the stunts. It's a losing battle.

Das Boot (The Director's Cut) (1981)

Starring: Jürgen Prochnow

Directed by: Wolfgang Petersen

The submarine movie to end all submarine movies gets the careful treatment it deserves on DVD. There is almost an hour of extra footage from the German TV version that brings the film to 209 minutes. But your enthusiasm won't drag as a German U-boat, with Prochnow as its conscience-stricken captain, embarks on perilous World War II missions that make the crew question the motives of the Nazi high command. The DVD re-creates the film's claustrophobic suspense with stunning accuracy, and the added character details bring the experience a strengthened humanity.

Hot Bonus: Many fascinating details, including how the U-boat was constructed from actual U-boat blueprints of the time.

Key Scene: That first moment when water pressure forces the rivets to pop.

Dawn of the Dead (The Ultimate Edition) (1978)

Starring: David Emge, Gaylen Ross, Ken Foree, Scott Reiniger

Directed by: George A. Romero

A DVD bonanza for horror fans. The four-disc set includes three versions of the classic film—the original *Dawn*, the extended *Dawn*, and the even gorier European *Dawn*. This color sequel to Romero's black-and-white 1968 landmark, *Night of the Living Dead*, focuses on a TV reporter (Ross), her traffic pilot boyfriend (Emge), and two SWAT cops (Foree and Reiniger) who hole up in a Pittsburgh shopping mall to protect themselves (ha!) from marauding zombies. Besides scares, the movie gives Romero a platform for a scathing satire of the malling of a sexist, racist America.

Hot Bonus: Everything you can think of, including home movies taken on the set between takes.

Key Scene: The zombies go shopping.

Dawn of the Dead (Unrated Director's Cut) (2004)

Starring: Sarah Polley, Ving Rhames, Jake Weber, Mekhi Phifer
Directed by: Zack Snyder

Here's a surprise—a big, glossy remake that pays tribute to the spirit of Romero's zombiefest and then takes off at its own bloody speed. Director Snyder also sets the film—his first—in a shopping mall (Milwaukee, this time, not Pittsburgh), but his living dead race around like sprinters. Whatever the film lacks in originality (plenty), it makes up for in zesty humor and nonstop gut-ripping. And it's preferable to Romero's 1985 *Day of the Dead*, a lifeless chapter three in his ongoing series.

Hot Bonus: The makeup tricks that turn actors into the undead.

Key Scene: The epilogue—don't stop watching the film till you see it.

Day for Night (1973)

Starring: Jacqueline Bisset, Valentina Cortese, Jean-Pierre Léaud
Directed by: François Truffaut

One of the most joyous and touching movies ever made about making movies hits DVD in shining splendor. Director Truffaut plays the director trying to make a light-as-air comedy in the south of France with a leading lady (Bisset) fresh from a nervous breakdown, a young star (Léaud) given to hissy fits, an Italian diva (Cortese) with a booze problem, and a screen Romeo (Jean-Pierre Aumont) who's a closet gay. The love of the filmmaking process emanates from every frame.

Hot Bonus: Bisset, sharing bittersweet memories of Truffaut, who died in 1984 and who once said he made films "to improve on life."

Key Scene: Cortese, Oscar nominated as Best Supporting Actress, trying futilely to remember her lines, which are pasted all over the set.

Day of the Jackal (1973)

Starring: Edward Fox, Michel Lonsdale, Delphine Seyrig, Cyril Cusack
Directed by: Fred Zinnemann

Frederick Forsyth's bestselling thriller is a grabber onscreen thanks to Fox's imperturbable portrait of the Jackal, the assassin hired to kill French President Charles De Gaulle (Adrien Cayla-Legrand is the spitting image). Director Zinnemann tightens the suspense as the Jackal preps for the big moment with a top cop (Lonsdale) at his heels

and the DVD more than up to doing justice to the globe-trotting action.

Hot Bonus: A trailer that is a model of its kind—it works up our interest without giving the game away.

Key Scene: The Jackal and gunsmith, played to perfection by Cusack.

Day the Earth Stood Still, The (1951)

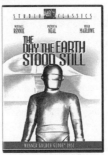

Starring: Michael Rennie, Patricia Neal, Billy Gray, Sam Jaffe
Directed by: Robert Wise

A seminal sci-fi film about a pacifist alien (Rennie) who lands in Washington, D.C., in a flying saucer to bring the message that all nuclear testing must stop. A killer robot named Gort helps him get that message across. The alien really learns about earthlings by living in a boarding house with a widow (Neal) and her young son (Gray). Director Wise keeps the film simple and to the point, which is why it still works and why people still remember the line, "klaatu baraada nikto," which must be uttered to stop Gort from obliterating the planet with his death-ray eye.

Hot Bonus: Wise discussing the film's subtext with director Nicholas Meyer, a fan who seems to know the movie better than he does.

Key Scene: The title sequence, set to Bernard Herrmann's jangling score.

Days of Heaven (1978)

Starring: Richard Gere, Brooke Adams, Sam Shepard, Linda Manz
Directed by: Terrence Malick

No film has better captured the beauty of the American plains, and the Oscar-winning cinematography of Néstor Amendros blooms gloriously on DVD. Director-writer Malick, a former MIT philosophy lecturer, sets up one gorgeous shot after another in this World War I–era love triangle about a hotheaded migrant worker (Gere) who encourages his lover (Adams) to pose as his sister and marry a wealthy farm owner (playwright Shepard in a striking acting debut) faced with a terminal illness. If Malick ultimately fails in giving the story the mythic heft of his images—though the rough-spoken narration spoken by Manz as Gere's real sister goes a long way toward achieving it—he succeeds triumphantly in every other department.

Hot Bonus: The images, from a train crossing a scaffold bridge silhouetted against the sky to threshers chomping through a golden wheat field—are bonus enough, especially as set to Ennio Morricone's haunting score.

Key Scene: Nature's climactic attack on the human landscape.

Days of Wine and Roses (1962)

Starring: Jack Lemmon, Lee Remick
Directed by: Blake Edwards

To see a blithe spirit like Lemmon immerse himself in the role of boozehound ad exec who marries a nondrinker (Remick) and hooks her with Brandy Alexanders (they taste like chocolate) until they're both in a hole that only he climbs out of is to witness an actor at the top of his game. He and Remick were both Oscar nominated for playing dramatically against type. The DVD not only preserves those tragedy-tinged performances, it shows how the film's superior black-and-white camerawork envelops the characters in an alcoholic haze. "They are not long the days of wine and roses," says Lemmon to Remick, reciting a poem—set to a hypnotic Henry Mancini melody—that catches the mood of the piece: "Out of a misty dream our paths emerge for a while then close within a dream."

Hot Bonus: Director Edwards talks frankly about his own drinking and Lemmon's and how they reacted while making the movie.

Key Scene: Lemmon's breakdown in the greenhouse.

Dazed and Confused (Flashback Edition) (1993)

Starring: Jason London, Wiley Wiggins, Matthew McConaughey
Directed and written by: Richard Linklater

No title better sums up the state in which high school leaves you—sometimes for life. Director-writer Linklater—whose cult hit, *Slacker* (about Texas dropouts), was resolutely right now—has gone retro. He sets his new social satire in 1976, with a soundtrack of great relics ranging from Aerosmith to ZZ Top. It's the last school day before summer and trying to get blitzed on grass, beer, music, brawling, and sex clearly transcends time. Pink (London) is in trouble for not signing the coach's pledge against drugs and alcohol. And eighth-grader Mitch (a terrific Wiggins) gets radically hazed. Linklater brings an anthropologist's eye to this hilarious celebration of the rites of stupidity. His shitfaced *American Graffiti* is the ultimate party movie on DVD—loud, crude, socially irresponsible, and totally irresistible.

Hot Bonus: Retro public-service announcements about the evils of partying.

Key Scene: McConaughey's monologue as a twentysomething grad who still hangs at the school because he may get older but the babes stay young.

Dead Man (1996)

Starring: Johnny Depp, Gary Farmer, Gabriel Byrne, Robert Mitchum
Directed and written by: Jim Jarmusch

A magical mystery tour of a movie that puts Depp, playing a Cleveland accountant, on a train out west, circa 1875, where an Indian named Nobody (Farmer) believes he is the reincarnation of British poet William Blake being chased by bounty hunters hired by Mitchum, whose son (Byrne) Depp has shot in a fight over a girl. Got that? If not, just go with the Jarmusch flow, which is enhanced by Robby Müller's evocative black-and-white photography and Neil Young's guitar score. This is a DVD to sink into.

Hot Bonus: Deleted scenes that are as weird as the ones they left in.

Key Scene: I have a problem erasing the images of Iggy Pop as an animal skinner in female drag and Lance Henriksen as a cannibal who raped and chowed down on his own parents. How about you?

Dead Man Walking (1995)

Starring: Sean Penn, Susan Sarandon, Raymond J. Barry, Celia Weston
Directed and written by: Tim Robbins

Sarandon won an Oscar for playing Sister Helen Prejean, a Louisiana nun who offers spiritual comfort to death row prisoners. Penn didn't win but should have for his dynamite turn as Matthew Poncelet, a racist with a Cajun accent and a bouffant hairdo awaiting lethal injection for participating in the murder of a teen couple. Based loosely on Sister Helen's autobiographical book, the film—while firmly anti-death penalty—offers a balanced look at a complex issue. As the DVD shows, Robbins directs with a keen eye for claustrophobic pressures on one man's body and conscience.

Hot Bonus: Robbins takes you through the movie with consummate care.

Key Scene: The flashback to the murders, as narrated by Penn, is as chilling as anything since *In Cold Blood*.

Dead Ringers (1988)

Starring: Jeremy Irons, Geneviéve Bujold
Directed by: David Cronenberg

In 1975, Stewart and Cyril Marcus, prominent gynecologists and identical twins, were found dead and partially decayed, surrounded by garbage and barbiturates in their fashionable Manhattan apartment. No one knows the true story. Director Cronenberg speculates that the doctors—one a drone, the other an extrovert (here called Beverly and Elliot Mantle and both played brilliantly by Irons)—shared careers, women, drugs, and a dependence that ended in a suicide pact. The tragedy begins when the shy doc's affair with a patient (Bujold) goes awry. The DVD heightens the film's obsessions with medical hardware and psychic dysfunction. It plays scarier than any Cronenberg horror film, including *Scanners*, as female patients are strapped helplessly into stirrups and subjected to verbal abuse. Cronenberg enlarges on these fears to make a movie that makes nightmares.

Hot Bonus: Fascinating inside stuff on how Irons managed to play both characters from a technical and emotional standpoint.

Key Scene: The opening credits, using obstetrical drawings and instruments, sets the tone with resonant creepiness.

Decalogue, The (Special Edition/Box Set) (1988)

Starring: Henryk Baranowski, Aleksander Bardini
Directed and co-written by: Krzysztof Kieslowski

Inspired by the Ten Commandments, Polish filmmaker Kieslowski and his co-writer Krzysztof Piesiewicz tell ten moral fables (around one hour each) set in a suburb of contemporary Warsaw. There is nothing rigidly biblical in any of the pieces. It's

the spirit behind the letter of each commandment that emerges from the film. To say anything more about the formal and emotional perfection of this epic—originally made for Polish TV and meticulously transferred to DVD—would be to cheat you of one of the great works of modern cinema.

Hot Bonus: A key interview with Kieslowski, who died in 1996, after completing his three-colors trilogy (*Red, Blue,* and *White*).

Key Scene: Impossible to pick, but the fifth fable, A Short Film about Killing, can stand as an individual masterpiece.

Deep End, The (2001)

Starring: Tilda Swinton, Goran Visnjic, Jonathan Tucker, Josh Lucas
Directed and written by: Scott McGehee and David Siegel

Buggery, blackmail, murder. What's a mom to do? That's the question Margaret Hall (the ever-amazing Swinton) asks herself in this supple, stealthy thriller. Margaret's life in Lake Tahoe unravels when she learns that her teen son (Tucker) has murdered the older man (Lucas) with whom he's having sex (there are videotapes to prove it). Now Margaret has to face a blackmailer (Visnjic). In adapting Elisabeth Sanxay Holding's novel *The Blank Wall* (Max Ophüls filmed the story in 1949 as *The Reckless Moment* with Joan Bennett as the mother and James Mason as the blackmailer), McGehee and Siegel springs surprises that entertain and provoke. Special praise to Giles Nuttgens's crisp camerawork, which looks super on DVD.

Hot Bonus: Rowdy commentary from the co-directors, including how they shot the gay sex video the day after Tucker turned eighteen.

Key Scene: The stirring of romance between mom and blackmailer. A lesser movie couldn't survive that twist, but Swinton and Visnjic pull it off.

Deep Red (1975)

Starring: David Hemmings, Daria Nicolodi
Directed by: Dario Argento

For those of you unfamiliar with gore maestro Argento, welcome to the peak of his perverse art. Uncut and restored to its original 126-minute length (from the butchered 98-minute version originally released in the United States), the film is a widescreen DVD beauty from Anchor Bay. There may be complaints from those who watch the English dub since the restored scenes are only available in the original Italian with English subtitles. My advice: stick with the Italian version all the way through. Hemmings stars as a jazz pianist on the trail of a killer. Nicolodi (Argento's wife and mother of their actress daughter Asia) plays a reporter who joins him on the chase. The violence, choreographed by Argento to an electronic score by Goblin, has a compositional sophistication that is scarily seductive.

Hot Bonus: A retrospective documentary in which Argento puts *Deep Red* in the context of his work and ranks it highly.

Key Scene: The puppet with a knife, coming right at us.

Deer Hunter, The (Two-Disc Legacy Edition) (1978)

Starring: Robert De Niro, Christopher Walken, John Savage, Meryl Streep
Directed by: Michael Cimino

A Best Picture Oscar went to one of the earliest films to deal with the effect of Vietnam on those who fought and those left behind. There are problems: Director Cimino takes a racist view of the North Vietnamese and invents a surreal game of Russian roulette to symbolize the terror inside the heads of men fighting a war they can't comprehend. But the film's intimate look at a Pennsylvania steel town and the friends—Michael (De Niro, the deer hunter of the title), Steven (Savage, a study in torment), and Nick (Walken, who won an Oscar as Best Supporting Actor)—who go to battle and come back damaged in ways they couldn't have imagined is still indelibly moving. The actors, including Streep as Nick's confused girl, are pitch perfect. The previous DVD was shockingly awful. Now, with remastered picture and sound, the power comes through.

Hot Bonus: Deleted scenes that add an hour to the running time. It's all fascinating, as is the audio commentary from cinematographer Vilmos Zsigmond.

Key Scene: The final group singing of "God Bless America," not as a sop to patriotism but as a ritual that might heal a few wounds.

Deliverance (1972)

Starring: Jon Voight, Burt Reynolds, Ned Beatty, Ronny Cox
Directed by: John Boorman

Poet James Dickey adapted his own 1970 novel (his first) for the screen and had the great good luck to have Boorman direct his tale of four Georgia buddies—three softies (Voight, Beatty, and Cox) and one macho man (Reynolds, of course)—

on a whitewater canoe trip that tests their mettle. Good luck, because Boorman keeps the adventure and the terror in the foreground and Dickey's mythical subtext bubbling underneath. The DVD hurtles you into the action, including a hillbilly rape scene, so be warned.

Hot Bonus: Boorman confides that he and Dickey fought like lions over particular scenes. See if you can guess which ones.

Key Scene: That first ride down the rapids to the tune of "Dueling Banjos."

Desperado (Special Edition) (1995)

Starring: Antonio Banderas, Salma Hayek, Joaquim de Almeida
Directed by: Robert Rodriguez

Banderas is the ultimate in sexy action cool as the guitarist and lover boy who has no problem with premature ejaculation except when it comes to guns. This killer mariachi can barely unholster before he's firing off. His chief target is Bucho (de Almeida), a Mexican drug baron who provides a string of thugs for our hero to pop while Carolina (Salma Hayek), the babe owner of a border-town bookstore that does no business, kisses his wounds. *Desperado* is writer, producer and director Rodriguez's sleek update of *El Mariachi*, the 1992 film that cost a puny seven thousand dollars. Now the Texas maverick gets Banderas, a score by Los Lobos, and a budget in the millions. The stunts dazzle on this kickass DVD, but you do miss the cost-conscious inventiveness of the original.

Hot Bonus: Lively commentary from Rodriguez.

Key Scene: Banderas and Hayek leaping from a rooftop, a stunt that lets Rodriguez indulge his first chance at high-end Hollywood fireworks.

Desperately Seeking Susan (1985)

Starring: Madonna, Rosanna Arquette
Directed by: Susan Seidelman

One of the few movies in which Madonna is actually not embarrassing, so you'll need this flamboyantly colorful DVD for your records. In fact, this class-clash comedy has held up well over the years with the Material Girl as a New York hipster who finds her identity stolen by a New Jersey housewife (a sprightly Arquette), so off she goes to suburbia. Director Seidelman gives the movie a goofy charm that's like attending a terrific loft party. It's different, it's infectious, and you never know who you'll run into next.

Hot Bonus: An alternate ending that provokes sexy questions.

Key Scene: Madonna trying on clothes in a downtown thrift shop. Those were the days.

Die Another Day
(Two-Disc Special Edition) (2002)

Starring: Pierce Brosnan, Halle Berry

Directed by: Lee Tamahori

The fourth and best of the James Bond movies with Brosnan—he looks like he has a stick up his ass in the other three—is full of wild stunts that are no substitute for the cool of Sean Connery's 007 but will do in a pinch when you're in the mood for DVD escapism done with flair. Director Tamahori knows his way around action, and it's fun to have Oscar-winner Berry playing a sexy NSA agent named Jinx. The plot starts in Korea and then trots off to Cuba, London, and Iceland as if the budget were limitless.

Hot Bonus: Brosnan is back with the stick on the commentary track, but the feature on staging the stunts is a winner.

Key Scene: Windsurfing off the glacier.

Die Hard
(Collector's Edition) (1988)

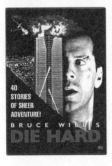

Starring: Bruce Willis, Alan Rickman

Directed by: John McTiernan

This is the no-frills kickoff to the series with Willis at his toughest and snarkiest as John Mc-Clane, the New York cop who rescues hostages from a Los Angeles highrise on Christmas Eve. The film has been copied so much (isn't *Speed* really *Die Hard* on a bus?) that you don't expect the DVD to have the same kick. But it does. Rickman makes a great

oily villain. And director McTiernan never cheats character for the sake of a cheap stunt.

Hot Bonus: McTiernan's comments are a film buff's dream.

Key Scene: A barefoot Willis walking on shattered glass.

Die Hard 2: Die Harder
(Collector's Edition) (1990)

Starring: Bruce Willis, William Sadler, Franco Nero

Directed by: Renny Harlin

Considered by many critics to be a slapdash knockoff of the original, the sequel—directed by Harlin—is packed with action that plays like gangbusters on DVD. It's set at Dulles Airport in Washington, D.C., where terrorists hold the whole place hostage. Not a minute of the movie is believable, but it's all brutal—sometimes too brutal—fun.

Hot Bonus: How'd they do those stunts? Here's how.

Key Scene: The shootout at the luggage carousel.

Die Hard With a Vengeance
(Collector's Edition) (1995)

Starring: Bruce Willis, Samuel L. Jackson, Jeremy Irons

Directed by: John McTiernan

No *Die Hard* movie looks better on DVD than number three in the series, with Willis's cop teaming up with Harlem store owner (Jackson) to take on the villainous Simon (a terrific Irons, sporting a blond dye job and a German accent). They do his bidding or bombs go off in New York—in subways and at landmarks from Wall Street to Yankee Stadium. Thanks to the teamwork of Willis and Jackson and the return of director McTiernan, the movie has a human touch. No matter how good the stunts—and these, to lift a McClane phrase, are "very cool stuff"—the audience needs characters to root for.

Hot Bonus: Screenwriter Jonathan Hensleigh reveals that his original script had nothing to do with the *Die Hard* series; it was adapted to fit.

Key Scene: Just when you think the nail-biting subway sequence is the high point, a giant ball of water chases McClane through an underground tunnel and spits him out on a geyser into midtown traffic. Very cool, indeed.

Diner (1982)

Starring: Kevin Bacon, Mickey Rourke, Steve Guttenberg, Daniel Stern

Directed and written by: Barry Levinson

It's great to hear Levinson's all-new intro to this charmer of a DVD. It kicked off his career as a director—he'd win an Oscar six years later for *Rain Man*—and showed an eye for detail as acute as his ear for dialogue. Pulled from his own experiences hanging out in a Baltimore diner circa 1959, the movie is smart and funny. The actors were all new faces then. Bacon is the guy who'll "do anything for a smile." Rourke is the ladykiller who sticks his dick through the bottom of a popcorn box and passes it to his date at the movies. Stern is the married one who can talk to the guys, but not his wife (Ellen Barkin). And Guttenberg is the football fanatic who won't marry his fiancée unless she passes a quiz about the Baltimore Colts. All the performances are remarkable, but the triumph is Levinson's. He captures both the surface and the soul of an era with candor and precision.

Hot Bonus: Fresh interviews with Levinson and the actors.

Key Scene: No contest. The debate over whether Frank Sinatra or Johnny Mathis provides the best make-out music.

Dirty Dancing (Two-Disc Ultimate Edition) (1987)

Starring: Patrick Swayze, Jennifer Grey

Directed by: Emile Ardolino

Teen girls still fantasize about being Baby (Grey), the seventeen-year-old daughter of a doctor (the late, great Jerry Orbach) who takes her on vacation to a Catskills resort, circa 1963, only to watch Baby bloom under the sexy tutelage of an ass-twitching dance instructor (Swayze in his career role) who teaches her moves Daddy never imagined. The newly remastered DVD gets all the sweaty bumps and grinds, and the songs, including the Oscar-winning "(I've Had) The Time of My Life," have never sounded better.

Hot Bonus: The cast tribute to director Ardolino, who died of AIDS in 1993, is touching, but Grey's screentest is the keeper.

Key Scene: The moment when Swayze says,

"Nobody puts Baby in a corner," and leads her to the dance floor.

Dirty Dozen, The (Collector's Edition) (1967)

Starring: Lee Marvin, Ernest Borgnine, Charles Bronson, John Cassavetes

Directed by: Robert Aldrich

Director Aldrich's brutal, cynical, and ragingly comic World War II action flick has been much imitated but never equaled. And this DVD transfer makes it look and sound as good as the day it premiered. Marvin chews vigorously on one of his iconic roles as a major assigned to destroy a French chateau where Nazi brass have gathered. It's a suicide mission, so Marvin recruits twelve prisoners. Jailed for rape, murder, and worse, the dirty dozen have nothing to lose. Cassavetes got the Oscar nomination, but Telly Savalas doing a psycho meltdown is the one you won't forget.

Hot Bonus: A promotional feature on the actors hanging out in swinging London during filming exerts a perverse fascination.

Key Scene: The training sequence must be seen to be believed.

Dirty Harry (Collector's Edition) (1971)

Starring: Clint Eastwood, Andy Robinson

Directed by: Don Siegel

Eastwood never won an Oscar for playing renegade San Francisco cop Harry Callahan, but the role is his true million-dollar baby. Back then our man Clint was pilloried for promoting police brutality. Harry did all the dirty jobs, including taking care of a psycho serial killer (Robinson) while the courts stood up for his rights. The widescreen DVD plays like gangbusters today thanks to Siegel's astute direction and Eastwood's uncanny ability to turn a squint and a sassy line ("That'll be the day") into lasting superstardom.

Hot Bonus: A short but incisive interview with Eastwood on the character he played in five movies. This one, the first, stands above them all.

Key Scene: Harry's last words to the killer: "I know what you're thinking. Did he fire six shots or only five? Well, to tell you the truth, in all the excitement, I've kind of lost track. But being as this is a .44 Magnum, the most powerful handgun in the world, and would blow your head clean off, you've got to ask yourself one question: 'Do I feel lucky?' Well, do ya, punk?"

Diva (1981)

Starring: Wilhelmenia Wiggins Fernandez, Frédéric Andréi

Directed by: Jean-Jacques Beineix

The first feature from French director Beineix put him on the map. Many of the scenes are like paintings, that is, if you stick with the DVD from Anchor Bay—newly transferred from original source material—and avoid the muddy disc from Fox Lorber. The plot is basic: A young Paris mailman, played with sly self-effacement by Andréi, secretly tapes the performance of an American opera diva (Wiggins, in a dazzling portrait of arrogance and beauty) who won't record her voice for fear of diluting her art. When two Taiwanese record pirates find out, the chase is on and then intensified when another tape, involving criminals, is dropped in the mailman's pouch.

Hot Bonus: A retrospective interview with Beineix.

Key Scene: A thrilling chase through the subways of Paris.

Do the Right Thing (Two-Disc Special Edition) (1989)

Starring: Spike Lee, Danny Aiello, John Turturro, Richard Edson, Bill Nunn

Directed and written by: Spike Lee

Lee's third movie—and still his best—gets the royal treatment from Criterion, which keeps the DVD pulsing with all the music, movement, humor, and heat that Lee built into the film. Set during one summer day in the black Bedford-Stuyvesant section of Brooklyn, the film simmers with anger. Lee plays Mookie, stuck making deliveries for Sal's Famous Pizza, a joint run by an Italian family—Sal (Aiello) and his sons, Pino (Turturro) and Vito (Edson). When Radio Raheem (Nunn) enters Sal's with his boom box playing Public Enemy's "Fight the Pow-er," Sal's temper flares. He smashes the radio that is Raheem's pride. Police are called. White police. Raheem, choked by a cop's nightstick, dies. The senseless killing releases pent-up fury as Lee offers a towering portrait of black America pushed to the limit.

Hot Bonus: Rehearsal footage, shot with a camcorder, speaks volumes.

Key Scene: Mookie hurling a garbage can through Sal's window.

Doctor Zhivago (Two-Disc Special Edition) (1965)

Starring: Omar Sharif, Julie Christie, Geraldine Chaplin, Rod Steiger

Directed by: David Lean

Freddie Young's Oscar-winning cinematography is superlatively served on this DVD transfer of director Lean's epic love story, based on the novel by Boris Pasternak. The pesky Russian Revolution keeps interfering with the love of poet-doctor Zhivago (a watery-eyed Sharif) and the luminous Lara (Christie), as does his wife (Chaplin) and her paramours (Steiger and the Oscar-nominated Tom Courtenay, in the film's strongest performances). Lean choreographs visual wonders, such as the good doctor's trek across the Russian steppes, but the mushy stuff—pounded into your head by Maurice Jarre's popular but grinding "Lara's Theme," also called "Somewhere My Love," can make you look for somewhere to hide.

Hot Bonus: The actors talk gibberish, but the production documentary that lets you see Lean at work—the film was shot in Spain and Finland—is well done.

Key Scene: Zhivago running through a cold empty house, rubbing the ice off the windows, for one last look at Lara as her carriage drives away.

Dodgeball: A True Underdog's Story (2004)

Starring: Ben Stiller, Vince Vaughn, Rip Torn

Directed and written by: Rawson Marshall Thurber

Guilty pleasures rarely come funnier or better packaged on DVD than this farce about debt-ridden gym owner (Vaughn) whose clientele of weaklings enter a dodgeball competition against a corporate gym giant (Stiller) and his team of steroidal freaks. Vaughn and Stiller spar with inspired lunacy, and writer-director Thurber makes you lap up the nonsense with pleasure.

Hot Bonus: "Dodgeball Boot Camp," a featurette on how the actors trained for their roles, is almost as giggle-inducing as the movie.

Key Scene: The peerlessly comic Torn, who plays Coach Patches O'Houlihan, toughening up his team by throwing wrenches at them instead of rubber balls. It's a wincingly hilarious Three Stooges moment.

Dog Day Afternoon (1975)

Starring: Al Pacino, John Cazale, Chris Sarandon
Directed by: Sidney Lumet

Pacino's mesmeric performance makes this New York true crime story a DVD must. As Sonny, Pacino robs a Brooklyn bank with his bumbling partner (Cazale, who played brother Fredo to Pacino's Michael in *The Godfather*) and takes hostages while the police swarm outside. Director Lumet keeps the atmosphere bursting with action and color, but it's Sonny on the phone to his transvestite lover (Sarandon), promising to buy him a sex-change operation, that allows Pacino and Sarandon to pierce the heart.

Hot Bonus: The DVD gives you the movie in full screen on one side and letterboxed on the other. This is one of those rare times that the full frame is preferable, letting a viewer get right into the actors' expressive faces.

Key Scene: Pacino chanting "Attica! Attica!" to rally the crowd to his side.

Dogville (2003)

Starring: Nicole Kidman, Paul Bettany, Lauren Bacall, James Caan
Directed and written by: Lars von Trier

Working for Danish loose cannon von Trier doesn't faze Kidman. She excels as Grace, a fugitive being pursued by gangsters and the police. The "good, honest folk of Dogville" (the words are spoken with caustic irony by narrator John Hurt) agree to hide her in exchange for Grace doing chores, which grow to include being yoked to a dog collar and serving as the town's unpaid prostitute. Shot on a soundstage in Copenhagen with no sets, just chalk marks to indicate the houses in a Rocky Mountain town during the Depression,

the film is von Trier's crushing critique of capitalist America. Despite the stagy set, the DVD makes for a riveting head trip.

Hot Bonus: Testy talk from von Trier, who has never visited the America he so roundly criticizes.

Key Scene: The violent climax, a daring stunt that forces us to detach from Grace and ends the film in a blaze of brutal glory.

Donnie Brasco (Special Edition) (1997)

Starring: Al Pacino, Johnny Depp
Directed by: Mike Newell

This DVD brings new life to a movie that never got props at the box office or at the Oscars. It's the true seventies-era story of how FBI agent Joe Pistone (Depp) went undercover in the mob as jewel fence Donnie Brasco to infiltrate the Bonanno family in Brooklyn, N.Y. His entrée is Lefty Ruggiero (Pacino), an aging, fading hood who takes in Donnie like a son and is taken in and betrayed in return. That is, until the FBI begins to question Donnie's loyalties. Based on the 1989 book by Pistone, the movie—astringently directed by Newell—blends the intensity of a docudrama with the intimacy of a character study. And Pacino and Depp riff off each other beautifully.

Hot Bonus: A featurette on the real Donnie Brasco.

Key Scene: The lesson in how to use the word "fuggedaboudit."

Donnie Darko (The Two-Disc Director's Cut) (2001)

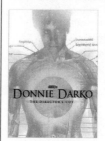

Starring: Jake Gyllenhaal, Drew Barrymore, Jena Malone

Directed and written by: Richard Kelly

The cult movie for the new century comes to DVD the way first-time filmmaker Kelly wanted it in the first place. Some may find the added twenty minutes a slog, but Darko fanatics will thrill to the new provocations in this story about teenaged Donnie (a terrific Gyllenhaal) and how his life changes after a jet engine crashes into his house in 1988. Donnie's visions of time travel and his acts of rebellion precipitated by conversations with Frank, a six-foot rabbit (James Duval) who tells him the world will end in twenty-eight days, worry his parents, his girl (Malone), and his teacher (Barrymore, who executive produced the film). As Donnie's actions grow violent and troubling, so does the film, which has been transferred to DVD with the care that will help make repeat viewers of us all.

Hot Bonus: Kelly, Gyllenhaal, Barrymore, other cast members, and filmmaker-actor Kevin Smith (way out of his Silent Bob mode) avoid the usual hype to comment directly on what the film means.

Key Scene: Donnie's room after the jet crash.

Don't Look Back (Special Edition–Director's Cut) (1967)

Starring: Bob Dylan
Directed by: D. A. Pennebaker

This raw and riveting documentary on the young Dylan is a landmark of the genre, and the DVD is worth celebrating. Pennebaker followed Dylan during his three-week concert tour in England during the spring of 1965. He got the songs ("They Times They Are A-Changin'," "Don't Think Twice, It's All Right," "Subterranean Homesick Blues") and shot handheld in black-and-white with an unobtrusive 16mm camera so he could film the young Dylan onstage and in private moments. with folkie girlfriend Joan Baez, road manager Bob Neuwirth, manager Albert Grossman) and musician pal Alan Price of the Animals. It's a remarkable portrait

Hot Bonus: Retrospective commentary from Pennebaker.

Key Scene: Dylan's meltdown in his hotel suite over a wine glass someone dropped out of a window.

Don't Look Now (1973)

Starring: Julie Christie, Donald Sutherland
Directed by: Nicolas Roeg

Get this DVD and you'll be holding the best movie thriller you've never heard of. It's based on a Daphne Du Maurier story about John (Sutherland), an art restorer, and his wife Laura (Christie). Both haunted by the accidental drowning of their daughter in England, they visit Venice where he works on a crumbling church and she meets two sisters with psychic abilities that may tie into their child's death. Director Roeg uses Venice to creep you out, and does he ever. Even the infamous sex scene between the two stars (rumor has it they did the deed for real) is intercut with before and after flashes that point to tensions in the marriage and chilling portents of what's to come.

Hot Bonus: A paltry trailer. But it took so long to get this classic to DVD–The Exorcist stole its glory in 1973–the transfer is bonus enough.

Key Scene: The figure in the red raincoat near the end. I still get nightmares.

Door in the Floor, The (2004)

Starring: Jeff Bridges, Kim Basinger, Jon Foster, Elle Fanning
Directed and written by: Tod Williams

Newcomer Williams had a ballsy idea for making a film of John Irving's 1998 novel A Widow for One Year: Shit-can the last two-thirds of the book and film the first 183 pages. The result captures the novel's essence while finding its own path. The film concerns children's book author Ted Cole (Bridges) and his wife Marion (Basinger), both haunted by the deaths of their two sons in a car crash. Ted hires Eddie (Foster), sixteen, as an assistant, mostly because he resembles their eldest son. Eddie lusts for the sad-eyed Marion, who is more embarrassed than shocked to catch him jerking off while staring at her underwear. Is the movie a tragedy of death and dismemberment, a stinging comedy, a tale of sexual betrayal and healing? All of the above, and all laid out beautifully on this DVD with Bridges giving a performance that burns in the memory.

Hot Bonus: A featurette on Irving.

Key Scene: The first image: the couple's four-year-old daughter Ruth (the remarkable Fanning) talking to framed photos of her dead brothers.

Doors, The (Two-Disc Special Edition) (1991)

Starring: Val Kilmer, Meg Ryan
Directed by: Oliver Stone

Jim Morrison, the lead singer and lyricist of the Doors, was equal parts poet and snake-oil salesman. You might say the same of Stone, who has turned Morrison's short life—he died of heart failure in 1971 at twenty-seven—into a film of wretched and splendid excess. Stone and Morrison, both products of the turbulent sixties, believed art should be violent and dangerous. The DVD delivers on that promise. The soundtrack should send Doors freaks into Dolby bliss. Kilmer, whose vocals are meshed with Morrison's in a few numbers, stalks the stage as the self-proclaimed "god of rock and cock," spitting out shocking lyrics ("Father, I want to kill you/Mother, I want to fuck you"). It's not art (Morrison's avant-garde posturing grows grating), but it is great theater. And a ball-of-fire DVD.

Hot Bonus: Stone being outrageous. He even disses Ryan's acting as Morrison's common-law wife, who OD'd in 1974.

Key Scene: Morrison's arrest at a 1969 Miami concert for exposing his private parts.

Double Indemnity (1944)

Starring: Barbara Stanwyck, Fred MacMurray, Edward G. Robinson
Directed by: Billy Wilder

DVD fans have a right to bitch that Wilder's classic film noir, with a killer script by Raymond Chandler from a James M. Cain short story, doesn't have a single bonus feature. I'm just pleased to have it at all, and you should be too. They really don't make them like this anymore, as a femme fatale Stanwyck plays MacMurray for a patsy and uses sex (she has a honey of an anklet) to get him to kill her husband for his insurance. Then a claims adjuster (Robinson) shows up. "I didn't get the money and I didn't get the woman," MacMurray tells Robinson. "Pretty, isn't it?"

Hot Bonus: The best print of the film currently available.

Key Scene: "Goodbye, baby"—the words that MacMurray (his career peak) shoots at Stanwyck just before he fires a gun at her.

Dr. No (Remastered) (1962)

Starring: Sean Connery, Ursula Andress, Joseph Wiseman, Lois Maxwell
Directed by: Terence Young

"Bond—James Bond." With those words (and John Barry's memorable theme music), Connery kicked off the first of the Bond films, based on Ian Fleming's novels about British agent 007. "What gives?" he asks his boss's secretary Miss Moneypenny (Maxwell). "Me—given an ounce of encouragement," she answers. Even though this DVD has been remastered, the Bond debut is far from the most elaborate. But Connery explodes off the screen, whether he's flirting with the bikini-clad Andress in Jamaica or taking on the villainous title character (Wiseman).

Hot Bonus: The profile of director Young shows how his own humor and roguish charm influenced Connery's performance.

Key Scene: The spider sticks in the memory, almost as much as Andress emerging from the water. On second thought, forget the spider.

Dr. Strangelove or: How I Learned to Stop Worrying and Love the Bomb (Special Edition) (1964)

Starring: Peter Sellers, George C. Scott, Sterling Hayden, Slim Pickens

Directed by: Stanley Kubrick

Writer Terry Southern's black comedy about nuclear annihilation found the perfect match in Kubrick, a director who knew how to play tragic stupidity for laughs. Sellers won an Oscar nomination for acting three parts: the U.S. president, an RAF captain, and the title role as a mad German scientist in a wheelchair (his hand instinctively rises up to salute the Führer). Hayden adds to the fun as the general who gives the order to drop the bomb, and Scott is a hoot as a gonzo militarist. The film's black-and-white picture is razor-sharp on DVD.

Hot Bonus: Many secrets are revealed, including why Kubrick cut the pie-throwing scene in the war room.

Key Scene: Pickens riding the bomb to mushroom-cloud glory. Yeee-hah!

Dracula (The Legacy Collection) (1931)

Starring: Bela Lugosi, Dwight Frye, Edward Van Sloan
Directed by: Tod Browning

This two-disc DVD is a must for buffs of the blood-sucking Count. Not only do you get the great Lugosi in the original—a DVD debut—you will find the Spanish version of *Dracula*, filmed at the same time and on the same sets with a different cast, as well as three sequels: *Dracula's Daughter* (1936), *Son of Dracula* (1943), and *House of Dracula* (1945). Take a bite, but the fun is seeing Lugosi in the cape, his tongue darting out of his mouth as he tells Renfield (Frye), "I never drink—wine." Director Browning gets the Transylvania atmosphere going, and the DVD gives you the choice of listening to the original score, mostly cribbed from *Swan Lake*, or new music by Philip Glass, performed by the Kronos Quartet.

Hot Bonus: An original documentary, *The Road to Dracula*, that compares the English version with its longer and lusher Spanish counterpart.

Key Scene: The Count expressing his delight in the howling of wolves: "Listen to them. Children of the night—what music they make."

Dreamers, The (The Unrated Director's Cut) (2003)

Starring: Eva Green, Louis Garrel, Michael Pitt
Directed by: Bernardo Bertolucci

Dream on if you think this unrated version means you're in for porn. You do get a vagina (full frontal) and two dicks (limp), but the film also resonates with ideas. The setting is Paris in 1968. Matthew (Pitt) is an American student who spends hours absorbing movie culture at the Cinematheque Francaise. Outside, young protesters take on the government. It's in this surging atmosphere that Matthew meets Isabelle (Green) and her twin brother, Theo (Garrel). He moves into their apartment and is pulled into their incestuous games. The early scenes of playful sexuality—the three in a tub, and Matthew gazing wonderingly up at Isabelle's crotch as he sucks her toes—take on a toxicity as jealousy kicks in. But there's no denying the thrill when the trio gets swept up in the street riots and a new world of danger.

Hot Bonus: A featurette on the events in 1968 France that inspired the film.

Key Scene: When the three re-create that exhilarating moment in Godard's *Band of Outsiders* when the lead actors race through the Louvre.

Dressed to Kill (Special Edition) (1980)

Starring: Michael Caine, Angie Dickinson, Nancy Allen, Keith Gordon
Directed and written by: Brian De Palma

This is De Palma at his most depraved and deliriously erotic, qualities the DVD is quick to show off. The director is a Hitchcock disciple, and this thriller is both reverent spoof and sexual tease. Dickinson gives her best film performance as a frustrated wife given to hitting on her shrink (Caine) as well as the occasional passing stranger. Allen (Mrs. De Palma at the time) also registers strongly as a hooker with an eye for art and Dickinson's teenaged son, nicely underplayed by Gordon. That's when throats start getting slashed—the

moment with the killer in an elevator is nerve frying.

Hot Bonus: A lovely appreciation from Gordon, now a director himself.

Key Scene: The long, sinuous sequence—oh, those gliding camera movements—when Dickinson and a stranger exchange hot looks at New York's Metropolitan Museum and the two tear at each other in a cab en route to his apartment can stand with screen's most erotic moments.

Drugstore Cowboy (1989)

Starring: Matt Dillon, Kelly Lynch, James LeGros, Heather Graham
Directed by: Gus Van Sant

Set in Oregon in the early seventies, this film about a quartet of druggies who rob pharmacies to feed their habit doesn't sound promising. But Van Sant's cult hit, transferred to DVD with attention paid to all the right details, has the humor and the smarts and the lyricism and the gravity to reward repeated viewings. For Bob (Dillon), his wife Dianne (Lynch), their pal Rick (LeGros), and Rick's teen girlfriend Nadine (Graham), the complex how-tos of stealing dope provide an exhilarating sense of purpose. When Nadine overdoses, Bob decides to withdraw from a world his wife won't leave. Dillon makes you feel Bob's ache for the drug life. For once, a movie sees the war on drugs by recognizing the enemy's power and allure.

Hot Bonus: Helpful commentary from Dillon and Van Sant.

Key Scene: When Lynch, in a criminally underrated performance, tells Bob: "You never fuck me, and I always have to drive."

Duck Soup (1933)

Starring: Groucho, Harpo, Chico, and Zeppo Marx
Directed by: Leo McCarey

This antiwar comedy from the funniest brother act in movies features Groucho as Rufus T. Firefly, the ruler of the barely map-worthy duchy of Fredonia who declares war on the neighboring Sylvania, well, just because he can. A satirical swipe at the rise of fascism, the film is widely considered the Marx Brothers' best, and the DVD transfer gives the picture and sound added snap, if not the full restoration it deserves.

Hot Bonus: As part of Universal's The Marx Brothers Silver Screen Collection, which also features *The Cocoanuts*, *Animal Crackers*, *Monkey Business*, and *Horse Feathers*, you get a booklet on the brothers and *Today Show* interviews with Groucho and Harpo from the 1960s and 1970s.

Key Scene: Groucho, Harpo, and Chico in the mirror pretending to be reflections of one another.

Duel in the Sun
(Roadshow Edition) (1946)

Starring: Gregory Peck, Jennifer Jones, Joseph Cotten, Lionel Barrymore

Directed by: King Vidor

Has there ever been a more flamboyantly erotic western? Martin Scorsese remembers getting hot under the collar while watching it. The DVD, with an eye-popping Technicolor transfer, may do the same for you. *Gone With the Wind* producer David O. Selznick cast his wife Jones as Pearl, the nympho half-breed who comes between two brothers—sensible Jesse (Cotten) and dark, dangerous Lewt (Peck, acting with his crotch and letting go as never before on screen—no wonder John Wayne got scared off by the role). Decried from pulpits that called it devil's work, the film had to be cut severely to even play in Philadelphia. Trust me—it's still irresistible.

Hot Bonus: Prelude, overture, and exit music not on the standard disc.

Key Scene: The climactic shootout between Jones and Peck plays like an orgasm set off by blood and bullets. Oh my.

E.T. the Extra Terrestrial
(Ultimate Gift Box Set) (1982)

Starring: Henry Thomas, Drew Barrymore, Robert MacNaughton

Directed by: Steven Spielberg

Check out this overpriced three-disc package—not because you need all the frou-frou (book, CD, collectible senitype, etc.)—but because it's the only way to get the original 1982 version of the movie (it's on Disc 2). The other DVDs available

feature Spielberg's 2002 upgrade with such nonimprovements as a modernized E.T. for a new century and the computerized removal of all guns and weapons so we can—what?—pretend there's no violence in the world. The Box Set also includes the 2002 abomination, but toss it for the DVD version that values simplicity above gloss. Melissa Mathison's deft script, about an alien creature trapped in a California suburb, kicks in when young Elliott (a funny and touching Thomas) helps E.T. get back to his spaceship. Elliott, his older brother (MacNaughton), and his impish younger sister (cutie-pie Barrymore) are—like Spielberg—children of divorce, living with their mom (Dee Wallace). The movie hints delicately at bruised emotions and the need for healing. That's what makes it a classic.

Hot Bonus: The conceptual drawings of the creature.

Key Scene: "E.T. phone home" and "Ouch"—two lines that conjure up the film's most moving moments.

East of Eden
(Two-Disc Special Edition) (1955)

Starring: James Dean, Julie Harris, Raymond Massey, Jo Van Fleet

Directed by: Elia Kazan

Fans of the broodingly intense Dean—he died in a car crash at twenty-four on September 30, 1955—have waited impatiently for the DVD debut of the film that made him a star and won him a posthumous Oscar nomination. They won't be disappointed in this new digital transfer from restored picture and audio elements. John Steinbeck's novel about California lettuce growers in California, circa 1917, was really a modern take on the Cain and Abel story with the troubled Cal (Dean) and his good twin Aron (Richard Davalos) fighting for the love of their Old Testament father (Massey, superb) and Aron's fiancée Abra (a tender and touching Harris). Director Kazan showcases Dean's bruised sensitivity, never more apparent than in his scenes with Oscar-winner Van Fleet as a brothel-owning mother he thought was dead.

Hot Bonus: Dean's screen-test footage and a doc, *Forever James Dean*.

Key Scene: Dean's breakdown when his father won't accept the money that could save his lettuce farm.

Easy Rider (Two-Disc Anniversary Deluxe Edition) (1969)

Starring: Peter Fonda, Dennis Hopper, Jack Nicholson

Directed by: Dennis Hopper

A movie of its time, and if you were there when it hit like a thunderbolt and gave movies the spirit of independent youth, this spiffed-up DVD is a real collector's item. With Fonda as Wyatt and Hopper as Billy, two hippie bikers trekking to New Orleans for Mardi Gras, the film is an indictment of America's failure to live up to its dream of tolerance. An Oscar-nominated Nicholson steals the show as a civil rights lawyer who says "Nic-nic-nic-fff–Indians!" whenever he takes a drink. Even for newbies, this road movie with a rock score remastered in Dolby Digital is a trip worth taking.

Hot Bonus: A retrospective documentary in which Hopper and Fonda tell how some of the drugs they used were real and how their friendship wasn't.

Key Scene: Nicholson's stoned monologue about Venusians who have landed on Earth and taken up positions of power.

Eclipse/L'Eclisse (Two-Disc Special Edition) (1962)

Starring: Alain Delon, Monica Vitti

Directed by: Michelangelo Antonioni

Criterion delivers a starkly beautiful black-and-white DVD transfer of Antonioni's take on Vittoria (a stunning Vitti), a translator who breaks up with her lover in the film's opening scenes and then takes up with Piero (Delon), a handsome young stock trader, in an attempt to feel something again. Set against the teeming background of modern Rome, the film is a study in Vittoria's growing alienation that completes the trilogy Antonioni began with L'Avventura and La Notte.

Hot Bonus: A piece on Antonioni, The Eye That Changed Cinema, which explains the director's style and profound influence.

Key Scene: The silent ending in which the lovers agree to meet but don't, and the camera studies the now-deserted places where they once did meet.

Ed Wood (Special Edition) (1994)

Starring: Johnny Depp, Martin Landau

Directed by: Tim Burton

With this biopic about a cross-dressing Hollywood filmmaker with an unrivaled rep for making cut-rate crap, director Burton doesn't do the expected. It's a cherishable trait that he shares with Depp, who wriggles into a skirt to play Ed Wood, the auteur of such classic clinkers as Glen or Glenda and Plan 9 From Outer Space. Burton insisted on shooting his film in Woodian black-and-white, which glows in tacky splendor on DVD. What gives the film an emotional core is the relationship between Wood and Bela Lugosi (Landau won a deserved Oscar), the Dracula star brought down by alcoholism and morphine addiction. Wood and Lugosi are easy targets that this sympathetic and endearing movie bravely resists.

Hot Bonus: Burton's commentary isn't always coherent, but the feature with Rick Baker on his makeup for Landau as Lugosi is a treat.

Key Scene: During night filming on Bride of the Monster, Lugosi retreats to a car to shoot up. It's a haunting image, intensified when Wood persuades the old man to sit in a cold swamp and wrestle a rubber octopus to get a shot. "OK," says Lugosi, ever the good soldier, "let's shoot this fucker."

Edward Scissorhands (Anniversary Edition) (1990)

Starring: Johnny Depp, Winona Ryder, Dianne Wiest, Vincent Price

Directed by: Tim Burton

Burton's update of the Frankenstein story is a haunting film fantasy that the DVD captures in its full pastel glory. The title character, touchingly played by Depp, is the work of an inventor–Price, in a lovely cameo–who creates a chalky-faced synthetic son, but dies before he can provide him with hands instead of shears. Enter Avon lady Peg (Wiest), who takes him home where he falls for her blond cheerleader daughter Kim (Ryder). The outsider, with a talent for sculpting the town's hedges into exotic topiaries, soon becomes the outcast as Edward is denounced as a freak.

Hot Bonus: Burton's commentary is erratic, but he clearly relates personally to how the townspeople's curiosity about Edward turns to suspicion and hostility (not unlike Hollywood's reaction to an innovative mind).

Key Scene: Edward creating ice sculptures while Kim dances in the flakes to Danny Elfman's engulfing score. When Kim reaches out to

Edward, he pulls back his cold hands until she tenderly wraps her arms around his chest.

Eight Men Out (1988)

Starring: John Cusack, David Strathairn, D. B. Sweeney, Clifton James
Directed and written by: John Sayles

Sayles digs into the true tale of how the Chicago White Sox, pissed at the skinflint tactics of team owner Charles Comiskey (James), threw the World Series for cash bribes in 1919. The action on the field has been transferred splendidly to disc. The cast was trained by White Sox outfielder Ken Berry, and it shows. Sweeney learned to bat left-handed to play Shoeless Joe Jackson. And Strathairn as pitcher Eddie Cicotte, who took the bribe, and Cusack as third baseman Buck Weaver, who protested his innocence, put human faces on a scandal that tarnished the game.

Hot Bonus: Just the trailer.

Key Scene: An epilogue showing Shoeless Joe playing under an assumed name with Weaver watching in the stands.

8 Mile (2002)

Starring: Eminem, Kim Basinger
Directed by: Curtis Hanson

In this corner: Eminem. The Detroit rapper who can rhyme fourteen syllables a line facing the challenge that has KO'd many before him: acting.

And in this corner: the hordes who want the artist formerly known as Marshall Mathers to fall flat on his misogynistic, homophobic, race-baiting, mother-hating, gun-toting, tattoo-flaunting ass. Sorry, hordes. In his film debut as aspiring rapper known as Rabbit, Eminem is on fire. He reads lines with an offbeat freshness that makes his talk and his rap sound interchangeable. Stuck in a trailer park with his broke mom (a splendid Basinger), Rabbit competes in freestyle verbal battles against black rappers at a local club. The DVD brings out the raw images and sound (Eminem won a Best Song Oscar for "Lose Yourself"). Director Hanson creates a Detroit world that teems with hip-hop energy.

Hot Bonus: Newly released rap battles showcase Eminem free-styling against local Detroit rappers who auditioned to appear in the movie.

Key Scene: Eminem taking on the reigning champ (Anthony Mackie) in a rap showdown where the words fly like fists.

8½ (Two-Disc Special Edition) (1963)

Starring: Marcello Mastroianni, Claudia Cardinale, Anouk Aimée
Directed by: Federico Fellini

Fellini's autobiographical masterpiece is brought home in DVD splendor by Criterion. The black-and-white picture shimmers as creatively stalled film director Guido Anselmi (Mastroianni at his most iconic) goes to a spa to stir his imagination and must deal with his wife (Aimée), his mistress (Sandra Milo), and his muse (Cardinale), as well as dreams of his boyhood, his first sexual initiation, and his uncertain future. Nino Rota's glorious score and Gianni Di Venanzo's camerawork helped Fellini create a movie milestone.

Hot Bonus: Film scholars blow hot air about the film's meanings, but it's an introduction from filmmaker and fan Terry Gilliam that sets the right mood.

Key Scene: Mastroianni as ringmaster trying to arrange his life the way he wants to remember it and freeze it on celluloid.

Election (1999)

Starring: Reese Witherspoon, Matthew Broderick, Chris Klein
Directed and co-written by: Alexander Payne

Payne's best film before *Sideways* uses an Omaha high school election to satirize the political and moral corruption at the heart of democracy. The intimacy of the DVD only increases admiration for Witherspoon's demonically fierce and funny performance as Tracy Flick, a young, female Tricky Dick Nixon who is willing to lie, cheat, steal, screw faculty, and even make cupcakes for voters to win the race for student council president against a jock (Klein) and the jock's lesbian sister (Jessica Campbell). One teacher (Broderick in his best role since *Ferris Bueller*) stands in the way of Tracy's fascist rise, and Payne and co-writer Jim Taylor make sure he pays dearly and hilariously.

Hot Bonus: Trenchant commentary from Payne.

Key Scene: Tracy at prayer, telling off God: "I really must insist that you help me win the election tomorrow."

he adds in a moment of exquisite heartbreak: "I must have been a great disappointment to her. I tried so hard to be good."

Elephant (2003)

Starring: Alex Frost, Eric Deulen
Directed by: Gus Van Sant

The title of Van Sant's look at a high school shooting spree modeled on Columbine refers to something metaphorically huge that we all see and we all choose to ignore. What Van Sant sees with piercing clarity are the bruises that come with being young in America. Set on a fall day at an unnamed high school in Portland, Oregon, the film uses real high school students who improvise their dialogue. The DVD does full justice to the cinematography of Harris Savides, whose camera pokes around, catching snippets of talk, observing the beauty of one young face and the desolation of another. Then two students, Alex (Frost) and Eric (Deulen), enter school and start shooting. This isn't a film about what turns kids into killers. It is a film that gets at the small things that drain a heart of feeling.

Hot Bonus: A "making of" featurette that truly informs.

Key Scene: "Most importantly, have fun," says Alex to Eric as they drive to school. It's a brushoff line they've heard too often. To those who see no purpose in this film, I say the purpose is learning not to turn a blind eye.

Elephant Man, The (1980)

Starring: John Hurt, Anthony Hopkins, Anne Bancroft
Directed by: David Lynch

Based on the true story of John Merrick, a Victorian-era freak hideously deformed since birth, the film finds this "elephant man" resigned to his life in a circus sideshow until he is rescued by a London surgeon (Hopkins) and introduced into London society by a famous stage actress (Bancroft). The power of the DVD owes much to resonant black-and-white cinematography of Freddie Francis. Hurt justly won an Oscar nomination, as did director Lynch, who captures the dark underside of a society that exploits its misfits.

Hot Bonus: An interview with makeup artist Christopher Tucker.

Key Scene: "Do you want to see a picture of my mother?" Merrick asks the doctor and his wife. Registering their surprise at how pretty she looks,

Elf (Two-Disc Special Edition) (2003)

Starring: Will Ferrell, Zooey Deschanel, James Caan
Directed by: Jon Favreau

There's a burst of holiday colors and good cheer on this DVD of a family-friendly comedy about a human baby who crawls into Santa's sleigh and winds up being raised by elves. Ferrell plays the grown-up doofus who must travel from the North Pole to Manhattan to find his real father (Caan), a hard-ass publisher of children's books, and teach him the true meaning of Christmas. OK, yuk. But Ferrell makes the damn thing work. Even though he can't get naked or use naughty words, there's a devil of comedy in Ferrell, and he lets it out to play. Favreau has the good sense to stand out of his way.

Hot Bonus: Elf Karaoke. Don't ask. Just laugh.

Key Scene: Ferrell, fully grown, sitting on the lap of a miniaturized elf, played by Bob Newhart.

Empire of the Sun (1987)

Starring: Christian Bale, John Malkovich, Miranda Richardson
Directed by: Steven Spielberg

Spielberg stunningly evokes the pre–Pearl Harbor Shanghai of 1941 when the Japanese invasion separates a British schoolboy (Bale) from his parents and leaves him in a Japanese prison camp. That evocation, stunningly rendered on DVD, is reason enough to prize the film playwright Tom Stoppard has deftly adapted from J. G. Ballard's autobiographical novel. Bale, who grew up to star in *Batman Begins* and *American Psycho*, is another; he gives one of the all-time best performances by a child actor.

Hot Bonus: A documentary that answers the question: How'd they do that?

Key Scene: The boy, silhouetted in front of a Japanese plane, caught between fear and admiration of his enemy.

Endless Summer, The (The Complete Three-Disc Box Set)

Directed by: Bruce Brown

Whether you watch one or all three of all these movies—1966's *Endless Summer*, 1994's *Endless Summer II*, and 2000's *The Endless Summer Revisited*—you will be watching some of the best and most exciting surfing footage ever committed to film or DVD. Brown and his son Dana have brought back the goods in their search for the perfect wave.

Hot Bonus: A scrapbook and new interviews with Bruce and Dana Brown conducted by Steve Pezman, publisher of *The Surfer's Journal*.

Key Scene: I could say the topless beach bunnies in *Endless Summer II*, but that would ignore the pow of surfing with sharks in Australia.

English Patient, The (Two-Disc Collector's Series) (1996)

Starring: Ralph Fiennes, Kristin Scott Thomas, Juliette Binoche

Directed by: Anthony Minghella

Elaine on *Seinfeld* couldn't understand what audiences or Oscar (it won Best Picture) saw in this intimate, nearly three-hour epic (from Michael Ondaatje's prizewinning novel of World War II) about a nurse (Binoche) who cares for a cartographer (Fiennes) who has been burned in a plane crash. In flashbacks, we learn the identity of this English patient and his love for a married woman (Kristin Scott Thomas). The DVD transfer is specular enough to make Elaine take a second look. Minghella proves that a movie love story can be smart, principled, and provoking, and still sweep you away.

Hot Bonus: More than you want to know, really, but a historical look at the real "English patient" is an eye-opener.

Key Scene: For romance, you can't beat Binoche (she won an Oscar) in the arms of Naveen Andrews, a Sikh officer in the British Army, as he swings her on a rope in an old cathedral to show her art work by torchlight.

Enter the Dragon (Two-Disc Special Edition) (1973)

Starring: Bruce Lee, Shih Kien

Directed by: Robert Clouse

This was the film Bruce Lee completed just before his death, and the bonus-loaded DVD, with deleted scenes, shows the benefits of a big budget. The sound has a kickass pop as Lee, playing an undercover agent, infiltrates a martial-arts tournament run by Asian crime lord Han (Shih Kien). Speaking English for the first time on screen and working for an American director, Lee showed a star quality that brought kung-fu into the mainstream.

Hot Bonus: Footage of Lee talking about his fight philosophy.

Key Scene: Lee taking on Han in the hall of mirrors.

Eraserhead (1978)

Starring: Jack Nance, Charlotte Stewart

Directed by: David Lynch

Lynch's debut as a director is such a cult film that you can only order the DVD from his Web site (DavidLynch.com). How can you not? Weirdness like this is special indeed. Stewart, who once starred on TV's *Little House on the Prairie*, plays Mary X, who with her factory-worker lover Henry (Nance) produces a premature baby, far more grotesque than Rosemary's. Besides the blood-spitting, gut-oozing horror, there's a little sci-fi, a little low comedy, some flying fetuses, a rolling severed head (later molded into an eraser), and stark, black-and-white images to haunt your dreams.

Hot Bonus: Lynch, in an exceedingly rare interview.

Key Scene: The lady in the radiator singing, "In heaven everything is fine."

Erin Brockovich (2000)

Starring: Julia Roberts, Albert Finney

Directed by: Steven Soderbergh

The DVD makes a case for this biopic as something more than an excuse to watch the highest-paid female star in Hollywood flash her ta-tas and talk dirty. Roberts won an Oscar playing the fiery title character—a twice-divorced mother of three with a hooker wardrobe. But it's file-clerk Erin who helps her lawyer boss Ed Masry (Finney in full, flinty vigor) take on Pacific Gas & Electric, the $30 billion company that contaminated the water supply of the people of Hinkley, California, and then lied about it. Thanks to Soderbergh's keen directorial eye, the film keeps the community front and center (part of the film was shot in Hinkley, next to the PG&E plant).

Hot Bonus: Interviews with real Brockovich and Masry.

Key Scene: It's gratifying to see Erin hand over a $5 million settlement to a cancer victim. But I winced when Roberts, who made $20 million for the film, says, "It's all you'll ever need and all your children will ever need."

Escape From New York (Two-Disc Special Edition) (1981)

Starring: Kurt Russell, Donald Pleasence, Isaac Hayes

Directed by: John Carpenter

It's weird now, watching a futuristic flick set in 1997. But Carpenter's headbanger looks better than ever on this DVD transfer. The United States has survived a war with Russia, and Manhattan is now a maximum-security prison with a thirty-foot-high wall around it. When the president (Pleasence) is kidnapped, eye-patch-wearing convict Snake Plissken (Russell, doing his best Clint Eastwood impression) is told he can win his freedom if he saves the prez. Gratuitous violence, sex, and implausibility ensue, all more entertaining than Carpenter's 1996 sequel, *Escape From L.A.*

Hot Bonus: It's a kick to watch the never-before-seen opening scene, the bank robbery that got Snake arrested, and then hear Carpenter and Russell bluntly admit it deserved to be cut. Score one for honesty.

Key Scene: Bad-guy Hayes cruising in a limo through the rotten Big Apple. Actually, most scenes were shot in St. Louis, but damn they look good.

Eternal Sunshine of the Spotless Mind (Two-Disc Collector's Edition) (2004)

Starring: Jim Carrey, Kate Winslet

Directed by: Michel Gondry

Charlie Kaufman's innovative script about two lovers—a subtly moving Carrey and a flamboyantly superb Winslet—who try to erase each other from their bruised memories combines with director Gondry's visual mastery to create a love story like no other. The DVD transfer gives every image and feeling it's striking due.

Hot Bonus: The infomercial for Lacuna, the firm that arranges for memory erasure in the film, is shown in full, and it's a doozy.

Key Scene: Carrey and Winslet in bed on a beach.

Europa Europa (1991)

Starring: Marco Hofschneider, Julie Delpy

Directed by: Agnieszka Holland

A German boy, Solly (the excellent Hofschneider), conceals his Jewish heritage from the Nazis only to be drafted as a member of Hitler Youth. Solly's attempts to hide his circumcised penis from the Aryan girl (Delpy) who comes on to him would be funny were it not for her comments: "If I ever catch a Jew, I'll cut his throat." Director Holland takes a deceptively light approach to the gravest of material, which in no way distracts from the film's devastating impact. Based on the story of Solomon Perel, who survived the war, the film comes to DVD with its images finely burnished.

Hot Bonus: English subtitles that are actually readable and coherent.

Key Scene: Solly catching a glimpse of a woman he thinks is his mother as he rides a trolley through the Lodz ghetto.

Everyone Says I Love You (1996)

Starring: Woody Allen, Goldie Hawn, Julia Roberts, Alan Alda

Directed and written by: Woody Allen

With his first musical, the Woodman wanted to prove a point: It's feeling that counts, not whether the actors can sing or dance. In reality, an actor with a thin voice or two left feet, like Allen himself, can be off-putting. Luckily, Everyone is a burst of exhilaration that rarely touches ground. The pin-size plot revolves around a wealthy Manhattan family: a liberal attorney (Alda), his do-gooder wife (Hawn), their kids, and her ex-husband (Allen), an author of racy novels who seduces a young babe (Roberts) by snooping on her shrink sessions. Everyone's love life is a mess, and everyone sings about it.

Hot Bonus: Techies complain about Allen DVDs with their mono sound and lack of bonus material. But Carlo DiPalma's camera puts a scrumptious sheen on New York that lights up the disc transfer.

Key Scene: Hawn singing "I'm Thru With Love" on a starry Paris night before joining Allen for a dance that leaves her literally walking on air. The scene is a trick done with wires that Allen transforms into romantic sorcery.

Evil Dead, The: The Book of the Dead (Limited Edition) (1983)

Starring: Bruce Campbell, Ellen Sandweiss

Directed by: Sam Raimi

College students. A cabin in the Tennessee woods. Demons on the prowl. This was *Spider-Man* director Raimi's first film. It's low-budget, grainy, and guaranteed to scare the bejesus out of you. Starting with the lumpy latex cover—face on the front, disembodied ear on the back—this DVD package is a horror buff's must-own. Campbell is clueless perfection as Ash, who hacks away at his zombified buddies when he's not cowering in a corner.

Hot Bonus: Footage of Campbell attending a horror-movie convention is almost as scary as the movie itself.

Key Scene: The game of cards.

Evil Dead II: Dead by Dawn (Remastered) (1987)

Starring: Bruce Campbell, Denise Bixler
Directed by: Sam Raimi

As funny as the first movie was fierce. Here's the rare sequel that equals the original. Ash, having some kind of acid flashback, returns to that cabin in the woods, opens *The Book of the Dead*, and starts hacking away at a new set of demons. Camp-

bell seems to enjoy reinventing Ash as a warrior. And the DVD reveals Raimi in a splatter mode that took on a new spin in 1993's *Army of Darkness* when Ash time-traveled to King Arthur's court.

Hot Bonus: Kickass commentary from Campbell and Raimi.

Key Scene: Ash fighting his own disembodied hand.

Excalibur (1981)

Starring: Nicol Williamson, Helen Mirren, Nigel Terry, Nicholas Clay
Directed by: John Boorman

Picture Camelot with gross-out gore and a Monty Python farce, and you'll have some idea of Boorman's retelling of King Arthur's search for the Holy Grail. Actually Arthur (Terry) and Lancelot (Clay) have to fight for attention since Boorman, who shot the film in Ireland—the visual splendor is rendered intact on the DVD—cares more about Merlin, played with bad-ass gusto by Williamson. The great Mirren almost matches him for eccentricity as the King's incestuous sister—she likes to have knights hanged from trees and watch birds peck their eyes out.

Hot Bonus: Boorman's comments about working with the famously uncontrollable Williamson are priceless.

Key Scene: It's a draw between the key moment that evokes what Boorman calls "man's lost oneness with nature" or the kinky sex involving naked women coupling with knights in spiky armor. Your call.

Exorcist, The (The Version You've Never Seen) (1973)

Starring: Ellen Burstyn, Linda Blair, Jason Miller, Max von Sydow
Directed by: William Friedkin

The template for demonic-possession movies, which inspired two inferior sequels and a lousy 2004 prequel, found its best DVD incarnation in this "never seen" version, released in 2000, that added 10 minutes to the 122-minute original. The scene with Blair as the possessed twelve-year-old girl doing her backwards crab-walk down a flight of stairs to the horror of her movie-star mother (Burstyn) got the most media attention, but the added discussion between the priests, Father Karras (Miller) and Father Merrin (von Sydow), about the roots of demonology and exorcism is even more worthwhile. The DVD is a testament to how well the film holds up, thanks to Friedkin's tense direction and the Oscar-winning screenplay by William Peter Blatty, who adapted the film from his bestselling novel.

Hot Bonus: The restored ten minutes.

Key Scene: Horror fans are torn among the girl's head-spinning, her puking (they used pea soup), her shocking language (dubbed by Mercedes McCambridge) to Karras ("Your mother sucks cocks in hell"), and the climactic levitation. But I'd choose the moment when Karras dares the demon to "come into me," and the film sparks debate over whether the girl is possessed by a demon or psychological forces closer to home.

Eyes Wide Shut (1999)

Starring: Tom Cruise, Nicole Kidman
Directed by: Stanley Kubrick

Several fellow critics have told me that my problems with Kubrick's final film would vanish over the years when its meanings would cohere and resonate with repeated viewings. I'm still waiting. But there's no denying the dazzling image and sound on the DVD transfer, preserving Kubrick's probing look at a marriage consumed by the sexual jealousy of the doctor husband (Cruise, over his head) and the sexual avidity of the wife (Kidman, combustibly effective). The DVD retains the full-screen format favored by Kubrick, which is fine, but also the cowardly R-rated version of the film released in theaters, which is not fine since using digital artifacts to block the naughty bits in an orgy scene hardly honors the memory of the great director.

Hot Bonus: Interviews with the then-married Cruise and Kidman about working with Kubrick, which fascinate in their details and frustrate in providing not nearly enough of them.

Key Scene: The wife's confession of her unrequited lust for a naval officer, sparking images in the husband's head that Kubrick films with an urgent eroticism missing in the rest of the movie.

Fabulous Baker Boys, The (1989)

Starring: Michelle Pfeiffer, Jeff Bridges, Beau Bridges
Directed by: Steve Kloves

A romantic mood piece makes the DVD transfer in high style thanks to Michael Ballhaus's dreamy cinematography and three actors who bring a needed edge to a script by Kloves, making his directing debut. Jeff Bridges plays Jack Baker, a womanizer who's been doing a piano lounge act for fifteen years with his married brother Frank (Beau Bridges). For spice, they add Susie Diamond (Pfeiffer), a professional escort turned singer. Jack falls hard. Who wouldn't with Pfeiffer as inspiration? The Bridges brothers shine, but it's Pfeiffer, doing her own singing, who delivers the "fabulous."

Hot Bonus: Ballhaus talks about fusing the look of the piece with the music.

Key Scene: Pfeiffer, atop a Steinway in a slinky red dress and singing "Makin' Whoopee," buckles your knees.

Face in the Crowd, A (1957)

Starring: Andy Griffith, Patricia Neal, Walter Matthau
Directed by: Elia Kazan

Griffith is a long way from Mayberry as Lonesome Rhodes, a cracker-barrel philosopher from Arkansas who gets the star treatment from Neal and Matthau. They don't realize until too late that they've helped to create a monster. Director Kazan and writer Budd Schulberg followed their On the Waterfront collaboration with this stinging indictment of megalomania. Griffith, in his film debut, is demonically powerful. The long-awaited debut of this powerhouse on DVD will shock fans of Sheriff Andy.

Hot Bonus: Harry Stradling's black-and-white cinematography is restored to its former luster.

Key Scene: Thinking the sound is off, Lonesome Rhodes ends his TV show by expressing his contempt for his audience while wearing a smile.

Face/Off (1997)

Starring: John Travolta, Nicolas Cage
Directed by: John Woo

If you want logic, skip this baby. Others can hop on for a hell of a DVD ride as an FBI agent (Travolta) undergoes surgery to switch his face and body type with a demented terrorist (Cage) to learn the location of a biological weapon set to destroy Los Angeles. Things get tricky when the terrorist pulls the same stunt. Woo, the Hong Kong action master, blends supercharged images of balletic brutality with an off-the-wall humor that allows Travolta and Cage to have the time of their lives parodying each other.

Hot Bonus: Travolta in a specially shot teaser for the film.

Key Scene: A classic Woo shootout at a chapel on the beach in which violence and sentiment collide with operatic intensity.

Fahrenheit 9/11 (2004)

Starring: Michael Moore, George W. Bush

Directed by: Michael Moore

Academy voters had a shot to make history by making Moore's broadside against the Bush administration the first documentary to be nominated as Best Picture. They blew it. Moore did not, as this DVD attests. His film measures the human toll taken by U.S. foreign policy after 9/11 and the war in Iraq. Moore isn't above a cheap laugh at the expense of Dubya's vocabulary, a pro-war Britney Spears, John Ashcroft warbling a patriotic ditty, or Deputy Defense Secretary Paul Wolfowitz vainly prepping for a TV interview. But he steps aside more often than not to let America speak for itself, notably Lila Lipscomb, the mother of a dead soldier. Moore has marshaled what's on the record and off into a stinging indictment.

Hot Bonus: A new sequence set outside Abu Ghraib Prison.

Key Scene: Moore rallies members of Congress to get their own children to enlist in the Marines. No chance.

Fall of the House of Usher, The (1960)

Starring: Vincent Price, Mark Damon, Myrna Fahey

Directed by: Roger Corman

The first of Corman's eight film adaptations of the works of Edgar Allan Poe is arguably the best. The widescreen DVD looks smashing, emphasizing the miracles achieved by Corman and art director Daniel Haller on a $350,000 budget. There's a fine script by sci-fi legend Richard Matheson, but the prize of the film is Price in the role that made him a horror icon. He is hauntingly good as Roderick Usher, a madman who will stop at nothing (even premature burial) to prevent his sister (Fahey) from marrying her suitor (Damon). Is it the family's tainted blood or Roderick's tainted desires?

Hot Bonus: A rare interview with Corman,

who reveals that he got the money for the film by telling the producers the house was the monster.

Key Scene: "The house lives!"—a deathless line as spoken by Price.

Fanny and Alexander (Five-Disc Special Edition) (1982)

Starring: Pernilla Allwin, Bertil Guve

Directed and written by: Ingmar Bergman

Bergman's autobiographical masterpiece gets the royal treatment from Criterion. There are high-definition digital transfers of both the 181-minute theatrical version of the film and the 312-minute version made for Swedish television. The DVD package uses five discs to conduct a master class on Bergman's filmmaking. It's impossible not to be engaged as young Alexander (Guve) and his younger sister Fanny (Allwin) find the sweet warmth of their lives chilled by the death of their theater-manager father and the marriage of their mother (Ewa Fröling) to a cold, exacting bishop (Jan Malmsjö). Before the children can escape to the home of their worldly actress grandmother (Gunn Wålgren), they must endure Dickensian hardships that allow Bergman to expose social and religious hypocrisies.

Hot Bonus: Bergman's feature-length documentary *The Making of Fanny and Alexander*, presented here for the first time on DVD.

Key Scene: Alexander's conversation with God.

Fantasia (Uncut Original Edition) (1940)

Narrated by: Deems Taylor

Directed by: Ben Sharpsteen

Even if you're one of those purists who finds Walt Disney's attempt to marry animation to great works of classical music a failed experiment in snob art—it was a box-office fizzle at the time of its release—this DVD is a demo disc to die for. No wonder the 1960s drug culture adopted it as its own. Pick the best parts—Tchaikovsky's "Nutcracker Suite" danced by fairies, flowers, and fish; Beethoven's "Pastoral Symphony" with its controversial cartoon nymphs; and Stravinsky's "Rites of Spring" with its dinosaurs—and let your home theater audio system show what it can do.

Hot Bonus: Archival interviews with Uncle Walt himself.

Key Scene: Nobody doesn't like Mickey Mouse and the dancing brooms in Paul Dukas's "The Sorcerer's Apprentice."

Fantasticks, The (Special Edition) (2000)

Starring: Joe McIntyre, Jean Louisa Kelly, Joel Grey, Brad Sullivan

Directed by: Michael Ritchie

The film version of the Off-Broadway musical, which ran a record-breaking forty years, was shot in 1995 by director Ritchie, and stayed on the shelf for five years until producer Francis Coppola recut it for a brief run in 2000. You'd have a right to expect a DVD disaster. Instead, you get a colorful charmer, shot by camera wiz Fred Murphy against the sweeping landscapes of the Arizona prairie where *Oklahoma!* was filmed. McIntyre, of New Kids on the Block, and Kelly catch just the right note of youthful yearning in their voices (digital wizardry allowed the actors to sing live) as the teens whose fathers (Grey and Sullivan) scheme to bring them together by keeping them apart. The dads' plan involves hiring a traveling magician, El Gallo (Jonathon Morris, no match for the late Jerry Orbach who created the role on stage), to stage a phony rape. Never mind. Even as the movie threatens to derail, the thrill of the score, by Tom Jones and Harvey Schmidt—"Try to Remember," "I Can See It"—keeps breaking through.

Hot Bonus: The deleted songs are a treat.

Key Scene: "Soon It's Gonna Rain"—a love song that lands like gossamer.

Far From Heaven (2002)

Starring: Julianne Moore, Dennis Quaid, Dennis Haysbert, Patricia Clarkson

Directed and written by: Todd Haynes

Cheers to the New York Film Critics Circle for choosing this haunting human drama as the year's Best Picture, while Oscar played it safe with *Chicago*. Haynes raises the chick flick to the level of art. Moore, as a girly-swirly Connecticut housewife (circa 1957), and Quaid, as her closet gay husband, give the performances of their careers. Haynes treats the 1950s like an exotic parallel universe. But this is no campfest, even when Quaid goes to a shrink for a "cure" that doesn't take. Moore's friend (a delicious, devious Clarkson) cuts her off when Moore lets down her guard with her handsome gardener (Haysbert). And since he is black, more scandal thunders into her life. Ed Lachman—in a glorious demonstration of all that cinematography can be—floods the screen with color. Coupled with the ravishing score by Elmer Bernstein, the DVD is a visual and aural knockout.

Hot Bonus: Hearing Haynes talk about the film's major influence, Douglas Sirk, the director who made his mark in Hollywood with a popular series of 1950s' women's pictures, such as *Imitation of Life*, that subversively attacked middle-class conformity.

Key Scene: Haysbert taking Moore for a drink and a dance at a "colored" restaurant. This imitation of life from half a century ago holds up a cracked mirror to the here and now.

Fargo (Special Edition) (1996)

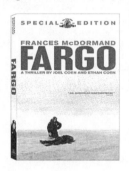

Starring: Frances McDormand, William H. Macy

Directed and written by: Joel and Ethan Coen

A contender for best movie of the 1990s. It's terrific in every particular, each one honed to perfection on the fully loaded DVD. Let's start with McDormand's Oscar-winning turn as Marge Gunderson, a hugely pregnant Minnesota sheriff tracking down a car salesman (Macy, sublimely smarmy) who hired two hoods (Steve Buscemi and Peter Stormare) to kidnap his wife. For the Coen brothers, who won a deserved Oscar for their script, the film revealed a heart beating beneath their macabre comic exterior. You feel for these people, even when you laugh at their patois ("Ya, be there in a jif—you betcha"). Camera wiz Roger Deakins can make lyric poetry out of a car emerging from a blinding snow. And the Coens go that one better: they make us see ourselves in the best and worst of human behavior.

Hot Bonus: The Coens talk, but don't believe a word they say—ever, including trying to pass off *Fargo* as a true story. The footage of the boys on set, communicating in a whispered secret language, rings truer.

Key Scene: The foot in the wood chipper is a classic. You betcha.

Fast and the Furious, The (Tricked-Out Edition) (2001)

Starring: Vin Diesel, Paul Walker, Michelle Rodriguez, Jordana Brewster

Directed by: Rob Cohen

Fast cars and faster women are a potent DVD combo. And engines that drown out dialogue.

Trust me, it helps. The cars look and sound sensational. Diesel, a great name for an actor in a film that showcases fuel, stars as the leader of a Los Angeles street-racing team that might be a front for a truck-hijacking racket. Walker co-stars as the cop who goes undercover as a racer to find out for sure. The women in the cast, including Brewster and Rodriguez, are used mostly as slut accessories to the chrome and beefcake. It isn't good, but it is fun, and seems better in retrospect when you consider the skid mark of a 2003 sequel, *2 Fast 2 Furious*, that Diesel and director Cohen has the good sense to skip out on.

Hot Bonus: Besides a feature on how to trick out a car, there's an Easter Egg if you go to the Bonus Materials and find the article that inspired the movie. Select that and you'll see a yellow steering wheel to click on which will provide cast interviews and scenes from the film.

Key Scene: The climactic race.

Fast Times at Ridgemont High (Special Edition) (1982)

Starring: Sean Penn, Jennifer Jason Leigh, Phoebe Cates, Judge Reinhold
Directed by: Amy Heckerling

Famous for Penn's performance as Jeff Spicoli, a surfer who looks at a wave and says, "Hey, Bud, let's party," this cult comedy about California teens with mall jobs reveals something deeper on DVD. Yes, Penn is still a hoot. Who can forget him flooring his teacher, Mr. Hand (Ray Walston), by ordering a pizza delivered to his history class? But on repeated viewings the script by Oscar-winner-to-be Cameron Crowe (*Almost Famous*) takes time to notice a fifteen-year-old (Leigh) considering an abortion and the sick feeling her brother (Reinhold) feels being named "head fryer" at a burger joint. Crowe and director Heckerling give you more reason to applaud this DVD other than the chance to freeze-frame Cates (she played the school's "woman of the world") with her top off.

Hot Bonus: A retrospective documentary that pulls you up short.

Key Scene: Spicoli, who his classmate says "has been stoned since the third grade," getting tricked back into the classroom. "You're wrong," he says, outraged. "There's no birthday party for me in here!"

Fatal Attraction (Special Collector's Edition) (1987)

Starring: Glenn Close, Michael Douglas, Anne Archer
Directed by: Adrian Lyne

"I'm not gonna be ignored," says Close to Douglas in the anti-date movie that gave many a married man pause about pursuing an affair with a sultry psycho. There's no depth to director Lyne's cautionary fable, but there is suspense, lots of it, especially when Close—Oscar nominated and a great roaring terror in the role—boils the Douglas family bunny. The DVD, a collectible for married guys who ever feel tempted to stray, contains an alternate ending that makes more sense than the original.

Hot Bonus: A look at the fuss the film stirred up as a cultural phenomenon.

Key Scene: The bathtub.

Fear and Loathing in Las Vegas (Two-Disc Special Edition) (1998)

Starring: Johnny Depp, Benicio Del Toro
Directed by: Terry Gilliam

The late, great Hunter S. Thompson's seminal book about his gonzo 1971 tear through Las Vegas, ingesting every detail (and every drug) that would get him closer to the truth about this American temple of desire and greed, became a movie that few understood and many frankly hated. Criterion counters with a first-class DVD package that pleads for re-consideration. Take in all the extras and you may see why Thompson, who ended his life with a gun in 2005, admired Gilliam's hallucinatory take on his book and Depp's all-or-nothing performance as his alter ego Raoul Duke, and Del Toro's take on Dr. Gonzo, his attorney and fellow prankster.

Hot Bonus: Thompson caught at home in Colorado.

Key Scene: Right at the start, as Depp and Del Toro drive down a desert highway in their red Chevy convertible, and Depp says in voice-over: "We were somewhere around Barstow when the drugs began to take hold."

Fearless (1993)

Starring: Jeff Bridges, Rosie Perez
Directed by: Peter Weir

Perhaps the most underrated film of the 1990s.

The ever-brilliant Bridges and an Oscar-nominated Perez play traumatized survivors of a jet crash (terrifyingly rendered), who teach each other how to live again. It sounds like an early take on the TV hit *Lost*, but this darkly comic and emotionally bruising film is alive with fresh provocations. Weir packs the film with astonishing images of beauty and terror that power the DVD.

Hot Bonus: While we wait for a letterboxed DVD with a commentary track, we can still appreciate the superb sound design in the crash sequence.

Key Scene: The opening in a cornfield. The scene looks eerily serene. Then sounds begin to filter through—a deep rumble, a high wailing noise. We see the remnants of a plane, an incinerated body still strapped to a seat, a woman screaming as a rescue crew drags her away from the wreckage.

Ferris Bueller's Day Off (1986)

Starring: Matthew Broderick, Mia Sara, Alan Ruck

Directed and written by: John Hughes

That wily charmer Broderick is still best known for playing the title role in this hit comedy about a Chicago scam artist who skips out on high school for a day with his pal (Ruck) and his girl (Sara). Ferris is a suburban Tom Sawyer, looking for action and trouble. The DVD captures the exhilaration of Ferris's freedom on the Chicago streets, especially when he leads a crowd in an impromptu version of "Twist and Shout."

Hot Bonus: Astute commentary from Hughes about his teen obsessions.

Key Scene: Ferris's first bit of talking to the camera: "This is my ninth sick day. It's getting pretty tough coming up with new illnesses. If I go for ten, I'm probably gonna have to barf up a lung."

Fiddler on the Roof (Special Edition) (1971)

Starring: Topol, Norma Crane, Leonard Frey

Directed by: Norman Jewison

One of the rare Broadway musical classics that made the trip to film without losing its power or its essence, both drawn from the Sholom Aleichem stories about Tevye (a hearty Topol), a poor Jewish milkman who only wants to marry off his four daughters and live modestly in the little village of Anatevka. Then a pogrom tears the village apart. Oswald Morris's Oscar-winning cinematography comes through crisply on DVD as does the score

by Sheldon Harnick and Jerry Bock which embraces the comic ("If I Were a Rich Man") and the heartbreaking ("Sunrise, Sunset").

Hot Bonus: Incisive commentary from director Jewison, who explains why he didn't hire Zero Mostel to reprise his landmark stage performance of Tevye (too broad, too comic). For me, it remains an opportunity missed.

Key Scene: "Tradition," the rousing opening number, nearly bursts the confines of your TV monitor with color and joyous movement.

Field of Dreams (Two-Disc Anniversary Edition) (1989)

Starring: Kevin Costner, Amy Madigan, Ray Liotta, Burt Lancaster

Directed and written by: Phil Alden Robinson

Frankly, the sentimentality of this hymn to baseball gives me acid reflux. But the baseball scenes themselves are kinetic and don't lose an ounce of spark on this DVD with remastered picture and sound. Costner plays the Iowa farmer who builds a baseball diamond in his cornfield because he heard a voice say, "If you build it, he will come." Is the "he" the ghost of Shoeless Joe Jackson (Liotta) of the Chicago "Black Sox," who was banned from the game after being wrongly accused of throwing the 1919 World Series for a bribe, or perhaps someone else?

Hot Bonus: A touching piece on how the movie's set on two farms in Iowa still inspires visits from baseball fans.

Key Scene: Shoeless Joe and his seven ghostly teammates stepping out of the misty cornfield to recapture "the sounds and the smells" of the game.

Fifth Element, The (Two-Disc Ultimate Edition) (1997)

Starring: Bruce Willis, Milla Jovovich, Chris Tucker

Directed by: Luc Besson

Besson's silly but stunning looking sci-fi adventure stars Willis as a twenty-third-century cabbie who hooks up with a beauty (Jovovich)—

she jumps off a building and into his airborne cab—who may be the diva chosen to save the planet from annihilation. Don't ask. The first disc contains the film in a high bit-rate picture and DTS sound. The second disc contains two hours of extras, but nothing to explain how to modify the screech of Tucker's voice—he plays a radio host—to a level that won't blow your eardrums.

Hot Bonus: There are four screen tests of Jovovich—Besson's love at the time—and she's a visual effect that never grows dull.

Key Scene: Want to demonstrate what your home theater system can do? Show the opening cityscape with flying cars whizzing past each other.

Fight Club
(Two-Disc Special Edition) (1999)

Starring: Brad Pitt, Edward Norton, Helena Bonham Carter
Directed by: David Fincher

Fincher's zeitgeist epic is one of the top-ten DVDs of all time, and an uncompromising American classic. How do you not relate to a movie that pulls you in, challenges your prejudices, rocks your world, and leaves you laughing in the face of an abyss? Norton gives his best performance to date as a white-collar work slave who meets his polar opposite, Tyler Durden (Pitt, never more dynamic). It's Tyler who introduces this insomniac "Ikea Boy" to Fight Club, where men get in touch with their feelings by pummeling each other to a bloody pulp. Based on a novel by Chuck Palahniuk, and adapted for the screen by Jim Uhls, the movie is much more than what meets and dazzles the eye. For clues, watch Bonham Carter as the twelve-step junkie who comes between the two men. And look for the telling details that define the relationship between Norton and Pitt and the true nature of a film that plumbs the violence of the mind to unearth even deeper truths.

Hot Bonus: All the extras are a template for what DVD can achieve when it seeks to illuminate instead of hype. Be warned: the revelations from Fincher, Pitt, and Norton are in strict violation of the first rule of Fight Club, which states that "you don't talk about Fight Club."

Key Scene: Norton beating himself up in front of his boss—a shocker that nonetheless goes directly to the heart of the film's mystery.

Filth and the Fury, The (2000)

Starring: Sid Vicious, Johnny Rotten, Paul Cook, Steve Jones, Glen Matlock
Directed by: Julien Temple

The rise and fall of the Sex Pistols, as chronicled by Temple in painful detail, is a rock doc for the time capsule. The interviews with surviving band members are emotional, testifying that punk was about community and friendship. But the live footage out of 1970s London is some of the scariest rock anarchy ever caught on film—all mad passion and dangerous guitars. The raw quality of the DVD picture and sound comes with the territory.

Hot Bonus: A look at the origins of the punk movement.

Key Scene: The Pistols cranking "Anarchy in the U.K.," young and hungry and meaning it, man.

Finding Nemo (Two-Disc Collector's Edition) (2003)

Starring: The voices of Albert Brooks, Ellen DeGeneres
Directed by: Andrew Stanton

If you think Pixar isn't where animation is at, check this knockout digital-to-digital DVD transfer. Kid stuff? You tell me. Little Nemo no sooner loses his mom than he's kidnapped, leaving his dad to find him before Sonny Boy is sold off or flushed. If the characters weren't fish, and deliciously comic, the damn thing would be traumatic. The voice work is exceptional, from Brooks as Marlin, the neurotic clownfish dad, to a howlingly funny DeGeneres as Dory, a blue tang with a short-term memory who travels with Marlin through the terrors of Australia's Great Barrier Reef until they find Nemo living in a fish tank owned by a dentist in Sydney. Co-writer and director Andrew Stanton, who also provides the surfer-dude voice of a surfer-dude turtle named Crush, makes miracles look easy.

Hot Bonus: "The Art of Nemo" narrated by the artists.

Key Scene: Watch for the dentist's young niece, Darla. She has braces as well as a nasty streak for fish, and she enters to the theme from *Psycho*.

Finding Neverland (2004)

Starring: Johnny Depp, Kate Winslet, Freddie Highmore
Directed by: Marc Forster

Depp as *Peter Pan* author J. M. Barrie was nominated for an Oscar for making, along with Winslet and Forster, screen magic that transfers elegantly to DVD. The plot kicks in when the married Barrie meets the widow (Winslet) and her four sons, notably Peter (Highmore). No truck is given to the pedophile rumors. As Barrie indulges the boys in their games, the film sparks with comic life, and *Peter Pan* is born. Barrie's conversations with the solemn little boy who can't accept his father's death are wonderfully touching, thanks to the interplay between Depp and Highmore. "I'm not Peter Pan—he is," says the boy, as Depp's face becomes a window into Barrie's soul.

Hot Bonus: On how the magic of the movie was created.

Key Scene: When Barrie brings the cast of *Peter Pan* to do a private performance for the ailing widow at her home.

Fish Called Wanda, A (1988)

Starring: John Cleese, Jamie Lee Curtis, Kevin Kline, Michael Palin
Directed by: Charles Crichton

The DVD is relatively bare bones, but the laughs come so hard and fast in this hilariously unhinged farce written by Cleese and directed by Crichton, seventy-eight at the time, that it's unthinkable not to own it. Cleese is at his best as a stuffy English barrister who falls under the spell of Wanda (a slinky, seductive Curtis), an American con artist who needs his unwitting help to finesse a diamond heist. Complications arise from her macho, mucho stupid lover (Kline won an Oscar for his inspired lunacy) and their stuttering accomplice (Palin) who loves the other Wanda, a goldfish. When Cleese develops genuine feelings for Curtis, a film that could have slid by on silliness takes on genuine heart.

Hot Bonus: It's Easter Egg time if you go to the Main Menu and click on the treasure chest, and you get your very own Wanda aquarium which you can use as a screen saver.

Key Scene: Cleese, stripped down for a tryst with Curtis, is discovered dancing in naked abandon by a nonplussed British family.

Fisher King, The (1991)

Starring: Robin Williams, Jeff Bridges, Mercedes Ruehl
Directed by: Terry Gilliam

Like all of Gilliam's films, this one is a visual knockout tailor-made for DVD. Watch in wonder as a flame-throwing red knight on horseback looms up on Manhattan's traffic-clogged streets to chase a homeless man (Williams). Gilliam is a master of a lost art—the grand gesture. Williams plays Parry, a former professor of medieval history who has escaped into a dream world rather than face the memory of his wife's violent death. The red knight is the manifestation of that horror. The improbable instrument of Parry's deliverance is Jack Lucas (the ever-surprising Bridges), the king of the radio shock jocks, escaping his own tragedy by holing up in the apartment of his wildcat girlfriend (Ruehl, who won an Oscar for her blazing performance). All this leads to one final bout of Gilliam sorcery.

Hot Bonus: Just the film alone, but immaculately presented.

Key Scene: Williams standing still in Grand Central Station, oblivious to the fact that the rest of the rush-hour crowd has broken into a waltz.

Five Easy Pieces (1970)

Starring: Jack Nicholson, Karen Black
Directed by: Bob Rafelson

Nicholson achieved greatness as Bobby Dupea, a classical pianist from a wealthy family whose feud with his father sends him on the road, working on oil rigs, hanging with rednecks, and dating a country-singing waitress named Rayette (a funny and touching Black). Then he learns his father is dying and returns to confront his past. Rafelson's film is a culture clash that requires contrasting colors and tones, all etched perfectly on this DVD.

Hot Bonus: The film is letterboxed on one side and in a full-frame format on the other. This is one of those rare times when the full frame has the edge.

Key Scene: Nicholson's famous rage at a waitress who refuses to serve him toast because it isn't on the menu: "Now all you have to do is hold the chicken, bring me the toast, give me a check for the chicken salad sandwich, and you haven't broken any rules." That's 1960s rebellion in a nutshell.

Fly, The (1958)

Starring: David Hedison, Patricia Owens, Vincent Price

Directed by: Kurt Neumann

A camp classic of its time about a scientist (Hedison) who invents a matter-transporting device and uses himself as a guinea pig. The botched result leaves him with a fly's head and arm and the fly with his head and arm. No wonder his wife (Owens) crushes him in a steam press. Price is left to sort out the ethical questions. All I know is the movie is a hoot, and the black-and-white picture looks pristine on DVD.

Hot Bonus: The inclusion of the film's 1959 sequel, *Return of the Fly*, which looks good in color but storywise is not so hot.

Key Scene: Caught in a spiderweb, the fly with the human head cries: "Help me! Help me!" to Price, who reported he ruined take after take by laughing.

Fly, The (Two-Disc Special Edition) (1986)

Starring: Jeff Goldblum, Geena Davis

Directed by: David Cronenberg

Cronenberg's graphic remake is scarier and more profound than the original. Goldblum as the shy scientist and Davis as the reporter he lets get close bring a touching human element to the story. The director's graphic display of a body's decay becomes a metaphor for disease in the AIDS era and touches areas of love and loss the campy original never investigated.

Hot Bonus: Incisive commentary from Cronenberg, plus deleted scenes and an alternate ending.

Key Scene: Goldblum's plea for death over life as someone (a monster?) Davis can no longer recognize or love.

Forbidden Planet (1956)

Starring: Walter Pidgeon, Anne Francis, Leslie Nielsen, Robby the Robot

Directed by: Fred M. Wilcox

A half century after its release, this sci-fi take on Shakespeare's *The Tempest* still stirs the imagination as Nielsen lands his spaceship on a planet where it appears no one lives except Dr. Morbius (Pidgeon doing his own take on Prospero), his daughter Altaira (Francis), and a friendly robot named Robby. Then the Krells make their appearance.

Hot Bonus: Seeing a widescreen transfer with its color restored instead of damagingly altered as it is on VHS. Don't touch your color controls, the

sky is supposed to be green, the sand pink, and moon in duplicate.

Key Scene: The attack of the invisible monster.

Forrest Gump (Two-Disc Collector's Edition) (1994)

Starring: Tom Hanks, Robin Wright, Gary Sinise

Directed by: Robert Zemeckis

Some critics will never forgive this "life is like a box of chocolates" tearjerker for winning the Best Picture Oscar over the groundbreaking *Pulp Fiction*. The striking DVD transfer reminds us what's to like, starting with Hanks as the sweet simpleton from the South who becomes a college football star, a Vietnam war hero, a shrimp tycoon, and even a father as he makes his pilgrim's progress from the fifties to the eighties. Zemeckis sees Forrest as a modern Candide, an optimist in the face of strong opposing evidence, but he blunts his satire with choking sentiment. Forrest is everything we admire in the American character—honest, brave, loyal—and the fierce irony is that no one can stay around him for long.

Hot Bonus: The "how to" stuff that makes it look like Forrest is talking with JFK, LBJ, Nixon, and other luminaries.

Key Scene: Forrest meets his son, played by a pre–*Sixth Sense* Haley Joel Osment, and the two watch TV in unforced, childlike wonder.

Forty Guns (1957)

Starring: Barbara Stanwyck, Barry Sullivan, John Ericson

Directed by: Samuel Fuller

This may be the best western you never heard of. It's certainly the most perversely nutty. For that, thank director Fuller, a risk-anything maverick who shot the damn thing in ten days in widescreen and black-and-white and packed in more sexual innuendo and phallic gun play than you'd get from a night at home reading Freud. Stanwyck has a high old time playing the whip-cracking Arizona cattle queen with forty penises, er guns, on her payroll. The DVD transfer looks amazing with its solid blacks and grays, the better to enjoy the action as Fuller makes his camera do incredible tricks. As a cowboy stares at his girl through a rifle's gunsight, we see her grinning like she's at the end of a tunnel. And the finale when Stanwyck is held hostage by her brother (Ericson), forcing the marshal (Sullivan) to fire on both of them, shows you why European critics went wild.

Hot Bonus: A trailer that's almost as much fun as the movie.

Key Scene: Sullivan stroking his gun in front of Stanwyck, who doesn't miss the phallic invitation. "Be careful," she says, after asking whether it's loaded, "that thing may go off in your face."

42nd Street (1933)

Starring: Ruby Keeler, Dick Powell, Warner Baxter

Directed by: Lloyd Bacon

Here's the ultimate backstage musical, presented on DVD in glorious black-and-white, with the new kid (Keeler) replacing the star on Broadway as a dying director (Baxter) tries for one last hit. It's fun to hear Powell sing those standards and put on her taps to clodhop through the title tune, but the genius of the film is in the dance routines choreographed by Busby Berkeley with an intricacy to match the battles in *The Lord of the Rings*.

Hot Bonus: The notes on Berkeley.

Key Scene: Baxter's last words to Keeler: "You're going out there a youngster, but you've got to come back a star!"

400 Blows, The (1959)

Starring: Jean-Pierre Léaud, Claire Maurier, Albert Rémy

Directed by: François Truffaut

Truffaut's autobiographical first film—one of the most remarkable debuts in cinema—stars Léaud as the filmmaker's alter ego Antoine Doinel, a role Léaud would play with distinction over two decades in *Love at Twenty*, *Stolen Kisses*, *Bed and Board*, and *Love on the Run*. Here Antoine is a troublemaking twelve, neglected by his mother (Maurier) and father (Rémy) and on his way to a life of petty crime. The Criterion name on the DVD guarantees that Henri Decae's black-and-white cinematography will not lose its lyrical beauty in the transfer or dull the poignancy of Truffaut's vision.

Hot Bonus: Brian Stonehill's commentary track discusses the film's parallels to Truffaut's life and its importance to the French New Wave.

Key Scene: The haunting freeze frame of Antoine at the end, caught between childhood and an uncertain future.

Four Weddings and a Funeral (1994)

Starring: Hugh Grant, Andie MacDowell, Kristin Scott Thomas

Directed by: Mike Newell

Here's the surprise hit (an Oscar nod for Best Picture, who knew?) that established Grant as the valuable man in a comedy. As Charles the bachelor, Grant stutters, stumbles, lets his hair flop about, and still emerges as a world-class charmer. So does the movie, dressed to kill on DVD. Grant watches a quartet of friends walk down the aisle—and loses one as well, quite unexpectedly—flirts with a sassy American (a miscast MacDowell), and entirely misses the romantic signals from a trusted ally (a touching Scott Thomas). The actors and director Newell rightly rely on Richard Curtis's champagne script—his lines keep their fizz even after repeated viewings.

Hot Bonus: Just a trailer, but a jolly good one.

Key Scene: The funeral, of all things, which resonates with genuine emotion and still gets off a killer line. "The recipe for duck a la banana fortunately goes with him to the grave."

Frailty (2002)

Starring: Bill Paxton, Matthew McConaughey, Powers Boothe

Directed by: Bill Paxton

They call this kind of cult hit a sleeper, but you won't get much sleep if you try to hit the sheets after watching this nerve-frying DVD. Not only does first-time director Paxton grab you, he gives his best performance to date as a Texas widower who truly believes God has chosen him to kill demons, even if they look like the good folks next door. To help him with his axe, Paxton chooses Fenton (Matt O'Leary), twelve, and Adam (Jeremy Sumpter), nine. They're his kids, and the film's probing of two powerful forces—faith and parenthood—raise *Frailty* far above the horror fray.

Hot Bonus: A "making of" documentary that sheds light on the film's shocking twists and turns.

Key Scene: The adult Fenton (a terrific McConaughey) telling his story at last to an F.B.I. agent (Boothe), who might have his own reasons to be worried.

Frankenstein (1931)

Starring: Boris Karloff, Colin Clive, Dwight Frye
Directed by: James Whale

The monster hasn't looked this good since lightning first woke him up in the lab of Dr. Frankenstein (Clive). The black-and-white picture is smashing (the sound less so, but why quibble?) as the doc and his helpful hunchback (Frye) rob graves and steal body parts to create a "man." Under Whale's commanding direction, Karloff brings rage and heart to the monster. And the DVD restores scenes and lines deemed too shocking in previous editions, such as the doctor saying, "Now I know what it feels like to be God."

Hot Bonus: A commentary track from Rudy Behlmer that traces the film's fascinating history, including what scenes were cut and why.

Key Scene: The monster and the little girl by the water.

Freaks (1932)

Starring: Wallace Ford, Olga Baclanova, Harry Earles, Henry Victor
Directed by: Tod Browning

Browning, the master director of *Dracula*, brought a Hollywood cast, led by Ford, together with actual circus freaks ("nature's mistakes") to create this scary and surprisingly moving film classic. Browning humanizes these freaks, from the bearded lady to the Siamese twins and the human skeleton. That's what makes their revenge so terrible when one of their own, a midget circus owner (Earles), marries gorgeous trapeze artist Cleopatra (Baclanova) who plots with her strongman lover, Hercules (Victor), to kill him for his money. How the freaks get even caused so much controversy that the film was severely cut in the United States and banned in Britain. Thanks to this vividly restored DVD, *Freaks* is whole again and wholly terrific.

Hot Bonus: A documentary that explains the film's strange history, including the deleted scene in which the freaks castrate the strongman.

Key Scene: The freaks chasing Cleopatra and Hercules in a driving rain is famous, but for infamous you can't beat the wedding reception at which the freaks welcome Cleopatra by shouting, "One of us! One of us!"

Freeway (Special Edition) (1996)

Starring: Reese Witherspoon, Kiefer Sutherland
Directed by: Matthew Bright

A cult movie that plays like a perverse take on *Little Red Riding Hood*. Witherspoon is a knockout, cast way against *Legally Blonde* type as a trailer-trash Lolita who hitches a ride to Grandma's house from Mr. Wolverton (a scary Sutherland), who just happens to be the serial killer patrolling Interstate 5. The poor fool doesn't know she's packing a handgun, and she doesn't know that he'll sue her for scarring his pretty face. The DVD catches the rot-in-the-sunlight essence of John Thomas's cinematography as the gifted Bright tweaks our obsession with crime.

Hot Bonus: Commentary from Bright explaining his satirical purposes.

Key Scene: Witherspoon watching the deformed wolf being wheeled into court and shouting: "Ho-lee shit . . . look who got beat with the ugly stick."

French Connection, The (Two-Disc Special Edition) (1971)

Starring: Gene Hackman, Roy Scheider, Fernando Rey
Directed by: William Friedkin

This Academy Award-winning Best Picture is mostly remembered today for its spectacular car chase under the elevated subway. But the movie is much more, starting with Hackman's Oscar turn as Popeye Doyle, the racist pig cop who wants to stop the heroin flow from Marseilles to the States. That means Doyle and his partner (Scheider) have to roust a strip bar, beat up on a few witnesses, and stand outside in the cold drinking coffee in a cardboard cup while the French drug kingpin (Rey) dines in luxury across the street. Director Friedkin shows an eye for telling detail, and this two-disc DVD package does him the favor of making sure each detail shines.

Hot Bonus: Friedkin compares his film with the real French Connection bust made by cops Eddie Egan and Sonny Grosso and bluntly shows how the facts and the film differ.

Key Scene: The car chase—the best since *Bullitt*—has Hackman trying to catch up with a hijacked elevated train and nearly wiping out every pedestrian in his path.

Friday Night Lights (2004)

Starring: Billy Bob Thornton, Tim McGraw, Derek Luke
Directed by: Peter Berg

The only fake thing in director Berg's film version of his cousin Pulitzer Prize–winner H. G. Bissinger's 1990 book is Thornton's hair. As Gary Gaines, the real-life coach of the Permian Panthers football team in Odessa, Texas, Thornton wears a piece and zips up his *Bad Santa* mouth. "Good gracious!" is the most you hear from Gary, even when his team loses its star running back, Boobie Miles (Luke), to an injury. It's a subtle, soulful performance. Chronicling the team's 1988 season, the film is red meat for rabid football junkies. Berg takes you deep into the action, and on the DVD you can hear the bones crunch.

Hot Bonus: A doc on the true story of the Permian team.

Key Scene: A personal one, involving Garrett Hedlund as tailback Don Billingsley and his abusive, alcoholic dad, played by country star McGraw (the son of the late major-league pitcher Tug McGraw), who proves a natural in the acting game. With Dad's glory days behind him, he tells his son, "After football, it's just babies and memories."

From Here to Eternity (1953)

Starring: Montgomery Clift, Burt Lancaster, Deborah Kerr, Frank Sinatra
Directed by: Fred Zinnemann

James Jones's sprawling novel about life on a Hawaiian army base just before the Japanese attack on Pearl Harbor won the Best Picture Oscar and another for its black-and-white cinematography, crisply transferred to the DVD. Clift hit a career peak as Prewitt, the lone-wolf private who gets hassled for refusing to box. Lancaster is the tough sarge having an affair with his captain's wife (a sizzling Kerr). Prewitt hooks up with Alma (Donna Reed in an Oscar-winning change of pace), a club hostess the novel bluntly called a hooker. The big news was Sinatra getting the role of Maggio against the wishes of studio chief Harry Cohn (an incident Mario Puzo borrowed for *The Godfather*).

Sinatra won an Oscar and a career comeback as the skinny hothead who takes on the sadistic Fatso (Ernest Borgnine). The film's power and scope haven't dated.

Hot Bonus: Zinnemann took his own movies during the shoot, and his color film provides an eye-popping contrast to what's on screen.

Key Scene: Lancaster and Kerr going at in the surf is still used as an example of the great movie sex scenes.

From Russia With Love (Special Edition) (1963)

Starring: Sean Connery, Lotte Lenya, Robert Shaw, Daniela Bianchi
Directed by: Terence Young

The second James Bond film, and pure pow thanks to Connery's no-bull 007, far closer to the British agent Ian Fleming created in his books than the gadget-fixated mannequin of the later Bond films with Pierce Brosnan. Connery takes on the evil SPECTRE, foils the former KGB agent Rosa Kleb (Lenya has her kicks as a killer lesbian with a poisonous blade in the tip of her shoe) and still has time to make time with a Soviet defector (Bianchi) as the film moves from Istanbul to Venice in full DVD splendor.

Hot Bonus: Good, dishy commentary from director Young.

Key Scene: Connery's punchfest with the villainous Red Grant (a bottle-blond Shaw) on the Orient Express is one of the great fight scenes in movies.

Fugitive, The (Special Edition) (1993)

Starring: Harrison Ford, Tommy Lee Jones
Directed by: Andrew Davis

Remastered for maximum impact on DVD, this kickass update on the 1960s TV series benefits from the ideal casting of Ford as the doctor who goes on the run after being wrongly accused of murdering his wife and Jones as the federal marshal who hunts him down. Jones blends mirth and malice so deliciously that he won the Oscar for Best Supporting Actor. Davis tightens the screws of suspense so expertly that you can't help being caught up.

Hot Bonus: In a retrospective documentary, Ford and Jones admit that they improvised a lot of their dialogue between the action set pieces.

Key Scene: The train wreck and Ford's escape.

Full Metal Jacket (1987)

STANLEY KUBRICK COLLECTION
DIGITALLY RESTORED AND REMASTERED

Stanley Kubrick's
FULL
METAL
JACKET

Starring: Matthew Modine, Vincent D'Onofrio, Lee Ermey

Directed by: Stanley Kubrick

An almost unbroken succession of unnerving images highlight this remastered edition of Kubrick's Vietnam epic (shot in England, by the way, since the reclusive director, who died in 1999, never left his home there). In the first half, the director concentrates on the Parris Island training of Marines, including Private Joker (Modine) and Private Gomer Pyle (D'Onofrio), under the brutal eye of drill instructor Hartman (real-life D.I. Lee Ermey is verbal TNT), who praises the marksmanship of former Marines and famous assassins Lee Harvey Oswald and Charles Whitman: "Those individuals showed what one motivated Marine and his rifle can do." In the second half, Kubrick follows the soldiers into combat with the film's ambiguity symbolized by the peace button and the words "Born to Kill" that Private Joker wears on his helmet. Kubrick's genius—and burden—is to see the insanity in all of us and to make it seem terrifyingly normal.

Hot Bonus: A new color transfer that honors the director's intentions.

Key Scene: D'Onofrio's meltdown is scarier than anything in *The Shining*.

Funny Face (1957)

Starring: Audrey Hepburn, Fred Astaire, Kay Thompson

Directed by: Stanley Donen

Aside from all its other virtues, this time-capsule-worthy DVD will provide a definition of class for future generations. Just watch Hepburn—dressed to the nines in a red Givenchy gown—descend a staircase. Or marvel at Astaire as he sweeps her off her feet to the lilt of a Gershwin tune ("He Loves and She Loves"). There is a plot: Astaire is fashion photographer, based on Richard

Avedon, and Hepburn is the gamine he turns into a top model. But this DVD isn't about plot, it's about enchantment.

Hot Bonus: A photo gallery that lets you look some more.

Key Scene: Astaire, Hepburn, and Thompson—as a fashion editor who "thinks pink"—singing "Bonjour Paris" as they tour the City of Light.

Funny Girl (1968)

Starring: Barbra Streisand, Omar Sharif

Directed by: William Wyler

Streisand won an Oscar for her debut screen performance in this musical biography of comedian Fanny Brice. It's still her best and most dynamic performance. She was twenty-six at the time and slickness had not yet had its way with the raw yearning in her voice. Sharif is just window dressing as Nicky Arnstein, the gambler who loved and left her. But as Fanny moves from ugly duckling to Ziegfeld headliner, master director Wyler showcases Streisand's talent with a great score by Jule Styne and Bob Merrill. When she sings "I'm the Greatest Star," it doesn't seem like an idle boast.

Hot Bonus: A detailed look at how the complex "Don't Rain on My Parade" number was planned, shot, and edited.

Key Scene: The finale, with Streisand singing Brice's signature song, "My Man," with nothing but a black backdrop and a voice for the ages.

Gangs of New York (Two-Disc Special Edition) (2002)

Starring: Daniel Day-Lewis, Leonardo DiCaprio, Liam Neeson

Directed by: Martin Scorsese

Here is a historical epic that fudges a few facts, tacks on a pandering love story, and trips on its own grand ambitions. And yet here is a film that is something better than perfect: It's thrillingly alive. The time is the mid-nineteenth century. The place is Manhattan's Five Points where immigrant tribes fight with knives, picks, axes, and shovels to carve out a piece of turf. The villain is Bill the Butcher, played by the brilliant Day-Lewis, who sets the screen ablaze as the leader of the Nativists; this killer with one glass eye is out to crush pope-loving Irish invaders. The hero is Amsterdam (an implosive DiCaprio) who vows vengeance on Bill for killing his father (Neeson). Scorsese sweeps through Old New York at the height of the Civil War when the new conscription act drafts any man who can't afford the three-hundred-dollar buyout. In one scarring image, immigrants off the boat are recruited while caskets of dead soldiers are lowered onto the docks. What Scorsese achieves here is defiantly untrendy: a triumph of pure craft and raw feeling.

Hot Bonus: Scorsese gives us a tour of Rome's Cinecittà Studio, where he gathered a huge cast on a mammoth set (bravo to Dante Ferretti's production design) to create a world without digital shortcuts or computer trickery.

Key Scene: The stunning opener when Neeson leads his Irish gang out of a dark tunnel and onto the hushed, snowy streets in a battle with the Butcher's men that leaves the snow colored red. Shot with a poet's eye by Michael Ballhaus, the scene knocks the breath out of you. It's the first of many.

Garden State (2004)

Starring: Zach Braff, Natalie Portman, Peter Sarsgaard

Directed and written by: Zach Braff

As actor, writer, and director, Braff wants to stuff his big feelings into one little movie; he wants to change the world. He doesn't totally pull it off, but it's a kick to watch him try. Braff plays Andrew, a waiter and L.A. actor wannabe who returns to his New Jersey home for his mom's funeral. The event prompts Andrew to drop his Zoloft habit, reconcile with his dad (Ian Holm), hook up with a school buddy (a terrific Sarsgaard), and find the love of his life in a sweet-crazy-sexy, Shins-loving pathological liar named Sam (an irresistible Portman). The DVD reveals Braff's debut feature as a filmmaker for what it is: a hilarious and heartfelt ode to twentysomething angst.

Hot Bonus: Braff's commentary addresses *The Graduate* references, but my suggestion is that you watch Mike Nichols's 1967 landmark to see for yourself. Nichols told me he was "flattered by Braff's imaginative homage" and confessed "I also stole from the films I loved."

Key Scene: The drug-fueled spin-the-bottle party.

General, The (1927)

Starring: Buster Keaton, Marion Mack

Directed by: Buster Keaton

Maybe you think you'd pass on a silent-film comedy set during the Civil War. Think again. Starring the deadpan Keaton as a Confederate railroad engineer who goes ballistic when Yankee spies steal his engine, nicknamed The General, and kidnap his lady love (Mack) who happens to be aboard, the film—digitally mastered from archival prints—is a masterpiece. And the DVD, featur-

ing the original musical score and sepia-tint that suggests a Matthew Brady photograph, is a perfect demo of Keaton's genius.

Hot Bonus: Keaton's silent shorts: 1921's *Playhouse* and 1922's *Cops.*

Key Scene: Keaton chopping wood on the back of a speeding train, oblivious to the battles raging around him.

Gentleman's Agreement (Collector's Edition) (1947)

Starring: Gregory Peck, Dorothy McGuire, John Garfield, Celeste Holm

Directed by: Elia Kazan

A magazine writer (Peck, the prince of goyim) passes as a Jew to do an expose on anti-Semitism. The film took the Best Picture Oscar over Edward Dmytryk's *Crossfire*—a better take on the same subject—and critics have retrospectively trashed the screen version of Laura Z. Hobson's novel as stiff and dated. Yeah, right—we sure have anti-Semitism licked. So pay heed to this remastered DVD. Despite some awkward passages, the film is still electrified by its crusading intentions, fierce direction from Kazan, and complex performances, especially by the great Garfield, as Peck's Jewish friend, and Holm, who won an Oscar as a fashion writer with a secret.

Hot Bonus: Pertinent, no-bull remarks from critic Richard Schickel.

Key Scene: Peck checking into a restricted hotel.

George Washington (2000)

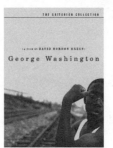

Starring: Donald Holden, Candace Evanofski

Directed and written by: David Gordon Green

The plot has nothing to do with our be-wigged first president. George (Holden) is a thirteen-year-old black kid living in a multiethnic town in North Carolina. He hangs with a handful of friends around a rusted-out railroad station. The film is narrated by Nasia (Evanofski), who has just broken up with Buddy (Curtis Cotton III) and sees quiet George as a romantic hero. It's a sharp contrast to the relationship between beefy Vernon (Damian Jewan Lee) and Sonya (Rachael Handy), a blond twig of a girl who helps Vernon steal a car. During a game, one of the kids is accidentally killed. A decision is made to hide the body, and Green—in a stunning debut as director and screenwriter—focuses on how that decision affects the lives of the kids. Using nonprofessional actors and mostly improvised dialogue, Green creates a dreamlike evocation of youth forced into maturity. The film's impact also relies on the delicacy of Ted Orr's widescreen camerawork, and Criterion has transferred to DVD with tender loving care.

Hot Bonus: Two of Green's short films, *Pleasant Grove* and *Physical Pinball*, that show their influence on his feature debut.

Key Scene: The moment when Nasia tells George, "I hope you live forever."

Get Carter (1970)

Starring: Michael Caine, John Osborne, Rosemarie Dunham
Directed by: Mike Hodges

One of the toughest, shrewdest crimes films ever. Caine is hard, cold steel as Jack Carter, a London hitman who goes home to Newcastle to find out who killed his brother and gets mixed up in a porno crime syndicate, run by Cyril Kinnear (*Look Back in Anger* playwright Osborne). On the train, Caine reads Raymond Chandler's *Farewell My Lovely*, which is a setup for gloves-off action. Hodges, making his debut as director and screenwriter, delivers the goods. And the DVD catches every grimy, bloody, juicy detail as Caine plays judge and executioner. Please do not confuse this gem with the twitty 2000 remake starring a horridly miscast Sylvester Stallone.

Hot Bonus: Caine and Hodges explain their reasons for the hardcore sex and violence. Hey, I wasn't complaining.

Key Scene: Caine killing two thugs with a shotgun. Nothing unusual there, except he's in the middle of shagging his landlady (Dunham).

Get Shorty (Two-Disc Special Edition) (1995)

Starring: John Travolta, Gene Hackman, Rene Russo, Danny DeVito
Directed by: Barry Sonnenfeld

Travolta gives one of his best performances as Chili Palmer, a Miami loan shark who links up with the sharks of the movie business and fits right in. Elmore Leonard's 1990 bestseller gets the A treatment—onscreen and on DVD—from director Sonnenfeld, writer Scott Frank, and a top-tier cast, including Hackman as a sleazy producer and DeVito as Martin Weir, a peewee egomaniac actor

who Chili needs to star in his project. Enter Karen (Russo), a B-movie queen and Martin's ex. Chili offers sincere praise of Karen's work in *Bride of the Mutant*: "Joan fuckin' Crawford wishes on her best day she had that much presence and charisma—not even in *Mildred Pierce*, which, by the way, was a better book than a movie." The awful and sometimes artful things movies do to books is *Get Shorty*'s bristling subtext. The result is a black comedy that gets everything right. Warning: The 2005 sequel, *Be Cool*, also based on a Leonard novel, gets everything wrong.

Hot Bonus: Leonard talks about his book's transition from page to screen.

Key Scene: Chili teaching an actor to play danger as spare, focused, and vividly real—the way Leonard sees it. "Look at me," says Chili, showing Martin the real thing. "Put it in your eyes: 'You're mine, asshole.'"

Ghost (1990)

Starring: Demi Moore, Patrick Swayze, Whoopi Goldberg
Directed by: Jerry Zucker

I call it the chick flick that won't die. But if you're in the right mood to watch Moore and Swayze do pottery in the nude to the tune of "Unchained Melody," this DVD will come in handy. Oh, I should mention, these two are chic New York marrieds. He banks, she sculpts. But when she says, "I love you," he can only answer, "Ditto." He finds it hard to express emotion. That is, until he's murdered. Then his feelings flow. But only a fake medium (Goldberg took home an Oscar for pumping in some funky humor) can hear him. Zucker pushes all the buttons—romance, thrills, laughs, tears—so just give in to the damn thing. The rest of the world has.

Hot Bonus: Director Zucker and screenwriter Bruce Jay Rubin look back at what they wrought. And they're damn funny about it.

Key Scene: The last dance, where Whoopi stands in for the ghost.

Ghost Dog: The Way of the Samurai (1999)

Starring: Forest Whitaker, Cliff Gorman, Henry Silva
Directed and written by: Jim Jarmusch

It's an uber-strange premise: A reclusive black dude named Ghost Dog (Whitaker)—he follows the samurai code—does hits for the mob when he isn't retreating to his New York rooftop to commune with his pigeons. They carry orders from his bosses, and the next target is the Dog himself. The DVD goes with Jarmusch's hypnotic flow. Couple that with Whitaker's haunting performance, and you're in for something truly original.

Hot Bonus: A production featurette in which Jarmusch, who says he wouldn't have made the film without Whitaker, elucidates on his themes.

Key Scene: The Dog telling a child to read *Rashomon* when she's older.

Ghost in the Shell (Special Edition) (1995)

Directed by: Mamoru Oshii

This adult-oriented, foul-mouthed, sci-fi anime from master Japanese innovator Oshii has a plot that's half *Blade Runner* and half incomprehensible. No matter. The images will floor you. An unnamed government, circa 2029, uses a robot force for espionage work. Kusanagi, a cybercop with silicon breasts, is asked to track down a hacker called The Puppet Master. Along with her partner Batô, Kusanagi faces treacherous enemies and doubts about the nature of identity that presage *The Matrix*.

Hot Bonus: Lots of background material on anime, but treat yourself to the 2004 sequel *Ghost in the Shell 2: Innocence* in which Oshii outdoes himself in anime sorcery as Batô investigates a series of murders relating to robots with sexual functions. It's only the botched subtitles on the DVD of *Shell 2* that makes me withhold a full recommendation.

Key Scene: Kusanagi's face-off with a tank.

Ghost World (2001)

Starring: Thora Birch, Scarlett Johansson, Steve Buscemi

Directed by: Terry Zwigoff

Daniel Clowes's cult comic book is filmed with its dark wit intact. If you haven't seen it yet, let this expertly executed DVD

catch you by surprise with its unsettling meditation on the life of two high school misfits after graduation. Extroverted Enid (a fiery Birch) and her polar opposite Rebecca, acutely observed by Johansson, live in a world of malls, franchises, and trendy pop-culture references that don't seem quite real to them. Each girl feels adrift and disaffected. Zwigoff directs the actors with artful delicacy. Watch Enid's cynicism fade when she meets Seymour (Buscemi), a fortyish record collector whose painful shyness can't disguise his passion for music. The two outcasts form a bond, spiritual and sexual, that is the heart of the movie. Buscemi has never been better, and Oscar should have noticed.

Hot Bonus: The deeply weird musical number Enid watches in spurts at the beginning of the film is presented in its entirety.

Key Scene: Seymour in his car, commenting on the annoying people he sees: "I can't relate to 99 percent of humanity."

Ghostbusters (Collector's Series) (1984)

Starring: Bill Murray, Dan Aykroyd, Harold Ramis, Sigourney Weaver

Directed by: Ivan Reitman

Murray and Aykroyd, teaming on screen for the first time since their *Saturday Night Live* days, play off each other with such prankish assurance that a comedy blockbuster was born, and reborn on DVD. Along with Ramis and Ernie Hudson, they play university parapsychologists tossed out of academia for their unorthodox ways. So they go into business to serve the public's "supernatural elimination" needs. Weaver is their first customer: the fridge in her apartment is the gateway to hell. They sure do raise spirits.

Hot Bonus: The Collector's Series includes the 1989 sequel, *Ghostbusters II*, which is not nearly as funny except when a sex-crazed Weaver asks Murray, "Do you want this body?" and he answers, "Is that a trick question?"

Key Scene: Anything with Murray saying: "It slimed me! It slimed me!"

Ghosts of the Abyss (Two-Disc Special Edition) (2003)

Directed by: James Cameron

Even the best home theater system can't capture the reach-out-and-touch experience of seeing *Ghosts* in digital 3-D on an IMAX screen. But this thrilling documentary hasn't lost its punch on DVD. *Titanic* director James Cameron goes two and a half miles beneath the Atlantic to explore the sunken ship that took fifteen hundred lives, and emerges with something historic and eye-popping. Cameron had used footage of the ship in his Oscar-winning 1997 film, but the technology didn't exist then for cameras to go deep into the ship. It does now. The ghost of the great ship that sunk in 1912 will haunt your dreams.

Hot Bonus: A new ninety-two-minute version of the sixty-one-minute film that adds fresh material on the Titanic's captain and the animal life found at the wreck site.

Key Scene: It's breathtaking to watch two small, remote-operated cameras—nicknamed Jake and Elwood—work their way into a stateroom where the furnishings seem preserved in watery amber, untouched by time.

Giant (Two-Disc Special Edition) (1956)

Starring: James Dean, Elizabeth Taylor, Rock Hudson

Directed by: George Stevens

Dean's last film before a car crash ended his life can make you a little crazy when he's stuck in old-age makeup and using Method Acting mumbles to play sour Texas tycoon Jett Rink. In his earlier scenes as the young Jett—a poor boy in love with the Virginia belle (Taylor) whom his ranch boss Bick Benedict (Hudson) has brought home as his wife—Dean had been magnificent. But a few downs among the ups are a small price to pay for the pleasure you get from this sprawling epic. Director Stevens won an Oscar for adapting Edna Ferber's novel to the screen. Taylor is beautiful. Hudson shines like never before, and Texas—with all its conflicts about cattle, oil, and race—looms as large as its legend.

Hot Bonus: The discs are stuffed with behind-the-scenes info, but what dazzles is seeing *Giant* restored to its former glory in picture and sound.

Key Scene: Jett strikes oil. Covered in the stuff, Dean delivers one of purest expressions of joy in the history of film.

Gilda (1946)

Starring: Rita Hayworth, Glenn Ford, George Macready

Directed by: Charles Vidor

What a kick to see this sexual snakepit of a movie restored in all its black-and-white sexiness on DVD. Critics love debating whether Ford's gambler and Macready's casino owner really have a thing for each other while they pretend to argue over Ford's alleged lust for Gilda, the owner's wife. It's all a moot point when Hayworth takes the screen as Gilda. Never more seductive, Hayworth established herself as the reigning movie love goddess. Spitting out lines that fly way past innuendo—"If I had been a ranch they would have called me the Bar Nothing"—Hayworth owns the screen.

Hot Bonus: A piece on Hayworth's career that will have fans drooling.

Key Scene: The "Put the Blame on Mame" number in which Hayworth, almost wearing a strapless gown, takes the stage to sing, strip off her gloves, and throw her hair around like a kitten with a whip. Hot! Hot! Hot!

Gimme Shelter (1970)

Starring: The Rolling Stones

Directed by: Albert Maysles, David Maysles, Charlotte Zwerin

Armed with cameras for the Rolling Stones' 1969 American tour, David and Albert Maysles and Charlotte Zwerin returned from the chaos and carnage of the final show at the Altamont Speedway free concert with a gripping chronicle of the Stones at their height. The fatal stabbing of Meredith Hunter at Jagger's feet by a Hell's Angel brought the peace-and-love sixties to a brutal close—and the Maysles brothers got it on film.

Hot Bonus: Never-before-seen footage of the Stones singing "Oh Carol" and "Prodigal Son."

Key Scene: Jagger in the cutting room, watching the footage of Hunter's murder in silent, haunted awe.

Gladiator (Three-Disc Special Edition) (2000)

Starring: Russell Crowe, Joaquin Phoenix, Connie Nielsen, Oliver Reed
Directed by: Ridley Scott

Are we not entertained by this colossus of rousing action and ferocious fun? It's hard not to be, debates aside over whether Scott's Roman epic deserved the Best Picture Oscar over *Crouching Tiger, Hidden Dragon* (it didn't). What matters most is Crowe, who truly deserved his gold statuette for firing up the role of Maximus, the general enslaved by an incestuous emperor—the dude has a thing for his sister (Nielsen), and Phoenix plays him to a twisted turn. Maximus gets his revenge by becoming a star gladiator under the tutelage of a slave owner (Reed, who died during production, went out on a high). Critics whined about all the digitalized battle scenes. Look, it works—the splendid DVD transfer testifies to that—and now there's the extra forty-six minutes.

Hot Bonus: Scott remains a model for how to do director's commentary. And he is—sound the trumpets—joined by Crowe, who never does these things. But Easter Egg fans should go to the Original Storyboards section on the second disc, find More, click on Rhino Fight, find the rhino, click on that, and you'll see test footage of a digital rhino who never made the movie.

Key Scene: Maximus in the rings with the tigers is demo-quality stuff.

Glengarry Glen Ross (Two-Disc Special Edition) (1992)

Starring: Jack Lemmon, Al Pacino, Kevin Spacey, Alec Baldwin
Directed by: James Foley

At the risk of sounding heretical, I think Foley's film version of David Mamet's play about real estate sharks is superior to its stage incarnation, which won a Pulitzer. Verbal dynamite is a bitch to transform into fluid cinema. Foley does it. The salesmen hang out in Chinese restaurants, bars, cars, and phone booths, but mostly in a grungy office that has just been robbed. And Foley's camera roams from face to face with a visual dexterity that the DVD enhances. Spacey and Baldwin (exceptional in a role not in the play) give the management side just the right doses of self-love and self-loathing. But it's Pacino's sharpie, Ricky Roma, and Lemmon's sagging old-timer, Shelley "the Machine" Levene, who cut deepest, dining on Mamet's gutter lyricism like the feast it is.

Hot Bonus: A.B.C. (*Always Be Closing*) compares Mamet's salesmen with the real-life variety.

Key Scene: Pacino in top form is something to see, especially when he generously encourages the Machine to relive a tough sale in a woman's kitch-en. Levene: "I'm eating her crumb cake." Roma: "Homemade or from the store?" Levene: "From the store." Roma: "Fuck her."

Glory (Two-Disc Special Edition) (1989)

Starring: Matthew Broderick, Denzel Washington, Morgan Freeman
Directed by: Edward Zwick

Praise is due Zwick's Civil War lesson about the first black fighting regiment in U.S. history,

the Fifty-Fourth Massachusetts Volunteer Infantry. Led by white officers, with Colonel Robert Gould Shaw (Broderick) in command, the Fifty-Fourth faced virulent racism but distinguished itself in battle (by war's end, they constituted 12 percent of the Union army). It's a great story, though sketchy characterizations, numbing dialogue, and the fact that we're watching another black story with a white guy at the center puts a hold on the hallelujahs. Among the actors, Freeman as a gravedigger and Washington as an angry runaway slave—he won a Best Supporting Actor Oscar for the role—make indelible impressions. But it's the battle scenes, photographed by Freddie Francis with a pungent clarity gloriously reproduced on DVD, that stir the blood and the conscience.

Hot Bonus: Freeman narrates a documentary about the real regiment.

Key Scene: The assault on South Carolina's Fort Wagner.

Go (1999)

Starring: Sarah Polley, Katie Holmes, Timothy Olyphant
Directed by: Doug Liman

The R rating is for drug use, topless nudity, bare butts, and violence. What else do you want from DVD escapism? Liman's followup to *Swingers* brashly borrows the structure of *Pulp Fiction* as it follows several stories: Polley and Holmes are L.A. supermarket checkers involved with a scary dealer (Olyphant, really good), who helps them sell Ecstasy to Scott Wolf and Jay Mohr as rave-bound soap actors being used by a scary cop (the fab William Fichtner) in a sting that links them to Polley's

Brit co-worker (Desmond Askew), who is tearing it up in Vegas with his pal (Taye Diggs). John August's script makes an art of contrivance. And Liman, who plays his young cast like a virtuoso, puts out with the adrenaline rush of pure cinema.

Hot Bonus: A "making of" featurette showing how Liman, who also shot the film, had to play by the rules to produce creative chaos.

Key Scene: Polley at the rave, trying to pass off allergy medicine and baby aspirin as Ecstasy to dumb teens who react like they had a real hit.

Godfather, The (1972)

Starring: Marlon Brando, Al Pacino, James Caan, John Cazale, Diane Keaton
Directed by: Francis Ford Coppola

It's only the greatest gangster epic of all time (my opinion). Technically, it's not the greatest DVD. The brownish tones and murky shadows that Coppola wanted from cinematographer Gordon Willis are harder to reproduce on a DVD transfer than a modern epic would be today. No matter. The DVD is a monumental achievement that preserves the film's resonant mood, stirring storytelling, haunting Nino Rota score, and gallery of career-defining performances. The Godfather won just three Oscars, including Best Picture. Amazingly, Coppola—who won for his screenplay—didn't win for directing (he lost to Bob Fosse for Cabaret). The third Oscar went to Brando for his iconic performance as Don Vito Corleone, the head of a New York Mafia family, first seen marrying off his only daughter (Talia Shire) but haunted by the legacy he would pass to his three sons: the hothead Sonny (Caan), the weakling Fredo (Cazale), and the outsider Michael (Pacino), a decorated soldier who wanted out and got pulled back in. The acting honor roll on this masterpiece extends to Robert Duvall as *consiglieri* Tom Hagen, Richard Castellano as the cannoli-loving Clemenza, Sterling Hayden as the crooked cop McCluskey, and Diane Keaton as Kay Adams, the woman with the bad luck to marry Michael. Watching the movie again on DVD, the realization hits that The Godfather is a movie without a false note. In adapting Mario Puzo's novel about a Mafia family torn apart by forces outside and inside, Coppola cut to the heart of the violence at the heart of the American character and turned a pulp bestseller into lasting cinema art. Don't even think of starting a DVD collection without this one on your list.

Hot Bonus: Coppola's commentary is packed with fascinating details: the real dilly is how he used the severed head of a real horse in the infamous scene with the Hollywood producer who won't cast the Godfather's favorite singer in a movie until the Don makes him an offer he can't refuse. If you buy the package containing all three Godfather films, you get an extra disc that's loaded with extras, including deleted scenes with Brando and Pacino and—mark this as a must—Robert De Niro auditioning to play Sonny.

Key Scene: From the opening monologue ("I believe in America") to the last image of Pacino accepting his father's mantle, The Godfather is a nonstop succession of wonders. For sheer suspense, it would have to be Michael in the restaurant just before he shoots two of his father's enemies.

Godfather, The: Part II (1974)

Starring: Al Pacino, Robert De Niro, Lee Strasberg, Michael V. Gazzo
Directed by: Francis Ford Coppola

Here's the rarest of all Hollywood birds: a sequel that equals the original. This time the Academy wised up and handed Coppola the Oscar for Best Director to go with the Best Picture prize. The sin of omission was Pacino who, let's face it, gives the performance of his life as Michael Corleone, now a slick businessman spreading his family's gambling interests to Nevada and Cuba. When Michael senses betrayal, be it from Jewish mobster Hyman Roth (Actors Studio founder Strasberg in a fierce portrayal) or from his own brother Fredo (Cazale at his most moving), he acts with a killer's instinct. It's Pacino's somber triumph to show the heart of Michael, and by extension the heart of corporate America, turn to stone. In contrast, Coppola flashes back to the young Vito Corleone (De Niro in an Oscar-winning performance that seems molded from Brando's DNA) as he leaves Sicily for New York to make his name. The DVD transfer stays alert to the frequent changes in look, sound, mood, and tone as the film spans decades with the unrushed confidence of a classic in the making.

Hot Bonus: More dish from Coppola, including his failure to negotiate an appearance from Brando in a flashback showing the whole family together in better days. Inspiration struck by having all the other characters—save Michael—leave the dinner table to greet their father at the door while the camera studies Michael—sitting alone—his isolation already eating his soul.

Key Scene: De Niro cold-bloodedly killing a neighborhood crime boss. He winces helplessly only when his feverish infant son cries in pain.

Godfather, The: Part III (1990)

Starring: Al Pacino, Andy Garcia, Joe Mantegna, Sofia Coppola

Directed by: Francis Ford Coppola

This one gets in on its pedigree, but there's no denying *Part III* is a major disappointment. Having mob corruption turn corporate worked in *Part II*, and it should work in *Part III* when a graying Michael Corleone (Pacino) buys his way into the spiritual sphere through loans to the Vatican bank. But the plot strands keep unraveling as Coppola turns Michael into a Mafia King Lear, hungry for respectability and forgiveness but heading for madness. "Just when I thought I was out, they pull me back in" is the line Michael famously utters as his plans go awry to turn his family's criminal interests over to mobster Joey Zasa (Joe Mantegna). For support, Michael leans on his bastard nephew Vincent (Garcia in the film's best performance). But Vincent makes the mistake of falling for Michael's daughter Mary. And Coppola makes the mistake of casting his unprepared daughter, Sofia, in that pivotal role. Aiming for operatic grandeur—the DVD is a fulsome rendering of image and sound—the film substitutes flourish for substance. It's only when Pacino lets us see flickers of humanity in Michael that *Part III* earns its place on *The Godfather* throne.

Hot Bonus: Coppola talks movingly about why he cast his daughter as Mary when Winona Ryder dropped out and how it hurt seeing her critically bashed. His wounds are still raw, despite Sofia Coppola's own recent success as a filmmaker with *The Virgin Suicides* and *Lost in Translation*.

Key Scene: Mary's final words and her father's scream on the steps of the opera house. It's everything that's right and wrong about this movie.

Gods and Monsters (Collector's Edition) (1998)

Starring: Ian McKellen, Brendan Fraser, Lynn Redgrave

Directed and written by: Bill Condon

Isn't this the movie with McKellen playing an old fruit horror director who tries to shag George of the Jungle? That's one way (the wrong way) of looking at a movie whose spell deepens on DVD. Director Condon won an Oscar for his screenplay in which McKellen etches a mesmerizing portrait of the gay British director James Whale who died, a suicide, in his Hollywood swimming pool in 1957, his heyday long past as the director of the 1931 *Fran-*

kenstein and its 1935 sequel, *Bride of Frankenstein.* Fraser excels as Clayton, the straight gardener Whale befriends and then repels with his advances. "Alone bad—friend good," said the monster in *Bride.* On a photo to Clay, Whale writes "Friend?" It's a question well worth a film asking.

Hot Bonus: Sharp commentary by Condon and intro to Whale's films that you should watch before viewing the main feature.

Key Scene: Clay in the rain, his body swaying stiffly in a Frankenstein dance that offers funny and touching tribute to Whale's creation.

Going Places (1974)

Starring: Gérard Depardieu, Patrick Dewaere, Miou-Miou, Jeanne Moreau

Directed by: Bertrand Blier

This French tragicomedy about sex is a shocker still. Depardieu and Dewaere star as petty thieves who hit the road and gets their dicks into anything they can, even each other. Miou-Miou plays the beautician they call frigid when they can't bring her to orgasm. And Moreau sizzles as an older woman, just out of prison and ready to pound some truth into these amoral young hard-ons about what a woman wants and what they want.

Hot Bonus: Restored from the original French negative, Blier's film seems fresher and more ferocious on this uncut DVD version.

Key Scene: The Moreau-Depardieu-Dewaere threeway, and its explosive climax—one you won't see coming.

Gold Rush, The (Two-Disc Special Edition) (1925)

Starring: Charlie Chaplin, Georgia Hale

Directed by: Charlie Chaplin

After years of watching this Chaplin classic on scratched, snowy videotapes, this stunning DVD restoration is like striking gold. That's the plot of the film as Chaplin's Little Tramp sets out to win his fortune in the Alaskan Gold Rush of 1898 only to be buffeted by blizzards, thieves, starvation, and the rejection of a dancehall girl (Hale). The comic setpieces—the cabin teetering on a cliff—are hilarious, but it's Chaplin grasp of the Tramp's loneliness that pierces the heart.

Hot Bonus: The DVD includes the ninety-six-minute silent original, and the sixty-nine-minute reissue version of the film, prepared by Chaplin in 1942, with his own musical score and narration. It's nice to have a choice, but the silent version is the keeper.

Key Scene: The famished Chaplin making

a Thanksgiving dinner for himself by cooking a tough old leather shoe with the laces on the side.

Goldeneye (Special Edition) (1995)

Starring: Pierce Brosnan, Sean Bean, Judi Dench, Izabella Scorupco
Directed by: Martin Campbell

Brosnan's debut film as James Bond may not keep Sean Connery up nights, but this DVD has all the bells and Dolby whistles to make your home theater system holler for mercy. Start with 007 bungee-jumping into a Russian weapons facility and blowing it up. Add Bean as the duplicitous 006, a new M in the person of Dench—the first dame to play Bond's boss, Scorupco as a Bond girl with computer skills, and Famke Janssen as Xenia Onatopp (really!), a Pussy Galore with castrating thighs. Nothing makes sense, but everything is demo-worthy.

Hot Bonus: Director Campbell explains how it's done—the rest is just promotional pap.

Key Scene: Bond runs after a small plane heading straight for a cliff: he leaps, climbs in, and steers it to safety just in the nick of time. It doesn't build character like Chekhov, but that's some stunt.

Goldfinger (1964)

Starring: Sean Connery, Honor Blackman, Gert Fröbe, Shirley Eaton
Directed by: Guy Hamilton

Speaking of how James Bond should be done onscreen and on DVD, here's the definitive answer. And don't tell me it lacks the punchy sound and picture you get in the Brosnan Bonds. Connery is 007 for the ages, and this DVD—mono soundtrack and all—shows him off in killer style. I'll take Fröbe's master villain as Goldfinger (he's out to rob Fort Knox), Eaton's gilded nudity, Blackman's innuendo as flygirl Pussy Galore, and Harold Sakata's lethal aim as the hat-throwing Oddjob over the techno tricks in the later films. And how about that gadget-loaded Aston-Martin, Shirley Bassey's title song, and director Hamilton's way of making it all look easy?

Hot Bonus: Home movies taken on the set, including a visit from Bond author Ian Fleming

Key Scene: Connery, strapped to a table with a laser beam heading right for his crotch: "Do you expect me talk?" he asks Fröbe's Goldfinger. "No, Mr. Bond," comes the now-famous reply, "I expect you to die."

Gone With the Wind (Four-Disc Collector's Edition) (1939)

Starring: Clark Gable, Vivien Leigh, Leslie Howard, Olivia De Havilland
Directed by: Victor Fleming

You know the plot: Leigh's fiery Scarlett loves Howard's wimpy Ashley but he loves De Havilland's also wimpy Melanie, and as for Gable's dashing Rhett, who marries Scarlett, he gets so fed up with her southern belle treacheries that frankly he doesn't give a damn. The Civil War is in there somewhere, but everyone loves this warhorse for the Leigh-Gable sparks. Producer David O. Selznick made sure that Rhett's words to Scarlett—"You should be kissed, and often, and by someone who knows how"—would rival the burning of Atlanta. Leigh grabbed an Oscar, as did the movie, director Fleming, and Hattie McDaniel as Mammy, Scarlett's backtalking maid. As Mammy would say, "It ain't fittin'" that Gable didn't win—he was robbed. But you won't be robbed making this DVD package a part of your collection. Under Warner's Ultra-Resolution process, the film is a burst of sound and color that hasn't looked this good since its Atlanta premiere.

Hot Bonus: All details are covered, except for the racism and sexism built into the piece, but the peek at how the restoration works had me glued.

Key Scene: That shot of Scarlett tending to a soldier as the camera pulls back on a crane to reveal a landscape of the wounded still produces shivers. But I'm sure I'll think of others. After all, tomorrow is another day.

Goodbye, Dragon Inn (2003)

Starring: Kang-sheng Lee, Shiang-chyi Chen
Directed by: Ming-liang Tsai

Call it a Taiwanese The Last Picture Show or Cinema Paradiso, but this DVD transfer of director Tsai's exquisitely rendered meditation on cinema and loneliness is a must for movie lovers. The rain lashes the Fu-Ho Theater in Taipei as a young projectionist (Lee) and the crippled ticket seller (Chen)—she secretly loves him—prepare for the theater's closing. The last picture show is King Hu's Dragon Inn, a 1966 sword-thrasher, which provides this film's only action. Tsai merely watches as a handful of patrons on their own wander into the theater. One gobbles popcorn, another sticks his dirty bare feet over the seat in front of him, yet another cruises for sex in the men's room. And Tsai's camera, almost immobile, simply watches as the nonevents that transpire make you smile or pierce your heart.

Hot Bonus: A short film by Tsai, The Skywalk Is Gone.

Key Scene: The camera picking out two patrons, played by Shih Chun and Tien Miao, the latter forcing back tears. They are the two stars of *Dragon Inn*, having one final look at their days of glory.

Good, the Bad, and the Ugly, The (Two-Disc Extended Version Collector's Set) (1966)

Starring: Clint Eastwood, Lee Van Cleef, Eli Wallach

Directed by: Sergio Leone

Here, fully restored with eighteen minutes of added footage, is the English-language version of the epic that defined the term "spaghetti western." The third piece in Leone's *Dollars* trilogy (*A Fistful of Dollars* and *For a Few Dollars More* were just warmups) starring Eastwood as the Man with No Name is set during the Civil War with three violent drifters—Eastwood (the good), Van Cleef (the bad), and scene-stealer Wallach (the ugly)—all hunting for buried Confederate treasure. Leone's compositions—faces in closeup with detailed landscapes in the background—play against Ennio Morricone's score. The film's brutality is nonstop (Van Cleef's sadist is a chilling creation), but this breathtaking DVD will help you see Quentin Tarantino's point when he called it "the best-directed movie of all time."

Hot Bonus: Background on the restoration with Eastwood and Wallach back in the dubbing studio in 2003 to add their voices to the new footage.

Key Scene: Eastwood's character showing his first glimmers of humanity as he offers a smoke to a dying soldier.

GoodFellas (Two-Disc Special Edition)(1990)

Starring: Ray Liotta, Joe Pesci, Robert De Niro, Lorraine Bracco

Directed by: Martin Scorsese

The only mob epic that can touch *The Godfather*—it's still galling that Kevin Costner's *Dances With Wolves* beat Scorsese's landmark for the Oscar—gets a new anamorphic digital transfer (the first DVD version was a washout). Writer Nicholas Pileggi tells the true story of Henry Hill (Liotta) from his 1950s rise in the mob with his buds, Jimmy the Gent (De Niro) and Tommy (Pesci), to his exile in the 1970s when he ratted the mob out and took cover in the Witness Protection Program. Pesci won a well-deserved Oscar for his "You think I'm funny" meltdown scene. Scorsese offers a visceral portrait of the mob underworld with virtuoso moments, including the introduction of the goodfellas at a bar and Liotta's cocaine hallucinations.

Hot Bonus: Hill talks about his experiences, not all of which are reflected in the movie.

Key Scene: Liotta taking his wife (Bracco at her best) to the Copacabana nightclub, with the camera tracking them through a surreptitious path down a dark hall, a stairway, through the kitchen, and finally into the light of a ringside table. In one justifiably famous shot, Scorsese creates a visual metaphor for the trip into hell that an amoral hood is willing to take to achieve a few moments of trashy, transient, ego-tripping glory.

Gosford Park (2001)

Starring: Maggie Smith, Helen Mirren, Clive Owen, Jeremy Northam

Directed by: Robert Altman

Upstairs, the mistress of the house boffs a young valet. Downstairs, a randy aristocrat bangs away at a plump kitchen maid. All the while, the police try to figure out who killed the lord of the manor. Set in an English country estate in 1932, the film appears to be a murder mystery. But slyboots director Altman, working from an Oscar-winning script by Julian Fellowes, knows better. He spikes the plot with wicked laughs, casts it with acting royalty (mostly British), and lets the social satire fly. Among the acting standouts is Smith as a snooty countess, Northam as singer Ivor Novello, and Mirren as a servant with a secret involving the valet played by Owen. Don't complain if you need a scorecard to keep track of the characters. Another visit to *Gosford Park* on this sumptuous DVD is twice the fun.

Hot Bonus: Twenty minutes of deleted scenes and, as usual with Altman, each minute counts.

Key Scene: The lovely moment when the servants, standing outside the drawing room, crane to hear snatches of the tune Northam sings.

Graduate, The (Special Edition) (1967)

Starring: Dustin Hoffman, Anne Bancroft, Katharine Ross

Directed by: Mike Nichols

"Ladies and gentlemen, we are about to begin our descent into Los Angeles." With those words—a comic preview of hell to college graduate Benjamin Braddock (Hoffman) as his plane returns him home to his materialistic parents, their questions about his future and one-word career advice from their friends ("Plastics")—director Nichols catches the confusion of a 1960s generation that seems just as pertinent today. The film that Buck Henry and Calder Willingham adapted from Charles Webb's novel isn't about Vietnam, feminism, or even the vintage Simon and Garfunkel songs that dot the soundtrack; it's a comedy of shocking gravity about being young and lost. Nichols deserved that Oscar for directing Hoffman to his career-making performance, for shaping Bancroft's Mrs. Robinson—the older woman who seduces Benjamin and then tries to destroy him for loving her daughter (Ross)—into a figure of pity and terror, and for creating a visual style that changed the way movies look, sound, and feel. This DVD makes those virtues shine in a manner that rewards repeated viewings.

Hot Bonus: There's a retrospective documentary, but it's Hoffman's comments on what the film meant then and mean now that cut deepest.

Key Scene: Hoffman and Ross reunited on the bus at the end and not knowing how to feel about it. Nichols told me the moment happened by accident. He had yelled at the actors to smile and they couldn't. And so one of the most resonant endings in movies was born.

Grand Illusion (Special Edition) (1937)

Starring: Jean Gabin, Pierre Fresnay, Eric von Stroheim, Marcel Dalio
Directed by: Jean Renoir

Criterion's digital transfer, in striking black-and-white, restores Renoir's antiwar masterpiece to a place of honor on DVD shelves. It's a World War I story about French POWs who are treated with respect by their German commandant (a superb von Stroheim). The prisoner played by Fresnay is an aristocrat who bonds strongly with his German peer, but also helps his friends—the working-class Gabin and the Jewish Dalio—plot an escape that leads to tragedy and the shattering of illusions about honor in time of war.

Hot Bonus: An interview with Renoir, who explains how an uncut print of his Nazi-banned film was found in Germany by American soldiers in 1945.

Key Scene: Von Stroheim inviting his prisoners to an elegant dinner.

Grapes of Wrath, The (1940)

Starring: Henry Fonda, Jane Darwell
Directed by: John Ford

A much-needed DVD restoration of Ford's seminal film—taken from the John Steinbeck novel—about the Joad family, Depression-era tenant farmers from Oklahoma's Dust Bowl who head out by rickety truck to find a future in California only to get body-and-spirit kicked by the forces of capitalism. Darwell won an Oscar as Ma Joad, but her "we're the people" uplift goes against the Steinbeck grit, captured in the stark camerawork of Gregg Toland. Fonda, as the eldest Joad son, gets closer to the mark when he lashes out, "Ma, there comes a time when a man gets mad."

Hot Bonus: A Movietone news report from 1934 rubs in the reality.

Key Scene: Fonda's goodbye to Ma—"Wherever there's a fight so hungry people can eat, I'll be there. . . . I'll be all around in the dark"—may be this actor's most moving screen moment.

Grease (1978)

Starring: John Travolta, Olivia Newton-John, Stockard Channing
Directed by: Randal Kleiser

Souped up for DVD till its colors shine like chrome, with a Dolby digital sound engine to pump the songs, the smash musical about 1950s hot rods and hotter chicks again proves the critics wrong: It's greased lightning. Playing the students at Rydell High—the oldest living teenagers on film—are Travolta (then twenty-four), all boyish charm behind the sexy swagger as Danny; Newton-John (then twenty-nine), all sugar till the final makeover as lousy-with-virginity Sandy; and Channing (then thirty-four), all makeout-queen sass as too-cool-for-school Rizzo. The songs ("You're the One That I Want," "Hopelessly Devoted to You") sparkle, the dances rock, and director Kleiser keeps the plot moving so fast you don't realize there isn't one.

Hot Bonus: Retrospective interviews with the stars.

Key Scene: The split-screen "Summer Nights" number in which Travolta and Newton-John give contrasting views on how close they got on vacation.

Great Escape, The (Two-Disc Collector's Edition) (1963)

Starring: Steve McQueen, James Garner, Richard Attenborough
Directed by: John Sturges

The first DVD version of this fact-based World War II prison-breakout saga was muddy and muted. Now, with this new high-definition transfer—remastered in Dolby digital to restore the thunder to Elmer Bernstein's score—the film achieves liftoff. McQueen gives a bust-out star performance as Captain Hilts, the baseball-obsessed "Cooler King," one of the Allied prisoners determined to break out of the "escape-proof" Stalag Luft North (the film was shot on location in Germany). Garner excels as "The Scrounger," who hustles supplies. And Attenborough is perfect as the British mastermind who devises the plan to build three tunnels. Director Sturges ratchets up suspense through painstaking detail.

Hot Bonus: A four-part History Channel show from 2001 shows how far the movie follows the facts before it goes (wonderfully) Hollywood.

Key Scene: McQueen's now-iconic escape on a motorbike.

Gremlins
(Special Edition) (1984)

Starring: Zach Galligan, Phoebe Cates, Hoyt Axton

Directed by: Joe Dante

With an all-new digital transfer and remastered sound, the movie seems even more mischievous and menacing. Galligan is a small-town bank clerk with a pretty girlfriend (Cates). His dad (Axton), home from Chinatown, brings them a mogwai: a cute, four-toed fuzzball he calls Gizmo. But mogwais come with rules: Never get them wet, never feed them after midnight, and always keep them away from bright lights. When the rules are broken, mogwais tend to multiply and morph into gremlins who kick your ass. The sudden violence rattles some people. Get over it. It's their bite that makes the gremlins memorable.

Hot Bonus: There's the usual commentary and deleted scenes, but the best treat—if you buy the double package—is *Gremlins 2: The New Batch*, the 1990 sequel that's less scary but way funnier.

Key Scene: The gremlins raising hell at a screening of Disney's *Snow White and the Seven Dwarfs*.

Grifters, The
(Collector's Series) (1990)

Starring: Anjelica Huston, John Cusack, Annette Bening

Directed by: Stephen Frears

Keep this DVD handy in case somebody asks for an example of great acting. Then show them Huston's gritty, groundbreaking performance as Lilly Dillon, a scam artist who works racetracks and works her way back into the life of Roy (Cusack), her estranged son. Roy is a small-time crook, until he meets Myra (a never-hotter Bening), a leggy sexpot who wants Roy to aim for higher scams. Based on Jim Thompson's hard-boiled novel, the film is a modern film noir and, as directed by Frears, a sly, stinging crime drama.

Hot Bonus: A profile on Thompson that you should watch before the film.

Key Scene: Huston's last confrontation with her son is as seductive and scary a meeting as anything Medea ever dreamed up. This is one of the finest displays of screen acting ever. How did she ever lose that Oscar?

Grosse Pointe Blank (1997)

Starring: John Cusack, Minnie Driver, Joan Cusack, Alan Arkin

Directed by: George Armitage

Cusack is brutally funny as Martin Q. Blank, a hitman with mixed feelings about going home to Grosse Pointe, Michigan—a swank suburb of Detroit—for his ten-year high school reunion. "What am I gonna say?" he asks his therapist (a dryly hilarious Arkin). "'I killed the president of Paraguay—how have you been?'" As star, co-producer, and co-writer of the film, Cusack takes aim at everything America holds dear: home, family, money, success—the things we're urged to kill for in an ethically clueless society. It's a grenade of black comedy tossed at the heartland.

Hot Bonus: Just a trailer, but one that gets the tone right.

Key Scene: Martin's assistant, played by Cusack's sister Joan, phones her boss while he's on the job—at a hotel window, aiming a rifle at his next victim—to urge her boss to attend the reunion. His shrink concurs, "Don't kill anybody for a few days," he says. "See what it feels like."

Groundhog Day
(Collector's Edition) (1993)

Starring: Bill Murray, Andie MacDowell, Chris Elliott

Directed by: Harold Ramis

Repeated viewings of this comedy gem on DVD only make it funnier and its implications deeper. Murray is reliably perfect as a snarky TV weatherman covering the February 2 Groundhog Day ceremony in Punxsutawney, Pennsylvania, only to discover that he is being forced by fate—

and a resonantly hilarious script by director Ramis and Danny Rubin—to repeat the same day over and over. With MacDowell as his producer and Elliott as his cameraman, Murray has just the right foils to transform his torture into a rehab experience in humanity.

Hot Bonus: *The Weight of Time*, a retrospective documentary in which Ramis suggests the original script was darker than the redemptive one here.

Key Scene: Murray's date with MacDowell, which he repeats so many times that he finally learns enough about her to seem impressively romantic.

Guns of Navarone, The (Special Edition) (1961)

Starring: Gregory Peck, David Niven, Anthony Quinn

Directed by: J. Lee Thompson

Old-school Hollywood action can still work like a charm, especially if its picture and sound get pumped up on DVD. Witness this World War II adventure, based on Alistair MacLean's novel, in which Peck heads up a force, including Niven as an explosives expert and Quinn as a Greek stalwart, to take down two German gun posts on the Mediterranean island of Navarone. If they fail, the British fleet is vulnerable. Director Thompson keeps the suspense cooking, though he complains on the commentary track that he would speed things up if he could make the movie today. Please, this DVD shows how effective a careful buildup can be.

Hot Bonus: A retrospective documentary, with Peck and Quinn, tells tales out of school—the best kind.

Key Scene: The destruction of the gun still has its wow factor.

Hair (1979)

Starring: Treat Williams, John Savage, Beverly D'Angelo

Directed by: Milos Forman

OK, so the Age of Aquarius seems like the Dark Ages by now, and "Let the Sun Shine In" got more airplay than it deserved even back in 1969 when the stage musical opened. But Czech-born director Forman turns this counterculture artifact into a fresh, fun movie. And the DVD transfer is a burst of color and sound that demands a reconsideration for the movie audiences ignored in 1979. Twyla Tharp's ingenious choreography (she even has horses dance in the park) is well integrated into the plot about Claude (Savage), an Oklahoma draftee who gets adopted by a group of Man-

hattan flower children, led by Berger (a very fine Williams), before the army ships him off to war.

Hot Bonus: A collection of thirty-six poster designs, showing how the studio tried to sell 1960s nostalgia to a new audience.

Key Scene: The movie is a definite up, but it's the sorrowful ending—with Berger singing "Flesh Failures" as young soldiers march into the belly of an air transport plane—that sticks with you.

Hairspray (1988)

Starring: Divine, Ricki Lake, Jerry Stiller

Directed and written by: John Waters

Waters, the king of shock in such films as *Mondo Trasho* and *Female Trouble*, went PG tame for the first time with this wholesome tale, set in Baltimore in 1962, of Tracy Turnblad (Lake), a fat teen who charms herself onto a TV dance program with her fancy footwork and then hustles to add black teens to the segregated show. Tracy wins the support of her mom Edna, played in a jumbo housedress by Divine. Born Harris Glen Milstead, Divine was a three-hundred-pound drag diva who brought heft and heart to many Waters films, but died of a heart attack just weeks after his first commercial hit in *Hairspray*, which was turned into a hit Broadway musical in 2002. The 1960s colors on this DVD transfer are eye-poppingly trashy.

Hot Bonus: Chat from Waters and Lake, who tell stories about Divine.

Key Scene: Divine changes into extra-large men's clothing to portray a racist station manager.

Halloween (Two-Disc Anniversary Edition) (1978)

Starring: Jamie Lee Curtis, Donald Pleasence

Directed by: John Carpenter

Michael Myers, a six-year-old in a Halloween mask, sees his sister and some dude having sex and stabs them both. Fifteen years later, Michael escapes from the loony bin and returns to his  hometown on Halloween night for more slashing. No one suspected at the time that this efficient, low-budget horror flick would spawn seven sequels. Director Carpenter merely set out to give "trick or treat" a new meaning. Did he ever. Curtis, then twenty, looks convincingly terrified as the babysitter who tangles with Michael. And Pleasence has a high old time as the bug-eyed shrink whose diagnosis runs to terms like "The Evil is loose!" It's still great fun, especially on this high-definition DVD transfer with a juiced-up sound mix.

Hot Bonus: A retrospective documentary, with Curtis and Carpenter exchanging fun factoids. Did you know Michael is wearing a William Shatner mask? To me, that makes it tons scarier.

Key Scene: After impaling a naked guy on a door, Michael tilts his head and just stares at his writhing victim. That head tilt kills me.

Hannah and Her Sisters (1986)

Starring: Woody Allen, Mia Farrow, Michael Caine, Dianne Wiest

Directed and written by: Woody Allen

A typically no-frills Allen DVD package, except that the transfer shows off the lush beauty of Manhattan and bruised feelings of its people. Allen's hypochondriac Mickey is the ex-husband of Hannah (Farrow), who is now married to Elliot (Caine), who is in lust for Hannah's sister Lee (a never lovelier Barbara Hershey) who is amazed when Mickey hits on their other sister Holly (Wiest), a cokehead actress wincing so hard from rejection that she strikes out at perfect Hannah who has a propensity for acquiring children by birth, adoption, and artificial insemination. Was Allen acting out on his then relationship with Farrow? You be the judge. Allen lets emotions run amok in a film that ranks as one of his very best.

Hot Bonus: The letterboxing of the image brings out the best in Carlo Di Palma's lyrical camerawork.

Key Scene: Wiest (who won an Oscar, as did Caine and Allen's screenplay) letting her sisters have it in a restaurant scene in which the camera circles the sisters, catching quicksilver emotions on the fly.

Hannibal (Two-Disc Special Edition) (2001)

Starring: Anthony Hopkins, Julianne Moore, Ray Liotta, Giancarlo Giannini

Directed by: Ridley Scott

Critics got all whiny about this sequel to 1991's *The Silence of the Lambs*. How dare Scott take over the directing from Jonathan Demme, and Moore take over the role of Agent Clarice Starling from Jodie Foster, and Hopkins agree to play the cannibal Hannibal Lecter again when his Oscar-winning colleagues wanted out? Get over it. As shown on this monstrously entertaining DVD, Scott merely shifted the tone from suspense to black comedy. Moving the plot from Florence (where Hannibal hides out) to Virginia (where he reenters Clarice's life), Scott even improves on the 1999 Thomas Harris novel that outraged readers with its love match between Hannibal and Clarice. Scott handles the romance by suggestion instead of by assault with a blunt tool. The scenes in Italy have a sinister allure that is heightened when Commandatore Pazzi (Giannini) comes sniffing around. Pazzi is being paid by Mason Verger (an uncredited Gary Oldman), an American billionaire and Hannibal's only surviving victim. With the help of his doctor, Cordell (Zeljko Ivanek), Mason plans to kidnap Hannibal and keep him alive on an IV drip while wild boars devour him from the toes up. And so it goes, with Hopkins's perverse perfection in the role that made him a star.

Hot Bonus: A nifty Easter Egg called "Flashframes," in which Moore is shown in several scenes after Scott has said, "Cut." To access this unusual feature, go to "Breaking the Silence," on Disc 2, find "Music," press the left arrow, and press "Enter" when the arrow turns blue.

Key Scene: Hannibal whipping up a gourmet feast that involves the sautéing of shallots, caper berries, and delicate slices from the prefrontal lobe of a cop (Liotta), who chows down as well. Don't ask. Just howl. Or hurl.

Happiness (Signature Series) (1998)

Starring: Lara Flynn Boyle, Philip Seymour Hoffman, Dylan Baker

Directed and written by: Todd Solondz

It's a copout to call Solondz (*Welcome to the Dollhouse*) an acquired taste. Some people won't ever cotton to his subversive satire. But his shock tactics have value. Just consider the implications in the lives of three sisters from New Jersey: Joy (Jane Adams) has split from her boyfriend (Jon Lovitz). Helen (Boyle) is a writer who invites her obscene caller (Hoffman) over to incite rape. And Trish (Cynthia Stevenson) is a happy housewife and mom until she realizes her shrink husband (played sympathetically by the astonishing Baker) is a pedophile who drugs and rapes the boys their son brings home for a sleepover. And I didn't mention the dog semen. It's all here on the DVD, which catches every perverse moment and is guaranteed to stir debate with anyone you watch it with.

Hot Bonus: Just a trailer, which doesn't begin to suggest the outrage ahead.

Key Scene: Baker talking calmly to his son (Rufus Read) about why he molests boys, and the son asking why Dad isn't attracted to him. In a suburban sitcom setting, Solondz spins the earth off its axis.

Happy Gilmore (1996)

Starring: Adam Sandler, Julie Bowen, Bob Barker, Ben Stiller

Directed by: Dennis Dugan

The essence of Sandler's goofball appeal can be found in this raucous farce about a hot-tempered hockey player who can't skate and his switch to being a hot-tempered golfer who can't putt. The reason? To save his grandma's house from the IRS. That's all there is, but the fun is constant, including Stiller's cameo as a nursing-home attendant. The DVD gets the colors to pop and the sound to soar as Gilmore drives a golf ball for four hundred yards.

Hot Bonus: A trailer that includes footage that never shows up in the film.

Key Scene: Sandler and Barker, of TV's *The Price Is Right*, going at it on the golf course is damn near classic comedy.

Hard Boiled (1992)

Starring: Chow Yun-Fat, Tony Leung

Directed by: John Woo

There are two DVDs of this Hong Kong action thriller on the market, and you want only the version from Criterion that delivers rich color and dimensional sound. Hong Kong megastar Chow Yun-Fat stars as the cop out for vengeance against the Triad that killed his partner. When one of the hoods turns out to be an undercover cop (Leung), the Woo action fireworks kick in.

Hot Bonus: A student film from Woo that shows you the roots of a master director of near-balletic violence.

Key Scene: The climactic shootout in a hospital is worth a triple wow!

Hard Day's Night, A (Two-Disc Collector's Series) (1964)

Starring: John Lennon, George Harrison, Paul McCartney, Ringo Starr

Directed by: Richard Lester

Fabness itself. Young director Lester managed to capture the Beatles' personality—they look prettier than Audrey Hepburn, talk funnier than the Marx Brothers, and strut sassier than Marlon Brando. The lads race from train to hotel to stage, leaving bitchy one-liners and gorgeous songs ("And I Love Her") in their wake. The film's kinetic energy—it was shot in black-and-white in just seven weeks—radiates from the DVD. Best line about Ringo: "He's very fussy about his drums. . . . They loom large in his legend."

Hot Bonus: There's an entire second disc devoted to extras, the best of which involves George Martin talking about producing the soundtrack. But someone please tell us: why no deleted scenes?

Key Scene: The opening montage of the Beatles running down the street to the title song, being chased by screaming fans.

Harder They Come, The (1972)

Starring: Jimmy Cliff, Bob Charlton

Directed by: Perry Henzell

You can practically inhale the Jamaican ganja on this vivid Criterion DVD transfer, but it's the reggae score that gets into your head. The legendary Cliff stars as Ivan, a country boy who comes to Kingston to be a reggae star and gets involved in a life of crime that only enhances his fame. OK, the story is familiar. It's the music, from the title song to "Many Rivers to Cross," that touches your soul.

Hot Bonus: Henzell discusses the class system in Jamaica and how it affected the content of the film and the difficulties in making it.

Key Scene: Cliff's face—the film is semiautobiographical—when he records his first song for a producer (Charlton) who is out to destroy him.

Harold and Maude (1971)

Starring: Ruth Gordon, Bud Cort, Vivian Pickles

Directed by: Hal Ashby

A true cult classic, a black comedy Ashby style in which the laughs stick in your throat. The film is a bizarre love story between Cort's Harold, twenty, and Gordon's Maude, seventy-nine. Given that premise, you might not want a DVD transfer that lets you see every detail. But these characters get to you: Harold with his staged suicide attempts to shock his mother (a hilarious Pickles) and Maude, the concentration-camp survivor with a hunger for life that is all visible in Gordon's wonderfully expressive eyes.

Hot Bonus: A new Dolby Digital track that brings out the best in the acoustic-driven Cat Stevens songs that help tell the story.

Key Scene: Maude, near death, telling Harold to "go out and love some more." By not going for cheap tears, the moment hits you harder.

Harry Potter and the Prisoner of Azkaban (2004)

Starring: Daniel Radcliffe, Emma Watson, Rupert Grint

Directed by: Alfonso Cuarón

Not only is this dazzler by far the best and most thrilling of the three Harry Potter movies to date, it's a film that can stand on its own even if you never heard of author J. K. Rowling and her young wizard hero. Director Cuarón, taking the reins from Chris Columbus, who made a slog of the first two films, scores a triumph by bringing lyricism, laughs, and dark magic to the party. You may wonder what the Mexican director of the erotic road movie *Y Tu Mamá También* would do with Harry (Radcliffe, fourteen), Hermione (Watson, fourteen) and Ron (Grint, fifteen) on the road to puberty. Snap out of it, freaks. Cuarón knows how to loosen up his pubescent wizards as they head for their third term at Hogwarts. They dress and sass like modern teens with hormones raging. With the help of his pals and Professor Lupin (the excellent David Thewlis), Harry must cope with an escapee from Azkaban prison (a haunting Gary Oldman) who may have been involved in the murder of Harry's parents. Everyone in this film has secrets (deep, dark Freudian ones) that rival the scary effects, which include a killer tree and soul-sucking creatures called Dementors. It's a great twisty ride, and the DVD transfer doesn't miss a turn or a trick.

Hot Bonus: A thrilling segment on how the Dementors were created.

Key Scene: Screenwriter Steve Kloves, ever faithful to Rowling, doesn't mess with overt sex, but it's hard not to laugh when Harry is first discovered under bedcovers playing with his wand.

Haunting, The (1963)

Starring: Julie Harris, Claire Bloom, Russ Tamblyn, Richard Johnson

Directed by: Robert Wise

One of the great haunted-house movies (and now DVDs) and not to be confused with the dreadful 1999 remake (a DVD disaster). Based on the Shirley Jackson story *The Haunting of Hill House*, the movie has a black-and-white picture that creeps you out big time. There are times you can hear the house breathe. Director Wise is great with creepy sounds and weird camera angles. He's not so great with the lesbian subtext bubbling under Harris and Bloom, as two women with ESP whom Dr. Markway (Johnson) has brought along to the haunted New England mansion inherited by Luke (Tamblyn). But the house knows how to seep into your bones.

Hot Bonus: Wise's script with his notes written in the margins is a treasure trove for those seeking the film's hidden meanings.

Key Scene: The spiral staircase. Don't say I didn't warn you.

Heat (Two-Disc Special Edition) (1995)

Starring: Al Pacino, Robert De Niro, Val Kilmer, Ashley Judd

Directed by: Michael Mann

Master L.A. cop Pacino chases master thief De Niro. That's it. And that's all you need as director Mann spins a crime film for the ages with layers of characters and insights that grow more compelling each time you watch the film—a prospect made all the more tempting by this pro DVD transfer. Mann stages a bank robbery that opens up into the streets with guns blazing, and the DVD adds an aural dimensionality that will have you ducking.

Hot Bonus: Eleven deleted scenes. That may seem like overkill for a film that already runs nearly three hours, but with this cast it all counts.

Key Scene: Pacino and De Niro—two groundbreaking actors in their only film together—meet for one historic scene in a coffeeshop. "Just like a couple of regular fellas," says Pacino's character. Yeah, right.

Heathers (THX Version) (1989)

Starring: Winona Ryder, Christian Slater

Directed by: Michael Lehmann

This startling satire of sex and suicide at Ohio's Westerburg High still soars on Lehmann's

inventive direction and Daniel Waters's diabolically clever script. The DVD pops with the bright colors of a teen sitcom. But surprise: what lies beneath is a tough core of toxic wit. Ryder hit her stride as an actress playing Veronica, handmaiden to three bitchy girls named Heather (Shannen Doherty, Kim Walker, and Lisanne Falk) who rule the school. That is, until newcomer J.D., seemingly cloned from a teenaged Jack Nicholson by Slater, starts Veronica on a plan to rig a few murders as suicides. "We should talk," says a teacher to a student. "Whether or not to kill yourself is one of the most important decisions a teenager can make."

Hot Bonus: A half-hour retrospective, *Swatch Dogs and Diet Coke Heads*, with observations from Ryder, Slater, Doherty, and Falk, shows why this film still rules the teen roost.

Key Scene: "You're not a rebel, you're a psycho," Veronica tells J.D. when he enters school like a walking time bomb. The ending is a copout, but a screenplay excerpt from the original ending shows how it should have been.

Heavenly Creatures (1994)

Starring: Kate Winslet, Melanie Lynskey
Directed by: Peter Jackson

Long before Jackson ever thought of Frodo, the New Zealander directed this amazing and appalling true story of two teenagers, Pauline Rieper (Linskey) and Juliet Hulme (Winslet, three years before she starred in *Titanic*), who had tea with Pauline's mother on a sunny afternoon in 1954 and then bashed Mum's skull with a brick stuffed in a stocking. Jackson's remarkable achievement, etched beautifully on this DVD, is the creation of the imaginary "Fourth World" these deluded, love-besotted girls retreated to when the world got too much. Forbidden by the courts to see each other again, the girls were released. Juliet has recently been identified as the British crime novelist Anne Perry.

Hot Bonus: Another ten minutes of footage not seen in the original cut.

Key Scene: The girls, brilliantly played by Winslet and Lynskey, whipping themselves into sexual hysteria while dancing in the woods as the voice of Mario Lanza, their favorite tenor, is heard warbling "Be My Love."

Hedwig and the Angry Inch (2001)

Starring: John Cameron Mitchell, Stephen Trask, Michael Pitt
Directed and written by: John Cameron Mitchell

An exuberant blast of rock & roll defiance, which Mitchell—the director, writer, and star—has adapted from his stage musical about an "internationally ignored" rocker from communist East Berlin who sings about his dick being cut off in a messy operation that leaves a one-inch mound of flesh where his penis used to be. Hence the name Angry Inch for the band of Eastern-bloc musicians with whom Hansel, now Hedwig, tours the pit stops of America. The brazen rock energy of Trask's score finds an ideal complement in Mitchell's screenplay, which manages to be tough, tender, and brutally funny. "What's that?" asks Tommy Gnosis (Pitt), the teen fan and Jesus freak who gets a shock when he first grabs Hedwig's crotch. "It's what I have to work with, honey," says Hedwig with a resignation that turns to fury when Tommy becomes a megastar by stealing his mentor's songs. The decision to sing live, exceedingly rare onscreen, creates a vivid immediacy that comes through like gangbusters on the DVD.

Hot Bonus: A feature-length documentary that traces the development of Hedwig from stage to screen.

Key Scene: The makeover anthem "Wig in a Box," sung by Hedwig with Cher-like gusto in a dingy trailer that turns into the ultimate arena fantasy stage. Is this a tour de force or what?

Hellraiser (Remastered) (1987)

Starring: Andrew Robinson, Sean Chapman, Clare Higgins
Directed by: Clive Barker

Acclaimed British horror novelist Barker makes his directing debut in fine, fierce style—just watch the blood flow on DVD—

as he opens the door to hell and out comes Pinhead, the leader of the Cenobites, who enjoys ripping bodies apart with fish hooks. That means big trouble for Larry (Robinson) and his new wife Julia (Higgins) who move into the home of his late brother Frank (Chapman). Actually, Frank is half alive upstairs thirsting for new blood to regenerate himself. Julia, his former flame in sexual deviancy, recruits the victims. Thanks to Barker, it's an artfully graphic grossout.

Hot Bonus: A retrospective doc about the film's impact and the rise of Pinhead, who starred in a number of sequels—some direct to video—that Barker didn't direct and you shouldn't go near.

Key Scene: Pinhead offering memorable advice to a new victim: "No tears, please. It is just a waste of good suffering."

Help! (1965)

Starring: John Lennon, George Harrison, Paul McCartney, Ringo Starr

Directed by: Richard Lester

The Beatles followup to A Hard Day's Night—this time in color, which the DVD does proud—makes even less sense but is no less enjoyable. A fan gives Ringo a ring that he can't get off. Then he learns the ring will enable him to rule the world? The plot is merely an excuse for the Fab Four to trot around the globe acting like monkeys and singing such hits as "Ticket to Ride," "You've Got to Hide Your Love Away," "You're Gonna Lose That Girl," and the title tune. Lester directs the lads with inspired lunacy.

Hot Bonus: Newsreels of the Beatles returning home after a concert tour.

Key Scene: Lennon fishing a ticket out of a bowl of soup. Actually, Lennon doing anything still has the power to pierce your heart for missing him.

Henry: Portrait of a Serial Killer (Director's Edition) (1986)

Starring: Michael Rooker, Tom Towles, Tracy Arnold

Directed and co-written by: John McNaughton

The movie doesn't shy away from gore, and neither does this DVD, which presents the uncut edition. Bodies are kicked, punched, slashed, shot, and dismembered. Director and co-writer McNaughton based the fictionalized script on Henry Lee Lucas, a convicted serial killer. Henry, rivetingly played by Rooker, shares a drab Chicago apartment with a prison buddy named Otis (a terrifying Towles). The plot trigger is the arrival of Otis's sister Becky (Tracy Arnold), a topless dancer. When Otis sees Henry snap the necks of two tarts they take parking, he joins Henry on his killing spree. McNaughton exposes a world stripped of standards. Far from glorifying Henry's fury, McNaughton rubs it in our faces. Sure we recoil. That's the point.

Hot Bonus: An interview with McNaughton in which he talks about his battle with the censors, who wanted the film cut. Plus deleted scenes and a retrospective documentary.

Key Scene: It's the one that prompted walkouts in theaters. Henry and Otis attack a suburban family and tape the deed. The video footage—grainy, unfocused, crazily angled—makes the carnage joltingly immediate.

Henry V (1989)

Starring: Kenneth Branagh, Derek Jacobi, Emma Thompson

Directed by: Kenneth Branagh

This is still the best Shakespeare and the best film Branagh has ever done as an actor and director. And in contrast to Laurence Olivier's 1944 film take on Henry, Branagh's ruler is not one to rally the troops to battle. He uncovers the inner struggle of the young king to inspire his soldiers to fight a war he cannot always justify to himself. The DVD captures everything the Belfast-born Branagh, then twenty-eight, poured into this hot-blooded, lively, and moving film to make it speak pertinently to a new generation.

Hot Bonus: Nothing much, besides a trailer. So please find Olivier's version of Henry V on Criterion (a superb transfer), shot during World War II to fire up the troops, and compare it to Branagh's antiwar interpretation.

Key Scene: Branagh, having just delivered the St. Crispin's Day speech ("God for Harry! England and Saint George!"), carries a body of a dead boy (Christian Bale, of all people) across the field of Agincourt where mud and blood mix in a stirring indictment of war.

Hero (2002)

Starring: Jet Li, Maggie Cheung, Tony Leung
Directed by: Yimou Zhang

No quarrel here with the raves for this Oscar nominee for Best Foreign Language Film. Director Zhang packs this visual feast with fierce action. Based on the king of Qin's attempts to unify the warring states of China in the third century B.C., the film stars Jet Li as Nameless, a sheriff who visits the Qin king (Daoming Chen) in his palace, claiming he has killed the king's three worst enemies. They are Sky (Donnie Yen), Snow (Maggie Cheung), and Broken Sword (Tony Leung). The story of their defeat is told in flashback. Actually there are four stories—each with its own color scheme—and Christopher Doyle's camerawork alone makes this a DVD must-own. The actors bring heat to the love triangle involving Snow, Broken Sword, and his servant Moon (gorgeous Zhang Ziyi). Audiences are left to decide the truth for themselves, as in Akira Kurosawa's 1950 masterwork *Rashomon*.

Hot Bonus: A conversation between Jet Li and Quentin Tarantino.

Key Scene: The soaring arrows—a true demo DVD moment.

High and the Mighty, The (Two-Disc Collector's Edition) (1954)

Starring: John Wayne, Claire Trevor, Jan Sterling, Robert Stack
Directed by: William A. Wellman

After decades in rights-dispute limbo—it was last seen on television after Wayne's death in 1979—this airborne nailbiter about a passenger plane experiencing mechanical problems on a run from Honolulu to San Francisco hits DVD in grand style. Loaded with extras and restored to widescreen glory, the movie and Wayne fly high. Trevor and Sterling won Oscar nominations as two of the passengers flying on this *Grand Hotel* in the sky, but it's Wayne's show. He plays pilot Dan Roman, an "ancient pelican" who survived a plane crash that killed his wife and child. Now he's reduced to co-piloting for the arrogant Stack. Director Wellman stages the action with such bravura skill that the film barely shows its age.

Hot Bonus: A piece on the film's restoration.

Key Scene: That last glimpse of Wayne, whistling the haunting title tune that won an Oscar for composer Dimitri Tiomkin. Wayne's family played it at his funeral. No fan of the Duke will watch it dry-eyed now.

High Fidelity (2000)

Starring: John Cusack, Jack Black, Todd Louiso, Iben Hjejle
Directed by: Stephen Frears

Top-five dream jobs? According to music freak Rob Gordon (Cusack), here's Number One: "Journalist for *Rolling Stone* magazine, 1976–1979." Rob was born too late to fulfill his dream. Instead he opened a music store in Chicago that specializes in LPs. Rob's girlfriend, Laura (Hjejle), has just dumped him for living his obsessions. "That's cold shit," says Rob. If you've been on either side of that argument, this film of Nick Hornby's fab 1995 novel will strike you as painfully hilarious even though the movie shifts the book's location from Eighties London to Y2K Chicago. No matter. The movie looks great on DVD, and sounds even better thanks to a kick-ass soundtrack. Rob floods his store with sounds, from the Clash to Beta Band. Even better, he hires two clerks: Louiso as the shy-guy Dick and Black, who is howlingly funny as Barry, the loudmouth who insults any "ass-muncher" customer who doesn't share his musical taste. Again working for Frears, who directed him in *The Grifters*, Cusack is note perfect and one of the top-five reasons that the film's imperfections don't matter. You're still smiling when it's over, so why go on with the list?

Hot Bonus: A cameo from Bruce Springsteen is enough for me, but the commentary from Cusack and Frears answers any question you can think of.

Key Scene: Cusack searching his memory for his desert-island, all-time, top-five split-ups and the songs that went with them. Think "I Hate You (But Call Me)," by the Monks.

High Noon (Collector's Edition) (1952)

Starring: Gary Cooper, Grace Kelly, Ian MacDonald
Directed by: Fred Zinnemann

A classic western gets it due on DVD with this digitally remastered black-and-white picture and sound. The screenwriter Carl Foreman was later blacklisted for making the script a veiled attack on McCarthyism. Marshal Will Kane, played by Cooper at his Oscar-winning best, has just married his Quaker bride (Kelly) and is ready to retire, when word comes that Frank Miller (Macdonald) is arriving on the noon train to take vengeance on Will, who no one in town is ready to help. Zinnemann creates unbearable tension as we watch clocks ticking, Cooper sweating (he had a bleeding ulcer), and Tex Ritter singing Dimitri Tiomkin's memorable theme ("Do Not Forsake Me").

Hot Bonus: The children of the filmmakers, including Cooper's daughter Maria, Zinnemann's son Tim, Foreman's son Jonathan, and Ritter's actor son John, share detailed memories of growing up around the film.

Key Scene: Cooper throwing away his badge in disgust at his fellow Americans. It took years for Cooper's pal John Wayne to forgive the actor.

Highlander
(The Immortal Edition) (1986)

Starring: Christopher Lambert, Sean Connery, Clancy Brown

Directed by: Russell Mulcahy

This cult fantasy, which spawned three godawful sequels and a TV series, travels from a sword fight in Madison Square Garden to another one in sixteenth-century Scotland. Critics went potty all over the tale of Connor MacLeod (Lambert), a Scottish highlander who discovers that he is one of a race of immortals who will walk the Earth until one of them wins by decapitating the rest. Got that? Few did when the film opened. Now on this two-disc DVD, with scenes added to restore logic and a soundtrack by Queen that never sounded better, *Highlander* emerges as a thrilling action epic as Connor races through the ages with the Kurgan (Brown) on his tail.

Hot Bonus: Having the uncensored director's cut with commentary by Mulcahy clears up a lot of questions.

Key Scene: Connery has a ball and great dialogue as the Spanish Peacock, the mentor who trains Connor for combat in the most exciting sequence.

His Girl Friday (1940)

Starring: Cary Grant, Rosalind Russell

Directed by: Howard Hawks

If someone asks you for the fastest-talking comedy of Hollywood's Golden Age, point them toward this madcap newspaper farce that actually improves on its source, Ben Hecht and Charles MacArthur's stage classic *The Front Page*, by casting the male role of star reporter Hildy Johnson with a woman (a never-better Russell). That makes the tricks pulled by Hildy's editor Walter Burns (Grant at his sublime best, which is saying something) to keep Hildy at his newspaper and in his life (they were once married) even funnier. Restored from the original negative, the DVD is time-capsule worthy.

Hot Bonus: Critic Todd McCarthy provides a commentary track that explains how screenwriter Charles Lederer adapted the play and how Hawks directed the actors to talk at 240 words a minute. Great stuff.

Key Scene: Russell on Grant's charm: "He comes by it naturally. His grandfather was a snake."

Homecoming, The (1973)

Starring: Vivien Merchant, Ian Holm, Terence Rigby, Michael Jayston

Directed by: Peter Hall

It's just a film of Harold Pinter's play, but what a play. And the DVD, released as part of the American Film Theater series, is a model of stage-to-screen adaptation. All the explosions are verbal as Pinter reveals a dysfunctional family imploding, with Jayston returning home with a wife (the brilliant Merchant, then Mrs. Pinter) who dad (Paul Rogers), uncle (Cyril Cusack), and brothers (Holm and Rigby) begin to treat like a whore. It's a nest of vipers, and director Hall keeps the tension crackling.

Hot Bonus: Cinematographer David Watkin talks about his techniques in making something cinematic of a claustrophobic atmosphere.

Key Scene: Merchant, in heels and black stockings, caressing her long legs in front of the men in a display of feminine power.

Honeymoon Killers, The (1970)

Starring: Shirley Stoler, Tony Lo Bianco, Mary Jane Higby

Directed by: Leonard Kastle

Leave it to Criterion to create a dazzling DVD transfer of a low-budget, documentary-style feature shot in black-and-white. But dazzle it does as Ray Fernandez (Lo Bianco) seduces and murders rich old ladies with the help of Martha Beck (Stoler), the two-hundred-pound nurse who loves him and poses as his sister. Martin Scorsese was fired from the film by screenwriter Kastle, who took up the directing reigns and delivers a striking take on this fact-based story from the 1940s. Stoler and Lo Bianco give indelible performances.

Hot Bonus: An illustrated essay on the real-life "Lonely Hearts Killers."

Key Scene: The murder of the widow, played by Higby, still startles.

Hotel Rwanda (2004)

Starring: Don Cheadle, Sophie Okonedo, Nick Nolte

Directed by: Terry George

In 1994, civil war broke out in Rwanda between the ruling Hutu tribe and the oppressed Tutsis. A million people were slaughtered while the world looked away. It's a huge subject for one film, leading director and co-writer George to focus on the true story of Paul Rusesabagina (Cheadle), the Hutu manager of the posh Milles Collines Hotel. Paul saved 1,268 Tutsis from the genocide. In playing an ordinary man who finds a core of heroism he never knew he had, Cheadle gives a haunting, Oscar-nominated performance. Paul's efforts to protect his children and his Tutsi wife (the stirring Okonedo, also Oscar nominated) soon extend to a broader family. George has been criticized for simplifying a complex story into an African *Schindler's List*. But this film of rare courage and heart deserves a long life on DVD.

Hot Bonus: Incisive commentary from Rusesabagina himself.

Key Scene: The bumps in the road that turn out to be slaughtered bodies as Paul drives home in darkness.

House of Flying Daggers (2004)

Starring: Zhang Ziyi, Takeshi Kaneshiro, Andy Lau

Directed by: Yimou Zhang

Here's a DVD that's loaded with demonstration-quality scenes. Prepare the eyes of your friends for popping as director Zhang Yimou's martial-arts fireball throws in head-spinning fights and dazzling surprises, not to mention a lyrical love story. Two Tang Dynasty officers—pretty-boy Jin (Kaneshiro) and rough-hewn Leo (Lau)—try to trick Mei (Zhang Ziyi), a blind dancer, into leading them to the Flying Daggers, a group of insurgents. Jin and Mei fall in love while Leo simmers with unrequited lust. The director of *Raise the Red Lantern*, a former insurgent himself in China, proves himself a poet of love and war. And don't be fooled by *Memoirs of a Geisha* star Zhang Ziyi's delicate beauty. This babe can kick your ass.

Hot Bonus: A featurette on the visual effects is an amazement.

Key Scene: The final duel in the snow.

House of Mirth, The (2000)

Starring: Gillian Anderson, Eric Stoltz, Dan Aykroyd

Directed by: Terence Davies

"With Edith Wharton, the gloves are off and there's blood on the walls." So says director Davies, who delivers the author's 1905 novel to the screen in all its full, flinty vigor, all of which shines anew on DVD. Anderson, light years from the X-Files, is delicate dynamite as Lily Bart, a social climber on the verge of a calamitous fall. She loves a lawyer (Stoltz) of limited prospects, but searches instead for a better catch only to be falsely accused of seducing a married tycoon (Aykroyd). In looking at old New York at the turn of the last century, Davies finds few things changed about sex and the city. Who's in and who's out among the filthy rich is still a killing game.

Hot Bonus: A different version, three minutes longer, of the film's opening.

Key Scene: "A girl must marry," says Lily to the lawyer, "but a man only if he chooses." She then blows a puff of cigarette smoke in his face. You've got to hand it to Anderson: Not since Bette Davis has an actress better used a cigarette as erotic punctuation. It's hotter than nudity and penetration.

House of Sand and Fog (2003)

Starring: Ben Kingsley, Jennifer Connelly, Shohreh Aghdashloo

Directed by: Vadim Perelman

Before it runs off course into excess, this brilliantly acted film version of the 1999 novel by Andre Dubus III moves with a stabbing urgency. Kingsley amazes as Behrani, a former colonel in the air force of the Shah of Iran. Now living in California, where he supports his wife, Nadi (Aghdashloo), and their teenage son (Jonathan Ahdout), by doing menial jobs, Behrani buys a house at auction that formerly belonged to Kathy (Connelly), a junkie who engages Behrani in a legal battle that speaks to issues of race and class. The DVD transfer honors cinematographer Roger Deakins, whose wizardry with light compliments director Perelman's keen feel for imploding emotions.

Hot Bonus: Commentary from Kingsley, Perelman, and Dubus that goes way beyond the usual self-congratulation.

Key Scene: On a visit to her former house, Kathy encounters Nadi, who offers her surprising sympathy. The Oscar-nominated Aghdashloo, an Iranian actress, has a face of elegant beauty on which emotions register with startling expressiveness. By merely serving tea, she creates a whole world.

House of Wax (1953)

Starring: Vincent Price, Phyllis Kirk, Charles Bronson
Directed by: Andre de Toth

Forget the 2005 remake with Paris Hilton. Here's the real deal in horror on a flamboyantly colorful DVD transfer that provides everything but the 3-D process in which it was introduced. Ironically, director De Toth was blind in one eye and had no depth perception. Price hams it up magnificently as Professor Henry Jarrod, a sculptor who has been wheelchair bound since a fire destroyed his wax museum. The professor reopens the place with an assistant named Igor (a young Bronson) and wins raves by pouring wax over dead bodies and passing them off as art.

Hot Bonus: The 1933 Michael Curtiz film *Mystery of the Wax Museum*, with Lional Atwill in the Price role, is included on the disc. It's nasty fun.

Key Scene: Kirk slapping Price's face. The wax falls off, revealing the fiend.

Howards End (Two-Disc Merchant-Ivory Collection) (1992)

Starring: Anthony Hopkins, Emma Thompson, Vanessa Redgrave
Directed by: James Ivory

A gorgeous DVD package. Academics usually squeeze the life out of E. M. Forster's classic 1910 novel by treating it as an allegory for the class war in Edwardian England. Rest assured, there is nothing pedantic about the movie version, which represents a career peak for producer Ismail Merchant, director James Ivory, and screenwriter Ruth Prawer Jhabvala, who also triumphed with

Forster's *A Room With a View*. Forster's effort to draw meaning and hope from a society divided by money, class, culture, and social irresponsibility is timelier than ever. The film serves Forster by taking to heart the book's epigraph: "Only connect." You can see it in Thompson's thrilling Oscar-winning performance. She makes virtue sexy as Margaret Schlegel, who is cheated of her inheritance of Howards End—a country estate bequeathed to her by Ruth Wilcox (Vanessa Redgrave)—by Ruth's ruthless husband Henry (Hopkins, reliably perfect) who she later marries and tries to reform. Subplots involving Margaret's bohemian sister Helen (Helena Bonham Carter) and the poor clerk (Sam West) she befriends and inadvertently helps to destroy cut to the problems Forster saw in rebuilding a society from the ashes of greed.

Hot Bonus: A new forty-five-minute documentary about the making of the movie features Merchant and Ivory going at each other over various details.

Key Scene: Hopkins proposing to Thompson on a staircase is uncommonly funny and touching—he lacks the romantic finesse to do it properly, and she is too filled with ardor to respond in more than monosyllables.

Hud (1963)

Starring: Paul Newman, Patricia Neal, Melvyn Douglas, Brandon de Wilde
Directed by: Martin Ritt

Is there a handsome actor with less vanity than Newman? Who else, at the peak of his career, would have played a son-of-a-bitch like Hud Bannon, a skirt-chasing, work-dodging modern cowboy who can't stop riding his cattle-ranching daddy (Oscar-winner Douglas) about his outdated principles. Yet Hud's nephew, Lon (De Wilde), idolizes him, and the sassy housekeeper Alma (Oscar-winner Neal) likes seeing him with his shirt off. But Hud, unbothered about raping a woman or the land, stays rotten—one reason, besides the mesmerizing Newman, that the film hasn't dated a bit.

Hot Bonus: Just seeing James Wong Howe's Oscar-winning cinematography in all its widescreen, black-and-white glory on DVD is enough.

Key Scene: Alma's goodbye to Hud at the bus station, slapping him verbally just as the bus door slams in his face.

Hunger, The (1983)

Starring: Catherine Deneuve, Susan Sarandon, David Bowie
Directed by: Tony Scott

OK, maybe you don't want to see Deneuve as

a vampire engaged in hot lesbo action with Sarandon as her new recruit. And maybe you don't care that these scenes have never looked or sounded better than they do on this DVD transfer. And maybe the sight of Deneuve and Bowie invading a chic disco in search of new blood to suck as Bauhaus sings "Bela Lugosi Is Dead" is way too hot for your cool tastes. Or maybe you're lying.

Hot Bonus: Director Scott is hilarious coming up with explanations about the film's serious intent. Yeah, right.

Key Scene: To get my mind off Deneuve and Sarandon for a moment, there is a great hospital sequence in which Bowie ages centuries in seconds.

Hunt for Red October, The (Special Edition) (1990)

Starring: Sean Connery, Alec Baldwin
Directed by: John McTiernan

DVD players are made to show off the special effects in movies like this, an efficient if hardly inspired adaptation of Tom Clancy's novel about a Russian submarine captain (Connery scoring points even with his Scots accent) who heads for the United States with Russian and American subs ready to waste him. Only C.I.A. agent Jack Ryan, nicely played by Baldwin before Harrison Ford inherited the role, thinks the Russian is out to defect, not to destroy. You may believe you've seen this all before, and you have. But McTiernan knows how to make models of subs look like the real thing.

Hot Bonus: McTiernan tells how he did it.
Key Scene: Thanks to the dimensionality of the DVD's sound design, anytime things go "Boom!" underwater is a pulse racer.

Hustler, The (1961)

Starring: Paul Newman, Jackie Gleason, Piper Laurie, George C. Scott
Directed by: Robert Rossen

With just a couple of balls on a table, director Rossen shows how you don't need a global canvas to produce an action epic. Newman hit his star stride as Fast Eddie Felson, the pool hustler who challenges champ Minnesota Fats (the great Glea-

son) and loses. Only after an affair with an alcoholic cripple (a haunting Laurie) and the machinations of a promoter (Scott is evil personified) does Eddie find the balls to take on Fats again. That match, shot in widescreen black-and-white by Oscar-winner Eugen Schüfftan, is a killer that seems to gain in tension on this gritty DVD transfer.

Hot Bonus: It's great to hear Newman, who won the Oscar for the same role in 1986's *The Color of Money*, recall the shooting. But the key extra is the picture-in-picture deconstruction of the pool shots by Mike Massey.

Key Scene: The glint and challenge in Newman's eyes when he regards Gleason and says: "Fat man, you shoot a great game of pool."

I ♡ Huckabees (Two-Disc Special Edition) (2004)

Starring: Jason Schwartzman, Jude Law, Naomi Watts, Mark Wahlberg
Directed by: David O. Russell

Director Russell's head-tripping comedy may drive you up the wall even on this special-edition DVD that tries to answer questions the film doesn't. It sounds silly to say that Schwartzman plays Albert, an environmentalist poet tormented with questions about the meaning of existence, especially his own. It sounds sillier to add that Albert hires the Jaffes, Bernard (Dustin Hoffman) and Vivian (Lily Tomlin), a married couple billed as existential detectives. Which brings us to Huckabees, the "everything store," repped by Albert's pretty-boy nemesis Brad (Law), who lives with Dawn (Watts), the Huckabees spokesmodel. Under Russell's shrewdly screwball direction, the actors go places they've never been before. Best of all is Wahlberg as Tommy, an angry post-9/11 firefighter so against Big Oil that he rides to fire scenes on his bike. Russell tosses so many big ideas in the air that it's not surprising a few crash and burn. Live with it. Russell is a rebel Pied Piper, and *Huckabees* is one more reason to follow him anywhere.

Hot Bonus: There are twenty-two deleted scenes that leave you just as amused and baffled.

Key Scene: When Isabelle Huppert as Caterine, the French nihilist, hands out her card, which reads: "Cruelty. Manipulation. Meaninglessness."

I Spit on Your Grave (Millennium Edition) (1978)

Starring: Camille Keaton, Eron Tabor
Directed by: Meir Zarchi

Critics once spit on this tale of rape and revenge. Today it has spawned a cult that this new digital letter-boxed DVD transfer will surely reinforce. A young Manhattan writer (Keaton, she is Buster Keaton's niece), working in a remote cabin in the woods, is beaten, raped, and left for dead by four men. The rape scenes are graphic, and so is the woman's revenge. But critics who accused director Zarchi of exploiting violence against the woman miss the point. This movie, which is antierotic, is about rage.

Hot Bonus: Zarchi, who married Keaton and hasn't talked about the film since its debut, defends his choices.

Key Scene: The most nonviolent moment, when the rape victim visits a church and asks forgiveness in advance for the revenge she is about to exact.

Ice Storm (1997)

Starring: Kevin Kline, Joan Allen, Christina Ricci, Elijah Wood
Directed by: Ang Lee

Here's a great movie about family. Just don't think Disney, since the parents indulge in adultery and wife swapping, and the kids, ages fourteen to sixteen, dry hump, mix drug cocktails, and contemplate suicide. The setting is the plush suburb of New Canaan, Connecticut. The time is Thanksgiving 1973. Nixon drones denials from every TV, and outside an ice storm makes the roads as treacherous as these broken relationships. In adapting Rick Moody's 1994 novel, Taiwanese director Lee uses a refined color palette that retains its delicacy on DVD, and elicits fine performances: Kline and Allen excel among the adults, and Ricci and Wood dig deep into teen angst.

Hot Bonus: The "making of" supplement offers astute comments on adaptation from Lee and Moody.

Key Scene: Kline outraged at catching his daughter (Ricci) having sex, while wearing a Nixon mask yet, walks her home in the snow, then carries her tenderly like he did when she was a child. In this single, transitory moment, Lee—without using dialogue—distills the timeless tension between the necessity and the heartbreak of growing up.

Igby Goes Down (2002)

Starring: Kieran Culkin, Ryan Phillippe, Claire Danes, Amanda Peet
Directed by: Burr Steers

Thank DVD for giving this darkly hilarious but little-seen heartbreaker a new life. Culkin, Macaulay's brother, touches a raw nerve as Igby, a rich Manhattan teen with a nutso dad (Bill Pullman), a dysfunctional mother (Susan Sarandon), and a young Republican brother (Phillippe). Like Holden Caulfield in J. D. Salinger's *The Catcher in the Rye*, Igby is adolescent rebellion incarnate. Igby crashes in a loft where his adulterous godfather (Jeff Goldblum) stashes his mistress (the sublime Peet). Igby is thrilled when she jumps his bones, but he can see she's a junkie with a fragile hold on her disguise as a free spirit. Steers, in a strong debut as director and screenwriter, clearly knows this world of privilege.

Hot Bonus: Steers and Culkin discuss Igby's origins.

Key Scene: Sarcasm is Igby's best weapon against emotional battering, and he's never better at it than he is with Danes as a know-it-all Bennington student who asks: "You call your mother Mimi?" Says Igby, "Heinous One is a bit cumbersome, and Medea was already taken."

Imitation of Life (1959)

Starring: Lana Turner, Sandra Dee, Susan Kohner, Juanita Moore
Directed by: Douglas Sirk

Guys who hate chick flicks need to get over it for this one. Director Sirk is a master of expressionism. Go ahead and laugh at the tearjerking plot—a black girl (Kohner) passes for white to the horror of her mother (Moore), a maid in the employ of a actress (Turner) who gives her a home and unthinking condescension. "It never occurred to me that you had any friends," says Turner, who believes Moore's life has been rightly devoted to caring for her and her daughter (Dee). Kohner and Moore were Oscar nominated, but the genius here isn't the acting; it's the way Sirk uses shadows and reflections and objects that separate people to show the greed and racism that make the American dream an imitation of life.

Hot Bonus: The DVD transfer is nowhere what it should be, but it will open your eyes to Sirk's gifts. The better bonus would be to watch Todd Haynes's 2002 tribute to Sirk, *Far From Heaven*.

Key Scene: It still stings to hear Kohner's white boyfriend (Troy Donahue) ask, before smacking her, "Is it true? Is your mother a nigger?"

In a Lonely Place (1950)

Starring: Humphrey Bogart, Gloria Grahame

Directed by: Nicholas Ray

A smashing Bogart film hardly anyone knows about. The DVD transfer in luscious black-and-white makes it even better. Bogie plays Dixon Steele (great name), a cynical Hollywood screenwriter who drinks hard and fights harder. Facing a murder charge involving a hatcheck girl, Dix gets involved with Laurel (Grahame), a neighbor in his apartment complex who provides him a false alibi and then wonders if he did it. So do we. Director Ray, whose marriage to Grahame was unraveling during filming, investigates themes of love and loneliness in true film noir fashion. A classic.

Hot Bonus: A fascinating segment on the film's restoration.

Key Scene: Grahame's good-bye: "I lived a few weeks while you loved me."

In Cold Blood (1967)

Starring: Robert Blake, Scott Wilson

Directed by: Richard Brooks

Now that Blake has beat his own murder rap, it's fascinating to watch him in the film role of his career as Perry Smith, the killer who entered the home of the Clutter family in Holcomb, Kansas, on November 15, 1959, and with the help of another ex-con, Dick Hickock (Wilson), massacred everyone for the sake of ten thousand dollars. Directed by Brooks with strict adherence to Truman Capote's nonfiction novel, the film is a haunted and haunting docudrama.

Hot Bonus: The film is left to speak for itself, but Conrad Hall's cinematography makes the transfer to DVD with its stark brilliance intact. Ditto the superb score by Quincy Jones.

Key Scene: The camera prowling the Clutter house in the aftermath of the killings.

In the Bedroom (2001)

Starring: Sissy Spacek, Tom Wilkinson, Marisa Tomei, Nick Stahl

Directed by: Todd Field

Here's a thriller, based on the Andre Dubus short story *Killings*, that transcends thrills to become a heart-stopping personal drama. A Maine doctor (Wilkinson) and his music-teacher wife (Spacek) don't approve of their son (Stahl) having an affair with an older woman (Tomei). Then he is murdered. Time passes but doesn't heal wounds; revenge, or at least the thought of it, does. If you want to see a master class in acting, watch Spacek and Wilkinson go at each other in scenes that shake the foundation of what appeared to be a solid marriage. Field, in a beautifully judged directing debut, denies audiences an easy out. That's part of the film's resonant power.

Hot Bonus: The addition of the French audio track wouldn't usually catch my attention, but try watching a few scenes that way, and the jarring effect illustrates how quintessentially American this film is.

Key Scene: The opening with Tomei and Stahl rolling in the high grass. It's the end of summer, and the small Maine village that runs on lobster and canning dollars exudes a shimmering Andrew Wyeth–like delicacy. Thanks to luminous camerawork from Antonio Calvache, the scene adds to the impact of what will follow. The DVD transfer doesn't miss a nuance.

In the Company of Men (1997)

Starring: Aaron Eckhart, Matt Malloy, Stacy Edwards

Directed and written by: Neil LaBute

Want to have an argument with a date? Pop this baby into your DVD player and get ready. Playwright LaBute, in his film-directing debut, watches as two execs—slick Chad (Eckhart) and nerdy Howard (Malloy)—decide to liven up a business trip by dating a deaf typist (Edwards), making her care, and then dumping her. Is it a revenge on the opposite sex or a reflection of something ever darker? Even on the DVD, you can see the sparks fly.

Hot Bonus: LaBute and the actors react to the way they think some critics and audiences misunderstood the film.

Key Scene: The moment when Chad reveals his real agenda.

In the Heat of the Night (1967)

Starring: Rod Steiger, Sidney Poitier
Directed by: Norman Jewison

OK, this racial drama didn't really deserve to beat *Bonnie and Clyde* and *The Graduate* for the Best Picture Oscar, but it still stirs up a heady brew of atmosphere and mystery—all in evidence on the

DVD. Steiger deserved his Oscar as the gum-chewing Mississippi redneck sheriff who arrests a black man (Poitier) for a local murder, only to find that he is Virgil Tibbs, a detective from Philadelphia who makes more in a week that the sheriff does in a month. "They call me Mr. Tibbs," says Poitier with all the tempered rage and nobility that made him a star. Jewison wisely doesn't push the film's racial politics, which makes it that much more powerful.

Hot Bonus: Jewison and Steiger entertainingly at cross purposes on separate commentary tracks.

Key Scene: The two cops, grudging comrades at last, saying good-bye at the railroad station. As Steiger's sheriff would say, "Oh, yeah."

In the Line of Fire (Special Edition) (1993)

Starring: Clint Eastwood, John Malkovich, Rene Russo

Directed by: Wolfgang Petersen

Along with *Unforgiven*, *Tightrope*, and *Million Dollar Baby*, this is the best acting of Eastwood's career. He plays Frank Horrigan, a Secret Service agent trying to protect the president from assassin Mitch Leary (Malkovich is venomously funny and scary). Frank is haunted by his failure to take a bullet for President Kennedy years ago. Director Petersen knows how to blend tension and humor, and the film benefits from the gifts of editor Anne Coates, cinematographer John Bailey, and composer Ennio Morricone. The DVD comes alive with their talents. But this is Eastwood's show. He

even hits on a female agent (the charming Russo) by playing jazz piano, claiming he once dueted with Nixon on "Moonglow."

Hot Bonus: Two documentaries on the Secret Service that you should watch before the movie.

Key Scene: In a menacing phone call, Mitch tells Frank he's going to shoot the prez right in front of the agent's eyes. "That's not gonna happen," says Frank in a terrific "make my day" Clintism.

In the Mood for Love (Two-Disc Special Edition) (2000)

Starring: Maggie Cheung, Tony Leung
Directed by: Kar Wai Wong

Has a movie ever smoldered more ravishingly with the promise of sex? And the fact that the gifted director Wong Kar-wai doesn't deliver any hardcore action only heightens the steamy atmosphere. The smallest details are eroticized on Criterion's resonant DVD transfer—the whisper of silk, the click of high heels, the splash of raindrops on a cheek. The place is Hong Kong, the time is 1962, and Chow (Leung), a journalist, and Li-zhen (Cheung), a secretary, have both moved into the same apartment building. There's a hitch. Chow and Li-zhen are married to other people. And another hitch: his wife and her husband are having an affair. In a movie justly prized for its look, it's still the tender longing written on the faces of Leung and Cheung that cuts deepest.

Hot Bonus: The documentary on the making of the film is a rare treat.

Key Scene: When Chow and Li-zhen rehearse what they will say to her husband and his wife and nearly break down in the process, the nearness of these two people in a crowded city works a potent spell.

Incredibles, The (Two-Disc Collector's Edition) (2004)

Starring: The voices of Craig T. Nelson, Holly Hunter, Jason Lee, Brad Bird
Directed by: Brad Bird

It's not every animated movie that deals with midlife crisis, marital dysfunction, child neglect, impotence fears, fashion faux pas, and existential angst. But this Pixar Oscar winner is not like any animated movie you've ever seen. And this electrifying DVD transfer proves it. For starters, there's no talking fish, insects, or toys. Director-writer Bird animates human beings. Take Mr. Incredible, voiced with beleaguered bluster by Nelson. This legend in spandex brushes off a kid fan who later becomes his archnemesis, Syndrome

(Lee never loses the hurt-boy tremor in his adult voice). Besieged by frivolous lawsuits from people who claim they never wanted to be rescued, Mr. Incredible enters a superhero-protection program and becomes Bob Parr, suburban slob, with wife Helen, the former Elastigirl (Hunter's vocal turn is a marvel of feisty comic nuance). But faking who they are puts pressure on the Parr kids. The baby just bawls. But teen daughter Violet (Sarah Vowell) hates hiding her ability to be invisible. And son Dash (Spencer Fox) itches to use his gift for supervelocity. The situation is primed to explode. And does it ever. When Mr. Incredible squeezes into his old costume, suddenly it's James Bond, Indiana Jones, and the X-Men all rolled into one kick-out-the-jams spectacle.

Hot Bonus: A new animated short, *Jack-Jack Attack.*

Key Scene: The entrance of short, sassy ball of fire Edna Mode (Bird does her voice, hilariously), the guru of fashion insults who designs indestructible costumes for the Incredibles that would drive Q, the old boy from the 007 films, back to his outmoded drawing board.

Independence Day (Two-Disc Special Collection) (1996)

Starring: Will Smith, Bill Pullman, Jeff Goldblum

Directed by: Roland Emmerich

Inane plot, incredible special effects. That's a no-brainer when it comes to acquiring a DVD that will blow all your system's whistles. Spaceships loom over the earth. The White House is destroyed, which pisses off the president (Pullman). It's up to a Marine pilot (Smith) and a computer genius (Goldblum) to take out those aliens by having Smith fly in to the mothership with a deadly computer virus devised by Goldblum. Oh, who cares? It's the special effects that count, and these doozies deservedly won an Oscar.

Hot Bonus: There's a whole extra disc full of them. But Easter Egg fans—true gluttons for punishment—will want to select "Data Console" on Disc 2. That will lead you to an alien ship, which will give you only seven seconds to type in a secret password (7-4 and Enter), which will lead to

hidden treasures, including—you guessed it—more explosions.

Key Scene: Boom goes New York. Boom, L.A. Boom, D.C. But my fave moment is when Smith punches an alien in his ugly-butt face.

Indiana Jones Trilogy, The (Box Set)

Starring: Harrison Ford
Directed by: Steven Spielberg

That's all three films so far about Indy and his adventures, plus a fourth disc filled with special features, including new interviews with director Spielberg, star Ford, and producer George Lucas that qualify as one truly hot bonus. As for the films themselves:

• *Raiders of the Lost Ark* (1981)—Here retitled *Indiana Jones and the Raiders of the Lost Ark*, the 1981 blockbuster presents in peak condition for DVD. Lucas wanted to do a film about a daredevil archeologist set in the 1930s and modeled on that era's cliffhangers. So he sketched a plot that pits his hero, Ford's Indiana Jones, against the Nazis, who are searching for the Ark of the Covenant—a golden chest said to contain the broken tablets of the Ten Commandments. Hitler is hot to have it. Indy, armed only with a bullwhip and his sharp-tongued lady love (Karen Allen), sets out to save the ark for democracy. Historical fact does not figure prominently in these proceedings, but fun does. Ford's satirical approach to macho is priceless. And Spielberg stages an exultantly good-humored, headon, rousing series of traps and escapes, raising movie escapism very near the level of art.

Hot Bonus: A segment on the stunts.

Key Scene: The opener with Indy being chased by a giant ball inside a jungle cave. A true demo classic

• *Indiana Jones and the Temple of Doom* (1984)—This film took a few hits from critics who complained about the gore in the 1984 sequel. Children are whipped and kicked, and one man's heart is torn out of his chest as a sacrifice. The public lapped it up anyway (the PG-13 rating was practically invented so this blockbuster wouldn't get an R rating). Tame by today's standards, the movie makes a lively DVD with Indy hooking up with singer Willie Scott (Kate Capshaw, the future Mrs. Spielberg) and Short Round (Ke Huy Quan), a twelve-year-old Vietnamese handful. They both help Indy restore a sacred stone to an Indian village. "Fortune and glory, kid," Indy tells Short Round, as succinct an explanation as you'll find for the film's appeal, and Indy's.

Hot Bonus: Some tough comments from Spielberg, who admits he may have gone overboard with this one.

Key Scene: Another knockout opener and DVD showstopper with Capshaw singing "Anything Goes," mostly in Chinese, at a Shanghai nightclub in 1935. Indy is among the listeners. A brawl ensues, causing Indy, Willie, and Short Round to flee via roadster, trimotor plane, life raft, and elephant.

• *Indiana Jones and the Last Crusade* (1989)–This installment found humor and heart to make up for the hyper and harsh *Temple of Doom*. The 1989 followup boasts a secret weapon: Sean Connery cast way against type as Indy's dad Dr. Henry Jones, a professor of antiquity whose nose was buried in musty parchments when his young, motherless son needed a guiding hand. When Dad goes missing while searching for the Holy Grail, it's Indy to the rescue. Sonny boy is barely through the window when Dad beans him with a vase. "Junior?" he asks. "Don't call me 'Junior,'" moans Indy. Ford and Connery have a mocking rapport that makes the film, along with Spielberg's nonstop stunts. Watch out for the plane in the tunnel.

Hot Bonus: A segment on the sound mix, at its peak in this episode.

Key Scene: Strafed by an enemy plane, Dad starts to chase a flock of sea birds with his umbrella. But Indy's exasperation turns to admiration when the rising flock blinds the pilot and sends the plane into a nosedive.

Infernal Affairs (2002)

Starring: Tony Leung, Andy Lau, Eric Tsang
Directed by: Andrew Lau and Alan Mak

This thrilling Hong Kong police thriller throbs with action and suspense that don't miss a beat on the DVD transfer. Yan (Leung) is a cop who has lived undercover in a triad gang for a decade and is near meltdown. Ming (Lau) is a gangster passing as a police officer and nearing his own breaking point. Neither realizes who the other is. But both the internal-affairs cops and the gang boss Sam (comic actor Tsang, in a menacingly effective change of pace) know a mole has infiltrated their midst. Yan turns to the only cop privy to his secret identity, his supervisor (the superb character actor Anthony Wong). It's a tribute to co-directors Lau and Mak that nothing about this movie follows the rules. Asian superstars Leung and Lau give bruising performances as the film prowls the night with a lit-by-neon intensity that illuminates those guilty of betrayal. This is a movie that gets its hooks into you early, and no chance is it letting go.

Hot Bonus: "Confidential File" offers a behind-the-scenes look at the film that spawned two sequels and an American remake directed by Martin Scorsese and starring Leonardo DiCaprio and Jack Nicholson.

Key Scene: The film rubs our noses in violence yet stings the most in the agonizing quiet of a climactic rooftop scene between Leung and Lau.

Innocents, The (1961)

Starring: Deborah Kerr, Pamela Franklin, Martin Stephens
Directed by: Jack Clayton

Ghost stories don't come scarier or kinkier than this stunning film co-adapted by Truman Capote from Henry James's *The Turn of the Screw*. It's taken years for Clayton's neglected classic to find its way to disc in its widescreen glory with black-and-white images from camera wiz Freddie Francis that will make you think you're seeing things, which is exactly the point. Kerr gives her best performance as Miss Giddens, the governess hired by a wealthy estate owner (Michael Redgrave) to care for his niece Flora (Franklin) and nephew Miles (Stephens). Without even a rustle of her Victorian petticoats, Kerr lets us see the erotic interest in Redgrave that Miss Giddens keeps repressed. When the angelic children start showing signs of being influenced by the "ghosts" of the previous governess Miss Jessel (Clytie Jessop) and the Irish groom Peter Quint (Peter Wyngarde)–depraved lovers found dead under mysterious circumstances–Kerr's repression erupts into sexual hysteria.

Hot Bonus: The beautiful DVD transfer is reward enough. But if this film grabs you as it did me, try finding *The Nightcomers* (available only on VHS, not DVD), the 1972 prequel in which no less an actor than the late Marlon Brando played the evil Quint. It's quite a ride.

Key Scene: The passionate kiss that Kerr forces on the little boy, who she believes is the reincarnation of Quint. It's a killer, whether you believe the ghosts are real or the figments of a deranged imagination.

Insider, The (1999)

Starring: Al Pacino, Russell Crowe, Christopher Plummer
Directed by: Michael Mann

60 Minutes producer Lowell Bergman (Pacino) and star correspondent Mike Wallace (Plummer) agree to back research scientist Jeffrey Wigand (Crowe), recently fired by the cigarette company Brown and Williamson, when Wigand agrees to go on TV and blow the whistle on his former bosses for maintaining nicotine at addictive levels.

Characters shed no blood, merely principles. But check out this visceral DVD and watch director Mann turn a moral issue into riveting suspense. Wigand didn't count on smear campaigns, death threats, and 60 *Minutes* refusing to air his interview out of fear that retaliation from Big Tobacco could kill the sale of CBS to Westinghouse. Crowe cuts to the heart of an isolated man. Like his acting, the film will pin you to your seat.

Hot Bonus: A breakdown of the scene in which Bergman and Wigand first meet, with comments from Crowe and Pacino.

Key Scene: A suicidal Wigand raging at Bergman, who in turn rails against Wallace for backing down. Says Wallace, "I'm seventy-eight years old, and I do not intend to spend the rest of my career wandering through the wilderness of National Public Radio." Ouch! No wonder Wallace protested.

Insomnia (2002)

Starring: Al Pacino, Robin Williams, Hilary Swank

Directed by: Christopher Nolan

Pacino stars as Will Dormer, an LAPD cop—shadowed by allegations of evidence tampering—who is sent to an Alaskan town to investigate the murder of a teenage girl. From the opener, with Will flying over a glacier, director Nolan establishes an atmosphere of cold unease, and the DVD transfer is so good you can feel the chill. Will, whose last name, Dormer, evokes sleep, isn't getting any. A local cop (Swank) tells Will this is the season of the midnight sun, when darkness just doesn't fall. Loosely based on an austere 1997 Norwegian film of the same name, the remake uses the sun as a metaphor for a conscience that won't sleep. This helps Williams, as a novelist suspected of the murder, push Will's buttons. A ravaged Pacino lets us see this alert cop come wrenchingly unglued. It's a brilliant performance in a film that will keep you up nights.

Hot Bonus: Something uniquely out-of-sync: Nolan presents another version of the film in the order he shot it, and makes comments accordingly.

Key Scene: A thrilling chase for cop and suspect across moving logs.

Internal Affairs (1990)

Starring: Richard Gere, Andy Garcia

Directed by: Mike Figgis

Critics can be asses. I sure was when I wrote off this firecracker as just another cop flick. Watch it again—that's what DVDs are for—and something darkly funny and disturbing emerges. British director Figgis has a ball with the deliciously untamed script by Henry Bean. Gere, in what is still his most riveting performance, plays a womanizing LAPD cop who has been married four times and has eight kids, with another on the way. As gentle as Mr. Rogers with the tykes, Gere heads a ring of rogue cops and moonlights as a hit man. It's up to Internal Affairs officer Garcia to catch him breaking the rules. What Figgis catches, with diabolical skill, is a vision of Los Angeles as hell with Gere as Satan with a badge. It's a killingly seductive portrait of bottomless evil.

Hot Bonus: No extras, but the DVD enhances appreciation for Figgis's score, which riffs as impressively as the script on the theme of corruption.

Key Scene: The chases and shootouts can't compare to Gere hurling the worst insult he can think of at Garcia: "You selfish yuppie."

Interview With the Vampire (Special Edition) (1994)

Starring: Tom Cruise, Brad Pitt, Kirsten Dunst

Directed by: Neil Jordan

Jordan's film of Anne Rice's bestseller is a major movie with major problems. But the good parts look spectacularly creepy on DVD. Rice initially resented the casting of Cruise as the blond, Byronic vampire Lestat, but relented when she saw the movie. The plot grabs you as soon as Lestat puts the bite on Louis de Pointe du Lac—that's Pitt as a Louisiana plantation owner. Pitt has the tougher role as the story's conscience, but his whining against the dying of the light is not as riveting as Lestat's wicked rage. Director Jordan uses his star duo to play characters willing to trade their souls for eternal youth and beauty. It's a sly joke that works for the movie, especially when they both end up in 1994 San Francisco, where Lestat gets hooked by his first earful of rock—Guns 'n' Roses sing the Stones.

Hot Bonus: Dunst talks proactively about making the film when she was only twelve, playing the child vampire who murders indiscriminately. "I want some more," says Claudia after her first taste of blood.

Key Scene: For controversy, you can't beat the homoerotic moment when Cruise first lifts Pitt in the air and bites into his throbbing artery.

Intolerance (Restored Version on Kino) (1916)

Starring: Lillian Gish, Constance Talmadge

Directed by: D. W. Griffith

Griffith's silent film contains the seeds of every cinematic epic from DeMille to Spielberg. Spanning four historical periods (ancient Babylon, Jerusalem at the time of Christ, France in 1572, and America in the early 1900s), the film means to show social and political intolerance through the ages. Released in several versions (Kino's DVD is the keeper), the film is a textbook on the possibilities of cinema. Griffith thought film had no limits. It's hard to watch this DVD and not catch his enthusiasm.

Hot Bonus: An introduction shot by Orson Welles in the 1980s.

Key Scene: The indelible shot of Gish rocking a cradle.

Invasion of the Body Snatchers (1956)

Starring: Kevin McCarthy, Dana Wynter

Directed by: Don Siegel

Classically subversive sci-fi and a barely veiled satire of the communist witch hunts run by Senator Joe McCarthy, as residents of the small town of Santa Mira, California, find themselves duplicated by alien pods if they make the mistake of falling asleep. It's the actor McCarthy's doctor who discovers the plot to colonize the world with glazed, unfeeling pod people. Director Siegal, criminally underrated, makes every one of the film's eighty minutes count—all crisply delivered on this black-and-white, widescreen DVD.

Hot Bonus: An interview with Kevin McCarthy, who tells about the framing device that had to be added to the film to explain things that needed no explanation. It's still as scary as hell.

Key Scene: The pod on the pool table, an amorphous mass that suddenly becomes—you!

Invasion of the Body Snatchers (1978)

Starring: Donald Sutherland, Brooke Adams, Leonard Nimoy

Directed by: Philip Kaufman

A remake that can stand with the original, thanks to Kaufman's deft direction and the blend of mirth and malice in the script by W. D. Richter. The film is shot in extravagant, nightmarish color that makes the transfer to DVD in high style.

This time Sutherland is the doc, a health inspector who finds the alien pods have spread to San Francisco. Leonard Nimoy shows up as the shrink who is on the pods' side. It figures. All that's missing is the symbolic subtext that gave the original that extra something.

Hot Bonus: Feature-length commentary by Kaufman.

Key Scene: Sutherland's final open-mouthed scream. Yike.

Iron Giant, The (Special Edition) (1999)

Starring: The voices of Vin Diesel, Jennifer Aniston, Eli Marienthal

Directed by: Brad Bird

Bird scored a huge box-office hit with *The Incredibles* five years later, but hardly anyone lined up for this animated gem. So get crackin' to this DVD. Based on a novella from Brit poet Ted Hughes, the film tells the story of Hogarth (child actor Marienthal), a boy from Maine—circa 1957, the Sputnik era—who befriends a fifty-foot robot from space. Diesel, of all people, grunts the giant with humor and heart, as Hogarth keeps his waitress mom (Aniston) and the feds at bay until he can pacify this war machine.

Hot Bonus: The segment on Diesel as the voice of the giant.

Key Scene: Hogarth saving the Giant from bumping into high-voltage wires.

Irreversible (2002)

Starring: Monica Bellucci, Vincent Cassel, Albert Dupontel

Directed by: Gaspar Noé

You can't see this shocker without arguing with whoever is watching it with you. Many DVD viewers will hit the eject button during the nine-minute scene in which Alex, played by the beautiful Bellucci, is beaten and anally raped in the lurid red light of a Paris underpass as Noé stations his camera and watches. But the film is too artfully crafted to write off as exploitation. French director Noé tells his story backward, beginning with Alex's lover (Cassel) and her ex-boyfriend (Dupontel) taking revenge on the rapist. We then watch Alex leave a party and head for the underpass. Noé then tracks further back to Alex and Marcus in bed, naked and tender with each other. Bellucci and Cassel, married in real life, give these scenes an erotic charge laced with affection and delicacy. It's this harmony that time destroys, except, of course, in Noé's film, where time is at the mercy of the filmmaker.

Hot Bonus: The movie leaves you too spent to have time for extras.

Key Scene: The rape. To see it is to absorb it, even against your will.

Italian Job, The (2003)

Starring: Mark Wahlberg, Charlize Theron, Edward Norton

Directed by: F. Gary Gray

It's a performance to remember: eager to please, thrumming, and able to negotiate every curve in the dumb script. And the bod, though relatively small and boxy, is still hot. Not bad when you think that this baby has been performing since the 1950s. The object of my affection is the Mini Cooper, the car that steals every scene in this tricked-out remake of a heist flick that was already flat and formulaic in 1969. Now it's Wahlberg behind the wheel of a new Mini—BMW relaunched the line in 2002—causing traffic hell in Los Angeles as he speeds off with gold bullion worth $34 million. Theron is the babe safecracker. And Norton, as the villain, gives the best performance by a noncar. But it's the Minis in action that make this DVD a winner.

Hot Bonus: What else? The Mighty Minis featurette.

Key Scene: Watching three Minis outrun a helicopter, burn rubber over the Hollywood Walk of Fame, and bump down stairs into a subway station is to experience this flick's DVD's one true kick.

It's a Wonderful Life (1946)

Starring: James Stewart, Donna Reed, Henry Travers

Directed by: Frank Capra

Struck from the original print—muddy duplicates have littered our TV screens for decades—this DVD lets you see Capra's classic with new and appreciative eyes. Stewart gives one of his most memorable performances as George Bailey, the small-town husband and father who sees himself as such a failure that he considers suicide on Christmas Eve. It takes an angel (Travers), out to earn his wings, to make George see the truth. This must be the darkest holiday film ever, which is why it's worth cherishing.

Hot Bonus: A documentary on the making of the film, just after Stewart and Capra returned from World War II.

Key Scene: When the bell rings and the angel gets his wings.

Jackie Brown (Two-Disc Special Edition) (1997)

Starring: Pam Grier, Robert Forster, Samuel L. Jackson, Robert De Niro

Directed by: Quentin Tarantino

Tarantino's hip, humane, and heartfelt film of Elmore Leonard's crime novel *Rum Punch* gives blaxploitation queen Grier another chance to strut her foxy stuff. Just to see her fill a red dress and fire a gun makes this a DVD event. As an aging flight attendant picked up by the feds for running scams for her lowlife boss (Jackson in peak form), Grier's Jackie is caught in a trap that brings her close to a surprisingly romantic bail bondsman (Forster, Oscar nominated). De Niro as a hood and Bridget Fonda as Jackson's stoner girl-toy both score points. But it's the relationship between Grier and Forster that anchors the film. Most audiences considered this a disappointing followup to *Pulp Fiction.* A close look at the DVD proves just how wrong they were.

Hot Bonus: Outrageous Tarantino commentary, including his reaction to criticism, notably from Spike Lee, about his use of the word "nigger."

Key Scene: The look on Forster's face as Grier simply walks toward him, but the Chicks with Guns video (expanded on Disc 2) is hard to resist.

Jacob's Ladder (1990)

Starring: Tim Robbins, Elizabeth Pena
Directed by: Adrian Lyne

The hallucinatory power of Lyne's psychological horror film comes through like gangbusters on this DVD transfer. Robbins is excellent as Jacob Singer, the divorced Vietnam vet working as a New York mailman and shacking up with a carnal co-worker (Pena). Then he starts having nightmare visions of war, personal tragedy, demons in the subway. Is this the result of army drug experiments or Jacob's own breakdown? Finding out is what makes repeated viewings of the film so rewarding and scary.

Hot Bonus: Three deleted scenes that actually add to the film's resonance.

Key Scene: The ending. Once seen, you can't stop arguing about it.

Jason and the Argonauts (1963)

Starring: Todd Armstrong, Nancy Kovack, Honor Blackman
Directed by: Don Chaffey

Don't let the stiff acting worry you. The DVD is a tribute to the monumental talents of stop-motion animator Ray Harryhausen. As Armstrong's Jason and his Argonauts sail the seven seas to find the mythical Golden Fleece, Harryhausen trots out a series of visual wonders that will knock you out.

Hot Bonus: A rare interview with Harryhausen by John Landis.

Key Scene: The monstrous seven-headed Hydra is a killer creation, but when the monster's teeth transform into living skeletons with thrusting swords, you are seeing Harryhausen at his peak.

Jaws (Two-Disc Thirtieth Anniversary Edition) (1975)

Starring: Roy Scheider, Richard Dreyfuss, Robert Shaw
Directed by: Steven Spielberg

Just when you thought it was safe to buy any old DVD version of Spielberg's landmark fish story—and that includes the spiffy Twenty-Fifth Anniversary Edition—along comes this killer-diller with a perfection of picture and dimensional sound that lays waste to all previous efforts. From the first thump of the John Williams score (his best) to the initial attack of the great white shark (we don't see Jaws, just his pretty victim zig-zagging in the water), the movie hits you hard and keeps on hitting. It doesn't matter if you know the story by heart: New England sheriff (Scheider) joins up with a fish expert (Dreyfuss, hilarious) and an old salt (Shaw, potently scary and hammy) to stop the great white from gobbling up the tourists. The DVD gives each terrifying moment a bracing freshness. Don't even bother to own a DVD player if you don't put this classic in your collection.

Hot Bonus: The retrospective documentary is detailed and dazzling, but the sight that really pleases is of Spielberg, then twenty-eight, making the movie that would make his career, despite being up against a production in which everything on set goes wrong, including the mechanical shark.

Key Scene: Scheider's face as he watches the shark—all twenty-five feet and three tons of him—rise out of the water. His deadpan remark to Shaw is perfect: "You're gonna need a bigger boat."

Jerry Maguire (Two-Disc Special Edition) (1996)

Starring: Tom Cruise, Renee Zellweger, Cuba Gooding Jr.
Directed and written by: Cameron Crowe

Cruise is at the top of his game as the me-first sports agent who learns a lesson in love from a single mom (Zellweger) and her young son (Jonathan Lipnicki). Sounds icky. Instead it's irresistible, thanks in part to the actors—Gooding won an Oscar as a manic football player who forces Jerry to repeat his mantra: "Show me the money!" And thanks mostly to Crowe. There are other lines that entered the culture, including Cruise telling Zellweger, "You complete me." But Crowe's talents as a writer and director don't come from one-liners. He knows how to get inside the heads of his characters. Nothing here to give your DVD system a workout, but what this gift of a romantic comedy does to your heart you won't forget.

Hot Bonus: Alert to Easter Egg fanatics: Hit the Title button on your remote any time during the film, and you'll get to watch the actors as they record their commentary tracks.

Key Scene: Cruise's climactic apology to Zellweger. She listens and then tells him, "You had me at hello."

JFK (Special Edition) (1991)

Starring: Kevin Costner, Tommy Lee Jones, Gary Oldman

Directed by: Oliver Stone

DVD is the best forum for digging into director Stone's exploratory, compulsively watchable attempt to prove that Lee Harvey Oswald (Oldman) did not act alone in gunning down John Kennedy as his motorcade passed through Dallas's Dealey Plaza on November 22, 1963. It's a grab bag of conspiracy theories, but no less riveting for that. Just don't mistake it for gospel. Costner stars as New Orleans DA Jim Garrison, who believes the Warren Commission covered up the involvement of a cabal of right-wing homosexuals, led by businessman Clay Shaw (a chilling Tommy Lee Jones). It's information overload when Stone mixes in the real (newsreels, photos, the shocking Zapruder film) with the imagined (reenactments staged on actual sites and shot from different angles and in varying speeds and tints). The camera work and editing are outstanding, creating a vast cyclorama that sets the mind reeling with possibilities and provocations.

Hot Bonus: *Beyond JFK: The Question of Conspiracy* continues the debate.

Key Scene: Garrison's final moment in court, in which he argues his case against Shaw, is a real barnburner. It's too bad it never happened: Garrison's assistant made the closing argument, and the DA wasn't even there to hear the swift verdict that cleared the defendant. Stone has turned what he considers the crime of the century into a dishonest search for truth.

Journey to the Center of the Earth (1959)

Starring: Arlene Dahl, James Mason, Pat Boone

Directed by: Henry Levin

A terrific adventure, based on a Jules Verne story, about a geologist (Mason, slyly witty) and his student (Boone—yes, he sings) who plan to explore the center of the earth through a volcano in Iceland. The gorgeous Dahl joins the expedition as a widow who knows how to get a rise out of Mason in ways you don't expect in family fare. Shot partly in the Carlsbad Caverns, the film has been restored to its colorful widescreen splendor

on DVD. And the score by the great Bernard Herrmann (*Vertigo*) provides an added kick.

Hot Bonus: A jaw-dropping documentary on the restoration.

Key Scene: The climax, involving a giant phallic funnel.

Jules and Jim (Two-Disc Special Edition) (1962)

Starring: Jeanne Moreau, Oskar Werner, Henri Serre

Directed by: François Truffaut

To see a great film honored by a great DVD transfer, which is what Criterion does to Truffaut's hilarious and heartbreaking love story in this restored high-definition transfer, supervised by cinematographer Raoul Coutard, is a special pleasure. Truffaut went mad crazy with the camera, just as Catherine (Moreau in a definitive portrayal of feminine mystery) goes mad crazy with Jules (Werner), a shy German writer, and Jim (Serre), his French counterpart. Set between the two world wars, this portrait of a three-way gone bewitchingly right and tragically wrong stands the test of time.

Hot Bonus: Among the many extras, the archival audio interview with Truffaut and a new one from Moreau are invaluable.

Key Scene: Catherine leaping into the Seine when Jules and Jim leave her out of their conversation about Strindberg. Then there's Moreau singing "Le Tourbillion," for no reason except enchantment.

Jurassic Park (Collector's Edition) (1993)

Starring: Sam Neill, Laura Dern, Jeff Goldblum, Richard Attenborough

Directed by: Steven Spielberg

Michael Crichton's speculative 1990 bestseller gives Spielberg a juicy two-pronged premise: What if dinosaur DNA extracted from mosquitoes trapped in amber allows extinct species to be cloned for a theme park? And what if these reconstituted behemoths don't like being exploited behind electrified fences? But who cares about plot? It's the dinosaurs that count, and on this spectacular DVD transfer they are up and breathing, honking, hunting, and stampeding. Stan Winston and his tech team use live-action models, puppets, hydraulics, and dazzling computer-generated imagery to get them there. Estimates of the film's cost range from $60 million to $100 million—big money back in 1993—but who's counting when a movie delivers a rush of pure elation? *Jurassic* is a grabber for the best of reasons: You won't believe your eyes.

Hot Bonus: Listening to Spielberg in a prepro-duction meeting telling his team how to make the dinosaurs look scary and real.

Key Scene: A twenty-foot T. rex picks up a tour-ist car in its jaws and hurls it into a tree before chas-ing after another vehicle like thunder on the hoof.

Kill Bill: Vol. 1 (2003)

Starring: Uma Thurman, Lucy Liu, Vivica A. Fox, Daryl Hannah

Directed and written by: Quentin Tarantino

Like a dick-swinging flasher, Tarantino whips out all his obsessions: kung-fu fighting, samu-rai flicks, spaghetti westerns, and babe-on-babe swordplay. And the DVD delivers the action with eye-popping vigor. Thurman is a gorgeous tower of power as the Bride, beaten and left for dead at her Texas wedding by her former boss, Bill (David Car-radine, heard but not seen), and her sisters at Di-VAS (Deadly Viper Assassination Squad), played by Liu, Fox, and Hannah. When the Bride wakes up from a coma four years later, she plots her ven-geance. The flashiest fight comes when Thurman takes on Liu and her yakuzas at the House of Blue Leaves, a nightclub that turns into a battlefield. Who else but Tarantino would pack a film with his fetishes for ultraviolence, Thurman's feet, and music from Nancy Sinatra to RZA? And who else could pull it off? *Vol. 1* is damn near as good as he thinks it is.

Hot Bonus: A "making of" documentary that leaves you hungry for more.

Key Scene: When O-Ren's teen bodyguard Gogo Yubari swings her mace, the sounds whiz around your head with all the muscle a DVD can muster. But that's just a warmup for the moment when the Bride cuts through O-Ren's army to face her nemesis alone. The scene is shot in the falling snow with a tenderness that belies the gore.

Kill Bill: Vol. 2 (2004)

Starring: Uma Thurman, David Carradine, Michael Madsen, Daryl Hannah

Directed and written by: Quentin Tarantino

The DVD powerhouse that is *Vol. 2* begins with Thurman's Bride looking glam in a top-down convertible, addressing the audience like an aveng-ing angel out of a 1940s Hollywood melodrama: "When I arrive at my destination, I am gonna kill Bill." You better believe it. Carradine, the hero of the 1970s TV series *Kung Fu*, invests the role with a purring, seductive danger. He and the siz-zling Thurman make the sexual tension between

Bill and the Bride palpable. Tarantino, stingy with dialogue in the action-mad *Vol. 1*, gives the actors words they can feast on. Madsen is killer good as Bill's kid brother, who buries the Bride alive. And Hannah mesmerizes as the eye-patch-wearing diva who engages Thurman in a showstopping cat-fight. Of course, all roads lead to the Bride's face-off with Bill and the daughter she didn't know she had. Tarantino builds the tension so artfully that we want to return to the film, both volumes, to shake out its secrets.

Hot Bonus: A great deleted scene featuring Bill in China.

Key Scene: The Bride's fight training under the cruel tutelage of Pai Mei, the white-bearded monk played by Chinese legend Gordon Liu. You might want to remember the five-point exploding-heart trick.

Killer, The (1989)

Starring: Chow Yun-Fat, Danny Lee, Sally Yeh

Directed by: John Woo

The Hong Kong bullet ballet that put director Woo on the map in America looks and sounds terrific on the Criterion DVD (the version on Fox Lorber is much inferior). Chow Yun-Fat, at his moody, menacing best, stars as a hit man who ac-cidentally blinds a singer (Yeh) during a nightclub shootout and then decides to pull one more job to pay for an operation to restore her sight. It's his magnificent obsession. One catch. A cop (Lee) is on his tail.

Hot Bonus: Commentary from Woo and pro-ducer Hark Tsui isn't always to easy to understand (due to accented English), but it's worth the effort.

Key Scene: The finale, set in a church, is charged with religious symbolism, over-the-top vi-olence—often in slow motion—and those signature Woo doves flying around dodging bullets. The scene, like the film, is masterful.

Killers, The (Double-Disc Set) (1964)

Starring: Lee Marvin, John Cassavetes, Angie Dickinson, Ronald Reagan

Directed by: Don Siegel

Loosely based on a short story by Ernest Hemingway, the movie was originally planned for television but was deemed too violent. So began its march into theaters and legend and now a DVD that looks deliciously lurid. The legend part involves Reagan in his last film role as a crime lord whose mistress (Dickinson) double-crosses him with a race-car driver (Cassavetes). This is Reagan's first and only villain role. He resisted doing the film, but he is fiercely good in it. Marvin, ever watchable, and Clu Gulager play hit men who knock off Cassavetes. When the target offers no resistance, the killers decide to find out why. That's how the story plays out. It's a grabber.

Hot Bonus: Criterion offers up Robert Siodmak's 1946 version of the Hemingway story, much different but equally good. And a twenty-minute take on the tale from then–film student Andrei Tarkovsky. Great stuff.

Key Scene: Reagan slapping around Dickinson must be seen to be believed. Reagan hated the film and quit acting to enter politics. Two years later he was elected governor of California.

Killing Fields, The (1984)

Starring: Sam Waterston, John Malkovich, Haing S. Ngor

Directed by: Roland Joffe

Based on the memoirs of *New York Times* reporter Sydney Schanberg, this devastating human drama centers on the U.S. evacuation of Phnom Penh when Schanberg (Waterston), working with photographer Al Rockoff (Malkovich), persuades his Cambodian translator Dith Pran (Ngor) to stay behind with him. A dangerous situation becomes worse when Dith falls into the hands of the genocidal Khmer Rouge. The DVD, which preserves the Oscar-winning cinematography of Chris Menges, holds you in thrall.

Hot Bonus: Director Joffe (this was his debut in features) relates the story of Ngor, himself a Cambodian doctor, who won an Oscar for reliving incidents of hiding, slave labor, and torture much like his own. In 1996, Ngor was shot to death outside his Los Angeles apartment by members of a street gang who demanded the locket around his neck. The locket contained a picture of his wife, who died in the gulag rather than betray him.

Key Scene: The killing fields themselves, showing the human toll taken by the Khmer Rouge. These scarring images are unshakable.

Kind Hearts and Coronets (1949)

Starring: Alec Guinness, Dennis Price, Joan Greenwood

Directed by: Robert Hamer

Robin Williams has been threatening for years to remake this classic Guinness farce from Ealing Studios. Please make him stop. Why remake perfection? Price plays the black sheep of an Edwardian family. He wants to inherit the dukedom but must first dispatch the eight relatives who stand in his way. Since they are all—men and women—played with black-comic brilliance by Guinness, the fun never stops. The DVD preserves it all.

Hot Bonus: A bio on Guinness, who became a global star with this movie.

Key Scene: Guinness as Lady Agatha.

King Creole (1958)

Starring: Elvis Presley, Dolores Hart, Walter Matthau, Carolyn Jones

Directed by: Michael Curtiz

One of the rare Presley movies that doesn't seem like it was made on his lunch hour while he was half asleep. The director's chair was occupied by Curtiz—just sixteen years after he gave us the immortal *Casablanca*—and the source material (Harold Robbins's *A Stone for Danny Fisher*) was unusually hard-boiled. Presley shows his dramatic chops as a hot-tempered club singer in New Orleans who gets a taste of evil from a hood (Matthau, playing it tough) and his boozing moll (Jones). It's all Elvis can do to stick with a good girl (Hart, who joined a cloistered convent five years later).

Hot Bonus: Not much by way of extras. The real bonus is the vivid rendering of the black-and-white picture on the DVD and erotic immediacy of the Elvis voice, not matched onscreen until 1964's *Viva Las Vegas*.

Key Scene: Presley singing "Trouble," with lyrics ("I was born standing up/and talkin' back") that bring out a demo-worthy fire in his eyes.

King Kong (Two-Disc Collector's Edition) (1933)

Starring: Fay Wray, Robert Armstrong, Bruce Cabot

Directed by: Merian C. Cooper and Ernest B. Schoedsack

This greatest of all creature features took forever to find its way to DVD as Warner worked on the black-and-white restoration and *Kong* freak Peter Jackson, whose own 2005 remake reflects a fan's passion (forget, please, the 1976 travesty) helped prepare the "making of" feature on this edition. To have the King on disc at last is a movie lover's dream. From the moment Hollywood filmmaker Carl Denham (Armstrong) lands on Skull Island with blonde starlet Ann Darrow (Wray), you are hooked whether this is the first time you see the film or the fiftieth. Leading man Cabot puts the moves on Ann, but she's Kong's girl—the beauty being offered as a bridal sacrifice to the beast. He wants only to protect her, even after Denham brings the fifty-foot ape to New York and exploits him as the Eighth Wonder of the World. Wray, who died in 2005, screams and sparks immortally with King, who generates romantic and erotic yearning through the stop-motion animation genius of Willis O'Brien. Max Steiner's score is a major asset as well. But it's Kong, whether taking on monsters, mechanical or human, who remains a classic screen creation. This belongs in every DVD collection.

Hot Bonus: A seven-part documentary, *RKO Production 601: The Making of Kong, the Eighth Wonder of the World*, vies for best in show with a deleted scene of Kong in a spider pit.

Key Scene: It has to be King atop the Empire State Building, putting down Wray after taking one last romantic sniff and swinging at World War I fighter planes that ultimately shoot him down. Or did they? As Denham says in the film's famous last line: "It was beauty killed the beast."

King of Comedy, The (1983)

Starring: Robert De Niro, Jerry Lewis, Sandra Bernhard

Directed by: Martin Scorsese

Here's a movie way ahead of its time, as was *Network*, receiving a long-overdue DVD transfer that makes it ripe for rediscovery. Scorsese and screenwriter Paul D. Zimmerman offer a caustic treatise on celebrity obsession. De Niro is crazed perfection as Rupert Pupkin, a comic wannabe who kidnaps a famous TV talk-show host (a hardnosed, revelatory Lewis) with the help of a neurotic rich girl (Bernhard, fiercely funny). His ransom demand: A spot on Lewis's talk show. Scorsese blurs fantasy and reality until we enter a deranged

world that has become shockingly like our own.

Hot Bonus: A retrospective documentary that includes deleted footage involving Lewis, who creates a wickedly accurate portrait of a celebrity exhausted and straitjacketed by success.

Key Scene: De Niro and Bernhard tying Lewis up in her candlelit Manhattan apartment, offering wild compliments to the man they are threatening.

King of New York (Special Edition) (1990)

Starring: Christopher Walken, Laurence Fishburne, David Caruso

Directed by: Abel Ferrara

Ferrara's visionary crime film—it's a bookend to *Scarface* that hardly anyone knows about—gets a DVD treatment that befits its New York gutter lyricism. Walken is astonishing as drug lord Frank White, just out of prison and setting up operation at Manhattan's Plaza Hotel (great to see it in pristine form before progress spoiled it). Frank has a hip wingman in Jimmy Jump (Fishburne, before he got grand) and three cops (Caruso, Wesley Snipes, and Victor Argo) breathing hotly down his neck. Ferrara makes the tensions—criminal, political, and racial—palpable. And Walken, whether he's doing a happy dance to freak out disloyal cohorts or finishing off a cop at another cop's funeral, gives a performance that deserves to be legendary.

Hot Bonus: A documentary that deals with Ferrara, a true maverick of the modern cinema, who is still lacking the respect he deserves. Get crackin'.

Key Scene: The finale set in Times Square. It's brutal poetry.

Kingpin (1996)

Starring: Woody Harrelson, Bill Murray, Randy Quaid

Directed by: Bobby and Peter Farrelly

There's something rowdy, crude, and hilarious about a Farrelly brothers movie, especially when they're not playing it safe (*Fever Pitch*). *Kingpin* dips delightfully low for laughs. Did you ever try milking a bull? Harrelson is a bowling champ until his right hand gets mangled by competitors, instigated by Murray (his drink of choice is Tanqueray and Tab), who is reason enough to buy the DVD. So Harrelson decides to manage an Amish farmer (Quaid) with a real bowling hand and take on Murray for big stakes in Reno. John Q. Public was deeply offended. You will be delighted.

Hot Bonus: The Farrellys speak, not always coherently. But their talk about Murray's ad-libs are priceless. And thanks for the dirty, deleted scenes.

Key Scene: Murray rolling a ball with his comb-over flying up in salute.

Kinsey (Two-Disc Special Edition) (2004)

Starring: Liam Neeson, Laura Linney, Peter Sarsgaard

Directed and written by: Bill Condon

Oscar snubbed *Kinsey*. Don't you make the same mistake. The DVD comes fully loaded with extras. But the movie is the thing. Back in 1948, Alfred Kinsey, a biology prof at Indiana University, published *Sexual Behavior in the Human Male*, a scientific tome that did *Harry Potter* numbers at bookstores. By the time his book on women arrived in 1953, the sexual revolution was born and Kinsey was blamed for the whole damned kinky mess. OK, that's a simplistic intro to a complex career. But it works to set up *Kinsey*, the scrappy biopic from director-writer Condon. Neeson is monumental as Kinsey. And Linney is his match as Clara, the student who marries her professor. Sex research puts a strain on marriage, especially when Kinsey associate Clyde Martin (the excellent Sarsgaard) beds the boss and then the wife. Kinsey wanted to snap the public out of sexual ignorance. So does Condon's movie. You'll be shocked at how far we haven't come.

Hot Bonus: Condon has more material here than one two-hour movie can hold, so we get twenty deleted scenes, plus an alternative ending.

Key Scene: The coda, in which various animals have sex in various ways to the tune of Cole Porter's "Let's Do It," speaks witty volumes.

Klute (1971)

Starring: Jane Fonda, Donald Sutherland

Directed by: Alan Pakula

Fonda was at the height of her politicized "Hanoi Jane" period when she stepped up to accept a well-deserved Oscar for playing a high-priced call girl stalked by a psychopath. Her acceptance speech was apolitical. Her movie is not. As the decades pass, *Klute* still speaks to the challenges facing women in terms of independence and exploitation. Not bad for a thriller, thanks to the psychological intricacies director Pakula builds into the story of a small-town detective (an implosive Sutherland) who treks to the Big Apple to get answers from Fonda, who wrote letters to his missing friend. The DVD transfer captures Pakula's resonant play of light and shadow.

Hot Bonus: A documentary about shooting the film in New York.

Key Scene: The film is famous for the moment of Fonda looking yawningly at her watch while a john sweats and grunts on top of her.

Knife in the Water (Two-Disc Special Edition) (1962)

Starring: Leon Niemczyk, Jolanta Umecka, Zygmunt Malanowicz

Directed by: Roman Polanski

Criterion pays homage to director Polanski's first feature film by bringing the black-and-white images a DVD sharpness that demands attention. Just as Polanski did in those days when this Polish wunderkind showed what he could do with only three roles—a writer, his wife, and the blond, boyish hitchhiker they pick up—and the boat on which the three take a sail. Sexual tension pours out of every frame until violence erupts. No fair telling how.

Hot Bonus: Disc 2 contains eight short films that Polanski made between 1958 and 1962. But the nonhot bonus—there have been many complaints—involves Polanski's insistence that the DVD scan function be disabled to preserve the momentum of the film. For true students of cinema, that lack of access is a misstep to which Criterion should never have agreed.

Key Scene: The first appearance of the hitchhiker's pocket knife. It's too bad that you can't stop the film and examine it.

Kundun (1997)

Starring: Tenzin Thuthob Tsarong, Tencho Gyalpo

Directed by: Martin Scorsese

Spirituality is at the heart of this delicate film, an anomaly in Scorsese's career. Working from a script by Melissa Mathison, Scorsese tells the tale of the fourteenth Dalai Lama from the time he is reincarnated in the body of a two-year-old boy and on through to the Chinese invasion of Tibet in 1950 and the Buddhist leader's eventual exile in India. Roger Deakins has photographed scenes of staggering beauty, and Scorsese links them in a manner that breaks all the rules of hurtling narrative that you find in *Raging Bull* and *GoodFellas*. *Kundun* builds slowly but is impossible to shake.

Hot Bonus: In addition to bringing these immaculate images to life, the DVD also adds dimension to Philip Glass's evocative score.

Key Scene: The Dalai Lama's haunting vision of being surrounded by the bodies of dead monks, who held to a pacifist ideal in the face of invasion.

L.A. Confidential (1997)

Starring: Russell Crowe, Guy Pearce, Kevin Spacey, Kim Basinger

Directed by: Curtis Hanson

One of the great movies of the 1990s is now one of the great DVDs of the new century. The film digs its way into Hollywood's criminal past, circa 1953, and locates parallels to the racial bonfires that still ignite present-day Los Angeles. Director Hanson keeps things blazing with action, eroticism, and humor. And Brian Helgeland's screenplay distills James Ellroy's 1990 novel without losing its crackle and density. Crowe is Bogart-tough as a loose-cannon cop who likes to beat up on men who beat up on women. Pearce plays his nemesis, a college-boy officer pushing for reform in the department but not above bedding a hooker (Oscar-winner Basinger), whose pimp (the excellent David Strathairn) decks out his girls to look like movie stars. Spacey steals every scene he's in as a sergeant with a knack for arresting celebrities and making himself a celeb in the process. The convoluted plot lines all intersect at the Nite Owl, where Pearce leads the attack against the black suspects, despite lack of evidence, and the precinct's captain (a diabolical James Cromwell) reveals his own dark secrets.

Hot Bonus: A "making of" featurette that really tells you something.

Key Scene: The deserted motel shootout will work your DVD sound system to the max. And remember the name Rollo Tomassi.

La Bamba (1987)

Starring: Lou Diamond Phillips, Esai Morales, Rosanna DeSoto

Directed by: Luis Valdez

DVD does full justice to the look and the sound of this biopic about singer Ritchie Valens (Phillips doing the acting superbly, Los Lobos doing the vocals likewise). Valens rose from the poverty of the California barrio, where he lived with

his mother (DeSoto) and hotheaded half-brother (Morales), to achieve stardom with the title song and such hits as "Donna," written for his wife, played by Danielle von Zerneck. Valens's young life was snuffed out in the same plane crash that killed Buddy Holly and the Big Bopper on February 3, 1959, which adds poignancy to the story.

Hot Bonus: One of the many commentary tracks features Phillips, who touchingly remembers his meeting with Valens's mother, who momentarily thinks he is her son reborn.

Key Scene: Phillips performing the title number is truly memorable and works even better on the extras in a video that intercuts Phillips on camera with Los Lobos doing the version that is heard but not seen onscreen.

La Cage Aux Folles (1978)

Starring: Ugo Tognazzi, Michel Serrault

Directed by: Edouard Molinaro

Serrault won the Cesar, France's Oscar, in this hugely successful comedy, playing an aging female impersonator in a St. Tropez nightclub, run by his lover (the relatively butch Tognazzi). Director Molinaro was Oscar-nominated for keeping the plot fizzing like a French farce. The colors come through explosively on DVD, as does the relationship between the gay lovers. The film became the source for a hit Broadway musical and an American remake (*The Birdcage*), but the original has its own charms.

Hot Bonus: English subtitles that you actually can read.

Key Scene: Tognazzi giving Serrault lessons on how to walk like a man.

La Dolce Vita (Two-Disc Collector's Edition) (1960)

Starring: Marcello Mastroianni, Anita Ekberg, Anouk Aimee

Directed by: Federico Fellini

Remastered and restored to the visual splendor that dazzled and shocked audiences five decades ago, Fellini's landmark film is in every way a DVD event. The film opens with the startling shot of a chopper carrying a statue of Jesus over the city of Rome and then descends to the party animals covered by a gossip writer (Mastroianni at his peak). The paparazzi (the name inspired by the photographer named Paparazzo in the film) chase a movie star (Ekberg) who Mastroianni follows around the monuments of Rome until her husband (Lex Barker, Ekberg's real husband back then) decks him. Fake visions of the Blessed Virgin vie with orgies and suicides in the great filmmaker's odyssey to find feeling in a world disconnected from it.

Hot Bonus: The extras on Disc 2 are more like glimpses into Fellini's world and nothing like in-depth analysis. But critic Richard Schickel offers trenchant comments about the film's themes and symbols, including the beach scene at the end featuring the dead fish with judgment in his stare.

Key Scene: No contest—Mastroianni and Ekberg in the Trevi fountain, an image of seductive decadence that has stood the test of time.

La Femme Nikita (Special Edition) (1990)

Starring: Anne Parillaud, Tcheky Karyo, Jean-Hugues Anglade

Directed by: Luc Besson

Here's a wildly seductive and erotic French thriller about a street punk (the dazzling Parillaud) who is turned into a government assassin in short skirts and heels. Bless the French. Forget the deadly 1993 American remake (*Point of No Return*) and the ill-cast TV series. Besson's original is the keeper as Nikita is trained to kill by Karyo—with an assist from the legendary Jeanne Moreau as a beauty consultant—and still manages a few romantic interludes with Anglade between assignments. Besson has a sexy way with action, which the Special Edition from MGM captures beautifully.

Hot Bonus: The extras aren't much, but there is an EasterEgg—an outtake—if you go to the Special Features menu and press the left arrow.

Key Scene: Nikita, decked out in leggy splendor at a restaurant, being forced to go into killing mode while wearing evening clothes.

La Strada (Two-Disc Special Edition) (1954)

Starring: Anthony Quinn, Giulietta Masina, Richard Basehart

Directed by: Federico Fellini

It's not that Criterion merely improves the look and sound of movies for DVD, it performs an act of resurrection. So often seen in unwatchable TV prints, Fellini's landmark love story emerges with all its brutal, heartbreaking spirit. And Nino Rota's haunting score is a gift to the ear. Masina (Fellini's wife) is perfection as Gelsomina, the simpleton sold by her mother to a circus strongman (Quinn, ideally cast as a raging bull) who treats her like a sex slave until he realizes he loves her. *La Strada* won the first competitive Oscar race for Best Foreign Film, but Masina—in an unforgettable performance—wasn't even nominated. Sheesh.

Hot Bonus: There is scholarly commentary from Peter Bondanella, but a fifteen-minute intro from Martin Scorsese cuts right to the chase.

Key Scene: Gelsomina beating her drum. Masina is born for the closeup, and here she rivals Chaplin.

Lady Eve, The (1941)

Starring: Barbara Stanwyck, Henry Fonda, Charles Coburn

Directed and written by: Preston Sturges

If anyone ever asks you why Sturges is such a celebrated maker of romantic comedies, show anyone this DVD and get out of the way. Just to watch Fonda, as a rich young rube who studies snakes, get suckered by Stanwyck and her card-shark father (the irreplaceable Coburn) is to experience delight that turns to a deeper pleasure when seen-it-all Stanwyck (never better or hotter, by the way) falls for the dope for real.

Hot Bonus: A video introduction from Peter Bogdanovich sets up the film beautifully. But the real treasure here is the digital transfer from Criterion that gives the black-and-white picture a bracing freshness.

Key Scene: Stanwyck extending her leg for Fonda to tie the strap on her shoe. Simple, huh? But in the hands of Sturges and two sublime stars, the moment packs an erotic charge that can leave you dizzy from the heat of it.

Lady From Shanghai, The (1947)

Starring: Orson Welles, Rita Hayworth, Everett Sloane

Directed and written by: Orson Welles

Everyone knows Welles's *Citizen Kane* is a masterpiece; now meet another one, admittedly lesser known, from the boy wonder of cinema. Welles plays an Irish sailor who hires on the yacht owned by Sloane, a wealthy lawyer with a hot wife (Hayworth) who'd like to see him dead and the sailor in her bed. The DVD transfer of this film noir captures all the Welles visual dazzle. But it's the subtext that draws you in. Welles's marriage to Hayworth was disintegrating at the time, and he did everything to expose her as a predator. He had her cut the long, red hair that helped make her a screen siren. The short blonde bob she wears in this film emphasizes what's artificial about her. And in the aquarium scene, he poses her next to killer fish. The wonderfully odd thing is that Welles's toxic valentine to his soon-to-be-ex-wife results in one of her best performances and his best films.

Hot Bonus: Commentary from Welles confidante Peter Bogdanovich.

Key Scene: The climax in the Hall of Mirrors, featuring a shootout involving Welles, Hayworth, and Sloane that finds the truth in shattered reflections. The sequence stands with the landmarks of film noir.

Lady Vanishes, The (1938)

Starring: Margaret Lockwood, Dame May Whitty, Michael Redgrave
Directed by: Alfred Hitchcock

A Hitchcock classic about a sweet old lady (the delightful Dame May) who disappears on a train bound for London from the Swiss Alps. Only one passenger (the lovely Lockwood) remembers seeing her. Everyone else, including Redgrave (dad to Vanessa and Lynn) as a music student, can't recall the old lady at all. Suspense master Hitchcock mixes one of his most exciting cocktails of mirth and menace. You'll find many cheap DVDs of this black-and-white film on the market, but the only beauty comes from Criterion, which does the master proud in terms of image and sound.

Hot Bonus: Film historian Bruce Eder discusses the plot, most helpfully when the topic turns to the political subtext in this pre–World War II release.

Key Scene: The writing on the train window.

Hit the freeze-frame button on your remote. It's a moment worth careful study.

Last Emperor, The (Director's Cut) (1987)

Starring: John Lone, Joan Chen, Peter O'Toole
Directed by: Bernardo Bertolucci

Bertolucci's epic about Pu Yi (Lone), who became the last Manchu emperor of China in 1908 at the age of three and ended his life as a park attendant in Beijing in 1967, won every Oscar it was nominated for, including Best Picture. But until this Director's Cut DVD, which now runs 218 minutes in comparison to the 160-minute theatrical release, no one has really seen the film or been able to fully appreciate Lone's extraordinary performance. Prepare to be wowed. With the blanks filled in, the film now resonates with rich detail, from the emperor's childhood in the Forbidden City (cameras were allowed to shoot inside), where he was tutored by a nonconformist Scot (O'Toole), to his playboy exile in Tianjin, where he sings "Am I Blue?" at a cocktail bar and watches his wife (Chen) develop a taste for opium and women, to his five years in a Russian prison camp, to his Communist reeducation and eventual return to China as an ordinary man. In tandem with cinematographer Vittorio Storaro, Bertolucci sweeps you up on waves of history and ravishing visuals.

Hot Bonus: Nothing, but that extra 58 minutes is a true gift.

Key Scene: It's hard to forget the young emperor toddling out of his palace to greet the huge army waiting to salute him.

Last House on the Left, The (1972)

Starring: David Hess, Lucy Grantham, Sandra Cassel
Directed by: Wes Craven

Twelve years before Craven dreamed up the nightmare of Freddy Krueger on Elm St., the director earned his hardcore props with this gory tale of two teen girls (Cassel and Grantham) who run into a gang of escaped cons led by Krug (Hess), and end up being tortured, raped, and murdered. The twist comes when the gang must seek help at a house that belongs to one of the dead girls' parents (Gaylord St. James and Cynthia Carr). A revenge ensues that upped the ante on gore for its time (you still want to turn away). What is even more surprising is how this crude, low-budget shocker—it's Craven's take on Ingmar Bergman's 1960 *The Virgin Spring*—can hit you so hard. The film still looks raw and rough-edged on DVD, which adds to its power.

Hot Bonus: For some, the never-before-seen footage of the disembowelment sequence will be a treat. I prefer the Craven commentary without pictures.

Key Scene: Craven intercutting the rape and murder with the parents planning a surprise party for their daughter.

Last of Sheila, The (1973)

Starring: James Mason, Raquel Welch, Dyan Cannon, Richard Benjamin

Directed by: Herbert Ross

One of those movies you probably never heard of that finds a home on DVD and wins a new audience. The DVD transfer captures the lush trappings of six Hollywood types invited on a yacht in the south of France by a producer (James Coburn) who is determined to nail one of them for the murder of his wife. But it's the cleverness of the script—by actor Anthony Perkins and legendary Broadway composer Stephen Sondheim—that draws you in. Director Ross gets the most of a juicy cast, notably Cannon as a killer agent, Welch as a bitchy movie star, Mason as a fading director, and Benjamin as the lowest man in the pecking order—a screenwriter.

Hot Bonus: Spiky commentary from Benjamin, Cannon, and Welch.

Key Scene: Benjamin with the puppets.

Last of the Mohicans, The (Expanded Director's Cut) (1992)

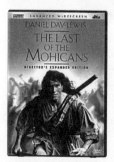

Starring: Daniel Day-Lewis, Madeleine Stowe

Directed by: Michael Mann

Director Mann adds scenes to make the DVD the final outpost for what he always wanted to see onscreen. From the

opening, in which Day-Lewis's Hawkeye fires his phallic rifle at the camera, you can tell Mann's film version of James Fenimore Cooper's classic 1826 novel will not be stuffy. Though Mann takes time to lay out the alliances of the French and Indian War—the Algonquin and New York's colonial militia with the British and the Huron with the French—the action is richly detailed and thrillingly staged. Hawkeye is the orphaned son of English settlers, raised by his adoptive Mohican father, Chingachgook (Indian activist Russell Means). Cooper scholars may be poleaxed to see Hawkeye talking street ("I ain't your scout, and I sure ain't no damn militia") and wet-kissing Cora Munro (Madeleine Stowe), the daughter of a redcoat colonel (Maurice Roeves) who wants him hanged for sedition. But the lithe Day-Lewis, sporting shoulder-length locks, is riveting. He and the radiant Stowe can make the cornball credible—even a farewell scene at a waterfall where he vows to find her again, "no matter how long it takes, no matter how far."

Hot Bonus: Nothing, except to the expanded footage. It's a fair trade-off.

Key Scene: The siege of Fort William Henry and the Huron ambush on the British are bloody marvels of action filmmaking.

Last Picture Show, The (Definitive Director's Cut) (1971)

Starring: Jeff Bridges, Timothy Bottoms, Cybill Shepherd, Ben Johnson

Directed by: Peter Bogdanovich

One of the seminal films of the 1970s is newly restored on DVD with seven additional minutes of footage. Shot in black-and-white by the brilliant Robert Surtees, the film is based on Larry McMurtry's novel about life in a small Texas town in 1951. Deemed a shocker at the time because of its depiction of naked pool parties and rampant sexuality, the film has aged into something more resonant and meaningful. Johnson won an Oscar as Sam the Lion, the town's conscience. Cloris Leachman also took home the gold as a coach's wife having an affair with a boy (Bottoms). All the performances hit the mark, with a special nod to Ellen Burstyn, as Shepherd's sexy, seen-it-all mama. Bogdanovich, paying tribute to his favorite directors—Howard Hawks, John Ford, Orson Welles—made a film that deserves classic status.

Hot Bonus: A retrospective documentary with the actors and Bogdanovich, a witty film historian who puts the film in fascinating context.

Key Scene: Bottoms and Bridges, who is about to leave for Korea, attend the last show at a moviehouse about to shut its doors as folks stay home with the TV. And as the boys watch a scene from

Hawks's Texas-set western, *Red River*, Bogdanovich sums up the end of an era with an aching tenderness.

Last Tango in Paris (1973)

Starring: Marlon Brando, Maria Schneider
Directed by: Bernardo Bertolucci

Presented uncut on DVD, the film that the late critic Pauline Kael famously called "the most powerfully erotic movie ever made" doesn't come as such a shock in the age of Internet porn. What still makes it devastating is Brando's Oscar-nominated performance (it was his followup to *The Godfather*) as Paul, a middle-aged American in Paris who takes up with Jeanne (Schneider), a twenty-year-old stranger who meets him for bouts of anonymous sex in an empty apartment. Pained by his wife's suicide, Paul is using sex as an escape. But as Bertolucci and cinematographer Vittorio Storaro move past the body heat to what simmers inside, Brando delivers a monologue on Paul's life that sounds much like his own. This is confessional cinema at its most raw and rending.

Hot Bonus: An eight-page booklet that talks about the controversy sparked by the film. Brando, who died in 2004, never did a commentary track.

Key Scene: Fans remember the "butter" sequence. And I can't forget the way Brando says, "Quo vadis, baby?" to Schneider as she exits the flat. Use your DVD remote to rerun the moment when Brando does that last tango in a Paris club, dropping his pants and all his defenses. His daring amazes.

Last Temptation of Christ, The (Special Edition) (1988)

Starring: Willem Dafoe, Harvey Keitel, Barbara Hershey
Directed by: Martin Scorsese

And you think Mel Gibson had problems with *The Passion of the Christ*? In filming Nikos Kazantzakis's 1955 novel about a "human" Jesus Christ who fantasizes about climbing down from the cross and rejoining the world of men as husband and lover to Mary Magdalene (Hershey), Scorsese sparked controversy, which Gibson did as well, and box-office rejection, which Gibson did not. It's doubtful that Scorsese's astounding film, with its violent, sexual Jesus (Dafoe in a towering performance) will ever gain mass acceptance. But this expertly transferred DVD—doing justice to Michael Ballhaus's camerawork and Peter Gabriel's score—should take it a step further. Scorsese and

screenwriter Paul Schrader use Christ's humanity and divinity to explore the eternal struggle of spirit and flesh. The attempt is not to titillate or blaspheme. The working-class accents of Judas (Keitel) and the apostles are meant to bring an immediacy to the film, even if they do jar the ear. But if Scorsese sometimes stumbles on his unorthodox journey through the gospels, he has still made a film of prodigious power, meeting every challenge with probing intelligence and passionate heart.

Hot Bonus: Incisive commentary from Scorsese, Dafoe, Schrader, and Jay Cocks, plus behind-the-scenes camcorder footage shot by Scorsese himself.

Key Scene: Besides the last temptation, the sequence in which Jesus throws the moneylenders from the temple has the visceral force of *Mean Streets*.

Last Waltz, The (Special Edition) (1978)

Starring: The Band
Directed by: Martin Scorsese

The last word on the unbeatable thrill of live rock & roll: Scorsese captures the 1976 farewell concert by the original lineup of the Band (Robbie Robertson, Richard Manuel, Rick Danko, Levon Helm, Garth Hudson). Featuring famous pals such as Bob Dylan, Neil Young, and Van Morrison, the film boasts kinetic, crisply lighted camerawork and foot-of-the-stage sound—all busting through gloriously on the DVD. When Band guitarist Robbie Robertson trades blazing licks with Eric Clapton in "Further On up the Road," you feel like you're in the crossfire. But this is also a movie about what it takes to make the music. In casual interviews, the Band talks about the madness and the miracles of touring: shoplifting food to stay alive, playing in shithole clubs, meeting bluesman Sonny Boy Williamson. The movie was supposed to be about the end of the road for the Band; instead, it celebrates—with grit and class—rock & roll as a way of life.

Hot Bonus: A dazzling transfer and audio remix, which also includes archival outtakes and scrappy commentary from Scorsese and Robertson.

Key Scene: The single-camera, slow-zoom sequence of Muddy Waters belting "Mannish Boy" and the Band's thundering version of "The Night They Drove Old Dixie Down."

Laura (1944)

Starring: Gene Tierney, Dana Andrews, Clifton Webb, Vincent Price
Directed by: Otto Preminger

It's impossible to think back on this most romantic and haunting of film noirs without hearing David Raksin's theme in your head ("Laura is a face in the misty night. . . .") and seeing that detective (Andrews) fall in love with the portrait of the murdered Laura (Tierney, never lovelier). The DVD transfer is the best friend this moody classic ever had. Webb's performance as Waldo Lydecker, the acid-tongued columnist who shaped Laura into a society darling, is a paradigm of stinging wit and twisted passion. Finding out who took a shotgun blast to the face of a beauty thought to be Laura is only part of the fun. You can feel the seeds of Hitchcock's *Vertigo* in every frame.

Hot Bonus: A biographical portrait of Tierney is almost as haunting as the film itself. And a sequence showing Laura's rise to fame—cut from the original release—has been restored to its teasing elegance.

Key Scene: The cop, in love with the portrait of the girl he thinks is a corpse, watching his dream girl walk right into his life.

L'Avventura (Two-Disc Special Edition) (1960)

Starring: Monica Vitti, Lea Massari, Gabriele Ferzetti
Directed by: Michelangelo Antonioni

Antonioni's immaculate realization of an enigma gets an immaculate DVD transfer from Criterion (one of the bonus features shows how the film was restored). The puzzle part relates to Massari, who disappears when she and her friends visit a remote island. They search until her lover (Ferzetti) and best friend (Vitti) drift into their own relationship. Antonioni is without peer at using landscapes to define characters and the emotional gaps between them. The film's slow pacing is a chore to some, but the images and their provocative subtext cast a lasting spell.

Hot Bonus: The essays and commentary go over old ground—pompously. But Jack Nicholson, who starred in Antonioni's *The Passenger*, offers his thoughts about the Italian master and reads from his writings.

Key Scene: Vitti, looking like an Italian Barbra Streisand, posed against a huge black rock—the very essence of existential angst.

Lawrence of Arabia (Two-Disc Special Edition) (1962)

Starring: Peter O'Toole, Alec Guinness, Omar Sharif
Directed by: David Lean

One of the most literate and jaw-droppingly stunning films ever made. The DVD looks great, but seeing this baby on a big screen the size of Pluto is even better. Working from a script by Robert Bolt, Lean tells the story of T. E. Lawrence (O'Toole), a British adventurer who united Arab tribes against the Turks during World War I. O'Toole's mesmerizing, mercurial performance holds you through vast chunks of history and Lawrence's collapse into sadism and delusion. One journalist (Arthur Kennedy) called him "the most shameless exhibitionist since Barnum and Bailey." With footage restored under Lean's supervision in 1989, the film dazzles you with its imagery (a lit match against a blazing sun). The Academy rewarded Freddie Young's cinematography and Maurice Jarre's score, plus an Oscar for Best Picture. If anyone asks you what epic filmmaking is, point here.

Hot Bonus: A retrospective doc offers insights into the restoration, but the archival materials on Lawrence are especially compelling after the movie.

Key Scene: The transfixing sight of Omar Sharif, as Sherif Ali, riding toward Lawrence across the desert, looking at first like a speck on the horizon and then slowly emerging as a figure to prodigious size.

League of Their Own, A (Two-Disc Special Edition) (1992)

Starring: Geena Davis, Tom Hanks, Madonna, Rosie O'Donnell
Directed by: Penny Marshall

Seen from a NOW perspective, this fact-based story of the All-American Girls Baseball League, begun in 1943 to sub for the men at war, has the makings of a sassy feminist manifesto. Not in this movie. Director Marshall keeps it light with lots of heart, which makes for a colorful, fun DVD. Davis stars as a dairy worker recruited by a caustic baseball scout (Jon Lovitz is pure joy in too brief a role) who wants players to be lookers. Madonna is also on the team as All-the-Way-Mae. She delivers a font of ball jokes in tandem with teammate O'Donnell. Hanks scores as their boozehound manager, who talks to the girls while taking the longest pee in film history. Marshall captures the camaraderie of these women in ways that rip the film out of its clichéd roots.

Hot Bonus: Forgive the Madonna music video. The rest of the extras are fine, especially the interviews with Marshall that deal with the real players. Though the teams continued playing ball until 1954, the girls mostly marched back into the kitchen when their Johnnies came marching home. It wasn't until 1988 that they were honored by the Baseball Hall of Fame.

Key Scene: Hanks helplessly screaming, "There's no crying in baseball," when he reduces one of his players to tears.

Leave Her to Heaven (1945)

Starring: Gene Tierney, Cornel Wilde, Jeanne Crain, Vincent Price

Directed by: John M. Stahl

Colors pop off this DVD with such clarity you might miss the plot points. They concern a psycho rich girl (an Oscar-nominated Tierney) who dumps her fiancé (Price) for a hunky author (Wilde), but can't drop her incestuous fascination with her dead daddy or her need to murder anyone who gets too close to Wilde. Stahl directs with melodramatic bravura. It's hard to forget Tierney on horseback, scattering her father's ashes to the wind in New Mexico. It's harder to forget the images for which cinematographer Leon Shamroy deservedly won an Oscar.

Hot Bonus: There's a solid feature on the color restoration, but give a listen to the bitchy commentary from actor Darryl Hickman, who played Wilde's handicapped brother. He royally disses Tierney's acting. Maybe he's still bitter about the scene in which she calmly watches him drown.

Key Scene: The drowning is a keeper, but so is Tierney throwing herself down a flight of stairs to abort her newborn baby.

Leaving Las Vegas (1995)

Starring: Nicolas Cage, Elisabeth Shue

Directed by: Mike Figgis

Who the hell wants to watch a DVD about a Vegas hooker who finds time between rough trade to fall for a screenwriter bent on taking the last booze train to oblivion? You do, if you want to experience a uniquely hypnotic and haunting love story sparked by Cage and Shue at their career best. He won an Oscar; she didn't, but should have. Directed by the gifted Figgis from an autobiographical 1991 novel by John O'Brien, who committed suicide two weeks after signing the deal to turn his novel into a film, *Vegas* is a tragedy that unspools with astonishing buoyancy and sneaky wit, as if no one told the lovers their story should be depressing. Uncut and unrated on DVD, the film plays like a neon-lit jazz piece (Figgis composed the evocative musical score) that resounds with an ardent defiance of despair.

Hot Bonus: A hidden page menu, featuring notes on the production.

Key Scene: By a motel pool, she sits on his lap, removes her swimsuit top and pours champagne over her breasts to entice him to her body with alcohol. It's the movie's saddest joke.

Leopard, The (Three-Disc Special Edition) (1963)

Starring: Burt Lancaster, Alain Delon, Claudia Cardinale

Directed by: Luchino Visconti

Criterion outdoes itself with this DVD presentation of Visconti's sumptuous epic of Italy in the 1860s. The film is based on Giuseppi di Lampedusa's acclaimed novel about the decline of the aristocracy as the middle class rises with Garibaldi's Risorgimento. Lancaster gives a towering performance as the powerful Sicilian prince known as Il Gattopardo (the Leopard). He arranges the marriage of his nephew (Delon) and a wealthy merchant's daughter (Cardinale) to hold on to a life that he knows is fading. The DVD shows off Delon and Cardinale at the height of their talent and beauty. Visconti, an aristocrat transformed by Marxism, creates a succession of dazzling images to illustrate the clash of cultures and the prince's loss. It's a joy to see the original 187-minute Italian version, restored in 1983, that honors the vision of Visconti and the camera genius of Giuseppe Rotunno.

Hot Bonus: Besides thorough, witty commentary by film scholar Peter Cowie, Criterion presents the alternate 161-minute English-language version that was released in the United States in 1963. The Italian version is much preferable, but hearing Lancaster's own voice somehow completes the picture.

Key Scene: The ball, a classic sequence that lasts nearly an hour and ends this masterpiece on a note of regret and lavish, richly detailed excess.

Lethal Weapon (Director's Cut) (1987)

Starring: Mel Gibson, Danny Glover

Directed by: Richard Donner

You can buy all four *Lethal Weapon* flicks in one DVD package, but the original says it best, especially in this Director's Cut, which adds seven minutes of footage. Glover plays Murtaugh, the family-guy L.A. detective assigned to work with Gibson's Riggs, a cop who is over the edge since the death of his wife of eleven years. Both men served in Vietnam, which means they get to Rambo themselves out of tight scrapes. That's the setup, and that's all you need. Gibson and Glover partner up perfectly, and Shane Black's script arms them with just the right wiseass ammunition.

Hot Bonus: One of the deleted scenes involves Gibson and a sniper. I can't understand why they ever cut it.

Key Scene: Gibson playing Russian roulette, a wildness spinning in his eyes that seems remarkably unfaked.

Lianna (1983)

Starring: Linda Griffiths, Jane Hallaren, Jon DeVries, Robyn Reeves

Directed and written by: John Sayles

It took decades for the early films of indie pioneer Sayles to get to DVD. Shot for three hundred thousand dollars in New Jersey, this unheralded gem has no explosions, just characters that mean more to Sayles than special effects. Griffiths, a touching Canadian actress, plays Lianna, the mother of two and wife of an English teacher (DeVries) who boffs his students. When Lianna begins a lesbian affair with a teacher (Hallaren), rat Hubby sues for custody of the kids. In her own apartment, Lianna bumps into a tenant (Sayles's longtime partner Maggie Renzi) in the laundry room. "I'm gay," Lianna blurts out. "I'm Sheila," comes the casual response. Long before lesbianism became the stuff of sitcoms, Sayles tread touchy territory with humor and feeling.

Hot Bonus: Solid commentary from Sayles, who gave himself the scene-stealing role of a film instructor who hits on Lianna on his morning jog. "Can I go now?" he asks, when she tells him her situation.

Key Scene: The employment office in a college town where Lianna learns the ropes from a hottie know-it-all, played with sassy verve by Reeves.

Like Water for Chocolate (1992)

Starring: Lumi Cavazos, Marco Leonardi

Directed by: Alfonso Arau

This cult hit from Mexico combines the hunger for food and sex into a tasty DVD dish that is part folktale, part magic realism. Director Arau, basing the film on the novel written by his then-wife Laura Esquivel, stays alert to every voluptuous image. Cavazos plays Tita, a young woman who defines herself through cooking. Her mother has decreed that Tita—the last of her three daughters—may never marry, which causes problems when handsome Pedro (Leonardi) comes sniffing around. Then the real cooking starts.

Hot Bonus: An alternate soundtrack dubbed into English, so subtitle haters can concentrate on the food and the fooling around.

Key Scene: Tita cuts her finger and lets her blood flow into a dish of quail simmered in rose-petal sauce. Unleashed passion never looked this good.

Limey, The (1999)

Starring: Terence Stamp, Peter Fonda, Lesley Ann Warren

Directed by: Steven Soderbergh

A terrific mood piece—the DVD excels with images, less so with sound—that evokes 1960s revenge dramas such as *Point Blank*. The Lem Dobbs script concerns Wilson, played with grizzled dignity by Stamp, a British gangster just out of jail and off to Los Angeles to find out how his daughter ended up dead. His suspicions fall on Valentine (sleazed to perfection by Fonda), a record producer living the kinky high life. Director Soderbergh layers the film with visual surprises that reward repeated viewings.

Hot Bonus: Soderbergh and Dobbs get into some heated commentary, but the hot extra for DVD techies is a side-by-side demonstration of a clip from *The Limey* in anamorphic and nonanamorphic widescreen.

Key Scene: A flashback to Wilson in his youth packs a real impact since it is taken from *Poor Cow*, a 1967 film starring Stamp in his prime.

Lion in Winter, The (1968)

Starring: Katharine Hepburn, Peter O'Toole, Anthony Hopkins
Directed by: Anthony Harvey

Think of a twelfth-century *Who's Afraid of Virginia Woolf?* with Hepburn's Eleanor of Aquitaine and O'Toole's King Henry II, her husband, aiming verbal darts at each other over Christmas Eve 1183. Henry has let his wife out of jail for the occasion so they can argue about which of their three sons should inherit the throne. "What shall we hang," Henry asks, "the holly or each other?" James Goldman adapts his 1966 play to the screen with cunning wit, and Harvey directs with an eye for the dirt and squalor that make a castle look lived in. The DVD transfer kicks up wonderful dust. But it's the sparks that fly between O'Toole and Hepburn—she won her third Oscar (in a tie with Barbra Streisand in *Funny Girl*)—that gives the film its lasting pull. "Well, what family doesn't have its ups and downs?" Eleanor comments dryly when patricide, treason, and sexual perversity are in the air.

Hot Bonus: Harvey's comments about working with the two divas.

Key Scene: In the bedroom, where plotters hide behind every drapery and the effect is a deft blend of murderous intrigue and French farce.

Lion King, The (Two-Disc Special Edition) (1994)

Starring: The voices of Matthew Broderick, Jeremy Irons, James Earl Jones
Directed by: Roger Allers and Rob Minkoff

Here's an animated film with a twist. Nobility rears it head—as it must with Disney—but there's also vulgar, violent life. For every cuddly creature there's an animal who'd like to bite his warm and fuzzy head off. *The Lion King* has no human characters and no familiar fairy tale as a source. If the original script borrows from anything, it's *Hamlet*. Simba, voiced by Jonathan Taylor Thomas as a cub and Broderick as a grown-up, is the lion of the melancholy mane. He thinks he's at fault in the death of his dad, King Mufasa (Jones), until the real culprit, Mufasa's brother, Scar (Irons), forces him into action. The father-son relationship is movingly rendered. And Elton John's songs, enhanced with African choral arrangements by Hans Zimmer, are terrific, especially "Hakuna Matata" (it's Swahili for *no worries*), sung by Nathan Lane as a sly meerkat and Ernie Sabella as a flatulent warthog.

Hot Bonus: A new song, "Morning Report," that adds to the mix.

Key Scene: Let's lionize the visual miracles by six hundred Disney artisans, who bring the African landscape to stunning life in the opening number, "Circle of Life." A stampede of wildebeests will really test your DVD system.

Little Big Man (1970)

Starring: Dustin Hoffman, Faye Dunaway, Chief Dan George
Directed by: Arthur Penn

Time, not to mention a knockout DVD transfer, can make a good movie seem even better. Such is the case with this revisionist epic, based on Thomas Berger's novel, about Jack Crabb, the 120-year-old survivor of Custer's Last Stand. Hoffman, in old-age makeup, plays the old man. He also plays the much younger Jack. Director Penn tells the rambling story of how this paleface is captured by the Cheyenne (called "human beings"), raised as a brave under the wise tutelage of Old Lodge Skins (the Oscar-nominated Chief Dan George), and then returned to white society where racist violence is the norm. The parallels to Vietnam come often and at times too bluntly. But Penn and Hoffman are tackling big themes with biting wit.

Hot Bonus: Nothing more than stunning picture and sound.

Key Scene: The battle of Little Big Horn staged by Penn as a prequel to the My Lai massacre with a deranged Custer (Richard Mulligan) ordering the genocidal slaughter of men, women, and children.

Little Shop of Horrors (1986)

Starring: Rick Moranis, Ellen Greene, Steve Martin, Bill Murray
Directed by: Frank Oz

The best man-eating-plant musical ever made comes to DVD with its songs and S&M intact. Moranis plays Seymour, a nerd who works at a flower shop and pines for Audrey (Greene, a vocal powerhouse), a ditzy flower arranger with a penchant for push-up bras and abusive men. Her latest is a biker dentist (a hilarious Martin), who enjoys torturing his patients. Murray does a great cameo as Martin's most masochistic patient. Enter Audrey II, a fly-trap plant that thrives on blood.

"Feed me, Seymour," sings this mean green mother from outer space in the potent voice of Levi Stubbs of the Four Tops. Seymour feeds Audrey II the dentist, and a monster is born. Screenwriter-lyricist Howard Ashman and composer Alan Menken contribute a sly, sassy score, and Oz directs with just the right touch of inspired silliness.

Hot Bonus: Comments from Oz that sound especially wise, maybe because Oz is also the voice of Yoda in the *Star Wars* series. Dull, he is not.

Key Scene: The "Skid Row" sequence is an aural marvel, but it's hard to resist the plant's last big number as he swallows most of the cast.

Local Hero (1983)

Starring: Peter Riegert, Burt Lancaster
Directed by: Bill Forsyth

Nothing flashy here, just pure DVD enchantment. Riegert plays a Texas oil conglomerate hotshot dispatched from Houston to sweet-talk residents of a Scottish coastal village into selling drilling rights to their land. With offbeat, idiosyncratic humor, Forsyth immerses Riegert and the audience in the hypnotic rhythm of a remote corner of the world. Some moments—when actors are silhouetted against the deep-blue twilight horizon, shimmering clear water, and distant mountains—verge on the mystical. Except for a few muted colors, the DVD captures the film's essence. The soundtrack, by Mark Knopfler of Dire Straits, also flows hauntingly.

Hot Bonus: A full-screen version of the film is included, as well as the widescreen version, for those who want to draw closer to the film's charms.

Key Scene: Riegert's boss (an outstanding Lancaster) choppers in to see paradise for himself and sets up an utterly transporting climactic twist.

Lolita (1962)

Starring: James Mason, Peter Sellers, Sue Lyon, Shelley Winters
Directed by: Stanley Kubrick

In the opening credit sequence, Mason's Humbert Humbert paints the toenails of Lolita (Lyon) with a fetishistic attention to detail. It's an erotic start to a film that otherwise lacks much heat because the censors put pressure on Kubrick to water down his film version of Vladimir Nabokov's 1955 novel about a British professor's sexual obsession with a twelve-year-old American nymphet. Nabokov wrote the script, which Kubrick altered by upping Lolita's age to fifteen. It's a compromise, but the film scores on the basis of Kubrick's wickedly dark wit and the pitch-perfect performances he draws from Mason, Winters as Lolita's mother, and Sellers as Quilty, a mad amalgam of TV writer and pedophile. Oswald Morris's black-and-white camerawork is justly honored on the expert DVD transfer.

Hot Bonus: A documentary on Kubrick's career sparks the Kubrick box set that includes *Lolita* and seven other of the director's films.

Key Scene: Humbert's first glimpse of a bikini-clad Lolita sucking a heart-shaped lollipop is a lewdly funny image that says what words can't.

Lone Star (1996)

Starring: Chris Cooper, Kris Kristofferson, Matthew McConaughey
Directed and written by: John Sayles

The place is the border town of Frontera, Texas. The time is 1957, when lawman Buddy Deeds (McConaughey) becomes Frontera's hero by forcing out the brutal, bigoted Sheriff Charlie Wade (a never-better Kristofferson) and taking his job. The time is also the present, when Buddy's son, Sam (Cooper), is sheriff. After a skeleton is discovered on an army rifle range, along with Charlie's rusted badge, Sam investigates a case that might prove his late father to be a murderer. Sayles uses the whodunit plot to expose Frontera's social, racial, and political hypocrisies. It sounds hifalutin, but Sayles's knack for edgy humor, ardent sexuality, and rough-hewn grace grounds the story in humanism. More than fifty characters people this multicultural tale of a town where the shift of power from Mexicans to Anglos is shifting again. This film, Sayles's best, is built to last.

Hot Bonus: The color transfer is a marvel of DVD production subtlety.

Key Scene: In an empty restaurant, beautifully lit by cinematographer Stuart Dryburgh, Sam and Pilar (Elizabeth Pena), the woman he loved and lost, slow-dance to a jukebox tune and glide out of frame and into their youth.

Long Goodbye, The (1973)

Starring: Elliott Gould, Nina Van Pallandt, Mark Rydell, Jim Bouton

Directed by: Robert Altman

Altman, bless him, had critics and audiences all riled up with his update on Raymond Chandler's 1953 novel featuring hardboiled private eye Philip Marlowe, here played by a never-better Gould as a shambling L.A. stoner with a moral conscience and a soft spot for his cat. His supermarket search for Curry brand cat foot finds dimensions in the role that Bogart never investigated. The DVD transfer stays alert to the visual and aural time warp established by Altman and camera wiz Vilmos Zsigmond as Marlowe helps a pal (Bouton, a pitcher turned credible actor) accused of murdering his wife. Enter the usual suspects: an alcoholic writer (a superb Sterling Hayden), his babe wife (Van Pallandt), his sinister shrink (Henry Gibson), a Jewish gangster (Rydell), and even Governator Schwarzenegger as a hood.

Hot Bonus: A smart, sassy retrospective documentary, Rip Van Marlow, features Altman and the actors discussing the film from every angle, including the contribution of screenwriter Leigh Brackett, who co-wrote *The Big Sleep* (with Bogie as Marlowe) and *The Empire Strikes Back.*

Key Scene: Besides the shocker ending, Rydell smashing a bottle on the head of his girl toy (Jo Ann Brody) can still make you jump out of your seat.

Long, Hot Summer, The (1958)

Starring: Paul Newman, Joanne Woodward, Orson Welles, Angela Lansbury

Directed by: Martin Ritt

The screen adaptation of three stories by William Faulkner received respectfully dismissive reviews. This gloriously torrid DVD resuscitation in Cinemascope reveals it for the goodie it is. Newman fires things up as Ben Quick, a Mississippi arsonist who goes to work for rich Will Var-

ner (Welles garbles his southern accent but still mesmerizes) and courts his standoffish daughter Clara (Woodward). Newman and Woodward married the same year, and the sparks that fly between them would be visible even in a bad DVD restoration. Anthony Franciosa and Lee Remick excel as Will's weak son and hottie daughter-in-law, as does Lansbury as Will's mistress. Ritt directs with a keen eye for erotic combustion and an ear for the cadences in the exceptionally fine script by Irving Ravetch and Harriet Frank Jr.

Hot Bonus: A retrospective documentary with Newman, Woodward, and Lansbury tells delightful tales out of school, especially about Welles.

Key Scene: At a picnic, so lushly shot you can inhale the magnolias, Newman aims his baby blues right at Woodward: "Go ahead, Miss Clara, run away, change your name, and maybe, just maybe, you'll get away from me." No barns burned in the making of this film give off more heat.

Long Kiss Goodnight, The (Remastered Special Edition) (1996)

Starring: Geena Davis, Samuel L. Jackson, Craig Bierko

Directed by: Renny Harlin

A sex- and action-charged B movie gets an A-class DVD transfer. Davis and director Harlin, then her husband, join up with ace screenwriter Shane Black to juggle jolts and jokes. Davis plays an amnesiac who woke up eight years ago, lost and two months' pregnant. She took the name Samantha Caine and settled down as a small-town teacher with a daughter. Now she's hired a shady private eye (Jackson) to dig for clues. He finds them: Samantha is really Charly Baltimore, the spy babe who came in from the 'burbs. Davis is a dazzler as Charly. She cuts her hair, dyes it blond, and offers a blow job to the private dick, who rejects it as a "white-woman, colored-man thing." The actors, including Bierko as a hottie from her secret past, deepen the mystery.

Hot Bonus: A "making of" doc does the minimum but does it well.

Key Scene: In the kitchen, a knife-tossing Davis slices and dices veggies like a pro. "Chefs do that," she says. She figures out her real job when a killer breaks in, and she twists his neck, cuts his throat, and licks his blood.

Longest Day, The (1962)

Starring: John Wayne, Henry Fonda, Robert Mitchum, Richard Burton

Directed by: Ken Annakin, Andrew Marton, Bernhard Wicki

Before Steven Spielberg did D-Day for the ages in *Saving Private Ryan*, producer Darryl F. Zanuck gathered forty-two international stars and three—count 'em, three—directors he could push around until the Allied invasion of Normandy beach on June 6, 1944, looked the way he wanted it to look, which was gray to match the weather. The black-and-white Cinemascope film has been immaculately transferred to DVD. You can see all of Zanuck's money ($10 million, a record at that time) on screen. The setup is a bit pokey, and all those stars—look, it's Sean Connery under that helmet—more than a bit hokey. But the battles, relatively bloodless compared to the Spielberg gore machine, have true epic scope.

Hot Bonus: One lousy trailer that looks like crap. But let me cheer the English subtitles when characters speak their native language. They run on a black bar at the bottom of the screen and don't get lost in the picture.

Key Scene: Cornelius Ryan's book offered detailed description, but seeing the midnight sky over Normandy fill up with parachutes is hard to beat.

Longest Yard, The (Widescreen Lockdown Edition) (1974)

Starring: Burt Reynolds, Eddie Albert
Directed by: Robert Aldrich

I'm going with the classic Burt model instead of the 2005 Adam Sandler remake, which is fun in itself but nowhere near as hilarious and hardass as the original, given new life on DVD. Reynolds, a former Florida State tailback, is a natural as Paul Crewe, the NFL pro who is jailed for stealing his girl's Maserati. Sandler, a former waterboy, can't match Reynolds's squint as he rebels against the sociopathic warden (Albert) who wants him to train a team of convicts—the Mean Machine—but then throw the game against the guards. The brutality of the film still shocks, since director Aldrich stuck it to the prison system and every other authoritarian target.

Hot Bonus: Reynolds chews the fat entertainingly with writer-producer Al Ruddy and offers insights about his football days and his relationship with Aldrich, a true movie maverick who died in 1983.

Key Scene: For my money, the climactic game—it lasts nearly a half hour—is the best football action ever committed to film. The DVD is a bone-cruncher.

Longtime Companion (1990)

Starring: Campbell Scott, Bruce Davison, Mary-Louise Parker
Directed by: Norman René

One of the first and best films to tackle the AIDS epidemic comes to DVD in a bare-bones transfer that still deserves attention. As written with delicacy and depth by playwright Craig Lucas (*Prelude to a Kiss*) and directed with like sensitivity by Rene, the film has been criticized for focusing on a group of white urbanites in Manhattan to the neglect of minorities. Personal and political anger would come later in Tony Kushner's *Angels in America*. Lucas, in fact, was writing what he knew. From the first *New York Times* article in 1981, mentioning a rare gay cancer, to the devastation exacted by the end of the decade, the film puts a human face on a plague. Davison won an Oscar nomination for the wrenching scene in which he tells his dying lover (Mark Lamos) to "just let go." But the other actors, notably Scott as a fitness instructor who panics after kissing the dying man and rushes to the bathroom to scrub himself free of possible contagion, also bring vivid, idiosyncratic life to the details of the period that are past forgetting.

Hot Bonus: A sensationalistic trailer that sells the film all wrong.

Key Scene: The ending, a dream vision of a world that unites the survivors and those who were robbed of their lives. Then as now, it wipes you out.

Lord of the Flies (Special Edition) (1963)

Starring: James Aubrey, Tom Chapin, Hugh Edwards
Directed by: Peter Brook

Forget the Americanized 1990 remake. The keeper is the Brook version of William Golding's novel about thirty British schoolboys who turn savage after a plane crash strands them on tropical island. Criterion's DVD transfer gives the black-and-white picture a raw documentary power and the contours of a living nightmare. Aubrey as the group leader, Chapin as a budding fascist, and Edwards as Piggy, the fat boy who tries to keep his head about him, are non-actors whose inexperience pays emotional dividends.

Hot Bonus: Brook's backstory is fascinating, but hearing Golding read excerpts from his novel puts the DVD in the time-capsule class.

Key Scene: The chilling chant of "Keerie-aye, keerie-o" as the boys go on the hunt for Piggy, who has lost his glasses (the last vestige of civilization).

Lord of the Rings, The: Fellowship of the Rings (Four-Disc Special Extended Edition) (2001)

Starring: Elijah Wood, Ian McKellen, Viggo Mortensen, Liv Tyler

Directed by: Peter Jackson

Jackson's monumental screen version of the massive tome that is J. R. R. Tolkien's *The Lord of the Rings* is the greatest epic trilogy in the history of cinema, not to mention the ultimate in DVD miracle-working. The bonus features aren't filler; they're endlessly informative. And the added footage only strengthens the trilogy's mythic resonance. *Fellowship*, the kickoff of the series, is the real deal, an eye-popping blockbuster that stays intimately attuned to character. Working in New Zealand, away from the Hollywood sharks, Jackson pulls off a directing coup that should give George Lucas pause. The script by Jackson, Fran Walsh (his wife), and Philippa Boyens never allows computer-generated marvels to overwhelm the personal story. A ring with the power to destroy the world has passed from the dark lord Sauron to Frodo Baggins (Wood). Frodo is a hobbit, a munchkin-short, sweet-natured, furry-footed species with a love of peace and of smoking pipeweed. Gandalf the good wizard (McKellen, the only actor in the trilogy to be Oscar nominated) tells Frodo it's his mission to travel east to Mordor to dump that ring into Mount Doom. Frodo takes along three fellow hobbits, Sam (Sean Astin), Pippin (Billy Boyd), and Merry (Dominic Monaghan); two human warriors, Aragorn (Mortensen) and Boromir (Sean Bean); the archer elf Legolas (Orlando Bloom); and the dwarf Gimli (John Rhys-Davies). Counting Gandalf, who's having his own problems with the corrupted wizard Saruman (the great Christopher Lee), that's nine in the fellowship. The good nine are being chased by nine Ringwraiths, dark riders on dark horses. Even scarier is the giant cave troll that knocks the bejesus out of Frodo and his boys when they enter the mines of Moria. Then there's the foul Orcs, with their rotting flesh and teeth. These action sequences play like gangbusters with the DVD designed to test your home theater system to the limit. What doesn't work? The love story between Arwen (Tyler), the elf princess, and who knows that if she marries the human Aragorn she will lose her immortality? Despite the lushness

of Andrew Lesnie's cinematography and the shimmering beauty of Howard Shore's music (a model in epic scoring), the romance falls flat. Even the reliably excellent Cate Blanchett lacks magic as the elf queen Galadriel; sadly, all the scenes in the elf land of Rivendell have that overlit theme-park tackiness. All is well again when Jackson plunges into darkness and the characters test their moral mettle against the power of the ring. Mortensen, in the film's best performance, brings heroic stature to Aragorn, befitting a man descended from kings. Aragorn's conflict with Boromir, given haunting complexity by Bean, strikes at the essence of brotherhood. Jackson wisely ends the film not with fireworks but with a small scene that cements the friendship between Frodo and Sam, a character of growing importance that Astin portrays with just the right notes of fun and feeling. Even on an extended DVD that runs a half hour longer than the theatrical version, Jackson leaves you wanting more.

Hot Bonus: Hot? They all sizzle, especially the commentaries. But for sheer Easter Egg fun, go to "Select a Scene" on the first disc and find "The Council of Elrod." Press the Down arrow until you find a gold ring. Hit Enter and you'll see the Elrod sequence as an uproarious MTV parody.

Key Scene: Gandalf, facing the winged demon Balrog on a bridge and thundering, "You shall not pass!" Even the Taliban would quake.

Lord of the Rings, The: The Two Towers (Four-Disc Special Extended Edition) (2002)

Starring: Elijah Wood, Sean Astin, Viggo Mortensen, Andy Serkis

Directed by: Peter Jackson

Jackson leaps into Part II with no patience for laggers. *The Two Towers*, shot at the same time as Part I and Part III, is spectacular in every sense of the word, even if you don't know an Orc from a Uruk-Hai. Running forty-four minutes longer than the theatrical release, which clocked in at three hours, the DVD version of the film stands as a testament to what the digital disc medium can accomplish as a technology and an art. Here's the plot tease: The fellowship has scattered. Frodo the Hobbit (Wood) still holds the all-powerful ring that he and Sam (Astin) must drop into Mount

Doom. Merry (Dominic Monaghan) and Pippin (Billy Boyd) are adrift in a forest talking to an Ent, a tree that talks back. The human warrior Aragorn (Mortensen, growing steadily impressive in the role) is still fighting the evil Saruman (Christopher Lee) with the help of elf archer Legolas (Orlando Bloom) and Gimli the dwarf (John Rhys-Davies). It's Aragorn who must release the Rohan king (a noble, moving Bernard Hill) from Saruman's spell and help save Middle-earth in a climactic clash at Helm's Deep. *The Two Towers* suffers a bit from being the middle chapter (no beginning, no end), but Jackson keeps the action percolating. The effects astonish, none more so than Gollum, a computer-generated creature, hauntingly voiced by Serkis. Gollum looks like a wasted junkie and speaks (with a rasp to rival Linda Blair's in *The Exorcist*) of the ring that corrupted him as "my precious." The battle between good and evil in this character catches the soul of the movie.

Hot Bonus: The commentaries by Jackson and his crew are as exemplary as ever. Ditto the behind-the-scenes documentaries. But my personal favorite is the material on the creation of Gollum, and how Serkis was used as a model on which to build the screen's most dazzling digital creation.

Key Scene: Helm's Deep ranks with the greatest battles in film (the parallels to the warring forces of democracy and fundamentalism are inescapable), and to see it play out in this extended cut enhances the experience.

Lord of the Rings, The: The Return of the King (Four-Disc Special Extended Edition) (2003)

Starring: Elijah Wood, Viggo Mortensen, Sean Astin, Liv Tyler, Andy Serkis

Directed by: Peter Jackson

At last, after two tries, an Oscar win for Best Picture, plus ten more gold statuettes which justly belong to the trilogy as a whole. Jackson does author J. R. R. Tolkien proud by turning his tome into a film epic by which all future film epics will be judged. Many reviewers who resisted the two previous films came aboard to hail *King*, as if the series had finally kicked in. Bull. All three films are equal and indispensable to the tale being told. There are missteps in *King*. Some of the computer-generated effects (the army of the dead, the ex-

ploding Mount Doom) look subpar. And Jackson inexplicably fails to show us that moment when the spark of kingship first lights in the eyes of Aragorn (Mortensen). I won't add to the clamor against the multiple endings (hell, they're in the book), but the rueful profundity the film needs for closure is spoiled by an orgy of hobbit hugging, with Frodo (Wood), Merry (Dominic Monaghan), and Pippin (Billy Boyd) jumping around in bed (the *Village Voice* called it "gayer than anything in *Angels in America*"). Still, Jackson's boldness rights all wrongs. He picks up with Gollum—the spindly, scary, schizoid, computer-generated villain, indelibly voiced by Serkis—as he tries to sabotage the plan of Frodo and Sam (Astin) to reach Mount Doom and destroy the ring. All roads lead to Minas Tirith, the seven-tiered capital city of Gondor where "the great battle of our time," according to the wizard Gandalf (McKellen), will hopefully distract the dark lord Sauron (now just one giant eye) from Frodo's mission. The plan pits monstrous Orcs, hulking elephants, and flying dragons against the forces of Gondor, under the mad stewardship of Denethor (John Noble), and the riders of Rohan, led by King Theoden (Bernard Hill, giving the role Shakespearean gravity). Theoden's niece Eowyn (Miranda Otto, all fire and grace in the film's strongest female role) sneaks into battle disguised as a man and proves her mettle. Her love for Aragorn is unrequited, but she makes it palpable. And Aragorn leading the final charge with the cry, "For Frodo," becomes the king we've all been waiting for. This is a film in which ideas resonate as well as action. And the bond between Frodo and loyal Sam cuts deep. It's a disgrace that Astin failed to win an Oscar nomination for a performance that is the soul of the movie. When Frodo, on the volcanic edge of Mount Doom, declares "I'm glad to be with you Samwise Gamgee, here at the end of all days"—the moment seizes your heart. So does the movie. Jackson is more than director, he's a wizard. After seven years, a $300 million budget and three films that add up to more than the sum of their parts, the *Rings* trilogy is more than a movie and the standard bearer of DVD achievement to date. It's a colossus on the march into legend.

Hot Bonus: It's an education in cinema to hear Best Director Oscar–winner Jackson—he beat out tough competition in Clint Eastwood for *Mystic River*—sum up a decade of work on the trilogy with every imaginable illustrative device needed to make his points.

Key Scene: OK, Sam saving Frodo from a giant spider is the scariest moment. But for sheer, tearful release, you can't beat the sequence in which every living character in the trilogy bows to the hobbits in respect and love.

Lost Boys, The (Two-Disc Special Edition) (1987)

Starring: Jason Patric, Kiefer Sutherland, Corey Haim
Directed by: Joel Schumacher

Critics put a stake in the heart of Schumacher's black-comic vampire flick. But catch the new digital transfer and you can see why it spawned a loyal cult. Patric and Haim play teens whose mom (Dianne Wiest) takes them to live with their gramps (Barnard Hughes) in the California town of Santa Clara. You might call the place sleepy, especially for vampires, led by Sutherland (the *24* star is an uber-cool menace with a mullet), who snooze all day, party all night, never grow old, and never die. It's an adolescent wet dream. A hottie (Jami Gertz) seduces Patric to the dark side, and Haim joins up with the vampire-slaying Frog brothers (scene-stealers Corey Feldman and Jamison Newlander). Here's a movie that sees the sex, drugs, and rock & roll of blood sucking. What's not to like?

Hot Bonus: Next to the retrospective documentary, the most fun comes in watching the deleted scenes.

Key Scene: The knockout bloodbath climax, followed by this immortal quote from Gramps: "One thing about Santa Clara I could never stomach was all the damn vampires."

Lost in America (1985)

Starring: Albert Brooks, Julie Hagerty, Garry Marshall
Directed and co-written by: Albert Brooks

No bonus features to dazzle you here, and the image and sound do the job—nothing more. But a DVD collection without this landmark Brooks comedy would be sorely lacking. Brooks as ad man David and Hagerty as his wife Linda play a Los Angeles couple in a Winnebago on the run from their upwardly mobile lives and workaholic jobs. They are determined to find themselves and "touch Indians." Says David: "Linda, this is just like *Easy Rider*, only now its *our* turn." If there is such a thing as despairingly hilarious, this is it.

Hot Bonus: OK, there is a trailer.

Key Scene: When Linda loses their savings at a Vegas roulette table, David tries futilely to use his persuasive skills to convince the casino owner (Marshall, a deadpan wonder) to give them the money back. The shot of Marshall's unbelieving face is an effect no computer could duplicate.

Lost in Translation (Special Edition) (2003)

Starring: Bill Murray, Scarlett Johansson, Giovanni Ribisi
Directed and written by: Sofia Coppola

Director Coppola's second feature—she won the Oscar for Best Original Screenplay—is a moonbeam that tickles you with laughs, teases you with romantic possibility, and then melts into heartbreak. The DVD transfer goes with the delicate flow. The film is a brief encounter in Tokyo between Bob Harris (a never-better Murray, playing for something way deeper than ha-ha), a middle-aged movie star in Japan to shoot a commercial, and Charlotte (Johansson, then eighteen and an actress of smashing loveliness and subtle grace), a Yale philosophy grad in Tokyo with her photographer husband (Ribisi). Bob and Charlotte find each other in an almost-love story that ends in a whisper between them that Coppola won't let the audience hear. She keeps her film as hushed and intimate as that whisper.

Hot Bonus: A featurette, *Lost on Location*, offers insights into Coppola's work methods and her skill at shooting on a low budget.

Key Scene: Murray's commercial gets the biggest laughs, but the opening shot of him floating in a limo bubble through the neon glitter of nighttime Tokyo catches the disconnect that comes from being a stranger in a strange land. Gifted cinematographer Lance Acord—shooting on high-speed film instead of the digital video fast becoming an indie cliché—gives that disconnect the seductive sheen of something exotic that's just out of reach.

Love Me or Leave Me (1955)

Starring: Doris Day, James Cagney
Directed by: Charles Vidor

This widescreen bio of 1920s torch singer Ruth Etting gives Day the role of her career. She's tough, sexy, and heartbreaking as a woman who marries the Chicago gangster Martin "The Gimp" Snyder (Cagney, Oscar-nominated and blazingly brilliant) who made her career and ends up hitting the bottle to dull her self-revulsion. Etting's love for the typically handsome Johnny (Cameron Mitchell) can't begin to rival the sparks that fly between her and the abusive, heartsick Snyder. The musical numbers, especially Day's show-stopping "Ten Cents a Dance," get vivid DVD treatment.

Hot Bonus: Two early Vitaphone short subjects show the real Etting singing and acting, and offers striking contrasts with Day's approach.

Key Scene: The exhilarating moment when

Cagney, watching Day dazzle on a nightclub stage, realizes that he doesn't have to pay audiences to applaud anymore is strikingly contrasted to the sequence when he pushes her on a bed and demands payment for her career boosting. Way bold for its time.

M
(Two-Disc Special Edition)(1931)
Starring: Peter Lorre
Directed by: Fritz Lang

Lang's first sound film stars Lorre in the performance of his career as a child molester and killer at loose in Berlin with both the police and underworld trying to catch him. Criterion's DVD transfer restores the film's artful play of light and shadow. And you watch Lorre, a fat little man with protruding eyes, take you into the mind of a psychopath whose actions are unthinkable (Lang only suggests the crimes, he never shows them) but whose twisted humanity ("I can't help myself," he cries) is impossible to ignore.

Hot Bonus: The scholarly commentaries set the film in context, but it's a conversation with Lang himself that makes the disc invaluable.

Key Scene: To seduce a little girl, Lorre buys a balloon from a blind man and whistles a tune (from Grieg's *Peer Gynt*) that will ultimately trap him.

M*A*S*H
(Two-Disc Special Edition) (1970)
Starring: Elliott Gould, Donald Sutherland, Sally Kellerman, Robert Duvall
Directed by: Robert Altman

Altman's antiwar comedy, set during the Korean conflict, is as subversively funny and influential as its subsequent TV spinoff was safe and comforting. The irreverent wit is evident from the opening theme ("Suicide Is Painless") to the camp public address system that announces the film's plot: "Follow the zany antics of our combat surgeons (Gould and Sutherland) as they cut and stitch their way along the front lines, operating as bombs and bullets burst around them, snatching laughs and loves between amputations." The cast is uniformly excellent, from Kellerman as Major Hot Lips O'Houlihan to Duvall as the holy roller major she screws. The DVD transfer does its best to keep up with Altman's overlapping dialogue and a picture that aims for grungy realism. The laughs count here because they stick in your throat.

Hot Bonus: The film's rebel spirit is caught in the making of documentary and Altman's tren-

chant comments, including how his rebel approach to filming so floored Gould and Sutherland that they tried to have him canned.

Key Scene: Hot Lips caught in the shower is classic, but the free-for-all football game pitting the MASH unit against military elite is the very essence of the film's comic stand against authoritarian hypocrisy.

Mad Max (1979)

Starring: Mel Gibson, Joanne Samuel
Directed by: George Miller

The Aussie headbanger movie that gave Gibson, then twenty-three, his first major role. He plays Max, a decent cop in a futuristic society. Max turns mad avenger when a punk biker gang kills his wife (Samuel) and child. Even on a laughably low budget, director Miller fills the screen with nifty, noisy car crashes that will blow your mind and your DVD speaker system. Followed by one knockout sequel (1981's *The Road Warrior*) and a followup (1985's *Mad Max: Beyond Thunderdome*) that lets the series down.

Hot Bonus: Car freaks will love this Easter Egg: Go to the Main Menu, press the Up arrow three times, and hit Enter when you see the words "Mad Max." You will then see images and descriptions of the cars used in the movie, including the Black Interceptor, Yellow Pursuit, and the Night Rider.

Key Scene: The final car chase and explosive crash set in the Outback.

Magnificent Seven, The (1960)

Starring: Yul Brynner, Steve McQueen, Eli Wallach, James Coburn
Directed by: John Sturges

What sounds like a goofball idea—remake Akira Kurosawa's *The Seven Samurai* as a western—turns out to be inspired in the hands of director Sturges and a well-chosen cast. Wallach (ever superb) and his bandits are intimidating a Mexican village, so the townsfolk hire seven badass desperados, led by Brynner, to take them down. For me, just hearing Elmer Bernstein's rousing theme—it really soars on the DVD as the seven ride together—is enough to get the blood pumping.

Hot Bonus: A retrospective 2001 documentary, *Guns for Hire*, delivers the gossipy goods. And it's great to hear that Kurosawa himself presented Sturges with a samurai sword in honor of the remake's achievement.

Key Scene: There's a Coburn knife fight that deserves repeated viewings, but the fun comes in watching then newcomer McQueen steal scenes without dialogue and right under star Brynner's nose.

Magnolia (Two-Disc Special Edition) (1999)

Starring: Tom Cruise, Julianne Moore, John C. Reilly, Jason Robards

Directed and written by: Paul Thomas Anderson

Anderson was only twenty-nine when he wrote and directed this startlingly mature human drama. And the DVD transfer preserves the widescreen elegance of the images and the aural sophistication of the sound design. Set in California's San Fernando Valley, *Magnolia* tells the stories of eleven principal characters whose lives intersect over the course of one day. The actors are perfection, starting with Reilly as a cop in love with a junkie (Melora Walters) whose father (Philip Baker Hall) is a dying game show host with a wife (Melinda Dillon) who turns a blind eye to his abuses. In another part of town, another dying father (Robards) is bedridden, cared for by a young wife (Moore) and a male nurse (Philip Seymour Hoffman) in the process of trying to locate the man's estranged son (Cruise), a sleazy motivational speaker who runs "Seduce and Destroy" seminars for women-hating men. Got that? Cruise is a revelation, fully deserving of his Oscar nomination. Whether he's teaching his audience to "respect the cock" or freezing out an interviewer on live television ("I'm sitting here silently judging you"), Cruise seethes with the chaotic energy of a wounded animal. Anderson takes risks that make you hopeful about the future of movies.

Hot Bonus: A production video diary that runs over an hour and really takes you behind the scenes to show Anderson working with the actors.

Key Scene: In a film of constant astonishments, the cast sing-along to a ballad by Aimee Mann is indelible, as is the climactic rain of frogs (check your Bible, Exodus 8:8) that serves as a millennial wake-up call.

Major Dundee (Extended Version) (1965)

Starring: Charlton Heston, Richard Harris
Directed by: Sam Peckinpah

Butchered by the studio and producer Jerry Bresler on its original release, Peckinpah's wildly ambitious Civil-War-era western comes to DVD with an additional twelve minutes of footage that clears up some but not all of the motivation (a half hour of film is still missing). This homage to a master is another validation for DVD. The plot still defies coherence as Heston's Dundee, a Yankee major, goes crackers by using prisoners in his stockade, including a Confederate captain (Harris), to launch a search for renegade Apaches in Mexico to restore his fading reputation. Parallels to Vietnam abound. And you can spot traces of the 1969 Peckinpah masterpiece, *The Wild Bunch*, in the ruins of this coulda-been, shoulda-been epic.

Hot Bonus: The DVD includes two scores: the original by Daniele Amfitheatrof, which Peckinpah hated, especially "The Major Dundee March" sung by Mitch Miller's Sing-Along Gang, and a new one by Christopher Caliendo that is more haunting than hyper.

Key Scene: Dundee crossing the Rio Grande into Mexico, with a ragtag group that suddenly coheres into a team as they rush into battle.

Malcolm X (Two-Disc Special Edition) (1992)

Starring: Denzel Washington, Spike Lee, Angela Bassett
Directed by: Spike Lee

Washington's monumental performance drives this biopic of Malcolm Little, the former thief and pimp who found his spirit in the Nation of Islam and later as an independent thinker and by-any-means-necessary force in the black liberation movement. His murder at New York's Audubon Ballroom on February 21, 1965—he was thirty-nine and known by his Muslim name, El-Hajj Malik El-Shabazz—martyred him to a contentious battle he left too soon. Lee's sweeping and heartfelt epic sometimes veers off course by trying to see this remarkable figure from every possible angle. But the film remains colorful and alive—the DVD bursts with the energy of Ernest Dickerson's camerawork—and the extras add valuable material to the package.

Hot Bonus: The inclusion of the Oscar-nominated 1972 documentary on Malcolm X with its newsreel footage is a stirring complement to the film.

Key Scene: The assassination of Malcolm X hits like a thunderbolt, and Lee directs it with eye for the chaos, the political motivation, and the emotional devastation as Malcolm's wife, Betty Shabazz (Bassett), holds her dying husband.

Maltese Falcon, The (1941)

Starring: Humphrey Bogart, Mary Astor, Peter Lorre, Sydney Greenstreet
Directed by: John Huston

Screenwriter Huston directs his first movie, and it's a classic. Bogart plays private eye Sam Spade and becomes a star for the ages. Dashiell Hammett sees his novel, about a nest of vipers willing to kill to attain the statue of a jewel-encrusted falcon, become the ultimate film noir. And Warner produces the best DVD transfer of the film yet, though they could still do better. But who's complaining, when you're watching Bogart blend cynical and honorable into one iconic package? And what a cast: Greenstreet is an all-time great villain as the Fat Man, Kasper Gutman. "I'm a man who likes talking to man who likes to talk," he tells Bogart. Astor is feminine deceit incarnate. And Lorre as pop-eyed, closet queen Joel Cairo, and Elisha Cook Jr. as the Fat Man's gunsel are priceless.

Hot Bonus: An original and fascinating look at Bogart's career as seen through the trailers for twelve of his movies.

Key Scene: Take your pick. They are all the stuff that film noir dreams are made of. I'll take Bogart's farewell to the treacherous Astor. He: "All we've got is that maybe you love me and maybe I love you." She: "You know whether you love me or not." He: "I'll have some rotten nights after I've sent you over, but that'll pass."

Mambo Kings, The (1992)

Starring: Antonio Banderas, Armand Assante
Directed by: Arne Glimcher

From its breathtaking opening shot in a Ha-

vana nightclub, *The Mambo Kings* runs on music and emotion. First-time director Glimcher does a service to Oscar Hijuelos's Pulitzer Prize–winning novel by not trying to cram too much in. The book spans three decades; the film zeroes in on the years from 1952 to 1955, when two Cuban musicians—Cesar (Assante) and his younger brother Nestor (Banderas)—come to New York . This extravagantly sexy film is a DVD stunner, suffused with romantic longing. Assante and Banderas are sensational as the loving, warring brothers. Their performances honor the dammed-up dreams of a culture long misunderstood by Hollywood. The tormented Nestor writes many versions of a song, "Beautiful Marfa of My Soul," to express his yearning for a lost love and his lost homeland. Here's a film that celebrates the mysterious power of a music that can make you feel like dancing and bring you to your knees.

Hot Bonus: A tribute to the now-deceased legends, bandleader Tito Puente and singer Celia Cruz, who have acting roles in the film.

Key Scene: Cesar and Nestor's first visit to New York's Palladium, where Puente's band is playing. Part of the seduction of mambo comes in dressing for the dance, and Glimcher gives the club a sensual, eye-popping opulence.

Man Who Fell to Earth, The (Two-Disc Special Edition) (1976)

Starring: David Bowie, Candy Clark, Buck Henry, Rip Torn
Directed by: Nicolas Roeg

Look for the Anchor Bay DVD, which has better picture and sound than the Fox Lorber edition, plus an extra disc of bonus features. Bowie is ideally cast as an ET who wants to get home to save his drought-stricken planet, but gets sidetracked by a lawyer (Henry) who makes him a corporate success and a sexy hotel clerk (Clark) who gets him addicted to gin and television while a chemistry prof (Torn) investigates his motivations. It's director Roeg's uber-cool imagery—amped by Bowie's awesomely watchable androgyny—that makes this movie sci-fi for the thinking person.

Hot Bonus: A retrospective documentary in which Roeg helps solves a few of the film's puzzles.

Key Scene: Bowie's arrival on Earth with a splash in a lake, and his stroll into a town that looks more alien than he does.

Man Who Knew Too Much, The (1956)

Starring: James Stewart, Doris Day, Christopher Olsen

Directed by: Alfred Hitchcock

This is supposed to be lesser Hitchcock. Ha! This DVD transfer, infused with suspense and vibrant color, gives the lie to that notion. Dr. Ben McKenna (Stewart) and his wife Jo (Day) are on vacation in French Morocco with their young son Hank (Olsen) when an Arab man staggers toward them in a bazaar, a knife in his back and a secret to whisper to Stewart. And that's just for starters, as Hank gets kidnapped and Stewart sedates his wife (now there's a psychological insight into their marriage) so he can find the culprits. Day's underrated performance is another reason for repeated DVD viewings.

Hot Bonus: A collection of photos, lobby cards, and posters set to the thrilling score by Bernard Herrmann.

Key Scene: The climax at London's Albert Hall is a masterful example of suspense choreography. As cymbals crash, Herrmann's score thunders, and the villains try to kill Hank, Doris saves the day by warbling "Que Sera, Sera"—the film's Oscar-winning song—at just the right moment.

Man Who Wasn't There, The (2001)

Starring: Billy Bob Thornton, Frances McDormand, James Gandolfini

Directed by: Joel Coen

Meditative pacing! Ironic detachment! Existential dread! Yup, director Joel Coen and his producer, brother Ethan, deliver everything that audiences run from. Bless them. Set in the sleepy California town of Santa Rosa during the doldrums of 1949, the film stars a subtle, precise Thornton as barber Ed Crane and McDormand as Doris, the wife who cheats on Ed with her married department-store boss, Big Dave (Gandolfini). What does Ed do? He smokes, stares and says nothing. Hooked yet? If you tune into the Coen vibe, you will be. *Man* traffics in blackmail, murder, bad barbering, and a blow job perpetrated on Ed by a teenage hussy (Scarlett Johansson). Shot in black-and-white by the great cinematographer Roger Deakins, the film transfers to DVD like the beauty it is.

Hot Bonus: The commentary from the Coens is hilariously unhelpful. Ditto seeing scenes that didn't make the cut, such as a table being set and hair being swept off the barber's floor. Gee thanks, guys.

Key Scene: The musical montage on haircuts and the alien visitation. What other film noirs give you that?

Man Who Would Be King, The (1975)

Starring: Sean Connery, Michael Caine, Christopher Plummer

Directed by: John Huston

A grand adventure film gets a DVD that preserves all its color and life. Based on a short story by Rudyard Kipling (Plummer), the movie stars the dream team of Connery and Caine as British soldiers—and expert scam artists—who care more about themselves than dying for England and Queen Victoria. They head for Kafiristan (a province in Afghanistan) and try to load up on treasure by pretending Connery is a god. That's when Connery starts believing it for real. Huston directs with enormous flair, blending action, comedy, and an attack on imperialism into high-style entertainment.

Hot Bonus: A "making up" feature that shows Huston at work with Connery and Caine, who later sued for their share of the film's jumbo profits.

Key Scene: The attack on the city of Sikandergul, once ruled by Alexander the Great, ending with the great moment when Connery pulls an arrow out of his chest. Let Indiana Jones top that.

Manchurian Candidate, The (Special Edition) (1962)

Starring: Frank Sinatra, Laurence Harvey, Angela Lansbury

Directed by: John Frankenheimer

A political thriller that satirizes Commies and right-wingers with equal malice. Frankenheimer directs this classic, much imitated but never equaled (see the failed 2004 remake), with a tension that carries over brilliantly on DVD. Based on Richard Condon's 1959 novel, the film focuses on Raymond Shaw (Harvey), a decorated Korean vet. "Raymond Shaw is the kindest, bravest, warmest, most wonderful human being I've ever known in my life," says Captain/Major Ben Marco (Sinatra), who knows something is wrong because he hated the son of a bitch. When Ben has nightmares about Korea, it becomes clear that he and the rest of his platoon have been brainwashed so that Raymond can be used for a top-level political assassination. Harvey catches both the cold snob and the lost boy in Raymond. And Sinatra hits an acting peak. But the movie belongs to the magnificent Lansbury as Raymond's monster mother, who does things to a son that . . . well, watch this DVD and let your jaw drop.

Hot Bonus: The commentaries, featuring Sinatra, Frankenheimer, and screenwriter George Axelrod, explain why the film was withdrawn after the JFK assassination.

Key Scene: The brainwashing, at which Ben, Raymond, and other soldiers have been conditioned to believe that they are waiting out a storm in the lobby of a small hotel where a meeting of the ladies' garden club is in progress. In fact, they are in Manchuria watching Raymond being trained to do unspeakable acts when triggered by producing a card, the Queen of Diamonds.

Manhattan (1979)

Starring: Woody Allen, Diane Keaton, Mariel Hemingway

Directed and co-written by: Woody Allen

The opening, with Manhattan shot by Gordon Willis in dreamy black-and-white to the rhapsodically romantic sounds of George Gershwin, would be reason enough to own this widescreen DVD and watch it regularly. But the beauty of it is just icing on the cake that is this trenchant, unexpectedly heartbreaking comedy. Allen, who co-wrote the deft script with Marshall Brickman, plays Isaac, a joke writer who wants to create a serious novel. *Manhattan* is Allen's attempt to raise his own game, and he succeeds triumphantly as Isaac, attracted to the neurotic Mary (Keaton), splits from Tracy (Hemingway, justly Oscar nominated), the teenager who loves him.

Hot Bonus: You won't mind the lack of extras. The Woodman's personal connection to the older man/younger woman theme will get you thinking.

Key Scene: At the soda fountain, with Hemingway choking back tears and a malted as a guilt-ridden Allen tells her they can no longer be together.

Manhunter (1986)

Starring: William Petersen, Brian Cox, Tom Noonan, Joan Allen

Directed by: Michael Mann

Yes, there is a two-disc limited edition Direc-

tor's Cut available, but don't avail yourself of it. The bare-bones theatrical version DVD looks much better and features insightful extras about this pulse-pounding prequel to *The Silence of the Lambs*, from the Thomas Harris novel *Red Dragon*. Brett Ratner directed a routine remake with that title in 2002, but Mann provides the real DVD deal. Predating his TV role on *CSI*, Petersen plays Will Graham, an F.B.I. agent who can get inside the heads of serial killers. Tracking the Tooth Fairy psycho Francis Dollarhyde (a terrifying Noonan), Will calls for help from the jailed cannibal Hannibal Lecter (the great Cox, before Anthony Hopkins's Oscar-winning take on the role). Allen scores as a blind girl who brings out the killer's softer side, but this DVD belongs on your shelf because of Mann's directorial inventiveness.

Hot Bonus: There are two retrospective documentaries, but the big news is an interview with ace cinematographer Dante Spinotti.

Key Scene: The blind girl and the tiger, which the killer has drugged so she can touch it and we can watch her touch it. Creepy as hell. Really.

Maria Full of Grace (2004)

Starring: Catalina Sandino Moreno, Yenny Paola Vega

Directed by: Joshua Marston

Moreno won a Best Actress Oscar nomination for her heartfelt and harrowing performance as Maria Alvarez, a seventeen-year-old Colombian girl who can't alleviate her family's poverty with the pittance she earns slaving in a flower factory. So she joins other Colombian girls (mules) who smuggle drugs into the United States. Debuting director Marston, who also wrote the taut screenplay, shows Maria being taught to swallow drugs wrapped in packets—she sips soup to make them go down without gagging. The DVD transfer sometimes betrays the film's low budget, but the human drama etched on Moreno's young, weary face gives Maria its potent punch.

Hot Bonus: Marston, a California native, provides detailed commentary on how he wound up making a film in Spanish with English subtitles.

Key Scene: The turbulent jet flight to New York. If the drugs in Maria's belly should seep she could be poisoned or arrested or both. The looks she exchanges with her friend Blanca (Paola Vega) build incredible tension.

Married to the Mob (1988)

Starring: Michelle Pfeiffer, Dean Stockwell, Mercedes Ruehl

Directed by: Jonathan Demme

With teased dark hair, a tarty wardrobe and a tawk-like-dis accent, blonde goddess Pfeiffer is almost unrecognizable as Mafia wife Angela De-Marco. The role seems to free her; she's funny, touching, and sumptuously sexy, and this DVD brings out all her assets. Ditto the movie's. When gangland boss Tony the Tiger (primo scene-stealer Stockwell) knocks off Angela's horndog hubby (Alec Baldwin), she grabs her son and decides to live straight—as a beautician—in Manhattan. Tony's jealous wife, a riotously funny Ruehl, stalks her and so does the F.B.I. in the person of a lanky romantic (Matthew Modine). Director Demme contrives to move the whole high-spirited and hilarious mess to Miami, where David Byrne's score and Tak Fujimoto's camera help Demme make an art of tackiness run amok.

Hot Bonus: A collectible booklet that puts an emphasis on Demme, an endlessly inventive director whose credits reward your DVD watching.

Key Scene: At the supermarket with the Mafia wives: "Try keeping Tony on a leash," Angela tells the don's wife. "I think you'll find one in aisle five."

Mask, The
(New Line Platinum Series) (1994)

Starring: Jim Carrey, Cameron Diaz

Directed by: Charles Russell

This is New Line's second shot at doing justice to this Carrey vehicle on DVD—and it works like a charm. The movie, Carrey's most underrated, is a lowbrow farce done with high-tech expertise by director Russell. Carrey plays nerdy bank teller Stanley Ipkiss, a dud who turns stud when he covers his face with a mask that he finds by chance. At the Coco Bongo club, where bank customer Tina (Diaz in a smashing film debut) sings, Stanley the loser puts on the mask and, zap, he's a green-faced human tornado in a zoot suit, who dances Tina into a sexual frenzy, grows guns out of his arms, mimics Dirty Harry, and unleashes all Stanley's innermost desires. "Ooooh, somebody stop me," he cries with a mad cackle. You won't want to.

Hot Bonus: Best of a great bunch, including an endearingly nervous Diaz auditioning, is Cartoon Logic, in which scenes from the film are compared to shots from cartoons by Tex Avery, the film's main influence.

Key Scene: Stanley getting so worked up watching Tina that his peepers pop, his jaw drops a foot, and his tongue slithers lasciviously across the table.

Mask of Zorro, The (Two-Disc Special Edition) (1998)

Starring: Antonio Banderas, Catherine Zeta-Jones, Anthony Hopkins

Directed by: Martin Campbell

One of the most exciting workouts you can ever give your home theater system. The picture is luminous, and the DTS sound has a head-spinning dimensionality. The movie's not bad either. First surprise: The dashing Banderas doesn't play Zorro. It's Hopkins in the role of Don Diego de la Vega, the nobleman who donned a mask and drew his sword to free Mexico from Spanish rule. Banderas plays Alejandro, a common thief. Don Diego has rotted in jail for twenty years, but he has escaped to find his daughter, Elena (the gorgeous Zeta-Jones), and plot his vengeance by training Alejandro to replace him as Zorro. Director Campbell makes the stunts a kick, even when it is indefensibly obvious that we're watching stunt doubles.

Hot Bonus: The Unmasking Zorro featurette digs deeply into the Zorro legend and the making of the film.

Key Scene: The finale with its duels and explosion shows off what DVD technology can do. But give me the eye-popping game of strip-fencing Banderas plays with Zeta-Jones.

Master and Commander: The Far Side of the World (Two-Disc Collector's Edition) (2003)

Starring: Russell Crowe, Paul Bettany

Directed by: Peter Weir

As sea-dog Captain Jack Aubrey, Crowe climbs the rigging of his fighting ship. He's pumped, alive to the moment.

That exhilaration courses through this rousing high-seas adventure that is rendered in vivid detail on DVD. In adapting two of the twenty novels that Patrick O'Brian wrote about Captain Jack, director Weir and co-screenwriter John Collee are faithful down to the splinters in the ship's wood. It's 1805, the Napoleonic Wars are raging, and Lucky Jack, as Aubrey is known in the British Navy, commands the HMS *Surprise*, with orders to intercept the French privateer *Acheron*. Weir introduces the officers, the crew, the lads—some as young as ten—who serve as midshipmen. We meet the ship's surgeon, Stephen Maturin (Bettany), a naturalist who also plays the cello, duetting with his friend Jack on violin during a calm in the storm. Yes, calm. This isn't a theme park; it's a movie with the confidence to let a story build. Bettany is a formidable match for Crowe, who is fierce, funny, and every inch the hero.

Hot Bonus: A detailed, behind-the-scenes look at the production runs for over an hour and could serve as a model for what a supplement should do.

Key Scene: The storm at sea, filmed in the same tank in Mexico where Titanic was shot, is a doozy. But an earlier sequence, superbly shot by Russell Boyd, in which the *Surprise* attacks the *Acheron* in a dense fog, makes you feel the rumble of cannon fire ripping through the decks.

Matrix, The
(The Ultimate Collection)

Starring: Keanu Reeves, Laurence Fishburne, Carrie-Anne Moss
Directed by: Andy and Larry Wachowski

A ten-disc whopper than rivals the *Alien, Lord of the Rings* and *Star Wars* packages for best-ever DVD status. The collection includes all three *Matrix* movies—with remastered picture and sound for the first one—*The Animatrix* (nine short films from anime directors), a feature-length documentary called *The Matrix Revisited*, highbrow discourse from philosophers Ken Wilber and Dr. Cornel West, footage from the *Enter the Matrix* video game, and 106 behind-the-scenes featurettes. That's thirty-five hours of extras. Except for the lack of audio commentary from the Wachowskis, college dropouts from Chicago who continue to give fans the silent treatment, the package covers everything, including critics bitching about not liking the series. I don't much like it either, except for its visual imagination, which is magisterial and well worth your time and attention even if the two sequels—*The Matrix: Reloaded* and *The Matrix Revolutions*, both released in 2003—are hot-air balloons that quickly deflate from all the deep-dish speechifying. But seeing them all together is an undeni-

able head trip. Not since *2001: A Space Odyssey* and the first *Star Wars* trilogy has the youth audience latched onto a cinematic vision of a future generation and mined it so vigorously for truth about its own. It's easy to see why. Thomas Anderson (Reeves) is a software wage slave when Morpheus (Fishburne) tells him that his reality—our reality—is an illusion. We all live in the Matrix, a program created to distract us with fantasies while evil machines suck out our life force. Hey, that's Hollywood's job. Morpheus thinks Thomas is Neo, the One who will save humans from machines. That means Neo gets to plug into the Matrix, dress in black, kick ass, dodge bullets in slo-mo, spout wisdom like a high priest, see what Trinity (Moss)—his high-kicking lady love—has got under that kinky latex and, oh yeah, save the world.

Hot Bonus: I liked having "bullet time" explained, but for fun you can't beat the wicked MTV parody in which Justin Timberlake's Neo is menaced by a replicating Seann William Scott, creating a "shitload of Stiflers."

Key Scene: I know you have your picks, these are mine—

- *The Matrix* (1999)—The much-imitated balletic fight in which Reeves, trained by Hong Kong wire-stunt master Yuen Wo Ping, flies and flips around a bullet that travels in slo-mo. Dude, that is so cool—still.

- *The Matrix: Reloaded* (2003)—Neo takes on the evil Agent Smith, played by Hugo Weaving, who sneers scarier and funnier than any movie robot. Suddenly, Smith morphs himself into a hundred all-kicking, all-sneering Smiths.

- *The Matrix Revolutions* (2003)—Humans climb into mechanical contraptions, like the one Sigourney Weaver used in *Aliens*, to face the attack of the clones (I mean, sentinels). It's a fourteen-minute sequence and the highlight of a movie that is otherwise clichéd, repetitive, and high on its own grandiosity.

McCabe & Mrs. Miller (1971)

Starring: Warren Beatty, Julie Christie
Directed by: Robert Altman

Altman's beautiful and haunting masterwork is honored by a DVD transfer that stays true to the director's raw vision of a Pacific Northwest mining town being carved out of the wilderness at the turn of the twentieth century. Beatty, in what is arguably his best performance, plays McCabe, a cocksure gambler who opens a whorehouse with the help of the hardnosed Mrs. Miller (the Oscar-nominated Christie), a madam and opium addict. McCabe hits it big, but doesn't know when to back down when the forces of capitalism come knocking. Altman deconstructs the usual frontier clichés to find the beating heart of greed that helped define America.

Hot Bonus: Altman's commentary is cherishably contentious as he talks about his arguments with the studio, with Beatty, and with anyone else who stood in the way to make a film that refused to play by Hollywood rules.

Key Scene: The climax in the snow, evocatively shot by Vilmos Zsigmond to the resonant songs of Leonard Cohen, as McCabe meets his fate and Mrs. Miller escapes into an opium haze as deep as the snowdrifts.

Mean Girls (2004)

Starring: Lindsay Lohan, Tina Fey, Rachel McAdams

Directed by: Mark Waters

Saturday Night Live's Tina Fey brings her sass as a writer and actress to this satire of high school bitchery. Lohan is pert perfection as Cady, a junior whose parents have home-schooled her in the African bush. So when Cady enters Chicago's North Shore High, she sees things in terms of savage animal behavior. She finds shelter with the outsiders: Janis Ian (Lizzy Caplan), a goth, and Damian (Daniel Franzese), who Janis calls "too gay to function." Her pals persuade naive Cady to infiltrate the Plastics, the hottie herd led by Regina (the acid-tongued McAdams is a wow). Sabotage is planned, then Cady decides she likes being cool. Adapting Rosalind Wiseman's *Queen Bees and Wannabes*, Fey reveals a keen ear for the intricacies of the insult. And the cast, including a hilarious Fey as a bumbling math teacher, tears into the wicked fun. The plot is flimsy, but director Waters trusts Fey's tart dialogue to carry the day. Wise man.

Hot Bonus: Fey talks with the same sass she invests in the script.

Key Scene: Janis and Damian show Cady the tribes of the cafeteria: the Asian nerds, the girls who eat their feelings, and the unfriendly black hotties.

Mean Streets (Special Edition) (1973)

Starring: Harvey Keitel, Robert De Niro, Amy Robinson

Directed by: Martin Scorsese

A seminal movie for the crime genre and for Scorsese, who defined it for a new generation. After years of settling for the muddy VHS version and the barely better laser disc, the DVD transfer gives the movie the look of something freshly minted with the dew still on it, which is just the

way you should watch *Mean Streets* to get an inkling of its impact. Set in New York's Little Italy, the film awakes with its protagonist, Charlie Cappa (a searingly subtle, impossibly youthful Keitel) to the sound of the Ronette's "Be My Baby." (Scorsese's mastery at using music has continued unabated.) Then Charlie's voiceover: "You don't make up for your sins in church. You do it in the streets." And there we are: Charlie dealing with Catholic guilt, his low-level job as a collector for his mobster uncle (Cesare Danova), and his love for Teresa (Robinson), an epileptic with a nutjob brother, Johnny Boy Civello (the young De Niro, practically ablaze). As Scorsese's camera patrols the streets, bars, and pool halls, pushing fierce humor up against fiercer violence, a world is laid out before us—a world in full.

Hot Bonus: Scorsese speaks of the film he wrote with Mardik Martin as autobiography (as if we didn't know), a feeling bolstered by "Back on the Block," a seven-minute trip with the director through his old neighborhood.

Key Scene: Johnny Boy, dancing in the street to "Mickey's Monkey," then heading to a rooftop where he shoots at street lights and gives the finger to heaven in a sequence of rage and exhilarating release that is indelible.

Medium Cool (1969)

Starring: Robert Forster, Verna Bloom, Marianna Hill, Peter Bonerz

Directed by: Haskell Wexler

Wexler, the noted radical and Oscar-winning cinematographer of *Who's Afraid of Virginia Woolf* and *Bound for Glory*, made his debut as a director by taking his camera to the 1968 Democratic Convention in Chicago and letting his cast play out a fictional story against the background of the protests and police riots. The result is unique and unforgettable. Forster stars as a TV news cameraman who stays emotionally distant from the events he photographs. This causes him difficulties with the woman (Hill) he lives with and later with the Appalachian widow (Bloom) he hits on—she is raising her young son (Harold Blankenship) in a Chicago slum. As the love story converges on the real-life violence being covered by John and his soundman Gus (Bonerz), the film—transferred to DVD with exacting verisimilitude—packs a wallop that hasn't softened with the years.

Hot Bonus: Wexler talks about the difficulties he encountered.

Key Scene: As tear gas is discharged during the demonstrations, we hear a crew member shout: "This is real, Haskell"—a warning to run.

Meet Me in St. Louis (Two-Disc Special Edition) (1944)

Starring: Judy Garland, Margaret O'Brien, Tom Drake

Directed by: Vincente Minnelli

Arguably the most beautiful movie musical ever, a fact not lost on this superior DVD transfer which treats ever brightly colored image and musical note like a found treasure. The year is 1903, and St. Louis is prepping for the World's Fair while the Smith family—four daughters, one son, and mother (Mary Astor)—is dealing with trauma of father (Leon Ames) being reassigned to New York. Esther, the daughter played by Garland at her loveliest, is merely falling for the boy next door (Drake) and singing ravishing tunes, including the heartbreaking ballad, "Have Yourself a Merry Little Christmas," to her kid sister (O'Brien, so cute you almost don't want to kill her). Minnelli, Garland's husband-to-be at the time, directs with a designer's flair and just the right amount of lump-in-the-throat emotion.

Hot Bonus: A documentary, narrated by Roddy McDowall, about the making of this near-perfect slice of Americana.

Key Scene: Has to be Garland's "The Trolley Song," a burst of light, warmth, and romantic energy that makes DVD magic.

Meet the Parents (Special Bonus Edition) (2000)

Starring: Robert De Niro, Ben Stiller, Blythe Danner, Teri Polo

Directed by: Jay Roach

Critics are always ragging on De Niro for betraying his dramatic art by doing low farce. Screw that. And embrace this DVD fluffball for allowing De Niro to once again show his comic gifts for ham (*Analyze This*) and wry (*Wag the Dog*). The former raging bull plays Jack Byrnes, a retired CIA operative (shush, it's a secret) whose daughter (Polo) comes home to Dad and Mom (Danner) to introduce Greg Focker (Stiller), the male nurse she wants to marry. Stiller is hilarious as the urban neurotic who feels as lost as Woody Allen in *Annie Hall* when Diane Keaton tells him sweetly,

"You're what Grammy Hall would call a real Jew." It's a goofball duel of wits, and De Niro and Stiller play the crazy hell out of it. The vulgar 2004 sequel, *Meet the Fockers*, made even more money, but lacked the original's style.

Hot Bonus: Thirty-five outtakes, including De Niro singing unplugged.

Key Scene: It's impossible not to laugh when Jack hooks up Greg to a home lie-detector ("Have you ever purchased pornographic material?").

Melvin and Howard (1980)

Starring: Paul LeMat, Jason Robards, Mary Steenburgen

Directed by: Jonathan Demme

A DVD find. Director Demme busted out of the B-movie ghetto with this lyrically comic folk tale about Melvin Dummar (LeMat), a Nevada milkman who claims he was the guy who picked up an old, scraggly, dying Howard Hughes (Robards) on the road to Las Vegas and that he should be the beneficiary of $156 million that the billionaire Hughes left in his will. Working from Bo Goldman's Oscar-winning script, Demme paints a warmly funny portrait of thwarted American dreamers. Steenburgen won a supporting Oscar as Melvin's go-go dancer wife. And watching her tap dancing to the Stones' "(I Can't Get No) Satisfaction," you can see why.

Hot Bonus: Demme's smart commentary provides info about the real Dummar, who does a cameo as a lunch counterman.

Key Scene: Melvin in the car with Howard (Robards, Oscar nominated) doing a duet to "Bye, Bye Blackbird" is pure filmmaking inspiration.

Memento (Two-Disc Limited Edition) (2001)

Starring: Guy Pearce, Carrie-Anne Moss, Joe Pantoliano

Directed by: Christopher Nolan

A mesmerizing mind-bender that stars Pearce in a tour de force as Leonard Shelby, a former insurance investigator who is out to find the man who killed his wife. Sound conventional? Think again. From the start—and cheers here to Wally Pfister's tricky camerawork that finds the perfect home on DVD—this jolting jigsaw puzzle of a movie grabs you and won't let go. The stunning opener involves a murder and a Polaroid of the body. Then Nolan runs everything backward. The photo slips back into the camera, a bullet is sucked back into a gun barrel, and Leonard starts living in reverse. A head injury sustained while he was trying to protect his wife has left him with short-term memory loss. To stay focused, the understandably paranoid Leonard takes pictures, writes notes to himself, and even tattoos messages on his body, such as "John G. raped and murdered your wife." Strangers, such as sexy bartender Natalie (Moss is pure femme fatale) and snarky undercover cop Teddy (Pantoliano), are a real hazard. Nolan's reverse action isn't a trick—it's a way to put us inside Leonard's head.

Hot Bonus: Nolan's commentary is also evasive, so go to the Easter Egg on Disc 2. You'll have to pass a test first involving arranging photos of a babe changing a tire. Put them in reverse order and *Memento* will play in chronological order. Neat trick.

Key Scene: Natalie using Leonard's affliction to take him to bed and screw with his psyche becomes a chilling moment of inhuman exploitation.

Men in Black
(Two-Disc Deluxe Edition) (1997)

Starring: Will Smith, Tommy Lee Jones, Linda Fiorentino

Directed by: Barry Sonnenfeld

DVD show-off stuff, plain and simple. Actually, Rick Baker's special effects are complicated; just check out those extras. What flows freely is the fun as Smith and Jones, working for an unofficial government agency (MiB), chase visitors from other planets away from ours. Putting on his Ray-Bans, Agent Smith cracks wise to Agent Jones: "You know the difference between you and me? I make this look good." Sonnenfeld deftly orchestrates their intricate comic byplay. It's too bad the magic disappeared in the 2002 sequel. But it works here as the agents interrogate a suspect with tentacles or blow the head off a man who then grows a new one. So why resist? To quote the film's wisest alien, who just happens to be occupying the body of an ugly-ass pug dog, "You don't like it, you can kiss my furry little butt."

Hot Bonus: You, the DVD owner, can re-edit three scenes, using various takes and outtakes to prove you're better than Sonnenfeld. Try it.

Key Scene: Smith getting wrapped up in a baby alien's giant tail and tossed around like a wet rag in spin dry.

Menace II Society (1993)

Starring: Larenz Tate, Tyrin Turner, Jada Pinkett

Directed by: Allen and Albert Hughes

Directed by the Hughes twins, then twenty-two, this groundbreaking film goes beyond its docudrama setting in the L.A. hood to explore the roots of gangsta violence among its fatherless homeboys. Caine (Turner), eighteen, grew up in Watts. He saw his mother OD and his father murder and be murdered. Tyger Williams's insightful script shows how hate closes off avenues of escape for Caine and his posse. Caine is surprised but hardly remorseful when his friend O-Dog (Tate) blows away a Korean grocer over a minor insult. The Hughes brothers bring a controlled intensity and maturity to their stunning feature debut. On a mere $2.5 million budget, whose limitations are barely visible on the DVD, they feel their way into madness and come up with an agonizing reflection of a generation at war with itself.

Hot Bonus: A ten-minute Hughes brothers interview is sharp but II short.

Key Scene: Caine visits a pal's women (Pinkett) and teaches her six-year-old son how to handle a gun. The pass-along brutality strikes a raw nerve.

Metallica: Some Kind of Monster
(Two-Disc Special Edition) (2004)

Starring: James Hetfield, Lars Ulrich, Kirk Hammett, Robert Trujillo

Directed by: Joe Berlinger and Bruce Sinofsky

A rock-doc window into the making of the Metallica album *St. Anger* that becomes a journey into the band's psychic inferno. Who knew? Certainly not filmmakers Berlinger and Sinofsky, who used Metallica songs in their documentary *Paradise Lost*, about three teens convicted of murder in Arkansas, while allegedly under the influence of the devil's music, heavy metal. The filmmakers thought it would be intriguing to film the process of making *St. Anger* after the departure of bassist Jason Newsted. Nearly three years and sixteen hundred hours of footage later, they emerged with a portrait of a dysfunctional band in crisis. Frontman James Hetfield hits rehab to fight his addictions (Metallica was dubbed "Alcoholica" in the 1980s) and feuds with Napster-hating drummer Lars Ulrich, as guitarist Kirk Hammett tries to play peacemaker. No luck there. That's when therapist and performance-enhancement coach Phil Towle is brought in, at forty thousand dollars a month, to ease the transition of these party animals turned middle-aged family men into a fresh creative force with the addition of bass player Robert Trujillo. Everything but blood is spilled in the process. What's on view for two hours and twenty minutes is a headbanger in every sense of the word. With its digital image and sonic surround boom, this is a thrashing, thrilling chunk of DVD gold.

Hot Bonus: More of everything, plus dishy talk from Berlinger and Sinofsky.

Key Scene: As relief from all the nonmetal screaming, let the music video of the band playing "Some Kind of Monster" rip through your system.

Metropolis (Restored Authorized Edition) (1927)

Starring: Brigitte Helm, Gustav Froelich
Directed by: Fritz Lang

Who wants to see some ancient silent film—in black-and-white yet—with actors you never heard of? You do. Lang's futuristic classic (set in 2026) has influenced films from *Star Wars* to *Blade Runner*. And Kino's DVD, from the German restoration released in 2002 with a new recording of the Gottfried Huppertz score, makes up for all the damaged prints that have plagued us for decades. The plot, about an industrialist's son (Froelich) who falls hard for a working girl (Helm, hailed by *The New York Times* as "the Kirsten Dunst of the Weimar Republic")—not to mention totalitarianism, class, mechanization, and men in lust with fembots—takes a backseat to the stunning visuals that are still being imitated.

Hot Bonus: A featurette on the digital restoration is astounding in its detail, making us hunger for the pieces of the film that are still missing.

Key Scene: The first glimpse of the soaring towers of the city with cars gliding through clouds makes a stark contrast to the workers crowding into the slums below.

Midnight Clear, A (1992)

Starring: Ethan Hawke, Gary Sinise, Frank Whaley, Ayre Gross
Directed by: Keith Gordon

A World War II film of startling delicacy. You heard me. Director Gordon, who adapted William Wharton's novel, sets the plot in motion during December 1944 in the Ardennes Forest, where six GIs wait in the snow for the German soldiers they are hunting to make a move. Instead, the enemy throws snowballs and sings Christmas carols, prompting both sides to try to work out a separate peace. Then violence erupts. Symbolism can weigh on a film in which one soldier (Sinise) is called Mother and another (Whaley) Father. But

under Gordon's astute direction, the cast—led by Hawke as the young Sarg—finds a moral center. The only complaint with the DVD is the pan-and-scan presentation of a film that demands a widescreen transfer.

Hot Bonus: Cogent commentary from Gordon and Hawke.

Key Scene: The shocking opener as Mother runs screaming from his foxhole, throws away his rifle, strips naked, and heads for the forest.

Midnight Cowboy (1969)

Starring: Jon Voight, Dustin Hoffman
Directed by: John Schlesinger

Best known as the only X-rated movie to win the Academy Award for Best Picture, this character piece deserves to stick for something less absurd. The remastered DVD is a chance to revel in its true qualities: The star turn from Voight as Joe Buck, a Texas dishwater who hits New York to service rich ladies. The acting brilliance of Hoffman as Ratso Rizzo, the crippled con artist who tries to pimp him ("You're beginning to smell, and for a stud in New York, that's a handicap."). The direction of Schlesinger, a Brit who sees America as dazzling and dehumanizing in equal doses. And the writing of Waldo Salt, who won an Oscar for adapting James Leo Herilihy's novel into a nonsexual love story between two losers. Add the Harry Nilsson soundtrack ("Everybody's Talkin'") and a devastating death scene on a Florida-bound bus and you have a DVD that reinvents itself each time you watch it.

Hot Bonus: A booklet of production notes, but where's the commentaries?

Key Scene: Ratso hitting a pushy cab and screeching "I'm walking here" as he and Joe cross a Manhattan intersection.

Midnight Express (Collector's Edition) (1978)

Starring: Brad Davis, John Hurt, Randy Quaid, Paul Smith
Directed by: Alan Parker

Not a pretty picture, though the DVD transfer does catch the grit in this harrowing true story of Billy Hayes (Davis, a solid actor who died of AIDS in 1991), an American who got busted in Turkey for trying to smuggle out two kilos of hashish. Despite repeated efforts to free him from prison, Hayes was subjected to almost five years of beatings, rapes, and harassment by guards, notably Hamidou (Smith), a peerless sadist. Quaid plays the hotheaded prison pal who plans their escape (called the midnight express), and Hurt steals the acting honors as a stoned Brit inmate. Oliver Stone won an Oscar for his brutally effective script (based on Hayes's book). Director Parker, goosed by Giorgio Moroder's propulsive score, puts you through the wringer in a movie that beats Nancy Reagan at the game of Just Say No.

Hot Bonus: A behind-the-scenes look that is too short at eight minutes.

Key Scene: Hayes and Hamidou in the torture room. Watch those spikes.

Mighty Wind, A (2003)

Starring: Eugene Levy, Catherine O'Hara, Fred Willard, Michael McKean

Directed and co-written by: Christopher Guest

Folk music numbs me. But the sheer exuberance of this satire, directed with mirth and mischief by Guest, who devised the story with fellow-actor Levy and let the cast improv the rest, had me begging for more. I can't think of a better recommendation to grab a DVD. Guest, McKean, and Harry Shearer make up the Folksman, an oddball trio that looks almost normal compared to Mitch & Mickey—the priceless Levy and O'Hara—a duo whose career and love breakdown precipitated Mitch's mental collapse. Then there's the New Main Street Singers, led by a former porn star (Jane Lynch) and a manager (Willard) who starred for two minutes on a TV series called *What Happened*, a phrase he thinks everyone remembers. The Guest stock company never gets a laugh wrong, and the songs, written for the film, bring parody hilariously close to truth. Take the title tune that ends: "Yes, it's blowin' peace and freedom/It's blowin' you and me."

Hot Bonus: Twenty-two minutes of deleted scenes, coupled with Guest-Levy commentary, are as funny as anything left in the movie.

Key Scene: Levy and O'Hara singing "A Kiss at the End of the Rainbow," a song that manages to be as heartbreaking as it is comically absurd.

Mildred Pierce (1945)

Starring: Joan Crawford, Ann Blyth, Eve Arden, Jack Carson, Zachary Scott

Directed by: Michael Curtiz

Crawford's Oscar-winning comeback vehicle is also a knockout film noir that belongs on every DVD shelf. Black-and-white cinematography (Ernest Haller) has rarely shimmered so seductively. Based on James M. Cain's hardassed novel about a waitress-turned-big-time-exec, the film transcends cliché as Crawford—under the subtle direction of Curtiz—gets to the heart of a woman whose daughter (Blyth, so good as a baddie) shoots the man (Scott) they both take to bed. Carson is slime personified, and Arden gives the wisecracking friend role her indelible stamp. But this is Crawford's show, and she holds you every step of the way.

Hot Bonus: A documentary on Crawford that explains how playing Mildred turned her career around.

Key Scene: Fur-clad Mildred on the pier at night, ready to jump in, until the sound of a cop's nightstick brings her back. It's noir in a nutshell.

Miller's Crossing (1990)

Starring: Gabriel Byrne, Albert Finney, Marcia Gay Harden, John Turturro

Directed by: Joel Coen

Gangsters. Prohibition. Forbidden love. Joel and Ethan Coen. Say no more, just watch the Coen brothers twist the genre into new shapes. The DVD gets the burnished browns of Barry Sonnenfeld's cinematography just right. The actors do the rest. Finney is tops as Leo, the Irish hood who doesn't know his wingman, Tom (Byrne), is screwing Leo's girl, Verna (Harden). He does know that his colleague Caspar (Jon Polito) wants Verna's brother, Bernie (Turturro), murdered for horning in on Casper's gambling interests. That's a dilemma that the Coens play for laughs and a surprising emotional gravity. Byrne anchors the film with devilish control.

Hot Bonus: A featurette on Sonnenfeld's outstanding camerawork

Key Scene: The woods. A fedora blowing in the wind. And Turturro giving the film's best performance as a marked man begging for his life.

Million Dollar Baby (Three-Disc Deluxe Edition) (2004)

Starring: Clint Eastwood, Hilary Swank, Morgan Freeman

Directed by: Clint Eastwood

Oscars for Best Picture, Actress, Supporting Actor, and Director. Welcome to the renaissance of Eastwood. In 2003, he directed *Mystic River* and

gave the piece a tragic poetry that seeps into *Million Dollar Baby*, a stunningly drawn map of the human heart disguised as a boxing yarn. Adapted by Paul Haggis from a story in the F. X. Toole collection *Rope Burns*, this emotional wallop of a movie focuses on Maggie Fitzgerald (Swank delivers the goods with ferocity and feeling), an uneducated waitress from the Ozarks who thinks she can be a fighter. Her dream brings her to the L.A. gym of Frankie Dunn (Eastwood), a fight trainer and cut man with zero patience for female warriors ("girlie tough is not enough"). The one person who thinks otherwise is Frankie's pal Scrap (the ever-magnificent Freeman), an ex-boxer who lost an eye in a fight for which Frankie was cut man. If you smell a setup for *Rocky* rah-rah, you don't know Eastwood. Even when calamity climbs in the ring and the script flirts with teary clichés (Maggie has an exploitative family, Frankie has an estranged daughter), Eastwood—a true film artist—never pummels you. His stripped-down performance—as powerful as anything he's ever done—has a rugged, haunting beauty. Ditto the movie.

Hot Bonus: The soundtrack CD with Eastwood's haunting score is a nice addition. But *Born to Fight*, a featurette that examines the parallels of Swank's role to real-life boxer Lucia Rijker, speaks volumes.

Key Scene: Great ring action, but seeing the two male legends spar over the socks Freeman was supposed to buy with Eastwood's money is magic.

Minority Report (Two-Disc Special Edition) (2002)

Starring: Tom Cruise, Colin Farrell, Samantha Morton

Directed by: Steven Spielberg

Spielberg's futuristic thriller, starring a focused, feeling Cruise as a D.C. cop who stops crime before it happens, is revved up on visionary action and a topical idea: how much freedom are we willing to sacrifice to feel secure at home?

Spielberg's source material is a 1956 short story by Philip K. Dick set in the year 2054. Cruise's John Anderton watched his life come apart when his son was kidnapped—divorce and drugs ensued—just as his Pre-Crime unit took off. Using the skills of a trio of psychics (precogs) who lie in a pool and see murders-to-be that computers turn into images, Anderton orchestrates visions into police action. Now Pre-Crime may go national, unless the Justice Department, led by an ex-seminarian (Farrell, excellent), screws things up for the boss-man (Max von Sydow). Anderton goes on the run when the precogs predict he will murder someone in thirty-six hours. Only Agatha (Morton), the most fragile precog, can prove him innocent.

Hot Bonus: Spielberg still has a thing about commentary tracks—he doesn't do them. But Disc 2 is crammed with special features, the best of which shows how Spielberg designed "the ugliest, dirtiest movie I've ever made."

Key Scene: The sequence with the mechanical spiders who perform retina scans is the film's funniest and most suspenseful.

Misery (Special Edition) (1990)

Starring: Kathy Bates, James Caan
Directed by: Rob Reiner

A Stephen King adaptation that makes you feel all oogie. The DVD makes you feel oogie as well, which is the point. Bates gives an Oscar-winning tour de force as nurse Annie Wilkes. She is a fan of the romance writer Paul Sheldon (Caan) and can't believe her luck when Paul (she calls him Mister Man) crashes his car in a blizzard on a road near her Colorado home. She splints his broken legs, props him up in her comfy bed and demands to know why he's killed off Misery Chastain, the nineteenth-century heroine of the eight novels Annie adores, and started on a serious book about ghetto life. Watch out for Annie's hammer. King is writing about his own attempts to get beyond the horror genre. In adapting the book, screenwriter William Goldman and director Reiner go for dark laughs and suspense over bonecrunching. But when the crunch comes, look out.

Hot Bonus: Conversations with Bates, Caan, and Reiner turn up interesting info, such as the fact that Warren Beatty was once set to play the writer.

Key Scene: The hobbling (ouch!) gets all the attention, but I prefer Bates in a fit of madness when Annie—to avoid profanity—refers to the "cocky-doodie car" and to Paul as "just another lying old dirty birdie!"

Mission: Impossible (Collector's Edition) (1996)

Starring: Tom Cruise, Jon Voight, Emmanuelle Beárt

Directed by: Brian De Palma

It's the stunts, stupid. They spark like firecrackers on DVD, long after you've stopped trying to figure why Cruise's Ethan Hunt was nearly wiped out with his crew during a mission in Prague. As a producer, Cruise seems determined to hire different quality directors to reimagine the old TV series in exciting new ways. I'm down with that, especially since he retains Lalo Schifrin's thrilling theme, now amped to the sonic stratosphere. When the convoluted plot doesn't sink him, De Palma turns out the action. Remember Cruise lowering himself by wire into CIA headquarters in Virginia?

Hot Bonus: The Dolby Digital track, which is such an improvement over the standard stereo surround option, you are forbidden not to use it.

Key Scene: The head-on between the chopper and a speeding train.

Mission: Impossible II (2000)

Starring: Tom Cruise, Thandie Newton, Dougray Scott, Anthony Hopkins

Directed by: John Woo

It's still the stunts that count. Hong Kong director Woo doesn't do the actors any favors, but the action, starting with Cruise scaling a cliff in Utah, is first class. Cruise's Ethan Hunt is out to find the renegade agent (Scott) who stole a virus and to do a little James Bond horndogging and globe-trotting with a babe (Newton) who takes him for a ride, literally and figuratively.

Hot Bonus: A featurette on the film's stunts and how they were done.

Key Scene: The motorcycle stuff runs a close second to the climactic fight between Cruise and Scott that has all the Woo chop-socky trademarks with the exception of doves flying in slo-mo.

Mister Roberts (Special Edition) (1955)

Starring: Henry Fonda, Jack Lemmon, James Cagney, William Powell, Betsy Palmer

Directed by: John Ford and Mervyn LeRoy

Fonda, repeating his stage role, is quietly devastating as Doug Roberts, the lieutenant who longs for combat but is stuck on a navy cargo ship as World War II rages elsewhere. In this comedy laced with touching gravity, Fonda's Mister Roberts stands up for his men against the tyrannical Captain (Cagney) with the help of the ship's Doc (the elegant Powell) and Ensign Pulver, played by the Oscar-winning Lemmon as a merry prankster. The DVD shows its age in spots, but otherwise the transfer looks smashing. The cast, having to deal with a director switch (Ford fell ill and was replaced by LeRoy) performs as a splendid unit. Whether reveling in farce—the exploding laundry, R&R with nurses led by the luminous Palmer—or revealing deeper feelings, the movie stands the test of time.

Hot Bonus: Lemmon speaks movingly about the bond among the actors.

Key Scene: The captain's beloved palm tree and what Pulver does to it after the ship is faced with tough news.

Modern Times (Two-Disc Special Edition) (1936)

Starring: Charlie Chaplin, Paulette Goddard

Directed by: Charlie Chaplin

Chaplin's last silent film receives a stunning DVD restoration from Warner as the Little Tramp takes on capitalism and the mechanization of modern society. Other than Chaplin's score, which includes the melodious "Smile," what we hear in the film comes from machines. The opening sequence that contrasts sheep with workers being herded into a factory is justly famous, as is the Tramp having a mental breakdown trying to keep up with an assembly line and the watchful eye of Big Brother. The master's voice is heard in a song "Nonsense," gibberish that constitutes the great man's teasing slap at talking pictures, which hereafter he would embrace. Goddard, Chaplin's then-wife, costars as the homeless (and underage) gamin he loves and tries to protect. She remains his best and liveliest leading lady.

Hot Bonus: The complete version of Chaplin's Nonsense song, including a karaoke version.

Key Scene: The gem of an ending with the two lovers (this would be the final appearance of the Little Tramp) walking arm and arm into a sunset.

Mommie Dearest (1981)

Starring: Faye Dunaway, Diana Scarwid, Mara Hobel

Directed by: Frank Perry

A camp classic. Paramount's widescreen DVD transfer is the icing on the cake of Dunaway's over-the-top and into the stratosphere portrait of Joan Crawford. Whether or not you believe that the late screen legend was guilty of the monstrous child abuse her adopted daughter Christina alleged in her bestselling 1978 hatchet job, you'll have to admire Dunaway's go-for-broke emoting. Dunaway often plays Crawford as Caligula—thrashing her daughter with closet implements ("No wire hangers—ever!"), pummeling her with a cleanser can, and chopping off her golden locks in a punishing rage. Astonishingly, Dunaway also provides insights into Crawford's fear of aging, poverty, and obscurity barely hinted at in Christina's book. Hobel and Scarwid are terrific playing Christina the child and the adult, respectively, but it's Dunaway, climbing the walls of this gaudy Hollywood exercise in self-flagellation, who makes her own kind of truth.

Hot Bonus: A gallery of photos from the movie that you can play while doing your own line-by-line readings of the atrocious dialogue. Dunaway, still embarrassed by the role, provides no audio commentary.

Key Scene: The wire hangers meltdown is classic, but so is Crawford facing down the Pepsi board (she was the widow of its chairman) with the immortal words: "Don't fuck with me, fellas. This ain't my first time at the rodeo."

Monsoon Wedding (2002)

Starring: Naseeruddin Shah, Vasundhara Das, Shefali Shetty, Vijay Raaz

Directed by: Mira Nair

Chaos—comic and otherwise—results when a large Indian family, whose members are scattered around the globe, assembles in contemporary New Delhi for an old-fashioned five-day ceremony of an arranged marriage. The DVD is alive with music and movement. Shah is magnificent as the harried father of the bride (Das), whose cousin (Shetty) harbors a dark secret against another wedding guest. The biggest laughs come from Raaz as a wedding planner. Director Nair choreographs this huge party with an eye for telling detail. She aims for pure joy and achieves it.

Hot Bonus: Nair talks with scrappy wit about filming in India.

Key Scene: The wedding night with the whole family dancing in the middle of a thunderstorm.

Monster (Special Edition) (2003)

Starring: Charlize Theron, Christina Ricci

Directed by: Patty Jenkins

You rub your eyes. This can't be Theron, the babe incarnate. As Aileen Wuornos, a prostitute executed in Florida in 2002 for murdering six men, Theron is transformed. Her flawless face is splotchy, her eyes heavy, her body thick and lumbering. Extra pounds, a dental prosthesis, and makeup magic (from Toni G.) add to the illusion. But the miracle Theron performs is more than a stunt to win her an Oscar (though she did win it). Theron gets into the skin of this woman whom the media called a monster. First-time director Jenkins strives hard—too hard—to explain away Wuornos's crimes. And Wuornos's graphic lesbo romance with Shelby (Ricci, hamstrung by an underwritten part) comes off like a lesser Boys Don't Cry. But Theron, like a force of nature, compels us to go beyond supposition and look Wuornos straight in the eye. DVD lets you do just that. Hit that freeze frame.

Hot Bonus: A look at how Theron achieved her physical transformation.

Key Scene: Wuornos in a car with a man (Pruitt Taylor Vince) she doesn't kill. It's a sequence of dangerous, quicksilver emotions, and Theron nails it.

Monster's Ball (Signature Series) (2001)

Starring: Halle Berry, Billy Bob Thornton, Peter Boyle, Heath Ledger

Directed by: Marc Forster

Berry made history by winning the Best Actress Oscar for this rubbed-raw drama. Thornton plays Hank, a guard on death row, who cares for his redneck dad (Boyle) and shares guard duty with his son (Ledger) as well as the same tired hooker, whom they both bang standing up. Nice, huh? Director Forster turns up the tension when Hank and Sonny supervise the execution of Lawrence Musgrove (a strong, understated Sean Combs), an event that brings Hank together with the dead man's waitress wife, Leticia (Berry), a hard case not above beating her grossly overweight son (Coronji Calhoun), when he sneaks candy. It's a welcome surprise when the film takes a tender turn and becomes the unlikeliest of love stories.

Hot Bonus: An "Anatomy of a Scene" is promised on the DVD box, but is nowhere on the disc. Try the section in which Forster talks about the film's score and how it subtly enhances the film's points.

Key Scene: The wham-bam sex sequence between Thornton and Berry is already notorious, but hardly anyone notices how these two actors find the ache of loneliness in their characters. Notice now.

Monsters Inc. (Two-Disc Collector's Edition) (2001)

Starring: The voices of John Goodman, Billy Crystal, Mary Gibbs

Directed by: Peter Docter

An unqualified treat, which is no surprise since this wow-worthy display of computer animation comes from the wizards at Pixar. For stars, we have Mike, a one-eyed green thingie hilariously voiced by Crystal, and Sulley, a giant blue furball voiced with wit and warmth by Goodman. The pair joins other monsters in a plot to scare kids by sneaking into their bedrooms. Of course, there are more laughs than scares in the script, which has three-year-old Boo (Gibbs) turn the tables by sneaking into the monster lair. Director Docter keeps the fun coming, but it's the Pixar animators who keep grown-ups as riveted as the kids with visual marvels that make the trip to DVD with their dazzle in full working order.

Hot Bonus: A tour of the Pixar Animation Studios really rocks.

Key Scene: The chase through what looks like a thousand closet doors.

Monterey Pop: The Complete Festival (Three-Disc Special Edition) (1968)

Starring: Janis Joplin, Jimi Hendrix, Otis Redding

Directed by: D. A. Pennebaker

Joplin wails "Ball and Chain," Hendrix literally sets fire to his guitar during "Wild Thing," Redding tears it up at the end of "Try a Little Tenderness." But the real star here is the audience, as

the camera lingers lovingly over a tribe of golden flower children.

Hot Bonus: Three packed discs include the full performances of Hendrix and Redding, plus sets from the Byrds and Buffalo Springfield that never made it into the film's theatrical release. Thank you, Criterion, for the impossibly crisp image and sound.

Key Scene: Country Joe and the Fish's "Section 43," waking up the sleeping campers with a psychedelic guitar attack.

Monty Python and the Holy Grail (Two-Disc Collector's Edition) (1975)

Starring: John Cleese, Eric Idle, Terry Jones, Michael Palin, Terry Gilliam, Graham Chapman

Directed by: Terry Gilliam and Terry Jones

Full disclosure: This is the movie that makes me laugh longer and harder than any other comedy. To have it digitally restored on DVD and jam-packed with extras is a gift. Does it look and sound better than ever? Hardly. It's never looked or sounded good. The Python troupe—five Brits and one American (Gilliam)—did it on the cheap (it was only their second movie). King Arthur (the late Chapman), with his servant Patsy (Gilliam) in tow, gathers his silly knights—Lancelot (Cleese), Galahad (Palin), Bedevere (Jones), and the not-so-brave Sir Robin (Idle)—and prances around the Middle Ages banging coconuts together to pretend his team has actual horses and begging others to join them in their search for the Holy Grail. "We already got one," says the French taunter (Cleese again), who blows his nose and farts in the general direction of these donkey-bottom biters. Then there's the Knights Who Say Ni and demand that Arthur gift them with a shrubbery ("make it a nice one and not too expensive"). And I haven't mentioned the Killer Rabbit, the Witch, the watery tart in the lake who hands Arthur a sword and supreme executive power, and a hundred hilarious lines I know by heart. No use my prattling on about how good it is or how Broadway has turned it into the hit musical *Spamalot* or how the more you watch the movie, the funnier its gets. The package contains a script and twenty-four seconds of new footage. Now that's a DVD holy grail.

Hot Bonus: Everything works, especially the general complaints and backbiting from Cleese, Idle, and Palin, the manual on how to use your own coconuts, the subtitles taken directly from the Bard's *Henry IV, Part II* for those who hate the film's dialogue, the "Hard of Hearing" control on the Menu that screams the film at you and—my personal favorite—the "Knights of the Round Table" song done with Lego men in a Lego castle.

Key Scene: If pushed to the wall, I can't live without the Black Knight who keeps fighting even after his arms and legs are hacked off.

Monty Python's Life of Brian (Special Edition) (1979)

Starring: John Cleese, Eric Idle, Terry Jones, Michael Palin, Terry Gilliam, Graham Chapman
Directed by: Terry Jones

Before Martin Scorsese and Mel Gibson riled up the religious right with their serious takes on the life of Christ, the Python troupe was out there pushing the envelope. Brian Cohen (Chapman) is born in a manger, just down the road from Jesus, and mistaken for the Messiah by not-so-wise men. Brian's mom, the Virgin Mandy (Jones in drag), doesn't think myrrh is much of a gift. Thirty years later, she and Brian keep mishearing Christ's pronouncements: "What did he say? 'The Greek shall inherit the Earth? Blessed are the *cheese*makers'?" A third party adds: "He's not talking literally. What he means to say is blessed are the manufacturers in general." You get the picture, which looks as good as it ever will, thanks to Criterion's DVD transfer. The satire may not be Swiftian, but with the Pythons playing dozens of roles each—all hail Cleese as a centurion giving lessons in Latin graffiti and Palin as a lisping Pontius Pilate—the laughs cut deep.

Hot Bonus: Seeing the Brit troupe at work on the film and then presenting the history of how the Pythons got started. Also give a listen to the British radio ads with the actors' mums pleading with listeners to see the movie.

Key Scene: Brian's crucifixion with Idle hanging on the cross next to him and chirping the song, co-opted for Broadway's *Spamalot*, "Always Look on the Bright Side of Life," with such immortal lyrics as "Life's a piece a shit/when you look at it." Sunday school was never like this.

Monty Python's The Meaning of Life (Two-Disc Special Edition) (1983)

Starring: John Cleese, Eric Idle, Terry Jones, Michael Palin, Terry Jones, Graham Chapman
Directed by: Terry Jones

Completing the Python circle (a rival to *The Lord of the Rings* trilogy in my warped mind) is this epic comic treatise on all that matters, done up proud on DVD. So what if it's just a series of sketches strung together about birth and death and all the fun stuff in between? Gilliam opens the curtain with his own animated pirate movie. Ingmar Bergman is royally tweaked as dinner guests die of food poisoning and face the Grim Reaper. A poor Catholic family is besieged by a stork—a real one—that keeps dropping off babies. Sperm gets its own song ("Hindu, Taoist, Mormon/Spill theirs anywhere/But God loves those who treat/their semen with more care").

Hot Bonus: As always, the Pythons shame all rivals in comic ingenuity. Besides a Director's Cut of the movie that inserts twenty minutes of deleted scenes, there's a soundtrack for people watching at home alone; Un Film de John Cleese, a hilarious trailer featuring only Cleese; and a new "making-of" segment with the surviving Pythons (Chapman died in 1989) offering naughty stories about making the film.

Key Scene: Just say the words, "Better bring the bucket," and images arise of Cleese's snob headwaiter feeding obscene quantities of rich French food to the obese Mr. Creosote (Jones), who projectile vomits all over the restaurant. Disgusting at first viewing, the sequence reduces you to helpless laughter each time you watch it again. Bring lots of buckets.

Moonstruck (Special Edition) (1987)

Starring: Cher, Nicolas Cage, Olympia Dukakis, Danny Aiello
Directed by: Norman Jewison

"I'm in love with you," says Cage. "Snap out of it," says Cher, slapping him hard across the face. That's amore, as seen by screenwriter John Patrick Shanley and director Jewison in a dazzling romantic comedy (the DVD transfer works hard to keep the dazzle) that believes, truly, that the moon watches over lovers. Even in Brooklyn. Even in an Italian American family where the daughter, Loretta (Cher), works in a funeral parlor and hardens herself to love (her husband was hit by a bus and died) and to the passion of Ronny (Cage), a one-armed baker whose brother (Aiello) is Loretta's fiancé. Loretta's mother, Rose (Dukakis), shares her daughter's skepticism. Her husband (Vincent Gardenia) cheats on her—she thinks it's because men fear death. Before this movie ends, the moon plays many more tricks—some sweet, some sad, and all of them as authentic as family.

Hot Bonus: Sassy talk from Cher, Jewison, and Shanley. But why, oh why, is the picture presented in full screen without an alternate letterboxed version?

Key Scene: The kitchen finale where the family tries to undo love's tangles. Cher and Dukakis won Oscars, and here you can see why. Both act without tearjerking, which makes the tears flow freely. Alla famiglia!

Motorcycle Diaries, The (2004)

Starring: Gael Garcia Bernal, Rodrigo de la Serna

Directed by: Walter Salles

Before he was executed in 1967, Argentina's Ernesto "Che" Guevara had become (at the side of Fidel Castro) an icon of guerrilla warfare. You won't find him in this mesmerizing look at an asthmatic, rich-boy medical student in the act of discovering his insurgent spirit on a 1952 motorcycle trip that Ernesto (Bernal), then twenty-three, took with his biochemist pal Alberto Granado (De la Serna), twenty-nine. Jose Rivera based his script on the diaries both men kept of their eight-month trip through South America (from the snows of the Andes to the heat of the Amazon). Cheers to Brazilian director Salles for shooting in the actual locations. The DVD captures the sights and sounds, including "Al Otro Lado del Rio," the Jorge Drexler theme that became the first song in Spanish to win an Oscar.

Hot Bonus: The filmmakers talk about the importance of Guevara, but I would have liked Salles to deal with the heat he took from critics who think the compassionate Ernesto doesn't jibe with the executioner he became.

Key Scene: The visit to the San Pablo leper colony. Ernesto (Bernal plays him like a gathering storm) feels an instant connection. His night swim (gasping for breath with each stroke) to join them is the film's true climax.

Moulin Rouge (Double Digipac) (2001)

Starring: Nicole Kidman, Ewan McGregor, Jim Broadbent

Directed by: Baz Luhrmann

For sound, light, color, and art direction for days, you can't beat the DVD of Luhrmann's musical, set in the Paris of 1900 but powered by contemporary pop and rock songs. Fatboy Slim provides a techno cancan; Beck reinvents David Bowie's "Diamond Dogs"; Christina Aguilera, Lil' Kim, Mya, and Pink cover "Lady Marmalade"; and, well, you get the deconstructionist drift. Watching the DVD, I felt less mauled than I did watching it in the theater. McGregor, he's dying of love, and the Oscar-nominated Kidman, she's dying of a nasty cough, can actually sing. Even better, they put human faces on the nonstop opulence. You can see every cent of the film's $52.5 million budget on these two discs. Luhrmann creates visual miracles with his wife, production designer Catherine Martin, but excess is his Achilles' heel.

Hot Bonus: Extras are everywhere, from commentaries to deleted scenes. But if ever a movie didn't need more, more, more, it's this one.

Key Scene: Kidman and McGregor on a Paris rooftop singing the "Elephant Love Medley," which practically swoons off the screen.

Mulholland Dr. (2000)

Starring: Naomi Watts, Laura Elena Harring

Directed and written by: David Lynch

Fanboys salivate when Watts and Harring strip down and rub titties. But don't reduce Lynch's mind teaser to hot lesbo action or a Freudian exercise. Let this DVD pull you in. Surrender to its visionary daring, swooning eroticism, and colors that pop like a whore's lip gloss. It opens in a fever dream, with a woman twisting and turning in bed. It's night in Los Angeles. A limo slithers along Mulholland Drive, carrying a gorgeous brunette amnesiac (Harring) who later links up with naïve Betty (Watts), an actress wannabe. The girls play detective and turn up a mysterious blue box, a dwarfish tycoon, a threatening cowboy, a hotshot director and—oh, yes—a rotting corpse. Watts digs into the juiciest role in ages for a young actress. Near the end, as identities shift, Lynch encourages us to put together the pieces of the puzzle. You can discover a lot about yourself by getting lost in this DVD. It grips you like a dream that won't let go.

Hot Bonus: Lynch provides ten clues to unlocking the mystery.

Key Scene: The audition is perversely brilliant. Betty reads lines with Jimmy (Chad Everett), an older actor. Earlier, with the brunette, Betty had spoken her dialogue like an innocent seduced by her dad's friend. But with Jimmy, Betty assertively takes charge, breathing in his ear, biting his lip, reading her dialogue ("Get out of here before I kill you") like a carnal invitation.

Mutiny on the Bounty (1935)

Starring: Clark Gable, Charles Laughton, Franchot Tone
Directed by: Frank Lloyd

Laughton's Captain Bligh is a walking sneer as he terrorizes his crew. No wonder First Officer Fletcher Christian (Gable) leads a mutiny. The great-granddaddy of all seafaring adventures (based on the Nordhoff-Hall book) won the Best Picture Oscar and still looks shipshape on DVD, despite its advanced age. That's because the Laughton-Gable combo puts the other actors who played the same roles—Marlon Brando and Trevor Howard in 1962, Mel Gibson and Anthony Hopkins in 1984—in the shadows.

Hot Bonus: A short subject on the real Pitcairn Island, where Mr. Christian and the Bounty crew settled after the mutiny.

Key Scene: Laughton's delicious villainy hits a peak when he addresses the ship's company: "I am your captain, your judge, and your jury." No wonder the crew put the captain to sea in leaky rowboat.

My Cousin Vinny (1992)

Starring: Joe Pesci, Marisa Tomei, Fred Gwynne, Ralph Macchio
Directed by: Jonathan Lynn

A lunatic farce gets top-tier DVD treatment. Bill (Macchio) and his college buddy just want out of Wahzoo City, Alabama, where they've been falsely arrested for killing a store clerk. So Bill phones home to Brooklyn for his lawyer cousin, Vinny (Pesci). Bill is shaken to learn that it took Vinny six tries to pass the bar and that he's never argued a case. Wahzoo City is a lot more shaken by the sight of Vinny and his babe Lisa (Tomei) in black leather. The judge (the late, great Gwynne) holds Vinny in contempt just for looking and talking the way he does. Lynn turns the actors loose. Pesci's mugging with the inimitable Gwynne is no less funny for being shameless. And Tomei is a sexy, comic wonder in an Oscar-winning performance.

Hot Bonus: Lynn's commentary is a detailed lesson in how to film comedy.

Key Scene: Lisa's reaction when Vinny criticizes the peekaboo outfits she wears to court: "Oh yeah, like you blend."

My Darling Clementine (1946)

Starring: Henry Fonda, Victor Mature, Walter Brennan, Cathy Downs
Directed by: John Ford

Wyatt Earp (Fonda) and Doc Holliday (Mature) gear up for the gunfight at the O.K. Corral. But unlike many westerns before and after, this landmark from director Ford is less interested in bullets than the social details of settling the Old West. Don't get me wrong. Marshal Earp has it out with the consumptive Doc as well as Old Man Clanton (Brennan) and his boys (they killed Wyatt's brother). But it's Earp's love for Clementine (Downs), the girl Doc left behind for a hooker named Chihuahua (Linda Darnell), that defines this most introspective of westerns. Joseph MacDonald's black-and-white camerawork lights every detail, such as Earp leaning back on the hind legs of a porch chair. It's a film of indelible images, caught beautifully on DVD.

Hot Bonus: An alternate version of the film, running seven minutes longer, is included, as well as commentary that explains the differences.

Key Scene: Clementine dancing with Earp (has Fonda ever been this awkwardly tender and moving?) at a church social—a moment that catches the civilizing influence of community on Ford's Wild, Wild West.

My Fair Lady (Two-Disc Special Edition) (1964)

Starring: Rex Harrison, Audrey Hepburn
Directed by: George Cukor

Eight Oscars, including one for Best Picture, greeted this lavish film version of the Lerner & Loewe Broadway musical version of George Bernard Shaw's *Pygmalion*. A sublime Harrison, in an Oscar-winning repeat of his stage triumph, acts and gloriously talk-sings the role of Henry Higgins, the arrogant professor who makes a bet that he can transform Cockney guttersnipe Eliza Dolittle (Hepburn, suffering unearned resentment for being given the role Julie Andrews created on stage) into a lady. The songs, from "I Could Have Danced All Night" (Hepburn dubbed by Marni Nixon) to "I've Grown Accustomed to Her Face," sound luscious. But it's the picture that will stun you. This stylish, Cukor-directed beauty hasn't just been transferred to DVD, it's been restored to thrilling life by Robert A. Harris and James C. Katz, who show you how on one of the copious extras.

Hot Bonus: An outtake of Hepburn singing "Wouldn't It Be Loverly" in her own small but charming voice is cherishable.

Key Scene: The Ascot racing number, in which the main characters converge, has a clarity that rivals any high-definition image.

My Favorite Year (1982)

Starring: Peter O'Toole, Mark Linn-Baker
Directed by: Richard Benjamin

Live television in the 1950s is lovingly and hilariously recalled. Benjy Stone (Linn-Baker), a novice writer for a comedy show, is assigned to the care and coddling of guest Alan Swann (O'Toole), a Hollywood star of many a swashbuckling epic who now gets most of his kicks from booze. The film is based on what happened to young jokesmith Mel Brooks when he squired Errol Flynn to Sid Caesar's show. The triumphantly mannered O'Toole—he was nominated for a Best Actor Oscar—walks off with the picture. But the DVD deserves praise for replicating the film's atmosphere, from the Rockefeller Center studios to the Stork Club nightlife.

Hot Bonus: Benjamin, an actor who turned director with this film, was a former NBC page. So he knew the period. It was directing that floored him, and his comments about bluffing his way through the process are priceless.

Key Scene: Swilling Scotch to allay his fears of the live TV camera, Swann excuses his behavior by declaiming, "I am not an actor—I am a movie star."

My Left Foot
(Special Collector's Edition) (1989)

Starring: Daniel Day-Lewis,
Brenda Fricker, Hugh O'Conor
Directed by: Jim Sheridan

Toss the previous DVD. The restored picture and sound on this new disc transfer wraps you up in the towering, Oscar-winning Day-Lewis performance as Christy Brown, a working-class Dubliner

who relished girls, brawls, drinking, painting and writing. The last two brought him fame. His autobiography, on which Sheridan's no-bull film is based, also details one hellish disability: Christy was born with cerebral palsy. His damaged brain allowed him control only over the movement of his left foot. Brown's dexterous toes could type, maneuver a paintbrush, wriggle to music, kick a soccer ball and even hold a razor in a failed attempt at suicide. Day-Lewis does nothing to tidy up Brown's illness. His head wobbles, his eyes roll, his mouth twitches and drools in a vein-swelling effort to produce even a few garbled words. At first we look away, but then the actor draws us in.

Hot Bonus: Footage of the real Christy Brown.

Key Scene: Christy's drunken, sex-crazed restaurant meltdown shows Day-Lewis expressing all of Christy's feelings, not just the acceptable ones.

My Little Chickadee (1940)

Starring: W. C. Fields, Mae West
Directed by: Edward Cline

This irreplaceable comic western brings together for the first and only time two movie icons, though Fields and West reportedly hated each other off the set. Fields plays Cuthbert J. Twillie, a con man who encounters West's Flower Belle Lee on a train traveling through Indian country. She's quite a shot. After kissing her hand ("Ah, what symmetrical digits") he lets her con him into marriage so her sinful ways won't scandalize Greasewood City, where she substitutes for the ailing schoolmarm. Seeing the words "I am a good boy. I am a good girl," written over and over on the blackboard, she scowls, "What is this, propaganda?" And so it goes. The DVD only looks and sounds reasonably good, but I can't live without it.

Hot Bonus: The movie comes as part of Fields DVD collection that also includes *The Bank Dick*, *You Can't Cheat an Honest Man*, *International House*, and *It's a Gift*. I'd call that a real bonus.

Key Scene: Fields's in bed with West on their wedding night, only it's not her. She's put in a replacement—a goat.

Mystery Train (1989)

Starring: Steve Buscemi, Masatoshi Nagase, Youki Kudoh, Nicoletta Braschi
Directed and written by: Jim Jarmusch

Jarmusch owes this one to Elvis. The King's voice, singing the title song, jump-starts this DVD tone poem. It opens with a train streaking into Memphis, Elvis's Memphis, where he took his first step into legend. Three stories are linked by a gunshot and the Arcade Hotel. Two teenage Japanese tourists, the glum Jun (Nagase) and his bubbly girl, Mitsuko (Kudoh), are on a pilgrimage. In another room, Luisa (Braschi), a young Italian widow, gets a visitation from Elvis's ghost. In the Arcade's tackiest room, the inept trio of Charlie (Buscemi), Johnny (Joe Strummer), and Will (Rick Aviles) plan a liquor store robbery. Jarmusch finds humor and poignancy in these people who never meet. His bracing, original comedy may be mostly smoke and air, but it insinuates itself into the memory and lingers on.

Hot Bonus: A thrilling anamorphic transfer. That's all. That's enough.

Key Scene: The Japanese lovers have sex under the portrait of Elvis. Later, listening to their idol sing "Blue Moon" on the radio, Jun gazes out the window at the neon-lit streets and distant train tracks. "This is cool," he says, a cigarette dangling from his lips and Memphis at his feet. With the help of Robby Müller's evocative camerawork, two foreigners have made Memphis the exotic, hip Mecca they want it to be.

Mystic River
(Three-Disc Deluxe Edition) (2003)

Starring: Sean Penn, Tim Robbins, Kevin Bacon, Laura Linney

Directed by: Clint Eastwood

Eastwood pours everything he knows about directing into this dark masterpiece. His film sneaks up, messes with your head, and then floors you. The script, a stunning distillation of Dennis Lehane's novel by Brian Helgeland, sounds like an ordinary police procedural: A girl is murdered, the cops investigate, a manhunt ensues. Three friends share a childhood secret that scars them as adults. Penn plays Jimmy, an ex-con whose teen daughter Katie (Emmy Rossum) has been murdered. Sean (Bacon) is the detective assigned to the case. And Dave (Robbins), married and a father yet visibly damaged by his past, is the prime suspect. There's a classic rigor to the DVD transfer as the camera sweeps over Boston, creating images that speak eloquently of class struggle and rogue justice. Eastwood, who composed the film's brooding score, takes his unflashy time to develop characters. The sheer brilliance of Penn's performance anchors the film. There's a

coiled intensity in Jimmy that even his wife (an outstanding Linney) can't touch. And Robbins, a strapping actor, seems to have shrunk himself outside and inside to play Dave. The script dodges a few raw spots, such as Dave's war with himself as a potential child molester. But Eastwood doesn't flinch from the guilt and the blood lust that drives these men, perhaps beyond redemption. His movie takes a piece out of you.

Hot Bonus: *Beneath the Surface* is the best of the lot, with Eastwood, the cast, and crew explaining how they prepped for such a challenging piece.

Key Scene: Penn and Robbins, both Oscar winners for performances that hit a peak on a back porch, as their characters take a moment away from a wake to share mutual, wrenching pain.

Naked
(Two-Disc Special Edition) (1993)

Starring: David Thewlis, Katrin Cartlidge, Lesley Sharp

Directed by: Mike Leigh

Criterion's DVD transfer does grunge justice to Leigh's nastiest piece of work, as the British writer-director slashes his way through London's displaced youth. It's a savagely witty bonfire, sparked by Thewlis as the homeless, horny, intellectually voracious Johnny—a no-hoper with a silver tongue and a knack for using women. Johnny is a Manchester boy in London to hook up with a former lover (Sharp), but willing to snog her junkie flatmate (Cartlidge) if it's convenient. As Johnny wanders the streets, the film becomes an odyssey of modern disconnection, and Leigh makes every moment literate, cinematic, and built to sing. Thewlis deserved the Oscar, for which he shamefully wasn't even nominated.

Hot Bonus: A fascinating intro by accused nihilist Neil LaBute is followed by audio commentary from Leigh, Thewlis, and the gifted Cartlidge, who died tragically in 2002, at forty-one, of pneumonia and septicemia.

Key Scene: Thewlis railing at Sharp for buying into pop culture: "You've had the universe explained to you, and you're bored with it. So now you just like cheap thrills—and plenty of them. And it doesn't matter how tawdry and vacuous they are as long as it's new, as long as it flashes and fucking beeps in five fucking different colors." It seems that Johnny missed his calling as a film critic.

Naked City, The (1948)

Starring: Barry Fitzgerald, Don Taylor, Howard Duff, Ted de Corsia
Directed by: Jules Dassin

The first studio feature to be shot on the streets of New York City won Oscars for cinematography and editing. Set your eyes on this superlative DVD transfer, and you'll see why. Director Dassin keeps the tension flowing docudrama style. Fitzgerald hams up a storm as a veteran cop teaching the ropes to his partner (Taylor) as they investigate the murder of a sleep-around blonde. Journalist Mark Hellinger, the film's producer, provides narration that goads along the bad guys (Duff and DeCorsia). Hellinger's sign-off spawned a 1950s TV series and countless imitations: "There are eight million stories in the naked city. This has been one of them."

Hot Bonus: Just a pristine black-and-white picture that age hasn't withered.

Key Scene: The climax on the Brooklyn Bridge deserves its classic status.

Naked Gun, The (1988)

Starring: Leslie Nielsen, O. J. Simpson, Priscilla Presley, Ricardo Montalban
Directed by: Jerry Zucker, Jim Abrahams, Pat Proft

DVD heaven for fans of the insanely stupid. Include me in. Director Zucker and his co-writers Jerry Zucker and Jim Abrahams turned their flop TV series *Police Squad* into a laugh machine that only looks slapdash. As in *Airplane!* they pile on the gags with relentless ingenuity. And when they run out of steam, Nielsen takes over in his career-crowning role as Frank Drebin, a police lieutenant who could give Inspector Clouseau lessons in how to screw up. Frank and his idiot team, including Simpson (insert your own joke here), must stop the villain (Montalban) from assassinating Queen Elizabeth II at a baseball game. The DVD looks and sounds great, but I'd watch through mud just to enjoy the walking sight gag that is Nielsen.

Hot Bonus: *The Naked Gun* gift set includes two sequels, *Naked Gun 2 1/2: The Smell of Fear* and *Naked Gun 33 1/3: The Final Insult*, that are nearly as good as the original because they all star Nielsen.

Key Scene: The opener with the squad car speeding through the Los Angeles streets, then into somebody's house, then into a shower with naked babes.

Naked Kiss, The (1964)

Starring: Constance Towers, Anthony Eisley, Michael Dante
Directed and written by: Samuel Fuller

Nobody springs surprises like Sam "The Man" Fuller. How many movies do you know that begin with a bald hooker (Towers) sticking it to her pimp with one of her spiked heels, putting on a wig, and heading out to the 'burbs to start living respectably. Ha! As our hooker (her name is Kelly) learns after taking a job as a pediatric nurse, men are exploiting women and children everywhere. Fuller pulls out all the stylistic stops, from kinky cops to pedophilia. And Towers gives him a killer heroine. Criterion builds the case for the film with an immaculate widescreen transfer that brings out the stark black-and-white camera wizardry of Stanley Cortez, who shot Orson Welles's *The Magnificent Ambersons*, among other masterworks.

Hot Bonus: An overcaffeinated trailer that makes a screaming promise to deliver "Emotional Violence!" They don't make them like that anymore.

Key Scene: The musical number featuring disabled kids leaning on crutches transcends camp in the hands of Fuller.

Naked Lunch (Two-Disc Special Edition) (1991)

Starring: Peter Weller, Judy Davis, Roy Scheider
Directed by: David Cronenberg

You can imagine the hallucinatory nightmares that result when you cross the cinematic visions of Cronenberg with the literary imaginings of William S. Burroughs. Actually, you don't have to imagine. Just get this DVD and let the games begin. Weller stars as Bill Lee, the exterminator whose wife Joan (Davis) is addicted to his bug powder. Soon Bill is addicted himself and taking orders from a giant bug that sends him to North Africa and into the mind-controlling clutches of Dr. Benway (Scheider, truly scary). You're on your own the rest of the way through this funny and frightening odyssey. The DVD guides you into the stunning, hellish imagery in high style.

Hot Bonus: An illustrated essay on the special effects (oh, those mugwumps) is almost as provocative as hearing Burroughs read excerpts from his book.

Key Scene: Bill's game of William Tell, in which he tries to shoot an apple off Joan's head and kills her, an incident taken from Burroughs's own life.

Napoleon Dynamite (2004)

Starring: Jon Heder, Efren Ramirez, Jon Gries, Aaron Ruell, Tina Majorino

Directed by: Jared Hess

Sweet. Cults have been springing up around this deadpan delight since it premiered at Sundance early in 2004. So the DVD—an elaborate sendoff for a very small film—is a must even if you end up hating it. To Napoleon Dynamite (Heder), a nerdy Idaho white boy in a red Afro, the word "sweet" signifies something sublime, like learning soul dancing. Or the time machine his crazy Uncle Rico (Gries) is building to revisit his days as a football hero. Or the ponytail his friend Deb (a fab Majorino) wears on the side of her head. Or the bootylicious mama, Lafawnduh (Shondrella Avery), that his brother Kip (Ruell) finds on the Internet. Or just the fact that his Mexican friend Pedro (Ramirez) is running for class president on a ticket of "Pedro offers you his protection." What's not sweet is anyone who is contemptuous of Napoleon's universe. First-time director Hess, who wrote the script with his wife, Jersuha, has been accused of ripping off *Welcome to the Dollhouse* and *Rushmore*. Nah. Hess and his terrific cast—Heder is geek perfection—make their own kind of deadpan hilarity. You'll laugh till it hurts. Sweet.

Hot Bonus: A wedding scene, filmed a year later, was added to the film after it went into wide distribution. So keep watching after the closing credits.

Key Scene: Napoleon's dance near the end will live forever.

Narc (2002)

Starring: Ray Liotta, Jason Patric

Directed by: Joe Carnahan

This compulsively watchable police thriller comes on like a speeding bullet with a cop (Patric) chasing a perp. Simple stuff, only a pregnant woman winds up dead. Director Carnahan—a ballsy find—gives the scene a breathless, handheld-camera urgency. It's a no-bull throwback to 1970s action films. The DVD looks gritty, just as it should. It zips along with B-movie verve while adding the rich details and go-for-broke acting that herald something special. Patric has his best role in years. And a beefed-up Liotta—firing on all cylinders—was robbed of Oscar attention as a cop you don't trust. Not if you're smart.

Hot Bonus: Caranhan explaining how the film happened with Tom Cruise producing. No explanation about how his deal to direct Cruise in *Mission: Impossible 3* fell through.

Key Scene: The informer in a chair, getting seriously worked over.

Nashville (1975)

Starring: Lily Tomlin, Keith Carradine, Ronee Blakley, Henry Gibson

Directed by: Robert Altman

Altman at the top of his game. Country music is the subject in the sense that country music is America in all its epic post-Watergate sprawl. Altman encouraged the actors to use Joan Tewkesbury's script as a spur to improvisation. Many of them wrote and sang their own songs. This is a movie that spills over with characters and ideas. The DVD transfer has to strain at times to keep up with the visual and aural chaos. Everything pivots around a presidential candidate (unseen) who is hustling the Nashville scene for support. He wants Barbara Jean (Blakley, Oscar-nominated)—a country legend on the verge of a Loretta Lynn breakdown—to perform at his rally. There's also the rightwinger (Gibson) who sings about how America "keeps a'goin," the wannabe (Gwen Welles) who stoops to stripping, the folkie (Carradine) who uses music as seduction, the married gospel choirist (Tomlin, also Oscar nominated) who sleeps with the folkie, and the runaway wife (Barbara Harris) who gets her chance to shine at a moment of tragedy. Just when you think you have these people pegged, Altman pulls the rug out. This kaleidoscope of a movie is powerfully moving.

Hot Bonus: Altman, reliably expansive and cranky, delivers a model commentary. No ass-kissing, just hype-free talk about how it all works.

Key Scene: Carradine singing the Oscar-winning song "I'm Easy" in a club filled with women, each of whom believes he is singing only to her. The story plays on their faces as Altman achieves his unique brand of artistry.

National Lampoon's Animal House (Double Secret Probation Edition) (1978)

Starring: John Belushi, Tim Matheson, Thomas Hulce, Stephen Furst

Directed by: John Landis

OK, maybe toga parties ("Toga! Toga!") are no longer the happening frat house thing. But Delta House, the least desirable destination for pledges during rush week at Faber College, circa 1962, was never the happening thing—except for the comic raunch delivered by director Landis and *Lampoon* writers Doug Kenney, Harold Ramis, and former Dartmouth man Chris Miller. As makeout king Otter, Matheson smoothly wrangles the losers, such as Pinto (Hulce) and Flounder (Furst). But the loudest, lowest laughs come from Belushi as Bluto. This dressed-up DVD makes the case for Belushi (he died in 1982) as a comic icon as he bashes a beer can against his forehead, nibbles Jell-O with his fingers, belches after a big gulp of Jack Daniels, and climbs a ladder to ogle sorority girl Mandy Pepperidge (Mary Louise Weller). Dean Wormer (John Vernon) invokes "double secret probation" to rid Faber of Bluto and the animals. Fat chance. As Bluto observes, that would be "seven years of college down the drain."

Hot Bonus: Behind-the-scenes footage of Belushi at work.

Key Scene: The food fight. How do you resist Belushi's imitation of popping a zit by stuffing his face with food, then squeezing his cheeks until the gunk spews out? Ah, nostalgia.

Natural, The (1984)

Starring: Robert Redford, Glenn Close, Barbara Hershey, Kim Basinger

Directed by: Barry Levinson

Too pretty by half (a virtue when you're showing off what a DVD can do), Levinson's oddly uplifting film version of Bernard Malamud's dark allegory hits its stride when it conjures up the mythic power of baseball. Young pitcher Roy Hobbs (Redford) is sidelined for years by a bullet from a female angel of death (Hershey). Cut ahead to 1939 with Roy coming back as a middle-aged slugger for the struggling New York Knights. Symbols from the Arthurian legend abound—Roy's mighty sword (he calls it Wonderboy, not Excalibur) is a bat that he carved out of a tree struck by lightning. Roy runs into evildoers—a nasty sportswriter (Duvall), a sexy siren (Basinger)—before he finds his pure lady (Close, Oscar nominated) and plays the big game for the Knights. Redford's deft underplaying and Randy Newman's tonally perfect score bring it all home.

Hot Bonus: A terrific documentary narrated by Baltimore Orioles legend Cal Ripken Jr., a real-life natural whose thoughts on the film carry weight.

Key Scene: The climactic moment: Redford at the plate with the season on the line, blood seeping through his shirt, his magic bat broken.

Natural Born Killers (1994)

Starring: Woody Harrelson, Juliette Lewis, Tommy Lee Jones

Directed by: Oliver Stone

Revolting movie. Riveting DVD, as long as we're talking technically. Stone says he operates from the gut, so maybe that's why this splatterfest plays like something he puked up. Lovebirds Mickey (Harrelson) and Mallory (Lewis) stomp, stab, and shoot their way through a murder spree in the Southwest that makes them worldwide stars and leaves fifty-two dead. Incoherent as drama or satire, the movie soars on its visual audacity. Shot on film and video, in color and in black-and-white, *Killers* serves as a compendium of visual styles from documentary crude to MTV flash. Violent images from movies, TV, and newspapers counterpoint the couple's rampage. There's even computer animation. Add sound to the fury with music producer Trent Reznor of Nine Inch Nails sampling the likes of Puccini (*Madame Butterfly*), and Lou Reed ("Sweet Jane"). Stone refracts the bloody tale of Mickey and Mallory through an optical and aural barrage. But don't look for a heartbeat.

Hot Bonus: The commentary is just Stone making excuses, but for those who want more gore, the disc offers sights deleted from the original release, such as the dismembered head of a prison warden (Jones).

Key Scene: Stone tells the story of how the lovers meet in the form of a lashing sitcom parody called *I Love Mallory*. The late comic Rodney Dangerfield plays Mallory's dad, a beer-guzzling slob who likes to jump in the shower with his daughter and wash her back.

Near Dark (Two-Disc Special Edition) (1987)

Starring: Adrian Pasdar, Jenny Wright, Bill Paxton, Lance Henriksen

Directed by: Kathryn Bigelow

A low-budget scare flick that looks like a billion bucks thanks to visual ingenuity of director Bigelow and cinematographer Adam Greenberg, plus a digital remastering that takes the breath away. It's bad luck for Oklahoma farm boy Caleb (Pasdar) to meet sweet blonde Mae

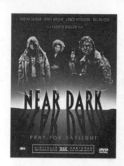

(Wright) licking an ice cream cone. She's a member of a marauding family (cowboys on bikes instead of horses), led by Henriksen, out to spread their disease through an exchange of bodily fluids. It isn't AIDS or drugs, except metaphorically. They're vampires, though no one mentions the word, and Bigelow turns their life as bloodsuckers into a thing of beauty and terror.

Hot Bonus: A retrospective documentary in which Henriksen's work process as an actor proves to be as scary as anything in the movie.

Key Scene: The massacre at a bar where the family chows down.

Network (1976)

Starring: Peter Finch, Faye Dunaway, William Holden, Beatrice Straight

Directed by: Sidney Lumet

Considered hyperbolic back in the day, Paddy Chayefsky's explosive satire of the boob tube now seems like a blueprint for reality TV. Finch won a posthumous Oscar as Howard Beale, the veteran news anchor who threatens to kill himself on the air when he's fired. When his threat is a ratings grabber, programming exec Diana Christensen (Dunaway, also an Oscar winner) gives him his own show. Holden, superb in every way, plays Max Schumacher, the old network hand who is appalled at Diana's desire to do shows with real bank robbers and terrorists, and appalled at himself for leaving his wife (Straight, another Oscar winner) for her: "You're television incarnate, Diana. Indifferent to suffering. Insensitive to joy. All of life reduced to the common rubble of banality." Lumet hit a career peak directing Chayefsky's Oscar-winning script. The DVD transfer is acceptable, no more, but the dialogue crackles better than special effects.

Hot Bonus: There is an Easter Egg that explains how the Nielsen ratings work, but it's a real killer to find. You're on your own.

Key Scene: Finch's Beale, near meltdown, telling his vast TV audience to go to their windows, open them, stick their heads out and yell: "I'm mad as hell and I'm not going to take it anymore." A moment for the time capsule.

Night Moves (1975)

Starring: Gene Hackman, Jennifer Warren, Edward Binns, Melanie Griffith

Directed by: Arthur Penn

One of the best detective movies you've never seen. The great Hackman plays Harry Moseby, a former football player in Los Angeles who decides to live the second half of his life as a private eye. His new case is to track a runaway teen nympho (Griffith is a pistol in one of her earliest roles) to the Florida Keys. But that's just the tip of a psychological mystery that keeps uncovering layers of corruption and betrayal, Watergate-style. Matching Hackman in brilliance is Warren as a sexy drifter Moseby meets in the Keys. She asks where he was when Kennedy was shot. "Which Kennedy?" he asks. "Any Kennedy," she answers. Director Penn mines every moral nuance in Alan Sharp's script. It took forever to get this baby on DVD. Grab it.

Hot Bonus: A vintage featurette on Penn, *The Day of the Director.*

Key Scene: The shocker of an ending, with Hackman in a boat going in circles and a killer drowning in a seaplane revealing the last clue.

Night of the Hunter, The (1955)

Starring: Robert Mitchum, Shelley Winters, Lillian Gish

Directed by: Charles Laughton

A cinema landmark, pure and simple. And if it's not in your DVD collection, don't bother to have one. This is the only film that actor Laughton ever directed, and the apathy it met with from critics and audiences then seems incomprehensible now. Based on a Gothic novel by Davis Grubb, which James Agee adapted and Laughton rewrote, the film concerns the Rev. Harry Powell (Mitchum in his greatest screen performance), a man of God doing the devil's work. The word "Love" is tattooed on the knuckles of one hand, "Hate" on the other. It's not love that motivates the Rev to marry a widow (Winters). He wants to know where her thief husband hid his stash. If he has to, Powell will kill her and her two children, John (Billy Chapin) and Pearl (Sally Jane Bruce), who jump a rowboat to escape this smiling, hymn-singing fiend. Screen legend Gish plays the savior who shelters the kids and takes on their nemesis. Blending Stanley Cortez's black-and-white images with Walter Schumann's haunting score, Laughton creates an expressionist tone poem that gets the luminous DVD transfer it deserves.

Hot Bonus: An eight-page production booklet. That's it. And *Miss Congeniality* gets a Deluxe Special Edition. Don't get me started.

Key Scene: A dead woman's body in a deep river, her hair billowing, creates one of many moments of clutching beauty that define the film.

Night of the Living Dead (Millennium Edition) (1968)

Starring: Duane Jones, Judith O'Dea, Russell Streiner

Directed by: George A. Romero

Not only the best flesh-eating zombie movie shot in Pittsburgh, it's the best flesh-eating zombie movie anywhere. Ignore the 1990 remake. And ignore Anchor Bay's Thirtieth Anniversary Edition DVD which mutilated the original and then rescored it. Elite's Millennium Edition is your baby. It preserves Romero's black-and-white imagery in all its ragged glory as a group of live ones hole up in a farmhouse as the dead come up to chow down. Jones, playing one of the first black heroes in the horror genre, must talk and sometimes slap sense into this panicky herd. Romero returned to the zombie scene in 1978's *Dawn of the Dead*, 1985's *Day of the Dead*, and 2005's *George A. Romero's Land of the Dead*, but the Dead have never been livelier or scarier than they are here where he built the mold.

Hot Bonus: A short interview with Jones, a truly nonviolent man, who always regretted doing the violent, gory film that made his name.

Key Scene: The cemetery opener in daylight always gets me, as O'Dea watches brother Streiner get bitten by a lurching zombie (Bill Heinzman).

Night to Remember, A (1958)

Starring: Kenneth More, David McCallum, Jill Dixon

Directed by: Roy Baker

Here's the British docudrama that delivers everything about the sinking of the *Titanic* on April 14, 1912, that James Cameron's 1997 epic skipped to spend more time with Kate and Leo. Criterion transfers the black-and-white picture with striking immediacy. Based on Walter Lord's book, the movie is a bear for details. A ship, the *Californian*, was only ten miles away yet took no action. The actors, led by More as Second Officer Herbert Lightoller, underplay to let the events take center stage. The result is electrifying.

Hot Bonus: A 1993 documentary about the film shows how models were used to achieve the amazing effects.

Key Scene: Hitting the iceberg, which left a three-hundred-foot gash in the unsinkable ship that took 1,513 passengers (out of 2,224) to the bottom with her.

Nightmare Before Christmas, The (Special Edition) (1993)

Starring: The voices of Danny Elfman, Chris Sarandon, Catherine O'Hara

Directed by: Henry Selick

The history-making stop-motion animation achieved by director Selick and his crew comes through brilliantly on DVD. Jack Skellington, the Pumpkin King of dreary Halloweentown, finds a secret passageway to Christmastown. Jack sandbags Santa and delivers presents in a coffin-shaped sleigh led by skeleton reindeer. Producer Tim Burton hatched the idea eleven years ago as a humble animator at Disney, a Conservativetown where such deviltry was quickly squashed. His later success with *Batman* prompted a reconsideration, despite some parents who raised hell over the film's dark mischief. Even Sally, Jack's rag-doll love, thinks he may be going too far. That leaves a gloomy Jack warbling a tune—one of ten composed by Elfman (who sings for Jack)—in the arms of a statue in a graveyard.

Hot Bonus: A look at how over one hundred crew members averaged only sixty seconds of film per week, taking three years to complete the project.

Key Scene: Jack unknowingly terrifying kids by delivering such presents as a shrunken head and a toy snake that devours Christmas trees.

Nightmare on Elm Street, A (1984)

Starring: Robert Englund, Heather Langenkamp, Johnny Depp

Directed by: Wes Craven

You can buy the original and all six sequels in a box set. But let's face it, Craven's first time at the Freddy Krueger party says it all. A little grain attacks the DVD transfer, but the scares come through just fine. Englund is now and forever known as Freddy, a scarfaced cadaver in a striped sweater and long, stiletto-like appendages on the ends of his fingers as if he had an overimaginative manicurist or perhaps an excessively iron-rich diet. He is out for blood, which he gets in vast, gushing quantities, by invading the dreams of horny teens. Langenkamp is the teen who fights back

Hot Bonus: Craven talks about how *Nightmare* pegged him as the horror guy, even after he directed Meryl Streep in the cloying *Music of the Heart*.

Key Scene: Depp, in his first movie role, being attacked by his bed.

No Way Out (1987)

Starring: Kevin Costner, Gene Hackman, Sean Young
Directed by: Roger Donaldson

A political thriller that gets a solid DVD transfer, though it's not anamorphic (a coding process that creates a more detailed picture on a widescreen TV). Costner gives a slyly confident performance as a naval hero working in Washington D.C. with the secretary of defense (the reliably fine Hackman). Their connection gets too close when Costner starts an affair with the secretary's mistress (Young) and she ends up dead. Donaldson directs with pleasurable smoothness and springs a surprise ending that makes you want to watch the film all over again to see just how you got fooled.

Hot Bonus: A "making of" booklet that makes you want to know more about the cinematographer John Alcott, to whom the film is dedicated.

Key Scene: A breathlessly erotic limo ride in which Costner and Young go at each other against a background of D.C. at night. The Washington Monument has never looked this phallic.

North by Northwest (1959)

Starring: Cary Grant, Eva Marie Saint, James Mason, Martin Landau
Directed by: Alfred Hitchcock

Peak Hitchcock, and beautifully served on DVD. Grant, never smoother or more iconic, plays a baffled New York ad man who is chased across America by spies and the cops for reasons that Hitch and screenwriter Ernest Lehman slowly make clear. Of course there is time for the director to add one of his trademarked cool blondes (Saint). Mason and Landau are great fun as homoerotic villains. But here the chase is all. Dangling from the face of Mt. Rushmore, Saint asks Grant why his two wives both dumped him.

His answer: "They said I led too dull a life." Not in this movie, baby.

Hot Bonus: An amazingly thorough retrospective documentary.

Key Scene: Grant alone in a cornfield until a cropduster appears. Classic.

Nosferatu (1922)

Starring: Max Schreck, Greta Schroeder
Directed by: F. W. Murnau

Murnau's silent take on Dracula can still scare you senseless. Schreck looks truly undead as Count Orlok. *Shadow of the Vampire*, released in 2000, implies that Schreck—played by Willem Dafoe—was a real vampire hired by Murnau to keep things real. Watch *Nosferatu* and you can almost believe it. Image's remastered edition has a few age-related pops and hisses. You get two audio choices: the old organ-based score or a New Agey update. Go with the organ. It sets just the right mood.

Hot Bonus: A look at the film's history, including how Murnau had intended to film Bram Stoker's *Dracula* without securing the rights. He changed the name, but the Stoker estate sued and prints were ordered destroyed. This DVD restoration was assembled from surviving elements.

Key Scene: The Count in his coffin in the cargo hold of a ship. We watch him rise as rats scurry about. You'll want to run with the rats.

Notorious (1946)

Starring: Cary Grant, Ingrid Bergman, Claude Rains
Directed by: Alfred Hitchcock

Only *Vertigo* beats this Hitchcock suspense landmark for obsessive eroticism. The Criterion transfer gives the black-and-white images the luxuriant feel of velvet. Grant plays an American agent who recruits Bergman—at her hottest—to spy on a group of post–World War II Nazis in Brazil. The job calls for her to sleep with the head spy (Rains), which she does. Grant, who has fallen hard for the lady, is torn apart by her willingness to do so. Grant and Bergman have never been sexier—their kiss may be the longest in screen history as Hitchcock circles them with his camera—in this love-hate duet that ends with a rescue of nerve-pounding tension.

Hot Bonus: Scene-by-scene analysis by Marian Keane.

Key Scene: A party at the Rains mansion in which the camera sweeps through the room in one unbroken movement to land on a closeup of Bergman's hand, holding a key that will unlock the film's central secret.

Notting Hill (Collector's Edition) (1999)

Starring: Julia Roberts, Hugh Grant, Rhys Ifans
Directed by: Roger Michell

A rom-com that raises the bar on fluff, thanks to a sharp script by Richard Curtis and deft teamwork from the two stars. Roberts plays Anna Scott, the biggest movie star in the world who glitters up the life of William Thacker (Grant), the owner of a London bookshop where Anna comes to browse. It's a matchup between Hollywood royalty and a commoner. Ifans is a hoot as Grant's slob roomie, but it's the chemistry between Roberts and Grant that sells it, plus a DVD transfer that glows with impossible pastel beauty.

Hot Bonus: Much jabbering by Curtis and by director Michell, but the funniest bit is Hugh Grant's Movie Tips in which the actor tells us how to dress on a movie set, deal with a visit from parents, and other emergencies.

Key Scene: Grant sneaking into a Roberts movie junket by pretending to be a reporter from *Horse and Hound*, a publication unlikely to have much interest in a space epic. "You are *Horse and Hound*'s favorite actress," he tells her with a straight face. "You and Black Beauty. Tied."

Nutty Professor, The (Special Collector's Edition) (1963)

Starring: Jerry Lewis, Stella Stevens
Directed and written by: Jerry Lewis

This Jekyll-and-Hyde farce won Lewis respect, and not just in France, for his acting, writing, and directing. The triple threat plays Professor Kelp, a buck-toothed nerd who invents a formula that turns him into hip, slick, obnoxious Buddy Love. To many critics, Love is Lewis's revenge on his former comedy partner Dean Martin. It's certainly wish fulfillment when the babe (Stevens) ends up preferring the naïve prof to his sleazy alter ego. The widescreen DVD transfer is a riot of color and movement, but it's the willingness of Lewis to cut deeper than laughs that makes this his best film.

Hot Bonus: Lewis offers trenchant commentary, categorically denying that Love is based on Martin: "I loved Dean. That character was a conglomeration of every unkind, nasty SOB I had seen all of my life."

Key Scene: The first appearance of Buddy Love, with Lewis—hair greased back—launching into a version of "That Old Black Magic" that floors the students with its narcissism. Lewis would play a version of his own dark side twenty years later

in Martin Scorsese's *King of Comedy*, a film that strengthens the argument that it's Lewis himself, not Martin, being skewered.

Nutty Professor, The (1996)

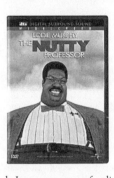

Starring: Eddie Murphy, Jada Pinkett
Directed by: Tom Shadyac

Murphy ups the ante on the Jerry Lewis original by making the Professor obese as well as dorky, and his rampaging alter ego Buddy Love even more of a slick prick. In one scene, Buddy viciously beats up a nightclub comic (Dave Chappelle, of all people) who once did fat jokes on Klump. There's a manic Jim Carrey quality to Buddy—maybe because director Shadyac also directed *Ace Ventura: Pet Detective*—that grows irritating. No wonder the babe (Pinkett) prefers the sweet, sad Klump. Murphy's tour de force won him the Best Actor prize from the high-toned National Society of Film Critics, but Lewis still gets pride of place.

Hot Bonus: Just production notes. You might want to rent the sadsack sequel, *Nutty Professor II: The Klumps*, to see how much better it all worked here.

Key Scene: Dinner with the Klumps, with Murphy (in wondrous Rick Baker makeup) playing the whole Klump family, except for a young boy who gets to laugh every time a Klump farts, which is way too frequently.

O Brother, Where Art Thou? (2000)

Starring: George Clooney, John Turturro, Tim Blake Nelson, Holly Hunter
Directed by: Joel Coen

On looks alone, this DVD earns the word spectacular. And the sound on the DTS track makes the ear-candy score of bluegrass, gospel, and country utterly transporting. No wonder the soundtrack album won a Grammy. The movie itself transports Homer's *Odyssey* to 1937 Mississippi with a live-wire star turn from Clooney as a vain escaped convict who wears a hairnet. Clooney's motor-mouthed Ulysses Everett McGill, jailed for practicing law without a license, escapes from a chain gang with fellow cons Pete (Turturro) and Delmar (Nelson) and embarks on an odyssey to reunite with his wife, Penny (Hunter). Homeric parallels include a one-eyed Bible salesman (John Goodman) who beats the boys up and three sirens who "love them up." The cons also find time to record a song, "I Am a Man of Constant Sorrow," that becomes a hit. It's a wild, whacked-out wonder.

Hot Bonus: Easter Egg alert: Insert the disc, then touch nothing and an instrumental—cut from the film—will play all the way through.

Key Scene: As the film swings from farce to fright, a striking Ku Klux Klan rally in which the Grand Wizard sings "O Death" is both.

Ocean's Eleven (2001)

Starring: George Clooney, Brad Pitt, Matt Damon, Julia Roberts
Directed by: Steven Soderbergh

What is Oscar-winning director Soderbergh doing remaking a 1960 Rat Pack flick best remembered for Frank Sinatra's orange sweaters and Dean Martin being Dino? Answer: having a ball. The remake borrows only the basics: a plan cooked up by Danny Ocean (Clooney) to rob three Vegas casinos owned by a prick (Garcia) who moved in on Danny's ex-wife (Roberts). The rest is meeting the eleven: Pitt is terrific as a cardsharp reduced to giving poker lessons to *Teen Beat* cover boys. Damon shares a great sting scene with Bernie Mac. Casey Affleck and Scott Caan are a pair of prime goofballs, and Don Cheadle, Eddie Jemison, and Shaobo Qin get in their licks, too. As for Clooney, his effortless star power is a thing of beauty. He'd own the movie if Elliott Gould and Carl Reiner didn't steal every scene they're in. Soderbergh treats these old pros with unforced affection. The coolness extends to the DVD transfer, which also gets the tone just right.

Hot Bonus: The commentaries are unusually dull. Better to watch the Sinatra version and make comparisons. Better not to go near the 2004 sequel *Ocean's Twelve*, in which all the charm evaporates.

Key Scene: The last look at the cast set to Debussy's "Clair de Lune."

Old School (Unrated) (2003)

Starring: Will Ferrell, Vince Vaughn, Luke Wilson
Directed by: Todd Phillips

Need a Ferrell fix? If so, keep this DVD handy. Ferrell's movies are mostly throwaways, but he is hilarious in all of them, even—gulp!—*A Night at the Roxbury*. In this eager-to-please mix of *Animal House* and *Jackass*, Ferrell, Vaughn, and Wilson play old guys (they're thirty-something) who open a frat house (Snoop Dogg is their house band). Director Phillips keeps the focus on Ferrell as the just-married Frank. He reverts to a party animal who recalls John Belushi's Bluto, only grosser. There are some movies that play better on DVD than they did at the multiplex. This is one of them.

Hot Bonus: The "Unrated" edition adds two more minutes of raunch, thirteen minutes of deleted scenes, and five minutes of bloopers.

Key Scene: Ferrell's streak down Main Street. Why he has this thing for exposing his flabby ass remains unanswered, even on the commentary track.

Oldboy (2005)

Starring: Min-sik Choi, Hye-jeong Gang, Ji-tae Yu
Directed by: Chan-wook Park

Korean movies rarely get wide distribution in the United States, so DVD is a great chance to catch this explosively exciting psychosexual revenge drama from Chan-wook Park. I won't spill the beans, but know this much: Min-sik Choi is a hell-raising wonder as Dae-su Oh, a skirt-chasing good old boy who is locked in a hotel room with a TV that tells him he's been accused of his wife's murder. Fifteen years later, Dae-su finds himself in a trunk on a rooftop—a free man. At a sushi bar—in the first of the film's scenes not for the squeamish—Dae-su chomps down on some live, wiggling squid. The sympathetic young waitress, Mi-do (Hye-jeong Gang in a strikingly vivid performance), takes him home, and he jumps her bones with the same vigor he showed the squid. In the bloody set pieces that follow, the mystery captor (Ji-tae Yu) gives Dae-su five days to figure out his identity, setting off a series of rampages that spray the screen with blood and shocking secrets.

Hot Bonus: Director's commentary that is fierce and funny. It seems all the suspects on Oh Dae-su's list are the director's filmmaking colleagues.

Key Scene: The fight in the corridor in which Oh Dae-su takes on a dozen men, pulls a knife out of his back, and still continues on.

Omen, The (Special Edition) (1976)

Starring: Gregory Peck, Lee Remick, Harvey Stephens

Directed by: Richard Donner

Damien. The name alone provokes a shiver. Or at least it did in the first of four films (the three sequels sucked) about a little boy anti-Christ. Donner gives the horror a class touch by casting Peck as the American ambassador to England, who pulls a fast one when his wife (Remick) has a stillborn baby. He substitutes a live one from a mother who died. Presto, Damien. Stephens plays the little devil with genuine menace. Couple that with a slick DVD transfer and Jerry Goldsmith's ubercreepy, Oscar-winning score (why no isolated music track?), and the scares seem mint fresh.

Hot Bonus: A retrospective documentary that runs around forty-five minutes called *666: The Omen Revealed*.

Key Scene: The lethal, decapitating sheet of glass. Ouch!

On Her Majesty's Secret Service (Special Edition) (1969)

Starring: George Lazenby, Diana Rigg, Telly Savalas

Directed by: Peter R. Hunt

The One Where James Bond Gets Married. That's right, 007 trades in the Bond girls for an Italian contessa, and Rigg plays her with such beauty and wit, you can't blame him. But who to blame for Lazenby, who filled in at the last minute when Sean Connery dropped out and left a vacuum where the great Scot's dangerous charm used to be? No matter. The ski stunts in the Swiss Alps as Bond chases the evil Blofeld (Savalas) look smashing on DVD, and Rigg does the heavy lifting with the acting. No 007 film is as touching and romantically resonant as this one.

Hot Bonus: A documentary in which director Hunt analyzes the stunts and pays much-deserved tribute to the aerial photography of John Jones.

Key Scene: The special effects must take a backseat to the final moment between Mr. and Mrs. Bond. It's incredibly wrenching, and having Louis Armstrong singing the gorgeous ballad, "We Have All the Time in the World," in ironic counterpoint can just wipe you out.

On the Waterfront (1954)

Starring: Marlon Brando, Eva Marie Saint, Karl Malden, Rod Steiger

Directed by: Elia Kazan

Many people believe that Brando gives the best and most emotionally intuitive performance ever captured on film in Kazan's Oscar-winning drama of the New York docks. No argument here, especially after watching this beautifully realized DVD transfer. From the first note of Leonard Bernstein's score to the last harrowing black-and-white image captured by Boris Kaufman's camera, this is a groundbreaking film. It mattered then. It matters now. Budd Schulberg's script pits the dock workers against union boss Johnny Friendly (Lee J. Cobb). Brando's Terry Malloy, an ex-fighter and brother of Friendly's mouthpiece (Steiger), finds himself morally implicated in the Friendly-ordered murder of someone close to the woman (Saint) he's beginning to love. Every performance shines, including Malden as the priest of the people. The argument still rages that having Terry turn informer was a convenient way for Kazan and Schulberg to excuse their naming names during the Commie witch-hunt led by Senator Joe McCarthy. The movie itself is bigger than politics. It's about conscience and how it grows.

Hot Bonus: A retrospective documentary deals with Kazan's shrewd decision to shoot in winter on the frozen docks of Hoboken, New Jersey, giving the film an unfakeable immediacy that can still be felt.

Key Scene: Brando pouring his heart out to Steiger in the taxi, two actors in a confined space creating an entire world: "You should've looked out for me," says Terry. "I could have had class. I coulda been a contender. I coulda been somebody, instead of a bum, which is what I am."

Once Upon a Time in America (Two-Disc Special Edition) (1984)

Starring: Robert De Niro, James Woods, Elizabeth McGovern

Directed by: Sergio Leone

After the film's debut in Cannes, the studio slashed two hours out of Leone's four-hour gangster epic to accommodate short American attention spans. The resulting mutilation damaged

the reputation of a cinematic landmark that has now been restored on this 229-minute Director's Cut. Despite minor grain and sound problems, this DVD transfer is found gold. As Noodles (De Niro) is stirred from his reverie by an insistently ringing phone (shades of *The Matrix*), Leone ferries us through memories of three time periods (1921, 1933, and 1968). Violence is the constant as Noodles and his friend Max (Woods)—Jewish immigrants making their names in crime on New York's Lower East Side—move through Prohibition and the consequences of its repeal. The DVD offers a lesson in the art of cinematography, editing, and scoring (Ennio Morricone, we salute you). Leone, the maestro of spaghetti westerns, never made another film. Thanks to DVD, we finally see it whole.

Hot Bonus: A retrospective documentary in which Woods's comments are particularly telling. I most valued the on-set photos of Leone at work.

Key Scene: The rape. We are watching a heart turn to stone as Noodles violates Deborah (McGovern), the girl he has loved since childhood (Jennifer Connelly made a striking film debut as the young Deborah).

Once Upon a Time in Mexico (2003)

Starring: Antonio Banderas, Salma Hayek, Johnny Depp
Directed by: Robert Rodriguez

In honor of spaghetti western master Sergio Leone, who did the "Dollars" trilogy with Clint Eastwood, Rodriguez ends the trilogy he started with the super-low-budget (seven-thousand-dollar) *El Mariachi* in 1992 and continued with *Desperado* in 1995 in epic style, even if he's shooting on high-def digital video. Banderas, looking every inch the romantic hero, is back as the mariachi. Brooding over a tragedy involving his wife (Hayek), the balladeer who hides guns in his guitar case is out to stop drug lord Barrillo (Willem Dafoe) from killing Mexico's El Presidente. That's all the plot you'll get here. Just let Rodriguez take you to popcorn-movie heaven.

Hot Bonus: Rodriguez lives and breathes film, and his commentaries are an uncontrolled high. He even takes you into his editing room, which

is actually his garage: "I believe home is where the dreams are."

Key Scene: Anything involving Depp as Sands, a rogue CIA agent who doesn't let a small thing like getting his eyes gouged out stop him from a gunfight. He slips on a pair of shades to hide the blood dripping from his peepers and hires a kid to tell him where to aim.

Once Upon a Time in the West (Two-Disc Special Edition) (1968)

Starring: Henry Fonda, Charles Bronson, Claudia Cardinale, Jason Robards
Directed by: Sergio Leone

What a beginning! What a middle! What an ending! Leone's masterpiece hits DVD restored to its full 165 minutes, remastered in 5.1 channel Dolby Digital sound (Ennio Morricone's classic score is pure aural excitement), and roadmapped with the faces of its extraordinary actors. The opening still stuns as Bronson steps off a train, plays a harmonica, and guns down the three assassins waiting to ambush him. Fonda sent them. And what Leone does to turn that beloved American icon into a cold-eyed killer still freezes the blood. The plot, cooked up by Leone, Dario Argento, and Bernardo Bertolucci, concerns the arrival of the railroad and major money to the Old West. Cardinale is the widow trying to survive with the help of Robards. This is a film of big themes and bigger close-ups. You watch this DVD stunned at the enormity of its scope and vision.

Hot Bonus: The analysis never quits, but it's a treat to hear whether a sequence was shot in Rome or Spain or in John Ford's Monument Valley.

Key Scene: Fonda smiling at a nine-year-old boy, just before he shoots him.

One False Move (1992)

Starring: Bill Paxton, Billy Bob Thornton, Cynda Williams, Michael Beach
Directed by: Carl Franklin

Three killers, played by Thornton, Williams, and Beach, leave Los Angeles after a bloody drug deal and head for Arkansas where two L.A. cops (Jim Metzler and Earl Billings) are waiting to set a trap. Paxton plays Hurricane, the local sheriff dismissed by the city slickers as a rube. Big mistake. This is one nest of vipers, and Franklin directs expertly as they uncoil and shoot venom. Thornton bugs out in high style, and the script he wrote with Tom Epperson revels in edgy suspense. The DVD transfer delivers the goods, especially for a low-budget film. It's an unfairly unheralded gem.

Hot Bonus: Franklin talks honestly about his fears making what would turn out to be his breakthrough film.

Key Scene: The surprise ending. Don't let anyone give it away.

One Flew Over the Cuckoo's Nest (Two-Disc Special Edition) (1975)

Starring: Jack Nicholson, Louise Fletcher, Brad Dourif, Danny De Vito

Directed by: Milos Forman

Thanks to the iconic power of Forman's film version of Ken Kesey's book, hardly any movie set in a mental institution is without a maverick hero like Randle Patrick McMurphy (a rip-roaring Nicholson) or a martinet like Nurse Ratched (Fletcher, a walking brick wall). It's just that nobody has done it better—before or since. The DVD is a revelation compared to the muted TV prints that have proliferated since the film won the top five Oscars (Picture, Actor, Actress, Director, Screenplay). Many of the actors, including Dourif, De Vito, Christopher Lloyd, and Will Sampson, made their first screen impact playing inmates.

Hot Bonus: Forman talks, along with producers Saul Zaentz and Michael Douglas, whose father, Kirk Douglas, tried for years to bring the book to the screen. My question: Why the DVD silence from Nicholson?

Key Scene: When Nurse Ratched forbids the inmates to watch the World Series on TV, Mc-Murphy stages an imaginary game. The moment captures Nicholson's enormous gifts as a physically expressive actor.

Open Water (2004)

Starring: Blanchard Ryan, Daniel Travis

Directed by: Chris Kentis

Shot on the cheap ($130,000) minus the safety net of stars, this shark tale will still scare the cynicism out of you. Writer-director-editor Kentis and his producer wife, Laura Lau, couldn't afford to build animatronic sharks. They had to use the real things. They took their two lead actors to the Bahamas, threw them in the ocean with a thin sheet of metal mesh to wear under their wet suits, told shark wranglers to throw bait in the water to stir up the fish, turned on the digital camera and called for "Action!" They got it. And so does the DVD, which pushes digital rawness to make everything look frighteningly real. Susan (Ryan) and Daniel (Travis) go diving, get left behind by their tour boat (it happened to a couple off Australia's Great Barrier Reef in 1998), and end up bitching, blubbering, and finally clinging to each other as the fins start circling. From the first bite—on Susan's leg (ouch!)—Kentis never lets up on the tension. You can feel the water, stretching against an unsheltering sky, seep into your bones.

Hot Bonus: Kentis and Lau deconstruct the shark myth. I'm not buying it.

Key Scene: That last look at Susan caps eighty sweat-job minutes of imaginative, jolting suspense.

Opposite of Sex, The (1998)

Starring: Christina Ricci, Lisa Kudrow, Martin Donovan, Ivan Sergei

Directed and written by: Don Roos

The special effects here are the verbal volleys tossed by an exceptional cast. Ricci is a fine piece of work as Dede, an unsweet sixteen who leaves her Louisiana home to barge in on her schoolteacher brother Bill (Donovan) and his gay lover Matt (Sergei), whom she promptly seduces. Dede narrates the movie, and writer-director Roos gives her an arsenal of zingers. "I don't have a heart of gold," she declares, "and I don't grow one later." I'll say. Her nemesis is Bill's friend Lucia (Kudrow), who doesn't buy Dede's claim that Matt is bisexual: "Please, I went to a bar mitzvah once. That doesn't make me Jewish." And so it goes. Kudrow won the Best Supporting Actress award from the New York Film Critics Circle. Having her performance—and Ricci's—preserved on DVD is reason to celebrate.

Hot Bonus: Deleted scenes, with Roos's commentary, are just as funny as anything Roos left in the movie.

Key Scene: Kudrow comparing the virtues of sex vs. a back rub.

Ordinary People (1980)

Starring: Mary Tyler Moore, Timothy Hutton, Donald Sutherland

Directed by: Robert Redford

Now that I'm over the fact that Redford's chamber piece beat Martin Scorsese's epically emotional *Raging Bull* for the Best Picture Oscar (actually, I'm not over it), this well-produced DVD allows an honest reconsideration of this adaptation (by Alvin Sargent) of the Judith Guest novel. In his directing debut, Redford showed a rare sensitivity with actors. Hutton, then nineteen, is a marvel as the son—guilty over his brother's accidental death—who finds comfort with a therapist (Judd Hirsch), a lovely girl (Elizabeth McGovern), and an understanding father (Sutherland), but only cold rejection from his mother (Moore). The hard edge of Moore's performance still cuts deep. Ditto the movie.

Hot Bonus: The widescreen DVD transfer, capturing the muted beauty of John Bailey's cinematography, makes up for the lack of extras.

Key Scene: The family photograph; it's a study in emotional tension.

Others, The (Two-Disc Special Edition) (2001)

Starring: Nicole Kidman, Fionnula Flanagan, Christopher Eccleston
Directed by: Alejandro Amenábar

It has spooky atmosphere, a wicked twist of an ending, and an ice-cold grabber of a performance by Kidman as Grace, a mother who isolates her two children in a Victorian mansion on the British isle of Jersey near the end of World War II. Grace, who fears her husband (Eccleston) has died in battle, keeps her two kids—Anne (Alakina Mann) and Nicholas (James Bentley)—in the dark. Literally. She tells the new housekeeper (the expert Flanagan) that daylight will cause fits in Anne and Nicholas. Curtains must always be drawn and doors firmly locked. Then the noises start, and the visions and the strange voices. *The Others* is the American feature debut of Amenábar, the gifted young Spanish director of *Open Your Eyes*, who knows how to hold an audience with artful stealth. Just watch the DVD.

Hot Bonus: A look at a family dealing with the disease of xeroderma pigmentosum portrayed in the movie.

Key Scene: A piano plays itself.

Out of Sight (Special Edition) (1998)

Starring: George Clooney, Jennifer Lopez, Albert Brooks
Directed by: Steven Soderbergh

Can bank robber Jack Foley (Clooney) find love with Karen Sisco (Lopez), the federal marshal assigned to put him away? Such is the plot focus for one of the screen's sexiest crime capers. Almost no one saw it. Enter the DVD in a superfine

anamorphic transfer with fleshtones to die for. And what flesh. Rumor has it that Clooney and Lopez didn't get along, but you'd never know it from the sparks they exchange here. Director Soderbergh, working from Scott Frank's tone-perfect adaptation of Elmore Leonard's novel, moves the story along from Florida to Detroit, where Richard Ripley (Brooks) has a stash of diamonds waiting to be robbed by a terrific cast of liars and thieves, including Don Cheadle, Steve Zahn, and Ving Rhames as a crook who keeps confessing his crimes to his sister, a nun, who dutifully keeps turning him in. Leonard's literary panache is beautifully served.

Hot Bonus: Soderbergh's commentary is reliably contentious, and the deleted scenes are so good you want to put them right back in the movie.

Key Scene: The first meeting of Clooney and Lopez, stuffed in the trunk of car (don't ask) and discussing the chemistry of Faye Dunaway and the young Robert Redford in *Three Days of the Condor*. Delicious.

Out of the Past (1947)

Starring: Robert Mitchum, Kirk Douglas, Jane Greer
Directed by: Jacques Tourneur

Arguably the ultimate film noir. Told in flashback as Mitchum's mysterious Jeff, now in hiding as a gas station owner in a nowhere town, tells how he was once a private eye sent to Mexico by a gangster (a quietly menacing Douglas) to track down Kathie (Greer), the dame who ran out on him with forty thousand dollars of his ill-gotten gains. Daniel Mainwaring's dialogue still crackles as Mitchum falls for Greer's irresistible femme fatale. She admits she's trouble. His answer: "Baby, I don't care." Mitchum is the quintessence of cool, even as he sinks into erotic quicksand. He doesn't buy her excuses: "Save it," he sneers, "you're like a leaf that blows from one gutter to another." But he's hooked. Tourneur lets light and shadow play around these characters with a haunting seductiveness. The fullscreen DVD transfer is near perfect. The movie is closer than that.

Hot Bonus: A surprisingly dry lecture on film noir from James Ursini.

Key Scene: That out-of-nowhere punch Mitchum throws while casually reaching to light his cigarette. Want to see "wow" in action? This is it.

Outlaw Josey Wales, The (Collector's Edition) (1976)

Starring: Clint Eastwood, Sondra Locke, Chief Dan George

Directed by: Clint Eastwood

Unlike *Unforgiven*, this is the classic Eastwood western that didn't win any Oscars. It should have. The Collector's Edition offers superior image and sound to the DVD that preceded it. Eastwood plays a Civil War–era Missouri farmer who turns vigilante when Redlegs (Union guerillas) burn down his farm and murder his family. Josey is pissed. But the film is more than a Clint rampage. It's the story of a man who builds a new family out of other disenfranchised loners, including a young soldier (Sam Bottoms), an old lady (Paula Trueman) and her purty granddaughter (Locke, Eastwood's then-galpal), and an Indian (the scene-stealing Chief Dan George). "I myself never surrendered," he tells Josey, "but they got my horse, and it surrendered."

Hot Bonus: A tasty documentary called *Hell Hath No Fury* that inexplicably ignores the issue that Eastwood fired director Philip Kaufman (*The Right Stuff*) and took over himself. What fury provoked that hell?

Key Scene: Josey vs. Ten Bears (Will Sampson). "Dyin' ain't so hard for men like you and me," Josey tells his adversary. "It's the livin' that's hard."

Outsiders, The (Two-Disc Special Edition) (1983)

Starring: C. Thomas Howell, Matt Dillon, Ralph Macchio, Patrick Swayze

Directed by: Francis Ford Coppola

Funny, touching, and revelatory as a restored DVD project with Coppola adding twenty-two minutes to the film, originally released at a scant ninety minutes. The DVD, with a gorgeous widescreen picture and completely remastered Dolby Digital 5.1 channel sound, is subtitled *The Complete Novel*. Coppola says that is in deference to admirers of the popular S. E. Hinton novel for young adults who thought he cheated the book

by cutting off the beginning and ending. Coppola restores those scenes, featuring many young actors (Tom Cruise, Rob Lowe, Emilio Estevez, Diane Lane) who went on to stardom. The film is now a complete picture of these 1960s Oklahoma teens who divide themselves into greasers and preppy Socs (pronounced so-shes). The focus is on Ponyboy (Howell), a fourteen-year-old orphan who lives with his older brothers (Lowe and Swayze) and gets involved in a murder committed by Johnny (Macchio), his best friend. With the help of greaser leader Dallas (a powerful Dillon), the boys hide out in an abandoned building until an act of unexpected heroism brings them to justice. The director has replaced the melodramatic score by his father Carmine Coppola with period music by Elvis Presley, Van Morrison, Jerry Lee Lewis, Carl Perkins, and others, while retaining "Stay Gold," the ballad Carmine wrote with Stevie Wonder. Even better, Coppola has given the film a fullness that blends ferocity and feeling in a way it never did before.

Hot Bonus: "Making of" featurettes abound, including Coppola's explanation of how a student petition from the Lone Star School in Fresno prompted him to make the film of Hinton's book.

Key Scene: Ponyboy, quoting Robert Frost's poem about how nothing gold (meaning youth) ever lasts, is set against an impossibly golden sunset that always threw me, as did much of the florid dialogue. This new DVD makes it clear that the scene and the entire film is being seen through Ponyboy, a writer wannabe with an intense love for reading *Gone With the Wind*. Coppola has directed the film as Ponyboy would see and hear it. That clarity results in a movie that will stay gold.

Pal Joey (1957)

Starring: Frank Sinatra, Rita Hayworth, Kim Novak

Directed by: George Sidney

Sinatra does little more than play himself as an arrogant nightclub singer who chases skirts and busts jaws. But what a kick to have a DVD that shows him at his cocky best, especially singing those Rodgers & Hart numbers ("I Could Write a Book," "I Didn't Know What Time It Was"). Even if the bitter cynicism of John O'Hara's story is softened by Hollywood, Sinatra's Joey is still a charming SOB, whether he's being kept by an older woman (Hayworth) or seducing an ingénue, played by Novak with just the right touch of corruptible innocence in her drunk scene. "Confidentially, I'm stacked," she purrs to Joey. Confidentially, this musical (beautifully shot on location in San Francisco) is a goodie. You mustn't kick it around.

Hot Bonus: The original "Hep Cat" theatrical trailer in which Sinatra gives lessons in Joey jargon, including such words as "gasser," which the singer incorporated into his own life as the leader of the Rat Pack.

Key Scene: Sinatra singing "The Lady Is a Tramp" is—hands down—the most erotically swinging moment he ever enjoyed onscreen.

Panic Room
(Three-Disc Special Edition) (2002)

Starring: Jodie Foster, Kristin Stewart

Directed by: David Fincher

A reference-quality DVD package. And the movie isn't bad either. It's Fincher's high-style testament to the cool things movies can do to make us jump out of our seats in the dark. So lights off when you watch this DVD, people. Foster is terrific as Meg, a recent divorcee who buys a four-story brownstone in Manhattan. That's one way she and her eleven-year-old daughter (Stewart) can stick it to rich daddy (Patrick Bauchau), who dumped them to boff a supermodel. What Meg and her daughter don't know yet is that three burglars (played by Jared Leto, Forest Whitaker, and Dwight Yoakam) have chosen to break in on the same rainy night they move in. Luckily, the brownstone has a panic room, a concrete bunker complete with surveillance monitors, a separate phone line, and a steel door that locks you in until the police show up. Unluckily, the phone doesn't work. The tension is nonstop, but watch the movie a second time, and it becomes a metaphoric battle between a bruised woman and her own despair.

Hot Bonus: From preproduction to post, no detail goes unexamined. You'll learn how the camera seems to glide through walls, swooping up and down four stories (OK, computer animation helped).

Key Scene: Things get bloodiest when mother grabs a sledgehammer.

Parallax View, The (1974)

Starring: Warren Beatty, Paula Prentiss
Directed by: Alan J. Pakula

A paranoid thriller that gives *All the President's Men* and *JFK* a run for their conspiracy money. Journalist Joe Frady (Beatty) gets a visit from a TV reporter (Prentiss) who witnessed the assassination of a senator three years before at the Seattle Space Needle. She says other witnesses are being eliminated one by one. Is she crazy? Joe thinks not, and he uncovers a plot that still feels scarily plausible. Beatty is a solid audience surrogate, but it's the literal and figurative spiderweb spun by director Pakula and cinematographer Gordon Willis that makes this widescreen DVD a winner.

Hot Bonus: Just a trailer, but even that works like a charm.

Key Scene: A political rally, shot from the roof of the arena, brings out the menace in public places with unparalleled tension.

Passion of the Christ, The (2004)

Starring: Jim Caviezel, Maria Morgenstern, Monica Bellucci

Directed by: Mel Gibson

Don't look here for a screed on why Gibson's hugely popular film version of the last twelve hours of Christ is offensive to Jews, a sop to the Christian right, and a selective reading of the Bible. We'll leave that to pundits on *Access Hollywood*. Gibson has directed a movie that is powerfully moving and fanatically obtuse in equal doses. But name another Hollywood star who would spend $30 million out of his own pocket to bring his personal obsession with Christ's agony to the screen and film it in Aramaic and Latin with English subtitles. Caviezel, who plays Jesus, doesn't so much give a performance as offer himself up as raw meat. So graphic are the torture scenes—flayings, a crown of thorns, whips with barbed metal tips, nails driven into hands and feet—that the clarity of the DVD transfer could be a liability for the squeamish. Gibson's immersion in the blood of Christ is an act of faith filmed with a zealot's rapture. But his *Passion* emerges as something contrary to Jesus' spirit: unforgiving.

Hot Bonus: None. But try this: mask off the English subtitles and watch the film as Gibson originally intended it—with no translation.

Key Scene: Christ in the garden of Gethsemane, praying quietly to his Father in heaven in a form both divine and human.

Paths of Glory (1957)

Starring: Kirk Douglas, Adolphe Menjou, George Macready, Ralph Meeker

Directed by: Stanley Kubrick

The greatest antimilitary film ever made is delivered to DVD with black-and-white images so potent they burn into your mind and heart (the mono sound needs work, though). This was only Kubrick's fourth film, but had he done no others *Glory* would still have established him as a master. Douglas stars as Colonel Dax, the French commander of a World War I regiment ordered to take an untakeable German fortress (the Ant Hill). While two of the fatcat generals, played by Menjou and Macready (both outstanding), sit in elegant chateaux, Kubrick's camera prowls through the trenches and the battlefield with relentless force. Later, three soldiers are court-martialed for cowardice, and Dax is charged with their defense. It's a losing game. The film, however, has a lasting power that calls for further DVD restoration.

Hot Bonus: A four-page booklet on the making of the film.

Key Scene: That first prowl through the trenches.

Patton (1970)

Starring: George C. Scott, Karl Malden

Directed by: Franklin Schaffner

Winner of seven Oscars, including Best Picture and a Best Actor trophy for Scott, who turned the damned thing down. When you're that good, you don't need a trophy to tell you. The film, sturdily directed by Schaffner, traces the career of General Patton ("Old Blood and Guts") through his World War II defeat of Rommel, the invasion of Sicily, D-Day, Bastogne, and the Battle of the Bulge. The DVD transfer delivers the goods in terms of widescreen fireworks.

But also credit the brilliant script by Edmund H. North and Francis Ford Coppola. Hearing Patton, on the battlefield, describing his feelings about war ("I love it. God help me, I do love it so"), you can't help but think of the napalm-loving Colonel Kilgore in Coppola's 1979 *Apocalypse Now.* Through it all is Scott, slapping a soldier for cowardice, threatening Hitler ("I'm gonna personally shoot that paper-hanging son of a bitch!"), and warning himself about fleeting glory. The achievement is monumental.

Hot Bonus: A retrospective documentary that includes Oliver Stone blaming the bombing of Cambodia on Nixon's love for *Patton.* Sheesh.

Key Scene: The opener with Scott's Patton addressing unseen troops against a ginormous American flag: "I want you to remember that no bastard ever won a war by dying for his country. He won it by making the other poor dumb bastard die for his country."

Peeping Tom (1960)

Starring: Carl Boehm, Anna Massey, Moira Shearer

Directed by: Michael Powell

Few movies are more influential than Powell's mesmeric look at a psycho (Boehm) who films his victims with a 16mm camera at the precise moment that he snuffs out their lives with the sharpened corner of his tripod. Powell was all but stoned in the streets of his native England for making a thriller that cut to the "Peeping Tom" nature of cinema itself. Seen today on this superior DVD color transfer from Criterion, the film still shocks but not without artful purpose. The script by Leo Marks takes pains to show how Boehm's character, named Mark, is befriended by Helen (Massey), a woman who recoils when Mark shows her black-and-white home movies of himself as a child being tormented by his psychologist father (Powell plays the role) as part of his study on fear. As a director, Powell achieves something more than a deep-dish provocation. He puts the idea of "watching" on trial.

Hot Bonus: *A Very British Psycho,* a U.K. documentary about the negative critical reaction to Marks and the film. Martin Scorsese, whose longtime editor Thelma Schoonmaker is Powell's widow, brought the uncut film to America in 1979. His reliably passionate comments would have been a fine alternative to the theoretical prattling of scholar Laura Mulvey.

Key Scene: The opening credits, which unspool against the background of Mark watching the film of the prostitute he has just murdered.

Pee-Wee's Big Adventure (1985)

Starring: Pee-Wee Herman (Paul Reubens), Elizabeth Daily

Directed by: Tim Burton

Pee-wee, with his red bowtie, white shoes, and baby brat smile, is a character that Paul Reubens developed for a standup comedy act and TV series. How could he carry a whole movie, with a skimpy plot about a stolen red bike that Pee-Wee hits the road to find (it's hidden at the Alamo)? Surprise, he does, only not alone. This is director Burton's first feature, and he makes colors and joy leap off the screen. It's a DVD lollipop. The script, co-written by Reubens and Phil Hartman, is juiced with Pee-Wee-isms ("I know you are, but what am I?"). Given Reubens's arrest in a porn theater in 1991, the character didn't survive for the kid fans. It gives Pee-Wee's line to his girl Dottie (Daily) a new ring: "There's things about me you don't know, Dottie. Things you wouldn't understand. Things you couldn't understand."

Hot Bonus: Danny Elfman's effervescent score has its own isolated track, and his comments add up to a valuable lesson about how music works in movies.

Key Scene: Pee-Wee meets Large Marge, who's been dead for ten years.

Pennies From Heaven (1981)

Starring: Steve Martin, Bernadette Peters, Jessica Harper, Christopher Walken

Directed by: Herbert Ross

An ambitious experiment, this Depression-era musical—based on Dennis Potter's acclaimed British TV series—met with public indifference. DVD provides a second chance. Take it. It's downbeat, but looks and sounds dazzling. Martin plays Arthur, a struggling sheet-music salesman. To escape his boring job and loveless marriage to Joan (Harper), he fantasizes a happier life with the help of period songs which he lip-syncs with gusto. But Potter wants no sympathy for this loser, who knocks up schoolmarm Eileen (Peters) and sends her off callously into a life of vice with a pimp, played by Walken, who stops the show with a dance number ("Let's Misbehave"). It all ends in murder and a hanging. Martin and Peters (an item at the time) dream themselves into an Astaire-Rog-

ers movie where life can be transformed by art, if only for a moment. Not built to warm the heart, *Pennies* excites the imagination in ways few musicals ever do.

Hot Bonus: A twentieth-anniversary reunion with Martin and the crew.

Key Scene: The title song, danced by Vernel Bagneris to Arthur Tracy's original recording. The setting is a diner out of an Edward Hopper painting with raindrops turning to gold coins. The DVD is worth owning just for this.

People vs. Larry Flynt, The (Special Edition) (1996)

Starring: Woody Harrelson, Courtney Love, Edward Norton

Directed by: Milos Forman

Much improved over the non–special edition DVD. The crisper the widescreen image and sound, the more you'll listen up. This is a fight for free expression seen through an unlikely biopic hero, *Hustler* publisher and porn king Larry Flynt, played by Harrelson in an Oscar-nominated tour de force. Working from a knowing script by Scott Alexander and Larry Karaszewski, Forman lets his top-tier cast make their points through laughs laced with gravity. Love won a deserved New York Film Critics Circle award for her role as Althea, Larry's bisexual stripper wife. She sticks with Larry even after a bullet from an unknown shooter leaves him in a wheelchair, paralyzed from the waist down. Forman follows Flynt through porn, drugs, religion, and the fight he and his lawyer (Norton) take to the Supreme Court. "If they'll protect a scumbag like me, then they'll protect all of you," says Flynt after his 1988 court victory. Amen to that, brother.

Hot Bonus: *Free Speech or Porn* is a behind-the-scenes free-for-all, including Love's screentest (hold on to your socks), interviews with big cheeses, plus watching Forman and the actors in action.

Key Scene: Flynt wheeling himself into the Supreme Court for the big fight.

Perfect Storm, The (Collector's Edition) (2000)

Starring: George Clooney, Mark Wahlberg, John C. Reilly, Diane Lane

Directed by: Wolfgang Petersen

The storm. I could go into painstaking detail about the film version of Sebastian Junger's best-selling nonfiction account of the six-man sword

boat crew of the *Andrea Gail* and the freak collision of three storm systems that took the boat down off the coast of Newfoundland in 1991. I could tell you about Clooney as Billy Tyne, the stalwart captain from Gloucester, Massachusetts, and director Petersen playing skipper behind the camera. But since the potential for a great movie goes frustratingly unrealized, all I can talk about is the storm, and how the wizards at Industrial Light and Magic cooked up a heaving wave to sweep you into digital and sonic overdrive.

Hot Bonus: How they created the storm.

Key Scene: The storm.

Perfect World, A (1993)

Starring: Kevin Costner, Clint Eastwood, T. J. Lowther

Directed by: Clint Eastwood

A box-office failure that is ripe for rediscovery on this immaculately produced widescreen DVD. On the surface, the film is a gripping manhunt with Eastwood as Texas Ranger Red Garnett, chasing Costner as escaped convict Butch Haynes. But John Lee Hancock's script unearths knotty matters of the heart. Set just days before the JFK assassination, the film is always on the edge of tragedy. It's that edge that Eastwood the director walks, drawing Costner's deepest, truest, most complex performance. Butch takes a hostage in fatherless, seven-year-old Phillip (Lowther). The two connect. Butch, also from a broken home, makes a charming and dangerous teacher in the art of guns and grand theft. Red, who sent Butch away as a juvenile, never loses sight of that lost boy in Butch. Neither does Eastwood, who guides the film to a shattering climax that indicts the legal system for helping to make career criminals of kids.

Hot Bonus: A trailer seems a puny extra for a film that demands discussion.

Key Scene: The startling sadism of Butch's attack on a black tenant farmer (Wayne Dehart), his wife (Mary Alice), and their grandson (Kevin Woods), who give Butch and Philip shelter. Seeing the farmer slap his grandson brings out the monster in Butch, and Eastwood lets us see it plain. This is American filmmaking at its toughest and least sentimental.

Persona (Special Edition) (1966)

Starring: Liv Ullmann, Bibi Andersson

Directed and written by: Ingmar Bergman

My favorite among Bergman masterpieces. An actress (Ullmann) stops speaking after a performance of *Electra*. She takes refuge at a seaside cottage, cared for only by a nurse (Andersson) who pours out her life story in a flow of words (English subtitles if you don't understand Swedish). Gradually, the two women begin to absorb each other's personalities. Bergman and cinematographer Sven Nykvist create one hypnotic image after another (returned to their stark perfection on this Special Edition DVD), culminating in the two women seeming to dissolve into one.

Hot Bonus: Ullmann and Andersson talk about the creative process and how Bergman blended its beauty and ugliness.

Key Scene: This magnificent acting duet finds its heart as Andersson tells an erotically detailed story of seducing a young boy on the beach and Ullmann's face reflects a sexual longing that turns words into flesh.

Peyton Place (1957)

Starring: Lana Turner, Diane Varsi, Russ Tamblyn, Terry Moore

Directed by: Mark Robson

An era of 1950s sexual hypocrisy is summed up in this film of Grace Metalious's then-notorious bestseller. It's a trip to watch the movie now when adultery, abortion, homosexuality, rape, and murder are the stuff of TV sitcoms. The movie still catches you up in its soap opera theatrics, thanks to a widescreen DVD transfer that captures this New England town in all its lush seasonal splendors. The Academy awarded Turner a nomination for playing a woman hiding a deep, dark secret: her daughter (Varsi) was born out of wedlock. The night Turner lost the Oscar she returned home to face a violent argument with her lover Johnny Stompanato, who was stabbed by Turner's protective daughter Cheryl Crane. Nothing in *Peyton Place* tops that.

Hot Bonus: Tamblyn and Moore look back on the film.

Key Scene: Varsi, the writer wannabe, giving the virginal Tamblyn his first kiss on a hillside above the town. The delicacy of their Oscar-nominated performances, set against Franz Waxman's score, is still something to see.

Philadelphia Story, The (Two-Disc Special Edition) (1940)

Starring: Katharine Hepburn, Cary Grant, James Stewart
Directed by: George Cukor

A timeless sophisticated comedy, from Philip Barry's play, gets digitally remastered and sent out in style to a new generation. Hepburn plays an heiress, on the eve of her wedding, who still loves ex-husband Grant but flirts with reporter Stewart. My guess is the star shine will never fade from these three legends. Grant and Hepburn spar like thoroughbreds under Cukor's astute direction. And Stewart won the Oscar for stating the obvious: "The prettiest sight in this fine pretty world is the privileged class enjoying its privileges." Even in black-and-white, the sight still astounds.

Hot Bonus: Documentaries on Hepburn and Cukor.

Key Scene: The dialogue sparkles: "South Bend?" says the great Kate. "It sounds like dancing." But the keeper is the silent opening encapsulating the breakup of Hepburn and Grant using a shove, a fist, and a bag of golf clubs.

PI (1998)

Starring: Sean Gullette, Mark Margolis, Ben Shenkman
Directed by: Darren Aronofsky

Not for the mathematically squeamish or those unwilling to go for a harsh, grainy black-and-white ride— the DVD is an exact transfer. Aronofsky cooked up this mindteaser on a puny budget (sixty thousand dollars) and unlimited imagination. Max (Gullette) locks himself in a room with his computers. He is convinced that numbers can solve any mystery, including nature, God, and the stock market. Exploitation and threat enter the equation when others start believing Max is on to something.

Hot Bonus: Aronofsky, who scored an impressive debut that won him the directing prize at Sundance, explains it all for you. Not really, but he tries.

Key Scene: The ants in Max's computer.

Pianist, The (2002)

Starring: Adrien Brody, Thomas Kretschmann
Directed by: Roman Polanski

Polanski's most personal and powerful film in years (he won the Oscar for it) tells the true story of young pianist Wladyslaw Szpilman (Brody), a Polish Jew who survived the Nazi invasion of Warsaw (where much of this film was shot) by hiding out and living like an animal. Szpilman is first seen playing Chopin for Polish radio when the Nazi bombs fall in 1939. For the rest, he is mostly alone, observing the horror through windows, hearing music only in his head. Brody, the Academy's choice as Best Actor, works miracles at showing bruises beyond words and tears.

Hot Bonus: Polanski's own story is told. Not the statutory rape charge that prompted the director to flee the United States in 1978, but his childhood in Poland (he escaped the Krakow ghetto, though his mother died in a concentration camp) and his soul-deep faith in the tender mercies of art.

Key Scene: Near the end of war, a Nazi officer (the superb Kretschmann) asks Szpilman to play, and the music pours out in waves. In a sensitive DVD transfer, the visual and aural highlight happens right here.

Piano, The (1993)

Starring: Holly Hunter, Harvey Keitel, Anna Paquin, Sam Neill
Directed by: Jane Campion

Mood pieces are notoriously difficult to transfer to DVD. The grays and browns can turn murky. But the hauntingly misty aura of Stuart Dryburgh's camerawork comes through relatively unscathed on disc. Without it, you cannot truly appreciate Campion's achievement in telling the story of Ada (Hunter), a headstrong woman who travels to New Zealand with her daughter (Paquin) and her piano for an arranged marriage to a farmer (Neill). Ada does not speak, her daughter never stops (both Hunter and Paquin won Oscars for their duet). But anger figures in the mix, especially when the farmer sells her piano to Baines (Keitel) and Ada compromises herself sexually to get it back. Or does she? The mysteries of this mesmerizer constantly fold back on each other, making repeat viewings a must.

Hot Bonus: Biographies of cast and crew are included. Check up on Campion. You'll want to see more of her movies.

Key Scene: Ada and the piano on a small boat, each trying not to go under.

Pickup on South Street (1953)

Starring: Richard Widmark, Jean Peters, Thelma Ritter, Richard Kiley
Directed by: Sam Fuller

Hardboiled doesn't begin to describe this Fuller crime odyssey through the mean streets of New York. With Criterion doing the DVD honors, the black-and-white picture is so sharp you could cut diamonds on it. Widmark is nail tough as the crook who lifts a purse on the subway. It belongs to Peters, who doesn't know she's carting around microfilm for her Commie boyfriend (Kiley). Fuller mixes crime and politics with wicked virtuosity. "Are you waving a flag at me?" Widmark asks the feds when they ask his help to catch a traitor. All the acting is aces. But Ritter's Oscar-nominated performance as Moe, an aging pickpocket, is the one you want to take home. Don't blame Moe for selling information. She's saving for a decent funeral. "If they bury me in Potter's Field, it would just kill me."

Hot Bonus: A terrific interview with Fuller.
Key Scene: The subway chase is thrilling and way brutal for its time.

Picnic (1955)

Starring: Kim Novak, William Holden, Rosalind Russell, Susan Strasberg
Directed by: Joshua Logan

Whether this widescreen DVD beauty is depicting a picnic morning or the moonglow floating down on dancers under the stars, something magical is always at work in Logan's screen translation of the Pulitzer Prize–winning play by William Inge. Holden is the sexy drifter who hops off a freight train into a small Kansas town and becomes an instant chick magnet for Novak as the town's beauty, her kid sister (Strasberg), and the aging schoolmarm (Russell) who ignores her suitor (Arthur O'Connell, Oscar nominated) to shoot Holden lustful looks (she even rips off his shirt). It's steamy stuff.

Hot Bonus: The vintage advertising is fun, but why no commentary? Novak, at her loveliest here, told me that the film was a nightmare for her due to what she perceived as Logan's favoritism toward Strasberg.
Key Scene: The Labor Day dance with James Wong Howe's cameras circling Novak and Holden as they move toward each in a slow dance to the "Moonglow" theme that topped the record charts. You can still see why.

Picnic at Hanging Rock (Special Edition) (1975)

Starring: Rachel Roberts, Dominic Guard, Helen Morse
Directed by: Peter Weir

A DVD to get lost in, just as gifted Aussie director Weir intended. The Criterion transfer, a widescreen director's cut with a 5.1 Dolby Digital soundtrack, does full justice to the erotic mystery at the film's core. It is Valentine's Day 1900—a time of sexual repression—and a teacher takes four of her girls on a picnic. While one girl naps, the others take off their shoes and prim stockings for a barefoot climb up Hanging Rock. They never return. Weir's camera probes the crevices with such scrutiny that we believe we see things, hear things, feel things. The film is a ravishment.

Hot Bonus: Intelligent liner notes from the late critic Vincent Canby.
Key Scene: The first glimpse of the girls in white dresses preparing for a trip that will change their lives. This is beauty, laced with foreboding.

Pillow Talk (1959)

Starring: Doris Day, Rock Hudson, Tony Randall, Thelma Ritter
Directed by: Michael Gordon

Long ago in a galaxy far away (the 1950s), Hollywood made movies about adult women who were virgins and adult men who needed to propose marriage to get them into bed. This fluffball is the paradigm. The DVD transfer decks it out with bright colors and sound (it's mono but serviceable). Day plays the virgin. She's done it many times, but this time she earned an Oscar nomination as an interior designer who can't stand the playboy (Hudson) with whom she shares a party line. In that galaxy far away there were no cellphones, and you had to share your line with another person who could listen in on your conversations. End of history lesson. For plot, we get Hudson pretending to be another guy so he can sweet-talk Jan into sexually compromising positions. Wags today like to comb the film for clues to Hudson being gay (his character writes Broadway musicals). But there's nothing fake about the Day-Hudson chemistry. It worked then, and now.

Hot Bonus: Having the film letterboxed is a must since the film frequently splits the screen to show Day on one line and Hudson on the other.

Key Scene: That split screen moment when Day is in her bathtub and Hudson is in his and they seem to be playing footsie.

Pink Flamingos (1972)

Starring: Divine, Mink Stole, Edith Massey, Danny Mills, David Lochary

Directed by: John Waters

The dirty movie that put Waters on the map. It's the one where the divine Divine (the three-hundred-pound transvestite whose real name is Glen Milstead) plays Babs Johnson. She's the filthiest person alive and eats dog doo to prove it. Having this sharp-looking DVD ups the gross level considerably. Babs lives in a trailer with her son Crackers (Mills), who cries "Do my balls, Mama," and her mom (Massey), who swallows eggs while sitting half-naked in a playpen. You can tell by now if this one's for you.

Hot Bonus: If you like Pink (and I do, I do), grab the John Waters Collection, which includes *Desperate Living, Female Trouble, Hairspray, Pecker, Polyester*, and the NC-17 version of *A Dirty Shame*. The Waters commentary on each is a treat all by itself.

Key Scene: Babs and Crackers licking the furniture of the Marbles (Lochary and Mink Stole), who dare to think they can beat Babs at her dirty game.

Pink Floyd: The Wall (Deluxe Edition) (1982)

Starring: Bob Geldof, Christine Hargreaves, Bob Hoskins

Directed by: Alan Parker

The Pink Floyd album is reimagined as a movie by director Parker, who throws at it every rock video trick in the book. Some of them stick, and the DVD (the Twenty-fifth Anniversary Edition) delivers the over-the-top images and sound with real digital pow. You're on your own with the plot, with rocker and Live Aid organizer Geldof playing Pink, a take on the band's Roger Waters as a rocker having a meltdown.

Hot Bonus: It's great to hear Waters and Parker on the commentary track discussing the differences they had making the movie. I also enjoyed

the option of having the lyrics on the bottom of the screen.

Key Scene: The animated sequences by political cartoonist Gerald Scarfe.

Pink Panther, The (1964)

Starring: Peter Sellers, David Niven, Capucine, Claudia Cardinale

Directed by: Blake Edwards

The movie that introduced Sellers as Inspector Clouseau deserves a place in any DVD collection. With his trenchcoat, shifty eyes, impossible French accent and utter hopelessness at crime solving, Sellers's deadpan creation is an immortal cure for the blues. The rest of the film, involving suave thief Niven trying to snag a diamond (the Pink Panther) from an Indian princess (Cardinale) while also boffing the inspector's wife (Capucine) is pretty filler—really pretty since the DVD transfer brings amazing freshness to the color and Henry Mancini's famous theme. But this is a Sellers show.

Hot Bonus: The commentary by director Edwards, a wiz at physical comedy, offers fascinating details about working with Sellers through four sequels, all of which are available on *The Pink Panther Collection*.

Key Scene: Clouseau playing the Stradivarius. He thinks the violin is a sexual lure. Not the way he plays it.

Pinocchio (Disney Gold Classic Collection) (1940)

Starring: The voices of Dickie Jones, Evelyn Venable, Cliff Edwards

Directed by: Ben Sharpsteen and Hamilton Luske

As long as you don't confuse this animated Disney classic with the deadly live-action 2002 version with Roberto Benigni, there are no strings about telling you to pony up for this elegantly restored beauty. What they can't do these days with DVD! Geppetto, voiced by Christian Rub, creates a wooden puppet, Pinocchio (Jones), who wants to be a real boy. The Blue Fairy (Venable) grants his wish, and he's off on a series of wonderful and sometimes scary adventures. "Always let your conscience be your guide," the Blue Fairy advises the boy. Jiminy Cricket (Edwards) takes the role of the conscience, and just a note or two from his song, "When You Wish Upon a Star," can bring memories of this movie flooding back. This was only Disney's second animated feature after *Snow White*. Funny how genius can come from something so simple.

Hot Bonus: We'll have to wait for the Platinum Edition.

Key Scene: Pinocchio inside the whale.

Pirates of the Caribbean: The Curse of the Black Pearl (Three-Disc Special Edition) (2003)

Starring: Johnny Depp, Geoffrey Rush, Orlando Bloom, Keira Knightley

Directed by: Gore Verbinski

What a DVD package: Anamorphic transfer. DTS sound. You almost forget the lack of fuel in the plot tank to power the visual fireworks in this Jerry Bruckheimer extravaganza. There's no depth, but there is Depp in his Oscar-nominated performance as Captain Jack Sparrow, a stoner pirate legend. In eye shadow and dreads, Depp swans through this swashbuckler with a scene-stealing gusto unseen since Marlon Brando in *Mutiny on the Bounty*. When the film goes long, there's always Depp to the rescue. The romantic rivalry between Captain Jack and prettyboy Will (Bloom) for the hand of the damsel (Knightley) makes the film seem longer than it is. But Depp achieves a fun rapport with Rush as Barbossa, captain of the undead pirates who look like skeletons in the moonlight and do much digital thrashing about under Verbinski's unassailably energetic direction.

Hot Bonus: More than you could wish for or stand. My favorite is the Easter Egg that lets you see Keith Richards give Depp hell for imitating him.

Key Scene: Depp's big pirate entrance in a rowboat that sinks under him.

Place in the Sun, A (1951)

Starring: Montgomery Clift, Elizabeth Taylor, Shelley Winters

Directed by: George Stevens

Clift, in a performance that influenced a generation of actors, plays a poor boy who sets his sights on a society beauty (Taylor, nineteen and smashing) only to have his plans thwarted when the factory girl (Winters) he's boffing tells him she's pregnant. Based on Theodore Dreiser's *An American Tragedy*, the film achieves artful potency through director Stevens, who won an Oscar for driving his actor to lyrical heights and creating images of seductive beauty. The sharpness of the full-screen DVD should win the film a new audience.

Hot Bonus: There's a discussion of the Stevens technique—he shoots countless takes. And Taylor's reaction to having her first grownup screen kiss with Clift is funny and touching. The two remained lifelong friends.

Key Scene: That kiss. Taylor pulls Clift off the dance floor and takes him outside. "Tell Mama, tell Mama all," she purrs. Stevens keeps their faces in a tight closeup as smothering as the kiss. The effect is swooningly erotic.

Planet of the Apes (Two-Disc Special Edition) (1968)

Starring: Charlton Heston, Roddy McDowall, Kim Hunter

Directed by: Franklin J. Schaffner

Forget the Tim Burton remake in 2001. The original is the real deal, and the widescreen DVD with its enveloping sound reminds you of that all over again. Heston stars as an astronaut who lands on a planet he doesn't recognize where the apes rule and humans are kept in cages and lobotomized if they dare to speak. Schaffner gets wonderfully expressive performances from the actors, especially McDowall and Hunter in John Chambers's Oscar-winning makeup. The whipsmart script is by *The Twilight Zone*'s Rod Serling. Jerry Goldsmith's score gets your pulse pounding in expectation of the still-famous twist ending.

Hot Bonus: McDowall, who died in 1998, takes you through the whole process of a movie fine enough to have spawned four sequels.

Key Scene: Heston speaks. You can feel the shockwaves when the silent human snaps, "Take your stinking paws off me, you damn dirty ape."

Platoon (Special Edition) (1986)

Starring: Charlie Sheen, Tom Berenger, Willem Dafoe

Directed by: Oliver Stone

Stone's intensely personal look at the trauma of Vietnam won the Best Picture Oscar. Sheen stars as Chris, a character much like Stone, a college dropout from a wealthy background who enlisted. Chris is caught between two sergeants—the compassionate Elias (Dafoe) and the murderous Barnes (Berenger)—surrogate fathers fighting for what Chris calls "possession of my soul." Stone re-creates the war with unnerving honesty. Many veterans have praised the sounds, the light, the texture. The gifted cinematographer Robert Richardson restores all of that on the superb DVD transfer. In a letter home to Grandma, Chris writes of his platoon: "They came from the end of the line, most of them. Small towns you never heard of. They're the unwanted, yet they're fighting for our society, and our freedom. It's weird, isn't it?" What's weird is that Stone thought it necessary to spell out his points in a way that reminds viewers that it's only a movie.

Hot Bonus: Stone goes past mere commentary to show how the movie is really a piece of his soul.

Key Scene: Dafoe's slo-mo execution gets all the attention, but it's the attack on a village, fueled by the platoon's rage over having lost two men, that captures the war at its most unreasoning.

Player, The (1992)

Starring: Tim Robbins, Vincent D'Onofrio, Fred Ward

Directed by: Robert Altman

Griffin Mill, the back-stabbing Hollywood exec brought to definitive life by Robbins, gets antsy with writers who can't describe a movie in twenty-five words or less. So let's try condensing *The Player*: Director Altman took an ax and gave his business forty whacks. And when he saw what he had done, he gave his audience forty-one. That leaves one word for a reaction, so let's try *bravo*. From a modest $8 million budget, Altman fashions a satire that leavens anger with cathartic wit. Michael Tolkin's admirably dark book often choked on bile: Altman's improvisatory style provides an exhilarating buoyancy, even when Griffin handles a disgruntled writer by killing him. There's no room to spell out the many characters and events in this toxic tapestry that transfers to DVD with all its pretty poison intact. Altman reveals a Hollywood where creativity is bad for business, marketing puts a seductive face on compromise, and success means having the clout to ski on the slopes of Aspen. It's a barren culture that's not hard to recognize as our own.

Hot Bonus: Altman and Tolkin bring a contentious vitality to the differences they had while making the film.

Key Scene: The opener: As a security chief (Ward) raves about Orson Welles's famous opening shot in *Touch of Evil*, Altman's camera swoops down on the studio lot, picking up snatches of conversation as Griffin takes story meetings with writers, including Buck Henry, who pitches a sequel to *The Graduate* ("Mrs. Robinson has a stroke"). Altman has used interlocking characters and overlapping dialogue before, but rarely as hilariously.

Point Blank (1967)

Starring: Lee Marvin, Angie Dickinson, John Vernon, Sharon Acker

Directed by: John Boorman

It's taken forever to get this crime classic to DVD. Now that it's here, you can start the cheering. Mel Gibson remade it as *Payback* in 1999, but that was sissy stuff compared to Boorman's brutal battering ram. Marvin is cool on two legs as Walker, a thief out for revenge on his wife (Acker) and his partner (Vernon). They shot him and left him for dead in his Alcatraz hideout. But he swam to shore. Now he's back, and plenty pissed. Boorman gives the violence a surreal ferocity. Cultists say that Walker is really dead and the revenge is what flashes through his mind in his last hours. OK. But the movie is the opposite of dead. It's a creative workout.

Hot Bonus: Boorman is interviewed by Steven Soderbergh, who knows he could never have made *The Limey* without seeing *Point Blank* first.

Key Scene: Marvin getting slapped silly by Dickinson (she's plays his wife's sister). He just takes his medicine in silence, like a sleepwalker.

Point Break (1991)

Starring: Keanu Reeves, Patrick Swayze, Lori Petty

Directed by: Kathryn Bigelow

Keanu plays Johnny Utah, an FBI agent who goes undercover as a surfer (dude!) to catch Bodhi (Swayze), the surfer-skydiver who just may be the leader of a gang that robs banks while wearing masks with the faces of presidents on them. Petty is the girl who comes between all the homoeroticism. The stupid plot was rejiggered with cars in *The Fast and the Furious*. I'll take the original, which Bigelow directs with a flair for action. The DVD keeps up with her, especially when you let that DTS track kick in.

Hot Bonus: A short featurette. Swayze did his own skydiving.

Key Scene: That last wave before the cop gets his man.

Poison Ivy (1992)

Starring: Drew Barrymore, Sara Gilbert, Tom Skerritt, Cheryl Ladd

Directed and co-written by: Katt Shea Rubin

As Ivy, the teen fatale of this low-budget find, Barrymore slips the tongue to a tomboy school chum, plays footsie with a man's crotch, has sex on the hood of a Mercedes (in the rain, yet) and kills . . . well, watch the darn thing. What sounds like B-movie trash is really an unsettling psychological thriller. Director and co-writer Shea Rubin keeps the atmosphere loaded as Ivy bonds with Coop (Gilbert), a loner who lives with her rich daddy (Skerritt) and invalid mother (Ladd). Things quickly turn sinister when Ivy seduces the dad, whose sex life ended with his wife's illness. Then Mom falls or is pushed from her balcony. Though the film can be read on several levels, it plays most provocatively when Ivy is seen as Coop's evil twin. As Ivy, Coop can express her repressed longings for her father and her hostility toward her mother. As herself, she cannot. That this doesn't come off as dimestore moralizing is a tribute to Shea Rubin's layered direction and the dynamic Gilbert-Barrymore teamwork. Coop's last words about Ivy—"I miss her"—become a poignant farewell to childhood.

Hot Bonus: The unrated version is included on the DVD as well as the R-rated edition released in theaters. Guess which you should watch.

Key Scene: Coop's first look at Ivy in a swing over a ravine as Phedon Papamichael's camera takes in this mystery creature from her pouty mouth to the peekaboo hole in her boot.

Poltergeist (1982)

Starring: Craig T. Nelson, JoBeth Williams, Heather O'Rourke

Directed by: Tobe Hooper

This DVD lets you add to the argument over who had the strongest impact on this haunted-house fable: director Hooper, the scaremeister behind *The Texas Chain Saw Massacre*, or co-producer and co-writer Steven Spielberg, known for his humanist touch. I'm going with Spielberg. Though ghosts do start appearing to little O'Rourke on her TV screen, alarming her parents (Nelson and Williams), the film avoids the blood and guts endemic to the genre. Zelda Rubinstein is responsible for the most scares as a four-foot-tall ghostbuster who engages in a tug-of-war with the poltergeists.

Hot Bonus: A trailer that reveals things not in the movie.

Key Scene: The house comes tumbling down in the big finale, but the stuff under the kid's bed had me going with no fx, just a fearful imagination.

Poseidon Adventure, The (1972)

Starring: Gene Hackman, Shelley Winters, Ernest Borgnine, Stella Stevens

Directed by: Ronald Neame

A tidal wave turns over a luxury cruise ship with passengers toppling everywhere. That's it. And it's enough. What is it about this potboiler—given THX certification to let you know the picture and sound are top-tier—that makes you want to watch it even with a big Hollywood remake on the way with state-of-the-art technology? Maybe it's because the characters actually get to you, and director Neame knows how to squeeze emotions, and, well, digital isn't everything. The entertaining result typifies the best of the 1970s disaster flicks, complete with an Oscar-winning song, "The Morning After," which the fat lady (Winters) fortunately doesn't sing.

Hot Bonus: The sound is mono, which has scandalized DVD buyers who want their speakers working double time. Sheesh, mono works just fine.

Key Scene: Winters performs a stirring underwater rescue as a Jewish lady who wants to visit her grandson in Israel. Critics made fat jokes ("It's like having a whale tell you you should love her because she's Jewish," sassed Pauline Kael). But Winters got the last laugh: an Oscar nomination.

Predator (Two-Disc Special Edition)(1987)

Starring: Arnold Schwarzenegger, Carl Weathers

Directed by: John McTiernan

Something wicked scary is in the jungle, and commando Schwarzenegger is heading for South America with his team to track it down. Boom,

boom, boom—they all get picked off, except for the Governator, who knows a girly predator when he sees one. Come on, the Thing wears a spacesuit to make itself invisible. Director McTiernan delivers more suspense and surprises then you'd ever think possible. And this new DVD package wipes out all earlier VHS and DVD versions with a supersonic presentation.

Hot Bonus: There are five hours of extras. Did you know Schwarzenegger looked so thin because of a bad run of the runs? The most touching feature is a tribute to Kevin Peter Hall, who played the predator and died in 1991.

Key Scene: Ah-nuld vs. the Predator. Did you think I was going to pick the moment that suggested the Predator was a symbol of U.S. imperialism?

Pretty Woman (Director's Cut) (1990)

Starring: Julia Roberts, Richard Gere
Directed by: Garry Marshall

Six minutes of extra footage enhances this Director's Cut DVD of a Cinderella story involving Edward (Gere), a corporate raider Prince Charming from Manhattan, and Vivian (Roberts), an L.A. streetwalker he picks up for the night. "You and I are such similar creatures," he tells her. "We both screw people for money." It's a sleazy plot redeemed by Marshall's light touch and the chemistry between the two leads. The megawatt starshine emanating from Roberts just keeps coming. She spars with Gere, looking great both in hooker raunch and the chic wardrobe he buys her for being his paid companion for the week. The Roberts smile melts all resistance, especially when she's in the bathtub listening to Prince.

Hot Bonus: Marshall delivers the kind of funny and informative commentary that makes to want to hear more.

Key Scene: The Roberts shopping spree on Rodeo Drive, paid for by Gere, is a wish-fulfillment fantasy that helped lift the film to mammoth grosses.

Prime of Miss Jean Brodie, The (1969)

Starring: Maggie Smith, Robert Stephens, Celia Johnson, Pamela Franklin
Directed by: Ronald Neame

"Little girls, I am in the business of putting old heads on young shoulders, and all my pupils are the crème de la crème. Give me a girl at an impressionable age and she is mine for life." To hear the great Maggie Smith utter such lines from the script that Jay Presson Allen adapted from the Muriel Spark novel makes this film a DVD essential. The time is 1932, and the place is Edinburgh (the city glows on DVD). Miss Brodie doesn't just teach her girls about art, life, and politics, she molds them into miniature Brodies. Good for some, deadly for others. Franklin fires up the role of Sandy, the student who takes vengeance on Brodie by seducing Teddy Lloyd (Stephens), the married art teacher Brodie loves. Smith won the Best Actress Oscar for her tour de force. It hardly seems enough.

Hot Bonus: Neame and Franklin recall their time together with Smith.

Key Scene: Brodie taking on Miss Mackay (Johnson), the headmistress who summons Brodie to her office at 3:15. "She seeks to intimidate me by her use of the quarter hour," Brodie tells her students. It's a declaration of war.

Prizzi's Honor (1985)

Starring: Jack Nicholson, Kathleen Turner, Anjelica Huston, William Hickey
Directed by: John Huston

Nicholson and Turner play lovers who find out they're both paid assassins. Brad Pitt and Angelina Jolie tried this trick in 2005's *Mr. & Mrs. Smith*. *Prizzi's Honor*, directed by Huston from Richard Condon's 1982 novel, shows how to do it right. Nicholson plays a trusted, if none too bright, enforcer for a Mafia don, deftly hammed by Hickey. Anjelica Huston, the director's daughter, won an Oscar for playing the don's malevolent granddaughter, jilted by Nicholson and plotting revenge when he hooks up with Turner. Why can't these two killers marry, set up house, and plan a family between planning jobs? Says Nicholson to Turner: "I look at you. I see what I want to see. That's what love is." They are two cobras with a nesting itch, and they mine the script (by Condon and Janet Roach) for every satirical poison dart aimed at the evil in everyday America

Hot Bonus: Having the widescreen version on a DVD with rich fleshtones is our reward. I'll take it.

Key Scene: Nicholson asking Huston about Turner: "Do I ice her? Do I marry her?" Huston votes against the icing. "Just because she's a thief and a hitter doesn't mean she's not a good woman in all the other departments."

Producers, The (Special Edition) (1968)

Starring: Zero Mostel, Gene Wilder, Kenneth Mars, Dick Shawn

Directed and written by: Mel Brooks

Before Brooks made *The Producers* a smash musical, he made it a movie—a comedy that ranks with the all-time greats. Now, with a DVD dressed up in widescreen and digital sound, it's time to flaunt it, baby, flaunt it. Mostel is larger-than-life perfection as Max Bialystock, a producer reduced to bedding old ladies to finance his shows. Wilder is smaller-than-life perfection as Leo Bloom, a whiny accountant with an idea that a flop could make money. Cue *Springtime for Hitler*, a musical no one could love, except the Nazi (Mars) who wrote it, the cross-dresser (Christopher Hewett) who directed it, and the LSD-addled hippie (Shawn) who plays the Fuhrer. Every time I watch *The Producers*, I look for a scene that isn't funny. No luck.

Hot Bonus: An retrospective documentary is full of Brooks patter, but check out the Easter Eggs. Go to Menu, find Play Movie, but don't click. Press the Left Arrow, and hit Enter when you see the number 18. Get ready for some hilarious outtakes.

Key Scene: Opening night of *Springtime for Hitler*, including Max bribing a critic, the audience covering their eyes and ears like monkeys as the chorus sings "Bombs falling from the sky again/ Deutschland is on the rise again," and the camera rising to show the dancers forming a swastika.

Professional, The (Uncut International Version) (1994)

Starring: Jean Reno, Natalie Portman, Gary Oldman

Directed by: Luc Besson

A good movie gets better with a smooth DVD transfer that adds twenty-four minutes of footage to develop the controversial relationship between hit man León (the reliably fine

Reno), Mathilda (Portman, extraordinary in her debut), a twelve-year-old girl whose family has just been wiped out by an on-the-take New York cop (Oldman). Leon takes the girl under his protection. To put it bluntly, he teaches her to "clean," namely kill a target, and she adds a level of sexual provocation to his fatherly concerns. Besson directs with a skilled hand at helping action define character.

Hot Bonus: The extra footage is the major deal.

Key Scene: On a rooftop, Leon hands Mathilda a rifle. He tells her to look through the scope and pick out a target. Then she pulls the trigger.

Psycho (Collector's Edition) (1960)

Starring: Anthony Perkins, Janet Leigh, Vera Miles, John Gavin

Directed by: Alfred Hitchcock

Close your eyes and you can hear the violin screams of Bernard Herrmann's score, see Leigh's Marion Crane driving in a blinding rain until she sees the sign "Bates Motel," watch her take a room from Perkins's Norman Bates—that peeping Tom with the demanding mother—and cringe when she steps into that shower. If you can do all that, why bother with a DVD? Because this transfer has produced a letterboxed version of Hitchcock's groundbreaking thriller that is even sharper and clearer than your memories.

Hot Bonus: New interviews with Hitchcock's daughter Patricia O'Connell, writer Joseph Stefano, and actress Leigh (she died in 2004), who talks about the role that won her only Oscar nomination and screen immortality.

Key Scene: It's not all about the shower, which the DVD allows you to play with or without music. Check out the murder of the detective (Martin Balsam), Norman's stuffed birds, Marion's car sinking in the swamp, the fruit cellar, and that last look at Mother, who wouldn't harm a fly.

Pulp Fiction
(Two-Disc Collector's Edition)
(1994)

Starring: John Travolta, Samuel L. Jackson, Uma Thurman, Bruce Willis

Directed and co-written by: Quentin Tarantino

Indisputably great. There's no question about owning this pow DVD transfer—the colors never looked this rich, the sound (on the DTS track) has never been this enveloping. The movie is an anthology that blends three stories and twelve principal characters into a mesmerizing mosaic of the Los Angeles scuzz world. Travolta won an Oscar nomination and revived his career as Vincent Vega, a hit man who isn't too busy to indulge in conversations with his partner Jules (a sublime Jackson) about quarter pounders with cheese and a guy who was murdered by their boss, Marsellus Wallace (Ving Rhames), for giving his wife Mia (Thurman) a foot massage. The debate on sexual etiquette is hilarious; they could be two pals driving to work, except their work is crime. "Let's get into character," says Jules, before he and Vincent take out their guns. Tarantino can do action like nobody's business, but it's second to his powerfully suggestive gift for language. Do yourself a favor with *Pulp Fiction*. Don't just watch; listen. Willis, as boxer Butch Coolidge, also digs into a tasty role. Marsellus sends Vincent to kill Butch for refusing to take a dive. They both wind up tied up by two hillbillies, a scene only rivaled by the mess when Vincent accidentally blows the head off a guy in the back seat of the car Jules is driving. The cleanup, supervised by a courtly mob facilitator called the Wolf (Harvey Keitel), takes place in the garage of Jules's pal Jimmie (a memorably manic Tarantino), who wants these gangsters out before his wife gets home. *Pulp Fiction* is ferocious fun without a trace of caution, complacency, or political correctness to inhibit its 154 deliciously lurid minutes.

Hot Bonus: All the extras are truly cool, but the four deleted scenes are monsters, notably Thurman with the video camera.

Key Scene: Mia and Vincent at Jack Rabbit Slim's, a diner filled with fifties-era movie memorabilia. Thurman, Oscar nominated, is seductively scrappy as she gets Vincent to enter a twist contest. Even playing a junkie reptile, Travolta exhibits amazing grace. His dance with Mia to a Chuck Berry oldie exudes down 'n' dirty eroticism and unexpected romantic longing.

Purple Rose of Cairo, The (1985)

Starring: Mia Farrow, Jeff Daniels, Danny Aiello

Directed and written by: Woody Allen

Back in the days when Woody and Mia were a couple instead of litigants, he gave her one of her best roles as Cecilia, a Depression-era waitress in New Jersey with no escape from her abusive husband (Aiello), except at the movies. In an inspired movie within a movie, Allen and camera god Gordon Willis create a 1930s black-and-white period film called *The Purple Rose of Cairo* that Cecilia watches continuously. The hero (Daniels) is a handsome adventurer enjoying a madcap Manhattan weekend. Farrow falls hard for the Daniels character, and when he steps off the screen to claim her, havoc ensues. To say more would spoil the surprise. Daniels is wonderfully endearing as the fictional hero and a true SOB as the actor who created him. Within the confines of this charming comedy, Allen wrestles with serious matters: the heart's propensity to be wounded and art's power to heal.

Hot Bonus: Just the movie, given a dream of a DVD transfer in color and in black-and-white.

Key Scene: The ending with Farrow seeking comfort at the movies, even when Fred Astaire does not step off the screen.

Q (Blue Underground Special Edition) (1982)

Starring: Michael Moriarty, David Carradine, Richard Roundtree

Directed and written by: Larry Cohen

It's possible you know nothing of Mr. Cohen, the auteur of such B-movie horrorshows as *It's Alive* and *The Stuff*. Your loss. Get up to speed with *Q*. The Blue Underground DVD transfer beats the pants off the previous one from Anchor Bay. The plot is easy to laugh at, so please do. It concerns Q or Quetzalcoatl, a mythical Aztec monster with wings and four claws who has been spotted on top of Manhattan's Chrysler Building—a good perch if you're in the mood to pounce on a bikini babe on a rooftop swimming pool. Good actors (Carradine, Roundtree) play cops who try to shoot Q for beheading citizens of the Big Apple. A great actor, Moriarty, takes the role of Jimmy Quinn, a small-time crook, who spots Q's nest (there's an egg) and decides to profit from it. Moriarty is flat-out fabulous as this twitchy loser. Between shots of the stop-motion monster, Moriarty plays jazz piano and sings. Only in a Cohen film, folks.

Hot Bonus: Cohen explains himself, and you don't want to miss it.

Key Scene: Quinn facing down the cops and holding the city for ransom ("A few minutes ago I was in the gutter,. Now I'm on top of the world"). Quinn and Q have a lot more in common than the same initial.

Quiz Show (1994)

Starring: Ralph Fiennes, John Turturro, Rob Morrow
Directed by: Robert Redford

DVD delivers a pitch-perfect transfer of an acclaimed film that never delivered at the box office. Time to play catch-up. In his fourth and finest movie as a director, Redford blows the dust off a 1950s scandal about rigged TV quiz shows and makes it snap with up-to-the-minute relevance. Redford puts television on trial and then raises the stakes by exploring the flaws in our national character that sucker us into buying the lies television tells. Charles Van Doren (Fiennes), a telegenic WASP bachelor who taught English at Columbia University, went on *Twenty-One*, a popular NBC quiz show, and electrified the nation by beating the reigning champ, Herbert Stempel (Turturro), a working-class ex-GI, who was described by one of the show's producers as "a fat, annoying Jewish guy with a sidewall haircut." What drama! What ratings! What a con job! A 1959 congressional investigation headed by Harvard lawyer Richard Goodwin (Morrow) exposed quiz shows, including *Twenty-One* and *The $64,000 Question*, as frauds. Redford sees the battle between Van Doren and Stempel as a microcosm of American class warfare: It's race vs. race, pretty vs. ugly, have vs. have not. *Twenty-One* is gone, but TV is still playing the game of reinforcing stereotypes and fudging facts in the name of entertainment.

Hot Bonus: We're waiting. Where's that Special Edition?

Key Scene: Van Doren and Stempel in their isolation booths, learning to lie in a front of a camera for a shot at fame. What's lost isn't American innocence—it's a sense of shame.

Raging Bull (Two-Disc Special Edition) (1980)

Starring: Robert De Niro, Joe Pesci, Cathy Moriarty
Directed by: Martin Scorsese

Given that Scorsese's bruising biopic of middleweight boxing champ Jake La Motta is one of the best movies of all time, the deluxe DVD treatment it gets here is as overdue as Scorsese's directing Oscar. Time has done nothing but burnish

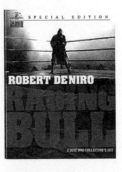

this film's brilliance. Using La Motta's 1970 autobiography as a base, screenwriters Paul Schrader and Mardik Martin craft a hot-blooded look at a Bronx street kid who could never confine his fury to a gym. Even the laughs in this movie are ferocious. Much has been made of De Niro gaining fifty pounds to show the champ's decline into bloat in the 1960s. But the weight of De Niro's performance isn't physical; it's the emotional heft he invests in this bull who repels the things he loves that puts this performance in the pantheon. Aided by Michael Chapman's black-and-white camerawork and Thelma Schoonmaker's editing, Scorsese keeps his 128-minute film at a fever pitch. The stylized, slo-mo fight scenes have a savage poetry. But they are only slightly more brutal than La Motta's emotional flare-ups with family, friends, and the Mob. As La Motta's sultry second wife Vickie, Moriarty, then twenty, hits the screen like a blonde Bronx goddess. And Pesci is De Niro's explosive match as Joey, the manager brother. Jake rages at him ("Did you fuck my wife?"), convinced he can solve anything with a fist. At the end, La Motta, fat and fiftyish, rehearses a monologue from *On the Waterfront* for his club act. It's a one-way ticket to Palookaville, painful to watch and, like the film, impossible to shake.

Hot Bonus: A shot-by-shot comparison of one of La Motta's fights with the Scorsese version.

Key Scene: La Motta in the ring, but seen by the camera as a man alone. He's still standing, but his jaw is slack, his eyes look black and drained of feeling. He's stalking, not like a man, like a predator.

Ragtime (1981)

Starring: James Cagney, Elizabeth McGovern, Howard E. Rollins
Directed by: Milos Forman

This outstanding DVD transfer should bring a second life to Forman's supremely elegant distillation of E. L. Doctorow's 1975 bestseller about America in 1906. Forman utilizes only a few crucial threads in Doctorow's vast weave of fictional and historical characters. But what remains is faithful in spirit to Doctorow's view of an archetypal small-town family—Mother (Mary Steenburgen), Father (James Olson), and Younger Brother (Brad Dourif)—that finds itself propelled into a twentieth century exploding with civil, political, and sexual conflict. In his last feature, the great Cagney, then eighty-two, plays a ramrod-straight New York police commissioner with a feisty top-of-the-world twinkle. And two new stars were born and Oscar nominated. The deliciously wicked Mc-Govern as Evelyn Nesbit, the beauty whose jealous husband shot her architect lover, Stanford White (a surprisingly adept Norman Mailer). As the black piano man Coalhouse Walker Jr., who initiates the film's climactic act of terrorism, Rollins shows the fire, dignity, and sex appeal of a young Sidney Poitier. Randy Newman's richly evocative score is another element that comes through beautifully on DVD.

Hot Bonus: The Forman commentary excels, especially when the director reveals how he coaxed Cagney out of a twenty-year retirement.

Key Scene: Cagney considering turning over the bigoted fire chief (Kenneth McMillan) to stop the bombing of the Morgan Library. "The library over there is worth millions," says Cagney, the old "you dirty rat" thunder rolling in his voice, "and people keep telling me you're a worthless piece of slime."

Rain Man (Special Edition) (1988)

Starring: Dustin Hoffman, Tom Cruise
Directed by: Barry Levinson

It's a setup for Oscar-begging schtick as Charlie (Cruise), a slick-dick used-car dealer from Los Angeles, travels to the Cincinnati mental institution that houses Raymond (Hoffman), the autistic brother he never knew he had. Charlie's plan is to kidnap his brother until he gets a share of the $3 million estate their father left only to Raymond. What keeps the movie free from overt tearjerking is Cruise's willingness to play a jerk and Hoffman's Oscar-winning turn as an idiot savant who knows numbers (he can count a pile of fallen toothpicks in the flick of an eye), but not emotions. Express love and he'll tell you, "I'm an excellent driver." Director Levinson makes sure the message about the blunt truths of autism is done subtly.

Hot Bonus: The commentary tracks from Levinson and the two screenwriters are a yawn. Be grateful for the widescreen DVD transfer.

Key Scene: The bittersweet climax that Hoffman had to fight to keep. The screenwriters wanted to turn on the waterworks with a happy ending.

Raising Arizona (1987)

Starring: Nicolas Cage, Holly Hunter, Trey Wilson
Directed by: Joel Coen

"Her womb was a rocky place in which my seed could find no purchase." That's Cage talking as H. I. McDonnough, an ex-con who marries prison photographer Edwina (Hunter)—they live in a trailer in the desert—only to find she can't have children. And if that bit of frisky Coen brothers dialogue doesn't tickle your funnybone, then by all means don't purchase this fine if nonanamorphic DVD. The screwball comedy kicks in when H.I. and Edwina learn that the wife of local tycoon Nathan Arizona (Wilson) has just welcomed quintuplets, and they decide to snatch one. A ransom plot develops with weird characters out of Coen world. Don't ask. Just go for it.

Hot Bonus: A trailer—do you think they could spare it?

Key Scene: When H.I. hands Edwina the stolen baby and she says, "I love him so much!" Actually she doesn't say it, she screams it like a banshee. Hunter's intensity and Cage's stoned bafflement somehow blend hilariously.

Rashomon (1950)

Starring: Toshiro Mifune, Machiko Kyo, Masayuki Mori, Takeshi Shimura
Directed by: Akira Kurosawa

The seminal Japanese film is a gift from Criterion to Kurosawa fans who can see his masterpiece in a high-definition digital transfer with restored image and sound. Set in the ninth century, the film deals with a rape and murder in the woods as witnessed by four people who each see it differently. Mifune became an international star as the bandit who allegedly raped Masako (Kyo) and murdered her husband (Mori). Shimura plays the woodcutter who claims to have witnessed it all. As the mystery unravels, Kurosawa reveals the nature of truth and human fallibility.

Hot Bonus: An introduction by Robert Altman points to the enormous influence that Kurosawa's technique had on an American film.

Key Scene: The fight between the husband and the bandit resonates with human exertion far removed from today's bloodless digital fight fantasies.

Ray (Special Edition) (2004)

Starring: Jamie Foxx, Kerry Washington, Regina King, Sharon Warren

Directed by: Taylor Hackford

It's not that Hackford's take on the joyous art and pained soul of Ray Charles doesn't look great on DVD; it's just that it sounds even better. A skilled pianist, Foxx does Charles proud on the keyboard. And though he only moves his lips to Charles's vocals on hits such as "I Got a Woman," "What'd I Say," "Unchain My Heart," and "Georgia on My Mind," the Oscar-winning Foxx gets so far inside the man and his music that he and Ray seem to breathe as one. When blindness overtook Ray at age seven, his laundress mama (Warren) taught him to lean on his other senses. Charles could flash a childlike smile to mask a harsh agenda. His wife Della Bea (Washington) had to endure his jones for junk and sleeping around. His volatile backup singer Margie Hendricks (King) has to face being dumped. Foxx wisely goes where the music takes him, and rides this winner to glory.

Hot Bonus: Footage of Foxx and Charles jamming in the studio.

Key Scene: Ray's first time on stage, going solo.

Reality Bites (Tenth Anniversary Edition) (1994)

Starring: Winona Ryder, Ben Stiller, Ethan Hawke, Janeane Garofalo

Directed by: Ben Stiller

Stiller's directorial debut was one of the first Gen X films. Many Gen Xers ragged on it hard, which means it works. Ryder is just out of college in Houston and looking for a job. She wants to do an unslick doc on her friends, including Garofalo who works at the Gap, and Hawke who works at his stoner musician look. Stiller plays the yuppie outsider, a slick MTV-ish producer, who falls for Ryder. Debuting screenwriter Helen Childress has a good ear for twentysomethings trying to pass for cool. And the DVD transfer—the Tenth Anniversary edition is a big improvement on the first DVD pass—really pumps out the color and that seventies retro sound ("My Sharona").

Hot Bonus: Stiller dealing honestly with the problem he had with Hawke.

Key Scene: Garofalo imagining her own funeral as done on *Melrose Place*.

Rear Window (Collector's Edition) (1954)

Starring: James Stewart, Grace Kelly, Thelma Ritter, Raymond Burr

Directed by: Alfred Hitchcock

Restored and remastered for DVD by people who know how, Hitchcock's disturbing study in voyeurism comes disguised as a thriller. And it's a doozy. A broken leg confines Stewart, a photographer, to his apartment in Greenwich Village. The people across the courtyard become his entertainment. His nurse (Ritter) thinks he's pushing it with the binoculars. But when Stewart believes a neighbor (Burr) has cut his wife into pieces, he brings in his fashion model girlfriend (Kelly, never cooler, blonder, or sexier) to sneak in a note: "What Have You Done With Her?" The devilish Hitchcock turns us all into peeping Toms to open up discussion on rear window-ethics. "In the old days, they used to put your eyes out with a red-hot poker," says Ritter.

Hot Bonus: A piece on the DVD restoration reveals a job well done.

Key Scene: Stewart hanging on for his life as the murderer proves snooping can have consequences. But as any movie fanatic will tell you, it's worth it.

Rebecca (Two-Disc Special Edition) (1940)

Starring: Laurence Olivier, Joan Fontaine, Judith Anderson

Directed by: Alfred Hitchcock

Shockingly, Hitchcock's first American thriller is the only film from the master of suspense to win the Best Picture Oscar. Producer David O. Selznick provided a lavish production, and Criterion rises to the occasion with this ritzy DVD package. "Last night, I dreamt I went to Manderley again," says Fontaine, famously kicking off the screen version of Daphne du Maurier's story in flashback. Fontaine is a mouse. "I'm not the sort of person men marry," the mouse tells Olivier's rich, haunted Maxim de Winter, who does marry her. He takes her home to Manderley where the aura of his dead first wife, Rebecca, is everywhere, especially on the housekeeper Mrs. Danvers (Anderson), who caresses Rebecca's things in a fetishistic lesbian swoon. Great stuff, superbly shot by George Barnes in rapturous black-and-white with a matching score by Franz Waxman. Just watch the mouse roar.

Hot Bonus: Screen tests of the other actresses who coveted Fontaine's star-making role, including *Gone With the Wind* Oscar-winner Vivien Leigh, then married to Olivier, who read with her. I'd love to know that backstory.

Key Scene: Mrs. Danvers burning the place down. This was Anderson's career role, and she runs with it.

Rebel Without a Cause (Two-Disc Special Edition) (1955)

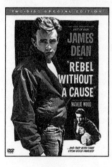

Starring: James Dean, Natalie Wood, Sal Mineo

Directed by: Nicholas Ray

This DVD package promises an enhanced digital transfer from restored picture and audio elements. Promise kept. After all these years, the movie still jumps out at you. Dean became a romantic symbol of confused 1950s youth as Jim Stark, the new troublemaker at school. Jim's pickup line to Judy (Wood), "You live here, don't you?" is lame compared to her reply: "Who lives?" After a knife fight, Jim and Judy bond against parents, cops, and the world, along with their misfit friend Plato (Mineo), in a deserted mansion. The violent climax started a cycle of teen flicks that continues. But no one did it like Dean—his death in a car crash turned him into a forever-young icon, but his talent was real. Wood and Mineo, both Oscar nominated, also met with tragic ends. But Ray gave *Rebel* humor and tenderness and an understanding of the violence wired into youth. He built it to last.

Hot Bonus: Tons of commentary, but Dean's "Drive Safely" commercial TV spot hits you hard.

Key Scene: The chickie run, in which Jim is challenged to compete with Buzz (Corey Allen). Both hop in souped-up jalopies and race toward the edge of a coastal cliff. The chickie is the one who jumps first.

Red Desert (1964)

Starring: Monica Vitti, Richard Harris, Carlo Chionette

Directed by: Michelangelo Antonioni

The first color film from Italian master Antonioni is a DVD must. Vitti stars as a woman who is driven to despair by the pollution of the industrial world around her. She sees her husband (Chionette), an engineer working on a project in Ravenna, as part of the problem. Her love for her young son can't alleviate the pressures. Neither can the sexual attentions of a manufacturing tycoon (Harris, dubbed) who seems to understand her. Even when the plot goes off onto psychological tangents, Antonioni and cinematographer Carlo Di Palma deliver haunting images of modern desolation.

Hot Bonus: A filmography of Antonioni that sets up *Red Desert* in the context of his work.

Key Scene: Vitti walking among machines and factories billowing smoke, looking like the last human in an alien world.

Red River (1948)

Starring: John Wayne, Montgomery Clift, John Ireland, Walter Brennan

Directed by: Howard Hawks

It's *Mutiny on the Bounty* on horseback as Wayne's Tom Dunson, the captain, and Clift's Matthew Garth, his second, herd their Texas cattle north. "Take 'em to Missouri, Matt," says Wayne in a scene that is justly famous as the men shout "Yeee-hah" and head into stampedes, sandstorms, and Indian attacks. Wayne is driven by madness, prompting a mutiny from Clift and the men, including a toothless Brennan. Wayne is powerfully good, as is Clift in his debut performance. Hawks's western has long been considered one of the greats. This DVD transfer confirms it. Those looking for sexual subtext should forget the kissy stuff with Joanne Dru and watch Clift with his pal Cherry (Ireland), comparing their guns and shooting them off. Yeee-hah!

Hot Bonus: No commentary, but revel in those sweeping black-and-white images shot by Russell Harlan and the rousing score by Dimitri Tiomkin.

Key Scene: The fight between Wayne, a wounded raging bull, and the skinny Clift is one of the longest and most exciting in screen history.

Red Shoes, The (1948)

Starring: Moira Shearer, Anton Walbrook, Marius Goring
Directed by: Michael Powell and Emeric Pressburger

Red is just for starters. The colors in this Criterion DVD transfer run riot. Even if you hate ballet, you can't resist the seductive assault on your senses conducted by those expressionist masters, Powell and Pressburger. Redheaded Shearer, trained at Sadler Wells, makes a stunning acting debut as a ballerina torn between her love for a young composer (Goring) and her devotion to the impresario (Walbrook) who demands that she live for art. Jack Cardiff's camerawork excels, especially in the ballet, from a tale by Hans Christian Andersen that Goring has put to music. It's about magical red-toe shoes that can make a ballerina dance like a dream. The catch is the wearer can't stop dancing and she can't take them off.

Hot Bonus: Martin Scorsese's collection of memorabilia from the movie supplements shrewd commentary from film scholar Ian Christie.

Key Scene: Shearer, unable to stop dancing, flying off stage onto the railroad tracks, followed by the announcement: "There will be no performance of *The Red Shoes* tonight."

Remains of the Day, The (1993)

Starring: Anthony Hopkins, Emma Thompson, James Fox
Directed by: James Ivory

Producer Ismail Merchant, who died in 2005, was famed for crafting stunning films on a shoestring. The miracles he accomplished for decades with his partners, director Ivory and screenwriter Ruth Prawer Jhabvala, come front and center in this implosive film of Kazuo Ishiguro's 1988 novel about a proper English butler, Stevens (a perfect Hopkins), who holds his politics and his emotions in check. Through two world wars, Stevens served Lord Darlington (Fox) at a country estate where guests included heads of state. But his lordship's efforts to appease Germany led to scandal after the rise of Hitler. Now it's 1958, and Stevens must admit his blindness in serving a dupe of the Nazis while the love of his life slipped away. She is Miss Kenton (Thompson, dazzlingly good), the spirited housekeeper whom Stevens is driving to meet. This love story between two people who never kiss or get beyond calling each other Mr. and Miss is suffused with regret but not self-pity. Ivory, whose direction is controlled but never chilly, shows how Stevens loses Miss Kenton through his devotion to a job that made him a witness to history without furthering his understanding of it.

Hot Bonus: Merchant is the liveliest commentator, talking frankly about the difficulties of persuading estate owners to turn their homes into a film set.

Key Scene: In a devastating gesture, Miss Kenton flirtatiously tries to grab a book from the butler's hand. Thompson gives the moment real heat; Stevens feels excited and cornered. But his wounded dignity drives her away.

Repo Man (Limited Edition) (1984)

Starring: Emilio Estevez, Harry Dean Stanton
Directed by: Alex Cox

A cult movie that should entice new members with a DVD transfer that flies on its punk soundtrack, remastered in Dolby Digital, and the energy of the actors. Estevez plays Otto, a Los Angeles punk who learns the art of repossessing cars from Bud (Stanton), the acknowledged master. Cox, who directed and wrote the script, is an Oxford-educated lawyer who split to study film in Los Angeles. That surreal decision permeates his debut movie, which thinks nothing of throwing in aliens and a neutron bomb. It all fits in Los Angeles, and Robby Müller shoots the City of Angels with a hallucinatory glee.

Hot Bonus: Cox tells you how it all happened, including his punk career.

Key Scene: That glowing thing in the trunk of the 1964 Chevy Malibu.

Requiem for a Dream (Director's Cut) (2000)

Starring: Ellen Burstyn, Jared Leto, Jennifer Connelly
Directed by: Darren Aronofsky

Aronofsky uses Hubert Selby Jr.'s 1978 novel to bend the world into new shapes. Set in Brooklyn, on the streets of Aronofsky's native Coney Island, the film stars Leto as Harry Goldfarb, a dreamer who gets hooked on drugs along with his girl, Marion (a shockingly good Connelly), who sells herself as a sex slave for a fix. Aronofsky, cinematographer Matthew Libatique, and editor Jay Rabinowitz assault the senses with jump cuts, split screens, and jarring, distorted images to show lives spiraling out of control. And the DVD transfer keeps up with them every step of the way. Leto, who lost twenty-five pounds for the role, excels in his scenes with Burstyn as Sara, Harry's widowed mother, a diet-pill freak with her own delusions. Burstyn's Oscar-nominated performance is as raw and riveting as the movie that contains it.

Hot Bonus: The Director's Cut is scarier and more erotic, and Aronofsky uses the commentary track to explain why.

Key Scene: Fixated on appearing on a TV game show, Sara diets down to fit into a red dress she wore in her youth. The speed leaves her crazed by hallucinations. A refrigerator seems to break free of the wall to crush her.

Reservoir Dogs (Two-Disc Special Edition) (1992)

Starring: Harvey Keitel, Tim Roth, Michael Madsen, Steve Buscemi

Directed and written by: Quentin Tarantino

A jewel robbery goes wrong. Real wrong. We never see how. But Tarantino, making the most impactful filmmaking debut since Scorsese, makes us think we see it. His writing and directing is that good. Tarantino also plays one of the team of strangers put together by Joe (veteran actor Lawrence Tierney). They meet first for a meal and discuss—hilariously—Madonna's "Like a Virgin" and tipping. Mr. Pink (Buscemi) won't tip. He gives his reasons to Mr. Brown (Tarantino), Mr. White (Keitel), Mr. Orange (Roth), Mr. Blonde (Madsen), Mr. Blue (Edward Bunker), and Joe's son, Nice Guy Eddie (Chris Penn). "Fork it over," says Joe. Even among thieves there's a code. It's that code that Tarantino deconstructs in the aftermath of the crime that leaves Mr. Orange bleeding from a bullet in the gut in their garage hideout and the survivors debating which Mr. ratted them out. But even as the body count rises, Tarantino keeps springing surprises. The narrative may owe a huge debt to Ringo Lam's City on Fire, but the Tarantino voice is uniquely and unforgettably his own.

Hot Bonus: Not to dissuade you from hearing my own commentary track on Disc 2, but there's an Easter Egg you have to see: Find "K-Billy Radio" on the Menu, chose the last channel, and there's "Reservoir Dolls," a puppet version of the grossest scene in the movie.

Key Scene: The grossest one, namely Madsen slicing off the ear of a cop (Kirk Baltz) while grooving to the sound of Stealer's Wheel on the radio with "Stuck in the Middle." For sheer iconic imagery, and no blood, try the credit sequence with the Dogs walking to the beat of "Little Green Bag."

Return of the Secaucus Seven (1980)

Starring: Jean Passanante, Gordon Clapp, Adam Lefevre, David Strathairn

Directed and written by: John Sayles

Not since John Cassavetes has any filmmaker done more to power American independent cinema than Sayles. His debut film, made for near nothing (sixty thousand dollars) with a cast of then-unknowns, preceded and outdid 1983's mainstream The Big Chill at showing 1960s student activists bumping their aging ideals against present-day realities. No DVD transfer could turn this small but generous-minded movie into a slick package. But Sayles' skill at blending raw feeling and acute observation is already apparent as the Seven, arrested in Secaucus back in the day, join their friends for a reunion in New Hampshire (Sayles drew most of his gifted cast from a summer stock company he helped run in North Conway during the 1970s).

Hot Bonus: The Sayles commentary is a model for young filmmakers who want to create an inexpensive calling card on talent fueled by ambition.

Key Scene: Passanante's multifaceted performance as Irene, a radical-turned-political flak, hits a strong current when her relationship with Chip (Clapp), a straitlaced outsider, goes awry. Clapp and Passanante have since won Emmys—he for NYPD Blue and she writing for As the World Turns.

Reversal of Fortune (1990)

Starring: Jeremy Irons, Glenn Close, Ron Silver

Directed by: Barbet Schroeder

Before the murder trials of O.J. and Robert Blake, there was Claus von Bülow (Irons), the Danish socialite who was charged and convicted of trying to murder his American-heiress wife, Sunny (Close), by injecting her with a near-fatal dose of insulin. (Sunny has been in an irreversible coma since 1980.) The media presented Claus as a charming, social-climbing leech, and Irons won an Oscar for playing him that way. Cinematographer Luciano Tovoli gives the trappings of wealth a perfumed allure that comes through powerfully on the DVD transfer. You don't just see wealth in this picture; you hear it purr. The movie is based on the book by Alan Dershowitz (Silver), the Harvard law professor and attorney who helped win Claus a retrial and an acquittal in 1985. This spellbinder paints a toxic portrait of an era in which everyone is presumed guilty where greed is concerned.

Hot Bonus: Retrospective commentary from Schroeder and screenwriter Nicholas Kazan catches us up on the von Bülow world.

Key Scene: During a lunch meeting at the kind of trendy restaurant Dershowitz abhors, von Bülow notes that until his trial, which he refers to as "the unpleasantness," he had always been shuttled off to the less-desirable tables; now headwaiters can't wait to seat him up front.

Right Stuff, The (Two-Disc Special Edition) (1983)

Starring: Sam Shepard, Scott Glenn, Ed Harris, Dennis Quaid, Fred Ward

Directed by: Philip Kaufman

Kaufman's film version of Tom Wolfe's nonfiction bestseller about the seven original Project Mercury astronauts puts you right in the cockpit And the DVD pumps the flying sequences with a full tank of digital fuel. The movie tells two stories: One is about test pilot Chuck Yeager, the first man to break the sound barrier; he is played, with the right cowboy touches, by playwright-actor Shepard, who won an Oscar nomination. The other story is about the astronaut program. Wolfe's point was to contrast the solitary courage and enterprise of men like Yeager with the illusions built around the astronauts by a public-relations machine eager to show up the Russians and their Sputnik. The actors dig in, including Glenn as Alan Shepard, Quaid as Gordo Cooper, Fred Ward as Gus Grissom, and Harris as John Glenn, the clean Marine who tamed this raucous group and became its public face.

Hot Bonus: Comments from Kaufman and Wolfe have a welcome blunt quality in contrast to a rah-rah featurette on John Glenn.

Key Scene: The shot of the X-1 on the runway with Yeager on horseback, the silent cowboy ready to push the envelope.

Ring, The (2002)

Starring: Naomi Watts, David Dorfman

Directed by: Gore Verbinski

Verbinski's Hollywood remake of Hideo Nakata's *Ringu*—a 1998 cult smash in Japan—creeps you out in high style, even if Nakata did it better. There's this cursed videotape (no, it's not a bootleg of Madonna's *Swept Away*). You watch it. The phone rings. A voice says, "Seven days." That means you have a week to live. Seattle reporter Rachel Keller decides to investigate. Luckily, she's played by Watts, who keeps you glued to the screen even when Verbinski lets the suspense slacken. Rachel's son (Dorfman) has this Haley Joel Osment-ish quality that's more weird than scary. But the tape itself, featuring skanky, stringy-haired Samara, a ghost girl whose mother drowned her in a well, is the stuff of nightmares.

Hot Bonus: A short film created by Verbinski exclusively for the DVD release reveals more secrets. I have one: *The Ring 2*, the 2005 sequel, sucks.

Key Scene: Samara's climactic leap out of a TV screen. Ooo-ee-oo.

Ringu (1998)

Starring: Nanako Matsushima, Miki Nakatani

Directed by: Hideo Nakata

Same as *The Ring*, except this one is in Japanese with English subtitles and has a better director. Nakata's skill at letting the dead run free delivers a subtle grace that is not in Gore Verbinski's bag of tricks. The tape that kills you in seven days is far less elaborate, but still does the trick. And don't tell me it's hard to locate the Japanese version. Find it. You have seven days.

Hot Bonus: I have two suggestions: For the ghost girl: Upgrade from video to DVD. For her victims: Get caller ID.

Key Scene: The well—it will have you climbing the walls.

Rio Bravo (1959)

Starring: John Wayne, Dean Martin, Ricky Nelson, Angie Dickinson

Directed by: Howard Hawks

The fine DVD transfer isn't showoffy, but then neither is the movie—a western that comes on so easy that only later do you realize how funny, touching, and vitally expressive it is. Wayne plays John T. Chance, the sheriff trying to stop the Burdette gang from breaking one of their own (Claude Akins) out of his jail. He's alone except for a barfly (Martin), an old cripple (Walter Brennan), a kid gunslinger (Nelson), and a leggy saloon babe named Feathers (Dickinson) who likes ruffling the sheriff. "I'm hard to get, John T," she says. "You're gonna have to say you want me." Hawks conceived the movie as a response to *High Noon*, in which Gary Cooper begged for help. Wayne and his ragtag group want to do it alone. They're a little shaky, but they're pros. Dino steals the acting honors as a reformed drunk who gets his pride back. But the whole cast excels at using action to define character. How many great movies do you know that blend comedy and tragedy and still have time for Martin and Nelson to sing a duet?

Hot Bonus: A fun trailer in which Nelson, a pop idol of his day, soft-sells the audience into seeing the movie.

Key Scene: The climatic shootout is so good, other directors keep stealing it. Did you see *Assault on Precinct 13?*

Ripley's Game (2002)

Starring: John Malkovich, Dougray Scott
Directed by: Liliana Cavani

Malkovich oozes sinister charm in this slithery and seductive thriller, which is delivered with a crisp image and truly enveloping DTS sound. Director Liliana Cavani (*The Night Porter*) updates Patricia Highsmith's 1974 novel to the present and gives Malkovich the juicy role of Tom Ripley, an American psychopath living in Italy who persuades a Brit family man (Dougray Scott), dying of leukemia, to join him in an assassination scheme. Malkovich oils himself around the plot—icy cool one moment, blazingly violent the next—with a master's finesse. Highsmith wrote five *Ripley* novels, and other actors have played the part, most recently and blandly Matt Damon in *The Talented Mr. Ripley.* But Malkovich plays it for keeps.

Hot Bonus: The skimpy extras may stem from the film never having had a U.S. theatrical release, denying Malkovich a shot at Oscar consideration.

Key Scene: The murder in a toilet aboard the Berlin-Dusseldorf Express.

Risky Business (1983)

Starring: Tom Cruise, Rebecca De Mornay, Joe Pantoliano
Directed by: Paul Brickman

A teenaged Cruise in Ray-Bans dancing in his underwear and air-guitaring to Bob Seger's "Old Time Rock & Roll" is the image that sticks. But screenwriter Brickman's sure-footed directing debut is a sex comedy with lots more on its mind. Like the posh Chicago home where Cruise's Joel Goodsen is letting his freak flag fly now that his parents are on vacation. He phones for a hooker, Lana, played with potent smarts and sexiness by De Mornay. Lana teaches Joel about free enterprise by inviting her friends over to meet his friends. She likes how they're "clean, polite, and quick." Pimping out a teenager is no shock when he's already been pimped out by his materialistic parents. Brickman's satire still has bite, and the slick DVD transfer makes it all look mighty tempting.

Hot Bonus: Production notes talk about the score by Tangerine Dream.

Key Scene: After the underwear, it's the opener in which Cruise dreams he's having sex in the shower and missing his college interview for Princeton.

River, The (1951)

Starring: Patricia Walters, Thomas E. Breen, Radha, Adrienne Corri
Directed by: Jean Renoir

Renoir's first film in English and in Technicolor still stands as a paradigm of beauty in any language. The Criterion DVD transfer sees to it that the serene purity of every frame is honored. Adapted from Rummer Godden's semiautobiographical novel about growing up in colonialist India, the film concerns Harriet (Walters) and her adolescent crush on Captain John (Breen), a wounded American soldier. Her two friends, Valerie (Corri) and the half-Indian Melanie (Radha), are also besotted. Renoir, the son of the legendary impressionist painter and uncle to Claude Renoir, the gifted cinematographer who shot *The River* on location along the Ganges, uses the slight plot as an excuse to steep himself in Indian culture. The film plays like a tone poem to a country and its customs.

Hot Bonus: Director Martin Scorsese, who helped precipitate the film's restoration, talks about the impact the film had on him as a child. "Its use of color seemed absolutely extraordinary to me. Practically every image in this film sings with color and light."

Key Scene: The film plays like one continuous scene that becomes a single painting. Another fine extra on this DVD, *Rumer Godden: An Indian Affair,* produced in 1995, details the novelist's feelings when she returned to India as an adult. Renoir distills his feelings in transcendent images.

River Runs Through It, A (1992)

Starring: Brad Pitt, Craig Sheffer, Tom Skerritt, Brenda Blethyn

Directed by: Robert Redford

Pitt fans usually dismiss this as his fishing movie, though the DVD makes both look gorgeous. Pitt resembles the young Redford, who directed this film of Norman Maclean's 1976 novella about families and the relation of fly-fishing to religion and art. Set in Montana between 1910 and 1935, the movie—shot by the great Philippe Rousselot—shimmers with the beauty of time remembered. "It was a world with the dew still on it," says Redford, who narrates with uncommon feeling. Norman (Sheffer) and his rebel brother Paul (Pitt) live in a home tended by their mother (Blethyn) but dominated by their father (Skerritt), a Presbyterian minister. Only when fishing the Blackfoot River using Dad's metronome casting rhythm are the men united. Faced with tragedy, the father still can't show his feelings. Pitt is the film's flamboyant center, but Redford sides with the ordinary people. He knows their heart.

Hot Bonus: Actor and director profiles.

Key Scene: The first sight of the boys fishing has a mystical delicacy.

River's Edge (1986)

Starring: Keanu Reeves, Crispin Glover, Ione Skye, Dennis Hopper

Directed by: Tim Hunter

Based on a number of real-life, teen-kills-teen cases, this still-powerful film—directed by Hunter from an incisive script by Neal Jimenez—takes on a knotty theme: the death of feeling. The DVD transfer preserves the muted urgency. Lumpish teen Samson (Daniel Roebuck) sits at the river's edge, the nude body of a strangled girl beside him. The boy's expression is blank. He confesses the murder to his friends. Clarissa (Skye) can only stare. Matt (Reeves) cares enough to want to call the police. But Layne (a twitchy Glover), the group leader, just pokes the corpse with a stick. Hopper plays Feck, a one-legged drug dealer who dances with a life-size sex doll and serves as mentor to the kids. He killed his own girlfriend years before in a fit of jealousy. "Did you love her?" Feck asks, looking for a shred of passion. Samson answers with chilling apathy, "She was OK."

Hot Bonus: No commentary, but on the back of the DVD box there's a quote from Hunter about how he filmed the Jimenez script "right off the page with minor trims." The film still has that immediacy.

Key Scene: Matt's twelve-year-old brother Tim (Joshua Miller) tossing a doll into the river. You can't help thinking, "What's next?"

Road to Perdition (2002)

Starring: Tom Hanks, Paul Newman, Jude Law, Daniel Craig

Directed by: Sam Mendes

A Depression-era crime drama with Hanks cast way against type as a hit man, fleeing with his twelve-year-old son (Tyler Hoechlin), both targets for death. The order comes from Newman, a crime boss who raised Hanks like a son, which Newman's blood son (Craig) violently resents. Hanks and the kid must also dodge an assassin, Maguire (a de-glammed Law), who doubles as a crime photographer. Mendes, working from a graphic novel by Max Allan Collins, reveals something elemental about fathers and sons. It's a thrill to watch Newman, his blue eyes switching in a snap from warmth to ice. Filmed in a harsh winter of rain, snow, and chilling darkness, *Road* will be long remembered for the artistry of cinematographer Conrad L. Hall. The DVD transfer stays alert to every nuance. There are breathtaking scenes of shootouts and bank robberies, but it's on the personal level that the film cuts deepest. Even the last words we hear—"He was my father"—evoke feelings too complicated for tears.

Hot Bonus: Mendes speaks passionately about what he was trying to achieve with each sequence.

Key Scene: The boy, hiding in a car trunk, witnessing for the first time his father on the job of killing a man.

Road Warrior, The (1981)

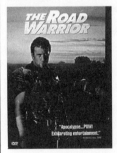

Starring: Mel Gibson, Bruce Spence, Kjell Nilsson

Directed by: George Miller

Miller's sequel to *Mad Max* outdoes the original in kinetic, postapocalyptic energy—and the DVD doesn't let you forget it. This is a future where men feed on men and only those mobile enough to scavenge for gasoline survive. Gibson is back as Max, the loner who saves a man's life in exchange for a tank of gas, then finds himself in an embattled outpost of civilization that has one last chance to thwart an attack by a gang of subhuman invaders, led by a bruiser called Humungus (Nilsson). Miller summons up a hellish, surreal quality that is haunting and provocative. Come on, why resist?

Hot Bonus: There is a cropped version of the

film on one side of the disc; don't go near it. The letterboxing is essential, especially at the start when the screen stretches before your eyes to take in Max's car and the highway.

Key Scene: Max's battle with a fleet of high-speed bikes is like nothing you've ever seen.

Robocop (Unrated Director's Cut) (1987)

Starring: Peter Weller, Nancy Allen, Ronny Cox, Miguel Ferrer

Directed by: Paul Verhoeven

You can buy the *Robocop* trilogy in its own DVD package. My advice is stick to the original—it's the only one that gets the tone right. And get Criterion's DVD transfer. Not only does it have extras; it has scenes not in the R-rated release version. Weller is quite good as Alex Murphy, a good-guy cop in futuristic Detroit who is killed by sadistic punks. What's left of him is reassembled into a cyborg, who fights crime with a hottie female partner (Allen), but still can't help wanting those punks punished and punished good. It's gory all right, but also keenly satirical and great fun.

Hot Bonus: Fascinating storyboards up the yin yang, and Dutch director Verhoeven, whose camera would peek up Sharon Stone's skirt in *Basic Instinct* five years later, reveals a kinky side in his commentary.

Key Scene: Robocop removes his helmet. What a great yuck moment!

Rock 'n' Roll High School (Special Edition) (1979)

Starring: P. J. Soles, Mary Woronov, Vincent Van Patten, the Ramones

Directed by: Allan Arkush

Soles is the coolest punk-rock girl at Vince Lombardi High School. She writes songs, and she totally loves the Ramones. So they come to rescue her from the evil principal (Woronov), with gabba-gabba live footage ("She's the One"), dialogue you want to carve into your arm, and a climactic scene of the band helping the kids blow up the school. It's the ultimate celebration of teen-girl fandom. Arkush directs on a shoestring budget provided by producer Roger Corman. But the DVD transfer looks and sounds super.

Hot Bonus: The Arkush commentary is good stuff, but the extra twenty minutes of the Ramones playing live—now that's real bonus anarchy.

Key Scene: I love the mice exploding, and Soles getting called into the principal's office and announcing, "I'm a teenage lobotomy."

Rocky (Special Edition) (1976)

Starring: Sylvester Stallone, Talia Shire, Carl Weathers, Burgess Meredith

Directed by: John G. Avildsen

What's left to say? Stallone wrote himself the role he was born to play (it may be the only one). Rocky Balboa is just another bum from the Philadelphia hood when he meets the right shy girl (Shire)—"Yo, Adrian!"—gets a shot at heavyweight champ Apollo Creed (Weathers), and trains himself bowlegged with his manager (Meredith). The Special Edition DVD makes the movie look better than its low-budget roots. Director Avildsen wisely used Bill Conti's rousing score at every available opportunity, and in Dolby Digital it really hits you. Corny as hell, sure, but there's no sense fighting this little engine that could win the Best Picture Oscar. Go ahead, throw a few punches at the four sequels, which ran the gamut of worse to much worse, but Stallone turned his Italian Stallion into one of the icons of American film.

Hot Bonus: Stallone leads a parade of showoff commentary. But the profile of cinematographer James Crabe reveals him as the real behind-the-scenes star of this underdog smash. Under Crabe's tutelage *Rocky* was the first film to use the Steadicam, which was invented by Garrett Brown.

Key Scene: Rocky in training (to Conti's "Gonna Fly Now"), culminating in his historic run up the steps of the Philly art museum.

Rocky Horror Picture Show, The (Two-Disc Special Edition) (1975)

Starring: Tim Curry, Susan Sarandon, Barry Bostwick, Richard O'Brien

Directed by: Jim Sharman

Name a bigger cult musical. You can't, so just give in to this eye-poppingly colorful DVD transfer that lifts the score by Richard O'Brien to Dolby Digital heaven. And now you can watch it anytime, not just at midnight in a theater crowded with singalong groupies. Just to hear Curry, decked out in fishnets and heels as Dr. Frank N. Furter, belt out "Sweet Transvestite" is to experience twisted bliss. The good doctor has just welcomed wholesome Brad (Bostwick) and Janet (Sarandon) into his time-warped den of iniquity where transsexuals have gathered to see Dr. Furter's latest creation for relieving his tension: Rocky. No, not Stallone. Peter Hinwood plays this bisexual body beautiful in gold lame jockeys. It's a sexual smorgasbord.

Hot Bonus: The whole movie is presented again in a theater with the audience doing lines and songs and making comments.

Key Scene: From a storm-tossed Brad and Janet singing "There's a Light" to Meat Loaf's "Hot Patootie" and Sarandon overheating to "Toucha Toucha Touch Me," there's too much choice. But I'm going with "Time Warp."

Roger Dodger (2002)

Starring: Campbell Scott, Jesse Eisenberg, Elizabeth Berkley, Jennifer Beals
Directed by: Dylan Kidd

Scott swings at the juiciest role of his career to date and knocks it out of the park. Adman Roger Swanson is a nightmare vision of the New York bachelor: a charming, acid-tongued predator. His boss (Isabella Rossellini) has dumped him, leaving Roger bitter when he decides to help his sixteen-year-old nephew, Nick (the excellent Eisenberg), lose the teen stigma of virginity. During a frenzied night in Manhattan—the expert handheld camerawork makes the transition to DVD with dizzying ease—Roger and Jesse hook up with two happy-hour babes (Beals and Berkley, both sublime), crash Roger's boss's party, and venture into an underground sex club. Roger's mouth never stops, and Scott gives every line a bruising comic snap. Writer-director Kidd creates a wild ride of a movie that keeps throwing fastballs. Unlike Roger, Kidd refuses to dodge the harsher truths.

Hot Bonus: Eisenberg conducts a walking tour of New York at night.

Key Scene: Nick getting kissed, and Roger getting left out in the cold, allowing Scott to show the bruised humanity in a relentless SOB.

Romancing the Stone (1984)

Starring: Michael Douglas, Kathleen Turner, Danny DeVito
Directed by: Robert Zemeckis

The man-eating crocodiles, the hair-raising jungle chase, the ride over the waterfall—all delivered by Zemeckis in the best cliffhanger tradition. And the DVD gets the look right even if it is non anamorphic. Turner plays a romance novelist who cries at the end of her own books. Her big love is her cat. Then her sister is kidnapped by thugs in South America and she flies in with the ransom, a treasure map. Douglas plays a drifter who meets Turner when she's about to be attacked by bad guys, including DeVito. Turner and Douglas spar with rollicking, tongue-in-cheek gusto.

Hot Bonus: To make up for the lack thereof, you could find the DVD of the 1985 sequel, *The Jewel of the Nile*, but it sucks.

Key Scene: Douglas finding a copy of *Rolling Stone* in the fuselage of a wrecked plane. "The Doobie Brothers broke up," he moans while poor Turner fights off a poisonous snake.

Romeo + Juliet (Special Edition) (1996)

Starring: Leonardo DiCaprio, Claire Danes
Directed by: Baz Luhrmann

An utterly gorgeous DVD with the kind of picture and sound that pulls you in even if you hate Shakespeare. DiCaprio, then twenty-one, and Danes, then seventeen, fill their classic roles with vital passion, speak the Elizabethan verse with unforced grace, find the spirited comedy of the play without losing its tragic fervor, and keep their balance when audacious Aussie director Luhrmann hurls them into a whirlwind of hardball action. Welcome to mythical Verona Beach, where the gangs fire on each other, and soldiers in choppers fire on them in a style that might be called retro-futuristic, since it encompasses castles and armor. The film reworks Shakespeare in a frenzy of jump cuts that makes most rock videos look like MTV on Midol.

Hot Bonus: A short piece with a pre-Titanic DiCaprio shows the actor's ease with the Bard. As his co-star Leguizamo, who plays Tybalt, has said in jest: "It came so easy to that little, blond, happy, golden-boy motherfucker."

Key Scene: When Romeo first sees Juliet at the costume ball, these "bright angels" steal looks at each other on opposite sides of a fish tank and steal a kiss. DiCaprio and Danes make the bandying of words a sly, erotic game.

Ronin (1998)

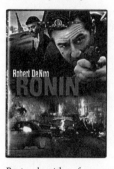

Starring: Robert De Niro, Jean Reno, Natascha McElhone, Sean Bean

Directed by: John Frankenheimer

Dolby Digital sound thunders out of this DVD. Directed at full-suspense throttle by Frankenheimer, *Ronin*—the title references a Japanese feudal term to describe shamed samurai who have failed in their warrior mission to protect their masters—sets up De Niro as Sam, a former CIA strategist who has turned mercenary since the dissolution of the Cold War deprived his killing skills of a higher purpose. Sam is the top gun among a dirty half-dozen international covert operatives, including Reno, Bean, Skipp Sudduth, Stellan Skarsgård, and the leggy McElhone as the Irish rep for the mysterious client (Jonathan Pryce), who barks orders by cell phone. These actors can toss a quip as deftly as a firebomb. But the star here is Frankenheimer, who doesn't stoop to hollow digital dazzle. Long, fluid camera movements emphasize that these are real cars we see racing through Paris tunnels in high-speed midnight chases that eerily evoke the death of Princess Diana. "Relax, darling, it's just a game," De Niro tells McElhone of the spy business. If so, Frankenheimer and De Niro are determined to play the game with honor. They're American samurai.

Hot Bonus: An alternate ending that has it all over they one they used.

Key Scene: The car chase through the narrow streets of Nice.

Room at the Top (1959)

Starring: Simone Signoret, Laurence Harvey, Heather Sears

Directed by: Jack Clayton

If a DVD can do the job of preserving Signoret's Oscar-winning performance, then that DVD belongs in your collection. Shot by Freddie Francis in a black-and-white so gritty you can smell the dirt, this stinging drama deals with Joe Lampton (Harvey), a social-climbing rat bastard who marries the boss's daughter (Sears) and dumps Alice (Signoret), the unhappily married older woman who brings out the last shreds of human warmth in him. Clayton, directing the award-winning script by Neil Paterson carved out of John Braine's novel, sticks it royally to the British class system. But it's Signoret you remember. She's unmissable.

Hot Bonus: The bio on Signoret, a French actress with a remarkable history.

Key Scene: Signoret with her back to the camera, extending her hand for a final wave in a gesture of heartbreaking resilience.

Room With a View, A (Two-Disc Special Edition) 1986

Starring: Maggie Smith, Helena Bonham Carter, Daniel Day-Lewis

Directed by: James Ivory

Director Ivory, producer Ismail Merchant, and screenwriter Ruth Prawer Jhabvala do E. M. Forster's 1908 novel proud. And the DVD follows suit in capturing the voluptuous colors of Italy that are lost on a group of Brits who visit Florence. Bonham Carter is chaperoned by her spinster cousin, acted with humor and anguished grace by Smith. Forster's point about the English is that they are always in England, closed off to any new culture afforded them. Then Bonham Carter meets Sands, a handsome Englishman traveling with his vulgarian father, beautifully played by Denholm Elliott. After witnessing a bloody stabbing in the piazza, she is passionately kissed by Julian Sands in the lush countryside. Shaken, she returns home and gets engaged to a prig (a brilliant Day-Lewis). Sands and Elliott make one last attempt to save her, exposing the hypocrisy festering under the elegant surfaces of Edwardian society. This is one of the best literary adaptations ever filmed.

Hot Bonus: A featurette showing Ivory and the late Merchant working, arguing, and making film magic stands as an exuberant tribute.

Key Scene: The shocking comic highlight is Bonham Carter discovering Sands, her brother (Rupert Graves), and a plump minister (Simon Callow) frolicking full-frontal naked in a muddy pond. A view, indeed.

Rose, The (1979)

Starring: Bette Midler, Alan Bates, Frederic Forrest, Harry Dean Stanton

Directed by: Mark Rydell

In her first starring role—a raw spin on a boozing, bisexual Janis Joplin—Midler won a well-deserved Academy Award nomination as Best Actress. Rose is almost burned out as the movie begins. After a country star (Stanton in a gem of a cameo) insults her talent and vulgar flirting with his son, Rose begs her manager (Bates) for time off, and then takes a hike with a chauffeur (Forrest, also Oscar nominated) who seems to understand her. Vilmos Zsigmond shoots this road odyssey, including a trip to a drag club where Rose sings with her male facsimile, with a feel for the light and shadow of Rose's life, astutely picked up on the DVD.

Hot Bonus: Commentary from director Rydell, but no talk from Miss M.

Key Scene: Rose's booze-and-drug-fueled concert performance of "Stay with Me," a song Midler hadn't yet performed for a live audience before filming. The sound and the performance are both enveloping.

Rosemary's Baby (1986)

Starring: Mia Farrow, John Cassavetes, Ruth Gordon, Sidney Blackmer

Directed by: Roman Polanski

Tannis root, anyone? That's the foul-tasting liquid those creepy neighbors the Castevets—Minnie (Gordon) and Roman (Blackmer)—give poor, pregnant Rosemary (Farrow). The DVD transfer is so vivid you want to gag. Polanski's magnificent horror show, based on Ira Levin's trashy novel, works so well and on so many levels that it's a kick to watch it over and over. Did Rosemary really get knocked up by the devil and give birth to the anti-Christ? Or is she just paranoid about being married to a selfish actor (Cassavetes) who isn't Catholic? Interpreting the movie as a lapsed Catholic fable yields many rewards. But however you see it, you marvel at Farrow's subtle performance, which shamefully failed to win her an Oscar nod, and the mesmeric mugging of Gordon, who did win the golden devil.

Hot Bonus: Farrow and Polanski working on the film in an old documentary.

Key Scene: The moment when Rosemary first sees her baby. Farrow covers her mouth and a violin shrieks like a banshee.

Rounders (Collector's Edition) (1998)

Starring: Matt Damon, Edward Norton, John Malkovich, Gretchen Mol

Directed by: John Dahl

With poker exploding in popularity, this special-edition DVD really is worth collecting. Set in the underground poker clubs of New York, the film stars a rock-solid Damon as Mike McDermott, a law student who blows thirty thousand dollars in tuition on a poker game with mad Russian Teddy KGB (Malkovich) and then futilely vows to kick the habit. *Rounders* (slang for players

who know all the angles) is stylish entertainment when director Dahl plays his strong suit (a gifted cast) instead of his weakest (a derivative plot). Mike's best pal Worm (a ratty, riveting Norton) is an ex-con whose knack for cheating reduces his options for staying alive. It's Worm who knows that no babe, not even Mol, can deter Mike from poker, especially in a can't-lose setup with trust-fund preppies in the burbs. "It's all-the-way nice," says Worm. Ditto the movie.

Hot Bonus: Pro poker players do the commentary. Addicts take note.

Key Scene: Anything with Malkovich. Splashing the pot with chips (a poker no-no) and speaking with a Russian accent that defies deciphering ("Ho-kay, Meester sum of a beech"), he soars so far over the top, he's passing Pluto.

Roxanne (1987)

Starring: Steve Martin, Daryl Hannah, Rick Rossovich

Directed by: Fred Schepisi

Most comics want to play Hamlet. Martin takes on Cyrano de Bergerac, updating the seventeenth-century soldier with a heart the size of his schnoz—that is to say, prodigious. Martin's C. D. Bales is a fire chief leading a troop of misfits in Washington State. When Chris (Rossovich), one of his firefighters, falls for Roxanne (Hannah), the dreamy astronomer C.D. loves, C.D. writes love letters for the tongue-tied lug that delivers Roxanne to the wrong guy's bed. Martin's warm and witty performance is topped only by his marvelous screenplay. And Schepisi provides a widescreen expansiveness that brings comic resonance to the movie and the DVD.

Hot Bonus: Filmographies, the best of which pays tribute to Michael Westmore who designed the nose, which is, well, hugely funny

Key Scene: Martin taking on a barroom heckler with a barrage of his own nose insults ("You could deemphasize your nose if you wore something larger, like Wyoming").

Royal Tenenbaums, The (Two-Disc Special Edition) (2001)

Starring: Gene Hackman, Ben Stiller, Gwyneth Paltrow, Bill Murray

Directed by: Wes Anderson

"It doesn't look good," says Hackman. He's not referring to this movie, which looks very good indeed on this Criterion DVD transfer. Hackman's Royal Tenenbaum—a prominent litigator until he was disbarred and briefly imprisoned—is referring to his marriage to Etheline (Anjelica Huston), the mother of their three prodigy children. The breakup of the marriage is the core of the film. The kids, now adults, are still dealing with Royal's neglect. Financial whiz Chas (Stiller), a widowed father of two, remembers how his dad shot him with a BB gun. Adopted sister Margot (Paltrow) is unhappily married to neurologist Raleigh St. Clair (Murray, hurray!). Retired tennis champ Richie (Luke Wilson) hides his love for his sister, who is having a woebegone fling with Richie's friend Eli Cash (Owen Wilson). In the words of the film's narrator (Alec Baldwin): "All memory of the brilliance of the young Tenenbaums had been erased by two decades of betrayal, failure, and disaster." The film plays like a *New Yorker* story that J. D. Salinger never wrote. Anderson, who crafted the script with his Texas chum Owen Wilson, has made something eccentric and hilarious that can suddenly—or maybe not for hours or even days later—choke you up with emotion.

Hot Bonus: On-the-set footage shot by Albert Maysles.

Key Scene: The great Hackman, robbed of an Oscar nod, teaching his grandkids the art of shoplifting, pelting cabs, and playing in traffic.

Rules of the Game (Two-Disc Special Edition) (1939)

Starring: Marcel Dalio, Julien Carette, Nora Gregor, Mila Parely

Directed by: Jean Renoir

You always hear critics raving about Renoir's French comedy of ill manners being the greatest thing since sound came in. Yet few people under thirty have ever seen it. Get cracking. Criterion makes it easy with a new DVD transfer featuring a restored image and new subtitles. The deep-focus photography that has influenced everything from *The Magnificent Ambersons* to *Gosford Park* is on immaculate display as characters run around a country estate hunting rabbits and chasing each other's mates and maids. Renoir, who also acts in the film as the likable clown Octave, keeps the comedy perking. But his subversive intent is to expose the blindness, racism, and pettiness of a ruling class that let itself be led into war and Nazi occupation. Everyone hated the film on its initial release. It was butchered, lost, and finally put back together again to reveal Renoir's genius at satirizing a society that didn't like what it saw in his mirror. That's why the film stays young and pertinent as it marches through time.

Hot Bonus: All the background and analysis you could wish for, plus a conversation between Renoir and the outstanding actor Dalio discussing the impact of the film in hindsight.

Key Scene: The slaughter of the rabbits.

Ruling Class, The (1972)

Starring: Peter O'Toole, Alastair Sim, Arthur Lowe, Carolyn Seymour

Directed by: Peter Medak

O'Toole plays a mad British earl who thinks he's Jesus Christ in the film's first half—there are song-and-dance numbers—and then switches to being Jack the Ripper, which the public and the peerage find far more acceptable. Criterion dresses it up nicely for a DVD that is explosive, perverse fun. Medak, working from a play by Peter Barnes, skewers every British institution from Parliament to the Church of England. Lowe is treasurable as a rebel butler, as is Sim as a bumbling bishop. But the show is O'Toole's. His wedding vows to Seymour include a vow of love "from the bottom of my soul to the tip of my penis." No wonder he won an Oscar nomination.

Hot Bonus: Medak took home movies on the set, which are fascinating.

Key Scene: Watching O'Toole climb on the cross he keeps in his living room, just to get in the mood.

Run Lola Run (1998)

Starring: Franke Potente, Moritz Bleibtreu, Herbert Knaup

Directed by: Tom Tykwer

Potente's flaming hair is reason enough to get this DVD. It will test your home-theater system's ability to hold all that bleeding red. Potente's Lola just wants to help her boyfriend Manni (Bleibtreu). He botched a drug deal, and if Manni can't come up with one hundred thousand marks in twenty minutes, he's going down. That's what gets Lola running. Not once. Not twice. But three times. Tykwer's concept is to show the three ways Lola tries to save Manni. Talk about making every minute count. This German film became a international hit. And no wonder. It's a breathless ride, er, run. And reading English subtitles is no trouble—there's hardly any dialogue.

Hot Bonus: Potente and Tykwer talk about the problems of getting this done without Potente collapsing from exhaustion.

Key Scene: Lola running by a store window only to see a cartoon version of herself running on a TV screen.

Runaway Train (1985)

Starring: Jon Voight, Eric Roberts, Rebecca De Mornay

Directed by: Andrei Konchalovsky

Voight and Roberts escape from an Alaskan prison, trudge through a blizzard, and climb aboard a train. Time to relax? Ha! The engineer has just dropped dead of a heart attack. De Mornay spots the cons and begs them to help as the train thunders toward the abyss. That's the movie, and Russian director Konchalovsky never takes his hand off the action throttle. Mindless escapism? Double ha! Voight and Roberts earned Oscar nominations, the script is by (get this!) Akira Kurosawa, and the DVD rides to glory on the camerawork of Alan Hume.

Hot Bonus: You'll have to settle for Voight quoting Nietzsche: "Whatever doesn't kill me makes me stronger."

Key Scene: Voight disconnecting a car from the train defines the phrase palm-sweating intensity.

Rush Hour (1998)

Starring: Jackie Chan, Chris Tucker

Directed by: Brett Ratner

Hong Kong cop Chan comes to Los Angeles on a kidnapping case and buddies up with Tucker, the cop assigned to babysit him. If you think that's original, in the 2001 sequel Tucker goes to Hong Kong. No matter. The main ingredients are Chan, who is hopeless with English, and Tucker, the motormouthed American comic who is hopeless with silence. All director Ratner has to do is stir and serve. When the plot thins, which is frequently, Ratner pulls out a new stunt. And the DVD, with its sharp images and dimensional sound, puts you right in the middle of the action. The whole film plays like a series of outtakes, and I mean that as a compliment.

Hot Bonus: There's an intriguing Easter Egg if you go to Chapter 3 and find Title 4. It's an early Ratner film called *Evil Luke Lee* that the director has good reasons for wanting to hide.

Key Scene: Chan, who does his own stunts, jumping from a double-decker bus to a Hollywood Boulevard road sign and then to a truck.

Rushmore (Special Edition) (1998)

Starring: Jason Schwartzman, Bill Murray, Olivia Williams

Directed and co-written by: Wes Anderson

A great movie that deserves the careful DVD transfer Criterion gives it. For starters, as Herman Blume, a steel tycoon with a cheating wife and teenage twin sons he hates almost as much as he hates himself, Murray artfully digs for signs of life in a character who thinks his soul is dead. Whether you see the film as a slowed-down farce or as a souped-up tragedy, it's packed with richly realized characters. Take Max Fischer, smashingly played by Schwartzman, a fifteen-year-old misfit who attends the snooty Rushmore Academy and puts on school dramas set in cities or jungles that always end in shootouts. Max and Herman, a school benefactor, both fall for first-grade teacher Rosemary Cross (the magnetic Williams), and try to kill each other. Anderson, who cowrote the deft script with Owen Wilson, fills each frame of his rigorously constructed fable with detail. On subsequent viewings, the plaintive subtext of even the funniest scenes becomes readily apparent.

Hot Bonus: The director's brother, Eric Chase Anderson, offers up a behind-the-scene program on the movie that speaks ironic volumes.

Key Scene: Murray cannily crowds a lifetime into one small moment. As Herman distractedly throws golf balls in the pool, he notices his wife flirting with the tennis pro. Cigarette dangling from the side of his mouth, Herman heaves his way to the diving board, casts a look of disdain at his family and jumps, the camera noting his sad isolation at the bottom of the pool.

Sabrina (1954)

Starring: Audrey Hepburn, Humphrey Bogart, William Holden
Directed by: Billy Wilder

The best Cinderella story ever. Screen goddess Hepburn shines like platinum on this sensational DVD transfer of Wilder's black-and-white film. Hepburn's Sabrina is the daughter of a chauffeur (John Williams) on a Long Island estate where she watches the rich from her perch in a tree. She moons over playboy son David Larabee (a charming Holden), who ignores her. Years later when the mouse returns from Paris as Sabrina the beauty, David pants for her. His brother Linus (Bogart in a romantic comedy—yikes!) tries to break them up by pretending to fall for Sabrina. And then he does. Who wouldn't? Wilder directs this soufflé with the fine hand of a master chef.

Hot Bonus: A retrospective documentary.

Key Scene: Sabrina's return from Paris, waiting at the railroad station dressed to the nines in Edith Head's Oscar-winning wardrobe, and David stopping his car to gawk without an idea of who he's gawking at.

Saddest Music in the World, The (2003)

Starring: Isabella Rossellini, Mark McKinney
Directed by: Guy Maddin

Maddin is not just a different kind of filmmaker; the Canadian innovator breathes another kind of air. That's what makes his formally experimental films (if you like this one, try *Dracula: Pages from a Virgin's Diary*) so perversely exciting. A double-amputee beer baroness (the delightful Rossellini) stages a contest in Depression-era Winnipeg to find the country that produces the saddest music. Then McKinney, a past lover of the baroness, enters the contest. It's a comedy with music and tragedy shot in a style to represent films of the era—silent and talkie. The DVD transfer gives Maddin's visual and aural flights of fancy a dream presentation.

Hot Bonus: The "making of" documentaries are terrific, but three Maddin shorts, including *Sissy Boy Slap Party*, put the icing on the cake.

Key Scene: When a lover drinks from the baroness's glass legs, which are filled with beer.

Safe (1995)

Starring: Julianne Moore, Xander Berkeley, Peter Friedman
Directed by: Todd Haynes

Carol White, the bored, sexually unfulfilled housewife played by the astonishing Moore, lives a sterile existence to which she develops an allergy. She's choking on her life. Haynes creates a visually arresting allegory that comes through thrillingly on DVD. Carol seeks a harbor at a New Age retreat in New Mexico run by an HIV-positive guru (Friedman) who wants to clear her viral load but just may be adding to it. The film is a mesmerizing, often hilarious minefield of emotional curveballs and striking imagery (check out that figure in the mask on the DVD box).

Hot Bonus: A scrappy conversation with Moore, Haynes, and producer Christine Vachon.

Key Scene: Carol, choking on fumes in traffic, pulling into a garage as the world seems to close in on her.

Salvador (Special Edition) (1986)

Starring: James Woods, James Belushi
Directed by: Oliver Stone

Stone's underrated look at political and moral chaos in Central America. At first, photojournalist Richard Boyle (Woods, dynamite and Oscar nominated) and his DJ buddy (Belushi) seem more interested in hooking up with whores in bars than getting the story of the 1980 civil war in El Salvador, but the wrenching stories they find grab hold. So does the movie. Stone, working with camera wiz Robert Richardson, thrusts you into the fray, and the DVD transfer catches that roiling immediacy.

Hot Bonus: A documentary, *Into the Valley of Death*, bashes the role of the Reagan administration with the kind of ferocity you expect from Stone.

Key Scene: The pile of bodies.

Saturday Night Fever (1977)

Starring: John Travolta, Karen Lynn Gorney, Donna Pescow, Barry Miller

Directed by: John Badham

More than a movie, *Fever* stands as an imperishable artifact of the 1970s disco era. Travolta's Tony Manero is an Italian teenager from Brooklyn who works in his father's paint store, lives with his parents, and dreams of making it in the Big Apple. His ticket out? At night, when he hits the 2001 Odyssey disco in a tight white suit, exuding animal heat and a panther's grace, he's a king. Gorney notices and picks him as her partner, which means Tony must dump his regular girl (a touching Pescow). Tony has his priorities: "When you make it with some of these chicks, they think you gotta dance with them." Says his priest brother: "You arrive and the crowd parts like the Red Sea." The movie had the same effect on audiences. Travolta became a star and earned an Oscar nomination, people bought white suits and wore them, and the soundtrack of Bee Gees songs took over the planet. Seen today, *Fever* is dated but still dazzling. The widescreen anamorphic DVD transfer is blemished by grain, but the Dolby Digital sound brings back the power of the music and the hot moves. Travolta's sad-eyed sensuality is appealing, but on the dance floor he stirs up a night fever that will live in screen history.

Hot Bonus: Badham's director commentary puts it all in perspective. And this time the deleted scenes are something you want to see.

Key Scene: A simple walk down the street that Travolta turns into a sexy swagger of a dance—the Bee Gees goosing him with "Staying Alive."

Saving Private Ryan (Special Edition) (1998)

Starring: Tom Hanks, Matt Damon, Ed Burns, Tom Sizemore, Vin Diesel

Directed by: Steven Spielberg

Raving about how great Spielberg's World War II epic looks on DVD, with the battle sounds roaring out of all your speakers, is to neglect the emotional resonance he was aiming for. But it's genuine emotions I do miss. Genuine is not what I'd call the slathering of sentiment in the prologue and epilogue when veterans visit the war dead. Genuine is not what I'd call a plot that has Captain John Miller (Hanks, excellent as usual) leading his squad (Sizemore, Burns, Diesel, Barry Pepper, Adam Goldberg, Jeremy Davies, and Giovanni Ribisi acquit themselves honorably) into France to find Private Ryan (Damon) and send him home because his three brothers have already died in battle. My guess is these scenes cost the film the Best Picture Oscar even when Spielberg justly won for the harrowing scenes of war.

Hot Bonus: Most moving are clips of the World War II movies made by Spielberg during his childhood years.

Key Scene: D-Day—nearly a half an hour is devoted to the Allied landing on Omaha Beach. It's the most brutal and bruising war footage ever filmed.

Say Anything . . . (Special Edition) (1989)

Starring: John Cusack, Ione Skye, John Mahoney, Lili Taylor

Directed and written by: Cameron Crowe

A teen romance, written by the keenest ear in the business in his auspicious directing debut. Crowe doesn't just craft dialogue; he shapes it to complement and sometimes contradict what we see. Even the names work. Cusack plays Lloyd Dobler, a guy in love with kickboxing who is now in love with Diane Court (Skye), the school brain. Lloyd lives with his sister (Joan Cusack, John's sister) and her kid. Diane lives with her father (Mahoney), who runs a nursing home and is being investigated for fraud. The relationships are complicated, and Crowe does nothing to gloss over the rough spots. And yet the movie—transferred to DVD with respect for its nuances—is exuberant. Crowe calls Lloyd a "warrior for optimism." His friend Corey (a priceless Taylor) writes sixty-five songs about the guy who dumped her, one song begins, "Joe lies." Crowe doesn't lie, his film and his actors—Cusack's Lloyd is officially a classic creation—speak the blunt truth, which is one of the reasons they so easily break our hearts.

Hot Bonus: Good talk from Crowe, who is joined by Cusack and Skye. They each confess an attraction back then that they never acted upon.

Key Scene: Lloyd holding up that boombox to Diane's window so she can hear Peter Gabriel's "In Your Eyes." It's like flying a flag.

Scarface
(Special Edition) (1983)

Starring: Al Pacino, Michelle Pfeiffer, Mary Elizabeth Mastrantonio

Directed by: Brian De Palma

Say 'ello to my leetle friend. Only the *Scarface* deluxe gift set isn't so leetle. For $59.98, you get a package trashy enough to please Tony Montana, the Cuban refugee turned Miami coke king hammed to the hilt by Pacino with an extra side of pineapple. The blood splatters better and redder than ever, thanks to digital remastering. And Pfeiffer, as Tony's sexy cokehead wife, makes an entrance that will have you down for the count. What floors Tony is his incestuous yen for his sister (Mastrantonio), that and the white stuff. Pacino, director De Palma, and screenwriter Oliver Stone talk about how the film was hammered by critics in 1983 only to be adopted by rap culture. Snoop Dogg himself advises: "Don't watch it just for the violence—watch it for the lessons. Watch it to see what Tony did right." Huh?

Hot Bonus: A monogrammed money clip is included, along with prints of the original lobby cards. Hold them up and cite such moralisms as "Don't get high on your own supply."

Key Scene: The big shootout after Tony's last climb on a mountain of coke.

Scary Movie (2000)

Starring: Anna Faris, Jon Abrahams, Carmen Electra, Shannon Elizabeth

Directed by: Keenen Ivory Wayans

The two sequels quickly ran out of steam, but the original had a low-comic blast at the expense of such horror flicks as *Scream* and *I Know What You Did Last Summer*. Too crude for satire and too busy for plot, the movie is just a raunchy series of ratings-defiant skits, cast with actors who are way too old to go to B.A. Corpse High School, where the female gym teacher, Ms. Mann, has a dick, which is used as a lethal weapon and with semen that gushes like an oil well. Electra is wet down in the first scene and stabbed in the boobs with a knife filled with silicone. You get the picture. It's gross in the extreme, and therefore a must DVD for those nights when only gross will do.

Hot Bonus: Six deleted scenes that should have been in the movie.

Key Scene: A woman in a theater is killed for talking during the movie, not just by one patron but by the entire audience. Amen to that, brother.

Schindler's List
(Collector's Edition) (1993)

Starring: Liam Neeson, Ralph Fiennes, Ben Kingsley

Directed by: Steven Spielberg

More than a movie, it's a rending historical document. Oskar Schindler, the Catholic war profiteer played by Neeson, saved more than twelve hundred Jews by giving him jobs in his factory in Poland. Spielberg's Oscar-winning film deserves the best in DVD picture and sound, and gets it, except for being a single disc that needs to be turned over. Shot in black-and-white by Janusz Kaminski, the film features deeply felt performances by Neeson as the unlikely hero, Kingsley as the Jewish accountant who helps him in his quest, and the brilliant Fiennes as the Nazi commandant Amon Goeth, who shoots Jews from his window as target practice. There are images of the Holocaust here that are past forgetting. Criticisms of the film—in the *New York Times*, Frank Rich complained that Spielberg has made the Jewish characters as "generic" and "forgettable" as "the chorus in a touring company of *Fiddler on the Roof*"—go beyond the board in terms of the larger picture.

Hot Bonus: The documentary *Voices From the List*, in which the men and women saved by Schindler talk about their experiences.

Key Scene: Schindler breaking down in a speech to the Jewish factory workers. The scene is important for two reasons: its emotional impact, and the fact that it never happened. Schindler was not a man to wear his emotions openly, but it fills Spielberg's need for a big heroic moment.

School of Rock
(Special Collector's Edition)
(2003)

Starring: Jack Black, Joan Cusack, Mike White

Directed by: Richard Linklater

Hail! Hail! Jack Black! He's the clown king of rock & roll. Black's Dewey Finn, newly booted from his rock band, signs on to substitute teach and throws away the curriculum (Principal Cusack's dismay is priceless) to instruct a class of ten-year-olds in the art of the Who, Van Halen, AC/DC, the Ramones, and Led Zep. Linklater and screenwriter Mike White, who plays Dewey's roommate, do nothing to soften the Black mojo. Cute kids don't exactly rub off on this headbanger. Even when Dewey enters his class in a Battle of the Bands contest, the goo level stays low. The DVD looks as bright as neon, though more pow in the sound would have been a plus.

Hot Bonus: Black's videotaped pitch to Led Zeppelin, notorious for refusing rights to their music, to use "The Immigrant Song" in the movie.

Key Scene: Black taking his kid band into battle.

Scream
(Collector's Edition) (1996)

Starring: Drew Barrymore, Neve Campbell, Courteney Cox, David Arquette

Directed by: Wes Craven

Craven and screenwriter Kevin Williamson rejuvenated the teen slasher flick with this knowing spoof of the genre. Campbell stars as a high school hottie whose mother was murdered a year before. Now her friends are getting picked off by a fiend in an Edvard Munch ghost mask who first asks his victims questions about horror movies. Campbell's boyfriend is a suspect, though Skeet Ulrich plays him like someone whose crimes stopped at stealing Johnny Depp's DNA. Cox puts on a tough act as a TV reporter, and Arquette (her real-life husband) looks perfectly clueless as the local law. The scene-stealer is Jamie Kennedy as a video junkie who knows the rules for surviving a horror movie: "Never have sex, never drink or do drugs, and never say, 'I'll be right back.'" The letterboxed Collector's Edition does its best by a hit that spawned two lesser sequels. From Barrymore's opening gambit in the kitchen, *Scream* produces what its title promises.

Hot Bonus: A behind-the-scenes look at the Barrymore sequence.

Key Scene: The guy watching *Halloween* on the tube and yelling to Jamie Lee Curtis to watch her back when he should be watching his own.

Seabiscuit
(Two-Disc Special Edition) (2003)

Starring: Tobey Maguire, Jeff Bridges, Chris Cooper

Directed by: Gary Ross

Bitch all you want about what's wrong. Unlike Laura Hillenbrand's dark, densely reported bestseller, Ross's movie version is rose-tinted, skin-deep, and wrinkle-free—more cotton candy than cutting edge. But how do you not love Seabiscuit, a puny, knobby-kneed Depression-era racehorse best known for napping and noshing until three men—all as dysfunctional as he is—changed his life and turned him into a champion? There's owner Charles Howard (Bridges), trainer Tom Smith (Cooper), and jockey Red Pollard (Maguire), forced to puke up his meals to stay thin for the game. The DVD transfer pumps real excitement into the races, as the gluepot (ten horses played Seabiscuit) takes to the track like Rocky on four skinny legs. Hipsters will be allergic; this is one for your inner sap.

Hot Bonus: The newsreel footage of the real Seabiscuit is a genuine thrill.

Key Scene: Tension is highest during the match race between Seabiscuit and Triple Crown–winner War Admiral—what with Red sidelined by a crippling leg injury and George "The Iceman" Woolf, sensationally played by Hall of Fame jockey Gary Stevens, riding the Biscuit.

Searchers, The (1956)

Starring: John Wayne, Jeffrey Hunter, Natalie Wood

Directed by: John Ford

The greatest western ever made. There I've said it, and the DVD transfer bears me out by blowing the dust off the old prints shown on TV until Ford's landmark film is resurrected for a new generation to behold. Wayne gives the performance of his life as Ethan Edwards, a Confederate soldier home from the Civil War and about to take on another mission: find his ten-year-old niece Debbie who's been kidnapped by the Comanches. Joined by Martin (Hunter), whose parents were murdered by Indians, Ethan spends the next seven years searching, his racism growing more bitter, his loneliness turning him slowly to stone. Ford's condemnation of bigotry is revolutionary in a western. When Ethan does find Debbie (Wood, exceptionally good), he's so churned up over what's happened to her sexually as "the leavins' of a Comanche buck" that you don't know whether he'll save her or kill her. The film's last shot of Ethan, isolated against a doorway, shut off from family and humanity, is an indelible screen image that will live as long there are movies.

Hot Bonus: A promotional featurette, done for TV at the time of the film's release, shows behind-the-scenes footage. But one longs for insightful commentary about the influence of *The Searchers* on films as diverse as *Taxi Driver* and *Star Wars*.

Key Scene: Ethan riding after his niece as she runs away in fear, then scooping her up in his arms. "Let's go home, Debbie," he says. It's a fleeting gesture of reconciliation from a man who will never be at peace.

Secretary (2002)

Starring: Maggie Gyllenhaal, James Spader
Directed by: Steven Shainberg

Mary Gaitskill's infamous short story comes to the screen as a film of startling humor and feeling, thanks to director Shainberg, who co-wrote the script with Erin Cressida Wilson. Gyllenhaal boldly steps into the role of Lee Holloway, fresh out of an institution (she cuts and burns herself) and eager to begin her job as secretary to bossy attorney E. Edward Gray (Spader, more twisted and terrific than he is on TV's *Boston Legal*). Mr. Gray gets right to her need to be spanked, handcuffed, and forced to deliver letters on all fours. Remarkably, the film is less an S&M wallow than a love story between two consenting adults with complementary sexual psychoses. And the DVD transfer stays attuned to how colors can be lurid and lyrical.

Hot Bonus: Shainberg explains the deeper meanings of getting spanked.

Key Scene: The moment when Spader's fear ("We can't do this twenty-four hours a day, seven days a week") lifts and Gyllenhaal sweetly asks, "Why not?"

Serial Mom (1994)

Starring: Kathleen Turner, Sam Waterston, Ricki Lake, Matthew Lillard
Directed and written by: John Waters

Waters and Turner bring out the sicko best in each other in this killingly funny spoof of crime and nonpunishment. Turner plays Baltimore's homicidal homemaker Beverly Sutphin. You'd better be nice to her nerdy dentist husband Eugene (Waterston), her lovelorn daughter Misty (Lake), and her horror-film fanatic son Chip (Lillard). Beverly kills in the name of family values. The colors on the DVD are bright and sitcom normal. But wait. Beverly sings along with Barry Manilow's "Daybreak" as she drives off to each kill. Nice touch. The grossest sight involves an internal organ that dangles on the end of the fire poker. And the funniest moment concerns a woman who gets whacked for wearing white shoes after Labor Day. Beverly considers it an unforgivable fashion faux pas.

Hot Bonus: Waters talks and talks—all of it hilarious.

Key Scene: The first one—Beverly swats a fly. In close-up, we see the squashed, bloody insect body. Superimposed over the gross image is a screen credit: written and directed by John Waters.

Servant, The (1963)

Starring: Dirk Bogarde, James Fox, Sarah Miles, Wendy Craig
Directed by: Joseph Losey

A study in delicious decadence as directed by Losey from a gravely satirical script by Harold Pinter that deconstructs the class system. Fox plays the British twit who takes a London townhouse and hires a butler (Bogarde at the top of his game) to run it, until the servant ends up running him. Sex is one of the tools Barrett uses, passing off his mistress as his sister (Miles, never more erotic) and having her seduce the master to get rid of the fiancée (Craig). Pinter's pungent dialogue finds its match in the noirish black-and-white camerawork of Douglas Slocombe, which gives off a perverse bloom on DVD. Like Bogarde's servant, the film grabs you and won't let go.

Hot Bonus: A Bogarde bio that should lead you to more films from the actor, who died in 1999 and left a legacy shockingly unavailable on DVD.

Key Scene: Fox in the revolving leather chair getting the ride of his life from Miles.

Se7en
(Two-Disc Special Edition) (1995)

Starring: Brad Pitt, Morgan Freeman, Kevin Spacey, Gwyneth Paltrow
Directed by: David Fincher

Fincher's seminal crime thriller is dark, moody, and rainy—notoriously difficult qualities to transfer to DVD. *Se7en* pulls it off in meticulous detail. Evocatively shot by Darius Khondji, the film is set in an unnamed modern city eroded by decay. Pitt stars as David Mills, a can-do detective just in from the sticks with his wife Tracy (Paltrow), to replace Lt. William Somerset (Freeman), a soul-sick cop ready to pack it in after thirty-four years of chasing scumbags. The case that brings the two together is a John Doe serial killer (Spacey at his malicious best) who bases his murders on the seven deadly sins. For gluttony, a fatso is forced to eat until he bursts. For pride, a model is brutally disfigured, and so on through greed, sloth, and lust. Envy and wrath are paired up for a twisted, gut-wrenching climax. Fincher wants to abrade, not ingratiate. It's not the identity of the killer that gives *Se7en* its kick—it's the way Fincher raises mystery to the level of moral provocation.

Hot Bonus: Four commentary tracks, and if any detail about the film's production is missed, it would take a crew member to find it.

Key Scene: The box, and what's in it.

Seven Beauties (1976)

Starring: Giancarlo Giannini, Shirley Stoler

Directed and written by: Lina Wertmüller

Newly restored and presented in 5.1 Surround Sound, Wertmüller's masterwork—she became the first Oscar-nominated female director—digs deep into the nature of survival. Giannini, also Oscar nominated, plays Pasqualino Frafuso, a small-time crook from Naples—he's the sole support of his seven wildly unattractive sisters—who ends up in a Nazi concentration camp during World War II. Petty cruelties grow to massive ones at the hands of the obese commandant (Stoler, magnifico). To save himself, Pasqualino will stoop to any low, and Wertmüller revels in each of them in a critique of her country that plays like slapstick tragedy.

Hot Bonus: An interview with the controversial director is included as a bonus on the six-disc Lina Wertmüller Collection, which presents five of her films, including Seven Beauties.

Key Scene: Pasqualino's sex scene with the commandant must be seen to be believed. Hit the still frame on the remote at your own risk.

Seven Days in May (1964)

Starring: Burt Lancaster, Kirk Douglas, Ava Gardner, Fredric March

Directed by: John Frankenheimer

The black-and-white cinematography in this crackling DVD transfer gives a docudrama feel to Frankenheimer's nerve-jangling thriller about a planned overthrow of the U.S. government by an enemy within: the military. Lancaster storms through the film as the general ready to launch a coup d'etat in seven days. Douglas plays the aide, who uncovers the plan and goes to the president (March). Gardner is Lancaster's former mistress, ready to reveal explosive love letters. It's a political thriller that still matters.

Hot Bonus: Frankenheimer gives the lowdown on the off-screen machinations to help get the film made, including cooperation from JFK.

Key Scene: The film owes much to the dialogue in Rod Serling's script, especially when the prez confronts the general: "Then, by God, run for office! You have such a fervent, passionate, evangelical faith in this country. . . . Why in the name of God don't you have any faith in the system of government you're so hell-bent to protect?"

Seven Samurai, The (1954)

Starring: Toshiro Mifune, Takashi Shimura

Directed by: Akira Kurosawa

The original *Magnificent Seven*. Kurosawa's seminal action film breaks new ground on a superior Criterion DVD transfer that freshens the sound and images of a classic and restores the running time to 208 minutes from the prevalent 160-minute version. Mifune is a towering presence as the veteran samurai who is hired to protect a town from bandits, and finds six more warriors to help him, including the implosive Takashi Shimura.

Hot Bonus: Film scholar Michael Jeck offers audio commentary on the film's meaning and impact.

Key Scene: The final battle in the pouring rain.

1776 (Director's Cut) (1972)

Starring: William Daniels, Howard da Silva, Ken Howard, Blythe Danner

Directed by: Peter H. Hunt

The funny and moving film version of the Broadway musical about the signing of the Declaration of Independence, with music and lyrics by Sherman Edwards and a script by Peter Stone, has been restored by director Hunt to a running time of 168 minutes (the butchered version on VHS ran 20 minutes shorter). I'll take all I can get, especially on this DVD transfer, which respects the miracles of lighting and design achieved by Hunt and his crew in re-creating a hot-as-hell Philadelphia. The actors play it for all it's worth—da Silva hams magnificently as the skirt-chasing, cootish old Ben Franklin; Ron Holgate outhams him as Virginia's Richard Henry Lee; Howard makes an ardent Thomas Jefferson, burning for his wife (Danner) while the Second Continental Congress burns for its Declaration; and Daniels is simply superb as John Adams, who practically railroads the Declaration into being while his wife (the beautiful Virginia Vestoff) writes letters that turn into passionate songs. Stirring stuff, and not just on the Fourth of July.

Hot Bonus: Hunt and Stone talk about controversies, including the removal of the conservative minuet, "Cool Considerate Men" (now restored), a song cut for political reasons in the 1970s when right-wing satire wasn't welcome.

Key Scene: The signing of the Declaration. The moment should come with DVD directions: Insert lump into throat.

Seventh Seal, The (Special Edition) (1957)

Starring: Max von Sydow, Gunnar Bjornstrand, Bengt Ekerot

Directed by: Ingmar Bergman

This is the film that put Swedish master Bergman on the international movie map. Von Sydow stars as a medieval knight heading home from the crusades. Visited by Death (Ekerot) in a black cloak, the knight tricks the reaper into more time by offering a game of chess. The two discuss the existence of God, which the knight's squire (Bjornstrand, the sins of the flesh incarnate) acutely denies. The argument continues through visions of plague and destruction, given graphic intensity on this restored version of the film from Criterion. Bergman's religious allegory burns with shocking images as the knight tries to save a juggler (Nils Poppe) and his wife (Bibi Andersson) from a death worse than fate.

Hot Bonus: The restoration demonstration is an eye-opener, though I'm disappointed the parodies by Woody Allen and Bill & Ted are not included.

Key Scene: The burning of the child witch.

7th Voyage of Sinbad, The (1958)

Starring: Kerwin Mathews, Kathryn Grant, Torin Thatcher

Directed by: Nathan Juran

A fantasy film for the ages, and it's all about the special effects and creatures created by the immortal Ray Harryhausen, the stop-motion animator working for the first time in color. The hues pop thrillingly on DVD, as does the musical score by Bernard Herrmann. There is a plot: Sinbad (Matthews) is sailing to Baghdad with his princess-bride-to-be (Grant) when a storm throws them into the clutches of a sorcerer (Thatcher), who is being chased by a Cyclops, whose magic lamp with the genie inside has been stolen by the sorcerer, who has also shrunk down the princess to iPod size, who. . . . Oh, who cares? Just watch the magic.

Hot Bonus: A featurette on Harryhausen's Dynamation process.

Key Scene: The sword fight with the skeleton, ripped off decades later in *Pirates of the Caribbean*.

Sex, Lies, and Videotape (1989)

Starring: James Spader, Andie MacDowell, Peter Gallagher, Laura San Giacomo

Directed and written by: Steven Soderbergh

No DVD visual fireworks, just the emotional kind. Written in eight days and shot over five weeks on a meager $1.2 million budget, this film put the juice back into American indie cinema. Soderbergh, then twenty-six, proved himself a writer and director of rare gifts. Filmed on location in Baton Rouge, Louisiana (Soderbergh's hometown), *Sex, Lies, and Videotape* begins with Ann (MacDowell) bitching to her shrink. Though her lawyer husband John (Peter Gallagher) is an inveterate womanizer, Ann claims to be more vexed by the garbage-disposal system and the upcoming visit of a stranger, John's college friend Graham (Spader). Unlike her bartender sister, Cynthia (Laura San Giacomo), who is boffing John on the sly, the gorgeous Ann finds sex overrated. It is left to Spader's Graham to make the others face the truth about one another and themselves. He comes to town with a collection of videotapes he's made over nine years of women confessing intimate sexual secrets. "I'm impotent," he tells Ann. "I can't get an erection in the presence of another person." Ann is intrigued; Cynthia is challenged. In a role of daunting demands, Spader amazes. Soderbergh, a professed movie obsessive, has constructed a loosely autobiographical film in which the key moments occur when a camera clicks off. Savor his triumph.

Hot Bonus: Soderbergh and filmmaker Neil LaBute discuss the issues the film raises in an exceptional commentary track.

Key Scene: Graham persuading the women to sit for his video camera. Formerly a compulsive liar, now filled with self-disgust, Graham has cut himself off from real life; only watching the tapes can arouse him.

Sexy Beast (2001)

Starring: Ben Kingsley, Ray Winstone, Amanda Redman

Directed by: Jonathan Glazer

A DVD transfer that can blind you with its visual and aural perfection. On Spain's Costa del Sol, the sun blazes down on Gary Dove (Winstone), a Cockney gangster, who sits by the pool while wife, Deedee (the trashy and terrific Redman)

hands him a beer. Then, boom! A boulder like something out of *Raiders of the Lost Ark* thunders down from the hills, barely missing Gary and landing in his pool with a tile-cracking crash. The boulder is the least of Gary's problems. It's the arrival of Don Logan (Kingsley) from London that really puts a dent in Gary's paradise. Don wants Gary back in the United Kingdom for one more job. Spouting profanity, staring daggers at any perceived enemy, and talking nuts to himself in a mirror like De Niro in a Cockney *Taxi Driver*, Kingsley creates an unforgettable monster. All credit to Glazer for keeping the script, by Louis Mellis and David Scinto, anchored to character.

Hot Bonus: Kingsley talks about working with first-time feature director Glazer, a boy wonder from commercials and music videos who restores the good name to his breed by trafficking in substance as well as style.

Key Scene: The London bank heist, in which gushing water from a Turkish bath nearly drowns the robbers and their booty in a bank vault.

Shadow of a Doubt (1943)

Starring: Joseph Cotton, Teresa Wright, Hume Cronyn
Directed by: Alfred Hitchcock

Hitchcock's favorite Hitchcock movie, and he's not far wrong. Thornton Wilder's script goes *Our Town* one better by adding a serial killer to the mix in the charming person of Uncle Charlie (Cotton). He comes home to Santa Rosa, California, to see his pretty niece (Wright), also named Charlie, and pick his next victim. Hitchcock has a great time defacing Norman Rockwell America. But Cotton, astoundingly good, goes deeper. His scenes with the terrific Wright have wit and warmth without sacrificing a bit of the terror.

Hot Bonus: Wright remembers Hitchcock.
Key Scene: The final struggle of the two Charlies on a speeding train.

Shadow of the Vampire (2000)

Starring: Willem Dafoe, John Malkovich, Catherine McCormack

Directed by: Elias Merhige

Here are the facts: In 1921, German director F. W. Murnau cast unknown actor Max Schreck to portray the undead Count Orlok in what would become the silent-film classic *Nosferatu*. As screenwriter Steven Katz wickedly sees it, Murnau, played to the creepy max by Malkovich, knew that Schreck (Dafoe) was a real vampire when he hired him, promising him the neck of leading lady Greta Schröder (McCormack) at the end of shooting if Schreck helped Murnau achieve cinematic immortality. It's a deal that most directors today would make in a snap if they could. That's the premise, and an exceptional cast, including Eddie Izzard as a hambone actor, gleefully plays variations on it. But Dafoe goes deeper. With the help of director Merhige, who evokes the silent-film era with a visionary brilliance brought home on the DVD transfer, Dafoe captures the humanity in the monster.

Hot Bonus: Merhige talks about seeing the movie camera as a vampire.
Key Scene: Dafoe advancing on the girl as the camera rolls and then, forgetting he's acting, going right for her pretty white neck.

Shaft (1971)

Starring: Richard Roundtree, Moses Gunn
Directed by: Gordon Parks

That Shaft, he's a bad muth . . . err. It's hard to think back on Parks's seminal blaxploitation film without also hearing Isaac Hayes's Oscar-winning theme in your head. Ya dig? I knew you would. The DVD transfer is not without grain, but the raw look only adds to the effect. Roundtree's John Shaft, besides being a sex machine to all the chicks, is a private eye hired by a Harlem hood (Gunn) to find his kidnapped daughter. The Sam Jackson remake in 2000 sure looked slicker, but this baby has the real cool.

Hot Bonus: A documentary, *Soul in Cinema: Filming Shaft on Location*, shows Parks directing and Hayes and his band jamming on the music.
Key Scene: The opener with Shaft walking out of the subway and onto Forty-second Street (the old, nasty Forty-second Street) with all those X-rated movie marquees and the propulsive Hayes score goosing him along. Indelible.

Shakespeare in Love (Special Edition) (1998)

Starring: Gwyneth Paltrow, Joseph Fiennes, Judi Dench, Ben Affleck

Directed by: John Madden

Oscars all around—Paltrow, Dench, Best Picture. It looked lovely at the multiplex, and it looks ever better on DVD with scene after scene suitable for freeze-framing. Fiennes plays the writer's blocked Bard, unable to finish *Romeo & Juliet* until a woman (Paltrow) disguises herself as a boy to audition for Romeo and gets Will Shakespeare delightfully confused and unblocked. The script by Tom Stoppard and Marc Norman is a literate delight. Paltrow is pure princess, and Dench steals every scene she's in by divine right, playing the queen. Madden directs like a man in love with theater, words, movies, make-believe, and love. Who's arguing?

Hot Bonus: Everyone talks about what a good time they had. For once, I believed them.

Key Scene: Fiennes unraveling Paltrow's boys' clothes to find the female underneath.

Shallow Grave (1994)

Starring: Kerry Fox, Ewan McGregor, Christopher Eccleston

Directed by: Danny Boyle

Three Glasgow flatmates—journalist Alex (McGregor), accountant David (Eccleston) and doctor Juliet (Fox)—are searching for a roommate and finally settle on Hugo (Keith Allen), a would-be novelist. It sounds like a Scottish sitcom, but there's nothing com about what director Boyle and screenwriter John Hodge have in mind. When the trio finds Hugo naked in his bed, dead of a drug overdose, they also find a suitcase full of money. What to do? Keep the cash, which requires slicing up Hugo for easy disposal. That's when everyone's head starts to unravel. Boyle turns the screws of the plot with perverse glee. And the DVD looks and sounds super, given the film's low budget.

Hot Bonus: Production notes, which reveal that Boyle had the actors live together in a rented flat to get the relationships right for the film.

Key Scene: Eccleston sealing himself up, with the money, in the apartment's ceiling and drilling holes to peep at what Fox and McGregor are doing.

Shampoo (1975)

Starring: Warren Beatty, Julie Christie, Goldie Hawn, Lee Grant

Directed by: Hal Ashby

"Want me to do your hair?" asks Beverly Hills hairdresser Beatty of Christie, who indeed does want him to do her. The time is November 4, 1968. Nixon is about to be elected, and the country is in moral freefall. Beatty's stud just wants to have sex with as many of his clients as possible, while pretending to be true to one (Goldie Hawn). He's also doing an older woman (Grant, who won the Oscar for Best Supporting Actress), who asks her husband (the superb Jack Warden) to help him open his own salon, not knowing that Beatty is doing her teen daughter (Carrie Fisher) and her husband is doing Christie. Got that? No matter. Director Ashby, working from a script by Beatty and Robert Towne, deftly orchestrates a hedonistic dance of beautiful people heading toward the abyss. This iconic 1970s sex farce, as much a part of the Watergate era as *All the President's Men*, transfers to DVD with its lewd, blow-dried palette intact.

Hot Bonus: A choice between widescreen and cropped versions of the film. In this case, the cropped version isn't bad at all.

Key Scene: At a Nixon victory party, Christie goes under the table to give Beatty a blow job, announcing her intentions to all her tablemates.

Shane (1953)

Starring: Alan Ladd, Jean Arthur, Van Heflin, Brandon de Wilde

Directed by: George Stevens

A mythic western with director Stevens setting up Shane (Ladd) as a knight who rides onto the Wyoming homestead of Heflin, his wife Arthur, and their young son de Wilde, ready to help them keep their land even if it means using the guns Shane had vowed to put down. The DVD transfer heightens the vistas that helped win an Oscar for cameraman Loyal Griggs. Stevens loads the film with unspoken emotions, such as Arthur's sexual attraction to Shane. This is Ladd's career role, especially in his scenes with de Wilde, whose cry of "Shane, Shane, come back!" still pierces the heart.

Hot Bonus: George Stevens Jr. (the director's son) offers inside info. This full-screen DVD is the way Stevens filmed it. On its initial release, Shane had the tops and bottoms of its picture chopped off to create the illusion that it was shot in widescreen, a format just getting popular at the time.

Key Scene: Shane's shootout with Jack Palance, as villainous a gunslinger as the movies have ever given us.

Shaun of the Dead (2004)

Starring: Simon Pegg, Nick Frost, Kate Ashfield

Directed by: Edgar Wright

Leave it to the Brits to find the joke in being gobbled by zombies. Shaun, played with comic zip by Pegg—he co-wrote the script with director Wright—is a twentyish bloke stuck in soul-sucking North London. Shaun tries to hold on, minus commitment, to his girlfriend (Ashfield), but he hangs happiest at the Winchester Pub, where he and the chubby, game-obsessed Ed (Frost) drink themselves into a stupor. That's why Shaun doesn't recognize the living dead—he looks like one of them. When the telly advises that you must remove the head to kill a zombie, Shaun and Ed bring out bats, shovels, and an LP collection. It turns out that the *Batman* soundtrack album is a handy decapitator. This blast of fright and fun knows that zombies shrieking, "We're coming to get you!" is an irresistible invitation.

Hot Bonus: Extended scenes and outtakes.

Key Scene: When everyone agrees that the pub is the ideal place to stand off against the undead. One catch: To get there through ghoul-clogged streets, they need to pass as zombies. It's the film's hilarity high point.

Shawshank Redemption, The (Deluxe Edition) (1994)

Starring: Morgan Freeman, Tim Robbins

Directed and written by: Frank Darabont

Based on a novella by Stephen King, *Shawshank* refers to a maximum-security prison in Maine, where inmate Andy Dufresne (Robbins), a Shawshank newcomer in 1946, strikes up a twenty-year friendship with a lifer named Red (Freeman). They're both in jail for the Big One: murder. Robbins and Freeman have the juice as actors to make figuring out whether Andy and Red really did it a riveting guessing game, especially if you're a sucker for prison melodramas. Writer Darabont, in his feature-directing debut, doesn't skimp on the caged-bird clichés, sadistic and sentimental. But the everyday agonies of prison life are meticulously laid out by cinematographer Roger Deakins. And the DVD transfer is so good, you can almost feel the frustration and rage seeping into the skin of the inmates.

Hot Bonus: Two documentaries, one detailing the making of the film and the other examining its impact as a Best Picture Oscar nominee.

Key Scene: When Andy, a banker convicted of murdering his wife and her lover, wins permission to expand the prison library by offering financial advice to the Shawshank elite. That includes the sadistic captain of the guards (Clancy Brown) and the fanatically religious warden (Bob Gunton).

Shining, The (Remastered Edition) (1980)

Starring: Jack Nicholson, Shelley Duvall, Danny Lloyd

Directed by: Stanley Kubrick

Stephen King, who never liked the film that Kubrick made of his novel, should grab this richly done DVD and eat his words. Nicholson is dynamite as Jack Torrance, a struggling writer prone to bouts of drinking and depression. Taking a job as winter caretaker of the Overlook Hotel, a summer resort in the Colorado mountains, Jack packs up wife Wendy (Duvall) and son Danny (Lloyd) and battens down the hatches against the storm outside and inside. Kubrick makes cabin fever palpable through music, shadow, and startling camera angles. Those Steadicam shots of Danny riding his bike through the winding corridors, deserted except for the ghosts of murdered children, are astounding. As Jack slowly communes with the evil forces of the hotel against his own family, Kubrick tightens the screws.

Hot Bonus: A documentary from the director's daughter, Vivian Kubrick.

Key Scene: Nicholson takes an axe: "Here's Johnny!"

Shock Corridor (1963)

Starring: Peter Breck, Constance Towers, James Best

Directed by: Samuel Fuller

No one does social satire like Fuller; to him it's a roller-coaster ride into hell. Criterion gives what used to be considered a black-and-white B-movie the A treatment on DVD. The great camerawork of Stanley Cortez really pops on disc. Breck plays a tabloid reporter, hungry for a Pulitzer, who gets himself checked into an asylum by pretending to be hot for his sister (Towers), a stripper who's really his girlfriend. He's investigating a murder, but the madness he encounters (the ills of society in hyperbolized microcosm) turns him loony tunes.

Hot Bonus: Rarely seen dream sequences in color.

Key Scene: The attack on Breck in the nympho ward is Fuller in a nutshell.

Short Cuts
(Two-Disc Special Edition) (1993)

Starring: Julianne Moore, Peter Gallagher, Lyle Lovett, Annie Ross

Directed by: Robert Altman

Altman weaves nine Raymond Carver short stories (plus one narrative poem) and twenty-two principal characters into 189 compulsively watchable minutes that leave you wrung out emotionally but still hungry for more. That's where DVD comes in—it allows you to rewatch and reassess. Carver, who died of lung cancer at fifty in 1988, wrote stories that expressed in plain, blunt language the desperation of ordinary people. His endings weren't happy but random and brutal. Altman saw a kindred spirit. The director and co-writer Frank Barhydt make startling additions, including the image of helicopters' spraying medflies that opens the film and the setting switch from Carver's Pacific Northwest to suburban California. The actors are solid gold, with special mention going to Jennifer Jason Leigh selling phone sex while diapering her baby; Lovett making something surprising of a lonely baker; Gallagher chainsawing everything in his ex-wife's house; Moore, naked from the waist down, telling her husband why she cheated; and Ross pouring out her bitterness in songs by Elvis Costello and Bono. They make this dark mirror on the world not hard to recognize as our own.

Hot Bonus: A making-of documentary that gets to the heart of what bonds Altman and Carver.

Key Scene: Fred Ward and his pals (Buck Henry and Huey Lewis) have just walked four hours to their favorite fishing spot when they spot the naked body of a beautiful girl floating lifeless in the water. They decide to leave her there for another day and keep fishing. She was dead, wasn't she?

Showgirls
(VIP Edition) (1995)

Starring: Elizabeth Berkley, Gina Gershon, Kyle MacLachlan

Directed by: Paul Verhoeven

Guilty pleasures don't come any guiltier than this. But why hide your enthusiasm for a DVD that waves its freak flag high, along with its NC-17 rating? Berkley, a decent actress stuck in career quicksand, is still trying to live down her role as Nomi Malone, a lethal looker who hits Vegas to make it as a showgirl, but first must make it with the johns on the lap-dancing circuit, get it on a with a bisexual show star (Gershon), recite appalling dialogue by Joe Eszterhas, and break someone's leg (not for good luck). Verhoeven directs with a real taste for sleaze, and the DVD delivers.

Hot Bonus: Buying the VIP Edition gets you *Showgirls* shot glasses, a deck of cards, party games, pasties and a blindfold (don't), and the film itself.

Key Scene: Berkley and pole. I rest my case.

Shrek
(Two-Disc Special Edition) (2001)

Starring: The voices of Mike Myers, Cameron Diaz, Eddie Murphy

Directed by: Andrew Adamson and Vicky Jenson

Based on a children's book by William Steig, the film won the first Oscar for Best Animated Feature. Shrek, voiced by Myers with a Scottish burr, is a big, green, stinking ogre who sticks close to his home in the swamps to avoid people who call him a big, green, stinking ogre. But then he rescues feisty Princess Fiona (Diaz) from a fire-breathing lady dragon who has her mojo going for Shrek's pal Donkey (brayed to comic perfection by Murphy). What matters about *Shrek* is the wonder of the photorealistic animation. Only God can make a tree, but a million digital polygons come damn close.

Hot Bonus: There's eleven hours worth, but go for the Easter Egg on Disc 2, accessed by finding Play and moving the Up Arrow before hitting Enter. Presto! You're in the Swamp Karaoke Party.

Key Scene: Shrek takes his first mud bath.

Shrek 2
(Special Edition) (2004)

Starring: The voices of Mike Myers, Cameron Diaz, Antonio Banderas

Directed by: Andrew Adamson, Kelly Asbury, and Conrad Vernon

Double the fun of the original, the sequel is also more technically assured. The DVD is glorious proof. Shrek (Myers) and his bride (Diaz) are called to the kingdom of Far Far Away—a sendup of Beverly Hills, with stores such as Farbucks and

Old Knavery—to meet Fiona's royal parents, royally voiced by John Cleese and Julie Andrews. Both are shocked that their daughter has married Shrek and turned full-time ogre herself. Now Dad conspires with Fairy Godmother, voiced by *Ab Fab*'s Jennifer Saunders, to kill Shrek. Call me twisted, but it's hard not to feel crazy love for an animated movie that pictures Cinderella's stepsister as bartending gorgon who offers tips on where to find a hit man and talks in a voice of pure Larry King gravel (King himself did the vocals).

Hot Bonus: The tech of *Shrek 2* is an insider's view of animated magic.

Key Scene: Anything with Puss In Boots, the feline assassin voiced by Banderas. With his Spanish accent and bedroom eyes for man, woman, and beast, Puss charms everyone except Donkey, who huffs that "the position of annoying talking animal is already taken."

Sid and Nancy (1986)

Starring: Gary Oldman, Chloe Webb
Directed by: Alex Cox

The dark side of the punk rock dream starring Oldman as doomed Sex Pistol bassist Sid Vicious and Webb as his punk muse, Nancy Spungen. They're a fabulous disaster, one of the screen's sickest romances. And the DVD transfer luxuriates in the lurid sights and sounds. Original title: *Love Kills.*

Hot Bonus: Commentary from Oldman and Webb, and a rare telephone interview from Vicious himself.

Key Scene: Vicious, near the end of his life, plays the clown for a jeering New York crowd, and we catch a glimpse of Johnny Rotten, sitting unnoticed and alone, in tears as he watches his old mate burn out.

Sideways (2004)

Starring: Paul Giamatti, Virginia Madsen, Thomas Haden Church, Sandra Oh
Directed by: Alexander Payne

Raise your glasses to a vintage American comedy that gets damn near everything right. The same goes for the nuance-alert DVD. Adapting

Rex Pickett's novel, director Payne co-wrote an Oscar-winning script with Jim Taylor that shapes dialogue into classic comic contours with the help of a quartet of actors who qualify as a cinematic dream team. Miles (Giamatti), a failed novelist, is taking his best pal, Jack (Haden Church), a former soap star, on a last fling before Miles serves as best man at Jack's L.A. wedding. Their destination is California's Santa Ynez Valley, where wine-snob Miles hopes to drink himself sideways on the local vino and wine-idiot Jack hopes to get his "bone smooched" by hottie waitresses. Enter Madsen as the wine-obsessed Maya, and Oh as Stephanie, a single mom who pours wine for tourists. *Sideways* is drunk on wine: its allure, its fragility, its vocabulary. Giamatti, a god among American character actors, has never been better. That he didn't win a Best Actor Oscar is bad enough; that he wasn't even nominated is a permanent blot on the Academy. Check back in a few years, and my guess is this special occasion of a film will have aged beautifully.

Hot Bonus: Giamatti and Haden Church have fun reliving the movie.

Key Scene: Payne gives Madsen and Giamatti the film's most transfixing moment—not in the novel—in which Miles sees himself as a temperamental pinot noir and Maya praises wine for how it evolves, gains complexity, and peaks.

Signs (2002)

Starring: Mel Gibson, Joaquin Phoenix
Directed by: M. Night Shyamalan

Here's the thing about Shyamalan: Any hack can work you over. Shyamalan turns the goosepimple genre on its empty head and fills it with emotionally bruised characters who add up to more than body count. Gibson gives one of his best and most surprising performances as Graham Hess, a Pennsylvania minister who turned in his collar six months earlier after blaming God for letting his wife die in an accident. Now Graham wakes up in a cold sweat. He races outside looking for his kids (Rory Culkin and Abigail Breslin). He finds them in a cornfield, staring in frightened awe. Us, too. Crop circles, huge ones, have been carved into the field. Is it a prank or a sign of something supernatural, maybe even an alien invasion? Something is moving out there (the Dolby Digital sound wraps you up in it), leaving Graham's younger sibling Merrill (a impressive Phoenix) to watch his rock of a brother crumble into a despairing crisis of faith.

Hot Bonus: Shyamalan takes you on a complete journey, from the film's inception as an idea to its marketing campaign.

Key Scene: A basement plunged into darkness and a little girl saying simply, "The monster is outside my room—can I have a glass of water?"

Silence of the Lambs, The (Special Edition) (1991)

Starring: Jodie Foster, Anthony Hopkins, Brooke Smith

Directed by: Jonathan Demme

Demme's Oscar-winning Best Picture comes in several DVD versions. Go with Criterion, which does the movie proud and packs it with extras. Based on Thomas Harris's best seller, the movie slams you like a sudden blast of bone-chilling terror. To catch a serial killer, F.B.I. trainee Clarice Starling (Oscar-winner Foster) uses another serial killer, Dr. Hannibal Lecter (Oscar-winner Hopkins), a former psychiatrist imprisoned in a Baltimore asylum for carving up nine people and cooking his favorite bits. Dr. Lecter, known as Hannibal the Cannibal, prides himself on having once eaten the liver of a census taker with some fava beans and a nice Chianti. You know the rest, and if you don't, just go with Demme's flow.

Hot Bonus: All the commentaries shine, but Foster is the most memorable in discussing her interpretation of Starling as a female warrior.

Key Scene: Starling's first sight of Lecter. Standing stone still, his close-cropped head tilted ever so slightly and the beams from his cold eyes sharp enough to pierce glass, he looms like a lion in a prison cell. It's the most frightening movie entrance ever, and Hopkins doesn't move a muscle.

Simple Plan, A (1998)

Starring: Bill Paxton, Billy Bob Thornton, Bridget Fonda, Brent Briscoe

Directed by: Sam Raimi

A small plane drops out of the sky into the Minnesota snow—one of the many visual stunners

on the DVD. Hardworking Hank Mitchell (Paxton), his dim brother Jacob (Thornton), and Jacob's boozer friend Lou (Briscoe) find the plane and $4 million inside. Simple plan: they should keep the cash. Hank's wife (Fonda) suggests they leave five hundred thousand dollars in the plane to avoid suspicion. Then greed sets in. Director Raimi, working from a script by novelist Scott B. Smith, generates deep psychological tension. Thornton was justly Oscar-nominated, but the whole cast is pitch-perfect.

Hot Bonus: A trailer that actually gets the feeling of the film right.

Key Scene: Thornton and Paxton's final confrontation in the woods.

Sin City (Two-Disc Special Edition/Recut and Extended) (2005)

Starring: Mickey Rourke, Bruce Willis, Clive Owen, Jessica Alba

Directed by: Robert Rodriguez and Frank Miller

The worst thing I can say about this savage, sexy, and ferociously funny screen translation of three stories from Frank Miller's *Sin City* series of graphic novels is that it's too much of a good thing. It makes your eyes go *boing* so often, you can use it as a demonstration-quality DVD. Shot by Rodriguez in black-and-white with the occasional splash of color from, say, a whore's lip gloss, the film mixes hard-boiled pulp fiction, 1940s film noir, and the dazzling monochrome of Miller's graphic design to explore the dark night of the soul. There are three overlapping stories, and Willis and Owen do fine by theirs. But Rourke is flat-out sensational as Marv, an ex-con with a Frankenstein jaw line who wakes up next to a dead hooker (Jaime King) and vows revenge, searching for "a soul to send screaming into hell."

Hot Bonus: Besides the restored, unrated footage, there's a behind-the-scenes thingie that explains how Rodriguez quit the Directors' Guild when it ruled that he couldn't co-direct with Miller, and then rubbed salt in the wound by bringing in pal Quentin Tarantino to direct a scene in a car featuring a talking corpse with a gun wedged in his forehead.

Key Scene: A foul-smelling, canary-yellow demon (Nick Stahl) makes Willis ball-ripping mad. "I take his weapons from him, both of them," says Willis as testicles are flung at the screen, and we wonder if the film escaped an NC-17 rating because the bastard's blood looks like cartoon custard.

Singin' in the Rain (Two-Disc Collector's Edition) (1952)

Starring: Gene Kelly, Debbie Reynolds, Donald O'Connor, Jean Hagen

Directed by: Gene Kelly and Stanley Donen

Near the summit of movie musicals, and you won't see it looking or sounding better than you do on this DVD special. Kelly plays a silent-movie hero making an easier transition to talkies than his siren-voiced co-star Hagen. The solution: have ingénue Reynolds dub Hagen's vocals. It's up to Kelly and pal O'Connor to make Reynolds a star on her own. Written by Betty Comden and Adolph Green, the plot is just an excuse to string together great songs by Arthur Freed and Nacio Herb Brown. Kelly and co-director Donen work miracles. O'Connor stops the show with "Make 'Em Laugh," and Hagen steals the acting honors. But just wait till Kelly starts dancing.

Hot Bonus: A retrospective documentary in which nearly everyone talks.

Key Scene: Kelly sings and dances the title song, splashing through puddles and into screen legend.

Singles (1992)

Starring: Matt Dillon, Bridget Fonda, Campbell Scott, Kyra Sedgwick

Directed and written by: Cameron Crowe

Twentysomethings, living in the same Seattle apartment building, fall in and out of love. It's a setup for a sitcom that Crowe transforms into gold through acute observation and a knack for blending fun and feeling. Fonda, a waitress considering breast augmentation, hooks up with Dillon, a rock musician with no talent for music. Sedgwick, who studies the environment, bonds with Scott, who studies traffic patterns. And so on, until the Seattle grunge scene set to music by Paul Westerberg of the Replacements comes alive on screen as it has not done before or since. It's a gift.

Hot Bonus: A deleted scene featuring talking magazine covers, freely giving romantic advice, should never have been cut.

Key Scene: A delusional Dillon posing by the grave of Jimi Hendrix.

Sisters (Special Edition) (1973)

Starring: Margot Kidder, Jennifer Salt

Directed by: Brian De Palma

Criterion puts its DVD restoration magic to work on De Palma's Hitchcock-like thriller, which even features a jangling score by Hitchcock regular Bernard Herrmann. Kidder takes on the dual role of Siamese twins, one of whom is a murderous psycho according to a reporter (Salt) who claims to have seen her in action. In a *Rear Window* touch, the reporter lives in the apartment across the way. The film is dated but still dazzling as a De Palma exercise in style, and there is no arguing with Kidder in sweet or sour mode.

Hot Bonus: A rare study of Siamese twins.

Key Scene: The "surprise" appearance of the other sister.

Sixteen Candles (High School Reunion Collection) (1984)

Starring: Molly Ringwald, Anthony Michael Hall, Michael Schoeffling

Directed by: John Hughes

Since the 1980s films written by Hughes, from *The Breakfast Club* to *Pretty in Pink*, are currently the retro rage at film festivals and midnight screenings, you might want to check out the teen comedy that started his career as a director. The DVD transfer looks pretty in every color. Ringwald, about to turn sixteen, pines for senior Schoeffling, but is stalked by Hall—killer funny as Ted the Geek. Worse, her entire family has forgotten her birthday in their excitement over her sister's wedding. This, right here, is when Hughes became the Neil Simon of teen angst.

Hot Bonus: The movie has been remastered with the original music. Financial or legal reasons forced the substitution of some songs ("Young Americans," "Kajagoogoo") in TV or tape versions.

Key Scene: Ringwald finding her scantily clad grandparents sleeping in her bedroom. Hughes sets the moment to the theme from *The Twilight Zone*.

Sixth Sense, The (Special Edition) (1999)

Starring: Bruce Willis, Haley Joel Osment, Toni Collette

Directed and written by: M. Night Shyamalan

"I see dead people," weird little duck Osment famously tells child psychologist Willis. The studio saw dollars—live ones—as Shyamalan's haunting film grew to become the most successful thriller of all time. The DVD transfer thrums with enveloping images (those people hanging in the kid's school) and DTS sound. Willis is outstanding as the shrink trying to help this eight-year-old boy deal with his divorced mother (Collette) and the ghosts who just won't shut up around him. The disc proves that Shyamalan's signature film is about more than a twist ending.

Hot Bonus: There's a great Easter Egg if you go to the Bonus Materials, looks for a jewelry box, hit Enter, and find a video: a short horror film that Shyamalan made when he was just eleven years old.

Key Scene: Osment relating a comforting message to Collette from her dead mother, just after a ghostly apparition with the back of her head blown off slides past Collette's car window looking mad as hell.

Slap Shot (Special Edition) (1977)

Starring: Paul Newman, Michael Ontkean, Lindsay Crouse, Jennifer Warren
Directed by: George Roy Hill

Player-coach Newman incites his third-rate hockey team to become storm-trooping maniacs. His dialogue is nearly as blue as his eyes, but the team and the movie end up winners. Here's another box-office reject that deserves to find a new life on DVD, where it looks ready for the ice and its profane language can run free. Newman's performance, which failed to win even a nomination from the Academy, remains one of his best. Just watch him lock horns with Ontkean as a rulebook player who objects to Newman bringing in the three Hanson brothers, who play as dirty as it gets.

Hot Bonus: Puck talk with the Hansons, who played minor league hockey.

Key Scene: The Hansons starting a fight even before the National Anthem.

Sleeper (1973)

Starring: Woody Allen, Diane Keaton, John Beck
Directed and co-written by: Woody Allen

The Woodman plays Miles Monroe, a Manhattan health store owner who gets zapped two hundred years into the future, where he must do battle with a big giant nose. Don't expect *Zelig*-tinged satire. This stylish farce—looking futuristically fresh on DVD—is more like a Bob Hope movie packed with one-liners: "My brain is my second favorite organ," says Miles, who hooks up with Keaton after disguising himself as her new house robot. Says she: "It's hard to believe you haven't had sex in two hundred years." Says he: "Two hundred four, if you count my marriage."

Hot Bonus: Production notes reveal that the film's witty costumes are the work of Joel Schumacher, who would soon become a director himself.

Key Scene: Woody's dazed joy as he exits the Orgasmatron, a machine where sex takes place without messing with human contact.

Slightly Scarlet (1956)

Starring: Arlene Dahl, Rhonda Fleming, John Payne
Directed by: Allan Dwan

Any DVD transfer that can capture the flaming tresses of redheads Dahl and Fleming belongs in the Technicolor time capsule. You can almost see the fire rise off your screen as Dahl, a kleptomaniac parolee, puts the moves on Payne to seduce him away from her goodie-goodie sister Fleming. Based on a novel of urban corruption by *Double Indemnity* author James M. Cain, the film resonates with director Dwan's noirish moods and compositions, often cited as a major influence on Martin Scorsese.

Hot Bonus: Mystery writer Max Allan Collins puts the film in context.

Key Scene: Dahl, all in black, getting picked up outside of prison and radiating enough come-on carnality to singe the screen.

Sling Blade (Two-Disc Director's Cut) (1996)

Starring: Billy Bob Thornton, Dwight Yoakam, Lucas Black, John Ritter
Directed and written by: Billy Bob Thornton

Thornton's screenplay won the Oscar, but what keeps you riveted is his nominated performance as the mentally challenged Karl Childers, back home in Arkansas after spending twenty-five years in a state mental hospital for killing his mother and her abusive lover. The weapon? "Some folks call it a Kaiser blade," he says of the instrument he used to kill the duo. "I call it a sling blade, uh-huh." Befriended by a boy (Black), whose widowed mother (Natalie Canerday) is involved with the belligerent Vaughn (a scarily effective Yoakam), Karl finds himself in a situation where history is likely to repeat itself. Thornton's direction is full of grace notes, particularly in his handling of the gay neighbor, beautifully played by the late Ritter.

Hot Bonus: The Director's Cut is a new anamorphic widescreen transfer with a 5.1 surround mix that adds about fifteen minutes of footage back into the film, and about seven hours of extras, including Thornton's commentary on the film and the new scenes he restored.

Key Scene: The confrontation between Karl and the bullying Vaughn simmers with violence, and the extended versions of the scene included here deepens the motivations of both characters.

Snatch
(Two-Disc Special Edition) (2000)

Starring: Brad Pitt, Benicio Del Toro, Dennis Farina

Directed by: Guy Ritchie

A crime caper that improves on Ritchie's testosterone-fueled 1998 debut, *Lock, Stock and Two Smoking Barrels*. The plot is a jumble, but a merry one. An eighty-six-carat diamond is stolen from a jeweler in Belgium. Del Toro plays a stylish Jewish jewel thief who is charged with delivering the diamond to Avi (Farina), his boss in New York. But when Del Toro stops off at a London bookie joint to bet on a boxing match run by a Russian gangster (Rade Serbedzija), the sting kicks in. Pitt has more fun than anybody as Mickey O'Neil, the boxer in question, an Irish gypsy mama's boy with an indecipherable accent on which Pitt plays hilarious variations. Despite dialogue that often requires a dictionary of British slang to negotiate, Ritchie makes a party of this gathering of geezers, pikers, and "mincey faggoty balls." The killer soundtrack shifts without shame from Oasis's "Fuckin' in the Bushes" to a snippet of "Hava Nagila."

Hot Bonus: A subtitling option for Pitt's dialogue.

Key Scene: What happens when the crooks think a dog has swallowed the diamond—ouch!

Snow White and the Seven Dwarfs
(Two-Disc Platinum Edition) (1937)

Starring: The voices of Adriana Caselotti, Harry Stockwell, Lucille LaVerne

Directed by: David Hand

The first Disney animated feature, as influential as any film ever made, is transferred to DVD with an unrivaled eye for what miracles can be achieved in restoring a classic to visual and aural

freshness. Whether or not you care about Snow White and the seven determined little men who whistle while they work day and night just for her to make sure that someday Ms. White's prince will come, this is a landmark movie and a landmark DVD.

Hot Bonus: From original storyboards to the film's restoration, this DVD package has all the details covered.

Key Scene: The Wicked Queen asking, "Mirror, mirror on the wall, who is the fairest of them all?" and not getting the answer she wants.

Soldier's Story, A (1984)

Starring: Howard E. Rollins, Denzel Washington, Adolph Caesar

Directed by: Norman Jewison

Jewison's screen version of Charles Fuller's Pulitzer Prize–winning play has looked so faded for so many years on TV prints that the crystal clarity of the DVD transfer is the equivalent of giving the movie a second life. Set at an army base in Louisiana near the end of World War II, the film opens with the murder of a black drill sergeant (all hail the Oscar-nominated Caesar), an aging, bantamweight bundle of muscle and malice who is contemptuous of his white superiors for keeping his black platoon functioning as a baseball team and out of the war. The film continues in flashback as a black army attorney (Rollins is outstanding) interrogates white and black suspects on the base, including Washington, all fire and ice as an embittered soldier.

Hot Bonus: Jewison talks about the problems he had getting the film made and the help he received from Bill Clinton, then the governor of Arkansas.

Key Scene: Caesar raising hackles, blaming his own race for the bigotry of white people: "You know the damage one ignorant Negro can do?"

Some Like It Hot
(Special Edition) (1959)

Starring: Marilyn Monroe, Tony Curtis, Jack Lemmon, Joe E. Brown

Directed by: Billy Wilder

For all the trouble Wilder had directing Monroe in his Roaring Twenties comedy classic, her performance as Sugar Kane, running wild as the singer in an all-girl band, is her most iconic. I'm not forgetting *The Seven-Year Itch* in which a gust from a subway grating lifted her skirt, but that's the only moment from that 1955 sex farce you remember. You remember everything about *Some*

Like It Hot, especially Monroe's byplay with Lemmon and Curtis, who go undercover as female musicians to escape gangsters. Curtis also disguises himself as a playboy with a Cary Grant accent to woo Monroe, whose bad luck with men ("I always get the fuzzy end of the lollipop") has driven her to drink. But it's the Oscar-nominated Lemmon who steals the picture. He gets so deep into drag that he believes he's a girl. The black-and-white DVD transfer is just like the movie: perfect.

Hot Bonus: Curtis looking back on the movie, and denying ever having said that kissing Monroe was like kissing Hitler.

Key Scene: Lemmon doing the tango with millionaire Joe E. Brown and then accepting his proposal. "Why would a guy want to marry a guy?" Curtis asks. Answers Lemmon: "Security."

Something Wild (1986)

Starring: Melanie Griffith, Jeff Daniels, Ray Liotta
Directed by: Jonathan Demme

Grab this brightly colored DVD at your own risk. You enter a funhouse and exit through chamber of horrors. The "something wild" of the title is Griffith. No sooner does this cunning cupcake meet a married yuppie exec (Daniels) at a New York diner than she's driving him off to a hot-sheets motel where she handcuffs him to a bed for a sexual workout. Just when you think you have the whole thing figured out, director Demme and screenwriter E. Max Frye throw in a toolbox full of monkey wrenches. The most surprising is Liotta in a smashing turn as Griffith's psycho of an ex-con husband. What started as a carnal comedy shifts into violent domestic drama. Demme resists easy categorization. Follow him anywhere.

Hot Bonus: The widescreen DVD transfer is the major reward.

Key Scene: Griffith taking Daniels to her high school reunion.

Something's Gotta Give (2003)

Starring: Jack Nicholson, Diane Keaton, Keanu Reeves, Amanda Peet
Directed by: Nancy Meyers

Keaton, Oscar nominated and looking smashing at fifty-seven, lands her sexiest, wittiest role in years as Erica Barry, a divorced playwright who has learned to do without men. Keaton nails every laugh and nuance in this tart, terrific romantic comedy from writer-director Meyers. It's a pleasure to watch Nicholson hand her the show.

Nicholson is hilarious as Harry Sanborn, a Viagra-popping record-company honcho (hip-hop, yet) who prides himself on never dating a babe over thirty—that includes Erica's daughter (a delicious Peet). It's only after Harry suffers a heart attack at Erica's beach house that he starts seeing her with flirty eyes. Even Harry's doctor (a relaxed, warmly funny Reeves) starts hitting on Erica. And Keaton's expression when she realizes both men are hot for her is a thing of beauty.

Hot Bonus: Meyers talks to Keaton, who is funny and touching, and with Nicholson, who is surprisingly serious and informative about his process.

Key Scene: Nicholson's reaction when he runs into a naked Keaton at her beach house defines comic timing.

Sophie's Choice (1982)

Starring: Meryl Streep, Kevin Kline, Peter MacNicol
Directed by: Alan J. Pakula

William Styron's best-selling novel was both overwhelming and overwrought. Pakula's faithful film version (he also wrote the script) shows the same strengths and weaknesses. But in Streep, Pakula finds an actress to make such criticism seem like nitpicking. Streep's Oscar-winning performance as Sophie, a Polish-Catholic survivor of Auschwitz who takes refuge in Brooklyn from the dark secrets of her past, shows uncanny emotional range, not to mention an unerring Polish accent. Kline brings charm and complexity to Nathan, an anguished Jew who befriends and berates Sophie in an all-consuming passion. As the film's narrator, Stingo, MacNicol spouts Styronisms ("In making love she was beating back death") better left unspoken. Even when Nestor Almendros's camera bathes Streep's face in shadow, the feelings come through. Streep, as this DVD proves, is lit from within.

Hot Bonus: Pakula talking frankly about his work with the actors.

Key Scene: The concentration camp sequence, shot in the starkest black-and-white, in which Sophie is forced to make her wrenching choice.

Sorrow and the Pity, The (Two-Disc Special Edition) (1970)

Directed by: Marcel Ophüls

A history lesson that strikes like lightning. Over four hours long, the Ophüls documentary does more than chronicle the small French city of Clermont-Ferrand during the Nazi occupation. It uses in-the-field interviews and newsreel clips about who collaborated and who resisted to re-create with shocking immediacy a time and a place. Ophüls records these memories and, when necessary, challenges them. The DVD transfer of this black-and-white document is far from perfect, but its rawness is its power.

Hot Bonus: A trailer that can barely suggest a subject so vast.

Key Scene: A French aristocrat casually confesses that "we were all a little thrilled by Hitler's show; it was like Cecil B. DeMille." But Britain's Anthony Eden provides another perspective: "One who has not suffered the horrors of an occupying power has no right to judge a nation that has."

South Park: Bigger, Longer & Uncut (1999)

Starring: The voices of Trey Parker and Matt Stone

Directed and co-written by: Trey Parker and Matt Stone

It's odd how the best musical of the last several decades involves Saddam Hussein boffing Satan. But that's Parker and Stone for you. Not content with outraging television with a *South Park* series featuring foul-mouthed third graders Stan, Kyle, Kenny, and Cartman, the co-directors have foisted their comic irreverence on the big screen. Bless them for that and for a DVD transfer that does full justice to this animated assault on a world of Disney dimness. Of course, the parents of South Park blame Canada for their mountain town kids trying to stop the persecution of Terrance and Philip—stars of *Asses of Fire*—in the name of free speech.

Hot Bonus: Three trailers, one of which takes on Disney directly.

Key Scene: The antiprofanity singalong, "It's Easy, MMMKay," which even tops "Uncle F**ker" for hummable perversity.

Soylent Green (1973)

Starring: Charlton Heston, Edward G. Robinson, Leigh Taylor-Young

Directed by: Richard Fleischer

An ultimate sci-fi cautionary fable for people who watch what they eat. It's 2022 and Heston is tracking a murderer on the overcrowded and polluted streets of the Big Apple and sharing a room with Robinson (the great ham in his film farewell). Like everyone else, they nosh on artificial food called Soylent Green, with Robinson waxing nostalgic for the good old days when a man could chew real celery. You may see where this is heading, but Fleischer still springs scary surprises, none scarier than a view of the future (check those colors on the DVD) from a 1970s perspective.

Hot Bonus: A documentary on the world of Soylent Green.

Key Scene: Heston being dragged away to meet his fate, screaming, "Soylent Green is . . ." You fill in the blank.

Spartacus (Two-Disc Special Edition) (1960)

Starring: Kirk Douglas, Peter Ustinov, Jean Simmons, Laurence Olivier

Directed by: Stanley Kubrick

Kubrick's thunderous epic of a 73–71 B.C. slave rebellion against ancient Rome comes to DVD restored by Criterion to its former glory, despite the director's disowning of the piece because he didn't control it. As the producer, Douglas reigned supreme. As Spartacus, the gladiator leader of the slave revolt, Douglas also looms like colossus with his clenched jaw and animal ferocity. But that doesn't stop a wily supporting cast from carving out their piece of the pie. Ustinov won an Oscar as the head of a gladiator school, Charles Laughton jaws delightfully as a senator, Simmons flirts sexily as Spartacus's slave love, and Olivier has a bisexual ball as the ambitious Crassus, with one eye on Simmons and the other on Tony Curtis as a singer of songs (their bath scene, in which Curtis is asked if he prefers snakes or snails, is restored for the DVD). Credit Douglas for fighting to hire blacklisted screenwriter Dalton Trumbo, who saw Spartacus as a timeless symbol of protest against oppression.

Hot Bonus: A "how'd they do that?" on the film's spectacular restoration.

Key Scene: Each slave risking his life to stand up and proclaim, "I'm Spartacus," rather than give up their leader to certain crucifixion.

Speed (Two-Disc Special Edition) (1994)

Starring: Keanu Reeves, Sandra Bullock, Dennis Hopper, Jeff Daniels

Directed by: Jan De Bont

A DVD with all the bells and whistles to up the rush factor. It's morning drive time in Los Angeles as a packed bus heads for the freeway. In a hideout, mad bomber Hopper (going full-tilt) phones

SWAT cop Jack Traven (Reeves) with a perverse pop quiz: "There's a bomb on the bus. Once the bus goes fifty miles per hour, the bomb is armed. If it drops below fifty, the bus blows up. Whaddya do, Jack?" It's *Die Hard* on a bus, with Reeves hoping on board to play savior. First-time director De Bont performs stunt marvels. But while Reeves and Hopper play a battle of wits, Bullock drives off with the picture. As Annie, a passenger whom Jack puts behind the wheel when the bus driver is shot, Bullock makes us believe the impossible and, better, makes us care. Jack and Annie even manage to strike up a convincing romance at hyperspeed and without taking their eyes off the road.

Hot Bonus: Producer Mack Gordon and screenwriter Graham Yost go at each other and the film with rare irreverence for a commentary track.

Key Scene: Bullock flooring the gas pedal to clear a fifty-foot gap in the freeway, then hurtling into city traffic for a nerve-rattling demolition derby.

Spider-Man
(Two-Disc Deluxe Edition) (2002)

Starring: Tobey Maguire, Kirsten Dunst, James Franco, Willem Dafoe

Directed by: Sam Raimi

DVD nirvana. The unlikely superhero that Stan Lee created at Marvel Comics in 1962 makes a perfect fit for Maguire, even if a stuntman squeezed into Spidey drag for the dangerous feats that aren't computer generated. Maguire's substantial accomplishment isn't acrobatic; he builds a real character out of the sketch that is Peter Parker, an orphan from Queens, New York. Peter has a high school geek's sense of the universe: he's getting screwed out of the good stuff, especially the teen angel next door, Mary Jane Watson (Dunst, taking adorable to a sexy

new dimension). Peter is the Average Joe incarnate. Even after that mutant spider bites him and he starts climbing walls, Peter still can't make the move that would get him into Mary Jane's pants. He feels resentful when his rich friend Harry (a brooding Franco) horns in on her, but says nothing. And Harry's dad, the scientist-mogul Norman Osborn (Dafoe), ignores him while staging shouting matches with his villainous alter ego, the Green Goblin. Some of the CGI isn't so hot, and the Goblin's mask looks like party plastic. But Raimi counters by showing a New York crowd booing the Goblin with a moving, post-9/11 fervor. Then there's the little things that float this $139 million balloon, including the upside-down kiss when Mary Jane slowly pulls down Spidey's mask for a smacker and nearly strips his face naked before he leaps away.

Hot Bonus: The material on the evolution of the comic book beats the strictly promotional commentary.

Key Scene: Peter testing his powers with small skips and jumps until he is leaping across rooftops defines Raimi's style: slow build, huge payoff.

Spider-Man 2
(Two-Disc Special Edition) (2004)

Starring: Tobey Maguire, Kirsten Dunst, James Franco, Alfred Molina

Directed by: Sam Raimi

My fear was that the follow-up would just repeat itself—built-in pressure for a hit that grossed $403 million to become the fifth-biggest box-office draw of all time. Instead, we get a sequel that one-ups the original. The computer effects are better. Ditto the widescreen camerawork and the DTS sound—all of which comes through powerfully on the DVD. Maguire gives us a sweaty and insecure Peter Parker, who chucks his Spidey costume when his powers fail him. It's an identity issue, but Peter thinks maybe he should just get it on with Mary Jane Watson (the ever-delicious Dunst) instead of mooning after her while she falls for an astronaut (Daniel Gillies). That's the setup for a sequel of twisted thrills and sly surprises (Spidey gets unmasked!) that lets director Raimi stage big-action moments. But the film's distinction is the love story that

Maguire and Dunst play with ravishing, romantic gravity. And let's hear it for the villain. Molina excels as a scientist gone mad when the mechanical tentacles he wears for a fusion experiment take over his brain and he becomes Doc Ock. Franco adds dimension to Harry, Peter's rich, tormented pal who uncovers secrets about the death of his goblin father. So what if it's a lure for *Spider-Man 3?* I'm in.

Hot Bonus: Sift through a daunting ten hours of new content to find the blooper reel—it's a hoot.

Key Scene: Spider-Man stopping a runaway train.

Spirited Away (Two-Disc Special Edition) (2001)

Starring: The voices of Daveigh Chase, Michael Chiklis, Lauren Holly

Directed by: Hayao Miyazaki

A ten-year-old girl, Chihiro (voiced by Chase), freaked out over moving to a new neighborhood with her parents (Chiklis and Holly), gets lost in an abandoned amusement park where Mom and Dad are transformed into pigs and Chihiro is left alone to explore a bathhouse where the gods come to play and bedevil interlopers. Winner of the Oscar for Best Animated Feature, *Spirited Away* is an embarrassment of comic, dramatic, and transporting riches from Japanese master Miyazaki.

Hot Bonus: *The Art of Spirited Away* offers ways of interpreting the subtext of the film.

Key Scene: Chihiro takes on the god of Stink.

Splash (Special Edition) (1984)

Starring: Tom Hanks, Daryl Hannah, John Candy, Eugene Levy

Directed by: Ron Howard

Hannah plays a mermaid who isn't little or regulation Disney. After rescuing Hanks when he takes a spill into the waters off of Cape Cod, she grows legs—long and lovely ones—and has sex with the guy in his bathtub. Good news: Age hasn't withered the charm of Howard's romantic comedy. The DVD delivers its colors with delicacy and warmth. Hannah is a luminous delight. And even if it takes a bit of adjustment to see the Oscar-laden Hanks as a callow youth, he does it well. Says Hanks after a scientist (Levy) exposes his sweetie's secret: "All my life I've been waiting for someone, and when I find her, she's a fish."

Hot Bonus: The audition tapes of Hanks and Hannah.

Key Scene: Hannah in a restaurant eating a live lobster, shell and all.

Splendor in the Grass (1961)

Starring: Natalie Wood, Warren Beatty, Pat Hingle, Barbara Loden

Directed by: Elia Kazan

Sexual repression finds its most haunting screen expression in Kazan's film of William Inge's original script about two teens fighting their natural urges while growing up, as Inge did, in Kansas, circa 1925. Deanie, played by a tremulous Wood in a performance that should have won her the Oscar for which she was nominated, loves Bud (Beatty in his screen debut) to the point of worship. Wood and Beatty make their carnal attraction palpable. But Deanie's mother (Audrey Christie) is a moral scourge. And wedlock is the last thing Bud's wealthy father (Hingle) wants for his strapping son, when Yale and easy women, like Bud's nympho sister (Loden, the future Mrs. Kazan), are out there for the taking. Bud's desertion drives Deanie to a suicide attempt and a breakdown. Her return to find a measure of peace is as close as this powerfully moving film comes to a happy ending.

Hot Bonus: Having a widescreen transfer, free of digital artifacts, makes up for the shameful lack of extras for this classic film by a great director.

Key Scene: Deanie's last visit to Bud, now happily married to an Italian waitress (Zohra Lampert). Looking virginal in a white dress and hat, Deanie recalls the Wordsworth poem she read in class, whose meaning she now understands: "Though nothing can bring back the hour/of splendor in the grass/of glory in the flower/we will grieve not/but rather find strength in what remains behind."

Spy Who Loved Me, The (Special Edition) (1977)

Starring: Roger Moore, Barbara Bach, Richard Kiel
Directed by: Lewis Gilbert

Of the seven times Moore stood at bat as James Bond, this was his shining two hours. Moore battles an evil shipping mogul (Curt Jurgens) who kidnaps nuclear submarines and threatens to blow up the world. Along the way, 007 meets a ravishing Russian agent (Bach, Mrs. Ringo Starr) for a fling in such erotic spots as Egypt and Sardinia. The usual gimmicks (supertankers, submersible cars) abound and are gorgeously photographed, much to the advantage of this superior DVD transfer. The real scene-stealer is the seven-foot-two-inch Kiel as Jaws, a shark-eating man with steel teeth. Carly Simon made a hit of the title tune, singing "nobody does it better." Did Carly never see Sean Connery play the role for keeps?

Hot Bonus: A documentary on the struggles to get the film made on such a large scale is a valuable lesson in Bond economics.

Key Scene: The spectacular ski jump off a cliff that opens the film.

Stagecoach (1939)

Starring: John Wayne, Thomas Mitchell, Claire Trevor, John Carradine
Directed by: John Ford

A stagecoach carrying six passengers, including a drunken doctor (Oscar-winner Mitchell) and a fallen woman (Trevor), rolls through Monument Valley with a driver (Andy Devine) on top next to a sheriff (George Bancroft) on the lookout for an escaped prisoner. When the felon shows up in the person of a startlingly young Wayne as the Ringo Kid, the plot takes off. Ford's seminal western is really a character study punctuated with Apache attacks. But when Mitchell tells Trevor, "We're the victims of a foul disease called social prejudice," Ford shows his ambitious hand. The DVD transfer captures the rugged beauty of Ford's sweeping West, just as Wayne's marriage proposal to the prostitute reveals his secret heart.

Hot Bonus: Production notes that reveal how Ford's return to the western after a dozen years rekindled a love affair that would last for life.

Key Scene: Wayne's incredible entrance, preceded by his rifle shot. He stands still as granite as the stagecoach and the law rush toward him.

Stand by Me (Special Edition) (1986)

Starring: Wil Wheaton, River Phoenix, Kiefer Sutherland
Directed by: Rob Reiner

Nostalgia without the goo. Based on a story by Stephen King (the nonscary kind), Reiner's film opens with a narrator (Richard Dreyfuss), a successful writer, reflecting on the death of one of his boyhood pals and the first time he saw a corpse, when he was twelve. The rest of the film is a flashback to that summer of 1959, when his memory takes him—in the form of Wheaton, then fourteen—on a trip through the Oregon countryside with three pals—Phoenix, Corey Feldman, and Jerry O'Connell—looking for the body that some older teens, led by Sutherland, allegedly saw from a stolen car. Accompanied by an oldies soundtrack, which sounds super on the DVD, the friends trade wisecracks. Dreyfuss points out that "finding new and preferably disgusting ways to describe a friend's mother was always held in high regard." Briefly forgetting their own problems at home, Wheaton and his pals touchingly seek refuge and reassurance in one another.

Hot Bonus: Reiner talks about directing young actors, including the gifted Phoenix who died seven years after this film opened. He also reveals that Wheaton's antagonistic relationship with his father was based in part on his difficulties with being the son of actor-director Carl Reiner.

Key Scene: The end, when Ben E. King's title song kicks in and Dreyfuss laments that he never had friends like the ones he had when he was twelve.

Standing in the Shadows of Motown (Two-Disc Special Edition) (2002)

Starring: The Funk Brothers
Directed by: Paul Justman

Long before hip-hop and Eminem, the Motor City of Detroit revved to the Motown sound. This beauty of a documentary pays long-overdue tribute to the Funk Brothers, the rotating studio musicians (not brothers at all) who played behind 1960s Motown legends from the Supremes to the

Temptations. Besides archival footage, featuring the late, great James Jamerson, Benny Benjamin, and Eddie "Bongo" Brown, the movie offers interviews with surviving Funkers, who play a concert of classics backing up the likes of Chaka Khan, Joan Osborne, and Bootsy Collins. It's a glorious DVD groove that leaves you wanting more. Ain't too proud to beg.

Hot Bonus: *The Ones Who Didn't Make It* is a tribute to the musicians who died before filming started.

Key Scene: James Jamerson Jr. demonstrating his late father's famous one-finger plucking technique on bass.

Star Is Born, A (Collector's Edition) (1954)

Starring: Judy Garland, James Mason, Jack Carson

Directed by: George Cukor

A glorious DVD restoration of a butchered masterpiece. Forget Barbra Streisand's vanity remake in 1976. It's the Garland version that counts, even if photos and audio snippets had to be used to get close to the complete picture. Garland's Vicki Lester is a singer on the way up. Mason's Norman Maine is a major actor (Mason gives a major performance) on the way to suicidal oblivion. Both leads received Oscar nominations. But credit director Cukor for providing the stylistic foundation and emotional resonance that allows Garland to soar. From the jazz simplicity of "The Man That Got Away" to the massive musical extravaganza of the "Born in a Trunk" number, the film is a explosion of talent and flamboyant creativity.

Hot Bonus: The telecast of the film's premiere is a show in itself.

Key Scene: Garland singing "It's a New World" quietly to Mason in their own room while the hit version of the song plays on the radio. It's an intimate moment that powers Garland famous last line: "Hello, everybody. I'm Mrs. Norman Mainer."

Star Trek II: The Wrath of Khan (Two-Disc Director's Edition) (1982)

Starring: William Shatner, Leonard Nimoy, Ricardo Montalban, Kirstie Alley

Directed by: Nicholas Meyer

At the risk of incurring the wrath of the Trekkers, the first *Star Trek* movie in 1979 was a snore.

The sequel has the real juice, namely a roaringly comic Montalban as the evil Khan, a role he created in the "Space Seed" episode of the TV series in 1967. His hair gone white and his skin like Corinthian leather, Montalban is a sight to see as he lures Admiral James T. Kirk (Shatner is ham on wry) from his desk job and back into command of the Starship *Enterprise*. Nimoy is back as Mr. Spock showing a half-interest in a half-Vulcan officer (Alley). But the longer Director's Edition lets Meyer dig into the tensions between Kirk and Khan. "Let them eat static," orders Khan when the *Enterprise* tries to establish radio communication.

Hot Bonus: A retrospective documentary that details the creative arguments over Montalban's character and the purported death of Spock.

Key Scene: Khan springing his secret weapon; it enters through the ear and makes the target "extremely susceptible to suggestion."

Star Trek IV: The Voyage Home (Two Disc Collector's Edition) (1986)

Starring: William Shatner, Leonard Nimoy, Catherine Hicks

Directed by: Leonard Nimoy

It starts off like the usual windbags at warp speed. A giant, cigar-shaped alien probe is threatening to vaporize Earth unless it can talk turkey with a humpback whale. But this is the twenty-third century, and humpbacks are extinct. That's the spur to send Kirk (Shatner), Spock (Nimoy), and the *Enterprise* crew to boldly go back to San Francisco, circa 1986, and steal two humpbacks to mollify the probe. Save the whales, and you'll save the Earth. It's a good joke with a pertinent kick, and director Nimoy has fun with the time-travel concept. It lets Shatner hook up with Hicks, a marine biologist, and Nimoy hook up with his sense of humor. This is by far the most entertaining of the billion *Star Trek* spinoffs out there. And the DVD transfer is a high-gloss reflection of the film's bright mischief.

Hot Bonus: Loved the outtakes.

Key Scene: Kirk, Spock, and the crew dealing with pizza, beer, health care, and other artifacts of a primitive time.

Star Wars: Episode I– The Phantom Menace (Two-Disc Special Edition) (1999)

Starring: Liam Neeson, Ewan McGregor, Natalie Portman, Jake Lloyd

Directed by: George Lucas

On a technical level—pristine picture, 5.1 channel Dolby Digital sound with EX enhancement, and special effects—Lucas's prequel return to the *Star Wars* trilogy that forged his legend is a dazzler. On a dramatic level—writing, directing, performance, and emotional resonance—the film is a dead thing that shows Lucas deserted by the force of creativity. The actors are wallpaper, the jokes are juvenile, there's no romance, and the dialogue lands with the thud of a computer-instruction manual. Neeson fares best as Qui-Gon Jinn, mentor to Obi-Wan Kenobi (McGregor, doing a young Alec Guinness) and Jedi protector of Queen of Naboo (Portman, doll-like and lifeless). Lloyd as Anakin Skywalker, the baby Darth Vader, is hopelessly bland. Jar-Jar Binks, the digital creation conceived as comic relief, became universally reviled, but the human actors are just as deadly. Even Darth Maul, the film's main menace, has a great satanic look (horns included), but there's no there there. Just like the movie.

Hot Bonus: Six hours worth that take you inside the Lucas dream factory and stir up more excitement than the film itself.

Key Scene: The Podrace, which has a videogame urgency that brings this sleeping giant to fitful life.

Star Wars: Episode II– Attack of the Clones (Two-Disc Special Edition) (2002)

Starring: Hayden Christensen, Natalie Portman, Ewan McGregor

Directed by: George Lucas

Is the magic back? Not without a price, baby. You have to trudge through nearly an hour of *Episode II* just to hear it cough and turn over. To alleviate his usual solemn mythmaking, Lucas throws in Jedi love (who knew Jedi knights take a vow not to screw?) between Portman, as queen-turned-senator Padmé Amidala, and Christensen, as hotheaded Jedi-in-training Anakin (Darth Vader's inside me somewhere) Skywalker. You won't find a more sexless, stiffly acted romance in modern cinema. Lucas compensates with asteroid showers, air speeders, swoop bikes, digital monsters, and the climactic clone battle. It's a grand digital design that looks fabulous on the DVD transfer. The big problem, aside from the fact that *The Matrix* and *The Lord of the Rings* outclassed Lucas at his own game, is talk, talk, talk. Lucas still can't write dialogue that doesn't induce projectile vomiting. And the film's visual snap (it was all shot digitally) leaves emotions at a chilly remove. What helps are the cool villains, notably the great Christopher Lee as Count Dooku and New Zealander Temuera Morrison as bounty hunter Jango Fett, the template for the clone army and daddy to Boba (Daniel Logan), the young son he loves and corrupts. The plot? Don't tell me you want to hear that there's unrest in the galactic senate, that Count Dooku's separatist movement is a threat to the limited number of Jedi knights, that . . . help, my eyes are glazing over.

Hot Bonus: Six hours of extras that outclass the film itself.

Key Scene: The climactic duel between Yoda (no longer a puppet but a digital warrior) and the Count. It's a treat to see that old troll stop stating the obvious ("Begun, this clone War has") and start kicking separatist ass.

Star Wars: Episode III– Revenge of the Sith (Two-Disc Special Edition) (2005)

Starring: Hayden Christensen, Natalie Portman, Ewan McGregor

Directed by: George Lucas

Drink the Kool-Aid. Wear blinders. Cover your ears. Because that's the only way you can totally enjoy the final and most futile attempt from skilled producer, clumsy director, and tin-eared writer Lucas to create a prequel trilogy to match the myth-making spirit of the original *Star Wars* saga. Heralded for its savagery (my God, it's rated PG-13), the film follows Anakin Skywalker (Christensen—to merely call him wooden is an affront to hand-carved puppets everywhere) as he loses his limbs and his conscience and takes on the evil mantle of Darth Vader. But thematic darkness is no excuse for dimness in all other departments, except the visual. To hear Anakin and his pregnant wife, Senator Padmé (the vivacious Portman rendered vacant), discuss their marriage is to redefine "stilted" for a new millennium. And yet, missing *Sith* is unthinkable, just for closure. It represents the last time Lucas will ever skywalk with the Skywalkers on the big screen (talk persists of a TV spinoff). Until the last half-hour, when Lucas actually does establish a emotional connection between the landmark he created in 1977 and the prequel investment portfolio he laid out in 1999, the movie is one spectacularly designed letdown after another. The one actor not defeated by the script is Ian McDiarmid as Supreme Chancellor Palpatine, the true badass of the piece. McDiarmid paints an insidious, seductive portrait of evil. To hail *Sith* as a satisfying bridge to a classic is not just playing a game of the Emperor's New Clothes; it's an insult to the original. The film's huge box-office success is no vindication. To paraphrase Padmé: This is how truth dies—to thunderous applause.

Hot Bonus: More hours of extras that show the artful work of craftspeople in the service of a flawed vision.

Key Scene: McGregor's Obi-Wan light-saber duel with Anakin on the lava planet, Mustafar. As Anakin nearly melts in lava, only to be put together Frankenstein-style in a lab while Lucas intercuts Padmé giving birth to the twins Luke and Leia, a link to genuine feeling is established at last.

Star Wars: Episode IV— A New Hope (1977)

Starring: Mark Hamill, Harrison Ford, Carrie Fisher, Alec Guinness

Directed by: George Lucas

Like breathing fresh air after the prequel trilogy. Here's the movie that reveals Lucas as a visionary to rank with Walt Disney. *A New Hope*, like *The Empire Strikes Back* and *Return of the Jedi*, is presented in a *Star Wars* trilogy DVD box that belongs in my personal time capsule. The late critic Pauline Kael once dismissed *A New Hope* as "an epic without a dream." I disagree. Lucas's dream is a grand one: to build a mythic futuristic fantasy out of the influences of his youth—the Bible, the Bard, H. G. Wells, Jack London, John Ford westerns, Flash Gordon serials, and long afternoons at the movies. He transformed pop culture into Pop Art. For those back then who originally criticized Hamill's Luke Skywalker, Fisher's Princess Leia, and Ford's Han Solo as lightweight dolts, all I can say is take another look at this classic on DVD and eat crow. From the opening crawl ("A long time ago in a galaxy far far away") to the last words a living Obi-Wan Kenobi (Oscar-nominee Guinness) speaks to Luke—"May the Force be with you"—you watch

this DVD with a sense of film history playing out before you. As well as rousing special effects and light-saber duels, the film has humor and heart. R2D2 and C-3PO are a Laurel-and-Hardy team of droids, Chewbacca makes Wookie magic, and Darth Vader, as voiced by James Earl Jones, emerges as the greatest villain in screen history. "I find your lack of faith disturbing," he tells a critic of his policies just before killing him. Han Solo's beat-up spaceship, the *Millennium Falcon*, defines the film's raw appeal. Can this cocky adventurer team up with Luke and Leia, who don't know they're siblings, take on the Death Star, and win? Of course they can. It's the movies.

Hot Bonus: A separate disc full of cool extras can't redeem Lucas in the eyes of some fans who think he betrayed them by sprucing up the special effects for DVD without also providing the film in its 1977 form.

Key Scene: Luke's space battle with the Death Star is a demo dazzler.

Star Wars: Episode V— The Empire Strikes Back (1980)

Starring: Mark Hamill, Carrie Fisher, Harrison Ford

Directed by: Irvin Kershner

The best of the bunch, the one with the most satisfying emotional payoff, was directed by Irvin Kershner (not Lucas) and written expertly by Lawrence Kasdan and Leigh Brackett (not Lucas). Hint, hint. This is the one with Master Yoda, voiced by the inimitable Frank Oz, instructing Hamill's Luke Skywalker in the way of the Jedi. This is the one with the romance between Ford's Han Solo and Fisher's Princess Leia. ("I love you," she tells him, just before he goes into carbon freeze. "I know," he says.) This is the one with Darth Vader telling Luke (in the powerful tones of James Earl Jones), "I am your father"—the line that sends a slam-bam space adventure into Freudian hyperspace. Every image, from the ice planet Hoth to the troops sent to wipe out the rebels, looks amazing. Every sound, from the rousing blare of the John Williams score to the comic yowl of Chewbacca, lands beautifully on the ear.

Hot Bonus: Despite his decision to stand back from the directing action, Lucas shows how much his influence was felt on a commentary track shared with Kershner, Kasdan, and Fisher.

Key Scene: For showing off, it's Han Solo navigating an asteroid field while C-3PO nags him about his dim chances. For sheer beauty, you can't beat Han saving Luke from freezing by cutting open the stomach of a snow camel and warming him inside.

Star Wars: Episode VI— Return of the Jedi (1983)

Starring: Mark Hamill, Carrie Fisher, Harrison Ford, Ian McDiarmid

Directed by: Richard Marquand

The end, the finale, that's all he wrote. The too-cute Ewoks are the only major blight on the fun as Lucas's epic turns into an intergalactic soap opera. The special effects really kick in on the DVD transfer, especially those involving what look like flying snowmobiles zooming through a forest. There's a gross new villain in Jabba the Hutt—he's a cross between Edward G. Robinson and a three-hundred-pound avocado—who kidnaps Princess Leia and chains her up in a harem outfit. This is as close as Lucas ever comes to kinky. Marquand is listed as the director, but he said having Lucas so involved was "like directing *King Lear* with Shakespeare in the next room." Maybe that's why the dialogue stiffens up so badly when the emperor, played by British stage actor McDiarmid, pushes Luke to the dark side. This scene delivers more impact after you watch the Emperor work over Luke's daddy in *Revenge of the Sith*. Maybe that's what Lucas had in mind all the time. There won't be a dry eye on your couch when the dying Vader reforms and says to his son, "Luke, help me take this mask off."

Hot Bonus: Four minutes of additional footage, which qualifies as found gold to *Star Wars* fanatics.

Key Scene: The class reunion at the end with all the characters taking a bow. Fanboys yowled like Wookies when Lucas dared to eliminate Sebastian Shaw, the actor who played the unmasked Vader in 1983. Lucas went in digitally and replaced Shaw on the DVD with Hayden Christensen, who would play Vader in the prequels. Talk about the dark side of technology.

Starship Troopers (1997)

Starring: Casper Van Dien, Denise Richards, Dina Meyer

Directed by: Paul Verhoeven

Dumb movie. Dynamite DVD. Your call. It's a war film with nudity—this is Verhoeven directing, and our troops (male and female) indulge in basic instincts. Then the enemy shows up. This isn't World War I or II; it's the future. The bad guys are giant bugs. The actors job

is to squash and squish them, which they do with enthusiasm. I don't remember the actors, just the bugs, and they're terrific. Pop in this DVD and show them to your friends. The transfer looks so crisp and real, you'll want to grab a flyswatter.

Hot Bonus: Verhoeven and screenwriter Edward Neumeir remind us that the source for the film is a respected sci-fi novel by Robert Heinlein. Funny they should remember it on the commentary. It's all but forgotten in the movie.

Key Scene: The army of bugs mobilizes.

Stepford Wives, The (Special Edition) (1975)

Starring: Katharine Ross, Paula Prentiss, Peter Masterson

Directed by: Bryan Forbes

Everything that went wrong with the 2004 Nicole Kidman remake goes wonderfully right in Forbes's version of Ira Levin's bestseller about Connecticut housewives who suddenly can't do enough for their men. Ross and Prentiss are the new Stepford wives, who suspect something is amiss when the women around them spend all day cleaning house and all night satisfying their man's every sexual need. The new DVD transfer brings the movie back to life, which is more than you can say for the wives. Screenwriter William Goldman finds just the right satirical tone for these fembots, making Stepford a household word for any woman with the mind sucked out of her by men frightened of the real thing.

Hot Bonus: A retrospective documentary with the actors talking about the film's relevance to the women's movement then and now.

Key Scene: Prentiss making coffee for Ross, who stabs her to make sure she's a robot. With her wires crossed, Prentiss goes berserk in the kitchen like a harried housewife having a meltdown.

Sting, The (Two-Disc Special Edition) (1973)

Starring: Paul Newman, Robert Redford, Robert Shaw

Directed by: George Roy Hill

No one back in 1973 seemed very surprised that this zippy, Depression-era flick about the ultimate con job managed to win the Best Picture Oscar over *American Graffiti*, *The Exorcist*, and *Cries and Whispers*. Nothing like the passing of time to provide perspective. Or perhaps it's just impossible for anyone to resist Newman and Redford oozing camaraderie. They look especially great on this much-needed Legacy disc, which restores the images to life after years of putting up with the dull original DVD. And now the *plink-plink-plink* of the wonderful Scott Joplin ragtime music comes through loud and clear. Director Hill does a lot to make this stylish entertainment. But seven Oscars was overkill. Amazingly, this froth remains the only time that Redford has received an Academy Award nomination for acting.

Hot Bonus: A retrospective documentary that fills in a lot of blanks.

Key Scene: Newman to Redford: "Glad to meet you, kid. You're a real horse's ass." They could be Butch and Sundance.

Stop Making Sense (1984)

Starring: Talking Heads

Directed by: Jonathan Demme

Demme's account of three nights with Talking Heads puts you in the front row of the Pantages Theater in Hollywood (audience shots—who needs 'em?), then dares you to stay on your ass. Singer David Byrne fills the screen in his Big Suit, but every Head is a star. This is a magnificent performance by America's greatest rainbow-funk art-and-party band, and Demme makes them play just for you. Sound and DVD picture are crystalline.

Hot Bonus: Byrne interviewing himself (a keeper) and bonus tracks of "Cities" and "I Zimbra/Big Business"

Key Scene: Byrne in the opening frames, alone with a boombox, yelping "Psycho Killer."

Stranger Than Paradise (1984)

Starring: John Lurie, Richard Edson, Eszter Balint

Directed by: Jim Jarmusch

Jarmusch demonstrates his hipster cool by filming a road movie in black-and-white and making sure nothing happens. It's actually quite fascinating watching a DVD transfer handle this series of long takes followed by blackouts. Lurie is a Hungarian living in a dismal corner of Manhattan. Then his sixteen-year-old cousin (Balint) visits from Budapest, stays ten days, and heads off to a dismal corner of Cleveland to live with their Aunt Lotte (the late, great Cecilia Stark). When Lurie and his pal Edson drive out to visit, all three decide to leave the cold for sunny Florida, a dismal corner of which they manage to find. Jarmusch makes a droll, fine time of it.

Hot Bonus: A seven-minute compilation of silent, 8mm color and black-and-white "behind the scenes" material shot by Jarmusch's brother during the Cleveland segment. It's as weird and unhinged as the movie.

Key Scene: "You know, you come some place new, and everything looks just the same," says Edson of his travels. The film proves his minimalist point.

Strangers on a Train (Two-Disc Special Edition) (1951)

Starring: Robert Walker, Farley Granger

Directed by: Alfred Hitchcock

Deliciously perverse Hitchcock. Granger's straight-arrow tennis ace Guy Haines meets Walker's charming psychopath Bruno Anthony on a train. Bruno spells out his plan: "Two fellows meet accidentally. Each one has someone that they'd like to get rid of, and they swap murders." Guy doesn't take Bruno seriously. Big mistake. The black-and-white picture sparkles on the DVD transfer, notably on such major set pieces as the murder in an amusement park (seen though broken glasses) and the runaway merry-go-round. But it's Walker who holds you spellbound.

Hot Bonus: Two versions of the movie are included: the final release version and the preview version, which is just a few minutes longer but shows more of the initial meeting of Guy and Bruno and heightens the homoeroticism. For a Hitchcock buff, this is nirvana.

Key Scene: The tennis match, with the crowd swinging their heads to follow Granger's ball and Walker staring straight ahead.

Straw Dogs (Two-Disc Special Edition) (1971)

Starring: Dustin Hoffman, Susan George

Directed by: Sam Peckinpah

Peckinpah—"Bloody Sam" to his fans—dishes out a film of brutal violence and provocative implications that come through like gangbusters on Criterion's impeccable DVD transfer. Hoffman stars as an American mathematician and pacifist who moves to a quiet Cornish village with his British wife, played by a super-sexy George. The feeling of serenity lasts for about five minutes, or until four local louts are hired to build a garage but spend more time ogling the wife. When Hoffman is sent on a decoy hunting expedition, two of the men rape the wife. The pacifist ultimately turns stone-cold killer in Peckinpah's potent allegory of the Vietnam era. "I care," he says, arming to protect his home. "This is where I live. This is me."

Hot Bonus: Film scholar Stephen Prince analyzes the film six ways from Sunday, but the prize extra is a retrospective on Peckinpah featuring family and actors who have worked with beloved Bloody Sam, who died in 1984.

Key Scene: The rape, which Peckinpah intercuts with Hoffman looking helpless in the woods. The wife's violation is edited in ways to suggest both hurt and willingness (a fear expressive of Hoffman's jealousy). Criterion has restored the scene to its original length before it was cut for ratings issues. It will be argued about as long as there are movies and DVDs to play them on.

Streetcar Named Desire, A (Director's Cut) (1951)

Starring: Marlon Brando, Vivien Leigh, Kim Hunter, Karl Malden
Directed by: Elia Kazan

Since Brando's death in 2004, a new generation has sparked to his films on DVD, looking for that one emblematic performance by the greatest film actor of his century. Here it is. As Stanley Kowalski, Brando burns up the screen in his ripped T-shirt calling for his wife ("Hey, Stella! Stella!") with an animal carnality that rivals steamy New Orleans. Brando made Stanley more than a brute that faded belle Blanche DuBois (Oscar-winner Leigh) could rail against. Having originated the role in the Tennessee Williams play on Broadway in 1947, Brando finds the character's charm, his shrewdness, his heat. No wonder Stella (Oscar-winner Hunter) stays with him and Mitch (Oscar-winner Malden) stays her friend. Leigh seized her finest film role since *Gone With the Wind*, and she's magnificent. But this is Brando's show, even if he's the only one of the four leads who didn't win an Oscar. (Humphrey Bogart won for *The African Queen*.) Check out this startling vivid DVD transfer, and see who you would have picked.

Hot Bonus: The Director's Cut adds three minutes of footage that the great Kazan had to cut to calm the censors.

Key Scene: Blanche, staring at Stanley, implores her sister Stella: "Don't hang back with the brutes." Brando understands fully why she does.

Strictly Ballroom (1992)

Starring: Paul Mercurio, Tara Morice, Bill Hunter
Directed by: Baz Luhrmann

Luhrmann cannot direct a movie that doesn't explode with color and vibrancy, both of which are in evidence on the DVD that celebrates his debut with this art-house crowd pleaser about ballroom dancing. The Aussie director gets these dance routines on their feet and kicking like a line of Rockettes. Will maverick dancer Scott Hastings (Mercurio) introduce new steps into a contest even though it's against the rules of old-fart judge Barry Fife (Hunter)? You bet. Will Scott choose an experienced dance partner or go for Fran (Morice)—a clumsy, four-eyed unknown—in the hope of turning her into Cinderella before the big championships? Stupid question. Even when you see every trick up the movie's sleeve, you still keep smiling.

Hot Bonus: A vivid documentary about the real dance competitions.

Key Scene: The finals. Will Scott and the transformed Fran win the top prize by doing the pasa doble, taught to them by Fran's Spanish father and grandmother? You'd have to be a movie illiterate to doubt it.

Stunt Man, The (Two-Disc Special Edition) (1980)

Starring: Peter O'Toole, Barbara Hershey, Steve Railsback
Directed by: Richard Rush

Rush's long-aborning labor of love gets an ideal sendoff on DVD with pristine picture and sound. O'Toole is his own DVD event as Eli Cross, a film director who brightly drives everyone to do his bidding on the set of the World War I film he is shooting on a California beach. When a fugitive (Railsback) wanders onto the set, O'Toole offers him protection from the law if he'll replace a stunt man who was accidentally killed. And so, as the stand-in stunt man sleeps with the unstable leading lady (Hershey) and does increasingly dangerous feats at O'Toole's urging, Rush blends illusion and reality into a hypnotic look at the comic anarchy of filmmaking.

Hot Bonus: A rip-roaring, off-the-wall feature-length documentary called *The Sinister Saga of Making the Stunt Man*.

Key Scene: O'Toole descending from a crane like a god (the actor said he was channeling his *Lawrence of Arabia* director David Lean) and declaring that if the police interfere with the film, "I'll kill them and I'll eat them."

Sugarland Express, The (1974)

Starring: Goldie Hawn, William Atherton, Michael Sacks, Ben Johnson

Directed by: Steven Spielberg

Spielberg was just twenty-eight when he made his extraordinary debut in features with this fact-based story. Lou Jean, played by a no-bull Hawn, and her fugitive husband Clovis (Atherton) bust out of jail, commandeer a squad car and a highway patrol cop (Sacks), and race across Texas to get back their infant son who's been adopted against their wishes. The movie is all chase with cops, media, and curiosity seekers following the fugitives to Sugarland, Texas. Spielberg is a wiz at choreographing cars, and just as good with people. The film deserves a better DVD than it got, but it's still a keeper.

Hot Bonus: A trailer that actually does a good job of suggesting the film's complex mix of emotions, from comedy to tragedy.

Key Scene: Hawn and the gold trading stamps.

Sullivan's Travels (Special Edition) (1942)

Starring: Joel McCrea, Veronica Lake, Robert Greig, Eric Blore

Directed and written by: Preston Sturges

A brilliant satire is brilliantly transferred to DVD by Criterion with a black-and-white picture that shimmers with a dewlike freshness. The great Sturges gives Hollywood a royal tweak as John L. Sullivan (McCrea in his best screen performance), a director of fluff (*Hey-Hey in the Hay*), decides to make a serious message picture about the Great Depression called *O Brother, Where Art Thou?* (a title the Coen brothers lifted for their 2000 comedy). As research, Sullivan goes out on the road as a homeless bum with only ten cents in his pocket to see how the poor really live. A pretty extra (Lake) goes with him, hotly pursued by a studio force occupied by, among others, his butler (Greig) and valet (Blore). When Sullivan loses his identity, the harsh realities hit home in ways that are hilarious and harsh.

Hot Bonus: A biography of Sturges and an interview with his widow add much to understanding this film and the rest of Sturges's work.

Key Scene: The prison camp that inspires Sullivan to return to making comedies that are "better than nothing in this cockeyed caravan."

Sunrise (1927)

Starring: Janet Gaynor, George O'Brien, Margaret Livingston

Directed by: F. W. Murnau

Want a DVD that defines gorgeous? Try this silent masterpiece from Murnau, which won the first Oscar ever for "Artistic Quality of Production." A farmer (O'Brien) and his wife (Oscar-winner Gaynor) find their idyllic life disrupted when a jazz-age city babe (Livingston) comes on to the farmer and provokes him to try to drown his wife. One amazing image flows into the other. Sit back and behold.

Hot Bonus: John Bailey, a superb cinematographer in his own right—be it *Ordinary People* or the musical version of *The Producers*—comments with invaluable lucidity on the film's production and design.

Key Scene: The reconciliation between husband and wife in a kiss that fades from crowded city traffic into lush fields.

Sunset Blvd. (Special Collector's Edition) (1950)

Starring: Gloria Swanson, William Holden, Erich von Stroheim

Directed by: Billy Wilder

So good in every detail that it fully deserves this superior DVD transfer. Holden is cynically perfect as Joe Gillis, the young screenwriter who narrates the film as a corpse in a swimming pool. The pool belongs to Norma Desmond (Swanson), the faded silent-screen star living like a hermit in a rotting Los Angeles mansion with Max (the marvelous von Stroheim), a butler who used to be her director and her husband. When the screenwriter wanders onto the scene, Norma seizes the moment. Joe will write her comeback project and become her lover. "I am big," she tells him. "It's the pictures that got small." Swanson's tour de force gives the film a tragic grandeur, but Wilder's black-comic enthusiasm for biting the Hollywood hand that feeds him makes the film a classic.

Hot Bonus: The film's original prologue, set in a morgue, is included as an extra. You can see why it was cut, but it's a joy nonetheless.

Key Scene: Norma's final descent down her staircase. The police are waiting to lock her up, but Max directs her surrender as one last close-up for "all those wonderful people out there in the dark."

Superman: The Movie (1978)

Starring:
Christopher Reeve,
Margot Kidder,
Marlon Brando,
Gene Hackman

Directed by:
Richard Donner

Picture and sound have been remastered to give the 1978 comic-book epic a twenty-first-century DVD sendoff, and there's eleven minutes of extra footage, but the film would even work without the improvements—thanks to Reeve. The actor, who died in 2004 after years of fighting the paralysis that resulted from a horseback riding accident, made an ideal Man of Steel and played his alter ego Clark Kent with a bumbling, bespectacled Cary Grant charm. The production looks lush, from the opening credits to the knockout special effects. And except for Brando, who walked through his high-priced cameo as Supie's dad, the actors manage to be more than cartoons, especially Kidder as reporter Lois Lane and Hackman as the villainous Lex Luthor. Director Donner gives the film just the right gung-ho spirit to go with Superman's line: "I'm here to fight for truth, justice, and the American way."

Hot Bonus: A retrospective interview with the wheelchair-bound Reeve.

Key Scene: Superman resealing the San Andreas Fault.

Superman II (1981)

Starring: Christopher Reeve, Margot Kidder, Gene Hackman

Directed by: Richard Lester

The novelty is gone and so, for better or worse, is Brando, but this film is more humane and hilarious than the original. The special effects, with nip-and-tuck rescues from Niagara Falls to the Eiffel Tower, provide the giddy sensation of daydreams fulfilled. And director Lester, replacing the axed Richard Donner, adds his own waggish style. The big surprise is how beautifully the love story comes through between Reeve's Superman and Kidder's Lois Lane. Reeve still seems blissfully right as Superman and Clark Kent. There's a disarming tickle in his performance that would disappear in the two additional sequels.

Hot Bonus: The theatrical trailer is a good one, but it's a stingy extra for such an epic film fantasy.

Key Scene: When Superman reveals his love and true identity to Lois, inciting a pull-out-the-stops romantic wallow.

Super Size Me (2004)

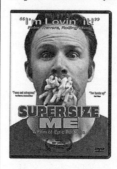

Starring: Morgan Spurlock

Directed and written by: Morgan Spurlock

Spurlock won the Best Director prize at the Sundance Film Festival for satirizing our fast-food obsession by eating at McDonald's for thirty days, with three doctors checking on his daily deterioration. But Spurlock's little movie that could is more than a Oscar-nominated documentary about the dangers of obesity. It's one of the blackest comedies to hit the screen since *Dr. Strangelove.* Spurlock proves himself a supersized talent; he makes you choke on every laugh.

Hot Bonus: An interview with Eric Schlosser, the author of *Fast-Food Nation,* which extends the film's political implications.

Key Scene: The shocking segment on how McDonald's and other fast-food companies market their product directly to children.

Sweet Hereafter, The (Special Edition) (1997)

Starring: Ian Holm, Sarah Polley, Tom McCamus, Bruce Greenwood

Directed by: Atom Egoyan

A lawyer, outstandingly played by Holm, comes to a Canadian town to offer help to some of its residents by suing for the deaths of their children in a school bus accident. "Let me direct your rage," he tells these bereaved parents In adapting the novel by Russell Banks, Egoyan gives the film a fragmented before-and-after structure that provokes us to carefully examine the residents of the town, including a father (McCamus) and daughter (the stunning Polley) whose relationship is not as caring as it first seems. The DVD transfer catches the cold, grave beauty of Egoyan's compositions.

Hot Bonus: Egoyan and Banks discussing the book's transfer to film.

Key Scene: The accident itself, shown at the film's midpoint, as the school bus skids off a road and into a frozen lake. Egoyan gives the sequence a haunting quality that resists exploitation to find a sorrowful truth.

Sweet Smell of Success (1957)

Starring: Burt Lancaster, Tony Curtis, Martin Milner, Susan Harrison

Directed by: Alexander Mackendrick

You wouldn't want to take a bite out of this movie; it's a cookie full of arsenic. It's also one of the nastiest, niftiest X-rays of the underbelly of New York show business ever captured on celluloid. The black-and-white picture on the DVD, despite minor flaws, gives Manhattan nightlife a seductively poisonous sheen. You can almost choke on the cigarette smoke at the chic restaurant table where Lancaster's J. J. Hunsecker holds court. "Match me, Sidney," he says, holding an unlit cigarette out to Curtis's Sidney Falco, a hungry press agent who avidly pursues J.J. to get his clients in Hunsecker's influential column. Things get brutal when J.J. asks Sidney to break up a relationship between a musician (Milner) and J.J.'s sister (Harrison). The columnist watches over his sibling like an incestuous hawk. Lancaster is a hard-assed wonder in the role, but the movie belongs to Curtis in his career performance. That neither actor was even nominated for an Oscar for these roles remains a blight on the Academy. Mackendrick directs the potently perverse script by Clifford Odets and Ernest Lehman with an eye for its darkest corners. James Wong Howe's cinematography and Elmer Bernstein's jazz score add just the right toxic tang.

Hot Bonus: A trailer does the film justice. But commentary from Curtis, who did a fine job on *Some Like It Hot*, would have been most welcome.

Key Scene: Watch Curtis's face when Lancaster tells him: "You're dead, son. Go get yourself buried."

Swept Away . . . By an Unusual Destiny in the Blue Sea of August (1974)

Starring: Giancarlo Giannini, Mariangela Melato

Directed by: Lina Wertmüller

Empty your mind of the Madonna remake in 2002, and check out this fiercely funny original starring Melato as a capitalist snob on a yachting trip who can't stop ridiculing the sweaty, communist deckhand, played by Giannini. When the two end up shipwrecked on a desert island, the merrily malicious Wertmüller turns the tables and puts Giannini in the dominant position. Forget the criticism of the film as antifeminist. Wertmüller is merely having scrappy fun with gender and class politics. The two stars have never looked better than they do on this newly restored DVD from Fox Lorber as part of the Lina Wertmüller Collection.

Hot Bonus: Wertmüller explains her position on the film in an interview, which is amplified in an essay by critic John Simon.

Key Scene: The moment in which she rings his penis with flowers and kisses his feet still gets audiences going. But Wertmüller isn't opting for feminist abasement. She's laughing at the cosmic joke behind the battle of the sexes.

Swing Time (1936)

Starring: Fred Astaire, Ginger Rogers

Directed by: George Stevens

The very best of the ten films that Astaire and Rogers made together, and that's saying something. He's a gambler named Lucky. She's a dance teacher named Penny. He's engaged to someone else. She tries to resist him. That's the plot, but director Stevens—a class act himself—keeps it bouncing through some of the finest song-and-dance numbers in screen history. With music by Jerome Kern and lyrics by Dorothy Fields, the hits just keep coming, from the funny duets ("Pick Yourself Up," "Let's Call the Whole Thing Off") to the Oscar-winning ballad ("The Way You Look Tonight") sung by Fred to Ginger when she's washing her hair. This long-awaited DVD brings a sheen to the picture and sound that "thrilling" is too puny a word to describe. The whole experience is pure bliss.

Hot Bonus: Commentary by John Mueller, author of *Astaire Dancing*.

Key Scene: "Never Gonna Dance" is by far the most erotic number in which Astaire and Rogers ever participated. He stands at the foot of staircase, refusing to move unless she comes back to him. Then slowly they begin to sway toward each other until the song and their bodies take orgasmic flight. If someone tells you movies can't be poetry, show them this sequence.

Swingers (Collector's Edition) (1996)

Starring: Vince Vaughn, Jon Favreau
Directed by: Doug Liman

Favreau, who wrote the hilariously unhip script, also plays Mike, a standup comic wannabe from Queens, New York, trying to make it in Los Angeles. A loser in love, Mike gets advice from best bud Trent (Vaughn, priceless), a party animal who teaches Mike how to be "money" by worshiping at the retro altar of Frank and Dean. For a low-budget movie, *Swingers* looks great on DVD. Liman directs Favreau's script with a keen eye for the weird and desperate as the guys take a trip to Vegas and try their "Jedi mind-shit" on women who aren't buying. I find it fall-on-the-floor funny.

Hot Bonus: Illustrated action commentary from Favreau and Vaughn.

Key Scene: Vaughn on his babe technique: "All I do is stare at their mouths and wrinkle my eyebrows, and somehow I turn out to be a big sweetie."

Switchblade Sisters (1975)

Starring: Robbie Lee, Joanne Nail, Monica Gayle, Kitty Bruce
Directed by: Jack Hill

A gang of teen girls, known as the Jezebels, goes to war with its rivals in one of the wildest B-movies ever to get a class-A treatment on DVD. Quentin Tarantino does the intros—he mainlines this stuff—and joins director Hill for a raucous commentary track that is just as entertaining as the movie. In addition to the hot lesbo action, the film parallels *Othello* as Patch (Gayle), the Iago figure, turns her boss Lace (Lee) against the gang's newest member, Maggie (Nail), by stirring up sexual jealousy.

Hot Bonus: Trailers from other Hill films, including three Pam Grier gems: *Coffy, Foxy Brown,* and *The Big Doll House.*

Key Scene: Inside the women's prison. I hope you did not think that Hill would skip the chance to cover this reliably racy territory.

Take the Money and Run (1969)

Starring: Woody Allen, Janet Margolin
Directed and co-written by: Woody Allen

The Woodman's first feature as director, writer, and star is a ramshackle comedy done in semi-documentary style. Allen plays Virgil Starkwell, a small-time crook who robs vending machines before switching to banks. In and out of jail, Virgil finds love with a laundress (Margolin), but no re-spect from his parents who are interviewed wearing Groucho Marx masks. This is Woody before he became an auteur, which makes this well-produced DVD shameless fun. Allen's stand-up comedy roots are clear from the dialogue. "I robbed a butcher shop," says Virgil. "I got away with 116 veal cutlets. Then I had to go out and rob a tremendous amount of breading."

Hot Bonus: Just the movie, presented in full-screen and letterbox formats. This is one of those rare cases when the full-screen edition plays better.

Key Scene: The illegible holdup note—"I am pointing a gub at you"—which creates a hilarious argument between Virgil and several bank tellers over the meaning of the word "gub."

Taking of Pelham One Two Three (1974)

Starring: Walter Matthau, Robert Shaw
Directed by: Joseph Sargent

A tremendously exciting thriller that hardly anyone knows about, making it a natural for DVD. Shaw makes a hell of a villain as Mr. Blue (an inspiration for the color-coded names in Quentin Tarantino's *Reservoir Dogs*). Blue and three henchmen hijack a New York subway train and threaten to start shooting passengers if a $1 million ransom isn't paid within the hour. Matthau is at his cranky-funny best at the transit cop negotiator. Sargent tightens the tension by shooting underground, and the DVD transfer uses the gritty realism to full advantage.

Hot Bonus: The MGM disc does wonders with the mono sound, notably in bringing out the jangle in David Shire's score.

Key Scene: The trick with the third rail is a real demo moment.

Talk to Her (2002)

Starring: Javier Cámara, Leonor Watling, Rosario Flores, Darío Grandinetti
Directed by: Pedro Almodóvar

Almodóvar, Spain's leading maverick, won the Best Original Screenplay Oscar for this haunting provocation that has been immaculately transferred to DVD. Marco (Grandinetti), a journalist, falls hard for a lady bullfighter, Lydia (Flores, so alive she seems to leap off the screen), who is gored in the ring. At the hospital where Lydia lies comatose, Marco meets Benigno (Cámara), a male nurse who takes special care of Alicia (Watling), a gorgeous ballerina who fell into a coma after a car accident four years earlier. Benigno tells Marco that talk is essential to these motionless women. Maybe, inside, they hear and understand. When Alicia becomes the victim of a crime, the film lurches into dark corners of the mind that Almodóvar navigates with uncanny skill and passionate heart. It's Cámara's tour-de-force performance, which anchors the film, that shocks and unnerves us.

Hot Bonus: Almodóvar talks to us, illuminating the film's subtext.

Key Scene: A dream sequence, done in silent-film style. Benigno, shrunk to fist size, bounces on Watling's lush naked body. Climbing up and over her breasts, he lands at the entrance to her vagina, into which he vanishes. The scene will later prove essential to unlocking the film's tragic mystery.

Tall Guy, The (1989)

Starring: Jeff Goldblum, Emma Thompson, Rowan Atkinson

Directed by: Mel Smith

A hoot and a half, and a pleasure to have on DVD since only about two people actually paid to see it at the multiplex. Goldblum stars as Dexter King, an American actor working in a London revue as the tall-guy stooge to a diminutive but hugely nasty Brit comic (Atkinson, in his element). "If you ever do anything funny in my show again—you're out," he tells Dexter. The script, by Richard Curtis—five years from international success with *Four Weddings and a Funeral*—moves from cheeky to hilarious when Dexter falls for a nurse (a delectable Thompson) and wins the lead in a London musical version of *The Elephant Man*. Theatrical satire has rarely been this delicious.

Hot Bonus: The stereo surround sound brings out every laugh in the parody score of *Elephant!*

Key Scene: Watching elephants fill the stage as Goldblum sings "I'm Packing My Trunk" is funny enough, but watching Thompson's priceless reactions to watching the show from a box seat is a show in itself.

Tarnation (2003)

Starring: Jonathan Caouette

Directed by: Jonathan Caouette

You might call this knockout debut from Caouette, then thirty, a documentary, since he put it together on a computer for $218 from home movies, photos, phone calls, and other artifacts of growing up gay and living in Texas and New York with a mentally damaged mother. From age eleven, Caouette sidesteps trauma with musicals, horror flicks, and pop-culture remnants that heal his psychic wounds. The full-screen DVD transfer keeps up with all the challenges of Caouette's mixed-media scrapbook of images and sounds. The film defies description. I'd call it some kind of miracle.

Hot Bonus: Great commentary from Caouette about the origins of the project and his planned sequel. Bring it on.

Key Scene: The mother's return home from the hospital after a lithium overdose. As she holds a pumpkin and sings a child's song, Caouette presents a picture of utter emotional desolation—hers and his.

Taxi Driver (Collector's Edition) (1976)

Starring: Robert De Niro, Jodie Foster, Harvey Keitel, Cybill Shepherd

Directed by: Martin Scorsese

The ultimate cinematic fever dream—a Scorsese masterpiece to rank with *Raging Bull* and *Good-Fellas*—finds a haven on this special-edition DVD, which damn near envelops you in the open sewer that is Manhattan in the eyes of De Niro's insomniac cabbie Travis Bickle. Paul Schrader wrote the script that became the blueprint for Scorsese's nightmare vision, and it still grabs you. Take this chunk of Travis narration: "All the animals come out at night—whores, scum, pussies, buggers, queens, fairies, dopers, junkies. Sick. Venal. Someday a real rain will come and wash all the scum off the street." Travis sees himself as that rain. He doesn't fit in otherwise. A date with a blonde campaign worker (Shepherd) misfires when he takes her to a porn movie. But this outsider, who calls himself "God's lonely man," figures that maybe he can make a difference. He can assassinate a double-talking politician or rescue a twelve-year-old hooker (Foster, indelibly brilliant) from her pimp (Keitel). Either way it's a bloodbath, but the gore can't make him feel clean. Referencing sources from the Old Testament to Dostoyevsky and *The Searchers*, Scorsese teams with a peak-performance De Niro to create a visceral celluloid that gets under your skin. The *Taxi Driver* DVD is dangerous. It leaves marks that don't go away.

Hot Bonus: A retrospective documentary shows how Scorsese, his cast, and his crew are still feeling those marks. This was the final score of the great Bernard Herrmann, and that last note—underlining that last look from Travis in his cab's rearview mirror—captures the film's ferocity and feeling.

Key Scene: De Niro in the mirror, repeating the phrase, "You talking to me?" Scorsese's film will talk as long as there are movies—and DVDs.

Team America: World Police (Uncensored and Unrated Special Collector's Edition) (2004)

Starring: The voices of Trey Parker and Matt Stone

Directed and co-written by: Trey Parker

Uncensored on DVD is just the way you want to view this outrageously, gut-bustingly hilarious movie. It's also a ruthlessly clever musical, a punchy political parody, and the hottest look ever at naked puppets. Those *South Park* mischiefmakers—director Trey Parker and co-screenwriter Matt Stone—have produced their own Jerry Bruckheimer epic (think *Armageddon* and *Pearl Harbor*) using Chiodo brothers string puppets. And for all the frat-boy humor, the film (shot by *Matrix* master Bill Pope) is a visual knockout, with design and costumes getting as many laughs as the script. The sex, tamped down at the multiplex, now includes the puppet golden shower. The six members of Team America are hell-bent on destroying terrorism, even as they obliviously wipe out world monuments. The songs, as in *South Park: Bigger, Longer and Uncut*, are uproarious, be it a country riff ("Freedom isn't free/There's a hefty fuckin' fee") or a power ballad ("*Pearl Harbor* sucked/Just a little bit more than I love you"). The film targets a clear and present danger: liberal Hollywood. Michael Moore, Sean Penn, Alec Baldwin, George Clooney, Tim Robbins, and (most ungallantly) Susan Sarandon are royally skewered, but only for the high crime of taking themselves seriously. Parker and Stone are too smart to make that mistake.

Hot Bonus: Ten deleted scenes and outtakes.

Key Scene: North Korean dictator Kim Jong Il, the film's scene-stealing villain as voiced by Parker, stops the show with "I'm Ronely."

10 Commandments, The (Two-Disc Special Edition) (1956)

Starring: Charlton Heston, Yul Brynner, Anne Baxter, Edward G. Robinson

Directed by: Cecil B. DeMille

Sure DeMille's 220-minute biblical epic is a kitsch marathon. But try resisting it as Heston's Moses blows harder than the wind of the Pharoah (Brynner) that drives the Jews out of Egypt. The script starts over the top and keeps flying from there. You haven't lived until you hear the Pharoah's wife, vamped for the ages by Baxter, tell Heston, "Oh Moses, Moses, you stubborn, splendid, adorable fool." The acting is all done in capital letters. Luckily, so are the special effects, which come through thunderously on DVD. Check out that plague of locusts.

Hot Bonus: A six-part documentary covers every aspect of the film.

Key Scene: Moses parts the Red Sea. Even after the decades of digital wonders that followed it, this is a moment that still pops your eyes.

Tender Mercies (1983)

Starring: Robert Duvall, Tess Harper, Betty Buckley, Ellen Barkin

Directed by: Bruce Beresford

Here's a DVD transfer that gets the smallest details right. Duvall stars as Mac Sledge, a boozy, burned-out country singer and songwriter tentatively taking a few steps back into music and life. Drinking and whoring had wrecked his first marriage to a country queen (a fiery Buckley), who retaliated by cutting him off from their daughter (Barkin). His salvation is the love of a Vietnam soldier's widow (the luminous Harper), who runs a shabby motel–gas station in Texas with the help of her young son (Allan Hubbard). Duvall gives Horton Foote's alert screenplay everything he has. His beery singing voice is revelation (he wrote two of the appealing songs), and his unfussy, brightly burnished acting is the kind for which awards are invented (deservedly, he won the Oscar). Credit for the film's many grace notes must also go to Beresford. That he is Australian only makes the singular American quality of this authentic film more remarkable.

Hot Bonus: A retrospective documentary with all-new interviews with Duvall, Harper, Hubbard, Foote, and Beresford.

Key Scene: The reconciliation between Mac and his daughter, which Duvall and Barkin play with the insinuating potency of a great country song.

Terminator, The (Special Edition) (1984)

Starring: Arnold Schwarzenegger, Linda Hamilton, Michael Biehn

Directed by: James Cameron

Long ago in a galaxy far, far, away when Schwarzenegger and Cameron worked on less-than-*Titanic* budgets, they came up with this tight, tense

sci-fi fable about a cyborg from the future sent to kill Sarah Connor (Hamilton), a woman set to give birth to the savior of humanity in a 2029 war against machines. Ah-nuld, far from his days as California's governor, isn't afraid to play badass, forcing Sarah to rely on a human time-traveler (Biehn) for protection. Like the movie, the DVD has real vitality in picture and sound.

Hot Bonus: A retrospective documentary offers many goodies, but go Easter Egg hunting in the Languages section, locate French, press the right arrow and then Enter, and you'll find five bonus featurettes.

Key Scene: Leaving a police station, the Terminator makes a promise no one who watches it forgets: "I'll be back."

Terminator 2: Judgment Day (Extreme Edition) (1991)

Starring: Arnold Schwarzenegger, Linda Hamilton, Edward Furlong

Directed by: James Cameron

For picture, sound, and extras by the ton, this 1991 blockbuster is still in the running for the best DVD of all time. And the movie itself isn't bad either, even though the run-in Schwarzenegger's Terminator, the T-800, had with a hydraulic press in the 1984 original would realistically have left him a waffle iron. Cameron gets around that by reprogramming the cyborg as a goody-goody to protect Sarah's son, John Connor, well played by fourteen-year-old Furlong. The bad Terminator (Robert Patrick) is a newer model T-1000—a hunk of liquid metal in human form (he looks like an Oscar with ears)—out to waste John and clear the way for nuclear war. John doesn't like killing, so Ah-nuld merely shoots the villains in the kneecaps. He even shows compassion. "What's wrong with your eyes?" he asks John as the boy cries. Soon he's the first cyborg to learn the meaning of a tear. The star has fun saying things like "Chill out, dickwad," and Hamilton comes into her own as an action hero, but this is Cameron's show. He's the reigning king of movie pow. T2 cost a reported $100 million, and you can actually see where the money went. The visual and makeup effects are state-of-the-art, and the demo-quality motorcycle chase will challenge your home-theater

system until it pants and begs for mercy. The Extreme Edition, following the Ultimate Edition in 2000, offers sixteen minutes of additional footage and images of jaw-dropping clarity and precision. What are you waiting for?

Hot Bonus: Too many to enumerate, plus Cameron's first-ever audio commentary, which is exhaustive and thoroughly entertaining.

Key Scene: Schwarzenegger to Patrick, just after issuing the coup de grace: "Hasta la vista, baby."

Terminator 3: Rise of the Machines (Two-Disc Special Edition) (2003)

Starring: Arnold Schwarzenegger, Nick Stahl, Claire Danes, Kristanna Loken

Directed by: Jonathan Mostow

Mostow's followup is not in the same league as James Cameron's one-two punch, but it has action moments no DVD freak will want to miss. Mostow propels the narrative with zippy B-movie energy. T3 may lack the mythic pow of the 1984 original and the visionary thrill of T2, but it's a potent popcorn movie that digs in its hooks and doesn't let go until an ending that ODs on apocalyptic hoo-ha. To catch you up, John Connor, now played by Stahl, is on the run from a new terminator, called T-X for Terminatrix, sent to dispatch him. As played by Loken, she shows up naked, ready to kill for clothes, for wheels, and for a weapon ("I like your gun," she tells a cop). Now there's dialogue to tax the film's two screenwriters. No matter. Loken brings sly wit and sexiness to an expressionless three-thousand-pound machine out to kill John and his veterinarian girlfriend (Danes). Enter T-101, the protector played by Schwarzenegger. He also comes in naked, stealing clothes from a leather-clad male stripper (nice touch). T-X's advanced alloy endoskeleton gives T-101 a jumbo inferiority complex. "I'm an obsolete design," he tells John. It's no "I'll be back," but it'll do until Mostow pumps out the action, highlighted by a car chase in which T-101 hangs from a hundred-ton crane.

Hot Bonus: Mostow does a good job explaining the film's effects.

Key Scene: The last fight between Terminator and Terminatrix—metal twisted into a parody of sexual positions—is both erotic and hilarious.

Terms of Endearment (1983)

Starring: Shirley MacLaine, Jack Nicholson, Debra Winger, Jeff Daniels

Directed and written by: James L Brooks

If this Oscar winner for Best Picture is soap opera, then bring on the suds. Screenwriter Brooks, in his directing debut, is a master at blending humor and heartbreak. Based on the 1975 novel by Texas writer Larry McMurtry, the film traces the relationship of Aurora Greenway (MacLaine) and her daughter Emma (Winger) from the daughter's birth to her bout with cancer as a thirty-year-old mother of three. MacLaine is a fierce and funny handful as the fading Texas widow whose love for Emma is not enough to reconcile their differences. She hates Emma's no-account husband, Flap (Daniels). It takes nymphet-chasing Garrett Breedlove (Nicholson), a former astronaut who lives next door, to loosen her up. "You need a lot of drinks," he tells Aurora, setting off a uniquely hilarious and touching relationship that won Oscars for both actors. Winger remains the soul of the movie. Her final exchange of looks—no dialogue—with MacLaine packs an emotional resonance that is totally devoid of manipulative sentiment.

Hot Bonus: The comments from Brooks and production designer Polly Platt are particularly appropriate since what the characters wear and how they live—details caught beautifully on the DVD—help define them.

Key Scene: MacLaine's fury at the hospital, demanding medication for her daughter, is acting at its riskiest. Here the risk pays off.

Texas Chain Saw Massacre, The (Special Edition) (1974)

Starring: Marilyn Burns, Gunnar Hansen, Paul A. Partain

Directed by: Tobe Hooper

A seminal horror film comes to DVD just in time to illustrate how Hooper, an expert director, can grip audiences in a vise of suspense without resorting to unrelenting gore. The 2003 remake, directed by Marcus Nispel, splattered so much blood in your face that you never felt it in your bones. You do here. Burns, her paralyzed brother (Partain), and a few of their friends visit the farmhouse where her grandfather used to live. Nearby, they encounter a family of slaughterhouse workers, including Leatherface (Hansen), so named because he wears a mask made of flesh. It's an unnerving setup for a film that plumbs the violence of the mind as it dissects a truly dysfunctional American family. Hooper relives the tension with humor, but his talent—caught perfectly on disc—is to imply what's lurking in the shadows.

Hot Bonus: Hooper, Hansen, and cinematographer Daniel Pearl talk about how they achieved their scares and show alternate footage that they believed revealed too much.

Key Scene: The first look at Leatherface, firing up his phallic chainsaw.

That's Entertainment Trilogy (Deluxe Four-Disc Collector's Edition) (1974, 1976, 1994)

Starring: The stars of over one hundred MGM musicals

Directed by: Jack Haley Jr., Gene Kelly, Bud Friedgen

All three movies are clip jobs, but what clips! Fred Astaire, Gene Kelly, Frank Sinatra, Judy Garland, Esther Williams, Jimmy Durante, Mickey Rooney, Ann Miller, Lena Horne, and dozens of others are seen doing musical numbers in films, from *The Hollywood Revue of 1929* to *Gigi*, that come alive again with picture restored and soundtracks digitally remastered. A true labor of love that deserves passing on to future generations.

Hot Bonus: A fourth disc filled with scenes from the cutting-room floor.

Key Scene: They are all key.

Thelma & Louise (Special Edition) (1991)

Starring: Geena Davis, Susan Sarandon, Brad Pitt, Harvey Keitel

Directed by: Ridley Scott

Beginning like *I Love Lucy* and ending with the impact of *Easy Rider*, the movie follows a bumpy path, and director Scott and first-time screenwriter Callie Khouri don't cushion the ride. This is DVD dynamite, detonated by Oscar-nominated performances from Davis and Sarandon in the title roles. Davis plays Thelma, a Arkansas housewife married to a cheating, verbally abusive salesman (Christopher McDonald). Sarandon plays Thelma's pal Louise, a waitress who is pushing forty and fed up with waiting for her musician boyfriend (subtly detailed by Michael Madsen) to stop roving and commit. They take a weekend trip, just two women putting drudgery and men behind them for a few days. That's before rape and murder enter the picture, and the cops, led by Keitel, start chasing them. As these female outlaws attempt to escape to a new life in Mexico, the movie offers vignettes that are comic, tragic, and surreal. They pick up J.D., a hitchhiking hunk charmingly played by Pitt. In bed with Thelma, J.D.—using a hair dryer as a gun—teaches Thelma the art of armed robbery. Then he robs her. The experience pushes Thelma into a life of crime. She won't go back to a cage. Neither will Louise. Are they feminist martyrs or bitches from hell? Neither. They're flesh-and-blood women out to expose the blight of sexism. This film isn't about rage or revenge; it's about waste.

Hot Bonus: Scott is enormously skilled at commentary tracks, and he proves it again by taking you inside his film as art and commerce.

Key Scene: That controversial up-up-and-away ending is now the stuff of screen legend and a provocation for endless discussion.

Them! (1954)

Starring: James Whitmore, Edmund Gwenn, Joan Weldon

Directed by: Gordon Douglas

The biggie among 1950s creature features concerns jumbo radioactive ants in the New Mexico desert, where atomic bomb tests are conducted. Hint. Hint. Nuclear paranoia was at its peak, so all the actors take things very seriously, including Whitmore as a state trooper, Gwenn as an ant scientist, and Weldon as his curvaceous (aren't they always?) daughter. When the ants take refuge in the Los Angeles drainage system and the good guys bring out the flamethrowers, it's hard not to get excited. The ants look terrific on this crisp black-and-white DVD transfer (the effects even won an Oscar nomination). You may laugh, but it's nearly impossible to turn away.

Hot Bonus: The outtakes, featuring malfunctioning ants, are a hoot.

Key Scene: The ants in their nest will give you the creepy-crawlies.

There's Something (More) About Mary (Two-Disc Collector's Edition) (1998)

Starring: Cameron Diaz, Ben Stiller, Matt Dillon

Directed by: Bobby Farrelly and Peter Farrelly

What's that jism doing in Stiller's hair? And why is Diaz rubbing the stuff in her blonde locks as a grooming aid? By now everyone knows about that notorious scene. But this new Collector's Edition of the Farrelly brothers hit adds ten more minutes to the party, plus dozens of extras. The picture looks sharp, with sound to match, so settle in for sensational, sicko fun. Diaz plays Mary with the beaming sexiness and sharp comic timing of a born star. The quest to win Mary sparks the script. Ted (Stiller), who has been obsessed with Mary since high school in Rhode Island, hires private eye Pat (Dillon) to find her. He traces Mary to Florida, where she's working in orthopedics, caring for her handicapped brother, and dating a disabled architect. There's a wicked twist in everything from the wry songs of Jonathan Richman to Stiller's romanticized version of a stalker. After Mary, the Farrellys lost their touch, but this was their shining two hours when they helped liberate comedy from the chains of timidity, banality, and censorship.

Hot Bonus: Terrifically funny footage of the Farrellys directing the actors.

Key Scene: Stiller will forever be known for his hair-gel moment and the penis-caught-in-his zipper moment, but I personally will never forget his fight with a dog he thought he had killed.

They Shoot Horses, Don't They? (1969)

Starring: Jane Fonda, Gig Young, Michael Sarrazin, Susannah York

Directed by: Sydney Pollack

During the Great Depression, the unemployed would often participate in punishing dance marathons, lasting hundreds of hours, dancing in circles until their feet bled for a shot at the grand prize. Director Pollack uses Horace McCoy's 1935 novel as an allegory for human suffering and resilience. After years of cropped TV prints, the widescreen DVD transfer is a revelation. So too are the performances. Fonda—in her first worthy dramatic role as the tough, despairing Gloria—is so good, she stings. And Young won an Oscar as the seedy emcee who keeps the dancers going to work the crowd. It's not a pretty picture, just an unforgettable one.

Hot Bonus: Nothing but a trailer, presumably the pristine sound and image were considered bonus enough.

Key Scene: The Derby, in which the dancers are forced to run faster and faster to bouncy music while hiding their physical pain and mental anguish.

Thief (Director's Cut) (1981)

Starring: James Caan, Tuesday Weld, Willie Nelson, Robert Prosky

Directed by: Michael Mann

Mann, in his feature directing debut, tells the story of an ex-con and jewel thief (Caan) who wants to get out of the crime game, except they keep pulling him back in. You've heard that before, but Mann makes you see and feel it as if for the first time. The DVD Director's Cut adds scenes not seen when the film opened and deletes others that were in the original version. Mann's gift for atmosphere and authenticity was there from the start, enhanced here by the cinematography of Donald Thorin and the electronic score by Tangerine Dream. Caan, in his best acting since *The Godfather*, is mesmeric in the title role, and gets strong support from Weld as the woman he marries, Prosky as the Chicago gangster who won't let him quit, and Nelson as the safecracker who taught him his trade.

Hot Bonus: Mann and Caan who kick around the film's issues with great humor, including the use of real thieves and cops in the film.

Key Scene: Caan cutting through a safe with a thermal lance.

Thief of Bagdad, The (1940)

Starring: Sabu, Rex Ingram, Conrad Veidt, Jon Justin June Duprez

Directed by: Ludwig Berger, Michael Powell, and Tim Whelan (uncredited: Zoltan Korda, Alexander Korda, and William Cameron Menzies)

An utterly beautiful DVD of a great Technicolor fantasy drawn from *The Arabian Nights*. And so what if it took six directors to do it? Sabu stars as Abu, the little thief of Bagdad who manages to save Prince Ahmad (Justin) and the Princess

(Duprez) he loves from the clutches of the evil Jaffar (a splendidly slimy Veidt). Abu does all this with the help of a fifty-foot genie (Ingram, magnificent), who grants Abu three wishes if Abu promises to free him from a bottle. What would you do?

Hot Bonus: The full-screen DVD transfer must be reward enough, since no one saw fit to explain the ins and outs of this troubled production, which won Oscars for art direction, cinematography, and special effects.

Key Scene: Sabu's magic carpet ride gets me every time.

Thin Blue Line, The (1988)

Directed by: Errol Morris

Leave it to the gifted Morris to make a documentary about the slippery nature of truth. It plays like a surreal whodunit. On November 27, 1976, Dallas policeman Robert Wood was shot five times and killed when he pulled over a vehicle being driven without lights. Hitchhiker Randall Adams is tried, convicted, and sentenced to die while Morris opens up the possibility that David Harris, then sixteen and now on death row for another murder, is the guilty party (Adams was later released). There is nothing cut-and-dried about Morris's approach to the material. His eerie closeups of smoking guns, bullet-wound diagrams, and flying milkshakes, set to a jangling score by Philip Glass, create a hypnotic sense of unease that seeps into the DVD transfer. The film confirms an attorney's description of the police as a thin blue line—a fragile barrier separating civilization from anarchy.

Hot Bonus: Nothing extra—it's all in the movie.

Key Scene: The reenactment of the murder done with actors as it merges with real-life testimony that throws objective facts out of sync.

Thin Red Line, The (1998)

Starring: Sean Penn, Nick Nolte, Jim Caviezel, Adrien Brody, Elias Koteas

Directed by: Terrence Malick

Released in the shadow of Steven Spielberg's heroic and reassuring *Saving Private Ryan*, this poetic and discursive World War II film—adapted by director Malick from the James Jones novel about the key American victory over the Japanese at Guadalcanal—offers raw fear, combat numbness, and moral uncertainty, plus assurances that war dehumanizes the men it doesn't kill. Malick tells us what we don't want to hear. No wonder it missed out on the Best Picture Oscar for which it was nominated. But don't miss out on this DVD, which turns the potent sound design and John Toll's artful camera lighting into a strikingly memorable disc. With the exceptions of Penn and Nolte—who have major roles and perform them superbly—the bigger names (John Travolta, George Clooney) mostly take small parts as a tribute to the reclusive Malick; *Line* is only his third film in twenty-five years. That leaves the focus on then lesser-known actors (Caviezel, Brody, Koteas), all of whom deliver nuanced performances. An army rifle company hits the beach at Guadalcanal expecting mass slaughter, only to find no initial resistance from the Japanese. Yet the scene is all the more terrifying coming after so much anxious waiting. Malick also shows the devastating effect of American and Japanese invaders on this serene island, from its Melanesian inhabitants to the shelling that obliterates vegetation and wildlife. Though the battle scenes rank with the greatest ever filmed, most prevalent are images of fragility, be they a bird's broken wing, a soldier's trembling blink, or a splash of blood on a blade of grass. In cutting an early six-hour version by more than half, Malick has left characters and plot strands dangling. But his haunting film shuns platitudes to expose war as a crime against nature.

Hot Bonus: The uncut version of the film would have been a DVD event, but Malick offers only the full versions of the Melanesian songs used in the film.

Key Scene: The sun following the backs of soldiers as they mount a hill—a wrenching counterpoint to the carnage ahead.

Thing From Another World, The (1951)

Starring: Kenneth Tobey, James Arness, Margaret Sheridan

Directed by: Christian Nyby

John Carpenter directed a far more graphic remake in 1982. But this thriller—set in an Arctic outpost where the air force joins scientists in a search for an alien aircraft buried in the ice—is far more effective for insinuating what Carpenter spells out. The black-and-white print shows only minor flaws on the DVD, which rewards repeated viewings. For movie detectives who suspect the film's legendary producer Howard Hawks really

directed the piece—Nyby was Hawks's editor on *Red River*—there is evidence aplenty. Just watch the Hawksian emphasis on men in groups and the sexual teasing between Tobey as an air force captain and Sheridan as a feisty member of the scientific team. Or just watch the men cut the Thing (Arness, before he became a TV star with *Gunsmoke*) out of the ice and scare yourself silly with the help of Dimitri Tiomkin's Theremin-based score.

Hot Bonus: The trailer, which sells the movie as pure horror.

Key Scene: When the ice melts, and the Thing emerges.

Third Man, The (Special Edition) (1949)

Starring: Orson Welles, Joseph Cotten, Alida Valli, Trevor Howard

Directed by: Carol Reed

Criterion does a classic proud on DVD. Enter the sewers of postwar Vienna where the black market thrives and American novelist Holly Martins (Cotten) searches for his friend Harry Lime (Welles). He finds him being lowered into his grave while Harry's lady love Anna (Valli) watches and a British major, Calloway (Howard), tells Holly that Harry was the crookedest of them all. Don't believe a word of it, except for the crooked part. Just revel in the delicious intrigue that director Reed and screenwriter Graham Greene lay out with the help of ace cinematographer Robert Krasker and the zither music by Anton Karas that you can never get out of your head.

Hot Bonus: A 1951 radio show, written by and starring Welles, in which he dramatizes the life of Harry Lime before his adventures on screen.

Key Scene: The delayed entrance of Welles as Harry in an abandoned amusement park. We hear the zither, see a cat crawl to his feet, and then that wonderful, smirking face as he justifies to Holly his corruption in a corrupt world: "In Italy for thirty years under the Borgias, they had warfare, terror, murder, and bloodshed. But they produced Michelangelo, Leonardo da Vinci, and the Renaissance. In Switzerland they had brotherly love, and they had five hundred years of democracy and peace. And what did that produce? The cuckoo clock."

Thirteen (2003)

Starring: Evan Rachel Wood, Nikki Reed, Holly Hunter

Directed by: Catherine Hardwicke

Thirteen-year-old Tracy (Wood) lives with her

single mom (Hunter), an at-home hairdresser, and mock studies for seventh grade while wondering what "cool" is. Motherless Evie (Reed), also thirteen, defines cool for Tracy. It means hoochie tops, body piercings, shoplifting, drugs, bad boys, oral sex, lap dances, and a three-way that Evie tries to negotiate with Tracy and a twentyish hunk (Kip Pardue). Every parent's nightmare about how girls go wrong is packed into this movie and onto Hunter's frazzled face as she watches her daughter deteriorate. The DVD transfer is up to every stylistic device used by Hardwicke, who won the directing prize at Sundance, to pack the film with raw vitality. Reed is strikingly good as Evie. She should be: She was thirteen when she wrote the semiautobiographical script with Hardwicke. Wood, then fifteen, makes Tracy's transformation harrowing and haunting. Brace yourself for *Thirteen*: it means to shake you, and does.

Hot Bonus: Ten deleted scenes that help flesh out the characters.

Key Scene: The opener in which Tracy and Evie—high on huffing—jump up and down on a bed, laughing and slapping each other until the slaps become punches, noses gush blood, and the film unspools in flashback.

Thirty Two Short Films About Glenn Gould (1993)

Starring: Colm Fiore
Directed by: Francois Girard

Half documentary, half meditation on the life of the Canadian pianist, who died of a stroke in 1982 at the age of fifty after building a reputation as an eccentric, reclusive musical genius (he retired from concert performance at age thirty-two). Director Girard uses Gould's famous recording of Bach's "Goldberg" Variations—music that Hannibal Lecter conducted in his jail cell in *The Silence of the Lambs*—to approximate the life of this unique figure, a piano prodigy from age four. The adult Gould, played with haunting expressiveness by Fiore, is seen in fragmentary vignettes—running from seconds to minutes—that show him preparing to go on stage by soaking his arms in hot water or making pronouncements on topics as diverse as numerology and Petula Clark. Girard's agile camera moves smoothly through these short films, and the DVD transfer retains all the grace notes that help put us inside Gould's head.

Hot Bonus: Bios of Girard and Fiore come in handy after watching the film.

Key Scene: Gould orchestrating the voices of diners at a truck stop.

39 Steps, The (1935)

Starring: Robert Donat, Madeleine Carroll, Peggy Ashcroft, John Laurie
Directed by: Alfred Hitchcock

An early Hitchcock gem gets a superior DVD picture and sound transfer from Criterion, making this comedy-thriller twice as inviting. Donat is the poor sucker who ruins his vacation in Scotland by getting mixed up in a spy ring. It's his good luck to get handcuffed to Carroll—their mutual hostility is a real turn-on—as they encounter a married couple (Ashcroft and Laurie—both marvelous) who wear invisible handcuffs. Hitchcock has a high old time, fading from a woman's scream to the sound of a shrieking train whistle and then setting his lovers on a search for a master spy (Godfrey Tearle) with a portion missing from a pinky finger on his right hand.

Hot Bonus: A solid featurette on Hitchcock's British films.

Key Scene: The confrontation with Mr. Memory (Wylie Watson), a music-hall performer who unlocks the mystery of the thirty-nine steps.

This Is Spinal Tap (Special Edition) (1984)

Starring: Christopher Guest, Michael McKean, Harry Shearer
Directed by: Rob Reiner

Here's the DVD proof that Reiner's fake documentary (it mocks the thing it loves) is the greatest rock movie ever. Low-budget and largely improvised, the film tells the tale of a bogus band of heavy-metal Brits: Guest's Nigel Tufnel, McKean's David St. Hubbins, and Shearer's Derek Smalls. Any DVD time capsule must include Nigel at the piano to play his fusion of Mozart and Bach, titled "Lick My Love Pump." Together with Reiner, who plays the documentarian Marty DiBergi, these comics came up with an unpredictably poignant portrait of rock and the people who live for it. It's not just a comedy; it's a love story. And it goes to Eleven.

Hot Bonus: Audio commentary from the band members who speak in character watching the film from a twenty-first-century perspective. They complain about how the film depicts them and lament the sorry state of their careers.

Key Scene: There's no sadder metaphor for the human condition than the band watching its eighteen-inch replica of Stonehenge get lowered to the floor of the stage, right between the dancing dwarves. Rock 'n' roll!

Three Colors Trilogy: Blue/ White/Red (1993/1994)

Starring: Juliette Binoche, Julie Delpy, Irène Jacob
Directed by: Krzysztof Kieslowski

This three-disc set contains all three parts of Polish director Kieslowski's trilogy—Blue, White, and Red—the three colors of the French flag, representing liberty, equality, and fraternity. Kieslowski died two years after completing the trilogy. He and his writing partner, Krzysztof Piesiewicz, wanted the trilogy to reflect the tug between humanism and consumerism in contemporary Europe. They succeeded brilliantly, using color, design, sound, and movement to play variations on their theme. The DVD trilogy comes loaded with extras that help you navigate the films, including interviews with Kieslowski's crew, insights from film scholars Geoff Andrew and Annette Insdorf, and comments from Polish director Agnieszka Holland. Kieslowski's career is thoroughly examined, from his student films to his filmed "cinema lessons." It's a remarkable collection.

Hot Bonus: Interviews with the lead actress in each film.

Key Scenes:

Blue: The moment when Bincohe reenters life, after the death of her composer husband and baby in a car crash, by leaving their country home for Paris, where a bustling, liberating city still can't free her from the sound of her husband's music and her nagging doubts about his fidelity.

White: The moment when Delpy dumps her impotent Polish husband (Zbigniew Zamachowski), a hairdresser who offers several funny and vengeful ways to put the marriage back on equal terms.

Red: The moment when Jacob, plagued by a possessive lover in Geneva, forms a platonic friendship with a retired judge (Jean-Louis Trintignant), whose dog she has just run over.

Three Kings (Special Edition) (1999)

Starring: George Clooney, Mark Wahlberg, Ice Cube, Spike Jonze
Directed and written by: David O. Russell

In this comedy of shocking gravity, Russell takes on the Persian Gulf War, Saddam Hussein, Bush Sr., and U.S. military hypocrisy. As ever, he pulls no punches. A rarely better Clooney stars as Archie Gates, a captain who enlists his sergeant buddies Wahlberg and Ice Cube in a scheme: A hillbilly private (*Being John Malkovich* auteur Jonze

in a credible acting debut) has dug a treasure map out of the ass of an Iraqi POW. With hostilities winding down, Clooney and company see a last chance at collecting some of that Kuwaiti loot. They grow a conscience when they see Iraqis abandoned by American forces who once promised them the moon. Watched now, in a post-9/11 world, the film offers further provocations.

Hot Bonus: Russell is a one-man band when it comes to commentary tracks. He holds nothing back, including his differences with Clooney. There is also a warning not to think your DVD player is on the fritz because Russell experiments with color, sound, and film stocks throughout the film.

Key Scene: A bullet going through a body—an MTV-ish technical trick that takes on human resonance when we see the toll taken in bodies.

3 Women (1977)

Starring: Sissy Spacek, Shelley Duvall, Janice Rule
Directed by: Robert Altman

Altman's haunting mood piece is a challenge for DVD, given its gauzy pastel colors and overlapping sound, but Criterion is up to the job. It took forever to get this enigmatic masterpiece on disc, and it's worth the wait. Duvall gives the performance of her life as Millie Lammoreaux—thoroughly modern Millie to those who mock her awkward attempts at cool. Spacek's Pinky Rose shows up out of nowhere to work alongside Millie at a spa for arthritic seniors in the California desert. They hit it off so well that Pinky moves in with Millie at an apartment complex for singles, run by Willie (Rule), a mute painter who does murals at the bottom of a swimming pool. Things get strange when the personalities of the women begin to merge. Altman and the three magical actresses hold you in thrall.

Hot Bonus: Audio commentary from Altman, who confesses the film emerged out of a dream he had about his wife.

Key Scene: Duvall's anal-neurotic preparations for a date—she's serving frozen shrimp cocktail—that goes hilariously, heartbreakingly wrong.

Thunderball (Collector's Edition) (1965)

Starring: Sean Connery, Claudine Auger, Adolfo Celi

Directed by: Terence Young

The fourth Bond film benefited from its biggest budget yet, and the color, sound, and Oscar-winning special effects show up beautifully on DVD. So does Connery, who exudes the charm and charisma to rise above the new influx of gimmicks that eventually spoiled the series. The underwater battles, as 007 races to the Bahamas to snatch a sunken nuclear bomb from the clutches of SPECTRE villain Largo (Celi) and his hottie mistress, Domino (Auger), are thrillingly staged. Connery must have enjoyed himself since he remade the same film as *Never Say Never Again* in 1983.

Hot Bonus: A profile of director Young, a stylish British chap who was reportedly more like Bond than the hardscrabble, working-class Connery.

Key Scene: Bond extricating himself from Largo's shark-infested pool. The credit sequence, with Tom Jones warbling the title song, isn't bad either.

THX 1138 (The George Lucas Director's Cut/ Two-Disc Special Edition) (1971)

Starring: Robert Duvall, Donald Pleasance, Maggie McOmie

Directed by: George Lucas

A great DVD to argue about. Lucas's debut film, based on a short he made in college, lit no fires at the box office. Critics called this futuristic cautionary fable slow and plodding. Look at it now, and you can still see Lucas's talent emerging in the story of Duvall, labeled THX 1138 in a robotic society that drugs its citizens to inhibit individual thinking and sexual desire, and his desire to escape with LUH 3417 (McOmie), the woman he loves, with the help of scientist SEN 5241 (Pleasance). You can also see that Lucas, following his lead with the first *Star Wars* trilogy on DVD, has altered his original film with enhanced computer effects without providing the original film for comparison. Heresy? Hu-

bris? You decide. But playing god with DVDs is a trend that needs tempering.

Hot Bonus: Lucas's original fifteen-minute student film is presented without digital tampering or remastering. Amen to that, brother.

Key Scene: The jail breakout of Duvall and McOmie.

Tightrope (1984)

Starring: Clint Eastwood, Genevieve Bujold

Directed by: Richard Tuggle

Eastwood gives one of his best and riskiest performances as Wes Block, a New Orleans homicide detective with enough kinky baggage to rival the serial killer of prostitutes currently plaguing the Big Easy. The city's dark-alley allure comes through potently on DVD. Deserted by his wife, who left him with their two daughters (Jennifer Beck and Clint's real daughter, Alison Eastwood), the sex-starved Wes starts seeking more than information from the hookers he questions. When several of these women turn up dead after he beds them, you may find it hard to reconcile the loving father with the man who likes to handcuff hookers to bedposts. A rape-crisis counselor, played with snappy authority by Bujold, tries to help, but Wes must grapple with his conscience alone. Director Tuggle, who wrote the script, shies away from the film's darker implications at the end. But until then, he really does keep the audience walking a tightrope.

Hot Bonus: Trailers for other Eastwood films are a poor excuse for extras, especially in a bold film like this that points the way to Eastwood's late-career renaissance with *Unforgiven*, *Mystic River*, and *Million Dollar Baby*. Rumor has it that Eastwood took over the direction from Tuggle early in the film—why no commentary on that?

Key Scene: Wes unmasks a killer and sees his own face.

Tin Cup (1996)

Starring: Kevin Costner, Rene Russo

Directed by: Ron Shelton

Check out this DVD for proof that it is possible to make golf sexy. Costner reteams with *Bull Durham* writer-director Shelton to play Roy McAvoy, a Texas slacker who runs a rundown driving range and doesn't think much past his next margarita until a sexy psychotherapist (Russo) shows up looking for lessons. Suddenly, Roy wants to enter the U.S. Open and win. Costner and Russo spark and spar like pros, and Shelton's golf footage is so energetic you may want to use your DVD remote for an instant replay.

Hot Bonus: Just a luscious widescreen DVD transfer.

Key Scene: Costner turning his instructions about a golf swing into a way of life: "Waggle it, and let the big dog eat."

Tin Drum, The (1979)

Starring: David Bennent, Mario Adorf
Directed by: Volker Schlöndorff

Günter Grass's novel about Oskar, a child who defies the Nazis by refusing to grow up, is Germany's finest postwar novel. Though great books often make disappointing films, director Schlöndorff–with Grass's collaboration on the screenplay–creates a stirring and sometimes shocking film that deservedly won the Oscar for Best Foreign Film. The parable about the dark side of human nature is rendered more charming and chilling by the use of a child as the protagonist. Bennent, then twelve, with his large, sunken eyes and stubborn mouth, is indelible as Oskar. And the letterboxed DVD transfer is alive with color and the sound of Maurice Jarre's memorably scary score.

Hot Bonus: Video interviews with Schlöndorff and young Bennett from the Cannes Film Festival, where the film won the top prize.

Key Scene: Oskar beating his tin drum to block out the world around him.

Titanic (Three-Disc Collector's Edition) (1997)

Starring: Leonardo DiCaprio, Kate Winslet, Billy Zane, Kathy Bates
Directed by: James Cameron

Since 1999, fans of the Oscar-winning Best Picture, which grossed $600 million to become the biggest box-office success of all time, had to content themselves with a single disc DVD with no extras. Now director Cameron has opened the floodgates with this Collector's Edition that looks and sounds as perfect as digital technology will allow. *Titanic* junkies can utilize a branching feature that allows viewers to access an hour of deleted scenes at the exact spot where the scenes were cut. A two-hour documentary features interviews with Cameron, DiCaprio, Winslet, and others. And that's just for starters. As for the movie itself, you know the story: DiCaprio and Winslet fall in love. The ship sinks. He dies. She lives. And Celine Dion sings about a heart that will go on and on. No one

cares anymore that Cameron's poet's eye for spectacle is almost blinded by his tin ear for dialogue. *Titanic* is simply the greatest romantic epic since *Gone With the Wind*, and everyone with a DVD player is going to own this Collector's Edition.

Hot Bonus: In addition to the above, Cameron includes interviews with studio executives who predicted the film would be a disaster.

Key Scene: The ship goes down.

To Catch a Thief (1955)

Starring: Cary Grant, Grace Kelly
Directed by: Alfred Hitchcock

The French Riviera looks impossibly glamorous. Grant and Kelly look even better. Do you need other reasons to grab this DVD? He plays a retired cat burglar trying to catch the new kid on the block. She's an American beauty, traveling with her mother (the invaluable Jessie Royce Landis). "Palaces are for royalty," Monaco's Princess-to-be tells Grant. "We're just common people with a bank account." Hitchcock has a ball mixing suspense and double entendres when Kelly takes Grant for a high-speed picnic drive on the twisty roads of the Riviera: "Do you want a leg or a breast?" she asks Grant teasingly. And so it goes. Hitchcock is taking a vacation from his more profound thrillers and inviting us along for the ride.

Hot Bonus: Rare glimpses of the director at work on the set.

Key Scene: The Grant-Kelly kiss that ends in an orgasmic fireworks display was destined to be imitated for decades by lesser filmmakers.

To Die For (1995)

Starring: Nicole Kidman, Matt Dillon, Joaquin Phoenix
Directed by: Gus Van Sant

Kidman's Suzanne Stone will kill for a TV career, even as a weather girl on the local ten-watt cable channel in Little Hope, New Hampshire, where she lives with her bartender husband Larry (Dillon). Larry wants kids, which would spoil her figure. Divorce would lose Suzanne her condo and cash. Better to just have her teen lover, Jimmy (Phoenix), kill Larry. Director Van Sant sets up the media as a poison piñata, and screenwriter Buck Henry, adapting the 1992 novel by Joyce Maynard, whacks at the target with the sharp edge of his wit, spilling the contents for observation and rude laughs. This is prime social satire sparked by a volcanically sexy and richly comic performance by Kidman, which this DVD preserves for a much-deserved immortality.

Hot Bonus: A full-screen version that improves on the letterboxed format (also provided) by conforming better to the shape of Suzanne's TV screen.

Key Scene: At the end when Suzanne gets hers, she also gets the last close-up: an eerily beautiful freeze frame that lingers long after the image dissolves into dots. Van Sant makes wicked sport of TV, but he doesn't underestimate its power to blind us to its faults and bring us to our knees.

To Have and Have Not (1944)

Starring: Humphrey Bogart, Lauren Bacall
Directed by: Howard Hawks

A Hemingway novel, adapted by William Faulkner, and starring Bogie and Bacall in roles that brought them together on and off screen. This belongs on the DVD shelf right next to the vintage wine. Bogart plays the skipper of a fishing boat in Martinique who tries to stay out of politics as France falls to the Nazis. But this is a Hawks picture, and a man has to take responsibility. He also has to find the right woman. Enter Bacall, in her smashing film debut. "I'm hard to get," she tells Bogart. "All you have to do is ask me."

Hot Bonus: A "making of" feature about how the stars fell in love on the set.

Key Scene: Bacall to Bogart after their first kiss: "You don't have to say anything and you don't have to do anything. Oh, maybe just whistle. You know how to whistle, don't you? You just put your lips together and blow."

To Kill a Mockingbird (Two-Disc Collector's Edition) (1962)

Starring: Gregory Peck, Mary Badham, Philip Alford, Robert Duvall
Directed by: Robert Mulligan

Peck's Oscar-winning performance as attorney Atticus Finch will endure as long as there are movies, not to mention DVDs. The Collector's Edition disc is a beauty, capturing the delicacy of Russell Harlan's black-and-white camerawork and Elmer Bernstein's score. Set in Alabama in the 1930s, this film adaptation (by Horton Foote) of Harper Lee's Pulitzer Prize–winning novel, concerns Atticus defending a black man (Brock Peters) accused

of raping a white woman. But the soul of the film resides in the relationship that Atticus, a widower, has with his two children—ten-year-old Jem (Alford) and six-year-old Jean Louise, known as Scout and played beautifully by Badham. He teaches them about racism and about the humanity in Boo Radley (Duvall in his film debut), a neighbor the kids have demonized. Mulligan's nuanced direction keeps preachiness at bay, and Peck keeps every emotion true.

Hot Bonus: An outstanding retrospective documentary, *Fearful Symmetry*, reunites the cast and presents a striking portrait of the South in the 1930s.

Key Scene: Atticus leaving the courtroom in defeat, not noticing the spectators in the upstairs gallery with his daughter. "Miss Jean Louise, stand up," a black minister instructs her. "Your father is passing."

Tokyo Story (Two-Disc Special Edition) (1953)

Starring: Chishu Ryu, Chieko Higashiyama
Directed by: Yasujiro Ozu

The artful simplicity of Ozu comes through with heart-piercing intimacy in Criterion's DVD of the Japanese director's most famous work. An old couple (Ryu and Higashiyama) leaves the country to visit their doctor son and hairdresser daughter in Tokyo. No fake contrivances intrude; we just see the aging parents buffeted by the city and busy lives that no longer have a place for them. Ozu's stationary camera can make an empty room resonate with the presence of a former occupant. He is a poet of cinema, and this newly restored digital transfer honors each image and sound that he creates.

Hot Bonus: A tribute to Ozu from directors as diverse as Aki Kaurismäki, Claire Denis, Paul Schrader, Wim Wenders, and Hsiao-Hsien Hou.

Key Scene: The parents, shuffled off to a crowded spa by their son and daughter, stand alone and isolated, wondering where they do belong.

Tom Jones (1963)

Starring: Albert Finney, Susannah York, Hugh Griffith, Edith Evans
Directed by: Tony Richardson

The Best Picture Oscar winner brims over with bawdy wit. Maybe a little less so on the DVD, for which director Richardson trimmed nearly ten minutes to speed up the pace for its release on disc. Bad idea. Watching John Osborne's literate and zesty adaptation of Henry Fielding's raucous

1749 novel only whets your appetite for more. Finney, a great actor captured here in his full, vigorous youth, plays the title character, a bastard by birth who roams England's backroads in search of adventure, mostly with thieves and wenches. Richardson uses every camera trick to hurtle the plot along, which introduces picture and sound problems in the DVD transfer, mostly grain in the darker scenes. No matter. You'll be too busy laughing as Tom falls for Sophie (York), the lovely daughter of Squire Western, delightfully played by Griffith as a lewd, unwashed, bewigged farm animal. His sister, acted with priceless indignation by Evans, is horrified to find him sleeping with his dogs in a drunken stupor. Finney, Griffith, and Evans joined Diane Cilento and Joyce Redman—as two of Tom's conquests—in the lineup of Oscar nominees. They were all robbed for not winning, though John Addison did grab a golden boy for his tinkling, ravishing score. Get the disc, and dig in.

Hot Bonus: Production notes with factoids, such as the info that Tom Jones was the last film that John F. Kennedy ever saw. The film was reportedly screened at the White House five days before his assassination.

Key Scene: The most erotic and witty eating sequence ever, featuring Finney and Redman ripping at their food, stuffing it into their mouths, and staring at each other with what can only be called sexual gluttony.

Tombstone (Two-Disc Collector's Edition) (1993)

Starring: Kurt Russell, Val Kilmer, Bill Paxton, Sam Elliott

Directed by: George P. Cosmatos

The umpteenth film version of the story of Wyatt Earp (Russell) heading for the famous shootout at the O.K. Corral with his brothers Morgan (Paxton) and Virgil (Elliott)

is more entertaining then it has any right to be. The scrappy integrity of Russell's performance helps, but it's Kilmer who wraps the movie up and takes it home as the preening, poetry-spouting, consumptive Doc Holliday, boozing and coughing up blood with time out to shoot a few bad guys. The Collector's Edition is a major step up from the former DVD model—with both 5.1 Dolby and DTS sound to pump up the action. Cosmatos, a lover of westerns since his boyhood in Italy, lets that love show through. Not bad for a guy who directed *Rambo*.

Hot Bonus: There are about five minutes of deleted scenes on this Director's Cut, including Doc reciting poetry in his hotel room on a stormy night.

Key Scene: The final shootout is a goodie, but give me the moment when Doc pecks out a little Chopin on a battered saloon piano.

Tommy (Superbit) (1975)

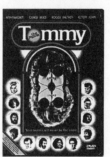

Starring: Roger Daltrey, Ann-Margret, Oliver Reed, Jack Nicholson

Directed by: Ken Russell

The Who's rock opera—let's hear it for Pete Townshend—gets the Russell treatment, which means your home-theater will have to go into overdrive to pump out the excess. Daltrey takes the title role as the deaf, dumb, and blind kid, reeling from a childhood trauma. The Who's John Entwistle appears as himself, and the late drummer Keith Moon has a ball fiddling about with the boy as Uncle Ernie. Tommy's sexpot mom, played by an Oscar-nominated Ann-Margret, and stepdad (Reed) take him to a doctor (Nicholson—yes, he sings!), but nothing helps until Tommy learns to play a mean pinball. Then he's the new messiah. The movie is not so much sung through as sung right at you. The DVD makes it an enveloping experience.

Hot Bonus: The Superbit process optimizes picture and sound, and when Daltrey sings "I'm Free," you'll get the full effect.

Key Scene: Tommy's defeat of the Pinball Wizard (Elton John) is the production number to end all production numbers.

Tootsie (1982)

"Marvelous fun."

Starring: Dustin Hoffman, Jessica Lange, Bill Murray

Directed by: Sydney Pollack

Hoffman and Pollack fought like bulls during the making of this classic comedy. Maybe all actors and directors should do that if the result is this good. *Tootsie* looks just fine on DVD, even if the impression lingers that the tech team could have done better. But the spirit of the movie, with a script by Larry Gelbart and Murray Schisgal, sparkles. Hoffman plays Michael Dorsey, an unemployed actor who wins the role of a hospital administrator on a TV soap opera by disguising himself as a woman he names Dorothy. Michael's roommate (an uproarious Murray) cocks an eyebrow: "It is just for the money, isn't it? It's not just so you can wear these little outfits?" And his agent (a sassy Pollack) is aghast: "God, I begged you to get some therapy." In a way he does. As Michael ultimately tells Julie (an Oscar-winning Lange), the soap queen he loves: "I was a better man with you as a woman than I ever was with a woman as a man." Hoffman's Dorothy is something less than a ten, but his performance is a true beauty.

Hot Bonus: A choice of watching the film letterboxed or full frame.

Key Scene: The live unveiling of Hoffman's identity on the medical soap. Watching at home, Murray quips, "That is one nutty hospital."

Top Gun (Two-Disc Special Collector's Edition) (1986)

Starring: Tom Cruise, Kelly McGillis, Val Kilmer, Anthony Edwards

Directed by: Tony Scott

The jangle of jingoism in the air made a box-office bell ringer out of this navy recruiting poster disguised as a movie. But as a widescreen DVD with a ton of flyboy action and a choice of stratospheric Dolby Digital or DTS sound, it's a top-tier demo disc. Cruise plays Maverick, a hotshot pilot graduated to Top Gun—read: the navy's elite Fighter Weapon School near San Diego. Maverick's world involves Goose (Edwards), a radar officer; Iceman (Kilmer), his chief pilot competition; and his improbably gorgeous female instructor in astrophysics (McGillis), who, being a civilian,

doesn't get a nickname. As the script struggles to make a lick of sense, Scott stages terrific aerial battles with the occasional cut to a closeup of Cruise.

Hot Bonus: There's a stuffy six-part documentary on the film, but for real fun, go find the 1994 movie *Sleep With Me* in which Quentin Tarantino explains the gay subtext in Top Gun regarding Maverick and Iceman.

Key Scene: Cruise, winking conspiratorially at the camera as he climbs into the cockpit and says, "I feel need, the need for speed."

Topsy-Turvy (1999)

Starring: Jim Broadbent, Allan Corduner

Directed and written by: Mike Leigh

Leigh's magnificently produced, directed, written, and acted biopic of librettist William Gilbert (Broadbent) and composer Arthur Sullivan (Corduner) doesn't have a dull scene in its entire 160-minute running time. These contentious partners, legends of the British stage, produced fourteen operettas, including *The Pirates of Penzance* and *The Mikado*; the creation of the latter in 1884 is what occupies Leigh and his sterling cast. The sumptuous look of the piece (the DVD is an absolute stunner) is as removed as can be from Leigh's working-class dramas (*Naked*, *Secrets and Lie*, *Vera Drake*), but the director's scrappy insistence on emotional authenticity shines through every frame. The entire cast excels, but Broadbent looms like a colossus playing a humorless man who writes with surpassing wit.

Hot Bonus: Leigh explains the way he works. During months of rehearsal, the actors help him write the script.

Key Scene: Gilbert rehearsing the actors with an attention to detail that serves as a celebration of the agony and inspiration that produces art.

Total Recall (Special Edition) (1990)

SPECIAL EDITION

SCHWARZENEGGER

TOTAL RECALL

Starring: Arnold Schwarzenegger, Sharon Stone, Rachel Ticotin

Directed by: Paul Verhoeven

Hugely entertaining sci-fi, based on a Philip K. Dick story. Ah-nuld plays a worker drone, married to Stone, who decides to chill out by taking a virtual vacation to Mars.

The crew at Rekall, Inc. hooks him to a chair, attaches wires to his skull, and there he is collecting memories, including a sexy love interest (Ticotin) in commando drag. Is it real or a dream? Verhoeven keeps you guessing through a visual assault that tests the limits of DVD technology. Mars looks like an overcrowded club where the owner (Ronny Cox) charges you just to breathe, and the clientele includes mutants and a three-breasted hooker. Kinky? Don't forget, Verhoeven gave us *Showgirls*.

Hot Bonus: In case the DVD packaging isn't enough—it's a round tin shaped like Mars—Schwarzenegger and Verhoeven chew the fat.

Key Scene: Schwarzenegger getting the best of a lively Stone in a bloody fight. "Consider this a divorce," he says, delivering the KO punch.

Touch of Evil (Restored) (1958)

Starring: Orson Welles, Charlton Heston, Janet Leigh, Marlene Dietrich
Directed by: Orson Welles

Now considered a masterpiece, Welles's film about a Mexican border town where Mike Vargas (Heston), a narcotics agent, tangles with the tangled morals of local cop Hank Quinlan (Welles) was originally recut by the studio and dumped on the market, which is hard to figure since every scene is a winner. Welles is monumental as the fat, sweaty Quinlan. "You're a mess, honey," says Tanya, the gypsy fortune teller played by Dietrich. The plot kicks in when Vargas's bride (Leigh) is kidnapped and Quinlan starts tampering with evidence to make his case. Russell Metty's black-and-white camerawork comes through strongly on the DVD transfer. But the film on disc is not what audiences saw in 1958. The restoration was done after Welles's death but in full accordance with the memo he left about how it should be edited. How about that Welles? Dead since 1985, he's still making waves. As Dietrich says in the film's last line: "He was some kind of a man."

Hot Bonus: The complete fifty-eight-page memo detailing Welles's editing wishes.

Key Scene: Check out the opener—a world-class crane shot in which the camera sweeps over the town until it finds a car with a trunk packed with explosives. In 1958, the credits ran over the sequence, along with Henry Mancini's score. Both are gone now, leaving the famous shot unblemished.

Touching the Void (2003)

Starring: Nicholas Aaron, Brendan Mackey
Directed by: Kevin Macdonald

Part documentary, part re-creation, Macdonald's movie makes the experience of climbing mountains palpable. It's a killer DVD, so sharp is the image that you can feel the frostbite. The movie is based on the book by Joe Simpson, whose 1985 climb up the Siula Grande in the Peruvian Andes with his partner Simon Yates nearly killed them both. Simpson and Yates do their own talking, while two actors—Aaron as Yates and Mackey as Simpson—participate in dramatizations on the actual locations.

Hot Bonus: A look at how the dramatizations were accomplished.

Key Scene: Simpson plunging through the ice, fracturing his leg, and setting off a chain of events that makes Yates leave him for dead.

Towering Inferno, The (1974)

Starring: Steve McQueen, Paul Newman, Fred Astaire, Faye Dunaway
Directed by: John Guillermin and Irwin Allen

Disaster films were all the rage in the 1970s—think *The Poseidon Adventure*. This epic about a burning San Francisco skyscraper—its owner boasts that it's the tallest building in the world (shades of the *Titanic*)—even won an Oscar nomination for Best Picture. That's pushing it, but you can see on the DVD what all the fuss was about. The fires and explosions come through convincingly, which is more than I can say for the all-star cast. McQueen as a fire chief and Newman as an architect fare best. Let's not mention O. J. Simpson as a security guard. Watching the film now, in the shadow of 9/11, McQueen's line ("One of these days they're gonna kill ten thousand people in these things") takes on unexpected heft.

Hot Bonus: Just a trailer, but it's so full of speckles and grain it makes you appreciate how good the movie itself looks.

Key Scene: The scenic elevator.

Toy Story (Two-Disc Anniversary Edition) (1995)

Starring: The voices of Tom Hanks, Tim Allen

Directed by: John Lasseter

All hail Pixar! The first totally computerized animated feature really digs the truth out of that cliché: for kids of all ages. A little boy named Andy hurts the feelings of his favorite toy, a cowboy Woody (voiced by Hanks), by getting all swoony about his birthday present, Buzz Lightyear (voiced by Allen), an astronaut toy with a human-sized ego. Director Lasseter is a visual wizard with the toys, which include a dinosaur, a piggy bank, a Slinky dog, and a traditional Mr. Potato Head with the untraditional voice of Don Rickles. Woody has a crush on Little Bo Peep–"What do you say I get someone else to watch the sheep tonight?" she asks, but Woody has Buzz business to deal with. So does the movie, which leaps off the screen on this anniversary edition, encoded with highest DVD bit-rate ever used for a Pixar film.

Hot Bonus: Deleted scenes that add to a full package of extras.

Key Scene: The vending machine with a mind of its own at Pizza Planet.

Toy Story 2 (1999)

Starring: The voices of Tom Hanks, Tim Allen

Directed by: John Lasseter

Even better than the original. Pixar keeps taking computer technology to new levels when it comes to animation. And it all looks and sounds smashing on DVD. Lasseter thickens the plot when Woody is kidnapped by Al, a toy collector voiced by Wayne Knight, and Buzz fires up the troops for a rescue mission. Woody must decide whether he wants to achieve immortality as a collectible or go back on Andy's shelf ("Do you really think Andy's gonna take you to college, or on his honeymoon?" he is asked). *Ouch!* Woody's new friend, cowgirl Jessie (voiced by Joan Cusack), remembers being outgrown by her little girl owner in the Oscar-nominated ballad "When She Loved Me" (sung by Sarah MacLachlan). Real emotion is at the heart of why both *Toy Story* movies are already classics.

Hot Bonus: There are some funny outtakes, but for the real deal in extras get hold of *Toy Story–The Ultimate Toy Box*, a three-disc Collector's Edition which contains both movies plus an entire disc devoted to bonus features.

Key Scene: The opener with Buzz doing his *Star Wars* thing as he takes on Zurg, his personal Darth Vader.

Traffic (Two-Disc Special Edition) (2000)

Starring: Michael Douglas, Catherine Zeta-Jones, Benicio Del Toro

Directed by: Steven Soderbergh

A real cannonball from Oscar-winner Soderbergh. This hard-ass drama about the drug trade that Soderbergh directs like a thriller gets the royal DVD treatment from Criterion. It deserves it. Besides a plot about drug trafficking between the United States and Mexico—sensitive toes are appropriately squished—this update on the 1989 British TV series is a free-form omnibus of interlocking story lines. Soderbergh, working from a propulsive screenplay by Stephen Gaghan, quickly gives us our bearings. Three characters take center stage: Ohio State Supreme Court Justice Robert Wakefield (Douglas), appointed by the president as the anti-drug czar, is oblivious that his teen daughter Caroline (Erika Christensen) is a junkie—that is, until he finds her zonked out and ravaged in a dealer's bed. Helena Ayala (Zeta-Jones), the pregnant wife of a San Diego drug lord (Steven Bauer), closes her eyes to how hubby makes his fat-cat living—that is, until he's arrested. Javier Rodriquez (Del Toro), a Mexican cop on the Tijuana border, tries to steer clear of the bribes and power plays—that is, until they cut close to home. Dozens of players swirl through Soderbergh's mosaic of willful blindness and systematic corruption. The hand-held camerawork—Soderbergh himself did the holding—provides a documentary feel that rivets attention. Among a terrific cast, Del Toro excels. The Academy rightly named him the year's Best Supporting Actor for finding the film's grieving heart.

Hot Bonus: Soderbergh explains how he manipulated colors to give each story a distinct feel.

Key Scene: The last closeup on Del Toro's face, watching baseball, a game that is fast giving way to drugs as the international pastime.

Training Day (2001)

Starring: Denzel Washington, Ethan Hawke

Directed by: Antoine Fuqua

Sometimes a great actor is all you need to turn a formula cop flick into a potent provocation. Oscar-winner Washington is a sparking, snapping live wire in the role of Detective Sgt. Alonzo Harris, the leader of an elite LAPD undercover narcotics squad. "King Kong ain't got shit on me," says Alonzo, a fact that greenhorn cop Jake Hoyt (a splendid Hawke) figures out during his training day. Everyday police work strikes Alonzo as a waste of time. He has a murder he needs to pin on someone. The DVD transfer is almost sharp enough to catch the tension in the air. In the final stretch, director Fuqua lets the action fly off the rails, stretching the long arm of coincidence in the David Ayer's script like Silly Putty. What saves the day is Washington. This is his tour de force, his *Scarface*, if you will, and his smiling, seductive monster is a thrilling creation that gives *Training Day* all the bite it needs.

Hot Bonus: An alternate ending that adds needed perspective.

Key Scene: Washington in a purring black Monte Carlo, pulling the white boy in beside him and proceeding to provide a street education that has Hawke's s head spinning. In minutes, Alonzo coaxes the kid into trying PCP as on-the-job training. "You gotta be a wolf to catch a wolf," he says.

Trainspotting
(Two-Disc Special Edition) (1996)

Starring: Ewan McGregor, Jonny Lee Miller, Ewen Bremner, Robert Carlyle

Directed by: Danny Boyle

Just what you need, right? An urban grunge flick from Scotland about four shoplifting, slum-dwelling Edinburgh junkies with accents as thick as their smack-addled heads. And hold on for the surreal sight of one lad sticking his head and finally his entire body down the filthiest toilet in Scotland to retrieve an opium suppository. Then there's the cold-turkey nightmare featuring the ghost of a dead baby. *Toy Story*, it ain't. Adapted from Irvine Welsh's 1993 cult novel, Boyle's visionary film—done up for DVD in an anamorphic widescreen transfer with a DTS soundtrack—declares war on the dull gravity of social realism. There's incendiary daring in it, a willingness to go for broke. Like the trainspotters in Britain who compulsively clock railroad comings and goings, these four mates impose a bogus order on their lives. Renton makes a ritual of shooting up. Sick Boy (Miller) obsesses about the films of Sean Connery. Spud (Bremner) uses speed to stay out of work and on the dole. Begbie (the amazing Carlyle) beats up on men and women. The film looks hard at the alternatives to living in oblivion. They're not as trendy as stealing and shooting up to a pulsating Brit-pop score (Elastica, Primal Scream, Pulp), but the film's flash can't disguise the emptiness of these blasted lives. *Trainspotting* is ninety minutes of raw power that

Boyle and a bang-on cast inject right into the vein.

Hot Bonus: Interviews with cast and crew, done then and now.

Key Scene: The needle injection is a killer, and the DVD allows you to see it from multiple angles. Knock yourself out.

Treasure of the Sierra Madre, The (Special Edition) (1948)

Starring: Humphrey Bogart, Walter Huston, Tim Holt, Alfonso Bedoya

Directed by: John Huston

Bogart's decision to play the vicious Fred C. Dobbs in Huston's film version of the B. Traven novel about gold prospectors in Mexico turned off his fans. *Treasure* wasn't a hit. It will have to settle for being vindicated by time as a certified classic. Spiffed up for this extra-packed Special Edition DVD, the disc qualifies as found gold. Bogart is a snarling marvel as Dobbs, the perfect contrast to his partners: the youthful Holt and the toothless geezer, played by Walter Huston, whose son John collected a pair of statuettes as the film's writer and director and won one for the old man as well. Greed is the poison that infects these men, and the director exults in watching the disease fester. The harshness extends to Bedoya's bandit. His line—"Badges? We don't need no stinking badges!"—has marched into screen legend.

Hot Bonus: A new documentary, *Discovering Treasure*, covers a lot of ground, and a feature on John Huston fills in the rest.

Key Scene: Walter Huston's manic dance when gold is discovered is one of the purest expressions of joy ever captured on film.

Triumph of the Will (Special Edition) (1935)

Directed by: Leni Riefenstahl

Why spare space for an infamous documentary that glorifies Hitler? Because separate the film from its toxic propaganda and you see a filmmaker whose talent is indisputable. Riefenstahl was given unprecedented access to Hitler's Nuremberg political rally in 1934. She didn't just film the crowds of workers and Hitler Youth, the torchlit parades, and the bombastic speeches in the stadium. Riefenstahl had the power and the budget to rearrange them, coddle them, intensify them, deify them. Images from her cinematic mythmaking have influenced films as diverse as *Star Wars* and *Gladiator*. By all means condemn Riefenstahl for her actions, but to deny her work is to deny film and the ways it can be corrupted.

Hot Bonus: Historian Anthony R. Santoro provides detailed commentary on the history of the Nazis. For details on the filmmaker, find the documentary *The Wonderful, Horrible Life of Leni Riefenstahl*, which doesn't shy from harsh truths about the woman who died in 2003, at the age of ninety-nine.

Key Scene: Hitler's first appearance, seemingly descending from the clouds.

True Grit (1969)

Starring: John Wayne, Kim Darby, Glen Campbell

Directed by: Henry Hathaway

If you think Wayne finally won his Oscar just for getting fat, wearing an eyepatch, and falling off his horse, you may resist the very real charms of this western. Wayne plays Rooster Cogburn, a gruff, hard-drinking U.S. marshal who helps fourteen-year-old Mattie Ross (Darby) catch the varmints who killed her daddy. Her hope is that Rooster has true grit. Can there be any doubt? Once director Hathaway clears the exposition out of the way—who needed to watch singer Campbell try to act?—Wayne takes off after the bad guy (Robert Duvall). The DVD picture is a riot of color, the better to revel in the sight of an American icon back in the saddle.

Hot Bonus: Personally, I loved the alternate French audio track. You haven't lived till you hear the Duke parlez vous in the language of love.

Key Scene: Wayne's face-off with Duvall. "Fill your hands, you son of a bitch," he hollers, riding toward his enemy with the reins in his teeth, a glint in his eye, guns blazing. True grit, indeed.

True Romance (Two-Disc Unrated Director's Cut) (1993)

Starring: Christian Slater, Patricia Arquette, Dennis Hooper, Gary Oldman

Directed by: Tony Scott

This savagely funny ride was the first script ever written by former video-store clerk Quentin Tarantino. But somehow Scott, a Britisher, got to direct. No matter. The true grunge of the script wins out over Scott's brand of slick. And the DVD—widescreen and Dolby sound—offers more of everything, including thirty minutes of deleted scenes. As Clarence Worley, Slater plays a kung-fu and Elvis worshiper much like Tarantino. No sooner does he meet Alabama Whitman (Arquette) than Clarence is proposing marriage and defending her honor against her dreadlocked, drug-crazed, mob-connected former boyfriend Drexl (Oldman in overdrive). Soon the newlyweds are fleeing Detroit for Los Angeles to sell Drexl's cocaine to Hollywood types. But first the couple stops to say goodbye to Clarence's security-cop dad (Hopper), who later runs into trouble with a mob hit man (Christopher Walken). Their blistering confrontation is pure Tarantino: a blast of bloody action and verbal fireworks. Arquette and Slater make a sexy pair of bruised romantics. Everyone shines, including Brad Pitt as a stoned innocent to Val Kilmer as the ghost of Elvis. But it's Tarantino's gutter poetry that pushes the detonator.

Hot Bonus: A much darker alternate ending favored by Tarantino.

Key Scene: Arquette giving a ballistic thrashing to the hood (James Gandolfini, of all people) who's just beaten the bejesus out of her.

Truman Show, The (Special Collector's Edition) (1998)

Starring: Jim Carrey, Laura Linney, Ed Harris, Noah Emmerich

Directed by: Peter Weir

Carrey's Truman Burbank, unbeknownst to him, has been bred since birth to star in his own TV show. Literally. All the people in his life are actors, including wife (Linney) and best friend (Emmerich). They get their contracts renewed, or not, by the televisionary (Oscar-nominee Harris) who calls the shots from his control room. Working from a prescient script by Andrew Niccol (is this not the ultimate in reality television?), director Weir puts sting in the satire and draws a subtly comic and touching performance from Carrey, who suggests reserves of hurt and anger in Truman when his eyes are finally opened. Keep your own eyes open for the marvels of color and design that emerge with remarkable clarity on this widescreen DVD transfer.

Hot Bonus: A documentary on how Truman's world—where everyone but Truman performs for hidden cameras—was created in Seaside, Florida.

Key Scene: The rain that falls just on Truman.

Tupac: Resurrection (Special Edition) (2003)

Directed by: Lauren Lazin

With Tupac's mom, former Black Panther Afeni Shakur, as executive producer, this approved take on the life of the rapper who was gunned down in 1996 sounds like another Tupac rehash, this one with the edges sanded off. A close look at this documentary on DVD silences those doubts. The film's producer and director, MTV veep Lazin (*Cribs, True Life*), had access to Tupac's MTV interviews, plus home movies, photographs, and letters. Lazin had enough material to let Tupac narrate his own history—and so he does. "This is my story," says Tupac, as if from the grave. It's eerie, especially when Tupac says, "I always knew I was gonna be shot." But this film portrait casts a spell, despite skimping on the misogyny and violence of his raps, his arrests for assault, the motive for his murder, and the killing of Biggie Smalls. The movie hits hard in showing Tupac transformed from the boy who wrote poetry, studied ballet, and tried out for TV sitcoms—he's almost a dork—to the thug activist of *All Eyez on Me* and *2Pacalypse Now*, and the agitating actor of *Juice* and *Gridlock'd*. Lazin's remarkable achievement is to catch Tupac in the act of discovering himself.

Hot Bonus: Four deleted scenes add more to the portrait.

Key Scene: "Runnin' (Dying to Live)," a single produced by Eminem for the film, brings Tupac and Biggie together one last time.

Twelve Monkeys (Collector's Edition) (1995)

Starring: Bruce Willis, Brad Pitt, Madeleine Stowe

Directed by: Terry Gilliam

Gilliam's beautifully despairing fantasy, based on Chris Marker's short film *La Jetée*, stars Willis as Cole, an asylum inmate who insists he's been sent from the future to stop a plague that has sent what's left of humankind underground. Pitt, Oscar nominated, plays a nutjob patient who may be a link to the army of the twelve monkeys, the group Cole believes started the plague. Stowe is the shrink who tries to cure Cole of his fantasies until she falls in love with him. The DVD transfer gives full reign to Gilliam's wild, poetic visions, including a frozen city inhabited only by wild animals who roam deserted skyscrapers and department stores. Gilliam, along with the gifted cinematographer Roger Pratt and production designer Jeffrey Beecroft, fashions a disturbing and dazzling lost world.

Hot Bonus: *The Hamster Factor*, a mesmerizing documentary shot during the production of the movie.

Key Scene: Cole's recurring dream of a young boy at an airport. The boy stands transfixed as a man with a suitcase rushes past him, followed by a blond woman who weeps by the man's side after the police gun him down. This dream is the soul of the film. Gilliam returns to it three times, adding more details until the dream links all the pieces in the puzzle.

21 Grams (2003)

Starring: Sean Penn, Naomi Watts, Benicio Del Toro

Directed by: Alejandro Gonzáles Iñárritu

In his first film in English, Mexican director Iñárritu (*Amores Perros*) crafts a scorching drama. Penn plays Paul, a math professor faced with the possibility of death after a heart transplant. Paul sees spirituality in terms of numbers, the twenty-one grams (the weight of a hummingbird, a chocolate bar, or a stack of five nickels) that leave our bodies at death. Is it the weight of the soul? Clearly, Iñárritu and screenwriter Guillermo Arriaga aren't afraid of tackling big issues or splintering a plot to make audiences work at putting the pieces together. They intensify the puzzle by adding two equally damaged characters. Ex-junkie Cristina (the Oscar-nominated Watts) is the widow of the man whose heart Paul carries. Jack (Del Toro), the cause of the heart donor's death, is an ex-con Jesus freak and alcoholic who loves and menaces his two kids and his wife (Melissa Leo, in a staggering portrayal of conflicted devotion). Acting is rarely this explosive. These characters, all kicked hard by fate, unite in a brutal, erotic, and tender dance of death.

Hot Bonus: Just the film, but the skill with which the DVD catches the seedy poetry of Rodrigo Prieto's camerawork is bonus enough.

Key Scene: Del Toro lecturing his kids on turning the other cheek.

24-Hour Party People (2002)

Starring: Steve Coogan, Lennie James, Shirley Henderson, Andy Serkis

Directed by: Michael Winterbottom

Real-life British pop impresario Tony Wilson made and lost a mountain of money in the 1980s and 1990s as the soul and brains of Factory Records, home to Joy Division, New Order, and

Happy Mondays. He is portrayed with endearing smarm and missionary lunacy by English comedian Coogan in this hilarious, loosely historical valentine to the drug-addled punk-and-dance-music glory days of Manchester. Shot on digital video by brilliant cinematographer Robby Müller, the movie transfers to DVD with a rough, grainy quality that totally fits the defiant mood. Like the music, the film is outspoken, roaringly funny, fiercely sexual, and relentlessly in your face. I can't wait to pop it in the DVD and watch it again.

Hot Bonus: Snarky talk from Wilson himself, and a piece on Manchester that actually adds to your knowledge and enjoyment of the movie.

Key Scene: Zoned on weed on a cold Manchester rooftop after losing his deal, Wilson sees God, who rides down from heaven to tell him, "You should have signed the Smiths."

25th Hour (2002)

Starring: Edward Norton, Barry Pepper, Philip Seymour Hoffman
Directed by: Spike Lee

One of the first films to deal directly with the emotional fallout from 9/11. This riveting, emotionally resonant New York drama about mostly Irish white guys is strange turf for Lee, who still manages to do the right thing by trusting the wildly ambitious script that David Benioff has adapted from his own novel. Lee is firing on all cylinders, and the actors match his energy. Norton excels as Brooklyn drug dealer Monty Brogan, a felon filling his last hours before going to prison for seven years. He hangs with his friends: Frank (Pepper), a Wall Street trader, and Jacob (Hoffman), a teacher who lusts after a teen student (Anna Paquin). Monty consoles his bar-owner dad, James (the great Brian Cox), and tortures himself with the idea that his girl, Naturelle (gorgeous Rosario Dawson), may have turned him in. Lee sets these relationships against a battered city—Frank's apartment looks out on Ground Zero—that the DVD captures with admirable restraint. In a restroom mirror, Monty launches into a love-hate attack on every race and institution in the five boroughs. Like the film, it's a defense against the unknown.

Hot Bonus: Lee and Benioff share thoughts about 9/11 and the characters.

Key Scene: In a long, indelibly moving dream sequence, Monty's dad imagines a future for his son outside of prison.

28 Days Later (Special Edition) (2002)

Starring: Cillian Murphy, Naomie Harris, Brendon Gleeson, Megan Burns
Directed by: Danny Boyle

The best zombie movie in, like, forever comes to DVD ready to rock. No slowpokes here. Director Boyle puts zip back in the zombie step. These buggers snap to at the scent of human flesh and take you down like a stealth bomber. Set in an evacuated London decimated by a virus, the film is shot with nerve-frying effectiveness on digital video. Twenty-eight days after the virus hits, Jim (Murphy) wakes up in a deserted hospital and wonders where everyone has gone. On the street, being chased by ghouls, he is rescued by Selena (a powerhouse Harris), a survivor who gives him the lowdown on the living dead: one of them bites you or even drools on you, and in twenty seconds you're a raging jungle beast. Along with cabbie Frank (the always-terrific Gleeson) and his teenage daughter Hannah (Burns), the two young strangers leave London in Frank's cab, facing major questions, such as Selena's to Jim: "Do you want us to find a cure and save the world, or just fall in love and fuck?" The movie loses steam at the end, when our group takes refuge at a fortress manned by sex-starved soldiers led by a kinky major (Christopher Eccleston). Until then, Boyle and screenwriter Alex Garland keep things visionary and scary.

Hot Bonus: Three different endings that move from bleak, bleaker and radical in that it takes the film in an entirely new direction.

Key Scene: The zombies in the church where crosses just don't do the trick.

20,000 Leagues Under the Sea (Two-Disc Special Edition) (1954)

Starring: Kirk Douglas, James Mason, Paul Lukas
Directed by: Richard Fleischer

Disney's live-action film of Jules Verne's 1870 fantasy about sea monsters and atomic submarines makes for a stunning DVD that hardly shows the film's age. Having survived a shipwreck, sailor Douglas and scientist Lukas are picked up by the *Nautilus*, a submarine ruled by the mad visionary Captain Nemo (Mason in smart-scary mode). The design of the sub, with its huge windows on the sea, is breathtaking. And Nemo's crazed plan to stop war by sinking warships keeps the action humming.

Hot Bonus: A retrospective documentary that misses no detail on how the film's effects were achieved.

Key Scene: The fight with the giant squid.

Twin Peaks: Fire Walk With Me (1992)

Starring: Sheryl Lee, Ray Wise, Kyle MacLachlan, Michael J. Anderson

Directed and co-written by: David Lynch

Lynch's big-screen prequel to his landmark 1990 TV series brought out that impulse in the arts to build idols and smash them. Boos greeted the film at Cannes. In two years, Lynch had gone from genius to leper. Good thing we have the DVD to show that Lynch had simply remained Lynch: a supreme stylist obsessed with working through the dark themes that matter to him. The film of *Peaks* is no match for the two-hour TV pilot, but Lynch draws us back into a uniquely hypnotic world. Events transpire during the week before the death of Laura Palmer, with actress Sheryl Lee tracing the character's downward trajectory of drugs and sex. Wise is more disturbing than ever as Laura's depraved father; Michael J. Anderson repeats his mesmerizing portrayal as the dwarf in Laura's dreams; and Lynch does a sly encore as a hearing-impaired FBI honcho. Though the movie ups the TV ante on nudity, language, and violence, Lynch never uses shock for its own sake. He is a poet of the unspeakable. His imagery here will haunt you.

Hot Bonus: Retrospective interviews with cast members.

Key Scene: Laura, prompted by incest or supernatural forces, telling her boyfriend, "The Laura you used to know doesn't exist anymore. There's only me." It's one of the most devastating moments in Lynch's work.

Twister (Special Edition) (1996)

Starring: Helen Hunt, Bill Paxton, Jami Gertz, Cary Elwes, Lois Smith

Directed by: Jan De Bont

There's a tornado of clichés ripping through this blockbuster, starring Hunt as a storm chaser who knows her husband (Paxton) still loves her even though he's leaving her for a pushy therapist (Gertz). But who cares about chunks of banality when you can pop in this remastered DVD and feel a tornado whoosh around your head with a dimensionality and pow that puts you right in the center of the action?

Hot Bonus: Commentary from De Bont that cuts to the chase on how the tornado effects were done.

Key Scene: The flying cow—it's so real you want to duck.

Two-Lane Blacktop (1971)

Starring: James Taylor, Dennis Wilson, Warren Oates, Laurie Bird

Directed by: Monte Hellman

When those two long-haired musical hunks—Sweet Baby James and Beach Boy Wilson—teamed up for a movie about cars and girls, thoughts of an Elvis-like box-office bonanza danced in executive heads. No one figured director Hellman would produce an existential art film. So a sure thing sank like a stone. My advice is to watch the film now on this spiffed-up DVD and honk if you think it's ripe for reevaluation. Taylor and Wilson don't say much as they drive their '55 Chevy across the Southwest looking for a money race. Even when the girl (Bird) they both have sex with dumps them for an older man (Oates in the film's knockout performance), the boys are more interested in the new GTO he drives and the cross-country race he challenges them to enter. The winner doesn't get the babe, he gets the other guy's car. Hellman's dark and meditative film, a study of loss and psychological dislocation, seems more pertinent now than ever.

Hot Bonus: A featurette on Hellman, directed by George Hickenlooper, will help you navigate this challenging road movie.

Key Scene: The ending, when Taylor and Wilson drive down another blacktop and the film burns in the camera, leaving only a blazing white light.

2001: A Space Odyssey (New Kubrick Collection) (1968)

Starring: Keir Dullea, Gary Lockwood

Directed by: Stanley Kubrick

Kubrick's masterpiece is, hands down, the most profoundly influential sci-fi epic ever made. DVD was invented to keep finding ways to present the film with optimum picture and sound. The remastered version from Warner, as part of the New Kubrick Collection, is currently the top choice. From the dawn of man episode to that look into the future through the eyes of an ambiguous star child, *2001*—based on a story by Arthur C. Clarke—dares to take on questions about the nature of technology, of faith, of language, of humans and machines, and of the place of both in the universe. The emotional connection we form is not with the two astronauts, played by Dullea and Lockwood, but with HAL (voiced by Douglas Rain), the computer who tries to kill them and who dies lamenting human error and singing the song, "Daisy," that was part of his original program. Kubrick reaches for the stars with this saga. This DVD challenges us to reach with him.

Hot Bonus: The interview with Clarke on the earlier MGM release has been dropped, but the Warner box set devotes an entire disc to Kubrick's career.

Key Scene: HAL eavesdropping on the astronauts by reading their lips strikes terror in our hearts, but for sheer visual grandeur it's hard to beat the moment when an ape throws a bone that morphs into a spaceship which floats among the stars in time to "The Blue Danube Waltz."

Umbrellas of Cherbourg, The (1964)

Starring: Catherine Deneuve, Nino Castelnuovo, Anne Vernon

Directed by: Jacques Demy

Drenched in color and dreamy melody, Demy's musical is so lovely it defies description, but fortunately not the skills of the DVD producers to render its multihued wonders and its heartfelt score by Michel Legrand with peerless precision. The film, sung through in French with English subtitles you have the option to remove, is a fairy tale. Deneuve, twenty-one and impossibly gorgeous, plays Geneviève. She works in the umbrella store owned by her mother (Vernon). Her night of love with Guy (Castelnuovo) ends with his being drafted and her being pregnant. Years later, having broken their mutual promise ("if it takes forever/I will wait for you"), they meet in Paris. Now married to others, their faces can't speak the feelings that pour out in the music. Demy had a genius for expressing romantic love and loss. This is the fullest expression of his gift.

Hot Bonus: Demy's widow, the director Agnès Varda, filmed a tribute to her husband—*The World of Jacques Demy*—that is aptly excerpted here.

Key Scene: The farewell at the gas station, in the snow.

Unbearable Lightness of Being, The (1988)

Starring: Daniel Day-Lewis, Lena Olin, Juliette Binoche

Directed by: Philip Kaufman

"Take off your clothes." It's a line Tomas (Day-Lewis), the womanizing Czech doctor, uses a lot, even after he marries Tereza (Binoche) and allegedly gives up his affair with Sabina (Olin), who enjoys having sex wearing only a bowler hat. Erotic farce? Hardly. Kaufman's adaptation of Milan Kundera's novel is a study of political and emotional commitment. The three actors give it their all. When Soviet tanks invade Prague in 1968 (newsreel footage is used), Tereza photographs the riots. Unlike Tomas, her consciousness is raised. "Life is very heavy for me, and it is so light for you," she says, before leaving him. The DVD does wonders in capturing Kaufman's use of color and light to show love and history converge.

Hot Bonus: Screenwriter Jean-Claude Carrière and editor Walter Murch join Kaufman and Olin on the commentary track to tease out meanings that sometimes prove elusive on the trip from page to screen.

Key Scene: Tomas's last and very different view of Sabina in her bowler hat. "Your hat makes me want to cry," he says.

Unbreakable
(Two-Disc Special Edition) (2000)
Starring: Bruce Willis, Samuel L. Jackson, Robin Wright Penn
Directed by: M. Night Shyamalan

Shyamalan's unfairly maligned followup to *The Sixth Sense* megahit is actually a more potent proposition. And the DVD has just the kind of picture and enveloping DTS sound to pull you into its diabolically clever web. Willis stars as David Dunn, a football stadium security guard with a wife (Wright Penn) who is alienated by his roving eye, and a twelve-year-old son (Spencer Treat Clark) who thinks Dad could have been superman if a car accident in college hadn't ended his football career. One day, David takes a train home to Philadelphia from New York. The train derails, killing all 118 passengers, save one. David is unbroken—not a scratch. Maybe he is superman, or something more mysterious. Then David meets Elijah Price (the estimable Jackson), who deepens his doubts. Elijah, who runs a gallery devoted to comic-book art, suffers from a bone disease that since birth has made him ultrasusceptible to injury. Fragile Elijah sees David as his polar opposite and accuses him of being afraid of the gift that might set him apart. Maybe you'll think the film's odd angles—characters glimpsed from ceilings or between cracks—are just arty showing off. But in modeling his film on a comic book's multiperspective frames, Shyamalan finds a style that stays organic to the dark and disturbing story being told.

Hot Bonus: The deleted scenes, each introduced by Shyamalan, and each adding in crucial ways to the understanding of film.

Key Scene: The train wreck—Shyamalan rejects the clichés of burning metal to let you feel the sheer, rocking terror of being inside a passenger car that is speeding out of control.

Under Siege (1992)

Starring: Steven Seagal, Tommy Lee Jones, Gary Busey
Directed by: Andrew Davis

The only Seagal movie in the DVD Top 1,000, and I make no apologies for putting it there. The ponytailed star plays Casey Ryback, a Navy SEAL reduced to chef duty on the USS *Missouri*.

When the battleship gets hijacked by terrorists, Seagal is thrust into a *Die Hard* situation to save the day. Funny how potent a cheap ripoff can be when the whole creative team is on fire. The smart-looking DVD transfer is powered by more than your barking subwoofer. Jones, disguised as a metal-head rocker, and Busey, in drag, are mad-crazy villains. Director Davis, who keeps the brutal action bubbling, would be in Oscar territory the following year with *The Fugitive*, for which Jones would actually win the darned thing. But it's the go-for broke intensity here that makes this perfect DVD escapism.

Hot Bonus: Production notes.

Key Scene: The climactic fight with the carving knife.

Unforgiven
(Two-Disc Special Edition) (1992)

Starring: Clint Eastwood, Gene Hackman, Morgan Freeman
Directed by: Clint Eastwood

An all-new digital transfer of Eastwood's Oscar-winning western beats the spurs off of previous DVD editions. The colors are rich and deep, and the sound is fully dimensional. In a directorial high-wire act, Eastwood crafts a film that is best understood as demythology. He plays widower William Munny, a reformed gunfighter who gets unreformed (he needs cash to save his farm and feed his kids). A braggart called the Schofield Kid (Jaimz Woolvett) dangles a tempting apple: a group of prostitutes from the town of Big Whiskey are offering a bounty of five hundred dollars each for the two cowboys who slashed and scarred one of their own. The sheriff, Little Bill Daggett (Hackman, in an Oscar-winning portrait of grinning evil), had let the culprits off with a fine, prompting the hookers to pool their money in a prefeminist call for justice. Munny enlists a pal, retired gunman Ned Logan (Freeman), to join him on the job. The graying gunfighters of David Webb Peoples's brilliant script are acutely observed. And Eastwood, aided by Jack N. Green's cinematography, gives the material a singularly rugged and sorrowful beauty. Often accused of dodging the consequences of violence in his work, Eastwood repeatedly shows the pain inflicted by even superficial wounds. In a horrifying scene, the panicky Kid shoots a man who is sitting on a toilet and tries to justify his action by saying the bastard had it coming. "We all have it coming, Kid," says Munny. When Daggett forces his hand, Munny's killer instinct overrides his conscience. This is the Eastwood hero the audience once cheered, but Eastwood the filmmaker is no longer cheering. By weighing Munny's rise to prosperity against his fall from grace, Eastwood puts his own filmmaking past in critical and moral perspective. In three decades of climbing into the saddle, Eastwood has never ridden so tall.

Hot Bonus: A retrospective documentary features Eastwood and the cast and crew discussing the film's attitude toward violence.

Key Scene: Munny, waiting for the burst of violence: "It's a hell of a thing killin' a man. You take away all he's got and all he's ever gonna have."

Untouchables, The (Special Collector's Edition) (1987)

Starring: Kevin Costner, Sean Connery, Robert De Niro

Directed by: Brian De Palma

The old TV crime series becomes a widescreen movie of incomparable color and design, and now a DVD that does all that creativity proud. Prohibition-era Chicago shines like an Art Deco fever dream. Costner's Eliot Ness and his unbribeable lawmen take on mobster Al Capone, flamboyantly played by De Niro with the help of a lethal baseball bat and mouthfuls of juicy David Mamet dialogue ("I want you to find that fancy boy Eliot Ness. I want him dead. I want his family dead. I want his house burned to the ground. I want to go there in the middle of the night, and I want to piss on his ashes"). Lucky for Ness, he has Connery on his side. The great Scot won a much-deserved Oscar for playing an Irish street cop who shows Ness the ropes ("You want to get Capone? Here's how you get him. He pulls a knife, you pull a gun. He sends one of yours to the hospital, you send one of his to the morgue. That's the Chicago way.") The De Palma way is to keep the shootouts coming between the Mamet-speak.

Hot Bonus: Four featurettes about how the film was conceived and shot.

Key Scene: As cops and hoods shoot it out at a Chicago train station, a baby buggy goes down the stairs evoking—with cheeky De Palma relish—the famous Odessa steps sequence from the Russian classic *Battleship Potemkin*.

Upside of Anger, The (2005)

Starring: Joan Allen, Kevin Costner, Mike Binder

Directed and written by: Mike Binder

All the fireworks you want on a DVD are available just by looking into the eyes of the reliably brilliant Allen. She plays Terry Wolfmeyer, a diva of the Detroit 'burbs who wants the best in schools, jobs, and men for her four daughters—Hadley (Alicia Witt), Emily (Keri Russell), Andy (Erika Christensen), and Popeye (Evan Rachel Wood). Terry is now royally pissed off. Her husband has split (she's sure it's with his Swedish secretary), and, using alcohol to fuel her fire, she's on the attack, starting with her family. Binder hits us with jokes that sting. Allen is the blaze that lights the film, but the whopper surprise is Costner. As Denny, a retired baseball star turned stoned radio DJ, he offers Terry a famous shoulder to rage on and laces the film with unforced charm and humor. Binder springs a contrived twist ending but otherwise keeps the emotions real. He also excels as Shep, Denny's radio producer who seduces young Andy and incurs her mother's wrath, for which he can find no upside.

Hot Bonus: Scrappy audio commentary from Binder and Allen, moderated by Rod Lurie, who directed them in *The Contender*.

Key Scene: Typical of the film's bold strokes is Terry at dinner, steaming at Shep for sleeping with her daughter, and imagining his head exploding, with blood all over the walls. The small smile on her face is delectable.

Urban Cowboy (1980)

Starring: John Travolta, Debra Winger, Scott Glenn, Madolyn Smith

Directed by: James Bridges

This is one honky-tonking DVD. Travolta stars as Bud, a modern Texan who punches clocks at a petrochemical planet by day and raises a ruckus by night doing a mean western two-step at the Houston-based club Gilley's. As Sissy, the hottie who marries Bud and heats up his jealous streak by riding the mechanical bull at Gilley's, Winger struts off with the movie in her star-making role. Smith is a distraction for Bud, and bad-boy Glenn does likewise for Sissy. The script by director Bridges and Aaron Latham, whose *Esquire* article inspired the film, hits more bumps than a butt on that bull, which is forced to bear more symbolic weight than Kubrick's monolith in *2001*. But when it sticks to the joyful noise at Gilley's, from the likes of the Charlie Daniels Band, Bob Seger, Boz Scaggs, Bonnie Raitt, and Kenny Rogers, *Urban Cowboy* actually does make you feel like dancing.

Hot Bonus: Travolta and Winger rehearsing their dance numbers.

Key Scene: Winger on that bull—work it, girl.

Usual Suspects, The (Special Edition) (1995)

Starring: Kevin Spacey, Gabriel Byrne, Benicio Del Toro, Stephen Baldwin

Directed by: Bryan Singer

This teasing puzzle of a movie makes an ideal DVD. Not only is it presented in a new high-definition transfer, you can return to it repeatedly to see how you were suckered by it. Five thieves, rounded up on suspicion of hijacking in New York, stand in a police lineup. Hockney (Kevin Pollak), the smartass, speaks first, then the simmering McManus (Baldwin) and his manic Latino partner Fenster (Del Toro). Then it's cool-hand Keaton (Byrne), an ex-cop gone bad. Last up is Kint (Spacey), spat on as a stoolie gimp with a debilitating palsy who is out of his league with these killers. They call him Verbal for short; he can't stop talking, especially if it'll save his ass. Six weeks later, talk will mean exactly that. The film's framing device is Verbal's testimony to U.S. customs agent Kujan (Chazz Palminteri). You say that "KOO-yan." In this mind-bender of a mystery, even pronunciation counts. Director Singer and screenwriter Christopher McQuarrie have crafted the funniest, scariest, and sneakiest crime thriller in ages. The point is to find the mastermind Keyser Söze. Verbal describes the mystery man as "the devil himself," not just a Turkish narcotics czar but a mythic creature of evil. The film is acted to sweet perfection, especially by Spacey. It's Verbal's torrent of words and the flickers of fear and cunning dancing in his stoolie eyes that keep us riveted as the plot goes its Byzantine way. Spacey's won the Oscar for his balls-out brilliance. This is just the film for an actor who's full of surprises and an audience fully up to the challenge.

Hot Bonus: Deleted scenes that help fill in the mystery.

Key Scene: The quick, devastating revelation of Söze. "Then like that," says Verbal, blowing a poof of air at Kujan, "he's gone."

Vampire's Kiss (1989)

Starring: Nicolas Cage, Jennifer Beals, Maria Conchita Alonso

Directed by: Robert Bierman

A real love-it-or-hate-it bloodsucker movie, with the DVD transfer providing appropriately pale fleshtones. As Manhattan literary agent Peter Loew, Cage goes so far out with his performance that you watch it like a tightrope act, done without a net. For kicks at the office, he browbeats his secretary (Alonso). At night, he picks up whatever's handy in spike heels. One evening *chez* Peter, a bat swoops in the window and takes the comely shape of Beals. Decked out in garter belt, clinging dress, and scads of mascara, she's just Cage's type. He hardly resists when she sinks in her fangs. Soon he's careening wildly through the streets, bashing into garbage cans and muttering, "I'm a vampire." He even eats a cockroach—for real. Is Peter a modern-day Dracula or just an old-school nut? Director Bierman is willing to go either way, giggles and goose flesh. I suggest you follow his lead.

Hot Bonus: An interview with Cage, who explains why he ate a cockroach.

Key Scene: Cage eating the cockroach.

Vanishing, The (1988)

Starring: Bernard Pierre Donnadieu, Gene Bervoets, Johanna Ter Steege

Directed by: George Sluizer

Warning: Do not confuse this hypnotic and haunting Dutch thriller—beautifully presented on the Criterion DVD in a new digital transfer—with Sluizer's disastrous 1993 Hollywood remake. Saskia (Ter Steege) and her lover Rex (Bervoets) are driving through France. They talk. They argue. They stop at a gas station. Saskia goes inside. She never comes out. Three years later, Rex still searches for her. That's when Sluizer introduces Raymond (Donnadieu), and we learn of his fiendish plan.

Hot Bonus: Much-improved picture and sound from its last DVD outing.

Key Scene: The claustrophobic finale.

Velvet Goldmine (1998)

Starring: Ewan McGregor, Jonathan Rhys-Meyers, Christian Bale

Directed by: Todd Haynes

Rhys-Meyers is not quite David Bowie, and McGregor is almost Iggy Pop in Haynes's imaginary biopic about the rise and flameout of a Ziggy Stardust–like rock god in glitter-mad early-seventies

London. Haynes evokes the bisexual electricity and illusory grandeur of glam with sumptuous spectacle and a knockout soundtrack of period classics by T. Rex and Roxy Music, as well as authentic re-creations featuring members of Sonic Youth and Radiohead.

Hot Bonus: Just the glam image and sound, smoothly transferred to DVD.

Key Scene: Rhys-Meyers and McGregor in full lip-lock, shot in aggressively tight focus and pregnant silence.

Verdict, The (1982)

Starring: Paul Newman, James Mason, Charlotte Rampling, Jack Warden

Directed by: Sidney Lumet

Newman won a sixth Oscar nomination for playing Frank Galvin, a chiseling, alcoholic Boston lawyer using a hospital malpractice suit as a last shot at regaining his integrity. There's nothing he can do about his looks (then fifty-seven, he was still a looker), but Newman captures the corruption and moral fatigue eating at his character. There are no fancy tricks on this DVD, except to show off actors to optimum advantage, and what actors. Besides Newman, director Lumet works magic with Mason as Galvin's high-priced legal adversary, Warden as his former partner, and Rampling as a love interest with interests of her own. David Mamet's script is unusually incisive for a courtroom drama, and Newman digs right in. To watch an actor gamble with his star image and come up aces is exhilarating.

Hot Bonus: Lumet's commentary is chatty and informative, and Newman stops in for a few minutes to put in his two cents.

Key Scene: Newman's tirade in the chambers of the canny judge, played by Milo O'Shea, reveals an actor holding nothing back.

Vertigo (Collector's Edition) (1958)

Starring: James Stewart, Kim Novak

Directed by: Alfred Hitchcock

Hitchcock's voyeuristic masterpiece about sexual obsession cuts to the heart of cinema itself. It's about how and why we watch movies and the blurred line between illusion and reality that makes the process so powerful. That's one reason this profoundly influential spellbinder tops the list of the greatest films Hitchcock or anyone else ever made. The DVD is also in the cream-of-the-crop category. Meticulously restored by Robert Harris and James Katz, this hallucinatory landmark returns to us on disc with the rich colors and enveloping surround sound that are essential in making Vertigo the ultimate film to get lost in. Stewart gives his most riveting and risky performance as Scottie Ferguson, a former San Francisco cop—his fear of heights retired him—hired by old school chum Gavin Elster (Tom Helmore) to follow his wife Madeleine (Novak), whose life is in danger, he says, "from someone out of the past, someone dead." Scottie tracks the cool blonde beauty down the hills of the city, into shops, an old hotel, a restaurant (Ernie's), a cemetery, and a museum where she stares for hours at a portrait of Carlotta, someone out of the past. These scenes are silent except for Bernard Herrmann's thrilling score (an engulfing experience in its own right). The dizzying reverie is broken only when Madeleine, in the shadow of the Golden Gate at Old Fort Point, jumps into the bay and Scottie rescues her. He brings her home to his bed, lost in her eyes, but his vertigo stops him from saving her later when she jumps from a mission bell tower. The zoom-in, dolly-out shot in the bell tower is justly famous. Madeleine's death drops Scottie into a deep depression. That is, until he meets Judy (also Novak), a trashy, raven-haired shopgirl. With a cruel perversity bordering on necrophilia, Scottie tries to transform Judy into Madeleine. Novak is the greatest camera subject Hitchcock ever had, and she gifts him with a quality that transcends acting to approach a state of grace. There is a twist ending that answers the easy questions. And critics have written for decades about how the film parallels Hitchcock's obsession with making over actresses into his own fetishistic ideal. But Vertigo goes beyond glib categorization to throw us into a world where we must confront our own demons. It's more than a movie; it's an imperishable work of art.

Hot Bonus: The restoration is laid out in fascinating detail.

Key Scene: Judy becomes Madeleine, as Novak walks dreamily and sorrowfully out of the shadows of a neon-lit room and into Stewart's arms.

Very Long Engagement, A (Two-Disc Special Edition) (2004)

Starring: Audrey Tautou, Gaspard Ulliel

Directed by: Jean-Pierre Jeunet

DVD does Jeunet proud, bringing visceral impact to his soaring visuals in this shattering film of Sébastien Japrisot's World War I–era novel. Jeunet reunites with his *Amelie* star, Tautou, in a film as harsh as *Amelie* was ethereal. Tautou is deeply affecting as Mathilde, a Frenchwoman—lame from polio—who refuses to believe her sweet, slender fiancé, Manech (Ulliel), is one of five soldiers killed in the trenches after being convicted of self-mutilation to avoid duty. She spends the war trying to track him down. It's unfair to reduce a dense plot, loaded with characters and incidents, to a quick summation, but the film is best met head-on. Jeunet the visionary and Tautou the force of nature take you to hell and back.

Hot Bonus: A fine featurette on the film's production.

Key Scene: In the trenches, as Jeunet captures the carnage of war with wrenching effectiveness.

Videodrome
(Two-Disc Special Edition) (1983)

Starring: James Woods, Deborah Harry

Directed by: David Cronenberg

You may not fully comprehend Cronenberg's hallucinatory riff on the business of selling pornography, torture, mutilation, and murder as entertainment. Not at first. But the minute you can peel your eyes off this admittedly shocking DVD, pop the disc back in for another look-see. Criterion's mind-bending transfer of the film is packed with enough extras to clear things up. Woods is pure sleazy energy as Max Renn, a cable TV programmer who picks up a show off a satellite dish that is practically a snuff film. It's called *Videodrome*, and Max loves it. "I think it's what's next," he says. So does Harry, a self-help guru who turns on Max by burning her breasts with a cigarette. Max gets more than he bargained for when he makes contact with the show's masterminds and their mind-control drugs. He grows a slot in his stomach where tapes are to be inserted (the movie came too early for DVD). Technology is made flesh in Cronenberg's provocative mix of dazzle and disgust. Cronenberg is onto something here. The fun part comes in deciding just what the hell it is.

Hot Bonus: *Forging the New Flesh* offers an in-depth look at the film's makeup and startling effects.

Key Scene: Max getting sucked into a television monitor that develops a fleshy, groaning, disturbingly erotic mind of its own.

Village of the Damned (1960)

Starring: George Sanders, Barbara Shelley, Martin Stephens

So Young. So Innocent. So Deadly.

Directed by: Wolf Rilla

A black-and-white B-movie that still has its scare mojo going. Heck, it was even parodied on *The Simpsons*. A mist invades the serene British village of Midwich and suddenly the women are pregnant, eventually giving birth to blonde, robotic children with glowing eyes, smartass attitudes, and dangerous ways of making good on their threats. Sanders, a professor, and his wife (Shelley) are parents to David (a chilling Stephens), the head of this telepathic posse. Turn on them with a gun or a moving vehicle, and they stare you down until you off yourself. Director Rilla, working from John Wyndham's novel *The Midwich Cuckoos*, builds a mood of quiet, churning terror that the DVD transfer sustains.

Hot Bonus: Commentary by horror analyst Steve Haberman. Skip the dim-bulb 1963 sequel, *Children of the Damned*, that comes with the package.

Key Scene: Sanders meets the children in the schoolhouse with a briefcase packed with dynamite. To keep them from reading his mind, he concentrates on a brick wall. Rilla shows the wall coming apart brick by brick.

Viva Las Vegas (1964)

Starring: Elvis Presley, Ann-Margret

Directed by: George Sidney

For the first and only time in his film career, Elvis met his match in a woman. There's an avid look in the King's eye when he's on-screen with the Swedish bombshell, and the competitive edge becomes him. He could outsing her, she could out-dance him. But their sizzle quotients are both off the charts. He races cars. She races pulses. She: "Can you help me? My engine's whistling." He: "I don't blame it." They're competing in a Vegas talent contest, which is good because it lets director Sidney put the musical numbers front and center. They share a sassy duet, "The Lady Loves Me" and dueling solos: Hers to "Appreciation," his to the title song—all of which makes for a hunka hunka burnin' DVD watching.

Hot Bonus: Seeing the film, at last, in widescreen instead of cropped beyond recognition, like it is on TV and on VHS tape.

Key Scene: The musical face-off to "Come On, Everybody," with Elvis swinging his pelvis onstage and Ann-Margret below, swinging everything from hair to hips. It's like sex with a beat you can dance to.

Wag the Dog (1997)

Starring: Dustin Hoffman, Robert De Niro, Anne Heche

Directed by: Barry Levinson

A wicked political satire that Levinson shot in less than a month as a throwaway. The topic is spin. The president has been caught fiddling with a Girl Scout. His aide (Heche) calls in fixer Conrad Brean (De Niro) to provide a distraction. Conrad decides America will go to war—with Albania. He hires Hollywood producer Stanley Motss (Hoffman) to stage the conflict, but just for the cameras. That's all that counts with Americans. The killer script by David Mamet and Hilary Henkin was Oscar nominated, as was Hoffman for his mercilessly funny parody of his producer pal Robert Evans. The fake footage of battle and nonexistent B-3 bombers has a grainy newsreel quality that comes through smashingly on DVD. The film has only one flaw: in today's tabloid world, a puny war would never distract the media from that Girl Scout scandal in the Oval Office.

Hot Bonus: Levinson and Hoffman have a scrappy good time talking about media manipulation. Hello, Grenada.

Key Scene: Shooting a clip for the nightly news involving an Albanian girl (Kirsten Dunst) fleeing the bombs with her kitten, which has been digitally created from a bag of Tostitos.

Wages of Fear, The (1953)

Starring: Yves Montand, Charles Vanel, Folco Lulli, Peter Van Eyck

Directed by: H. G. Clouzot

Criterion restores Clouzot's black-and-white suspense classic to vivid life on DVD. To put out a raging oil fire in a poverty-stricken town in Central America, Montand and three cohorts take on the suicide mission of driving two trucks filled with nitroglycerine across impossibly rough terrain. It's a sweat job as all kinds of obstacles—boulders, swamp, fear—get in their way. Avoid *Sorcerer*, the 1977 Hollywood remake. This is the real deal.

Hot Bonus: Scenes deleted from the original American release.

Key Scene: Watching the trucks cross a shaky suspension bridge. The DVD audio lets you hear every groan.

Waiting for Guffman (1996)

Starring: Christopher Guest, Eugene Levy, Parker Posey

Directed and co-written by: Christopher Guest

Borrowing the style of *This Is Spinal Tap*, in which he played Nigel Tufnel, actor-director-writer-composer Guest kicked off a priceless series of mockumentaries (*Best in Show*, *A Mighty Wind*) with this priceless gem about the citizens of Blaine, Missouri, staging a musical to celebrate the town's 150th anniversary. Guest loads an arsenal of laughs into a deceptively small package. Wearing bangs and speaking in a lisp, Guest swans through the role of Corky St. Clair, back in Blaine after a failed go at Broadway. He wins the job of directing *Red, White, and Blaine*—despite the fact that Corky's recent production of *Backdraft* burned newspapers in the air vent, hitting audiences with hot ash so they could feel the fire. Guest's wicked cohorts, many from SCTV, include Levy as a singing dentist, and Catherine O'Hara and Fred Willard as travel agents with a yen for greasepaint. Posey shines as a Dairy Queen doll who does a slutty version of Doris Day's "Teacher's Pet." This outrageously funny DVD is comic nirvana.

Hot Bonus: Guest and Levy provide audio commentary and deleted scenes.

Key Scene: I lost it just watching Corky show off such memorabilia as *My Dinner With Andre* action figures and a *Remains of the Day* lunch box.

Waking Life (2001)

Starring: Wiley Wiggins, Ethan Hawke, Julie Delpy

Directed and written by: Richard Linklater

Linklater's dreamscape is strikingly original. The film's protagonist—Wiggins from Linklater's *Dazed and Confused*—sleepwalks around asking essential questions about existence, identity, the nature of the universe, and whether it's a big,

"Strikingly original... nothing short of amazing."
—Peter Travers, ROLLING STONE

stupid risk to make a plotless movie about dreams. That the Texas-based Linklater chose to express his ideas through animation shows he has guts. That he pulls off the innovative feat with hypnotic assurance is nothing short of amazing. This isn't your dad's animation, or even Disney's. Having first shot the film digitally with live actors in Texas and New York, Linklater and art director Bob Sabiston asked thirty-one artists to computer-paint over that footage in their own distinct styles, assigning different characters and vignettes to each artist. The result is a DVD magic-carpet ride the likes of which has not been seen since the head-tripping *2001: A Space Odyssey* and *Yellow Submarine*. But don't label the movie "For Stoners Only." Linklater's cerebral provocations allow for tickling visuals—check out that car-boat—and lively humor.

Hot Bonus: Seeing the real actors go through the action before they get computer-painted.

Key Scene: Watching Hawke and Delpy, repeating their roles in Linklater's *Before Sunrise* and *Before Sunset*, pillow talk about reincarnation.

Walkabout (1971)

Starring: Jenny Agutter, David Gulpilil, Lucien John
Directed by: Nicolas Roeg

Images of shocking gravity and beauty are the thrust of Roeg's remarkable solo directing debut. And the Criterion DVD—the unedited director's cut—polishes each one until it shines anew. The film begins as a father abandons his two children—a teen girl (Agutter) and her younger brother (John, the director's son)—in the Australian outback and promptly shoots himself. Their savior is a young Aborigine boy (Gulpilil) on his walkabout—akin to an initiation into manhood. The attraction between Gulpilil and Agutter sparks a disaster that allows Roeg to walk the thin line between primitivism and civilization in ways that will haunt you long after the film ends.

Hot Bonus: In retrospective interviews, Roeg and Agutter share illuminating memories of what the filming was like.

Key Scene: The revelation that accompanies the return to civilization.

Wall Street (1987)

Starring: Michael Douglas, Charlie Sheen, Daryl Hannah, Sean Young
Directed by: Oliver Stone

Good and evil fight for the soul of Charlie Sheen. The same struggle that went on in Stone's *Platoon* moves from Vietnam to Wall Street in the writer-director's still timely look at buying, selling, and insider trading. Sheen's Bud Fox betrays the values of his father (his own father, Martin Sheen, plays the role) to work at the pampered feet of financial killer Gordon Gekko. Douglas, hair slicked back, his suits even slicker, makes Gekko a seductive icon of Me Decade corruption. His performance won him a Best Actor Oscar and a place in the pantheon of fatcat villains. Stone takes a moral stance in his script, but he can't resist showing us what Gekko's money can buy, including women, represented by Hannah and Young. The DVD transfer is so lush you can feel your feet sink in Gekko's carpeting. Temptation comes alive in this movie, and its power hasn't abated.

Hot Bonus: In a retrospective documentary, Stone discusses his father's career on Wall Street, and Douglas credits the director for having to bully his award-winning performance out of him.

Key Scene: Gekko delivering his "greed is good" speech to appreciative stockholders. "Greed is right," he says. "Greed works."

War of the Roses, The (Special Edition) (1989)

Starring: Michael Douglas, Kathleen Turner, Danny DeVito
Directed by: Danny DeVito

"What fresh hell is this?" asks Turner, her eyes bulging with trepidation. She is playing Barbara Rose, a neglected wife who wants out of her seventeen-year marriage to her lawyer husband, Oliver (Douglas). There's a catch: both Roses want to keep the elegant Washington, D.C., house in which they watched their love turn to indifference and then open hatred. Packing their two teenagers off to school, the Roses divide their home into a battle zone. The letterboxed framing of the DVD transfer is exactly right for showing the gap between these combatants. Under the astute direction of DeVito, who does a sly turn as Oliver's attorney, this acid-dipped epic of revenge is killingly funny and dramatically daring. Turner and Douglas delineate the conquest of emotion over reason with chilling exactitude.

Hot Bonus: DeVito's acerbic commentary, plus juicy deleted scenes.

Key Scene: The chandelier-swinging finale that takes this "war" to its dark but logical conclusion. The daring of DeVito's choice still astonishes.

War of the Worlds (Special Edition) (2005)

Starring: Tom Cruise, Dakota Fanning
Directed by: Steven Spielberg

Spielberg's mastery of film technique is a guarantee of DVD magic. H. G. Wells might not recognize his 1898 alien-invasion novel in Spielberg's updated film version. But Wells could relate to the ensuing fear and panic. Unlike the campy 1953 film rendition with its primitive Martians, Spielberg's *War* is set in a real world seized by a terrorist attack. Divorced dad Ray Ferrier (Cruise, complex and vulnerable), a New Jersey dockyard worker, is a screw-up with his daughter (Fanning) and his teen son (Justin Chatwin). So when huge, hostile alien Tripods rise out of the ground during an electrical storm and start laying waste, Ray grabs the kids and runs. Stealing a car that the aliens haven't immobilized, the Ferriers hit the road to Boston to find the kids' remarried mom (Miranda Otto) and a safe haven. That road trip, by car and foot, inspires Spielberg to create extraordinary images of a frayed family in a frayed civilization. The 9/11 parallels are unmistakable, as the streets of America are littered with bodies and the next threat comes without reason or mercy.

Hot Bonus: Spielberg lets us in on a few secrets.

Key Scene: When the Tripods capsize a ferry, spilling bodies into watery graves. It's a sequence that rivals *Titanic*.

Warriors, The (Two-Disc Special Edition) (1979)

Starring: Michael Beck, James Remar, Roger Hill, Deborah Van Valkenburgh
Directed by: Walter Hill

Hill's movie deserves to spawn a cult and just might get it from this Special Edition DVD that puts the previous single disc in the shadows. The dogs of virtue were all over this film in 1979 when it was accused of glamorizing gang violence. But now you can see it for the surreal visual trip it is with its neon-lit New York and its rival gangs in gaudy dress and goth makeup. Hill borrows the plot from Xenophon's *Anabasis*, in which ten thousand Greek warriors fought their way across Persia in 401 B.C. Hill's warriors, led by Beck, make the long subway trip from Coney Island to the Bronx for a meeting of the city's gangs, only

to be wrongly accused of assassinating a would-be messiah (Hill) who wants to unite the gangs. It's war, and Hill keeps the action throbbing with the city's raw energy.

Hot Bonus: A new introduction from Hill sets up four featurettes that cover the film's development.

Key Scene: The battle between the Warriors and the Furies, a rival gang who paint their faces orange and whack anyone who laughs at them because they wear baseball uniforms. Big mistake. They also carry bats.

Way We Were, The (Special Edition) (1973)

Starring: Barbra Streisand, Robert Redford
Directed by: Sydney Pollack

The chick flick that guys secretly love. As for the DVD transfer: hello, gorgeous. Widescreen, color to die for, and dimensional sound (the better to wallow in Marvin Hamlisch's Oscar-winning music and title song). Streisand gives her best dramatic performance as Katie Morosky, the Jewish firebrand who falls for Hubbell Gardner (Redford), the godlike WASP prince without a political thought in his head. It's *Annie Hall* in reverse, and just as irresistible. Redford brings a wounded self-awareness to Hubbell. A line from a story he writes says it all: "He was like the country he lived in. Everything came too easily to him." The Arthur Laurents script, astutely directed by Pollack, moves from the 1930s to the 1950s as Katie and Hubbell fight, marry, have a baby, divorce, and find others. If this is soap opera, it sure is a classy one.

Hot Bonus: A terrific retrospective documentary, all but Redford participating, plus deleted scenes about the Hollywood blacklist that were cut just before the film's original release.

Key Scene: That heartbreaker ending. The two meet again outside Manhattan's Plaza Hotel. She's distributing "Ban the Bomb" leaflets, he's on his way to a new job. He asks about their daughter, whom he rarely sees. Out of habit, she brushes his hair back from his brow. For a moment, their eyes meet and hold in a flood of memories. "See ya, Katie," he says, waving good-bye. "See ya, Hubbell," she answers. Cue the music and the tears.

Wayne's World (1992)

Starring: Mike Myers, Dana Carvey
Directed by: Penelope Spheeris

Don't spew or hurl. But the laughter that still bubbles up when you watch this spinoff comedy on DVD is proof that the characters Myers and Carvey created on *Saturday Night Live* have not passed their sell-by date. (Note: This does not apply to *Wayne's World 2*, the 1993 sequel, which sours quickly.) So party on, dudes, as teens Wayne Campbell (Myers) and Garth Algar (Carvey) run a public-access TV show out of Wayne's mom's basement in Aurora, Illinois. Sample discussion: "Did you ever find Bugs Bunny attractive when he put on a dress and played a girl bunny?" Trouble invades their pop culture paradise when a sleazy TV exec (Rob Lowe) wants to take the show big-time and steal Wayne's girl (Tia Carrere, schwing!). If Cassandra were president, says Garth, "she'd be BABE-raham Lincoln."

Hot Bonus: Director Spheeris tells of the hell of a time she had trying to keep Myers and Carvey in line.

Key Scene: Wayne, Garth, and friends in a car singing along to Queen's "Bohemian Rhapsody." Truly excellent.

Wedding Crashers, The (Special Edition) (2005)

Starring: Vince Vaughn, Owen Wilson, Rachel McAdams
Directed by: David Dobkin

Sometimes a movie comedy just clicks. Welcome to one of those times. *Wedding Crashers* is an indisputable laugh riot that rewards repeated viewing on DVD. Wilson's John Beckwith and Vaughn's Jeremy Grey are divorce mediators out of Washington, D.C., who crash weddings to scam babes and bridesmaids. Wilson's stoner drawl and Vaughn's snappy patter blend perfectly. They're a comedy dream team. The script, by newbies Steve Faber and Bob Fisher, is a solid blueprint. And director Dobkin allows the boys to improv until the dialogue purrs. Love, of course, intervenes. John is besotted at first sight by a bridesmaid named Claire (the showstopping McAdams), and Jeremy enjoys a quickie with her sister Gloria (Isla Fisher), who announces it's her first time. Jeremy wants to run. "I've got a stage-five clinger," he tells John. There is no running. Both girls are the daughters of Treasury secretary and presidential wannabe William Cleary (Christopher Walken), who insists the guys join the family for a weekend at his beach house. The film is bawdy as hell and unafraid of naked carnality. It's that anything-goes sass that crashes the movie into the realm of comic gold.

Hot Bonus: Dobkin gives the lowdown on directing Vaughn and Wilson.

Key Scene: In one inspired quick-speed montage, John and Jeremy fall into bed one by one with wedding hotties—Jewish, Italian, Chinese, Irish, Hindu—in a trampoline dance of bare butts and bouncing breasts that reminds us what trippy turn-ons movies can be.

Weekend (1967)

Starring: Mireille Darc, Jean Yanne
Directed by: Jean-Luc Godard

Godard's outrageous, surreal satire comes to DVD as a jumble of noises and images that the disc helps to assemble into coherence. After a seminaked session with her shrink, Corinne (Darc) drives out of Paris with her husband Roland (Yanne) for a weekend visit with her parents. The roads are littered with burning cars and corpses as well as rapists, cannibals, black militants, historical figures from Emily Bronte to Mao, and hippies with guns. The gifted cinematographer Raoul Coutard manages visual miracles as Godard skewers middle-class consumerism run amok in a world without values.

Hot Bonus: Coutard discusses the challenges of the filming.

Key Scene: The justly famous ten-minute take as the camera sweeps over a traffic jam is a nightmare vision that is one for the time capsule.

Welcome to the Dollhouse (1995)

Starring: Heather Matarazzo, Brendan Sexton Jr.
Directed and written by: Todd Solondz

Solondz takes us on a hair-raising trip into the mind of Dawn Wiener (Matarazzo), a four-eyed, mouth-breathing pariah of such desperate geekiness that her fellow New Jersey seventh-graders call her "Wiener Dog." It is the purpose of the film—and Solondz and Matarazzo accomplish it triumphantly—to make us see ourselves in Wiener Dog and to feel every insult, even the funny ones, like an arrow into our own hearts. And yet Dawn perseveres. Her chief school tormentor (Sexton) reaches out in his own dysfunctional way: "Tomorrow you get raped," he tells her. "Be there." Solondz should be pleased with the DVD transfer, which catches every painfully hilarious detail of Dawn's life with queasy verisimilitude.

Hot Bonus: Production notes, which tell you enough to know that Solondz grew up as the male equivalent of Dawn.

Key Scene: As her brother's band practices in the family garage, Dawn sits outside on a car hood gazing dreamily at the hunk lead singer (Eric Mabius) and swaying to the music. She's so uncool that she is cool.

West Side Story (Two-Disc Special Edition) (1961)

Starring: Natalie Wood, Richard Beymer, Rita Moreno, George Chakiris
Directed by: Robert Wise and Jerome Robbins

The Oscar-winning film version of the Broadway musical phenom that transported *Romeo and Juliet* from Verona to the mean streets of New York hurtles toward you on DVD in a rush of color, song, and thrilling dance. The heat is on from the second those street gangs—the anglo Jets, led by Riff (Russ Tamblyn), and the Puerto Rican Sharks, led by Bernardo (Chakiris), stop walking toward the camera and start dancing. The acrobatic ballet of Robbins's choreography is as electric as the day he first set it in motion. Chakiris and Moreno, as Anita the passionate chica who galvanizes the "America" number, both won supporting Oscars. As Maria and Tony, the star-crossed lovers, Wood and Beymer are poorly dubbed, but their natural appeal enhances the soaring Leonard Bernstein music and Stephen Sondheim lyrics. Wood, taking Maria from lilting innocence ("I Feel Pretty") to tragic muse ("Somewhere") brings the role an iconic power.

Hot Bonus: A retrospective documentary deals with the reasons that Wise had to be brought in to direct the nonmusical scenes. Robbins showed a genius for dance that translated into budget-busting spending. Both won Oscars for co-directing. Also included: Wood's own recording of the songs before Marni Nixon was brought in to dub her with professional polish. Big mistake from the sound of it. Wood's thin, sweet voice resonates with feeling.

Key Scene: The opening ballet achieves screen immortality. But the rumble and the preparations for it are a near match as each of the main characters reprises "Tonight" with his and her own spin on what the rumble means.

Whale Rider (Special Edition) (2002)

Starring: Keisha Castle-Hughes, Rawiri Paratene, Vicky Haughton
Directed by: Niki Caro

A crowd-pleaser in the best sense of the word: It wins you over without cheating. You look at the remarkable face of Best Actress Oscar nominee Castle-Hughes, only eleven when the film was shot, and you're hooked. She plays Pai, a Maori girl being raised by her grandparents, Koro (Paratene) and Nanny Flowers (Haughton), in contemporary New Zealand. Her father ran off after his wife died giving birth to Pai and her twin brother, who also died. That will leave the tribe without a leader when Koro dies, since girls are considered unfit to lead. Pai has other ideas. As Koro educates local boys in ancient mysticism and the martial arts, Pai trains in secret, evoking the anger of Koro, whose ancestor, legend has it, arrived in their village on the back of a whale. Director Caro, who adapted Witi Ihimaera's novel, has made a film of female empowerment that resonates deeply. The DVD provides the crisp picture and dimensional sound to bring it all home.

Hot Bonus: Caro speaks eloquently and wittily about being a woman director working with a male crew, paralleling the story being told on-screen.

Key Scene: The moment that brings the title to life on film.

Whatever Happened to Baby Jane? (1962)

Starring: Bette Davis, Joan Crawford, Victor Buono
Directed by: Robert Aldrich

The infamous off-screen feud between Davis and Crawford makes watching this horror classic—campy and compelling in equal doses—twice the fun. This DVD of Aldrich's black-and-white film is so sharp you can practically feel the rot eating away at the old house where gorgonish ex–child star Baby Jane Hudson (Davis) tends to the care, feeding, and torture of her wheelchair-bound sister Blanche (Crawford), a screen glamorpuss crippled in a mysterious accident. When Jane overhears Blanche's plans to ship her off to the loony bin, the sadism begins. That includes serving Blanche brochette of rat and glazed parakeet. The stars go at it hammer and tongs, with Davis snagging the Oscar nomination for malevolence above and beyond the call of duty. When her sister moans that she wishes she wasn't in a wheelchair, Jane's line—"But cha aah, Blanche, ya ahh in that chair!"—brings Davis a scary new kind of screen immortality.

Hot Bonus: Production notes set up the Davis-Crawford feud.

Key Scene: Desperate to revive her career, Jane hires Edwin Flagg (Oscar nominee Buono), a fat, mama's-boy pianist, to accompany her on "I've Written a Letter to Daddy"—the song that turned

Baby Jane into a kiddie phenom. Davis makes the sight of Jane tearing into that song wearing a girl's dress, blonde curls, and grotesque makeup frightening and poignant.

What's Eating Gilbert Grape? (1993)

Starring: Johnny Depp, Leonardo DiCaprio, Juliette Lewis, Darlene Cates
Directed by: Lasse Hallström

Hallström's disarmingly eccentric film succeeds by locating beauty in unlikely places, and the DVD transfer lavishes full attention on that beauty. Depp plays Gilbert, the eldest son of an Iowa household that includes his couch-bound five-hundred-pound Momma (Cates), two sisters, and Arnie (DiCaprio), a severely retarded younger brother, who likes to climb the water tower. Dad's a suicide, so responsibility falls on Gilbert, who ekes out a living at the local grocery store. He doesn't complain, but you sense the turmoil inside. Becky (Lewis), a visitor in town, senses it too. She falls for Gilbert and stirs dreams in him of a world outside. There's a sweet modesty to Depp's performance. The same goes for the film, adapted by Peter Hedges from his novel. Hallström directs the actors with an eye to revealing the humanity we share with these quirky characters. Cates, a newcomer discovered on a TV show about overweight couch potatoes, is remarkable for her spirit and dignity. And Oscar nominee DiCaprio is fearless in letting us see Arnie as joy and burden, especially when Gilbert gives him a bath.

Hot Bonus: A trailer that deserves study for how well it captures the tone of this complex, multilayered film.

Key Scene: Momma leaves the house, rousing herself to protect Arnie.

What's Love Got to Do With It? (1993)

Starring: Angela Bassett, Laurence Fishburne
Directed by: Brian Gibson

Who wants to see a musical biopic about Anna Mae Bullock from Nutbush, Tennessee? You do, because Anna Mae grows up to become Tina Turner, the international star who made her name touring with her abusive husband, Ike, until she broke free and soared even higher as a solo. Director Gibson, working with a script adapted by Kate Lanier from *I, Tina,* the memoir Turner wrote with Kurt Loder, is trapped in a biopic format. But nothing can trap the Oscar-nominated performances of Bassett as Tina and Fishburne as Ike. Bassett lip-syncs to Turner's numbers, from "Proud Mary" to "River Deep, Mountain High," and storms across the stage with her own athletic energy. Fishburne performs the sly trick of finding the flawed human being in a character the script treats like a monster. The DVD transfer catches every shift in their electrifying dynamic.

Hot Bonus: Look for the live stage performance by the real-life Turner at the end of the film.

Key Scene: Tina's brutal battle with Ike in the back of a limo.

When Harry Met Sally . . . (Special Edition) (1989)

Starring: Meg Ryan, Billy Crystal
Directed by: Rob Reiner

The movie begins with a man and a woman in a car, and the car doesn't crash. That's the first thing that wins you over. Reiner and screenwriter Nora Ephron start the plot whirling in 1977. Sally (Ryan) is giving Harry (Crystal), her friend's lover, a ride from Chicago to New York. He's too pushy and vulgar for her; she's too hoity-toity for him. Harry thinks a man and woman can't be friends without sex becoming an issue. Crystal and Ryan— in her star-making performance—make an ideal team. For the next eleven years, Harry, a political consultant, and Sally, a journalist, labor to stay in friendship and out of each other's bed. Reiner breaks up the story by interviewing older couples who tell what brought them together. My fave is the woman who says you know a great relationship like "you know a great melon." A similar instinct applies to movies on DVD. You can tell this one is a winner by the way it leaves a smile on your face that lasts for days.

Hot Bonus: A retrospective documentary with Reiner, Ephron, and Crystal.

Key Scene: Ryan in a deli showing Crystal how easy it is to fake an earth-shaking orgasm. "I'll have what she's having," says a customer, neatly played by Estelle Reiner, the director's mother.

When We Were Kings (1996)

Starring: Muhammad Ali, George Foreman
Directed by: Leon Gast

Gast's Oscar-winning documentary does much more than document the legendary 1974 title fight in Zaire between Ali and Foreman. The so-called Rumble in the Jungle involved many factors, including the African Woodstock—featuring the likes of B. B. King and James Brown—organized around the fight by young promoter Don King

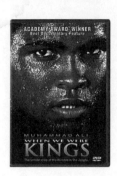

and Ali's decision to fight in a police state—against a younger, fiercer opponent—to send a message of brotherhood to the world. This from a conscientious objector during the Vietnam conflict. Gast uses photographs; interviews with Norman Mailer, George Plimpton, and Spike Lee; and stunning fight footage to put the "rumble" in a global perspective that makes this DVD historic.

Hot Bonus: Gast explains the legal wrangling that took him nearly two decades to surmount to get his documentary out there.

Key Scene: The ring footage of Ali using his Rope-a-Dope defense, taking enormous punishment from Foreman in order to outlast him.

Where the Boys Are (Special Edition) (1960)

Starring: Dolores Hart, George Hamilton, Paula Prentiss, Yvette Mimieux

Directed by: Henry Levin

A spring-break sex comedy that sums up the genre and an entire pre-sixties generation. The colors, the sound, the yearning title tune by Connie Francis (who also makes her acting debut) all combine on the DVD to make *Boys* provocative time-capsule material. Hart, Prentiss, Francis and Mimieux are college friends who join the exodus to Fort Lauderdale, Florida, where winter clothes are shed along with inhibitions. For the girls, the trick is to hook up with an Ivy Leaguer. Tall-girl Prentiss flirts sweetly with Jim Hutton (Timothy's dad), while Hart has a tougher time keeping slick-dick Hamilton at bay. For Mimieux, eagerness opens the door to date rape. Watch how director Levin and the actors sidestep the script's moralistic traps to come up with something funny, touching, and insightful.

Hot Bonus: Prentiss, who suffered a nervous breakdown in 1964 and mostly withdrew from acting, provides a deeply felt retrospective commentary. She remembers her co-stars, including Hutton, who died in 1979, and recalls a visit to Hart, who entered a cloistered convent. Hamilton stayed tan.

Key Scene: That last sweeping pan across the beach as Hart and Hamilton forge a truce that may end in an actual relationship.

White Heat (Special Edition) (1949)

Starring: James Cagney, Edmond O'Brien, Margaret Wycherly

Directed by: Raoul Walsh

Cagney's gangster movie peak, and a more exciting and surreal explosion of perverse psychology you won't find anywhere. The DVD image is so hot, it's damn near flammable. Cagney plays Cody Jarrett, trained to rob and kill at the hands of an expert—his mother (Wycherly). If you want examples of Academy idiocy, point to the fact that neither of these landmark performances was even nominated. Loosely based on the story of Ma Barker and her son Doc, this Freudian film noir will have you rubbing your eyes in disbelief as Cody sits on his ma's lap. He has a wife (Virginia Mayo), but it's his mother fixation that gives him migraines, not the undercover cop (O'Brien) posing as his cellmate. Her death sends convict Cody memorably berserk. Cagney and director Walsh are absolutely fearless.

Hot Bonus: The film's psychology is examined by Dr. Drew Casper and director Martin Scorsese.

Key Scene: "Made it, Ma—top of the world!"—Cagney's last words before burning oil tankers blow him sky high.

Who Framed Roger Rabbit (Two-Disc Collector's Edition) (1988)

Starring: Bob Hoskins, Christopher Lloyd, Kathleen Turner

Directed by: Robert Zemeckis

An innovative combo of animation and live-action that gets a DVD treatment guaranteed to make your eyes go *boinnnnnng*! Director Zemeckis shrewdly opens the movie with an old-fashioned, two-dimensional cartoon. Baby Herman crawls toward a cookie jar, narrowly escaping disaster thanks to a protector rabbit named Roger. Then Zemeckis pulls the rugs out. Baby Herman and Roger walk off the screen into the real world. The time is 1947. The place is Toontown, a Hollywood studio where humans and toons interact, often nastily. The whiskey-voiced baby chomps on a stogie and grabs at script girls. Roger is suspected of murdering a studio mogul (Stubby Kaye) who has been "playing pattycake" with Roger's sexpot wife, Jessica. She is also a toon but drawn in human form and gifted with the sultry voice of Turner. Roger hires Eddie Valiant (Hoskins), a down-at-the-heel detective, to clear his name before Judge Doom (Lloyd) kills more beloved cartoon characters by dropping them in a bubbling acid solution he dubs the Dip. Led by Hoskins, who interacts with what's not there better than any actor in the business, the movie is historic entertainment.

Hot Bonus: An Easter Egg for the twisted. Use the Still Frame feature to stop Jessica during her accident scene, and you'll find three frames that reveal more of this hot number than the official Disney version would allow.

Key Scene: Jessica slinking toward Eddie: "I'm not bad," she says. "I'm just drawn that way." Apparently so, if you follow the instructions above.

Wicker Man, The (Two-Disc Special Edition) (1973)

Starring: Christopher Lee, Edward Woodward, Britt Ekland

Directed by: Robin Hardy

Anchor Bay has done a superior job of restoring this mesmerizing mix of horror and suspense to its rightful place in the cult pantheon. Woodward stars as Sergeant Howie, a Scottish cop of good Christian principles (he's an impotent, aging virgin) who investigates the case of a missing girl on a remote island. He finds that the place is run by Lord Summerisle (the great Lee), according to ancient pagan sex rituals, which Ekland, among others, amply demonstrate. The crisp DVD picture really comes in handy here. It's a shame that the eleven minutes of restored footage is from a damaged print. But the script by Anthony Shaffer (*Sleuth*) is clever, erotic, and insightful, and Hardy directs like he knows he's onto something. He is.

Hot Bonus: The special edition comes in a nifty wooden box, but it's the documentary, *The Wicker Man Enigma*, that shows how the film was nearly lost forever in bureaucratic quicksand.

Key Scene: The ending is a real surprise, but for fun you can't beat Lee arguing against the existence of a Christian God: "He's dead, he can't complain. He had his chance and, in the modern parlance, he blew it."

Wild at Heart (Special Edition) (1990)

Starring: Nicolas Cage, Laura

Dern, Diane Ladd

Directed by: David Lynch

Lynch's kinky fairy tale is a triumph of startling images and comic invention. In adapting Barry Gifford's book *Wild at Heart* for the screen, Lynch does more than tinker. Starting with the outrageous and building from there, he ignites a slight love-on-the-run novel into a bonfire of a movie. Lynch paints with color and sound, and this DVD with its upgraded picture and sound is his canvas. The story revolves around the love of Sailor Ripley (Cage) and Lula Pace Fortune (Dern). "Jeez Louise, Sailor," says Lula after one of their marathon sex bouts, "you are something else." They're just two sweet, horny kids, except for their Lynch-load of psychological baggage. Raped at thirteen by her father's business partner, Lula has a monster mother, Marietta (Oscar-nominee Ladd is Dern's real mother). And Sailor, despite his tender way with a Presley ballad ("Treat me like a fool/Treat me mean and cruel/But love me"), has a hidden past and a rebel streak. Lynch keeps us eager to follow these lovers on their yellow brick road to the unexpected. "This whole world is weird on top and wild at heart," says Lula. And who better to chart such a world than Lynch? Even over the rainbow, he finds his own kind of truth.

Hot Bonus: Lynch rarely participates in DVD commentaries. This time he does, making the disc essential for any serious film enthusiast.

Key Scene: Sailor and Lula encounter the staggering victim of a car wreck (Sherilyn Fenn), and the moment resonates with a ghostly, poetic terror.

Wild Bunch, The (Director's Cut) (1969)

Starring: William Holden, Ernest Borgnine, Robert Ryan, Edmond O'Brien

Directed by: Sam Peckinpah

An essential DVD; don't even think of not owning it. And make sure it's the 144-minute Director's Cut—the way Peckinpah intended you to see his brutal, elegiac western. "We've got to start thinking past our guns," Holden's Pike Bishop tells his men. "Those days are closing fast." It's 1913. Pike and the bunch, including Borgnine, O'Brien, Warren Oates, Jaime Sanchez, and Ben Johnson, are leaving Texas for a new job of killing in Mexico, with a little whoring on the side. The toll of this life is written on the lined face of Holden, an actor who reached the pinnacle of his mature talent with this film and *Network*. Peckinpah shows these outmoded warriors in near-balletic displays of destruction and bloodshed. But their time is passing. One of their own, Deke Thornton (a superb Ryan), has betrayed them to collect a bounty. A car sprays dust in the eyes of their horses. But the bunch holds to its fading code of honor among killers. And Peckinpah, heightening his vision through the lighting genius of cinematographer Lucien Ballard, takes us into battle with them. Turning a poet's eye on conflicting notions of good and evil, he creates something monumental.

Hot Bonus: The documentary, *Wild Bunch: An Album in Montage*, offers invaluable footage of Peckinpah at work, along with discussions of the art of the filmmaker known affectionately as Bloody Sam.

Key Scene: It's hard to beat the opener as the bunch ride into a Texas border town, past children laughing as they watch red ants devour a dying scorpion, only to face an ambush that becomes a symphony of slow-motion carnage.

Willy Wonka and the Chocolate Factory (Widescreen Special Edition) (1971)

Starring: Gene Wilder, Peter Ostrum, Jack Albertson

Directed by: Mel Stuart

With all respect to Tim Burton and Johnny Depp's 2005 take on Roald Dahl's landmark fairy tale for twisted children of all ages, Stuart's musical version still deserves props. The chief reason is Wilder, whose plays candy man Willy Wonka with just the right mix of sweet mirth and wicked malice. Wonka has opened his secret chocolate factory to five children—and one relative of choice. The kids are uber-brats, all but poor boy Charlie Bucket (Ostrum) and his Grandpa Joe (Albertson), who behave in marked contrast to gluttonous Augustus Gloop, spoiled Veruca Salt, gum-chewing Violet Beauregarde, and television-obsessed Mike Teevee. Other treats, besides tasty songs by Leslie Bricusse and Anthony Newley, are the spun-sugar sets that look good-enough-to-eat

on this anamorphic widescreen transfer. Oompa-Loompa, doopity do, I've got another puzzle for you: What's wrong with this DVD? Absolutely nothing.

Hot Bonus: The now-adult actors who played the kids all reunite to share memories that all surprisingly scrappy.

Key Scene: The "Pure Imagination" number in which Wonka greets his guests with the loveliest ballad in the score, and then can't hide his pleasure when greedy Augustus nearly drowns in a river of chocolate.

Winchester '73 (1950)

Starring: James Stewart, Stephen McNally, Shelley Winters

Directed by: Anthony Mann

This is the first of five landmark "psychological westerns" Stewart did with director Mann (followed by *Bend of the River*, *The Man From Laramie*, *The Naked Spur*, and *The Far Country*). It's a visual and emotional knockout, with Stewart's great edge-of-madness performance on a par with his crazed bounty hunter in *The Naked Spur* (still a DVD holdout). As Lin McAdams, Stewart is in relentless pursuit of Dutch (McNally), the villain who stole the rare Winchester '73 rifle (one of only one thousand) that he won in a shooting contest. Mann creates images of spare, rugged brutality, but the real subject here is the violence of the mind.

Hot Bonus: Stewart, who died in 1997, contributes a priceless audio commentary over the film's ninety-two-minute running time. It's an amazement that no genuine fan of the star and his film should dream of missing.

Key Scene: The final shootout in the mountains is justly famous.

Winged Migration (Special Edition) (2001)

Directed by: Jacques Perrin

A documentary about birds of every feather who migrate across forty countries and seven continents? Really? Yes. With the help of many cinematographers, director Perrin gets so close to the intimate beauty of flight, you feel privileged. The result is a movie miracle that soars even higher on a DVD of dazzling clarity and dimensional sound.

Hot Bonus: The "how they did it" stuff is remarkable, right down to hanging cameras from balloons to catch the birds in flight.

Key Scene: The birds fleeing an avalanche.

Wings of Desire (Special Edition) (1987)

Starring: Bruno Ganz, Otto Sander, Solveig Dommartin, Peter Falk

Directed by: Wim Wenders

There is a beauty beyond words—but thankfully not beyond this DVD transfer—in Wenders's visual tone poem about two angels (Ganz and Sander) who watch over Berlin. Particular attention is paid to a pretty trapeze artist (Dommartin), an elderly poet (Curt Bois), and an American TV star (Falk). Your attention will also be riveted by the artful cinematography of Henri Alekan, who moves from the black-and-white rigor of daily Berlin to bursts of color when Ganz's angel achieves his wish to become human and experience feelings. To fully appreciate the film's brilliance, get the DVD of *City of Angels*, the disastrous 1998 Hollywood remake with Nicolas Cage.

Hot Bonus: A retrospective documentary with Wenders and Falk that describes the film's gestation and ultimate impact.

Key Scene: Angels on the Berlin subway, listening to the thoughts of the passengers that begin to blend in a symphony of sound.

Winslow Boy, The (1999)

Starring: Jeremy Northam, Rebecca Pidgeon, Nigel Hawthorne

Directed by: David Mamet

Many were shocked when playwright Mamet, the poet king of American street talk, decided to write and direct a film of Terence Rattigan's very British and very proper play about a thirteen-year-old cadet (Guy Edwards) expelled from the Royal Naval Academy in 1910 for petty theft. The boy's father (Hawthorne) risks everything to sue the Admiralty, hiring Sir Robert Morton (Northam) to take the case. The family is basically ruined in its search for justice. Mamet exults in the language of the law and the passions roiling beneath tight collars and stiff upper lips. This is one of his best and most subtly powerful films, and the clarity of the DVD transfer does every nuance justice. Northam's performance, whether playing hard-

ball with the boy or flirting outrageously with his suffragette sister Catherine (Pidgeon, Mrs. Mamet), deserves to be legendary.

Hot Bonus: Mamet talks about his intentions, as well as the influence that the O. J. Simpson murder case had on his wanting to make this film.

Key Scene: Sir Robert's final exchange with Catherine, drawing a battle line between the sexes by telling her that feminism is a lost cause. Catherine: "Do you really think so, Sir Robert? How little you know about women. Good-bye. I doubt that we shall meet again." Sir Robert: "Do you really think so, Miss Winslow? How little you know about men."

Winter Kills (Two-Disc Special Edition) (1979)

Starring: Jeff Bridges, John Huston

Directed by: William Richert

One of the great political conspiracy thrillers of the 1970s gets a full-scale, roll-out-the-extras DVD treatment to make up for being kicked to the curb on its original release. Based on a novel by Richard Condon (*Winter Kills*), this blackest of black comedies stars the reliably superb Bridges as Nick Kegan, the stepbrother of an assassinated president who bears more than a passing resemblance to JFK. Nick accidentally discovers a second shooter behind his sibling's death nineteen years ago. The trail of deceit extends to his womanizing father, Pa Kegan, played by Huston with a surreal burst of energy that fits in just fine with Richert's direction. Shot by Vilmos Zsigmond, the film is authentically gorgeous as well as authentically nuts. Check out those cameos from Toshiro Mifune as a houseboy and Elizabeth Taylor as a madam with a dirty mouth.

Hot Bonus: A thirty-eight-minute featurette, *Who Killed Winter Kills?*, examines behind-the-scenes conspiracies that will curl your hair.

Key Scene: Huston's last hurrah, involving an American flag and a shocking moment of revelation.

With a Friend Like Harry (2000)

Starring: Sergi López, Laurent Lucas, Mathilde Seigner, Sophie Guillemin

Directed by: Dominik Moll

Here's a suspense mind-teaser you want to see again, pronto. Hello, DVD. There are things to consider about this tale of Michel (Lucas), a failed writer driving to a country getaway with his wife (Seigner) and three kids. The car is hot, the kids are noisy. Then he meets Harry (López), who says he's an old school friend. Harry's car is cool, his girlfriend (Guillemin) is hot, he wants to help. Invited for dinner, Harry recites poetry his friend wrote in school. There are gifts he can give Michel, problems he can eliminate. Murder is mentioned. Dread mixes with dark humor to suggest forbidden wish fulfillment. It's a French version of Hitchcock's *Strangers on a Train*.

Hot Bonus: The film is offered in French with English subtitles, so you must never watch the English dubbed version. Never.

Key Scene: The meeting of Michel and Harry in a highway restroom. The camera sees them both as a reflection in a mirror. That's a clue.

Witness (Special Collector's Edition) (1985)

Starring: Harrison Ford, Kelly McGillis, Lukas Haas

Directed by: Peter Weir

From its brutal opening in a Philadelphia train station to its meltingly romantic conclusion outside an Amish family farm, this movie is a spellbinder. The new DVD transfer brings out rich colors and sound like never before, allowing director Weir to mix the exotic and the mundane to devastating effect. A young Amish boy (Haas, then nine) witnesses a murder in a railway restroom. Suddenly he and his widowed mother (McGillis) are swept up in a big-city nightmare of cops and corruption. Their rescuer is detective John Book, played by Ford in an Oscar-nominated performance. Hiding out among the Amish until he can finger the guilty parties, Ford's cop finds himself inside a nonviolent world that hasn't changed in two hundred years. The Amish are a plain people, but far from unfeeling. McGillis gives her attraction to Ford a lyrical urgency. Two worlds collide and, for a moment, mesh.

Hot Bonus: A documentary, *Between Two Worlds: The Making of Witness.*

Key Scene: One night, helping Ford repair his car, McGillis hears the radio crackle with a song ("Don't know much about history/don't know much biology"). As Ford moves his body to the kind

of arousing backseat music that has been forbidden to her, McGillis is caught up and led into a dance.

Wizard of Oz, The (Three-Disc Collectors' Edition) (1939)

Starring: Judy Garland, Ray Bolger, Bert Lahr, Jack Haley, Margaret Hamilton

Directed by: Victor Fleming

Long available on DVD, but never like this digital reproduction of the Technicolor presentation. Many claim this classic film of Frank Baum's novel looks better than it did in 1939—the new clarity reveals a never-before-seen pimple on Garland's lip, and maybe a few drunken Munchkins. "Toto, I've a feeling we're not in Kansas anymore," says Garland's Dorothy to her dog, as the journey to the Emerald City begins. The Good Witch Glinda (Billie Burke) points Dorothy toward the yellow brick road to Oz, where the Wizard (Frank Morgan) can help Dorothy return home and find a brain for the Scarecrow (Bolger), a heart for the Tin Man (Haley), and some nerve for the Cowardly Lion (Lahr). The main obstacle is the Wicked Witch (Hamilton) who wants Dorothy's ruby slippers. "I'll get you, my pretty," says Hamilton in her iconic cackle, "and your little dog, too!"

Hot Bonus: A newly restored transfer of the 1925 silent version of *Wizard of Oz* starring Oliver Hardy.

Key Scene: The simplest. Garland by a haystack—in glorious black-and-white—singing "Over the Rainbow," the cream of Harold Arlen's score.

Wolf Man, The (Classic Monster Collection) (1941)

Starring: Lon Chaney Jr., Claude Rains, Bela Lugosi, Maria Ouspenskaya

Directed by: George Waggner

"Whoever is bitten by a werewolf and lives becomes a werewolf himself." So says gypsy woman Ouspenskaya to Chaney—and what she says goes. He plays Sir John Talbot, the American-educated British heir who confounds his father (Rains) and his girlfriend (Evelyn Ankers) by howling at the moon as soon as Lugosi puts the bite on him. The black-and-white picture looks astoundingly sharp on DVD for a film this age. A newly remastered audio track adds to the thrill quotient.

Hot Bonus: A documentary features commentary by film historian Tom Weaver illustrates the superior makeup effects by Jack Pierce.

Key Scene: The first transformation, as Talbot grows fur, paws, and a snout and leaps out a window in search of prey.

Women in Love (1969)

Starring: Glenda Jackson, Alan Bates, Oliver Reed, Jennie Linden

Directed by: Ken Russell

D. H. Lawrence's novel of falling sexual barricades in 1920s England collides with the locomotive that is Russell. Amazingly, both survive. Russell's blazing images (the DVD transfer gets them wonderfully right) mostly serve to illuminate the Lawrence text. Jackson won an Oscar as Gudrun, the artist and free spirit—she dances topless before bulls—who shocks her lover Gerald (Reed) and her schoolteacher sister Ursula (Linden), but not Birkin (Bates), who loves Ursula but aspires to a kind of bisexual purity. Got that? No matter. Just let the images lap against your eyeballs.

Hot Bonus: Russell and gay screenwriter Larry Kramer, then closeted, let their own sexual feelings hang out.

Key Scene: Bates and Reed nude wrestling by a fire.

Women on the Verge of a Nervous Breakdown (1988)

Starring: Carmen Maura, Antonio Banderas, Rossy De Palma

Directed by: Pedro Almodóvar

Almodóvar's breakthrough film is a screwball sex farce that typifies the riot of color and passion you expect from Spain's wild man. The DVD can barely contain his visual ideas. Almodóvar gives the film the high-style look of a typical Hollywood comedy of the 1950s—say, *Pillow Talk*. But the merry malice with which he approaches sex, politics, and religion has nothing in common with Doris Day fluff. Maura is a force of nature as Pepa, a TV commercial actress and film dubber who goes over the edge when her cheating lover (Fernando Guillen) dumps her. Pregnant and miserable, she wrecks their penthouse apartment, which quickly fills up with the oddest characters since the Marx Brothers phoned room service. There's the lover's gun-toting ex-wife (Julieta Serrano), his grown son (Banderas), the son's girl (De Palma), and a collection of daffy cops, repairmen, and taxi drivers. There's also the doped gazpacho to explain. Just go with the wanton flow.

Hot Bonus: The film is presented in Spanish with clearly legible English subtitles, which means you should ignore the badly dubbed English version.

Key Scene: Maura burns the king-size bed in a blaze lit by jealousy.

Woodstock (Director's Cut) (1970)

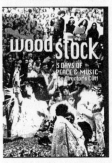

Directed by: Michael Wadleigh

The 1969 three-day concert is the mother of all rock-festival films. Director Wadleigh's risky mix of wide-pan vistas and split-screen editing (courtesy of Martin Scorsese, among others) nails the overwhelming whole of the 1960s last great party: the peace as well as the rain-soaked chaos; hippie frolicking and slay-'em-in-their-sleeping-bags performances by the Who, Santana, and Sly and the Family Stone.

Hot Bonus: The director's cut adds forty minutes of footage.

Key Scene: Jimi Hendrix in buckskin, sending the stragglers home to the scorched remains of "The Star Spangled Banner."

Working Girl (1988)

Starring: Melanie Griffith, Harrison Ford, Joan Cusack, Sigourney Weaver

Directed by: Mike Nichols

Mixing jobs and sex may be bad for business, but it can be great for comedy. Just look at this frisky farce from director Nichols, screenwriter Kevin Wade, and a class-act cast. It's a piñata of brightly colored surprises that come through niftily on DVD. Griffith is irresistible as Tess McGill, an ambitious (she attends night school) secretary at a Manhattan brokerage firm. When Tess's boss (a hilariously bitchy Weaver) steals her ideas and pitches them to hunkish broker Jack Trainer (Ford, becomingly relaxed), Tess vows revenge. She persuades Jack she's the boss, while he tries to persuade her into bed. Looking for sparkle? This is it. Griffith, Weaver, Cusack, Nichols, and the movie won Oscar nominations, and Carly Simon took the prize for her catchy song, "Let the River Run."

Hot Bonus: Three TV spots for the film that sell it three different ways.

Key Scene: Griffith, just sitting on a bar stool flirting with Ford, is the kind of erotic poetry in fluid motion that can't be achieved digitally. "I have a head for business," she tells him, "and a bod for sin."

Written on the Wind (1956)

Starring: Rock Hudson, Lauren Bacall, Robert Stack, Dorothy Malone
Directed by: Douglas Sirk

Want to see a great director turn soap opera into art? Watch Sirk go to work on this sordid story of a dysfunctional Texas oil family. Oscar-winner Malone plays a nymphomaniac who pants after geologist Hudson, who pants after secretary Bacall, who is married to Malone's playboy brother Stack, who is impotent. When Bacall becomes pregnant, what's written on the wind hits the fan. Sirk works with subtext, with light and shadow, with every technique at his command to turn what looks like trash into a scathing social satire of how a capitalist America squeezes out human emotion.

Hot Bonus: A Sirk filmography that analyzes his work and methods.

Key Scene: Malone's last moment, caressing a miniature oil derrick that her dead oil tycoon father holds in the portrait hanging on the wall above her, is phallic and Freudian in ways that must be seen to be believed.

Wuthering Heights (1939)

Starring: Laurence Olivier, Merle Oberon, David Niven, Geraldine Fitzgerald
Directed by: William Wyler

Romantic yearning hits its cinematic height in Wyler's stunning adaptation of Emily Brontë's novel. Olivier's Heathcliff, a lowly servant, burns with consuming passion for Oberon's Cathy. But fate intervenes. She marries Edgar Linton (Niven) for wealth and, out of anger, he turns to Edgar's sister Isabella (Geraldine Fitzgerald)—decisions that lead to tragedy. Gregg Toland won an Oscar for his black-and-white cinematography—etched hauntingly on the DVD—that transforms a California backlot into a re-creation of the English moors that would have fooled Bronte.

Hot Bonus: An interview with Fitzgerald that points to less-than-ideal relationships among Wyler and the actors.

Key Scene: Buffeted by the winds, the young Heathcliff and Cathy stand on the rocks above Wuthering Heights, the manor that Heathcliff will later buy. As the narrator Ellen Dean (Flora Robson) says of the dead, "There is a force that brings them back, if their hearts were wild enough in life." And so, through the force of this DVD, that wildness is back.

X-Men 1.5 (Two-Disc Collector's Edition) (2000)

Starring: Hugh Jackman, Patrick Stewart, Ian McKellen, Halle Berry
Directed by: Bryan Singer

A few fans bitched about this deluxe 1.5 edition. They loved all the new extras and the ten minutes of deleted scenes that could be watched separately or incorporated into the film as a whole. They hated having to buy the DVD again, having already purchased the stripped-down first edition. Welcome to the world of DVD, where reselling us the same movie in new packages is standard procedure. Luckily, X-Men 1.5, armed with superior color and sound, is worth the price. Adapted from Stan Lee's Marvel Comics series by co-writer and director Singer, the movie has enough smarts and special effects to let you forgive the choppy editing. As various misfits and mutants seek shelter with Professor X (Stewart), who wants to integrate them into human society, his counterpart, Magneto (McKellen), plans to destroy humanity and create an X society. Among the X-men, Jackman's Wolverine takes pride of place with his long metal claws and short temper. No complaints either about eyeballing the shape-shifting Mystique (Rebecca Romijn-Stamos), the weather-changing Storm (Berry), and the telekinetic Jean Grey (Famke Janssen), the professor's babe apprentice who gets Wolvie's claws rising. Singer knows enough to just turn them loose.

Hot Bonus: The piece on how they did effects is a keeper.

Key Scene: The stopping of a speeding bullet, a train-station Armageddon, and the fight between Wolverine and himself all earn cheers.

X2: X-Men United (Two-Disc Special Edition) (2003)

Starring: Hugh Jackman, Patrick Stewart, Ian McKellen, Alan Cumming
Directed by: Bryan Singer

A rarity—a sequel that betters the original. The first X-Men set up the story; now it's ready to rock and roll. Everyone is pumped up and pissed off, starting with director Singer, who reportedly kicked chairs and screamed at the crew. His mood fits the movie. Jackman is again in fierce, lupine form as Wolverine. Pushing the bounds of PG-13 intensity, Wolvie stabs his spikes into Deathstrike (the dazzling Kelly Hu), whose talons are twice the size of his. The two mutant camps—one led by Professor X (Stewart), the other by Magneto (McKellen)—unite against Stryker (a terrific Brian Cox), a military psycho with a genocidal rage against mutants. Romance also trips up the X-Men. Wolverine is losing telepathic Jean Grey (Famke Janssen) to laser-eyed Cyclops (James Marsden). On the junior X team, Iceman (Shawn Ashmore) has an itch for Rogue (Anna Paquin, sporting gray streaks) that requires safe scratching, since a mere touch from her can put him in a coma. "We love what you've done with your hair," says Magneto, lobbing the line at Rogue like a bitchy Cupid. Fun stuff. And the DVD transfer looks great with a fully dimensional DTS soundtrack that plays ping-pong with your head. The only problem is overload: Do we need the steel guy, the screamer, the girl who passes through walls, and the kid with the forked tongue?

Hot Bonus: The rehearsal footage of the Wolverine fight with Deathstrike.

Key Scene: In the White House. We hear a sound—bampf!—and there stands Nightcrawler (zesty scene-stealer Cumming), a blue-skinned, yellow-eyed, fork-tailed demon who teleports past security, almost stabs the prez, and behaves unlike the gentle soul he is, a German acrobat who enjoys deep religious dish with Storm (Berry). It's a demo moment from fx heaven.

Y Tu Mamá También (Unrated Edition) (2001)

Starring: Gael Garcia Bernal, Diego Luna, Maribel Verdü

Directed by: Alfonso Cuarón

Road movies don't come hotter, and this unrated DVD doesn't miss a wisp of erotic steam. Unlike American sex comedies, where screwing a pie is always a handy option, Y Tu Mamá También is a film that uses sex to unlock emotional secrets. Two teens—rich-boy Tenoch (Luna) and middle-class Julio (Bernal)—take off for a hidden beach with Luisa (Verdü), twenty-eight, a knockout who learns her husband is cheating and decides, in an act of revenge, to go along for the joyride. The politics and poverty of present-day Mexico City don't mean much to the guys; they just want to get laid. Director Cuarón spins a script with his brother Carlos that takes unexpected comic and dramatic turns. With the help of gifted cinematographer Emmanuel Lubezski, Cuarón gives the sex scenes an exhilarating, unforced carnality. At a motel, Tenoch hops out of a shower, grabs a towel, then finds a pliant Luisa waiting for him to drop it. When she brushes her face against the boy's wet crotch, the scene has a sensuality that is neither mechanical nor pornographic. No wonder Julio, who peeks at the two of them, is both turned on and jealous. Later, when Julio is alone with Luisa in the car, he gropes her like a panting adolescent. She teaches him to channel that frenzy into something more lasting. The film is in Spanish with English subtitles. Don't worry. Very little gets lost in the translation.

Hot Bonus: Deleted scenes—the more the merrier.

Key Scene: The moment when the boys find the beach—the place is being decimated by developers. What they discover opens their eyes to Luisa, to each other, and to the world.

Yankee Doodle Dandy (Two-Disc Special Edition) (1942)

Starring: James Cagney, Joan Leslie, Walter Huston, Rosemary DeCamp

Directed by: Michael Curtiz

Cagney gives his best performance (he thought so, too) in this musical about the life of song-and-dance man George M. Cohan. Who'd have thought the actor who squashed a grapefruit in Mae Clark's face in Public Enemy and immortalized the line, "You dirty rat," would win his only Oscar for dancing across a stage and singing "Give My Regards to Broadway" in a distinctive, rat-a-tat croak that puts a big grin on your face and keeps it there? This tribute to vaudeville and Yankee Doodle Cohan's Irish cockiness is expertly directed by Curtiz. Huston, DeKamp, and Jeanne Cagney (the actor's sibling) are all terrific as the mother, father, and sister that Cohan thanked after every performance—as is Leslie as the girl he married—but it's Cagney you can't stop watching. Thanks to this richly detailed DVD transfer, you can see him in the full bloom of his talent. Bravo.

Hot Bonus: Documentaries on the making of the movie and Cagney's career.

Key Scene: Cagney dancing down the steps of the White House after visiting FDR and whistling Cohan's patriotic anthem "Over There," while outside a parade to support World War II troops marches past singing the same song ("and we won't come home till it's over, over there").

Year of Living Dangerously, The (1983)

Starring: Mel Gibson, Sigourney Weaver, Linda Hunt

Directed by: Peter Weir

Even in a DVD transfer that is less than it could be, Weir's fever dream of political and sexual betrayal leaps off the screen. The director creates a palpable sense of time and place. The year is 1965. Indonesia is on the verge of civil war as plans emerge to overthrow God-King Sukarno, who lives in palatial splendor while his people starve. Gibson plays the Aussie journalist ready to get the story, even it means wangling secret documents out of the British attaché (Weaver) he is sleeping with. The sexual heat between Gibson and Weaver is white-hot. But Hunt, a woman cast in the male role of a Chinese-Australian photographer Billy Kawn, is the film's conscience. The diminutive Hunt won an Oscar for playing the only character tall enough to see over the issues to find the real face of Asia.

Hot Bonus: A four-page booklet. Weir chose Hunt for the role because he said he wanted to "disturb something between what is male and female."

Key Scene: Images, hallucinatory and horrific, crowd for attention, including hookers cruising a graveyard, diplomats and press gorging on oysters a stone's throw away from a starving crowd, and a mass assassination briefly glimpsed at an airport.

Yellow Submarine (1968)

Starring: The music of the Beatles

Directed by: George Dunning

A animated head trip for kids and stoners of all ages. The Blue Meanies are in danger of invading Pepperland and draining everyone of color. Time for the Beatles to hop in their yellow submarine

and put a stop to all that. The Day-Glo mix of Peter Max and Andy Warhol (let's hear it for the 1960s) and movie looks splendiferous on this restored DVD, and such Beatle songs as "Lucy in the Sky with Diamonds," "Nowhere Man," and "All You Need Is Love" have been remastered from mono into sumptuous Dolby stereo. It's true that the speaking voices of the Fab Four are done by others, but that's the lads singing and showing up for the film's live-action coda.

Hot Bonus: The "Hey Bulldog" number has been returned to the movie, but the real treat is the "music only" option that drops the dialogue and lets you just look and listen.

Key Scene: There is something so Lennonesque about the Nowhere Man (voiced by Dick Emery) saying his favorite line: "Ad hoc, ad hoc, and quid pro quo/So little time, so much to know."

Young Frankenstein (Special Edition) (1974)

Starring: Gene Wilder, Peter Boyle, Marty Feldman, Cloris Leachman

Directed and co-written by: Mel Brooks

After *The Producers*, this my favorite Brooks movie. It's a laugh riot that also evokes—and boy does the DVD transfer get this right—the artful style of the original black-and-white *Frankenstein* movies directed by James Whale. Wilder digs right into the role of Freddy Frankenstein. "That's Fronk-en-steen," he says, trying to distance himself from the "doo-doo" experiments of his infamous grandfather. No chance. When Freddy inherits the old-boy's place in Transylvania, he quickly builds his own monster (Boyle) with the help of Igor (the bug-eyed and brilliant Feldman), whose hunchback keeps switching positions; Frau Blücher (Leachman), whose name said aloud scares the horses; and two love interests (Teri Garr and Madeline Kahn), who inspire a chorus of tit and dick jokes.

Hot Bonus: Brooks provides a running commentary that is manic, disorganized, and utterly irresistible.

Key Scene: Wilder and Boyle are fall-on-the-floor-funny as Freddy introduces his monster to the public by performing a "Puttin' on the Ritz" song-and-dance routine in white tie and tails.

Z (1969)

Starring: Yves Montand, Irene Papas, Jean-Louis Trintignant
Directed by: Costa Gavras

This Oscar winner for Best Foreign Language Film is a political firecracker dressed up as a thriller. As such, director Costa Gavras makes his points with subversive force. Montand stars as the deputy, a character clearly based on Gregorios Lambrakis, the Greek liberal who was assassinated by right-wing factions in 1963 while the police stood idly by. Papas, she of the dark, haunted eyes, plays his wife. And Trintignant excels as the judge who decides to investigate the case he was appointed to cover up. Restored to its former widescreen glory on DVD, Z offers a tale of sanctioned murder and corruption that sadly hasn't lost its relevance to the here and now.

Hot Bonus: A fascinating piece on how the film was restored.

Key Scene: The assassination itself is thrillingly staged, as Montand moves through crowded streets with danger lurking in sun and shadow.

Zelig (1983)

Starring: Woody Allen, Mia Farrow
Directed and written by: Woody Allen

Allen's mock documentary, set in the Depression era, tells the tale of Leonard Zelig (Allen), whose desperation to be liked is so overwhelming he develops the ability to emulate whomever he is with. The KKK, intones the narrator Patrick Horgan, considers him "a triple threat because he's a Jew who can turn into a Negro or an Indian." This chameleon becomes a human exhibit loved only by his psychiatrist (Farrow). The old newsreel style is beautifully mimicked, right down to the dust and speckles on the picture—don't adjust your DVD controls, it's meant to look aged by time. Zelig blends seamlessly with real vintage film of such figures as Babe Ruth and William Randolph Hearst, allowing Allen to make statements about celebrity and conformity that cut deep for a comedy.

Hot Bonus: A collectible booklet on the production is included.

Key Scene: Zelig among the crowds at Nuremberg, cheering the Führer.

Zoolander (Special Collector's Edition) (2001)

Starring: Ben Stiller, Owen Wilson, Will Ferrell
Directed and co-written by: Ben Stiller

Bracing comic stupidity that gets funnier each time you watch it. Prep those DVD players. This flick looks smashing, and well it should. The topic is male models. Stiller, the director and co-writer, stars as Derek Zoolander, the infantile, breathy supermodel who still forgets to turn at the end of a runway. Derek sucks in his cheeks to rehearse his pouty new look; he calls it Magnum. His two previous looks (Blue Steel and Ferrari) are each indistinguishable from the other. Superficiality has rarely been treated with such comic depth. Derek hits crisis mode when he loses the model-of-the-year award to surfer-dude newbie Hansel (Wilson, making performance art out of preening). "Hansel is so hot right now," says Mugatu (the great Ferrell), a designer who secretly turns models into assassins. Even when the plot is pounded thinner than veal scaloppini, it flies on pure silliness.

Hot Bonus: The deleted scenes are welcome, but try the Easter Egg (find the spinning M in the Photo Galleries section) that allows you to access Stiller and Wilson practicing their form on the catwalk.

Key Scene: Derek's return home to the Pennsylvania mining town that spawned him. His grimy dad (Jon Voight) cringes when a TV at the local bar blares a commercial featuring Derek as a tail-flipping merman.

MOVIES BY GENRE

ACTION

Bourne Identity, The
Bourne Supremacy, The
Bring Me the Head of Alfredo Garcia
Clear and Present Danger
Cliffhanger
Crimson Tide
Day of the Jackal
Deliverance
Desperado
Die Another Day
Die Hard
Dirty Dozen, The
Dr. No
Enter the Dragon
Escape from New York
Excalibur
Fast and the Furious, The
Fight Club
French Connection, The
From Russia with Love
Get Carter
Ghost Dog: The Way of the Samurai
Gladiator
Goldeneye
Goldfinger
Great Escape, The
Guns of Navarone, The
Hard Boiled
Hero
House of Flying Daggers
In the Line of Fire
Italian Job, The
Kill Bill, Vol. 1
Kill Bill, Vol. 2
Killer, The
La Femme Nikita
Long Kiss Goodnight, The
Mad Max
Mission Impossible
Natural Born Killers
Oldboy
Once Upon a Time in Mexico
One False Move

Panic Room
Professional, The
Rush Hour
Sexy Beast
Shaft
Shawshank Redemption, The
Spy Who Loved Me, The
Sugarland Express, The
Switchblade Sisters
Taking of Pelham One Two Three
Thief
Thunderball
Under Siege
Wages of Fear, The
White Heat

ADVENTURE

Adventures of Robin Hood, The
Aguirre, The Wrath of God
Air Force One
Apollo 13
Bill & Ted's Excellent Adventure
Bridge on the River Kwai, The
Butch Cassidy and the Sundance Kid
Cast Away
Crimson Tide
Crouching Tiger, Hidden Dragon
Escape from New York
Gold Rush, The
Great Escape, The
Harry Potter and the Prisoner of Azkaban
Hero
High and the Mighty, The
Hunt for Red October, The
Incredibles, The
Indiana Jones and the Last Crusade
Indiana Jones and the Temple of Doom
Italian Job, The
Jaws
Last of the Mohicans, The
Mad Max
Man Who Would Be King, The
Mask of Zorro, The

Master and Commander: The Far Side
    of the World
Mission: Impossible
Motorcycle Diaries, The
Mutiny on the Bounty
North by Northwest
Open Water
Pee-Wee's Big Adventure
Perfect Storm, The
Pirates of the Caribbean: The Curse
    of the Black Pearl
Point Break
Poseidon Adventure, The
Raiders of the Lost Ark
Ripley's Game
Road Warrior
Ronin
Run Lola Run
Runaway Train
Speed
Spirited Away
Stand by Me
Sting, The
Sullivan's Travels
Team America: World Police
Titanic
Top Gun
Touching the Void
Towering Inferno, The
Treasure of the Sierra Madre, The
20,000 Leagues under the Sea
Twister
Wages of Fear, The
Walkabout
Warriors, The
Winged Migration
Wizard of Oz, The

ANIMATION

Akira
Beauty and the Beast
Fantasia
Finding Nemo
Ghost in the Shell
Incredibles, The
Iron Giant
Lion King, The
Monsters Inc.
Nightmare before Christmas, The
Pinocchio
Shrek
Shrek 2
Snow White and the Seven Dwarfs
South Park: Bigger, Longer & Uncut
Spirited Away
Toy Story

Toy Story 2
Waking Life
Yellow Submarine

BIOPICS

Ali
Amadeus
American Splendor
Apollo 13
Aviator, The
Backbeat
Baadasssss!
Bird
Bonnie and Clyde
Born on the Fourth of July
Boys Don't Cry
Braveheart
Bugsy
Chariots of Fire
Chopper
Coal Miner's Daughter
Crumb
Dead Man Walking
Donnie Brasco
Doors, The
Ed Wood
Eight Men Out
Elephant Man, The
Erin Brockovich
Finding Neverland
Funny Girl
Gods and Monsters
Goodfellas
Heavenly Creatures
Hotel Rwanda
In Cold Blood
Killing Fields, The
Kinsey
Kundun
La Bamba
Last Emperor, The
Lawrence of Arabia
Love Me or Leave Me
Malcolm X
Melvin and Howard
Mommie Dearest
Monster
Motorcycle Diaries, The
My Left Foot
Passion of the Christ, The
Patton
People vs. Larry Flynt, The
Pianist, The
Raging Bull
Ray
Reversal of Fortune
Right Stuff, The

Schindler's List
Seabiscuit
Sid and Nancy
Spartacus
Topsy-Turvy
Tupac: Resurrection
24-Hour Party People
What's Love Got to Do with It?
Yankee Doodle Dandy

COMIC-BOOK HEROES

Batman
Batman Returns
Blade II
Men in Black
Sin City
Spider-Man
Spider-Man 2
Superman: The Movie
Superman II
Terminator, The
Terminator 2: Judgment Day
Terminator 3: Rise of the Machines
Unbreakable
X-Men 1.5
X2: X-Men United

CRIME AND PUNISHMENT

American History X
Anatomy of a Murder
Asphalt Jungle, The
Bad Day at Black Rock
Bad Education
Bad Lieutenant
Band of Outsiders
Beverly Hills Cop
Bicycle Thief, The
Big Sleep, The
Blood Simple
Blow
Blow Out
Blow-Up
Bonnie and Clyde
Bottle Rocket
Boyz N the Hood
Breathless
Bugsy
Bullitt
Butch Cassidy and the Sundance Kid
Caged Heat
Chinatown
Chopper
City of God
Clockwork Orange, A

Collateral
Conversation, The
Crash
Crimes and Misdemeanors
Croupier
Dead Man Walking
Deep End, The
Die Hard
Dirty Harry
Dog Day Afternoon
Dogville
Donnie Brasco
Double Indemnity
Dressed to Kill
Face/Off
Fargo
Fight Club
400 Blows, The
Frailty
Freeway
French Connection, The
Fugitive, The
Gangs of New York
Get Shorty
Godfather, The
Godfather, The: Part II
Godfather, The: Part III
GoodFellas
Grifters, The
Grosse Pointe Blank
Heat
Heathers
Heavenly Creatures
Honeymoon Killers
In Cold Blood
In the Heat of the Night
Infernal Affairs
Insomnia
Internal Affairs
Irreversible
Italian Job, The
Jackie Brown
Killers, The
L.A. Confidential
Laura
Lethal Weapon
Limey, The
Long Goodbye, The
M
Mean Streets
Memento
Menace II Society
Mystic River
Naked City, The
Narc
Natural Born Killers
Night of the Hunter, The
Oldboy
Once Upon a Time in America
One False Move

Out of Sight
Out of the Past
Panic Room
Peeping Tom
Perfect World, A
Point Blank
Point Break
Prizzi's Honor
Professional, The
Pulp Fiction
Rashomon
Requiem for a Dream
Reservoir Dogs
Reversal of Fortune
Ripley's Game
Road to Perdition
Ronin
Run Lola Run
Scarface
Se7en
Shallow Grave
Silence of the Lambs, The
Simple Plan, A
Sin City
Sting, The
Sugarland Express, The
Sunrise
Taking of Pelham One Two Three
Taxi Driver
Thief
Tightrope
To Catch a Thief
Touch of Evil
Traffic
Training Day
True Romance
Under Siege
Untouchables, The
Usual Suspects, The
Verdict, The
Weekend
White Heat
Winter Kills
With a Friend Like Harry
Z

DOCUMENTARY

Bowling for Columbine
Broadway: The Golden Age
Buena Vista Social Club
Capturing the Friedmans
Don't Look Back
Fahrenheit 9/11
Ghosts of the Abyss
Gimme Shelter
Last Waltz, The

Metallica: Some Kind of Monster
Sorrow and the Pity, The
That's Entertainment
Thin Blue Line, The
Touching the Void
Triumph of the Will
When We Were Kings
Winged Migration
Woodstock

DRAMA

American Beauty
Angels in America
Atlantic City
Being There
Bicycle Thief, The
Birth
Children of Paradise
Cinema Paradiso
Citizen Kane
Contempt
Cries and Whispers
Crimes and Misdemeanors
Days of Heaven
Days of Wine and Roses
Decalogue, The
East of Eden
Eclipse/L'Eclisse
Face in the Crowd, A
Faces
Fearless
Five Easy Pieces
400 Blows
Glengarry Glen Ross
Hannah and Her Sisters
Homecoming, The
House of Mirth, The
House of Sand and Fog
Howards End
Ice Storm
In the Bedroom
In the Company of Men
Insider
L'Avventura
La Dolce Vita
La Strada
Last Picture Show, The
Leaving Las Vegas
Lianna
Lord of the Flies
Magnolia
Man Who Wasn't There, The
Midnight Cowboy
Million Dollar Baby
Monster's Ball
Mystery Train

Nashville
Network
Night Moves
One Flew over the Cuckoo's Nest
Opening Night
Ordinary People
Persona
Peyton Place
Piano, The
Picnic
Picnic at Hanging Rock
Prime of Miss Jean Brodie, The
Quiz Show
Ragtime
Rain Man
Red Desert
Red Shoes, The
Remains of the Day, The
Requiem for a Dream
Return of the Secaucus Seven
River, The
River Runs through It, A
Romeo + Juliet
Room at the Top
Room with a View, A
Rounders
Royal Tenenbaums, The
Rules of the Game
Ruling Class, The
Safe
Servant, The
Shadows
Shock Corridor
Short Cuts
Sling Blade
Sophie's Choice
Stranger Than Paradise
Straw Dogs
Stunt Man, The
Sweet Hereafter, The
Sweet Smell of Success
Talk to Her
Tender Mercies
Terms of Endearment
Thelma & Louise
They Shoot Horses, Don't They?
Three Colors Trilogy: Blue/ White/Red
3 Women
To Kill a Mockingbird
Tokyo Story
21 Grams
25th Hour
Upside of Anger, The
Whale Rider
What's Eating Gilbert Grape?
Winslow Boy, The
Woman under the Influence, A

FANTASY

Amelie
Being John Malkovich
Big
Brazil
City of Lost Children, The
Crow, The
E.T. the Extra Terrestrial
Edward Scissorhands
Elf
Eraserhead
Eternal Sunshine of the Spotless Mind
Fantasia
Field of Dreams
Finding Neverland
Fisher King, The
Harry Potter and the Prisoner of Azkaban
Heavenly Creatures
Highlander
It's a Wonderful Life
Jason and the Argonauts
Journey to the Center of the Earth
Lord of the Rings, The: Fellowship of the Ring
Lord of the Rings, The: Return of the King
Lord of the Rings, The: Two Towers
Mulholland Dr.
Naked Lunch
Purple Rose of Cairo, The
Seventh Seal, The
7th Voyage of Sinbad, The
Sin City
Splash
Stepford Wives, The
Thief of Bagdad, The
Truman Show, The
Who Framed Roger Rabbit
Willy Wonka and the Chocolate Factory
Wings of Desire
Wizard of Oz, The
Zelig

FILM NOIR

American Friend, The
Asphalt Jungle, The
Big Sleep, The
Body Heat
Double Indemnity
Gilda
Grifters, The
In a Lonely Place
Lady from Shanghai, The
Laura
Maltese Falcon, The
Mildred Pierce
Notorious

Out of the Past
Pickup on South Street
Shadow of a Doubt
Strangers on a Train
Sunset Blvd.
Sweet Smell of Success
Touch of Evil

GUILTY PLEASURES

Basic Instinct
Bride of Chucky
Caged Heat
Crimes of Passion
Dodgeball: A True Underdog's Story
Fast and the Furious, The
Freeway
Hannibal
Mommie Dearest
Pink Flamingos
Q
Showgirls

HORROR

American Werewolf in London, An
Army of Darkness
Birds, The
Black Christmas
Blair Witch Project
Blob, The
Bram Stoker's Dracula
Bride of Chucky
Bride of Frankenstein, The
Carnival of Souls
Carrie
Cat People
Darkman
Dawn of the Dead
Deep Red
Dracula
Evil Dead, The: The Book of the Dead
Evil Dead II: Dead by Dawn
Exorcist, The
Fall of the House of Usher, The
Fly, The
Frankenstein
Freaks
Gremlins
Halloween
Hellraiser
House of Wax
I Spit On Your Grave
Innocents
Interview with the Vampire
Invasion of the Body Snatchers

Last House on the Left, The
Lost Boys, The
Near Dark
Nightmare on Elm Street, A
Night of the Living Dead
Omen, The
Others, The
Poltergeist
Predator
Psycho
Q
Ring, The
Ringu
Scary Movie
Scream
Shadow of the Vampire
Shaun of the Dead
Shining, The
Sixth Sense, The
Texas Chain Saw Massacre, The
Them!
28 Days Later
Village of the Damned
Wicker Man, The

LAUGHS (DUMB)

Airplane!
American Pie
Anchorman
Austin Powers: International Man of Mystery
Austin Powers: The Spy Who Shagged Me
Austin Powers in Goldmember
Back to School
Bad Santa
Bananas
Beetlejuice
Bill & Ted's Excellent Adventure
Billy Madison
Birdcage, The
Blazing Saddles
Caddyshack
Dodgeball: A True Underdog's Story
Duck Soup
Elf
Ghostbusters
Happy Gilmore
Kingpin
Longest Yard, The
Mask, The
Meet the Parents
My Cousin Vinny
My Little Chickadee
Naked Gun, The
Napoleon Dynamite
National Lampoon's Animal House
Nutty Professor, The

Old School
Pink Flamingos
Pink Panther, The
Repo Man
Serial Mom
Showgirls
Snatch
Take the Money and Run
There's Something (More) about Mary
Wayne's World
Wedding Crashers
Zoolander

LAUGHS (SMART)

Adaptation
After Hours
All about Eve
Apartment, The
Barton Fink
Best in Show
Big Lebowski, The
Bob Roberts
Brazil
Broadcast News
Bringing Up Baby
Bullets over Broadway
Chasing Amy
Citizen Ruth
Clerks
Clueless
Dazed and Confused
Diner
Election
Fargo
Fish Called Wanda, A
Get Shorty
Ghost World
Gold Rush, The
Gosford Park
Graduate, The
Grosse Pointe Blank
Groundhog Day
Hairspray
High Fidelity
I ♡ Huckabees
Kind Hearts and Coronets
King of Comedy, The
Local Hero
Lost in America
Manhattan
Married to the Mob
Mask, The
Mean Girls
Mighty Wind, A
Modern Times
Monty Python and the Holy Grail

Monty Python's Life of Brian
Monty Python's The Meaning of Life
O, Brother, Where Art Thou?
Opposite of Sex, The
Philadelphia Story, The
Player, The
Raising Arizona
Roger Dodger
Royal Tenenbaums, The
Rules of the Game
Rushmore
Sideways
Sleeper
Sullivan's Travels
Tootsie
Wag the Dog
Waiting for Guffman
War of the Roses, The
Welcome to the Dollhouse
Working Girl

MUSICALS

All That Jazz
Band Wagon, The
Beauty and the Beast
Buena Vista Social Club
Cabaret
Carousel
Chicago
Coal Miner's Daughter
Dancer in the Dark
Everyone Says I Love You
Fabulous Baker Boys, The
Fantasia
Fantasticks, The
Fiddler on the Roof
42nd Street
Funny Face
Funny Girl
Grease
Hard Day's Night, A
Harder They Come, The
Hedwig and the Angry Inch
King Creole
La Bamba
Lion King, The
Little Shop of Horrors
Love Me or Leave Me
Mambo Kings, The
Meet Me in St. Louis
Mighty Wind, A
Moulin Rouge
My Fair Lady
Nashville
Nightmare before Christmas, The
Pal Joey

Pennies from Heaven
Ray
Rose, The
Saturday Night Fever
Singin' in the Rain
South Park: Bigger, Longer & Uncut
Star Is Born, A
Swing Time
Tall Guy, The
Team America: World Police
Tender Mercies
Topsy-Turvy
Umbrellas of Cherbourg, The
Viva Las Vegas
Waiting for Guffman
West Side Story
What's Love Got to Do with It?
Willy Wonka and the Chocolate Factory
Wizard of Oz, The
Yankee Doodle Dandy
Yellow Submarine

MYSTERY

Anatomy of a Murder
Big Lebowski, The
Big Sleep, The
Chinatown
Conversation
Crash
Dogville
In the Heat of the Night
JFK
L.A. Confidential
Lady Vanishes, The
Laura
Maltese Falcon, The
Memento
Mildred Pierce
Mystic River
Oldboy
Rashomon
Rear Window
Rebecca
Se7en
Sixth Sense, The
Soldier's Story, A
Third Man, The
39 Steps, The
Usual Suspects, The
Vertigo
Witness
Z

POLITICS

All the King's Men
All the Presidents Men
American History X
Angels in America
Believer, The
Bob Roberts
Bowling for Columbine
China Syndrome, The
City of God
Do the Right Thing
Dr. Strangelove or: How I Learned to Stop
   Worrying and Love the Bomb
Election
Fahrenheit 9/11
Gentleman's Agreement
JFK
Killing Fields, The
Lone Star
Longtime Companion
Manchurian Candidate, The
Medium Cool
Midnight Express
On the Waterfront
Parallax View, The
Seven Days in May
Team America: World Police
Traffic
Wag the Dog
Winter Kills

ROCK 'N' ROLL

Almost Famous
Backbeat
Commitments, The
Don't Look Back
Doors, The
8 Mile
Filth and the Fury, The
Gimme Shelter
Hard Day's Night, A
Hedwig and the Angry Inch
Help!
High Fidelity
Last Waltz, The
Metallica: Some Kind of Monster
Monterey Pop: The Complete Festival
Rock 'n' Roll High School
Rose, The
School of Rock
Sid and Nancy
Stop Making Sense
This Is Spinal Tap
Tommy
24-Hour Party People

Velvet Goldmine
Woodstock

ROMANCE

Age of Innocence, The
All That Heaven Allows
Annie Hall
Apartment, The
As Good As It Gets
Before Sunrise
Before Sunset
Birdcage, The
Bull Durham
Casablanca
Charade
Chasing Amy
City Lights
Crouching Tiger, Hidden Dragon
Crying Game
Day for Night
Dirty Dancing
English Patient, The
Eternal Sunshine of the Spotless Mind
Far from Heaven
Garden State
Gilda
Gold Rush, The
High Fidelity
House of Flying Daggers
Igby Goes Down
Jackie Brown
Jerry Maguire
La Cage Aux Folles
Lady Eve, The
Leaving Las Vegas
Like Water for Chocolate
Long, Hot Summer, The
Lost in Translation
McCabe & Mrs. Miller
Moonstruck
Moulin Rouge
Notting Hill
On Her Majesty's Secret Service
Out of Sight
Philadelphia Story, The
Picnic
Pillow Talk
Place in the Sun, A
Pretty Woman
Rebecca
Remains of the Day, The
Room with a View, A
Roxanne
Rushmore
Sabrina
Say Anything . . .
Shakespeare in Love

Sid and Nancy
Sideways
Singles
Sixteen Candles
Something's Gotta Give
Splash
Strictly Ballroom
Swing Time
Titanic
To Catch a Thief
To Have and Have Not
True Romance
Upside of Anger, The
Way We Were, The
When Harry Met Sally . . .
Winslow Boy, The
Witness
Wuthering Heights
Year of Living Dangerously, The

SCI-FI

A.I.: Artificial Intelligence
Abyss, The
Akira
Alien Quadrilogy
Back to the Future
Barbarella
Blade Runner
Brazil
Clockwork Orange, A
Close Encounters of the Third Kind
Day the Earth Stood Still, The
Donnie Darko
E.T. the Extra Terrestrial
Fifth Element, The
Forbidden Planet
Independence Day
Invasion of the Body Snatchers
Jurassic Park
Man Who Fell to Earth, The
Matrix Trilogy
Men in Black
Metropolis
Minority Report
Planet of the Apes
Predator
Robocop
Soylent Green
Spider-Man
Spider-Man 2
Starship Troopers
Star Trek II: The Wrath of Kahn
Star Trek IV: The Voyage Home
Star Wars: Episode I—The Phantom Menace
Star Wars: Episode II—Attack of the Clones
Star Wars: Episode III—Revenge of the Sith
Star Wars: Episode IV—A New Hope

Star Wars: Episode V—The Empire Strikes
Back
Star Wars: Episode VI—Return of the Jedi
Terminator, The
Terminator 2: Judgment Day
Terminator 3: Rise of the Machines
THX 1138
Total Recall
Twelve Monkeys
2001: A Space Odyssey
Videodrome
War of the Worlds
X-Men 1.5
X2: X-Men United

SEXUAL OBSESSION

. . . And God Created Woman
Bad Education
Barbarella
Basic Instinct
Belle du Jour
Blue Velvet
Body Heat
Boogie Nights
Bound
Breaking the Waves
Carnal Knowledge
Chinatown
Closer
Crimes of Passion
Don't Look Now
Door in the Floor, The
Dreamers, The
Duel in the Sun
Eyes Wide Shut
Freeway
From Here to Eternity
Going Places
Innocents
In the Mood for Love
Jules and Jim
Klute
La Dolce Vita
Lady from Shanghai, The
Last Tango in Paris
Laura
Lolita
Manhattan
Monster's Ball
Mulholland Dr.
Naked
Naked Kiss, The
Notorious
Poison Ivy
Risky Business
Roger Dodger
Secretary

Servant, The
Sex, Lies & Videotape
Shampoo
Sin City
Slightly Scarlet
Something Wild
Splendor in the Grass
Streetcar Named Desire, A
Sunrise
Sunset Blvd.
Talk to Her
Team America: World Police
Tightrope
To Die For
Twin Peaks: Fire Walk with Me
Unbearable Lightness of Being, The
Vertigo
Wild at Heart
Women in Love
Written on the Wind
Y Tu Mamá También

SPORTS

Any Given Sunday
Bend It Like Beckham
Big Wednesday
Bull Durham
Caddyshack
Chariots of Fire
Cliffhanger
Color of Money, The
Dodgeball: A True Underdog's Story
Eight Men Out
Endless Summer, The
Fast and the Furious, The
Field of Dreams
Fight Club
Friday Night Lights
Hustler, The
Jerry Maguire
Kingpin
League of Their Own
Longest Yard, The
Million Dollar Baby
Natural, The
Point Break
Raging Bull
Rocky
Rounders
Seabiscuit
Slap Shot
Tin Cup
Touching the Void
When We Were Kings

SUSPENSE/THRILLERS

American Psycho
Black Christmas
Blow Out
Blow-Up
Cape Fear
Chinatown
Croupier
Deep End, The
Diva
Dressed to Kill
Fargo
Fight Club
Henry: Portrait of a Serial Killer
In the Heat of the Night
Insomnia
Jaws
King of New York
Klute
Lady from Shanghai, The
Leave Her to Heaven
M
Manchurian Candidate, The
Memento
Naked Kiss, The
Night Moves
Night of the Hunter, The
North by Northwest
Notorious
No Way Out
Psycho
Rear Window
Rebecca
Reservoir Dogs
Se7en
Shadow of a Doubt
Shining, The
Shock Corridor
Signs
Silence of the Lambs, The
Sisters
Sixth Sense, The
Strangers on a Train
Straw Dogs
Third Man, The
39 Steps, The
Touch of Evil
Twin Peaks: Fire Walk with Me
Unbreakable
Usual Suspects, The
Vanishing, The

TEENS

American Graffiti
American Pie
Better Tomorrow, A

Big
Bill & Ted's Excellent Adventure
Billy Elliott
Boyz N the Hood
Camp
Clockwork Orange, A
Clueless
Dazed and Confused
Dirty Dancing
Donnie Darko
Dreamers, The
Election
Fast Times at Ridgemont High
Ferris Bueller's Day Off
George Washington
Ghost World
Grease
Harry Potter and the Prisoner of Azkaban
Heathers
Last Picture Show, The
Lost Boys, The
Maria Full of Grace
Mean Girls
Menace II Society
Napoleon Dynamite
Outsiders, The
Poison Ivy
Rebel without a Cause
Risky Business
River's Edge
Rock 'n' Roll High School
Romeo + Juliet
Rushmore
Saturday Night Fever
Say Anything . . .
Sixteen Candles
South Park: Bigger, Longer & Uncut
Splendor in the Grass
Stand by Me
Warriors, The
Wayne's World
Whale Rider
What's Eating Gilbert Grape?
Where the Boys Are
Willy Wonka and the Chocolate Factory
Y Tu Mamá También

WAR

Apocalypse Now Redux
Barry Lyndon
Battle of Algiers, The
Big Red One, The
Braveheart
Bridge on the River Kwai, The
Bridges at Toko-Ri, The
Battleship Potemkin
Caine Mutiny, The

Das Boot
Deer Hunter, The
Dirty Dozen, The
Europa, Europa
From Here to Eternity
Full Metal Jacket
General, The
Glory
Gone with the Wind
Grand Illusion
Great Escape, The
Henry V
Hotel Rwanda
Killing Fields, The
Lawrence of Arabia
Longest Day, The
M*A*S*H
Mister Roberts
Paths of Glory
Patton
Pianist, The
Platoon
Salvador
Saving Private Ryan
Schindler's List
Spartacus
Thin Red Line, The
Three Kings
Tin Drum, The
Very Long Engagement, A

WESTERNS

Dances with Wolves
Dead Man
Duel in the Sun
Forty Guns
Good, the Bad and the Ugly, The

HIGH NOON

Last of the Mohicans, The
Little Big Man
Lone Star
Magnificent Seven, The
Major Dundee
My Darling Clementine
Once Upon a Time in Mexico
Once Upon a Time in the West
Outlaw Josey Wales, The
Red River
Rio Bravo
Searchers, The
Shane
Stagecoach
Tombstone
True Grit
Unforgiven
Wild Bunch, The
Winchester '73

ACKNOWLEDGMENTS

Wenner Books honcho Robert Wallace, my longtime friend and colleague, pushed hard for this book and then pushed me harder to write it. He brought in the estimable Nicholas Weir-Williams to ride herd on every detail. And what a gift to have Bob Land around to wrangle the copy into shape. If you find any mistakes, we'll take full responsibility and then blame each other. The creative support of designer Mayapriya Long, as well as Nina Pearlman, Corey Seymour, Tom Maloney, Kate Rockland, Henry Groskinsky, Elias Ravin, Adem Tepedelen, Lauren Bans, Rebecca Raber, and Fred Kennedy would do any book division proud. At *Rolling Stone*, Kent Brownridge, John Dragonetti, Will Dana, Kevin O'Donnell and copy editor supreme Tom Walsh have always been there to speed me on and watch my back. Add a huge shout out to Kerry Smith—you try doing the research on 1,000 DVDs. And a salute from the heart to Jann S. Wenner for giving me the enviable job of writing about movies for the best magazine in the world.